"When The Gavel Falls"
"All"

KING JAMES VERSION | AMPLIFIED BIBLE

KJV | AMP

PARALLEL BIBLE

LARGE PRINT

Published by Zondervan
Grand Rapids, Michigan 49530, U.S.A.

www.zondervan.com

Library of Congress Control Number 2004111016

08 09 10 11 12 13 14 15 /DCI/ 12 11 10 9 8 7 6 5

KJV | AMP

PARALLEL BIBLE

LARGE PRINT

Contents

PUBLISHERS' PREFACE, vi

King James Version

Preface, vii
Epistle Dedicatory, viii

The Amplified Bible

Preface, ix
Introduction, ix

THE OLD TESTAMENT

THE NEW TESTAMENT

Publishers' Preface

The first edition of *The Amplified New Testament* was released in 1958, followed by the complete text in 1965. Twenty-two years later, Zondervan Publishing House and The Lockman Foundation presented *The Amplified Bible, Expanded Edition,* the present standard text of this unique Bible version. The purpose of the textual amplification is to reveal multiple meanings of the original languages. This is a luxury denied other Bible translations, as traditional translation methods force scholars to select the meaning that best suits the style and interpretation of their particular rendering. *The Amplified Bible* is not meant to copy or replace other Bible translations, but rather to be used in conjunction with them, thus clarifying and illuminating God's Word. With this in mind, the publication of a parallel Bible placing the amplified text together with another translation was natural.

Grounded in the best scholarship of its day and combined with its impressive, eloquent style, *The King James Version* has been a beloved translation for centuries. Based on their similarities of format and language, the *Amplified* and the *KJV* are a classic match. Combined, their value multiplies as each enhances the content of the other in a manner sure to aid all readers in their study of Scripture.

In addition to being an indispensible study tool, larger type makes the *KJV/Amplified Parallel Bible, Large Print* easier to read as you delve into God's Word. We hope and pray that this *KJV/Amplified Parallel Bible, Large Print* will be a reliable, invaluable resource for you in your Christian walk.

THE PUBLISHERS

King James Version

PREFACE TO THE KING JAMES VERSION
1873 EDITION

The most time-honored and widely used edition of the English Bible is the translation of 1611, commonly known as the Authorized Version or King James Version (KJV). But though it has served as the standard translation for millions of users through nearly four centuries, there has never been a standard edition to which all printings are conformed.

No two early printings of the KJV were identical—not even the two printings of 1611—and no two modern settings are identical, either. These differences are due to accidental human error as well as to intentional changes by printers and editors, who sought to eliminate what they judged to be the errors of others and to conform the text to their standards of English usage. This said, most differences involve only spelling, punctuation, and italics, and few variations materially affect the meaning of the text.

As early as 1616 there were systematic attempts to revise and standardize the KJV. Other important early editions were issued by Cambridge in 1629 and 1638. In the eighteenth century, the two great English universities (who were also officially chartered printers) commissioned thorough and systematic revisions. The edition of Dr. F. S. Paris was published by Cambridge in 1762 and that of Dr. Benjamin Blayney by Oxford in 1769. Though far from perfect, these remained the standard editions until *The Cambridge Paragraph Bible* of 1873.

The Cambridge Paragraph Bible began with the simple plan of arranging the text of the KJV according to the sense of the literature: arranging the prose sections into paragraphs and the poetic sections into parallel lines. This simple plan, however, was enhanced by the editor's desire to create the most thorough standardization of the text ever attempted. To this task Dr. F. H. A. Scrivener devoted seven laborious years: 1866 to 1873.

Because the translators' original manuscript no longer exists, the KJV text must be established by consulting the earliest settings. Dr. Scrivener compared at least 15 early settings and important revisions, including both settings of 1611; Bibles of 1612, 1613, 1616, 1617, 1629, 1630, 1634, 1638, 1640; and the significant editions of Drs. Paris (1762) and Blayney (1769).

In his 120-page introduction, Dr. Scrivener addressed the various features of the KJV he worked to standardize:

Italic type. Italic type was used in the KJV, as in the Geneva Bible, to indicate words in the English translation that have no exact representative in the original language. Dr. Scrivener, following many earlier scholars, noted that the KJV translators were noticeably inconsistent in their use of italics, sometimes even in the same paragraph and verse. To cite one small pattern from the 1611 edition, Leviticus 11:20 has "upon all foure," while for the same

Hebrew 11:21 and 42 have "upon *all* foure," and 11:27 has "on *all* foure."

Dr. Scrivener carefully analyzed why italic type was used throughout the KJV, reduced this analysis to 14 major principles, and then applied these principles with meticulous consistency throughout the entire Bible. A substantial portion of the editor's "seven laborious years" was devoted to this significant improvement.

Punctuation. Later printings of the KJV added a great deal of punctuation to the editions of 1611. Dr. Scrivener restored the major punctuation (periods, colons, parentheses, question marks) of 1611, and used commas and semicolons to help divide longer sentences into more manageable units for reading.

Spelling and capital letters. Spelling of proper names and common words was very fluid in the sixteenth and seventeenth centuries: "Inquire" and "enquire" were interchangeable, as were "ceiling," "cieling," and "sieling." Most differences between modern settings of the KJV and early settings involve standardization of spelling. Dr. Scrivener's general rule was that whenever a word was spelled more than one way, he conformed all occurrences to the standard spelling of the late nineteenth century. Proper names, on the other hand, vary according to their spelling in the original languages, so "Elijah" throughout 1 and 2 Kings and in Malachi 4:5 becomes "Elias" throughout the New Testament, as in Matthew 11:14 and 17:3. For the benefit of modern readers, three spelling patterns are changed in this edition that are not changed in Scrivener's edition: twenty-nine occurrences of "mo" and "moe" are conformed to "more"; four occurrences of "unpossible" are conformed to "impossible"; and "neesed" in 2 Kings 4:35 is spelled "sneezed."

Paragraphs. According to Dr. Scrivener and other scholars, the paragraph marks (¶) were unequally and inconsistently distributed, and they disappear altogether after Acts 20:26. So, while consulted, the original marks were not always followed in *The Cambridge Paragraph Bible*.

With the *KJV-AB Parallel Bible*, Zondervan continues to conform its settings of the King James or Authorized Version to its most highly regarded edition: *The Cambridge Paragraph Bible* of 1873, edited by F. H. A. Scrivener. As in the case of the first edition of the version of 1611, this is done out of "zeal to promote the common good, whether it be by devising any thing ourselves, or revising that which hath been laboured by others" ("The Translators to the Reader," the preface to the version of 1611). With the original translators, we hope our efforts will be "welcomed," not "with suspicion" but with "love," and that the reissue of this edition will contribute to improvement of this great treasure of the English-speaking church.

JOHN R. KOHLENBERGER III

King James Version

TO THE MOST HIGH AND MIGHTY PRINCE

JAMES

BY THE GRACE OF GOD
KING OF GREAT BRITAIN, FRANCE, AND IRELAND
DEFENDER OF THE FAITH, &c.

The Translators of the Bible wish Grace, Mercy, and Peace
through JESUS CHRIST our Lord

Great and manifold were the blessings, most dread Sovereign, which Almighty God, the Father of all mercies, bestowed upon us the people of *England*, when first he sent Your Majesty's Royal Person to rule and reign over us. For whereas it was the expectation of many, who wished not well unto our *Sion*, that upon the setting of that bright *Occidental Star*, Queen *Elizabeth* of most happy memory, some thick and palpable clouds of darkness would so have overshadowed this Land, that men should have been in doubt which way they were to walk; and that it should hardly be known, who was to direct the unsettled State; the appearance of Your Majesty, as of the *Sun* in his strength, instantly dispelled those supposed and surmised mists, and gave unto all that were well affected exceeding cause of comfort; especially when we beheld the Government established in Your Highness, and Your hopeful Seed, by an undoubted Title, and this also accompanied with peace and tranquility at home and abroad.

But among all our joys, there was no one that more filled our hearts, than the blessed continuance of the preaching of God's sacred Word among us; which is that inestimable treasure, which excelleth all the riches of the earth; because the fruit thereof extendeth itself, not only to the time spent in this transitory world, but directeth and disposeth men unto that eternal happiness which is above in heaven.

Then not to suffer this to fall to the ground, but rather to take it up, and to continue it in that state, wherein the famous Predecessor of Your Highness did leave it: nay, to go forward with the confidence and resolution of a Man in maintaining the truth of Christ, and propagating it far and near, is that which hath so bound and firmly knit the hearts of all Your Majesty's loyal and religious people unto You, that Your very name is precious among them: their eye doth behold You with comfort, and they bless You in their hearts, as that sanctified Person who, under God, is the immediate Author of their true happiness. And this their contentment doth not diminish or decay, but every day increaseth and taketh strength, when they observe, that the zeal of Your Majesty toward the house of God doth not slack or go backward, but is more and more kindled, manifesting itself abroad in the farthest parts of *Christendom*, by writing in defence of the Truth, (which hath given such a blow unto that man of sin, as will not be healed,) and every day at home, by religious and learned discourse, by frequenting the house of God, by hearing the Word preached, by cherishing the Teachers thereof, by caring for the Church, as a most tender and loving nursing Father.

There are infinite arguments of this right Christian and religious affection in Your Majesty; but none is more forcible to declare it to others than the vehement and perpetuated desire of accomplishing and publishing of this work, which now with all humility we present unto Your Majesty. For when Your Highness had once out of deep judgment apprehended how convenient it was, that out of the Original Sacred Tongues, together with comparing of the labours, both in our own, and other foreign Languages, of many worthy men who went before us, there should be one more exact Translation of the holy Scriptures into the *English Tongue;* Your Majesty did never desist to urge and to excite those to whom it was commended, that the work might be hastened, and that the business might be expedited in so decent a manner, as a matter of such importance might justly require.

And now at last, by the mercy of God, and the continuance of our labours, it being brought unto such a conclusion, as that we have great hopes that the Church of *England* shall reap good fruit thereby; we hold it our duty to offer it to Your Majesty, not only as to our King and Sovereign, but as to the principal Mover and Author of the work: humbly craving of Your most Sacred Majesty, that since things of this quality have ever been subject to the censures of illmeaning and discontented persons, it may receive approbation and patronage from so learned and judicious a Prince as Your Highness is, whose allowance and acceptance of our labours shall more honour and encourage us, than all the calumniations and hard interpretations of other men shall dismay us. So that if, on the one side, we shall be traduced by Popish Persons at home or abroad, who therefore will malign us, because we are poor instruments to make God's holy Truth to be yet more and more known unto the people, whom they desire still to keep in ignorance and darkness; or if, on the other side, we shall be maligned by self-conceited Brethren, who run their own ways, and give liking unto nothing, but what is framed by themselves, and hammered on their anvil; we may rest secure, supported within by the truth and innocency of a good conscience, having walked the ways of simplicity and integrity, as before the Lord; and sustained without by the powerful protection of Your Majesty's grace and favour, which will ever give countenance to honest and Christian endeavours against bitter censures and uncharitable imputations.

The Lord of heaven and earth bless Your Majesty with many and happy days, that, as his heavenly hand hath enriched Your Highness with many singular and extraordinary graces, so You may be the wonder of the world in this latter age for happiness and true felicity, to the honour of that great GOD, and the good of his Church, through Jesus Christ our Lord and only Saviour.

The Amplified Bible

PREFACE TO THE AMPLIFIED BIBLE

In 1958 The Lockman Foundation and Zondervan Publishing House issued the first edition of The Amplified New Testament after more than 20,000 hours of research and prayerful study. Some four years later the first of two Old Testament volumes appeared (The Amplified Old Testament, Part Two—Job to Malachi), followed in 1964 by the publication of The Amplified Old Testament, Part One—Genesis to Esther. The next year (1965) The Amplified Bible came out in one volume.

Now, twenty-two years later, Zondervan Bible Publishers and The Lockman Foundation are pleased to present The Amplified Bible, Expanded Edition. The purpose of all the characters in the story of the making of The Amplified Bible is still relevant today: to communicate the Word of God to people and to exalt Jesus Christ. This has been the fourfold aim of The Lockman Foundation from the beginning:

1. That it should be true to the original Hebrew and Greek.
2. That it should be grammatically correct.
3. That it should be understandable to the masses.
4. That it should give the Lord Jesus Christ His proper place, the place which the Word gives Him.

From the days of John Wycliffe (1329-1384) and the first English Bible to the present, translators have worked diligently on English versions designed to faithfully present the Scriptures in contemporary language. The Amplified Bible is not an attempt to duplicate what has already been achieved, nor is it intended to be a substitute for other translations. Its genius lies in its rigorous attempt to go beyond the traditional "word-for-word" concept of translation to bring out the richness of the Hebrew and Greek languages. Its purpose is to reveal, together with the single English word equivalent to each key Hebrew and Greek word, any other clarifying meanings that may be concealed by the traditional translation method. Perhaps for the first time in an English version of the Bible, the full meaning of the key words in the original text is available for the reader. In a sense, the creative use of the amplification merely helps the reader comprehend what the Hebrew and Greek listener instinctively understood (as a matter of course).

Take as an example the Greek word *pisteuo*, which the vast majority of versions render "believe." That simple translation, however hardly does justice to the many meanings contained in the Greek *pisteuo*: "to adhere to, cleave to; to trust, to have faith in; to rely on, to depend on." Consequently, the reader gains understanding through the use of amplification, as in John 11:25: "Jesus said to her, I am [Myself] the Resurrection and the Life. Whoever believes in (adheres to, trusts in, and relies on) Me, although he may die, yet he shall live."

In the words of the apostle Paul, "And we are setting these truths forth in words not taught by human wisdom but taught by the [Holy] Spirit. . . [that His glory may be both manifested and recognized]" (1 Cor 2:13; Phil 1:11).

INTRODUCTION TO THE AMPLIFIED BIBLE

ABOUT THE AMPLIFIED BIBLE

The story of the Amplified Bible is a remarkable story of faith, hope, and love. It's the story of a woman, a foundation, a committee, and a publisher. Commitment, energy, enthusiasm, giftedness—these are the words that paint the picture, the picture of the making of a translation.

Frances Siewert (Litt. B., B.D., M.A., Litt. D.) was a woman with an intense dedication to the study of the Bible. It was Mrs. Siewert (1881-1967) who laid the foundation of the Amplified Bible, devoting her life to a familiarity with the Bible, with the Hebrew and Greek languages, and with the cultural and archaeological background of Biblical times, which would result in the publication of this unique translation.

Every vision need visionaries willing to follow the cause. The story of this dream is no different. Mrs. Siewert's vision was seen by a California non-profit foundation called The Lockman Foundation, made up of Christian men and women who through their commitment, their expertise, and their financial support undergirded Mrs. Siewert's monumental translation project. The Lockman Foundation's purpose remains today what is was then: to promote Bible translation, Christian evangelism, education, and benevolence.

Commitment, energy, enthusiasm, giftedness—the things visions are made of—describes the efforts of the committee appointed by The Lockman Foundation to carefully review the impressive work of Mrs. Siewert. This Editorial Board, made up of dedicated people, lent credibility and organization to this unprecedented attempt to bring out the richness of the Hebrew and Greek languages within the English text itself.

One chapter yet remained to bring the vision into reality. A publishing house in Grand Rapids, Michigan, on its way to becoming a major religious publishing firm, seized the opportunity to participate in a project which all visionaries involved strongly believed would be used by God to change lives. The Zondervan Publishing House joined the team, and the dream became reality with the publication of The Amplified New Testament in 1958, followed by the two-volume Amplified Old Testament in 1962 and 1964, and the one-volume Amplified Bible in 1965.

FEATURES OF THE AMPLIFIED BIBLE

The Amplified Bible, Expanded Edition, features the text of The Amplified Bible, with explanatory and devotional footnotes; a reference system contained within the text; a comprehensive bibliography of original sources cited in the footnotes.

THE TEXT OF THE AMPLIFIED BIBLE

The text of the Amplified Bible is easy to understand, and is made even easier to understand by the inclusion of informative footnotes which often alert readers to different textual readings and give insight into Greek grammar and translation. Numerous Bible translations are among the sources cited in the footnotes, as well as some of the greatest lexicographers of all time and some of the best of Bible commentators.

To help readers achieve the greatest possible clarity and understanding in their reading of the text of The Amplified Bible, some explanation of the various markings within the text is necessary:

Parentheses ( ) signify additional phases of meaning included in the original word, phrase, or clause of the original language.

Brackets [ ] contained justified clarifying words or comments not actually expressed in the immediate original text, as well as definitions of Hebrew and Greek names.

Italics point out:

1. certain familiar passages now recognized as not adequately supported by the original manuscripts. This is the primary use of italics in the New Testament, so that, upon encountering italics, the reader is alerted to a matter of textual readings. Often these will be accompanied by a footnote. See as an example Matthew 16:2-3.

2. conjunctions such as "and," "or," and the like, not in the original text, but used to connect additional English words indicated in the same original word. In this use, the reader, upon encountering a conjunction in italics, is alerted to the addition of an amplified word or phrase. See as an example Acts 24:3.

3. words which are not found in the original Hebrew or Greek but implied by it.

Capitals are used:

1. in names and personal pronouns referring to the Deity. See as an example Psalm 94.

2. in proper names of persons, places, specific feasts, topographical names, personifications, and the like. See as an example Proverbs 1:2; John 7:2.

Abbreviations may on occasion be encountered in either the text or in the footnotes.

cf.,	compare, confer
ch., chs.	chapter, chapters
e.g.	for example
etc.	and so on
i.e.,	that is
v., vv.	verse, verses
ff.	following
ft.	foot
c.	about
KJV	King James Version
RV	Revised Version
ASV	American Standard Version

THE REFERENCE SYSTEM

The reference system of the Amplified Bible is contained within the text. The Scripture references are placed within brackets at the end of a verse, and are intended to cover any part of the preceding verse to which they apply. If a verse contains more than one Scripture reference, the list of references is in Biblical order. A sensitivity to the prophecy-fulfillment motif is indicated by such references as [Fulfilled in. . .]; [Foretold in. . .].

THE BIBLIOGRAPHY

A comprehensive, though not exhaustive, bibliography of original sources cited in the footnotes is included in the back of the Bible. The bibliography lists basic information such as author or editor/editors, book or periodical title, publisher (and location of publisher), and date of publication. For more information on the bibliography, see the introduction to the bibliography.

The Old Testament

King James Version	Amplified Bible

THE FIRST BOOK OF MOSES, CALLED

Genesis

THE FIRST BOOK OF MOSES, COMMONLY CALLED

Genesis

1 In the beginning God created the heaven and the earth.

2 And the earth was without form, and void; and darkness *was* upon the face of the deep. And the Spirit of God moved upon the face of the waters.

3 ¶ And God said, Let there be light: and there was light.

4 And God saw the light, that *it was* good: and God divided the light from the darkness.

5 And God called the light Day, and the darkness he called Night. And the evening and the morning were the first day.

6 ¶ And God said, Let there be a firmament in the midst of the waters, and let it divide the waters from the waters.

7 And God made the firmament, and divided the waters which *were* under the firmament from the waters which *were* above the firmament: and it was so.

8 And God called the firmament Heaven. And the evening and the morning were the second day.

9 ¶ And God said, Let the waters under the heaven be gathered together unto one place, and let the dry *land* appear: and it was so.

10 And God called the dry *land* Earth; and the gathering together of the waters called he Seas: and God saw that *it was* good.

11 And God said, Let the earth bring forth grass, the herb yielding seed, *and* the fruit tree yielding fruit after his kind, whose seed *is* in itself, upon the earth: and it was so.

12 And the earth brought forth grass, *and* herb yielding seed after his kind, and the tree yielding fruit, whose seed *was* in itself, after his kind: and God saw that *it was* good.

13 And the evening and the morning were the third day.

14 ¶ And God said, Let there be lights in the firmament of the heaven to divide the day from the night; and let them be for signs, and for seasons, and for days, and years:

15 And let them be for lights in the firmament of the heaven to give light upon the earth: and it was so.

1 IN THE beginning God (prepared, formed, fashioned, and) created the heavens and the earth.

2 The earth was without form and an empty waste, and darkness was upon the face of the very great deep. The Spirit of God was moving (hovering, brooding) over the face of the waters.

3 And God said, Let there be light; and there was light.

4 And God saw that the light was good (suitable, pleasant) *and* He approved it; and God separated the light from the darkness.

5 And God called the light Day, and the darkness He called Night. And there was evening and there was morning, one day.

6 And God said, Let there be a firmament [the expanse of the sky] in the midst of the waters, and let it separate the waters [below] from the waters [above].

7 And God made the firmament [the expanse] and separated the waters which were under the expanse from the waters which were above the expanse. And it was so.

8 And God called the firmament Heavens. And there was evening and there was morning, a second day.

9 And God said, Let the waters under the heavens be collected into one place [of standing], and let the dry land appear. And it was so.

10 God called the dry land Earth, and the accumulated waters He called Seas. And God saw that this was good (fitting, admirable) *and* He approved it.

11 And God said, Let the earth put forth [tender] vegetation: plants yielding seed and fruit trees yielding fruit whose seed is in itself, each according to its kind, upon the earth. And it was so.

12 The earth brought forth vegetation: plants yielding seed according to their own kinds and trees bearing fruit in which was their seed, each according to its kind. And God saw that it was good (suitable, admirable) *and* He approved it.

13 And there was evening and there was morning, a third day.

14 And God said, Let there be lights in the expanse of the heavens to separate the day from the night; and let them be signs *and* tokens [of God's provident care], and [to mark] seasons, days, and years,

15 And let them be lights in the expanse of the sky to give light upon the earth. And it was so.

King James Version

16And God made two great lights; the greater light to rule the day, and the lesser light to rule the night: *he made* the stars also.

17And God set them in the firmament of the heaven to give light upon the earth,

18And to rule over the day and over the night, and to divide the light from the darkness: and God saw that *it was* good.

19And the evening and the morning were the fourth day.

20 ¶ And God said, Let the waters bring forth abundantly the moving creature that hath life, and fowl *that* may fly above the earth in the open firmament of heaven.

21And God created great whales, and every living creature that moveth, which the waters brought forth abundantly, after their kind, and every winged fowl after his kind: and God saw that *it was* good.

22And God blessed them, saying, Be fruitful, and multiply, and fill the waters in the seas, and let fowl multiply in the earth.

23And the evening and the morning were the fifth day.

24 ¶ And God said, Let the earth bring forth the living creature after his kind, cattle, and creeping thing, and beast of the earth after his kind: and it was so.

25And God made the beast of the earth after his kind, and cattle after their kind, and every thing that creepeth upon the earth after his kind: and God saw that *it was* good.

26 ¶ And God said, Let us make man in our image, after our likeness: and let them have dominion over the fish of the sea, and over the fowl of the air, and over the cattle, and over all the earth, and over every creeping thing that creepeth upon the earth.

27So God created man in his own image, in the image of God created he him; male and female created he them.

28And God blessed them, and God said unto them, Be fruitful, and multiply, and replenish the earth, and subdue it: and have dominion over the fish of the sea, and over the fowl of the air, and over every living thing that moveth upon the earth.

29 ¶ And God said, Behold, I have given you every herb bearing seed, which *is* upon the face of all the earth, and every tree, in the which *is* the fruit of a tree yielding seed; to you it shall be for meat.

30And to every beast of the earth, and to every fowl of the air, and to every *thing* that creepeth upon the earth, wherein *there is* life, *I have given* every green herb for meat: and it was so.

Amplified Bible

16And God made the two great lights—the greater light (the sun) to rule the day and the lesser light (the moon) to rule the night. He also made the stars.

17And God set them in the expanse of the heavens to give light upon the earth,

18To rule over the day and over the night, and to separate the light from the darkness. And God saw that it was good (fitting, pleasant) *and* He approved it.

19And there was evening and there was morning, a fourth day.

20And God said, Let the waters bring forth abundantly *and* swarm with living creatures, and let birds fly over the earth in the open expanse of the heavens.

21God created the great sea monsters and every living creature that moves, which the waters brought forth abundantly, according to their kinds, and every winged bird according to its kind. And God saw that it was good (suitable, admirable) *and* He approved it.

22And God blessed them, saying, Be fruitful, multiply, and fill the waters in the seas, and let the fowl multiply in the earth.

23And there was evening and there was morning, a fifth day.

24And God said, Let the earth bring forth living creatures according to their kinds: livestock, creeping things, and [wild] beasts of the earth according to their kinds. And it was so.

25And God made the [wild] beasts of the earth according to their kinds, and domestic animals according to their kinds, and everything that creeps upon the earth according to its kind. And God saw that it was good (fitting, pleasant) *and* He approved it.

26God said, Let Us [Father, Son, and Holy Spirit] make mankind in Our image, after Our likeness, and let them have complete authority over the fish of the sea, the birds of the air, the [tame] beasts, and over all of the earth, and over everything that creeps upon the earth.

27So God created man in His own image, in the image *and* likeness of God He created him; male and female He created them.

28And God blessed them and said to them, Be fruitful, multiply, and fill the earth, and subdue it [using all its vast resources in the service of God and man]; and have dominion over the fish of the sea, the birds of the air, and over every living creature that moves upon the earth.

29And God said, See, I have given you every plant yielding seed that is on the face of all the land and every tree with seed in its fruit; you shall have them for food.

30And to all the animals on the earth and to every bird of the air and to everything that creeps on the ground—to everything in which there is the breath of life—I have given every green plant for food. And it was so.

King James Version

31And God saw every thing that he had made, and behold, *it was* very good. And the evening and the morning were the sixth day.

2 Thus the heavens and the earth were finished, and all the host of them.

2And on the seventh day God ended his work which he had made; and he rested on the seventh day from all his work which he had made.

3And God blessed the seventh day, and sanctified it: because that in it he had rested from all his work which God created and made.

4 ¶ These *are* the generations of the heavens and of the earth when they were created, in the day that the LORD God made the earth and the heavens,

5And every plant of the field before it was in the earth, and every herb of the field before it grew: for the LORD God had not caused it to rain upon the earth, and *there was* not a man to till the ground.

6But there went up a mist from the earth, and watered the whole face of the ground.

7And the LORD God formed man *of* the dust of the ground, and breathed into his nostrils the breath of life; and man became a living soul.

8 ¶ And the LORD God planted a garden eastward in Eden; and there he put the man whom he had formed.

9And out of the ground made the LORD God to grow every tree that is pleasant to the sight, and good for food; the tree of life also in the midst of the garden, and the tree of knowledge of good and evil.

10And a river went out of Eden to water the garden; and from thence it was parted, and became into four heads.

11The name of the first *is* Pison: that *is it* which compasseth the whole land of Havilah, where *there is* gold;

12And the gold of that land *is* good: there *is* bdellium and the onyx stone.

13And the name of the second river *is* Gihon: the same *is it* that compasseth the whole land of Ethiopia.

14And the name of the third river *is* Hiddekel: that *is it* which goeth toward the east of Assyria. And the fourth river *is* Euphrates.

15And the LORD God took the man, and put him into the garden of Eden to dress it and to keep it.

16And the LORD God commanded the man, saying, Of every tree of the garden thou mayest freely eat:

Amplified Bible

31And God saw everything that He had made, and behold, it was very good (suitable, pleasant) *and* He approved it completely. And there was evening and there was morning, a sixth day.

2 THUS THE heavens and the earth were finished, and all the host of them.

2And on the seventh day God ended His work which He had done; and He rested on the seventh day from all His work which He had done.

3And God blessed (spoke good of) the seventh day, set it apart as His own, and hallowed it, because on it God rested from all His work which He had created and done.

4This is the history of the heavens and of the earth when they were created. In the day that the Lord God made the earth and the heavens—

5When no plant of the field was yet in the earth and no herb of the field had yet sprung up, for the Lord God had not [yet] caused it to rain upon the earth and there was no man to till the ground,

6But there went up a mist (fog, vapor) from the land and watered the whole surface of the ground—

7Then the Lord God formed man from the [a]dust of the ground and breathed into his nostrils the breath *or* spirit of life, and man became a living being.

8And the Lord God planted a garden toward the east, in Eden [delight]; and there He put the man whom He had formed (framed, constituted).

9And out of the ground the Lord God made to grow every tree that is pleasant to the sight *or* to be desired—good (suitable, pleasant) for food; the tree of life also in the center of the garden, and the tree of the knowledge of [the difference between] good and evil *and* blessing and calamity.

10Now a river went out of Eden to water the garden; and from there it divided and became four [river] heads.

11The first is named Pishon; it is the one flowing around the whole land of Havilah, where there is gold.

12The gold of that land is of high quality; bdellium (pearl?) and onyx stone are there.

13The second river is named Gihon; it is the one flowing around the whole land of Cush.

14The third river is named Hiddekel [the Tigris]; it is the one flowing east of Assyria. And the fourth river is the Euphrates.

15And the Lord God took the man and put him in the Garden of Eden to tend and guard *and* keep it.

16And the Lord God commanded the man, saying, You may freely eat of every tree of the garden;

AMP notes: a The same essential chemical elements are found in man and animal life that are in the soil. This scientific fact was not known to man until recent times, but God was displaying it here.

King James Version

¹⁷But of the tree of the knowledge of good and evil, thou shalt not eat of it: for in the day that thou eatest thereof thou shalt surely die.

¹⁸ ¶ And the LORD God said, *It is* not good that the man should be alone; I will make him a help meet for him.

¹⁹And out of the ground the LORD God formed every beast of the field, and every fowl of the air; and brought *them* unto Adam to see what he would call them: and whatsoever Adam called every living creature, that *was* the name thereof.

²⁰And Adam gave names to all cattle, and to the fowl of the air, and to every beast of the field; but for Adam there was not found a help meet for him.

²¹And the LORD God caused a deep sleep to fall upon Adam, and he slept: and he took one of his ribs, and closed up the flesh instead thereof;

²²And the rib, which the LORD God had taken from man, made he a woman, and brought her unto the man.

²³And Adam said, This *is* now bone of my bones, and flesh of my flesh: she shall be called Woman, because she was taken out of Man.

²⁴Therefore shall a man leave his father and his mother, and shall cleave unto his wife: and they shall be one flesh.

²⁵And they were both naked, the man and his wife, and were not ashamed.

3 Now the serpent was more subtil than any beast of the field which the LORD God had made. And he said unto the woman, Yea, hath God said, Ye shall not eat of every tree of the garden?

²And the woman said unto the serpent, We may eat of the fruit of the trees of the garden:

³But of the fruit of the tree which *is* in the midst of the garden, God hath said, Ye shall not eat of it, neither shall ye touch it, lest ye die.

⁴And the serpent said unto the woman, Ye shall not surely die:

⁵For God doth know that in the day ye eat thereof, then your eyes shall be opened, and ye shall be as gods, knowing good and evil.

⁶And when the woman saw that the tree *was* good for food, and that it *was* pleasant to the eyes, and a tree to be desired to make *one* wise, she took of the fruit thereof, and did eat, and gave also unto her husband with her; and he did eat.

Amplified Bible

¹⁷But of the tree of the knowledge of good and evil *and* blessing and calamity you shall not eat, for in the day that you eat of it you shall surely die.

¹⁸Now the Lord God said, It is not good (sufficient, satisfactory) that the man should be alone; I will make him a helper meet (suitable, adapted, complementary) for him.

¹⁹And out of the ground the Lord God formed every [wild] beast *and* living creature of the field and every bird of the air and brought them to Adam to see what he would call them; and whatever Adam called every living creature, that was its name.

²⁰And Adam gave names to all the livestock and to the birds of the air and to every [wild] beast of the field; but for Adam there was not found a helper meet (suitable, adapted, complementary) for him.

²¹And the Lord God caused a deep sleep to fall upon Adam; and while he slept, He took one of his ribs *or* a part of his side and closed up the [place with] flesh.

²²And the rib *or* part of his side which the Lord God had taken from the man He built up *and* made into a woman, and He brought her to the man.

²³Then Adam said, This [creature] is now bone of my bones and flesh of my flesh; she shall be called Woman, because she was taken out of a man.

²⁴Therefore a man shall leave his father and his mother and shall become united *and* cleave to his wife, and they shall become one flesh.

²⁵And the man and his wife were both naked and were not embarrassed *or* ashamed in each other's presence.

3 NOW THE serpent was more subtle *and* crafty than any living creature of the field which the Lord God had made. And he [Satan] said to the woman, Can it really be that God has said, You shall not eat from every tree of the garden?

²And the woman said to the serpent, We may eat the fruit from the trees of the garden,

³Except the fruit from the tree which is in the middle of the garden. God has said, You shall not eat of it, neither shall you touch it, lest you die.

⁴But the serpent said to the woman, You shall not surely die,

⁵For God knows that in the day you eat of it your eyes will be opened, and you will be like God, knowing the difference between good and evil *and* blessing and calamity.

⁶And when the woman saw that the tree was good (suitable, pleasant) for food and that it was delightful to look at, and a tree to be desired in order to make one wise, she took of its fruit and ate; and she gave some also to her husband, and he ate.

King James Version

⁷And the eyes of them both were opened, and they knew that they *were* naked; and they sewed fig leaves together, and made themselves aprons.

⁸And they heard the voice of the LORD God walking in the garden in the cool of the day: and Adam and his wife hid themselves from the presence of the LORD God amongst the trees of the garden.

⁹And the LORD God called unto Adam, and said unto him, Where *art* thou?

¹⁰And he said, I heard thy voice in the garden, and I was afraid, because I *was* naked; and I hid myself.

¹¹And he said, Who told thee that thou *wast* naked? Hast thou eaten of the tree, whereof I commanded thee that thou shouldest not eat?

¹²And the man said, The woman whom thou gavest *to be* with me, she gave me of the tree, and I did eat.

¹³And the LORD God said unto the woman, What *is* this *that* thou hast done? And the woman said, The serpent beguiled me, and I did eat.

¹⁴And the LORD God said unto the serpent, Because thou hast done this, thou *art* cursed above all cattle, and above every beast of the field; upon thy belly shalt thou go, and dust shalt thou eat all the days of thy life:

¹⁵And I will put enmity between thee and the woman, and between thy seed and her seed; it shall bruise thy head, and thou shalt bruise his heel.

¹⁶Unto the woman he said, I will greatly multiply thy sorrow and thy conception; in sorrow thou shalt bring forth children; and thy desire *shall be* to thy husband, and he shall rule over thee.

¹⁷And unto Adam he said, Because thou hast hearkened unto the voice of thy wife, and hast eaten of the tree, of which I commanded thee, saying, Thou shalt not eat of it: cursed *is* the ground for thy sake; in sorrow shalt thou eat *of* it all the days of thy life;

¹⁸Thorns also and thistles shall it bring forth to thee; and thou shalt eat the herb of the field;

¹⁹In the sweat of thy face shalt thou eat bread, till thou return unto the ground; for out of it wast thou taken: for dust thou *art*, and unto dust shalt thou return.

²⁰And Adam called his wife's name Eve; because she was the mother of all living.

Amplified Bible

⁷Then the eyes of them both were opened, and they knew that they were naked; and they sewed fig leaves together and made themselves apronlike girdles.

⁸And they heard the sound of the Lord God walking in the garden in the cool of the day, and Adam and his wife hid themselves from the presence of the Lord God among the trees of the garden.

⁹But the Lord God called to Adam and said to him, Where are you?

¹⁰He said, I heard the sound of You [walking] in the garden, and I was afraid because I was naked; and I hid myself.

¹¹And He said, Who told you that you were naked? Have you eaten of the tree of which I commanded you that you should not eat?

¹²And the man said, The woman whom You gave to be with me—she gave me [fruit] from the tree, and I ate.

¹³And the Lord God said to the woman, What is this you have done? And the woman said, The serpent beguiled (cheated, outwitted, and deceived) me, and I ate.

¹⁴And the Lord God said to the serpent, Because you have done this, you are cursed above all [domestic] animals and above every [wild] living thing of the field; upon your belly you shall go, and you shall eat dust [and what it contains] all the days of your life.

¹⁵And I will put enmity between you and the woman, and between your offspring and her ᵃOffspring; He will bruise *and* tread your head underfoot, and you will lie in wait *and* bruise His heel.

¹⁶To the woman He said, I will greatly multiply your grief *and* your suffering in pregnancy *and* the pangs of childbearing; with spasms of distress you will bring forth children. Yet your desire *and* craving will be for your husband, and he will rule over you.

¹⁷And to Adam He said, Because you have listened *and* given heed to the voice of your wife and have eaten of the tree of which I commanded you, saying, You shall not eat of it, the ground is under a curse because of you; in sorrow *and* toil shall you eat [of the fruits] of it all the days of your life.

¹⁸Thorns also and thistles shall it bring forth for you, and you shall eat the plants of the field.

¹⁹In the sweat of your face shall you eat bread until you return to the ground, for out of it you were taken; for dust you are and to dust you shall return.

²⁰The man called his wife's name Eve [life spring], because she was the mother of all the living.

King James Version

[21] Unto Adam also and to his wife did the LORD God make coats of skins, and clothed them.

[22] And the LORD God said, Behold, the man is become as one of us, to know good and evil: and now, lest he put forth his hand, and take also of the tree of life, and eat, and live for ever:

[23] Therefore the LORD God sent him forth from the garden of Eden, to till the ground from whence he was taken.

[24] So he drove out the man; and he placed at the east of the garden of Eden Cherubims, and a flaming sword which turned every way, to keep the way of the tree of life.

4 And Adam knew Eve his wife; and she conceived, and bare Cain, and said, I have gotten a man from the LORD.

[2] And she again bare his brother Abel. And Abel was a keeper of sheep, but Cain was a tiller of the ground.

[3] And in process of time it came to pass, that Cain brought of the fruit of the ground an offering unto the LORD.

[4] And Abel, he also brought of the firstlings of his flock and of the fat thereof. And the LORD had respect unto Abel and to his offering:

[5] But unto Cain and to his offering he had not respect. And Cain was very wroth, and his countenance fell.

[6] And the LORD said unto Cain, Why art thou wroth? and why is thy countenance fallen?

[7] If thou doest well, *shalt thou* not be accepted? and if thou doest not well, sin lieth at the door. And unto thee *shall be* his desire, and thou shalt rule over him.

[8] And Cain talked with Abel his brother: and it came to pass, when they were in the field, that Cain rose up against Abel his brother, and slew him.

[9] And the LORD said unto Cain, Where *is* Abel thy brother? And he said, I know not: *Am* I my brother's keeper?

[10] And he said, What hast thou done? the voice of thy brother's blood crieth unto me from the ground.

[11] And now *art* thou cursed from the earth, which hath opened her mouth to receive thy brother's blood from thy hand.

[12] When thou tillest the ground, it shall not

Amplified Bible

[21] For Adam also and for his wife the Lord God made long coats (tunics) of skins and clothed them.

[22] And the Lord God said, Behold, the man has become like one of Us [the Father, Son, and Holy Spirit], to know [how to distinguish between] good and evil *and* blessing and calamity; and now, lest he put forth his hand and take also from the tree of life and eat, and live *a*forever—

[23] Therefore the Lord God sent him forth from the Garden of Eden to till the ground from which he was taken.

[24] So [God] drove out the man; and He placed at the east of the Garden of Eden the *b*cherubim and a flaming sword which turned every way, to keep *and* guard the way to the tree of life.

4 AND ADAM knew Eve as his wife, and she became pregnant and bore Cain; and she said, I have gotten *and* gained a man with the help of the Lord.

[2] And [next] she gave birth to his brother Abel. Now Abel was a keeper of sheep, but Cain was a tiller of the ground.

[3] And in the course of time Cain brought to the Lord an offering of the fruit of the ground.

[4] And Abel brought of the firstborn of his flock and of the fat portions. And the Lord had respect *and* regard for Abel and for his offering,

[5] But for *c*Cain and his offering He had no respect *or* regard. So Cain was exceedingly angry *and* indignant, and he looked sad *and* depressed.

[6] And the Lord said to Cain, Why are you angry? And why do you look sad *and* depressed *and* dejected?

[7] If you do well, will you not be accepted? And if you do not do well, sin crouches at your door; its desire is for you, but you must master it.

[8] And Cain said to his brother, *d*Let us go out to the field. And when they were in the field, Cain rose up against Abel his brother and killed him.

[9] And the Lord said to Cain, Where is Abel your brother? And he said, I do not know. Am I my brother's keeper?

[10] And [the Lord] said, What have you done? The voice of your brother's blood is crying to Me from the ground.

[11] And now you are cursed by reason of the earth, which has opened its mouth to receive your brother's [shed] blood from your hand.

[12] When you till the ground, it shall no longer

AMP notes: *a* This sentence is left unfinished, as if to hasten to avert the tragedy suggested of men living on forever in their now fallen state.   *b* Cherubim are ministering spirits manifesting God's invisible presence and symbolizing His action (E. F. Harrison et al., eds., *Baker's Dictionary of Theology*).   *c* In bringing the offering he did, Cain denied that he was a sinful creature under the sentence of divine condemnation. He insisted on approaching God on the ground of personal worthiness. Instead of accepting God's way, he offered to God the fruits of the ground **which God had cursed.** He presented the product of his own toil, the work of his own hands, and God refused to receive it (Arthur W. Pink, *Gleanings in Genesis*).   *d* The Hebrew omits this clause, but various other texts show that it was originally included. Matt. 1:23; Luke 1:31; Rom. 16:20; Gal. 4:4; Rev. 12:17.

King James Version

henceforth yield unto thee her strength; a fugitive and a vagabond shalt thou be in the earth.

¹³And Cain said unto the LORD, My punishment *is* greater than *I* can bear.

¹⁴Behold, thou hast driven me out *this* day from the face of the earth; and from thy face shall I be hid; and I shall be a fugitive and a vagabond in the earth; and it shall come to pass, *that* every one that findeth me shall slay me.

¹⁵And the LORD said unto him, Therefore whosoever slayeth Cain, vengeance shall be taken on him sevenfold. And the LORD set a mark upon Cain, lest any finding him should kill him.

¹⁶And Cain went out from the presence of the LORD, and dwelt in the land of Nod, on the east of Eden.

¹⁷And Cain knew his wife; and she conceived, and bare Enoch: and he builded a city, and called the name of the city, after the name of his son, Enoch.

¹⁸And unto Enoch was born Irad: and Irad begat Mehujael: and Mehujael begat Methusael: and Methusael begat Lamech.

¹⁹And Lamech took unto him two wives: the name of the one *was* Adah, and the name of the other Zillah.

²⁰And Adah bare Jabal: he was the father of such as dwell in tents, and *of such as have* cattle.

²¹And his brother's name *was* Jubal: he was the father of all such as handle the harp and organ. *His music influenced the Rebellion of Noah's Time*

²²And Zillah, she also bare Tubal-cain, an instructor of every artificer in brass and iron: and the sister of Tubal-cain *was* Naamah.

²³And Lamech said unto his wives, Adah and Zillah, Hear my voice; ye wives of Lamech, hearken unto my speech: for I have slain a man to my wounding, and a young man to my hurt.

²⁴If Cain shall be avenged sevenfold, truly Lamech seventy and sevenfold.

²⁵And Adam knew his wife again; and she bare a son, and called his name Seth: For God, *said she,* hath appointed me another seed instead of Abel, whom Cain slew.

²⁶And to Seth, *to* him also there was born a son; and he called his name Enos; then began *men* to call upon the name of the LORD.

5 This *is* the book of the generations of Adam. In the day that God created man, in the likeness of God made he him;

²Male and female created he them; and

Amplified Bible

yield to you its strength; you shall be a fugitive and a vagabond on the earth [in perpetual exile, a degraded outcast].

¹³Then Cain said to the Lord, My punishment is ᵃgreater than I can bear.

¹⁴Behold, You have driven me out this day from the face of the land, and from Your face I will be hidden; and I will be a fugitive and a vagabond *and* a wanderer on the earth, and whoever finds me will kill me.

¹⁵And the Lord said to him, ᵇTherefore, if anyone kills Cain, vengeance shall be taken on him sevenfold. And the Lord set a ᶜmark *or* sign upon Cain, lest anyone finding him should kill him.

¹⁶So Cain went away from the presence of the Lord and dwelt in the land of Nod [wandering], east of Eden.

¹⁷And Cain's wife [one of Adam's offspring] became pregnant and bore Enoch; and Cain built a ᵈcity and named it after his son Enoch.

¹⁸To Enoch was born Irad, and Irad was the father of Mehujael, and Mehujael the father of Methusael, and Methusael the father of Lamech.

¹⁹And Lamech took two wives; the name of the one was Adah and of the other Zillah.

²⁰Adah bore Jabal; he was the father of those who dwell in tents and have cattle *and* purchase possessions.

²¹His brother's name was Jubal; he was the father of all those who play the lyre and pipe.

²²Zillah bore Tubal-cain; he was the forger of all [cutting] instruments of bronze and iron. The sister of Tubal-cain was Naamah.

²³Lamech said to his wives, Adah and Zillah, Hear my voice; you wives of Lamech, listen to what I say; for I have slain a man [merely] for wounding me, and a young man [only] for striking *and* bruising me.

²⁴If Cain is avenged sevenfold, truly Lamech [will be avenged] seventy-sevenfold.

²⁵And Adam's wife again became pregnant, and she bore a son and called his name Seth. For God, she said, has appointed for me another child instead of Abel, for Cain slew him.

²⁶And to Seth also a son was born, whom he named Enosh. At that time men began to call [upon God] by the name of the Lord.

5 THIS IS the book (the written record, the history) of the generations of the offspring of Adam. When God created man, He made him in the likeness of God.

²He created them male and female and

AMP notes: ᵃ Some ancient versions read, "too great to be forgiven!" ᵇ Some versions read, "Not so!" ᶜ Many commentators believe this sign not to have been like a brand on the forehead, but something awesome about Cain's appearance that made people dread and avoid him. ᵈ C. H. Dodd (cited by Adam Clarke, *The Holy Bible with A Commentary*) shows that it would have been possible for Adam and Eve, in the more than 100 years he estimates may have elapsed since their union, to have had over 32,000 descendants at the time Cain went to Nod, all of them having sprung from Cain and Abel, who married their sisters.

King James Version

blessed them, and called their name Adam, in the day when they were created.

³And Adam lived an hundred and thirty years, and begat *a son* in his own likeness, after his image; and called his name Seth:

⁴And the days of Adam after he had begotten Seth were eight hundred years: and he begat sons and daughters:

⁵And all the days that Adam lived were nine hundred and thirty years: and he died.

⁶And Seth lived an hundred and five years, and begat Enos:

⁷And Seth lived after he begat Enos eight hundred and seven years, and begat sons and daughters:

⁸And all the days of Seth were nine hundred and twelve years: and he died.

⁹And Enos lived ninety years, and begat Cainan:

¹⁰And Enos lived after he begat Cainan eight hundred and fifteen years, and begat sons and daughters:

¹¹And all the days of Enos were nine hundred and five years: and he died.

¹²And Cainan lived seventy years, and begat Mahalaleel:

¹³And Cainan lived after he begat Mahalaleel eight hundred and forty years, and begat sons and daughters:

¹⁴And all the days of Cainan were nine hundred and ten years: and he died.

¹⁵And Mahalaleel lived sixty and five years, and begat Jared:

¹⁶And Mahalaleel lived after he begat Jared eight hundred and thirty years, and begat sons and daughters:

¹⁷And all the days of Mahalaleel were eight hundred ninety and five years: and he died.

¹⁸And Jared lived an hundred sixty and two years, and he begat Enoch:

¹⁹And Jared lived after he begat Enoch eight hundred years, and begat sons and daughters:

²⁰And all the days of Jared were nine hundred sixty and two years: and he died.

²¹And Enoch lived sixty and five years, and begat Methuselah:

²²And Enoch walked with God after he begat Methuselah three hundred years, and begat sons and daughters:

²³And all the days of Enoch were three hundred sixty and five years:

²⁴And Enoch walked with God: and he *was* not; for God took him.

²⁵And Methuselah lived an hundred eighty and seven years, and begat Lamech:

²⁶And Methuselah lived after he begat Lamech seven hundred eighty and two years, and begat sons and daughters:

²⁷And all the days of Methuselah were nine hundred sixty and nine years: and he died.

Amplified Bible

blessed them and named them [both] Adam [Man] at the time they were created.

³When Adam had lived 130 years, he had a son in his own likeness, after his image; and he named him Seth.

⁴After he had Seth, Adam lived 800 years and had other sons and daughters.

⁵So altogether Adam lived 930 years, and he died.

⁶When Seth was 105 years old, Enosh was born.

⁷Seth lived after the birth of Enosh 807 years and had other sons and daughters.

⁸So Seth lived 912 years, and he died.

⁹When Enosh was 90 years old, Kenan was born to him.

¹⁰Enosh lived after the birth of Kenan 815 years and had other sons and daughters.

¹¹So Enosh lived 905 years, and he died.

¹²When Kenan was 70 years old, Mahalalel was born.

¹³Kenan lived after the birth of Mahalalel 840 years and had other sons and daughters.

¹⁴So Kenan lived 910 years, and he died.

¹⁵When Mahalalel was 65 years old, Jared was born.

¹⁶Mahalalel lived after the birth of Jared 830 years and had other sons and daughters.

¹⁷So Mahalalel lived 895 years, and he died.

¹⁸When Jared was 162 years old, Enoch was born.

¹⁹Jared lived after the birth of Enoch 800 years and had other sons and daughters.

²⁰So Jared lived 962 years, and he died.

²¹When Enoch was 65 years old, Methuselah was born.

²²Enoch walked [in habitual fellowship] with God after the birth of Methuselah 300 years and had other sons and daughters.

²³So all the days of Enoch were 365 years.

²⁴And Enoch walked [in habitual fellowship] with God; and he was not, for God took him [home with Him].

²⁵When Methuselah was 187 years old, Lamech was born to him.

²⁶Methuselah lived after the birth of Lamech 782 years and had other sons and daughters.

²⁷So Methuselah lived 969 years, and he died.

King James Version

²⁸And Lamech lived an hundred eighty and two years, and begat a son:

²⁹And he called his name Noah, saying, This *same* shall comfort us concerning our work and toil of our hands, because of the ground which the LORD hath cursed.

³⁰And Lamech lived after he begat Noah five hundred ninety and five years, and begat sons and daughters:

³¹And all the days of Lamech were seven hundred seventy and seven years: and he died.

³²And Noah was five hundred years old: and Noah begat Shem, Ham, and Japheth.

6 And it came to pass, when men began to multiply on the face of the earth, and daughters were born unto them,

²That the sons of God saw the daughters of men that they *were* fair; and they took them wives of all which they chose.

³And the LORD said, My spirit shall not always strive with man, for that he also *is* flesh: yet his days shall be an hundred and twenty years.

⁴There were giants in the earth in those days; and also after that, when the sons of God came in unto the daughters of men, and they bare *children* to them, the same *became* mighty *men* which *were* of old, men of renown.

⁵And GOD saw that the wickedness of man *was* great in the earth, and *that* every imagination of the thoughts of his heart *was* only evil continually.

⁶And it repented the LORD that he had made man on the earth, and it grieved him at his heart.

⁷And the LORD said, I will destroy man whom I have created from the face of the earth; both man, and beast, and the creeping thing, and the fowls of the air; for it repenteth me that I have made them.

⁸But Noah found grace in the eyes of the LORD.

⁹ ¶ These *are* the generations of Noah: Noah was a just man *and* perfect in his generations, *and* Noah walked with God.

¹⁰And Noah begat three sons, Shem, Ham, and Japheth.

¹¹The earth also was corrupt before God, and the earth was filled *with* violence.

¹²And God looked upon the earth, and behold,

Amplified Bible

²⁸When Lamech was 182 years old, a son was born.

²⁹He named him Noah, saying, This one shall bring us relief *and* comfort from our work and the [grievous] toil of our hands due to the ground being cursed by the Lord.

³⁰Lamech lived after the birth of Noah 595 years and had other sons and daughters.

³¹So all the days of *a*Lamech were 777 years, and he died.

³²After Noah was 500 years old, he became the father of Shem, Ham, and Japheth.

6 WHEN MEN began to multiply on the face of the land and daughters were born to them,

²The sons of God saw that the daughters of men were fair, and they took wives of all they desired *and* chose.

³Then the Lord said, My Spirit shall not forever dwell *and* strive with man, for he also is flesh; but his days shall yet be 120 years.

⁴There were giants on the earth in those days—and also afterward—when the sons of God lived with the daughters of men, and they bore children to them. These were the mighty men who were of old, men of renown.

⁵The Lord saw that the wickedness of man was great in the earth, and that every imagination *and* intention of all human thinking was only evil continually.

⁶And the Lord regretted that He had made man on the earth, and He was grieved at heart.

⁷So the Lord said, I will destroy, blot out, *and* wipe away mankind, whom I have created from the face of the ground—not only man, [but] the beasts and the creeping things and the birds of the air—for it grieves Me *and* makes Me regretful that I have made them.

⁸But Noah found grace (favor) in the eyes of the Lord.

⁹This is the history of the generations of Noah. Noah was a just *and* righteous man, blameless *in* his [evil] generation; Noah walked [in habitual fellowship] with God.

¹⁰And Noah became the father of three sons: Shem, Ham, and Japheth.

¹¹The earth was depraved *and* putrid in God's sight, and the land was filled with violence (desecration, infringement, outrage, assault, and lust for power).

¹²And God looked upon the world and saw how degenerate, debased, *and* vicious it was,

---

AMP notes: *a* It is now well known that the age of mankind cannot be reckoned in years from the facts listed in genealogies, for there are numerous known intentional gaps in them. For example, as B. B. Warfield (*Studies in Theology*) points out, the genealogy in Matt. 1:1-17 omits the three kings, Ahaziah, Jehoash, and Amaziah, and indicates that Joram (Matt. 1:8) begat Uzziah, who was his great-great-grandson. The mistaking of compressed genealogies as bases for chronology has been very misleading. So far, the dates in years of very early Old Testament events are altogether speculative and relative, and the tendency is to put them farther and farther back into antiquity.

King James Version

it was corrupt; for all flesh had corrupted his way upon the earth.

[13]And God said unto Noah, The end of all flesh is come before me; for the earth is filled *with* violence through them; and behold, I will destroy them with the earth.

[14]Make thee an ark of gopher wood; rooms shalt thou make *in* the ark, and shalt pitch it within and without with pitch.

[15]And this *is the fashion* which thou shalt make it *of: the* length of the ark *shall be* three hundred cubits, the breadth of it fifty cubits, and the height of it thirty cubits.

[16]A window shalt thou make to the ark, and in a cubit shalt thou finish it above; and the door of the ark shalt thou set in the side thereof; *with* lower, second, and third *stories* shalt thou make it.

[17]And behold, I, even I, do bring a flood of waters upon the earth, to destroy all flesh, wherein *is* the breath of life, from under heaven; *and* every *thing* that *is* in the earth shall die.

[18]But with thee will I establish my covenant; and thou shalt come into the ark, thou, and thy sons, and thy wife, and thy sons' wives with thee.

[19]And of every living *thing* of all flesh, two of every *sort* shalt thou bring into the ark, to keep *them* alive with thee; they shall be male and female.

[20]Of fowls after their kind, and of cattle after their kind, of every creeping thing of the earth after his kind, two of every *sort* shall come unto thee, to keep *them* alive.

[21]And take thou unto thee of all food that is eaten, and thou shalt gather *it* to thee; and it shall be for food for thee, and for them.

[22]Thus did Noah; according to all that God commanded him, so did he.

7 And the LORD said unto Noah, Come thou and all thy house into the ark; for thee have I seen righteous before me in this generation.

[2]Of every clean beast thou shalt take to thee by sevens, the male and his female: and of beasts that *are* not clean by two, the male and his female.

[3]Of fowls also of the air by sevens, the male and the female; to keep seed alive upon the face of all the earth.

[4]For yet seven days, *and* I will cause it to rain

Amplified Bible

for all humanity had corrupted their way upon the earth *and* lost their true direction.

[13]God said to Noah, I intend to make an end of all flesh, for through men the land is filled with violence; and behold, I will [a]destroy them and the land.

[14]Make yourself an ark of gopher *or* cypress wood; make in *it* rooms (stalls, pens, coops, nests, cages, and compartments) and cover it inside and out with pitch (bitumen).

[15]And this is the way you are to make it: the length of the ark shall be 300 cubits, its breadth 50 cubits, and its height 30 cubits [that is, 450 ft. x 75 ft. x 45 ft.].

[16]You shall make a roof or [b]window [a place for light] for the ark and finish it to a cubit [at least 18 inches] above—and the [c]door of the ark you shall put in the side of it; and you shall make it with lower, second, and third stories.

[17]For behold, I, even I, will bring a flood of waters upon the earth to destroy *and* make putrid all flesh under the heavens in which are the breath *and* spirit of life; everything that is on the land shall die.

[18]But I will establish My covenant (promise, pledge) with you, and you shall come into the ark—you and your sons and your wife and your sons' wives with you.

[19]And of every living thing of all flesh [found on land], you shall bring two of every sort into the ark, to keep them alive with you; they shall be male and female.

[20]Of fowls *and* birds according to their kinds, of beasts according to their kinds, of every creeping thing of the ground according to its kind—two of every sort shall come in with you, that they may be kept alive.

[21]Also take with you every sort of food that is eaten, and you shall collect *and* store it up, and it shall serve as food for you and for them.

[22]Noah did this; he did all that God commanded him.

7 AND THE Lord said to Noah, Come with all your household into the ark, for I have seen you to be righteous (upright and in right standing) before Me in this generation.

[2]Of every clean beast you shall receive *and* take with you seven pairs, the male and his mate, and of beasts that are not clean a pair of each kind, the male and his mate,

[3]Also of the birds of the air seven pairs, the male and the female, to keep seed [their kind] alive over all the earth *or* land.

[4]For in seven days I will cause it to rain upon

AMP notes: [a] Enoch had warned these people (Jude 14, 15); Noah had preached righteousness to them (II Pet. 2:5); God's Spirit had been striving with them (Gen. 6:3). Yet they had rejected God and were without excuse. [b] Noah's ark possibly had a window area large enough to admit light and provide ventilation. [c] "Here can only be meant an entrance which was afterward closed, and only opened again at the end of the flood. And since there were three stories of the ark, the word is to be understood, perhaps, of three entrances capable of being closed, and to which there would have been constructed a way of access from the outside" (J. P. Lange, *A Commentary on the Holy Scriptures*).

King James Version

upon the earth forty days and forty nights; and every living substance that I have made will I destroy from off the face of the earth.

⁵And Noah did according unto all that the LORD commanded him.

⁶And Noah *was* six hundred years old when the flood of waters was upon the earth.

⁷And Noah went in, and his sons, and his wife, and his sons' wives with him, into the ark, because of the waters of the flood.

⁸Of clean beasts, and of beasts that *are* not clean, and of fowls, and of every *thing* that creepeth upon the earth,

⁹There went in two and two unto Noah into the ark, the male and the female, as God had commanded Noah.

¹⁰ ¶ And it came to pass after seven days, that the waters of the flood were upon the earth.

¹¹In the six hundredth year of Noah's life, in the second month, the seventeenth day of the month, the same day were all the fountains of the great deep broken up, and the windows of heaven were opened.

¹²And the rain was upon the earth forty days and forty nights.

¹³In the selfsame day entered Noah, and Shem, and Ham, and Japheth, the sons of Noah, and Noah's wife, and the three wives of his sons with them, into the ark;

¹⁴They, and every beast after his kind, and all the cattle after their kind, and every creeping thing that creepeth upon the earth after his kind, and every fowl after his kind, every bird of every sort.

¹⁵And they went in unto Noah into the ark, two and two of all flesh, wherein *is* the breath of life.

¹⁶And they that went in, went in male and female of all flesh, as God had commanded him: and the LORD shut him in.

¹⁷And the flood was forty days upon the earth; and the waters increased, and bare up the ark, and it was lift up above the earth.

¹⁸And the waters prevailed, and were increased greatly upon the earth; and the ark went upon the face of the waters.

¹⁹And the waters prevailed exceedingly upon the earth; and all the high hills, that *were* under the whole heaven, were covered.

²⁰Fifteen cubits upward did the waters prevail; and the mountains were covered.

²¹And all flesh died that moved upon the earth, *both* of fowl, and of cattle, and of beast,

Amplified Bible

the earth forty days and forty nights, and every living substance *and* thing that I have made I will destroy, blot out, *and* wipe away from the face of the earth.

⁵And Noah did all that the Lord commanded him.

⁶Noah was 600 years old when the flood of waters came upon the earth *or* land.

⁷And Noah and his sons and his wife and his sons' wives with him went into the ark because of the waters of the flood.

⁸Of ᵃclean animals and of animals that are not clean, and of birds *and* fowls, and of everything that creeps on the ground,

⁹There went in two and two with Noah into the ark, the male and the female, as God had commanded Noah.

¹⁰And after the seven days the floodwaters came upon the earth *or* land.

¹¹In the year 600 of Noah's life, in the seventeenth day of the second month, that same day all the fountains of the great deep were broken up *and* burst forth, and the windows *and* floodgates of the heavens were opened.

¹²And it rained upon the earth forty days and forty nights.

¹³On the very same day Noah and Shem, Ham, and Japheth, the sons of Noah, and Noah's wife and the three wives of his sons with them, went into the ark,

¹⁴They and every [wild] beast according to its kind, all the livestock according to their kinds, every moving thing that creeps on the land according to its kind, and every fowl according to its kind, every winged thing of every sort.

¹⁵And they went into the ark with Noah, two and two of all flesh in which there were the breath *and* spirit of life.

¹⁶And they that entered, male and female of all flesh, went in as God had commanded [Noah]; and the Lord shut him in *and* closed [the door] round about him.

¹⁷The flood [that is, the downpour of rain] was forty days upon the earth; and the waters increased and bore up the ark, and it was lifted [high] above the land.

¹⁸And the waters became mighty and increased greatly upon the land, and the ark went [gently floating] upon the surface of the waters.

¹⁹And the waters prevailed so exceedingly *and* were so mighty upon the earth that all the high hills under the whole sky were covered.

²⁰[In fact] the waters became fifteen cubits higher, as the high hills were covered.

²¹And all flesh ceased to breathe that moved upon the earth—fowls *and* birds, [tame] animals, [wild] beasts, all swarming *and* creeping

AMP notes: ᵃ Noah had many years in which to interest travelers in securing these animals for him. The five extra pairs of clean animals were for food, and for sacrifice later.

King James Version

and of every creeping thing that creepeth upon the earth, and every man:

²²All in whose nostrils *was* the breath of life, of all that *was* in the dry *land,* died.

²³And every living substance was destroyed which *was* upon the face of the ground, both man, and cattle, and the creeping things, and the fowl of the heaven; and they were destroyed from the earth: and Noah only remained *alive,* and *they* that *were* with him in the ark.

²⁴And the waters prevailed upon the earth an hundred and fifty days.

8 And God remembered Noah, and every living thing, and all the cattle that *was* with him in the ark: and God made a wind to pass over the earth, and the waters assuaged;

²The fountains also of the deep and the windows of heaven were stopped, and the rain from heaven was restrained;

³And the waters returned from off the earth continually: and after the end of the hundred and fifty days the waters were abated.

⁴And the ark rested in the seventh month, on the seventeenth day of the month, upon the mountains of Ararat.

⁵And the waters decreased continually until the tenth month: in the tenth *month,* on the first *day* of the month, were the tops of the mountains seen.

⁶And it came to pass at the end of forty days, that Noah opened the window of the ark which he had made:

⁷And he sent forth a raven, which went forth to and fro, until the waters were dried up from off the earth.

⁸Also he sent forth a dove from him, to see if the waters were abated from off the face of the ground;

⁹But the dove found no rest for the sole of her foot, and she returned unto him into the ark, for the waters *were* on the face of the whole earth: then he put forth his hand, and took her, and pulled her in unto him into the ark.

¹⁰And he stayed yet other seven days; and again he sent forth the dove out of the ark;

¹¹And the dove came in to him in the evening; and lo, in her mouth *was* an olive leaf pluckt off: so Noah knew that the waters were abated from off the earth.

¹²And he stayed yet other seven days; and sent forth the dove; which returned not again unto him any more.

¹³ ¶ And it came to pass in the six hundredth and first year, in the first *month,* the first *day* of the month, the waters were dried up from off the earth: and Noah removed the covering of

Amplified Bible

things that swarm *and* creep upon the land, and all mankind.

²²Everything on the dry land in whose nostrils were the breath *and* spirit of life died.

²³God destroyed (blotted out) every living thing that was upon the face of the earth; man and animals and the creeping things and the birds of the heavens were destroyed (blotted out) from the land. Only Noah remained alive, and those who were with him in the ark.

²⁴And the waters prevailed [mightily] upon the earth *or* land 150 days (five months).

8 AND GOD [earnestly] remembered Noah and every living thing and all the animals that were with him in the ark; and God made a wind blow over the land, and the waters sank down *and* abated.

²Also the fountains of the deep and the windows of the heavens were closed, the gushing rain from the sky was checked,

³And the waters receded from the land continually. At the end of 150 days the waters had diminished.

⁴On the seventeenth day of the seventh month the ark came to rest on the mountains of Ararat [in Armenia].

⁵And the waters continued to diminish until the tenth month; on the first day of the tenth month the tops of the high hills were seen.

⁶At the end of [another] forty days Noah opened *a* window of the ark which he had made

⁷And sent forth a raven, which kept going to and fro until the waters were dried up from the land.

⁸Then he sent forth a dove to see if the waters had decreased from the surface of the ground.

⁹But the dove found no resting-place on which to roost, and she returned to him to the ark, for the waters were [yet] on the face of the whole land. So he put forth his hand and drew her to him into the ark.

¹⁰He waited another seven days and again sent forth the dove out of the ark.

¹¹And the dove came back to him in the evening, and behold, in her mouth was a newly sprouted *and* freshly plucked olive leaf! So Noah knew that the waters had subsided from the land.

¹²Then he waited another seven days and sent forth the dove, but she did not return to him any more.

¹³In the year 601 [of Noah's life], on the first day of the first month, the waters were drying up from the land. And Noah ᵃremoved the cov-

---

AMP notes: ᵃ Possibly overhanging eaves which prevented the rain from coming through the perforated window space had also prevented Noah from seeing the mountaintops. It is well to remember that the Architect of Noah's ark was the omniscient Scientist Whose "ways are past finding out," though men have learned much from them through the

King James Version

the ark, and looked, and behold, the face of the ground was dry.

¹⁴And in the second month, on the seven and twentieth day of the month, was the earth dried.

¹⁵And God spake unto Noah, saying,

¹⁶Go forth of the ark, thou, and thy wife, and thy sons, and thy sons' wives with thee.

¹⁷Bring forth with thee every living thing that *is* with thee, of all flesh, *both* of fowl, and of cattle, and of every creeping thing that creepeth upon the earth; that they may breed abundantly in the earth, and be fruitful, and multiply upon the earth.

¹⁸And Noah went forth, and his sons, and his wife, and his sons' wives with him:

¹⁹Every beast, every creeping thing, and every fowl, *and* whatsoever creepeth upon the earth, after their kinds, went forth out of the ark.

²⁰ ¶ And Noah builded an altar unto the LORD; and took of every clean beast, and of every clean fowl, and offered burnt offerings on the altar.

²¹And the LORD smelled a sweet savour; and the LORD said in his heart, I will not again curse the ground any more for man's sake; for the imagination of man's heart *is* evil from his youth; neither will I again smite any more every *thing* living, as I have done.

²²While the earth remaineth, seedtime and harvest, and cold and heat, and summer and winter, and day and night shall not cease.

9 And God blessed Noah and his sons, and said unto them, Be fruitful, and multiply, and replenish the earth.

²And the fear of you and the dread of you shall be upon every beast of the earth, and upon every fowl of the air, upon all that moveth *upon* the earth, and upon all the fishes of the sea; into your hand are they delivered.

³Every moving thing that liveth shall be meat for you; *even* as the green herb have I given you all *things*.

⁴But flesh with the life thereof, *which is* the blood thereof, shall you not eat.

⁵And surely your blood of your lives will I require; at the hand of every beast will I require it, and at the hand of man; at the hand of every man's brother will I require the life of man.

⁶Whoso sheddeth man's blood, by man shall his blood be shed: for in the image of God made he man.

Amplified Bible

ering of the ark and looked, and behold, the surface of the ground was drying.

¹⁴And on the twenty-seventh day of the second month the land was entirely dry.

¹⁵And God spoke to Noah, saying,

¹⁶Go forth from the ark, you and your wife and your sons and their wives with you.

¹⁷Bring forth every living thing that is with you of all flesh—birds and beasts and every creeping thing that creeps on the ground—that they may breed abundantly on the land and be fruitful and multiply upon the earth.

¹⁸And Noah went forth, and his wife and his sons and their wives with him [after being in the ark one year and ten days].

¹⁹Every beast, every creeping thing, every bird—and whatever moves on the land—went forth by families out of the ark.

²⁰And Noah built an altar to the Lord and took of every clean [four-footed] animal and of every clean fowl *or* bird and offered burnt offerings on the altar.

²¹When the Lord smelled the pleasing odor [a scent of satisfaction to His heart], the Lord said to Himself, I will never again curse the ground because of man, for the imagination (the strong desire) of man's heart is evil *and* wicked from his youth; neither will I ever again smite *and* destroy every living thing, as I have done.

²²While the earth remains, seedtime and harvest, cold and heat, summer and winter, and day and night shall not cease.

9 AND GOD pronounced a blessing upon Noah and his sons and said to them, Be fruitful and multiply and fill the earth.

²And the fear of you and the dread *and* terror of you shall be upon every beast of the land, every bird of the air, all that creeps upon the ground, and upon all the fish of the sea; they are delivered into your hand.

³Every moving thing that lives shall be food for you; and as I gave you the green vegetables *and* plants, I give you everything.

⁴But you shall not eat flesh with the life of it, which is its blood.

⁵And surely for your lifeblood I will require an accounting; from every beast I will require it; and from man, from every man [who spills another's lifeblood] I will require a reckoning.

⁶Whoever sheds man's blood, by man shall his blood be shed; for in the image of God He made man.

centuries. Nothing was lacking in Noah's ark to keep it from being suited for all that was required of it. The comfortable, light, well-ventilated, watertight, perfectly planned boat, large enough to accommodate all the original land animals intelligently and to permit the four human couples to live separately and in peace, needs no apology today. "In 1609 at Hoorn, in Holland, the Netherlandish Mennonite, P. Jansen, produced a vessel after the pattern of the ark, only smaller, whereby he proved it was well adapted for floating, and would carry a cargo greater by one-third than any other form of like cubical content" (J. P. Lange, *A Commentary*). It revolutionized shipbuilding. By 1900 every large vessel on the high seas was definitely inclined toward the proportions of Noah's ark (as verified by "Lloyd's Register of Shipping," *The World Almanac*). Later, ships were built longer for speed, a matter of no concern to Noah.

King James Version

7And you, be ye fruitful, and multiply; bring forth abundantly in the earth, and multiply therein.

8 ¶ And God spake unto Noah, and to his sons with him, saying,

9And I, behold I establish my covenant with you, and with your seed after you;

10And with every living creature that *is* with you, of the fowl, of the cattle, and of every beast of the earth with you; from all that go out of the ark, to every beast of the earth.

11And I will establish my covenant with you; neither shall all flesh be cut off any more by the waters of a flood; neither shall there any more be a flood to destroy the earth.

12And God said, This *is* the token of the covenant which I make between me and you and every living creature that *is* with you, for perpetual generations:

13I do set my bow in the cloud, and it shall be for a token of a covenant between me and the earth.

14And it shall come to pass, when I bring a cloud over the earth, that the bow shall be seen in the cloud:

15And I will remember my covenant, which *is* between me and you and every living creature of all flesh; and the waters shall no more become a flood to destroy all flesh.

16And the bow shall be in the cloud; and I will look upon it, that I may remember the everlasting covenant between God and every living creature of all flesh that *is* upon the earth.

17And God said unto Noah, This *is* the token of the covenant, which I have established between me and all flesh that *is* upon the earth.

18 ¶ And the sons of Noah, that went forth of the ark, were Shem, and Ham, and Japheth: and Ham *is* the father of Canaan.

19These *are* the three sons of Noah: and of them was the whole earth overspread.

20And Noah began *to be* a husbandman, and he planted a vineyard:

21And he drank of the wine, and was drunken; and he was uncovered within his tent.

22And Ham, the father of Canaan, saw the nakedness of his father, and told his two brethren without.

23And Shem and Japheth took a garment, and laid *it* upon both their shoulders, and went backward, and covered the nakedness of their father; and their faces *were* backward, and they saw not their father's nakedness.

24And Noah awoke from his wine, and knew what his younger son had done unto him.

Amplified Bible

7And you, be fruitful and multiply; bring forth abundantly on the earth and multiply on it.

8Then God spoke to Noah and to his sons with him, saying,

9Behold, I establish My covenant *or* pledge with you and with your descendants after you

10And with every living creature that is with you—whether the birds, the livestock, or the wild beasts of the earth along with you, as many as came out of the ark—every animal of the earth.

11I will establish My covenant *or* pledge with you: Never again shall all flesh be cut off by the waters of a flood; neither shall there ever again be a flood to destroy the earth *and* make it corrupt.

12And God said, This is the token of the covenant (solemn pledge) which I am making between Me and you and every living creature that is with you, for all future generations:

13I set My bow [rainbow] in the cloud, and it shall be a token *or* sign of a covenant *or* solemn pledge between Me and the earth.

14And it shall be that when I bring clouds over the earth and the bow [rainbow] is seen in the clouds,

15I will [earnestly] remember My covenant *or* solemn pledge which is between Me and you and every living creature of all flesh; and the waters will no more become a flood to destroy *and* make all flesh corrupt.

16When the bow [rainbow] is in the clouds and I look upon it, I will [earnestly] remember the everlasting covenant *or* pledge between God and every living creature of all flesh that is upon the earth.

17And God said to Noah, This [rainbow] is the token *or* sign of the covenant *or* solemn pledge which I have established between Me and all flesh upon the earth.

18The sons of Noah who went forth from the ark were Shem, Ham, and Japheth. Ham was the father of Canaan [born later].

19These are the three sons of Noah, and from them the whole earth was overspread *and* stocked with inhabitants.

20And Noah began to cultivate the ground, and he planted a vineyard.

21And he drank of the wine and became drunk, and he was uncovered *and* lay naked in his tent.

22And Ham, the father of Canaan, glanced at *and* saw the nakedness of his father and told his two brothers outside.

23So Shem and Japheth took a garment, laid it upon the shoulders of both, and went backward and covered the nakedness of their father; and their faces were backward, and they did not see their father's nakedness.

24When Noah awoke from his wine, and knew the thing which his youngest son had done to him,

King James Version

²⁵And he said, Cursed *be* Canaan; a servant of servants shall he be unto his brethren.

²⁶And he said, Blessed *be* the LORD God of Shem; and Canaan shall be his servant.

²⁷God shall enlarge Japheth, and he shall dwell in the tents of Shem; and Canaan shall be his servant.

²⁸And Noah lived after the flood three hundred and fifty years.

²⁹And all the days of Noah were nine hundred and fifty years: and he died.

10 Now these *are* the generations of the sons of Noah, Shem, Ham, and Japheth: and unto them were sons born after the flood.

²The sons of Japheth; Gomer, and Magog, and Madai, and Javan, and Tubal, and Meshech, and Tiras.

³And the sons of Gomer; Ashkenaz, and Riphath, and Togarmah.

⁴And the sons of Javan; Elishah, and Tarshish, Kittim, and Dodanim.

⁵By these were the isles of the Gentiles divided in their lands; every one after his tongue, after their families, in their nations.

⁶ ¶ And the sons of Ham; Cush, and Mizraim, and Phut, and Canaan.

⁷And the sons of Cush; Seba, and Havilah, and Sabtah, and Raamah, and Sabtecha: and the sons of Raamah; Sheba, and Dedan. *Let us rebell.*

⁸And Cush begat Nimrod: he began to be a mighty *one* in the earth.

⁹He was a mighty hunter before the LORD: wherefore it is said, *Even* as Nimrod the mighty hunter before the LORD.

¹⁰And the beginning of his kingdom was Babel, and Erech, and Accad, and Calneh, in the land of Shinar. *→ Iraq*

¹¹Out of that land went forth Asshur, and builded Nineveh, and the city Rehoboth, and Calah,

¹²And Resen between Nineveh and Calah: the same *is* a great city.

¹³And Mizraim begat Ludim, and Anamim, and Lehabim, and Naphtuhim,

¹⁴And Pathrusim, and Casluhim, (out of whom came Philistim) and Caphtorim.

¹⁵And Canaan begat Sidon his firstborn, and Heth,

¹⁶And the Jebusite, and the Amorite, and the Girgashite,

¹⁷And the Hivite, and the Arkite, and the Sinite,

¹⁸And the Arvadite, and the Zemarite, and the

Amplified Bible

²⁵He exclaimed, Cursed be Canaan! He shall be the ªservant of servants to his brethren!

²⁶He also said, Blessed be the Lord, the God of Shem! *And* blessed by the Lord my God be Shem! And let Canaan be his servant.

²⁷May God enlarge Japheth; and let him dwell in the tents of Shem, and let Canaan be his servant.

²⁸And Noah lived after the flood 350 years.

²⁹All the days of Noah were 950 years, and he died.

10 THIS IS the history of the generations (descendants) of the sons of Noah, Shem, Ham, and Japheth. The sons born to them after the flood *were:*

²The sons of Japheth: Gomer, Magog, Madai, Javan, Tubal, Meshech, and Tiras.

³The sons of Gomer: Ashkenaz, Riphath, and Togarmah.

⁴The sons of Javan: Elishah, Tarshish, Kittim, and Dodanim.

⁵From these the coastland peoples spread. [These are the sons of Japheth] in their lands, each with his own language, by their families within their nations.

⁶The sons of Ham: Cush, Egypt [Mizraim], Put, and Canaan.

⁷The sons of Cush: Seba, Havilah, Sabtah, Raamah, and Sabteca; and the sons of Raamah: Sheba and Dedan.

⁸Cush became the father of Nimrod; he was the first to be a mighty man on the earth.

⁹He was a mighty hunter before the Lord; therefore it is said, Like Nimrod, a mighty hunter before the Lord.

¹⁰The beginning of his kingdom was Babel, Erech, Accad, and Calneh, in the land of Shinar [in Babylonia].

¹¹Out of the land he [Nimrod] went forth into Assyria and built Nineveh, Rehoboth-Ir, Calah,

¹²And Resen, which is between Nineveh and Calah; all these [suburbs combined to form] the great city.

¹³And Egypt [Mizraim] became the father of Ludim, Anamim, Lehabim, Naphtuhim,

¹⁴Pathrusim, Casluhim (from whom came the Philistines), and Caphtorim.

¹⁵Canaan became the father of Sidon his firstborn, Heth [the Hittites],

¹⁶The Jebusites, the Amorites, the Girgashites,

¹⁷The Hivites, the Arkites, the Sinites,

¹⁸The Arvadites, the Zemarites and the

AMP notes: ª The language of Noah here is an actual prophecy and not merely an expression of personal feeling. That Noah placed a curse on his youngest grandchild, Canaan, who would naturally be his favorite, can only be explained on the ground that in the prophetic spirit he saw into the future of the Canaanites. God Himself found the delinquency of the Canaanites insufferable and ultimately drove them out or subdued them and put the descendants of Shem in their place. But Noah's foresight did not yet include the extermination of the Canaanite peoples, for then he would have expressed it differently. He would not merely have called them "the servant of servants" if he had foreseen their destruction. The form of the expression, therefore, testifies to the great age of the prophecy (J. P. Lange, *A Commentary*).

King James Version

Hamathite: and afterward were the families of the Canaanites spread abroad.

¹⁹And the border of the Canaanites was from Sidon, as thou comest to Gerar, unto Gaza; as thou goest unto Sodom, and Gomorrah, and Admah, and Zeboim, even unto Lasha.

²⁰These *are* the sons of Ham, after their families, after their tongues, in their countries, *and* in their nations.

²¹ ¶ Unto Shem also, the father of all the children of Eber, the brother of Japheth the elder, even to him were *children* born.

²²The children of Shem; Elam, and Asshur, and Arphaxad, and Lud, and Aram.

²³And the children of Aram; Uz, and Hul, and Gether, and Mash.

²⁴And Arphaxad begat Salah; and Salah begat Eber.

²⁵And unto Eber were born two sons: the name of one *was* Peleg; for in his days was the earth divided; and his brother's name *was* Joktan.

²⁶And Joktan begat Almodad, and Sheleph, and Hazarmaveth, and Jerah,

²⁷And Hadoram, and Uzal, and Diklah,

²⁸And Obal, and Abimael, and Sheba,

²⁹And Ophir, and Havilah, and Jobab: all these *were* the sons of Joktan.

³⁰And their dwelling was from Mesha, as thou goest unto Sephar, a mount of the east.

³¹These *are* the sons of Shem, after their families, after their tongues, in their lands, after their nations.

³²These *are* the families of the sons of Noah, after their generations, in their nations: and by these were the nations divided in the earth after the flood.

11 And the whole earth was *of* one language, and *of* one speech.

²And it came to pass, as they journeyed from the east, that they found a plain in the land of Shinar; and they dwelt there.

³And they said one to another, Go to, let us make brick, and burn *them* thoroughly. And they had brick for stone, and slime had they for morter.

⁴And they said, Go to, let us build us a city and a tower, whose top *may reach* unto heaven; and let us make us a name, lest we be scattered abroad upon the face of the whole earth.

⁵And the LORD came down to see the city and the tower, which the children of men builded.

⁶And the LORD said, Behold, the people *is* one, and they have all one language; and this

Amplified Bible

Hamathites. Afterward the families of the Canaanites spread abroad

¹⁹And the territory of the Canaanites extended from Sidon as one goes to Gerar as far as Gaza, and as one goes to ᵃSodom, Gomorrah, Admah, and Zeboiim, as far as Lasha.

²⁰These are the sons of Ham by their families, their languages, their lands, and their nations.

²¹To Shem also, the younger brother of Japheth and the ancestor of all the children of Eber [including the Hebrews], children were born.

²²The sons of Shem: Elam, Asshur, Arpachshad, Lud, and Aram.

²³The sons of Aram: Uz, Hul, Gether, and Mash.

²⁴Arpachshad became the father of Shelah; and Shelah became the father of Eber.

²⁵To Eber were born two sons: the name of one was Peleg [division], because [the inhabitants of] the earth were divided up in his days; and his brother's name was Joktan.

²⁶Joktan became the father of Almodad, Sheleph, Hazarmaveth, Jerah,

²⁷Hadoram, Uzal, Diklah,

²⁸Obal, Abimael, Sheba,

²⁹Ophir, Havilah, and Jobab; all these were the sons of Joktan.

³⁰The territory in which they lived extended from Mesha as one goes toward Sephar to the hill country of the east.

³¹These are Shem's descendants by their families, their languages, their lands, and their nations.

³²These are the families of the sons of Noah, according to their generations, within their nations; and from these the nations spread abroad on the earth after the flood.

11 AND THE whole earth was of one language and of one accent *and* mode of expression.

²And as they journeyed eastward, they found a plain (valley) in the land of Shinar, and they settled *and* dwelt there.

³And they said one to another, Come, let us make bricks and burn them thoroughly. So they had brick for stone, and slime (bitumen) for mortar.

⁴And they said, Come, let us build us a city and a tower whose top reaches into the sky, and let us make a name for ourselves, lest we be scattered over the whole earth.

⁵And the Lord came down to see the city and the tower which the sons of men had built.

⁶And the Lord said, Behold, they are one people and they have ᵇall one language; and this is

---

AMP notes: ᵃ Surely no greater proof is needed of the great antiquity of this portion of Genesis than the fact that it mentions as still standing these four cities of the plain, which were utterly destroyed in Abraham's time (Gen. 19:27-29; Deut. 29:23). ᵇ Some noted philologists have declared that a common origin of all languages cannot be denied. One, Max Mueller (*The Science of Language*), said "We have examined all possible forms which language can assume,

King James Version

they begin to do: and now nothing will be restrained from them, which they have imagined to do.

Angels

⁷Go to, let us go down, and there confound their language, that they may not understand one another's speech.

⁸So the LORD scattered them abroad from thence upon the face of all the earth: and they left off to build the city.

⁹Therefore is the name of it called Babel; because the LORD did there confound the language of all the earth: and from thence did the LORD scatter them abroad upon the face of all the earth.

¹⁰ ¶ These *are* the generations of Shem: Shem *was* an hundred years old, and begat Arphaxad two years after the flood:

¹¹And Shem lived after he begat Arphaxad five hundred years, and begat sons and daughters.

¹²And Arphaxad lived five and thirty years, and begat Salah:

¹³And Arphaxad lived after he begat Salah four hundred and three years, and begat sons and daughters.

¹⁴And Salah lived thirty years, and begat Eber:

¹⁵And Salah lived after he begat Eber four hundred and three years, and begat sons and daughters.

¹⁶And Eber lived four and thirty years, and begat Peleg:

¹⁷And Eber lived after he begat Peleg four hundred and thirty years, and begat sons and daughters.

¹⁸And Peleg lived thirty years, and begat Reu:

¹⁹And Peleg lived after he begat Reu two hundred and nine years, and begat sons and daughters.

²⁰And Reu lived two and thirty years, and begat Serug:

²¹And Reu lived after he begat Serug two hundred and seven years, and begat sons and daughters.

²²And Serug lived thirty years, and begat Nahor:

²³And Serug lived after he begat Nahor two hundred years, and begat sons and daughters.

²⁴And Nahor lived nine and twenty years, and begat Terah:

²⁵And Nahor lived after he begat Terah an hundred and nineteen years, and begat sons and daughters.

²⁶And Terah lived seventy years, and begat Abram, Nahor, and Haran.

Amplified Bible

only the beginning of what they will do, and now nothing they have imagined they can do will be impossible for them.

⁷Come, let Us go down and there confound (mix up, confuse) their language, that they may not understand one another's speech.

⁸So the Lord scattered them abroad from that place upon the face of the whole earth, and they gave up building the city.

⁹Therefore the name of it was called Babel—because there the Lord confounded the language of all the earth; and from that place the Lord scattered them abroad upon the face of the whole earth.

¹⁰This is the history of the generations of Shem. Shem was 100 years old when he became the father of Arpachshad, two years after the flood.

¹¹And Shem lived after Arpachshad was born 500 years and had other sons and daughters.

¹²When Arpachshad had lived 35 years, he became the father of Shelah.

¹³Arpachshad lived after Shelah was born 403 years and had other sons and daughters.

¹⁴When Shelah had lived 30 years, he became the father of Eber.

¹⁵Shelah lived after Eber was born 403 years and had other sons and daughters.

¹⁶When Eber had lived 34 years, he became the father of Peleg.

¹⁷And Eber lived after Peleg was born 430 years and had other sons and daughters.

¹⁸When Peleg had lived 30 years, he became the father of Reu.

¹⁹And Peleg lived after Reu was born 209 years and had other sons and daughters.

²⁰When Reu had lived 32 years, he became the father of Serug.

²¹And Reu lived after Serug was born 207 years and had other sons and daughters.

²²When Serug had lived 30 years, he became the father of Nahor.

²³And Serug lived after Nahor was born 200 years and had other sons and daughters.

²⁴When Nahor had lived 29 years, he became the father of Terah.

²⁵And Nahor lived after Terah was born 119 years and had other sons and daughters.

²⁶After Terah had lived 70 years, he became the father of [at different times], *ª*Abram and Nahor and Haran, [his firstborn].

---

and now we ask, can we reconcile with these three distinct forms, the radical, the terminational, the inflectional, the admission of one common origin of human speech? I answer decidedly, 'Yes'." *The New Bible Commentary* says, "The original unity of human language, though still far from demonstrable, becomes increasingly probable."   *ª* Abram is only mentioned first by way of dignity. Noah's sons also are given as "Shem, Ham, and Japheth" in Gen. 5:32, although Shem was not the oldest, but for dignity is named first, as is Abram here (Adam Clarke, *The Holy Bible with A Commentary*).

King James Version

27 ¶ Now these *are* the generations of Terah: Terah begat Abram, Nahor, and Haran; and Haran begat Lot.

28 And Haran died before his father Terah in the land of his nativity, in Ur of the Chaldees.

29 And Abram and Nahor took them wives: the name of Abram's wife *was* Sarai; and the name of Nahor's wife, Milcah, the daughter of Haran, the father of Milcah, and the father of Iscah.

30 But Sarai was barren; she had no child.

31 And Terah took Abram his son, and Lot the son of Haran his son's son, and Sarai his daughter in law, his son Abram's wife; and they went forth with them from Ur of the Chaldees, to go into the land of Canaan; and they came unto Haran, and dwelt there.

32 And the days of Terah were two hundred and five years: and Terah died in Haran.

12 Now the LORD had said unto Abram, Get thee out of thy country, and from thy kindred, and from thy father's house, unto a land that I will shew thee:

2 And I will make of thee a great nation, and I will bless thee, and make thy name great; and thou shalt be a blessing:

3 And I will bless them that bless thee, and curse him that curseth thee: and in thee shall all families of the earth be blessed. ➤Through Jesus Christ!

4 So Abram departed, as the LORD had spoken unto him; and Lot went with him: and Abram *was* seventy and five years old when he departed out of Haran.

5 And Abram took Sarai his wife, and Lot his brother's son, and all their substance that they had gathered, and the souls that they had gotten in Haran; and they went forth to go into the land of Canaan; and into the land of Canaan they came.

6 And Abram passed through the land unto the place of Sichem, unto the plain of Moreh. And the Canaanite *was* then in the land.

7 And the LORD appeared unto Abram, and

Amplified Bible

27 Now this is the history of the descendants of Terah. Terah was the father of Abram, Nahor, and Haran; and Haran was the father of Lot.

28 Haran died before his father Terah [died] in the land of his birth, in *a*Ur of the Chaldees.

29 And Abram and Nahor took wives. The name of Abram's wife was Sarai, and the name of Nahor's wife was Milcah, the daughter of Haran the father of Milcah and Iscah.

30 But Sarai was barren; she had no child.

31 And Terah took Abram his son, Lot the son of Haran, his grandson, and Sarai his daughter-in-law, his son Abram's wife, and they went forth together to go from Ur of the Chaldees into the land of Canaan; but when they came to Haran, they settled there.

32 And Terah lived 205 years; and Terah died in Haran.

12 NOW [in Haran] the Lord said to Abram, Go for yourself [for your own advantage] away from your country, from your relatives and your father's house, to the land that I will show you.

2 And I will make of you a great nation, and I will bless you [with abundant increase of favors] and make your name famous *and* distinguished, and you will be a blessing [dispensing good to others].

3 And I will bless those who bless you [who confer prosperity or happiness upon you] and *b*curse him who curses *or* uses insolent language toward you; in you will all the families *and* kindred of the earth be blessed [and by you they will bless themselves].

4 So Abram departed, as the Lord had directed him; and Lot [his nephew] went with him. Abram was seventy-five years old when he left Haran.

5 Abram took Sarai his wife, and Lot his brother's son, and all their possessions that they had gathered, and the persons [servants] that they had acquired in Haran, and they went forth to go to the land of Canaan. When they came to the land of Canaan,

6 Abram passed through the land to the locality of Shechem, to the oak *or* terebinth tree of Moreh. And the Canaanite was then in the land.

7 Then the Lord appeared to Abram and said, I

AMP notes: *a* Abram's home town was Ur of the Chaldees. As the result of extensive archaeological excavations there by C. Leonard Woolley in 1922-34, a great deal is known about Abram's background. Space will not permit more than a glimpse at excavated Ur, but a few items will show the high state of civilization. The entire house of the average middle-class person had from ten to twenty rooms and measured forty to fifty-two feet; the lower floor was for servants, the upper floor for the family, with five rooms for their use; additionally, there was a guest chamber and a lavatory reserved for visitors, and a private chapel. A school was found and what the students studied was shown by the clay tablets discovered there. In the days of Abram the pupils had reading, writing, and arithmetic as today. They learned the multiplication and division tables and even worked at square and cube root. A bill of lading of about 2040 B.C. (about the era in which Abram is believed to have lived) showed that the commerce of that time was far-reaching. Even the name "Abraham" has been found on the excavated clay tablets (J. P. Free, *Archaeology and Bible History*). *b* To look with disfavor on the Jews was to invite God's displeasure; to treat the Jews offensively was to incur His wrath. But to befriend the Jews was to bring down upon one's head the rewards of a promise that could not be broken.

King James Version

said, Unto thy seed will I give this land: and there builded he an altar unto the LORD, who appeared unto him.

⁸And he removed from thence unto a mountain on the east of Beth-el, and pitched his tent, *having* Beth-el on the west, and Hai on the east: and there he builded an altar unto the LORD, and called upon the name of the LORD.

⁹And Abram journeyed, going on still toward the south.

¹⁰ ¶ And there was a famine in the land: and Abram went down into Egypt to sojourn there; for the famine *was* grievous in the land.

¹¹And it came to pass, when he was come near to enter into Egypt, that he said unto Sarai his wife, Behold now, I know that thou *art* a fair woman to look upon:

¹²Therefore it shall come to pass, when the Egyptians shall see thee, that they shall say, This *is* his wife: and they will kill me, but they will save thee alive.

¹³Say, I pray thee, thou *art* my sister: that it may be well with me for thy sake; and my soul shall live because of thee.

¹⁴And it came to pass, that, when Abram was come into Egypt, the Egyptians beheld the woman that she *was* very fair.

¹⁵The princes also of Pharaoh saw her, and commended her before Pharaoh: and the woman was taken into Pharaoh's house.

¹⁶And he entreated Abram well for her sake: and he had sheep, and oxen, and he asses, and menservants, and maidservants, and she asses, and camels.

¹⁷And the LORD plagued Pharaoh and his house with great plagues because of Sarai Abram's wife.

¹⁸And Pharaoh called Abram, and said, What *is* this *that* thou hast done unto me? why didst thou not tell me that she *was* thy wife?

¹⁹Why saidst thou, She *is* my sister? so I might have taken her to me to wife: now therefore behold thy wife, take *her,* and go thy way.

²⁰And Pharaoh commanded *his* men concerning him: and they sent him away, and his wife, and all that he had.

13 And Abram went up out of Egypt, he, and his wife, and all that he had, and Lot with him, into the south.

Amplified Bible

will give this land to your posterity. So Abram built an altar there to the Lord, Who had appeared to him.

⁸From there he pulled up [his tent pegs] *and* departed to the mountain on the east of Bethel and pitched his tent, with Bethel on the west and Ai on the east; and there he built an altar to the Lord and called upon the name of the Lord.

⁹Abram journeyed on, still going toward the South (the Negeb).

¹⁰Now there was a famine in the land, and Abram ᵃwent down into Egypt to live temporarily, for the famine in the land was oppressive (intense and grievous).

¹¹And when he was about to enter into Egypt, he said to Sarai his wife, I know that you are beautiful to behold.

¹²So when the Egyptians see you, they will say, This is his wife; and they will kill me, but they will let you live.

¹³Say, I beg of you, that you are ᵇmy sister, so that it may go well with me for your sake and my life will be spared because of you.

¹⁴And when Abram came into Egypt, the Egyptians saw that the woman was very beautiful.

¹⁵The princes of Pharaoh also saw her and commended her to Pharaoh, and she was taken into Pharaoh's house [harem].

¹⁶And he treated Abram well for her sake; he acquired sheep, oxen, he-donkeys, menservants, maidservants, she-donkeys, and ᶜcamels.

¹⁷But the Lord scourged Pharaoh and his household with serious plagues because of Sarai, Abram's wife.

¹⁸And Pharaoh called Abram and said, What is this that you have done to me? Why did you not tell me that she was your wife?

¹⁹Why did you say, She is my sister, so that I took her to be my wife? Now then, here is your wife; take her and get away [from here]!

²⁰And Pharaoh commanded his men concerning him, and they brought him on his way with his wife and all that he had.

13 SO ABRAM went up out of Egypt, he and his wife and all that he had, and Lot with him, into the South [country of Judah, the Negeb].

AMP notes: ᵃ Some books on archaeology frequently allude to the critical view that strangers could not have come into Egypt in earlier times, quoting Strabo and Diodorus to that effect; but later archaeological discoveries show that people from the region of Palestine and Syria were coming to Egypt in the period of Abraham. This is clearly indicated by a tomb painting at Beni Hassan, dating a little after 2000 B.C. It shows Asiatic Semites who had come to Egypt. Furthermore, the archaeological and historical indications of the coming of the Hyksos into Egypt around 1900 B.C. provided another piece of evidence that strangers could come into that land (J. P. Free, *Abraham in Egypt*). ᵇ Sarai was Abraham's half sister. They had the same father, but different mothers (Gen. 20:12).   ᶜ Critics have set aside the statement that Abraham had camels in Egypt as an error. But archaeological evidence, including some twenty objects ranging from the seventh century B.C. to the period before 3000 B.C., proves the authenticity of the Bible record concerning Abraham. It includes not only statuettes, plaques, rock carvings, and drawings representing camels, but also "camel bones, a camel skull, and a camel hair rope" (J. P. Free, *Archaeology and Bible History*).

King James Version

2And Abram *was* very rich in cattle, in silver, and in gold.

3And he went on his journeys from the south even to Beth-el, unto the place where his tent had been at the beginning, between Beth-el and Hai;

4Unto the place of the altar, which he had made there at the first: and there Abram called on the name of the LORD.

5And Lot also, which went with Abram, had flocks, and herds, and tents.

6And the land was not able to bear them, that they might dwell together: for their substance was great, so that they could not dwell together.

7And there was a strife between the herdmen of Abram's cattle and the herdmen of Lot's cattle: and the Canaanite and the Perizzite dwelled then in the land.

8And Abram said unto Lot, Let there be no strife, I pray thee, between me and thee, and between my herdmen and thy herdmen; for we *be* brethren.

9*Is* not the whole land before thee? separate thyself, I pray thee, from me: if *thou wilt take* the left hand, then I will go to the right; or if *thou depart to* the right hand, then I will go to the left.

10And Lot lifted up his eyes, and beheld all the plain of Jordan, that it *was* well watered every where, before the LORD destroyed Sodom and Gomorrah, *even* as the garden of the LORD, like the land of Egypt, as thou comest unto Zoar.

11Then Lot chose him all the plain of Jordan; and Lot journeyed east: and they separated themselves the one from the other.

12Abram dwelled in the land of Canaan, and Lot dwelled in the cities of the plain, and pitched his tent toward Sodom.

13But the men of Sodom *were* wicked and sinners before the LORD exceedingly.

14 ¶ And the LORD said unto Abram, after that Lot was separated from him, Lift up now thine eyes, and look from the place where thou *art* northward, and southward, and eastward, and westward:

15For all the land which thou seest, to thee will I give it, and to thy seed for ever.

16And I will make thy seed as the dust of the earth: so that if a man can number the dust of the earth, *then* shall thy seed also be numbered.

17Arise, walk through the land in the length of it and in the breadth of it; for I will give it unto thee.

18Then Abram removed his tent, and came and dwelt in the plain of Mamre, which *is* in Hebron, and built there an altar unto the LORD.

14 And it came to pass in the days of Amraphel king of Shinar, Arioch king of Ellasar, Chedorlaomer king of Elam, and Tidal king of nations;

Amplified Bible

2Now Abram was extremely rich in livestock and in silver and in gold.

3And he journeyed on from the South [country of Judah, the Negeb] as far as Bethel, to the place where his tent had been at the beginning, between Bethel and Ai,

4Where he had built an altar at first; and there Abram called on the name of the Lord.

5But Lot, who went with Abram, also had flocks and herds and tents.

6Now the land was not able to nourish *and* support them so they could dwell together, for their possessions were too great for them to live together.

7And there was strife between the herdsmen of Abram's cattle and the herdsmen of Lot's cattle. And the Canaanite and the Perizzite were dwelling then in the land [making fodder more difficult to obtain].

8So Abram said to Lot, Let there be no strife, I beg of you, between you and me, or between your herdsmen and my herdsmen, for we are relatives.

9Is not the whole land before you? Separate yourself, I beg of you, from me. If you take the left hand, then I will go to the right; or if you choose the right hand, then I will go to the left.

10And Lot looked and saw that everywhere the Jordan Valley was well watered. Before the Lord destroyed Sodom and Gomorrah, [it was all] like the garden of the Lord, like the land of Egypt, as you go to Zoar.

11Then Lot chose for himself all the Jordan Valley and [he] traveled east. So they separated.

12Abram dwelt in the land of Canaan, and Lot dwelt in the cities of the [Jordan] Valley and moved his tent as far as Sodom *and* dwelt there.

13But the men of Sodom were wicked and exceedingly great sinners against the Lord.

14The Lord said to Abram after Lot had left him, Lift up now your eyes and look from the place where you are, northward and southward and eastward and westward;

15For all the land which you see I will give to you and to your posterity forever.

16And I will make your descendants like the dust of the earth, so that if a man could count the dust of the earth, then could your descendants also be counted.

17Arise, walk through the land, the length of it and the breadth of it, for I will give it to you.

18Then Abram moved his tent and came and dwelt among the oaks *or* terebinths of Mamre, which are at Hebron, and built there an altar to the Lord.

14 IN THE days of the kings Amraphel of Shinar, Arioch of Ellasar, Chedorlaomer of Elam, and Tidal of Goiim,

King James Version

²*That these* made war with Bera king of Sodom, and with Birsha king of Gomorrah, Shinab king of Admah, and Shemeber king of Zeboiim, and the king of Bela, which *is* Zoar.

³All these were joined together in the vale of Siddim, which *is* the salt sea.

⁴Twelve years they served Chedorlaomer, and *in* the thirteenth year they rebelled.

⁵And in the fourteenth year came Chedorlaomer, and the kings that *were* with him, and smote the Rephaims in Ashteroth Karnaim, and the Zuzims in Ham, and the Emims in Shaveh Kiriathaim,

⁶And the Horites in their mount Seir, unto El-paran, which *is* by the wilderness.

⁷And they returned, and came to En-mishpat, which *is* Kadesh, and smote all the country of the Amalekites, and also the Amorites, that dwelt in Hazezon-tamar.

⁸And there went out the king of Sodom, and the king of Gomorrah, and the king of Admah, and the king of Zeboiim, and the king of Bela (the same *is* Zoar); and they joined battle with them in the vale of Siddim;

⁹With Chedorlaomer the king of Elam, and *with* Tidal king of nations, and Amraphel king of Shinar, and Arioch king of Ellasar; four kings with five.

¹⁰And the vale of Siddim *was* full of slimepits; and the kings of Sodom and Gomorrah fled, and fell there; and they that remained fled to the mountain.

¹¹And they took all the goods of Sodom and Gomorrah, and all their victuals, and went their way.

¹²And they took Lot, Abram's brother's son, who dwelt in Sodom, and his goods, and departed.

¹³And there came one that had escaped, and told Abram the Hebrew; for he dwelt in the plain of Mamre the Amorite, brother of Eshcol, and brother of Aner: and these *were* confederate with Abram.

¹⁴And when Abram heard that his brother was taken captive, he armed his trained *servants,* born in his own house, three hundred and eighteen, and pursued *them* unto Dan.

¹⁵And he divided himself against them, he and his servants, by night, and smote them, and pursued them unto Hobah, which *is* on the left hand of Damascus.

¹⁶And he brought back all the goods, and also brought again his brother Lot, and his goods, and the women also, and the people.

¹⁷ ¶ And the king of Sodom went out to meet him after his return from the slaughter of Ched-

Amplified Bible

²They made war on the kings Bera of Sodom, Birsha of Gomorrah, Shinab of Admah, Shemeber of Zeboiim, and the king of Bela, ᵃthat is, Zoar.

³The latter kings joined together [as allies] in the Valley of Siddim, which is [now] the [Dead] Sea of Salt.

⁴Twelve years they had served Chedorlaomer, but in the thirteenth year they rebelled.

⁵And in the fourteenth year, Chedorlaomer and the kings who were with him attacked *and* subdued the Rephaim in Ashteroth-karnaim, the Zuzim in Ham, and the Emim in Shaveh-kiriathaim,

⁶And the Horites in their Mount Seir as far as El-paran, which is on the border of the wilderness.

⁷Then they turned back and came to En-mishpat, which [now] is Kadesh, and subdued all the country of the Amalekites, and also the Amorites who dwelt in Hazazon-tamar.

⁸Then the kings of Sodom, Gomorrah, Admah, Zeboiim, and Bela, that is, Zoar, went out and [together] they joined battle [with those kings] in the Valley of Siddim,

⁹With the kings Chedorlaomer of Elam, Tidal of Goiim, Amraphel of Shinar, and Arioch of El-lasar—four kings against five.

¹⁰Now the Valley of Siddim was full of slime *or* bitumen pits, and as the kings of Sodom and Gomorrah fled, they fell (were overthrown) there and the remainder [of the kings] fled to the mountain.

¹¹[The victors] took all the wealth of Sodom and Gomorrah and all the supply of provisions and departed.

¹²And they also took Lot, Abram's brother's son, who dwelt in Sodom, and his goods away with them.

¹³Then one who had escaped came and told Abram the Hebrew [one from the other side], who was living by the oaks *or* terebinths of Mamre the Amorite, a brother of Eshcol and of Aner—these were allies of Abram.

¹⁴When Abram heard that [his nephew] had been captured, he armed (led forth) the 318 trained servants born in his own house and pursued the enemy as far as Dan.

¹⁵He divided his forces against them by night, he and his servants, and attacked *and* routed them, and pursued them as far as Hobah, which is north of Damascus.

¹⁶And he brought back all the goods and also brought back his kinsman Lot and his possessions, the women also and the people.

¹⁷After his [Abram's] return from the defeat *and* slaying of Chedorlaomer and the kings who were with him, the king of Sodom went out to

AMP notes: ᵃ One of the notable proofs of the antiquity of the early sections of Genesis is that many of the original names of places about which they speak were so old that Moses, the writer, had to add an explanation in order to identify these ancient names so that the Israelites returning from Egypt might recognize them. Chapter 14 alone contains six such explanatory notes (Gen. 14:2, 3, 7, 8, 15, and 17).

King James Version

orlaomer, and of the kings that *were* with him, at the valley of Shaveh, which *is* the king's dale.

¹⁸And Melchizedek king of Salem brought forth bread and wine: and he *was* the priest of the most high God.

¹⁹And he blessed him, and said, Blessed *be* Abram of the most high God, possessor of heaven and earth:

²⁰And blessed *be* the most high God, which hath delivered thine enemies into thy hand. And he gave him tithes of all.

²¹And the king of Sodom said unto Abram, Give me the persons, and take the goods to thyself.

²²And Abram said to the king of Sodom, I have lift up mine hand unto the LORD, the most high God, the possessor of heaven and earth,

²³That I will not *take* from a thread even to a shoelatchet, and that I will not take any thing that *is* thine, lest thou shouldest say, I have made Abram rich:

²⁴Save only that which the young men have eaten, and the portion of the men which went with me, Aner, Eshcol, and Mamre; let them take their portion.

15 After these things the word of the LORD came unto Abram in a vision, saying, Fear not, Abram: I *am* thy shield, *and* thy exceeding great reward.

²And Abram said, Lord GOD, what wilt thou give me, seeing I go childless, and the steward of my house *is* this Eliezer of Damascus?

³And Abram said, Behold, to me thou hast given no seed: and lo, one born in my house is mine heir.

⁴And behold, the word of the LORD *came* unto him, saying, This shall not be thine heir; but he that shall come forth out of thine own bowels shall be thine heir.

⁵And he brought him forth abroad, and said, Look now towards heaven, and tell the stars, if thou be able to number them: and he said unto him, So shall thy seed be.

⁶And he believed in the LORD; and he counted it to him *for* righteousness.

⁷And he said unto him, I *am* the LORD that brought thee out of Ur of the Chaldees, to give thee this land to inherit it.

⁸And he said, Lord GOD, whereby shall I know that I shall inherit it?

Amplified Bible

meet him at the Valley of Shaveh, that is, the King's Valley.

¹⁸Melchizedek king of Salem [later called Jerusalem] brought out bread and wine [for their nourishment]; he was the priest of God Most High,

¹⁹And he blessed him and said, Blessed (favored with blessings, made blissful, joyful) be Abram by God Most High, Possessor *and* Maker of heaven and earth,

²⁰And blessed, praised, *and* glorified be God Most High, Who has given your foes into your hand! And [Abram] gave him a tenth of all [he had taken].

²¹And the king of Sodom said to Abram, Give me the persons and keep the goods for yourself.

²²But Abram said to the king of Sodom, I have lifted up my hand *and* sworn to the Lord, God Most High, the Possessor *and* Maker of heaven and earth,

²³That I would not take a thread or a shoelace or anything that is yours, lest you should say, I have made Abram rich.

²⁴[Take all] except only what my young men have eaten and the share of the men [allies] who went with me—Aner, Eshcol, and Mamre; let them take their portion.

15 AFTER THESE things, the word of the Lord came to Abram in a vision, saying, Fear not, Abram, I am your ᵃShield, your abundant compensation, *and* your reward shall be exceedingly great.

²And Abram said, Lord God, what can You give me, since I am going on [from this world] childless and he who shall be the owner *and* heir of my house is this [steward] Eliezer of Damascus?

³And Abram continued, Look, You have given me no child; and [a servant] born in my house is my heir.

⁴And behold, the word of the Lord came to him, saying, This man shall not be your heir, but he who shall come from your own body shall be your heir.

⁵And He brought him outside [his tent into the starlight] and said, Look now toward the heavens and count the stars—if you are able to number them. Then He said to him, So shall your descendants be.

⁶And he [Abram] believed in (trusted in, relied on, remained steadfast to) the Lord, and He counted it to him as righteousness (right standing with God).

⁷And He said to him, I am the [same] Lord, Who brought you out of Ur of the Chaldees to give you this land as an inheritance.

⁸But he [Abram] said, Lord God, by what shall I know that I shall inherit it?

AMP notes: ᵃ The reference is to the Lord as Abram's King.

King James Version

9And he said unto him, Take me a heifer of three years old, and a she goat of three years old, and a ram of three years old, and a turtledove, and a young pigeon.

10And he took unto him all these, and divided them in the midst, and laid each piece one against another: but the birds divided he not.

11And when the fowls came down upon the carcases, Abram drove them away.

12And when the sun was going down, a deep sleep fell upon Abram; and, lo, a horror of great darkness fell upon him.

13And he said unto Abram, Know of a surety that thy seed shall be a stranger in a land *that is* not theirs, and shall serve them; and they shall afflict them four hundred years; EGYPT

14And also that nation, whom they shall serve, will I judge: and afterward shall they come out with great substance.

15And thou shalt go to thy fathers in peace; thou shalt be buried in a good old age.

16But *in* the fourth generation they shall come hither again: for the iniquity of the Amorites *is* not yet full.

17And it came to pass, that, when the sun went down, and it was dark, behold a smoking furnace, and a burning lamp that passed between those pieces.

18In the same day the LORD made a covenant with Abram, saying, Unto thy seed have I given this land, from the river of Egypt unto the great river, the river Euphrates:

19The Kenites, and the Kenizzites, and the Kadmonites,

20And the Hittites, and the Perizzites, and the Rephaims,

21And the Amorites, and the Canaanites, and the Girgashites, and the Jebusites.

16 Now Sarai Abram's wife bare him no *children:* and she had a handmaid, an Egyptian, whose name *was* Hagar.

2And Sarai said unto Abram, Behold now, the LORD hath restrained me from bearing: I pray thee, go in unto my maid; it may be that I may obtain children by her. And Abram hearkened to the voice of Sarai.

3And Sarai Abram's wife took Hagar her maid the Egyptian, after Abram had dwelt ten years in the land of Canaan, and gave her to her husband Abram to be his wife.

4And he went in unto Hagar, and she con-

Amplified Bible

9And He said to him, Bring to Me a heifer three years old, a she-goat three years old, a ram three years old, a turtledove, and a young pigeon.

10And he brought Him all these and cut them down the middle [into halves] and laid each half opposite the other; but the birds he did not divide.

11And when the birds of prey swooped down upon the carcasses, Abram drove them away.

12When the sun was setting, a deep sleep overcame Abram, and a horror (a terror, a shuddering fear) of great darkness assailed *and* oppressed him.

13And [God] said to Abram, Know positively that your descendants will be strangers dwelling as temporary residents in a land that is not theirs [Egypt], and they will be slaves there and will be afflicted *and* oppressed for 400 years. [Fulfilled in Exod. 12:40.]

14But I will bring judgment on that nation whom they will serve, and afterward they will come out with great possessions.

15And you shall go to your fathers in peace; you shall be buried at a good old (hoary) age.

16And in the *a*fourth generation they [your descendants] shall come back here [to Canaan] again, for the iniquity of the *b*Amorites is not yet full *and* complete.

17When the sun had gone down and a [thick] darkness had come on, behold, a smoking oven and a flaming torch passed between those pieces.

18On the same day the Lord made a covenant (promise, pledge) with Abram, saying, To your descendants I have given this land, from the river of Egypt to the great river Euphrates—the land of

19The Kenites, the Kenizzites, the Kadmonites,

20The Hittites, the Perizzites, the Rephaim,

21The Amorites, the Canaanites, the Girgashites, and the Jebusites.

16 NOW SARAI, Abram's wife, had borne him no children. She had an Egyptian maid whose name was Hagar.

2And Sarai said to Abram, See here, the Lord has restrained me from bearing [children]. I am asking you to have intercourse with my maid; it may be that I can obtain children by her. And Abram listened to *and* heeded what Sarai said.

3So Sarai, Abram's wife, took Hagar her Egyptian maid, after Abram had dwelt ten years in the land of Canaan, and gave her to her husband Abram to be his [secondary] wife.

4And he had intercourse with Hagar, and she

AMP notes: *a* This prophecy was literally fulfilled. Moses, for example, who led the Israelites back to Canaan after their 400 years in Egypt, was "in the fourth generation" from Jacob—Levi, Kohath, Amram, Moses.   *b* The most important and powerful group of that region. The name "Amorite" later became virtually synonomous with that of the inhabitants of Canaan generally.

King James Version	Amplified Bible

ceived: and when she saw that she had conceived, her mistress was despised in her eyes.

5And Sarai said unto Abram, My wrong *be* upon thee: I have given my maid into thy bosom; and when she saw that she had conceived, I was despised in her eyes: the LORD judge between me and thee.

6But Abram said unto Sarai, Behold, thy maid *is* in thy hand; do to her as it pleaseth thee. And when Sarai dealt hardly with her, she fled from her face.

7And the angel of the LORD found her by a fountain of water in the wilderness, by the fountain in the way to Shur.

8And he said, Hagar, Sarai's maid, whence camest thou? and whither wilt thou go? And she said, I flee from the face of my mistress Sarai.

9And the angel of the LORD said unto her, Return to thy mistress, and submit thyself under her hands.

10And the angel of the LORD said unto her, I will multiply thy seed exceedingly, that it shall not be numbered for multitude.

11And the angel of the LORD said unto her, Behold, thou *art* with child, and shalt bear a son, and shalt call his name Ishmael; because the LORD hath heard thy affliction.

12And he will be a wild man; his hand *will be* against every man, and every man's hand against him; and he shall dwell in the presence of all his brethren.

13And she called the name of the LORD that spake unto her, Thou God seest me: for she said, Have I also here looked after him that seeth me?

14Wherefore the well was called Beer-lahai-roi; behold, *it is* between Kadesh and Bered.

15And Hagar bare Abram a son: and Abram

became pregnant; and when she saw that she was with child, she looked with contempt upon her mistress *and* despised her.

5Then Sarai said to Abram, May [the responsibility for] my wrong *and* deprivation of rights be upon you! I gave my maid into your bosom, and when she saw that she was with child, I was contemptible *and* despised in her eyes. May the Lord be the judge between you and me.

6But Abram said to Sarai, See here, your maid is in your hands *and* power; do as you please with her. And when Sarai dealt severely with her, humbling *and* afflicting her, she [Hagar] fled from her.

7But *a*the Angel of the Lord found her by a spring of water in the wilderness on the road to Shur.

8And He said, Hagar, Sarai's maid, where did you come from, and where are you intending to go? And she said, I am running away from my mistress Sarai.

9The Angel of the Lord said to her, Go back to your mistress and [humbly] submit to her control.

10Also the Angel of the Lord said to her, I will multiply your descendants exceedingly, so that they shall not be numbered for multitude.

11And the Angel of the Lord continued, See now, you are with child and shall bear a son, and shall call his name Ishmael [God hears], because the Lord has heard *and* paid attention to your affliction.

12And he [Ishmael] will be as a *b*wild ass among men; his hand will be against every man and every man's hand against him, and he will live to the east *and* on the borders of all his kinsmen.

13So she called the name of the Lord Who spoke to her, You are a God of seeing, for she said, Have I [not] even here [in the wilderness] looked upon Him Who sees me [and lived]? *Or* have I here also seen [the future purposes or designs of] Him Who sees me?

14Therefore the well was called Beer-lahai-roi [A well to the Living One Who sees me]; it is *c*between Kadesh and Bered.

15And Hagar bore Abram a son, and Abram

AMP notes: *a* "The Angel of the Lord" or "of God," or "of His presence" is readily identified with the Lord God (Gen. 16:11, 13; 22:11, 12; 31:11, 13; Exod. 3:1-6 and other passages). But it is obvious that the "Angel of the Lord" is a distinct person in Himself from God the Father (Gen. 24:7; Exod. 23:20; Zech. 1:12, 13 and other passages). Nor does the "Angel of the Lord" appear again after Christ came in human form. He must of necessity be One of the "three-in-one" Godhead. The "Angel of the Lord" is the visible Lord God of the Old Testament, as Jesus Christ is of the New Testament. Thus His deity is clearly portrayed in the Old Testament. *The Cambridge Bible* observes, "There is a fascinating forecast of the coming Messiah, breaking through the dimness with amazing consistency, at intervals from Genesis to Malachi. Abraham, Moses, the slave girl Hagar, the impoverished farmer Gideon, even the humble parents of Samson, had seen and talked with Him centuries before the herald angels proclaimed His birth in Bethlehem." *b* "Nothing can be more descriptive of the wandering, lawless, freebooting life of the Arabs than this. From the beginning to the present they have kept their independence, and God preserves them as a lasting monument of His providential care and an incontestable argument of the truth of divine revelation. Had the books of Moses no other proof of their divine origin, the account of Ishmael and the prophecy concerning his descendants during a period of nearly 4,000 years would be sufficient. To attempt to refute it would be a most ridiculous presumption and folly" (Adam Clarke, *The Holy Bible with A Commentary*). *c* This, "it is between Kadesh and Bered," is further proof of the antiquity of the original names, since the place had to be identified to the reader in the time of Moses.

King James Version

called his son's name, which Hagar bare, Ishmael.

¹⁶And Abram *was* fourscore and six years old, when Hagar bare Ishmael to Abram.

17 And when Abram was ninety years old and nine, the LORD appeared to Abram, and said unto him, I *am* the Almighty God; walk before me, and be thou perfect.

²And I will make my covenant between me and thee, and will multiply thee exceedingly.

³And Abram fell on his face: and God talked with him, saying,

⁴*As for* me, behold, my covenant *is* with thee, and thou shalt be a father of many nations.

⁵Neither shall thy name any more be called Abram, but thy name shall be Abraham; for a father of many nations have I made thee.

⁶And I will make thee exceeding fruitful, and I will make nations of thee, and kings shall come out of thee.

⁷And I will establish my covenant between me and thee and thy seed after thee in their generations for an everlasting covenant, to be a God unto thee, and to thy seed after thee.

⁸And I will give unto thee, and to thy seed after thee, the land wherein thou art a stranger, all the land of Canaan, for an everlasting possession; and I will be their God.

⁹And God said unto Abraham, Thou shalt keep my covenant therefore, thou, and thy seed after thee in their generations.

¹⁰This *is* my covenant, which ye shall keep, between me and you and thy seed after thee; Every man *child* among you shall be circumcised.

¹¹And ye shall circumcise the flesh of your foreskin; and it shall be a token of the covenant betwixt me and you.

¹²And he that is eight days old shall be circumcised among you, every man *child* in your generations, he that is born in the house, or bought with money of any stranger, which *is* not of thy seed.

¹³He that is born in thy house, and he that is bought with thy money, must needs be circumcised: and my covenant shall be in your flesh for an everlasting covenant.

¹⁴And the uncircumcised man *child* whose

Amplified Bible

called the name of his son whom Hagar bore *ᵃ*Ishmael.

¹⁶Abram was eighty-six years old when Hagar bore Ishmael.

17 WHEN ABRAM was ninety-nine years old, the Lord appeared to him and said, I am the Almighty God; walk *and* live habitually before Me and be perfect (blameless, wholehearted, complete).

²And I will make My covenant (solemn pledge) between Me and you and will multiply you exceedingly.

³Then Abram fell on his face, and God said to him,

⁴As for Me, behold, My covenant (solemn pledge) is with you, and you shall be the father of many nations.

⁵Nor shall your name any longer be Abram [high, exalted father]; but your name shall be Abraham [father of a multitude], for I have made you the father of many nations.

⁶And I will make you exceedingly fruitful and I will make nations of you, and *ᵇ*kings will come from you.

⁷And I will establish My covenant between Me and you and your descendants after you throughout their generations for an everlasting, solemn pledge, to be a God to you and to your posterity after you.

⁸And I will give to you and to your posterity after you the land in which you are a stranger [going from place to place], all the land of Canaan, for an everlasting possession; and I will be their God.

⁹And God said to Abraham, As for you, you shall therefore keep My covenant, you and your descendants after you throughout their generations.

¹⁰This is My covenant, which you shall keep, between Me and you and your posterity after you: Every male among you shall be circumcised.

¹¹And you shall circumcise the flesh of your foreskin; and it shall be a token *or* sign of the covenant (the promise or pledge) between Me and you.

¹²He who is eight days old among you shall be circumcised, every male throughout your generations, whether born in [your] house or bought with [your] money from any foreigner not of your offspring.

¹³He that is born in your house and he that is bought with your money must be circumcised; and My covenant shall be in your flesh for an everlasting covenant.

¹⁴And the male who is not circumcised, that

AMP notes: ᵃ Ishmael was the first person whom God named before his birth (Gen. 16:11). Others were: Isaac (Gen. 17:19); Josiah (I Kings 13:2); Solomon (I Chron. 22:9); Jesus (Matt. 1:21); and John the Baptist (Luke 1:13). *ᵇ* This prophecy and promise has been literally fulfilled countless times—for example, by all of the kings of Israel and Judah.

King James Version

flesh of his foreskin is not circumcised, that soul shall be cut off from his people; he hath broken my covenant.

15And God said unto Abraham, *As for* Sarai thy wife, thou shalt not call her name Sarai, but Sarah *shall* her name *be*.

16And I will bless her, and give thee a son also of her: yea, I will bless her, and she shall be *a mother* of nations; kings of people shall be of her.

17Then Abraham fell upon his face, and laughed, and said in his heart, Shall *a child* be born unto him that is an hundred years old? and shall Sarah, that is ninety years old, bear?

18And Abraham said unto God, O that Ishmael might live before thee!

19And God said, Sarah thy wife shall bear thee a son indeed; and thou shalt call his name Isaac: and I will establish my covenant with him for an everlasting covenant, *and* with his seed after him.

20And as for Ishmael, I have heard thee: Behold, I have blessed him, and will make him fruitful, and will multiply him exceedingly; twelve princes shall he beget, and I will make him a great nation.

21But my covenant will I establish with Isaac, which Sarah shall bear unto thee at this set time in the next year.

22And he left off talking with him, and God went up from Abraham.

23 ¶ And Abraham took Ishmael his son, and all that were born in his house, and all that were bought with his money, every male among the men of Abraham's house; and circumcised the flesh of their foreskin in the selfsame day, as God had said unto him.

24And Abraham *was* ninety years old and nine, when he was circumcised *in* the flesh of his foreskin.

25And Ishmael his son *was* thirteen years old, when he was circumcised in the flesh of his foreskin.

26In the selfsame day was Abraham circumcised, and Ishmael his son.

27And all the men of his house, born in the house, and bought with money of the stranger, were circumcised with him.

18 And the LORD appeared unto him in the plains of Mamre: and he sat *in* the tent door in the heat of the day;

2And he lift up his eyes and looked, and lo, three men stood by him: and when he saw *them,* he ran to meet them from the tent door, and bowed himself toward the ground,

3And said, My Lord, if now I have found favour in thy sight, pass not away, I pray thee, from thy servant:

4Let a little water, I pray you, be fetched, and

Amplified Bible

soul shall be cut off from his people; he has broken My covenant.

15And God said to Abraham, As for Sarai your wife, you shall not call her name Sarai; but Sarah [Princess] her name shall be.

16And I will bless her and give you a son also by her. Yes, I will bless her, and she shall be a mother of nations; kings of peoples shall come from her.

17Then Abraham fell on his face and laughed and said in his heart, Shall a child be born to a man who is a hundred years old? And shall Sarah, who is ninety years old, bear a son?

18And [he] said to God, Oh, that Ishmael might live before You!

19But God said, Sarah your wife shall bear you a son indeed, and you shall call his name Isaac [laughter]; and I will establish My covenant *or* solemn pledge with him for an everlasting covenant and with his posterity after him.

20And as for Ishmael, I have heard *and* heeded you: behold, I will bless him and will make him fruitful and will multiply him exceedingly; He will be the father of twelve princes, and I will make him a great nation. [Fulfilled in Gen. 25:12-18.]

21But My covenant, My promise and pledge, I will establish with Isaac, whom Sarah will bear to you at this season next year.

22And God stopped talking with him and went up from Abraham.

23And Abraham took Ishmael his son and all who were born in his house and all who were bought with his money, every male among [those] of Abraham's house, and circumcised [them] the very same day, as God had said to him.

24And Abraham was ninety-nine years old when he was circumcised.

25And Ishmael his son was thirteen years old when he was circumcised.

26On the very same day Abraham was circumcised, and Ishmael his son as well.

27And all the men of his house, both those born in the house and those bought with money from a foreigner, were circumcised along with him.

18 NOW THE Lord appeared to Abraham by the oaks *or* terebinths of Mamre; as he sat at the door of his tent in the heat of the day,

2He lifted up his eyes and looked, and behold, three men stood at a little distance from him. He ran from the tent door to meet them and bowed himself to the ground

3And said, My lord, if now I have found favor in your sight, do not pass by your servant, I beg of you.

4Let a little water be brought, and you may

King James Version

wash your feet, and rest yourselves under the tree:

⁵And I will fetch a morsel of bread, and comfort ye your hearts; after *that* you shall pass on: for therefore are ye come to your servant. And they said, So do, as thou hast said.

⁶And Abraham hastened into the tent unto Sarah, and said, Make ready quickly three measures of fine meal, knead *it*, and make cakes upon the hearth.

⁷And Abraham ran unto the herd, and fetcht a calf tender and good, and gave *it* unto a young man; and he hasted to dress it.

⁸And he took butter, and milk, and the calf which he had dressed, and set *it* before them; and he stood by them under the tree, and they did eat.

⁹And they said unto him, Where *is* Sarah thy wife? And he said, Behold, in the tent.

¹⁰And he said, I will certainly return unto thee according to the time of life; and lo, Sarah thy wife shall have a son. And Sarah heard *it in* the tent door, which *was* behind him.

¹¹Now Abraham and Sarah *were* old *and* well stricken in age; *and* it ceased to be with Sarah after the manner of women.

¹²Therefore Sarah laughed within herself, saying, After I am waxed old shall I have pleasure, my lord being old also?

¹³And the LORD said unto Abraham, Wherefore did Sarah laugh, saying, Shall I of a surety bear *a child,* which am old?

¹⁴Is any thing too hard for the LORD? At the time appointed I will return unto thee, according to the time of life, and Sarah shall have a son.

¹⁵Then Sarah denied, saying, I laughed not; for she was afraid. And he said, Nay; but thou didst laugh.

¹⁶ ¶ And the men rose up from thence, and looked toward Sodom: and Abraham went with them to bring them on the way.

¹⁷And the LORD said, Shall I hide from Abraham *that thing* which I do;

¹⁸Seeing that Abraham shall surely become a great and mighty nation, and all the nations of the earth shall be blessed in him?

¹⁹For I know him, that he will command his children and his household after him, and they shall keep the way of the LORD, to do justice and

Amplified Bible

wash your feet and recline *and* rest yourselves under the tree.

⁵And I will bring a morsel (mouthful) of bread to refresh *and* sustain your hearts before you go on further—for that is why you have come to your servant. And they replied, Do as you have said.

⁶So Abraham hastened into the tent to Sarah and said, Quickly get ready three measures of fine meal, knead it, and bake cakes.

⁷And Abraham ran to the herd and brought a calf tender and good and gave it to the young man [to butcher]; then he [Abraham] hastened to prepare it.

⁸And he took curds and milk and the calf which he had made ready, and set it before [the men]; and he stood by them under the tree while they ate.

⁹And they said to him, Where is Sarah your wife? And he said, [She is here] in the tent.

¹⁰ᵃ[The Lord] said, I will surely return to you when the season comes round, and behold, Sarah your wife will have a son. And Sarah was listening *and* heard it at the tent door which was behind Him.

¹¹Now Abraham and Sarah were old, well advanced in years; it had ceased to be with Sarah as with [young] women. [She was past the age of childbearing].

¹²Therefore Sarah laughed to herself, saying, After I have become aged shall I have pleasure *and* delight, my lord (husband), being old also?

¹³And the Lord asked Abraham, Why did Sarah laugh, saying, Shall I really bear a child when I am so old?

¹⁴Is anything too hard *or* too wonderful ᵇfor the Lord? At the appointed time, when the season [for her delivery] comes around, I will return to you and Sarah shall have borne a son.

¹⁵Then Sarah denied it, saying, I did not laugh; for she was afraid. And He said, No, but you did laugh.

¹⁶The men rose up from there and faced toward Sodom, and Abraham went with them to bring them on the way.

¹⁷And the Lord said, Shall I hide from Abraham [My friend and servant] what I am going to do,

¹⁸Since Abraham shall surely become a great and mighty nation, and all the nations of the earth shall be blessed through him *and* shall bless themselves by him?

¹⁹For I have known (chosen, acknowledged) him [as My own], so that he may teach *and* command his children and the sons of his house after him to keep the way of the Lord and to do

---

AMP notes: ᵃ One of the three guests was the Lord, and since God the Father was never seen in bodily form (John 1:18), only the "Angel of the covenant," Christ Himself, can be meant here; see especially Gen. 18:22 and also the footnote on Gen. 16:7. ᵇ The word "Lord" as applied to God is obviously the most important word in the Bible, for it occurs oftener than any other important word—by actual count more than 5,000 times. **Nothing** is "too hard *or* too wonderful" for Him when He is truly made Lord.

King James Version

judgment; that the LORD may bring upon Abraham that which he hath spoken of him.

²⁰And the LORD said, Because the cry of Sodom and Gomorrah is great, and because their sin is very grievous;

²¹I will go down now, and see whether they have done altogether according to the cry of it, which is come unto me; and if not, I will know.

²²And the men turned their faces from thence, and went toward Sodom: but Abraham stood yet before the LORD.

²³ ¶ And Abraham drew near, and said, Wilt thou also destroy the righteous with the wicked?

²⁴Peradventure there be fifty righteous within the city: wilt thou also destroy and not spare the place for the fifty righteous that *are* therein?

²⁵That be far from thee to do after this manner, to slay the righteous with the wicked: and that the righteous should be as the wicked, that be far from thee: Shall not the Judge of all the earth do right?

²⁶And the LORD said, If I find in Sodom fifty righteous within the city, then I will spare all the place for their sakes.

²⁷And Abraham answered and said, Behold now, I have taken upon me to speak unto the Lord, which *am but* dust and ashes:

²⁸Peradventure there shall lack five of the fifty righteous: wilt thou destroy all the city for *lack of* five? And he said, If I find there forty and five, I will not destroy *it.*

²⁹And he spake unto him yet again, and said, Peradventure there shall be forty found there. And he said, I will not do *it* for forty's sake.

³⁰And he said *unto him,* Oh let not the Lord be angry, and I will speak: Peradventure there shall thirty be found there. And he said, I will not do *it,* if I find thirty there.

³¹And he said, Behold now, I have taken upon me to speak unto the Lord: Peradventure there shall be twenty found there. And he said, I will not destroy *it* for twenty's sake.

³²And he said, Oh let not the Lord be angry, and I will speak yet but *this* once: Peradventure ten shall be found there. And he said, I will not destroy *it* for ten's sake.

³³And the LORD went his way, as soon as he had left communing with Abraham: and Abraham returned unto his place.

19 And there came two angels to Sodom at even; and Lot sat in the gate of Sodom: and Lot seeing *them* rose up to meet them; and he bowed himself with his face toward the ground;

Amplified Bible

what is just and righteous, so that the Lord may bring Abraham what He has promised him.

²⁰And the Lord said, Because the shriek [of the sins] of Sodom and Gomorrah is great and their sin is exceedingly grievous,

²¹I will go down now and see whether they have done altogether [as vilely and wickedly] as is the cry of it which has come to Me; and if not, I will know.

²²Now the [two] men turned from there and went toward Sodom, but Abraham still stood before the Lord.

²³And Abraham came close and said, Will You destroy the righteous (those upright and in right standing with God) together with the wicked?

²⁴Suppose there are in the city fifty righteous; will You destroy the place and not spare it for [the sake of] the fifty righteous in it?

²⁵Far be it from You to do such a thing—to slay the righteous with the wicked, so that the righteous fare as do the wicked! Far be it from You! Shall not the Judge of all the earth execute judgment *and* do righteously?

²⁶And the Lord said, If I find in the city of Sodom fifty righteous (upright and in right standing with God), I will spare the whole place for their sake.

²⁷Abraham answered, Behold now, I who am but dust and ashes have taken upon myself to speak to the Lord.

²⁸If five of the fifty righteous should be lacking—will You destroy the whole city for lack of five? He said, If I find forty-five, I will not destroy it.

²⁹And [Abraham] spoke to Him yet again, and said, Suppose [only] forty shall be found there. And He said, I will not do it for forty's sake.

³⁰Then [Abraham] said to Him, Oh, let not the Lord be angry, and I will speak [again]. Suppose [only] thirty shall be found there. And He answered, I will not do it if I find thirty there.

³¹And [Abraham] said, Behold now, I have taken upon myself to speak [again] to the Lord. Suppose [only] twenty shall be found there. And [the Lord] replied, I will not destroy it for twenty's sake.

³²And he said, Oh, let not the Lord be angry, and I will speak again only this once. Suppose ten [righteous people] shall be found there. And [the Lord] said, I will not destroy it for ten's sake.

³³And the Lord went His way when He had finished speaking with Abraham, and Abraham returned to his place.

19 IT WAS evening when the two angels came to Sodom. Lot was sitting at Sodom's [city] gate. Seeing them, Lot rose up to meet them and bowed to the ground.

King James Version

2And he said, Behold now, my lords, turn in, I pray you, into your servant's house, and tarry all night, and wash your feet, and ye shall rise up early, and go on your ways. And they said, Nay; but we will abide in the street all night.

3And he pressed upon them greatly; and they turned in unto him, and entered into his house; and he made them a feast, and did bake unleavened bread, and they did eat.

4But before they lay down, the men of the city, *even* the men of Sodom, compassed the house round, both old and young, all the people from every quarter:

5And they called unto Lot, and said unto him, Where *are* the men which came in to thee this night? bring them out unto us, that we may know them.

6And Lot went out at the door unto them, and shut the door after him,

7And said, I pray you, brethren, do not *so* wickedly.

8Behold now, I have two daughters which have not known man; let me, I pray you, bring them out unto you, and do ye to them as *is* good in your eyes: only unto these men do nothing; for therefore came they under the shadow of my roof.

9And they said, Stand back. And they said *again,* This one *fellow* came in to sojourn, and he will needs be a judge: now will we deal worse with thee, than with them. And they pressed sore upon the man, *even* Lot, and came near to break the door.

10But the men put forth their hand, and pulled Lot into the house to them, and shut to the door.

11And they smote the men that *were at* the door of the house with blindness, both small and great; so that they wearied themselves to find the door.

12And the men said unto Lot, Hast thou here any besides? son in law, and thy sons, and thy daughters, and whatsoever thou hast in the city, bring *them* out of *this* place:

13For we will destroy this place, because the cry of them is waxen great before the face of the LORD; and the LORD hath sent us to destroy it.

14And Lot went out, and spake unto his sons in law, which married his daughters, and said, Up, get ye out of this place; for the LORD will destroy this city. But he seemed as one that mocked unto his sons in law.

15And when the morning arose, then the angels hastened Lot, saying, Arise, take thy wife, and thy two daughters, which are here; lest thou be consumed in the iniquity of the city.

16And while he lingered, the men laid hold upon his hand, and upon the hand of his wife, and upon the hand of his two daughters; the

Amplified Bible

2And he said, My lords, turn aside, I beg of you, into your servant's house and spend the night and bathe your feet. Then you can arise early and go on your way. But they said, No, we will spend the night in the square.

3[Lot] entreated *and* urged them greatly until they yielded and [with him] entered his house. And he made them a dinner [with drinking] and had unleavened bread which he baked, and they ate.

4But before they lay down, the men of the city of Sodom, both young and old, all the men from every quarter, surrounded the house.

5And they called to Lot and said, Where are the men who came to you tonight? Bring them out to us, that we may know (be intimate with) them.

6And Lot went out of the door to the men and shut the door after him

7And said, I beg of you, my brothers, do not behave so wickedly.

8Look now, I have two daughters who are virgins; let me, I beg of you, bring them out to you, and you can do as you please with them. But only do nothing to these men, for they have come under the protection of my roof.

9But they said, Stand back! And they said, This fellow came in to live here temporarily, and now he presumes to be [our] judge! Now we will deal worse with you than with them. So they rushed at *and* pressed violently against Lot and came close to breaking down the door.

10But the men [the angels] reached out and pulled Lot into the house to them and shut the door after him.

11And they struck the men who were at the door of the house with blindness [which dazzled them], from the youths to the old men, so that they wearied themselves [groping] to find the door.

12And the [two] men asked Lot, Have you any others here—sons-in-law or your sons or your daughters? Whomever you have in the city, bring them out of this place,

13For we will spoil *and* destroy [Sodom]; for the outcry *and* shriek against its people has grown great before the Lord, and He has sent us to destroy it.

14And Lot went out and spoke to his sons-in-law, who were to marry his daughters, and said, Up, get out of this place, for the Lord will spoil *and* destroy this city! But he seemed to his sons-in-law to be [only] joking.

15When morning came, the angels urged Lot to hurry, saying, Arise, take your wife and two daughters who are here [and be off], lest you [too] be consumed *and* swept away in the iniquity *and* punishment of the city.

16But while he lingered, the men seized him and his wife and his two daughters by the hand,

King James Version

LORD being merciful unto him: and they brought him forth, and set him without the city.

17 And it came to pass, when they had brought them forth abroad, that he said, Escape for thy life; look not behind thee, neither stay thou in all the plain; escape to the mountain, lest thou be consumed.

18 And Lot said unto them, Oh, not so, my Lord:

19 Behold now, thy servant hath found grace in thy sight, and thou hast magnified thy mercy, which thou hast shewed unto me in saving my life; and I cannot escape to the mountain, lest some evil take me, and I die:

20 Behold now, this city is near to flee unto, and it is a little one: Oh, let me escape thither, (is it not a little one?) and my soul shall live.

21 And he said unto him, See, I have accepted thee concerning this thing, that I will not overthrow this city, for the which thou hast spoken.

22 Haste thee, escape thither; for I cannot do any thing till thou be come thither. Therefore the name of the city was called Zoar.

23 The sun was risen upon the earth when Lot entered into Zoar.

24 Then the LORD rained upon Sodom and upon Gomorrah brimstone and fire from the LORD out of heaven;

25 And he overthrew those cities, and all the plain, and all the inhabitants of the cities, and that which grew upon the ground.

26 But his wife looked back from behind him, and she became a pillar of salt.

27 And Abraham gat up early in the morning to the place where he stood before the LORD:

28 And he looked toward Sodom and Gomorrah, and toward all the land of the plain, and beheld, and lo, the smoke of the country went up as the smoke of a furnace.

29 And it came to pass, when God destroyed the cities of the plain, that God remembered Abraham, and sent Lot out of the midst of the overthrow, when he overthrew the cities in the which Lot dwelt.

30 ¶ And Lot went up out of Zoar, and dwelt in the mountain, and his two daughters with him;

Amplified Bible

for the Lord was merciful to him; and they brought him forth and set him outside the city and left him there.

17 And when they had brought them forth, they said, Escape for your life! Do not look behind you or stop anywhere in *a*the whole valley; escape to the mountains [of Moab], lest you be consumed.

18 And Lot said to them, Oh, not that, my lords!

19 Behold now, your servant has found favor in your sight, and you have magnified your kindness and mercy to me in saving my life; but I cannot escape to the mountains, lest the evil overtake me, and I die.

20 See now yonder city; it is near enough to flee to, and it is a little one. Oh, let me escape to it! Is it not a little one? And my life will be saved!

21 And [the angel] said to him, See, I have yielded to your entreaty concerning this thing also; I will not destroy this city of which you have spoken.

22 Make haste and take refuge there, for I cannot do anything until you arrive there. Therefore the name of the city was called Zoar [little].

23 The sun had risen over the earth when Lot entered Zoar.

24 Then the Lord rained on Sodom and on Gomorrah brimstone and fire from the Lord out of the heavens.

25 He overthrew, destroyed, and ended those cities, and all the valley and all the inhabitants of the cities, and what grew on the ground.

26 But [Lot's] wife looked back from behind him, and she *b*became a pillar of salt.

27 Abraham went up early the next morning to the place where he [only the day before] had stood before the Lord.

28 And he looked toward Sodom and Gomorrah, and toward all the land of the valley, and saw, and behold, the smoke of *c*the country went up like the smoke of a furnace.

29 When God ravaged and destroyed the cities of the plain [of Siddim], He [earnestly] remembered Abraham [imprinted and fixed him indelibly on His mind], and He sent Lot out of the midst of the overthrow when He overthrew the cities where Lot lived.

30 And Lot went up out of Zoar and dwelt in the mountain, and his two daughters with him,

---

AMP notes: *a* The valley which Lot had once so much coveted (Gen. 13:10, 11).   *b* Lot's wife not only "looked back" to where her heart's interests were, but she lingered behind; and probably overtaken by the fire and brimstone, her dead body became incrusted with salt, which, in that salt-packed area now the Dead Sea, grew larger with more incrustations—a veritable "pillar of salt." In fact, at the southern end of the Dead Sea there is a mountain of table salt called Jebel Usdum, "Mount of Sodom." It is about six miles long, three miles wide, and 1,000 feet high. It is covered with a crust of earth several feet thick, but the rest of the mountain is said to be solid salt (George T. B. Davis, *Rebuilding Palestine According to Prophecy*). Somewhere in this area Lot's wife looked back to where her treasures and her heart were, and "she became a pillar of salt." Jesus said, "Remember Lot's wife" (Luke 17:32).
c Not only were Sodom and Gomorrah blazing ruins, but also Admah and Zeboiim (Deut. 29:23; Hos. 11:8), as well as all the towns in the Valley of Siddim; Zoar was the lone exception.

King James Version

for he feared to dwell in Zoar: and he dwelt in a cave, he and his two daughters.

31And the firstborn said unto the younger, Our father *is* old, and *there is* not a man in the earth to come in unto us after the manner of all the earth:

32Come, let us make our father drink wine, and we will lie with him, that we may preserve seed of our father.

33And they made their father drink wine that night: and the firstborn went in, and lay with her father; and he perceived not when she lay down, nor when she arose.

34And it came to pass on the morrow, that the firstborn said unto the younger, Behold, I lay yesternight with my father: let us make him drink wine this night also; and go thou in, *and* lie with him, that we may preserve seed of our father.

35And they made their father drink wine that night also: and the younger arose, and lay with him; and he perceived not when she lay down, nor when she arose.

36Thus were both the daughters of Lot with child by their father.

37And the firstborn bare a son, and called his name Moab: the same *is* the father of the Moabites unto *this* day.

38And the younger, she also bare a son, and called his name Ben-ammi: the same *is* the father of the children of Ammon unto *this* day.

20 And Abraham journeyed from thence toward the south country, and dwelled between Kadesh and Shur, and sojourned in Gerar.

2And Abraham said of Sarah his wife, She *is* my sister: and Abimelech king of Gerar sent, and took Sarah.

3But God came to Abimelech in a dream by night, and said to him, Behold, thou *art but* a dead man, for the woman which thou hast taken; for she *is* a man's wife.

4But Abimelech had not come near her: and he said, Lord, wilt thou slay also a righteous nation?

5Said he not unto me, She *is* my sister? and she, even she herself said, He *is* my brother: in the integrity of my heart and innocency of my hands have I done this.

6And God said unto him in a dream, Yea, I know that thou didst this in the integrity of thy heart; for I also withheld thee from sinning against me: therefore suffered I thee not to touch her.

7Now therefore restore the man *his* wife; for

Amplified Bible

for he feared to dwell in Zoar; and he lived in a cave, he and his two daughters.

31The elder said to the younger, Our father is aging, and there is not a man on earth to live with us in the customary way.

32Come, let us make our father drunk with wine, and we will lie with him, so that we may preserve offspring (our race) through our father.

33And they made their father drunk with wine that night, and the older went in and lay with her father; and he was not aware of it when she lay down or when she arose.

34Then the next day the firstborn said to the younger, See here, I lay last night with my father; let us make him drunk with wine tonight also, and then you go in and lie with him, so that we may preserve offspring (our race) through our father.

35And they made their father drunk with wine again that night, and the younger arose and lay with him; and he was not aware of it when she lay down or when she arose.

36Thus both the daughters of Lot were with child by their father.

37The older bore a son, and named him Moab [of a father]; he is the father of the Moabites to this day.

38The younger also bore a son and named him Ben-ammi [son of my people]; he is the father of the Ammonites to this day.

20 NOW ABRAHAM journeyed from there toward the *a*South country (the Negeb) and dwelt between Kadesh and Shur; and he lived temporarily in Gerar.

2And Abraham said of Sarah his wife, She is my sister. And Abimelech king of Gerar sent and took Sarah [into his harem].

3But God came to Abimelech in a dream by night and said, Behold, you are a dead man because of the woman whom you have taken [as your own], for she is a man's wife.

4But Abimelech had not come near her, so he said, Lord, will you slay a people who are just *and* innocent?

5Did not the man tell me, She is my sister? And she herself said, He is my brother. In integrity of heart and innocency of hands I have done this.

6Then God said to him in the dream, Yes, I know you did this in the integrity of your heart, for it was I Who kept you back *and* spared you from sinning against Me; therefore I did not give you occasion to touch her.

7So now restore to the man his wife, for he is

AMP *notes:* *a* "Primitive geographic expressions such as 'the South country (the Negeb)' (Gen. 12:9; 13:1, 3; 20:1; 24:62) and 'the east country' (Gen. 25:6) are used in the time of Abraham . . . After the time of Genesis they have well-known and well-defined names; I submit that they were written down in early days, and that no writer after Moses could have used such archaic expressions as these" (P. J. Wiseman, *New Discoveries in Babylonia About Genesis*).

King James Version

he *is* a prophet, and he shall pray for thee, and thou shalt live: and if thou restore *her* not, know thou that thou shalt surely die, thou, and all that *are* thine.

⁸Therefore Abimelech rose early in the morning, and called all his servants, and told all these things in their ears: and the men were sore afraid.

⁹Then Abimelech called Abraham, and said unto him, What hast thou done unto us? and what have I offended thee, that thou hast brought on me and on my kingdom a great sin? thou hast done deeds unto me that ought not to be done.

¹⁰And Abimelech said unto Abraham, What sawest thou, that thou hast done this thing?

¹¹And Abraham said, Because I thought, Surely the fear of God *is* not in this place; and they will slay me for my wife's sake.

¹²And yet indeed *she is* my sister; she *is* the daughter of my father, but not the daughter of my mother; and she became my wife.

¹³And it came to pass, when God caused me to wander from my father's house, that I said unto her, This *is* thy kindness which thou shalt shew unto me; at every place whither we shall come, say of me, He *is* my brother.

¹⁴And Abimelech took sheep, and oxen, and menservants, and womenservants, and gave *them* unto Abraham, and restored him Sarah his wife.

¹⁵And Abimelech said, Behold, my land *is* before thee: dwell where it pleaseth thee.

¹⁶And unto Sarah he said, Behold, I have given thy brother a thousand *pieces* of silver: behold, he *is* to thee a covering of the eyes, unto all that *are* with thee, and with all *other:* thus she was reproved.

¹⁷So Abraham prayed unto God: and God healed Abimelech, and his wife, and his maidservants; and they bare *children.*

¹⁸For the LORD had fast closed up all the wombs of the house of Abimelech, because of Sarah Abraham's wife.

21 And the LORD visited Sarah as he had said, and the LORD did unto Sarah as he had spoken.

²For Sarah conceived, and bare Abraham a son in his old age, at the set time of which God had spoken to him.

³And Abraham called the name of his son that was born unto him, whom Sarah bare to him, Isaac.

⁴And Abraham circumcised his son Isaac being eight days old, as God had commanded him.

⁵And Abraham *was* an hundred years old, when his son Isaac was born unto him.

Amplified Bible

a prophet, and he will pray for you and you will live. But if you do not restore her [to him], know that you shall surely die, you and all who are yours.

⁸So Abimelech rose early in the morning and called all his servants and told them all these things; and the men were exceedingly filled with reverence *and* fear.

⁹Then Abimelech called Abraham and said to him, What have you done to us? And how have I offended you that you have brought on me and my kingdom a great sin? You have done to me what ought not to be done [to anyone].

¹⁰And Abimelech said to Abraham, What did you see [in us] that [justified] you in doing such a thing as this?

¹¹And Abraham said, Because I thought, Surely there is no reverence *or* fear of God at all in this place, and they will slay me because of my wife.

¹²But truly, she is my sister; she is the daughter of my father but not of my mother; and she became my wife.

¹³When God caused me to wander from my father's house, I said to her, This kindness you can show me: at every place we stop, say of me, He is my brother.

¹⁴Then Abimelech took sheep and oxen and male and female slaves and gave them to Abraham and restored to him Sarah his wife.

¹⁵And Abimelech said, Behold, my land is before you; dwell wherever it pleases you.

¹⁶And to Sarah he said, Behold, I have given this brother of yours a thousand pieces of silver; see, it is to compensate you [for all that has occurred] and to vindicate your honor before all who are with you; before all men you are cleared *and* compensated.

¹⁷So Abraham prayed to God, and God healed Abimelech and his wife and his female slaves, and they bore children,

¹⁸For the Lord had closed fast the wombs of all in Abimelech's household because of Sarah, Abraham's wife.

21 THE LORD visited Sarah as He had said, and the Lord did for her as He had promised.

²For Sarah became pregnant and bore Abraham a son in his old age, at the set time God had told him.

³Abraham ᵃnamed his son whom Sarah bore to him Isaac [laughter].

⁴And Abraham circumcised his son Isaac when he was eight days old, as God had commanded him.

⁵Abraham was a hundred years old when Isaac was born.

AMP notes: ᵃ See footnote on Gen. 16:15.

King James Version

⁶And Sarah said, God hath made me to laugh, *so that* all that hear will laugh with me.

⁷And she said, Who would have said unto Abraham, that Sarah should have given children suck? for I have born *him* a son in his old age.

⁸And the child grew, and was weaned: and Abraham made a great feast the *same* day that Isaac was weaned.

⁹And Sarah saw the son of Hagar the Egyptian, which she had born unto Abraham, mocking.

¹⁰Wherefore she said unto Abraham, Cast out this bondwoman and her son: for the son of this bondwoman shall not be heir with my son, *even* with Isaac.

¹¹And the thing was very grievous in Abraham's sight because of his son.

¹²And God said unto Abraham, Let it not be grievous in thy sight because of the lad, and because of thy bondwoman; in all that Sarah hath said unto thee, hearken unto her voice; for in Isaac shall thy seed be called.

¹³And also of the son of the bondwoman will I make a nation, because he *is* thy seed.

¹⁴And Abraham rose up early in the morning, and took bread, and a bottle of water, and gave *it* unto Hagar, putting *it* on her shoulder, and the child, and sent her away: and she departed, and wandered in the wilderness of Beer-sheba.

¹⁵And the water was spent in the bottle, and she cast the child under one of the shrubs.

¹⁶And she went, and sat her down over against *him* a good way off, as it were a bowshot: for she said, Let me not see the death of the child. And she sat over against *him,* and lift up her voice, and wept.

¹⁷And God heard the voice of the lad; and the angel of God called to Hagar out of heaven, and said unto her, What aileth thee, Hagar? fear not; for God hath heard the voice of the lad where he *is.*

¹⁸Arise, lift up the lad, and hold him in thine hand; for I will make him a great nation.

¹⁹And God opened her eyes, and she saw a well of water; and she went, and filled the bottle *with* water, and gave the lad drink.

²⁰And God was with the lad; and he grew, and dwelt in the wilderness, and became an archer.

Amplified Bible

⁶And Sarah said, God has made me to laugh; all who hear will laugh with me.

⁷And she said, Who would have said to Abraham that Sarah would nurse children at the breast? For I have borne him a son in his old age!

⁸And the child grew and was ᵃweaned, and Abraham made a great feast the same day that Isaac was weaned.

⁹Now Sarah saw the son of Hagar the Egyptian, whom she had borne to Abraham, mocking [Isaac].

¹⁰Therefore she said to Abraham, Cast out this bondwoman and her son, for the son of this bondwoman shall not be an heir with my son Isaac.

¹¹And the thing was very grievous (serious, evil) in Abraham's sight on account of his son [Ishmael].

¹²God said to Abraham, Do not let it seem grievous *and* evil to you because of the youth and your bondwoman; in all that Sarah has said to you, do what she asks, for in Isaac shall your posterity be called.

¹³And I will make a nation of the son of the bondwoman also, because he is your offspring.

¹⁴So Abraham rose early in the morning and took bread and a bottle of water and gave them to Hagar, putting them on her shoulders, and he sent her and the ᵇyouth away. And she wandered on [aimlessly] and lost her way in the wilderness of Beersheba.

¹⁵When the water in the bottle was all gone, Hagar caused the youth to lie down under one of the shrubs.

¹⁶Then she went and sat down opposite him a good way off, about a bowshot, for she said, Let me not see the death of the lad. And as she sat down opposite him, ᶜhe lifted up his voice and wept *and* she raised her voice and wept.

¹⁷And God heard the voice of the youth, and the angel of God called to Hagar out of heaven and said to her, What troubles you, Hagar? Fear not, for God has heard the voice of the youth where he is.

¹⁸Arise, raise up the youth and support him with your hand, for I intend to make him a great nation.

¹⁹Then God opened her eyes and she saw a well of water; and she went and filled the [empty] bottle with water and caused the youth to drink.

²⁰And God was with the youth, and he developed; and he dwelt in the wilderness and became an archer.

AMP notes: ᵃ This was probably when the child was about three years of age. Samuel served in the sanctuary from the time that he was weaned (I Sam. 1:22-28). A Hebrew mother is quoted in II Maccabees 7:27 as saying to her son that she gave him "suck three years." ᵇ Ishmael was born when Abraham was eighty-six years old (Gen. 16:16), so Ishmael was fourteen when Isaac was born. Isaac was weaned (Gen. 21:8) at least three years later probably (II Chron. 31:16; II Maccabees 7:27). ᶜ The Hebrew says, "she lifted up her voice." *The Septuagint* (Greek translation of the Old Testament) says "he . . ."—which the next verse seems to support. The circumstances allow either.

King James Version

²¹And he dwelt in the wilderness of Paran: and his mother took him a wife out of the land of Egypt.

²² ¶ And it came to pass at that time, that Abimelech and Phichol the chief captain of his host spake unto Abraham, saying, God *is* with thee in all that thou doest:

²³Now therefore swear unto me here by God that thou wilt not deal falsely with me, nor with my son, nor with my son's son: *but* according to the kindness that I have done unto thee, thou shalt do unto me, and to the land wherein thou hast sojourned.

²⁴And Abraham said, I will swear.

²⁵And Abraham reproved Abimelech because of a well of water, which Abimelech's servants had violently taken away.

²⁶And Abimelech said, I wot not who hath done this thing: neither didst thou tell me, neither yet heard I *of it*, but to day.

²⁷And Abraham took sheep and oxen, and gave *them* unto Abimelech; and both of them made a covenant.

²⁸And Abraham set seven ewe lambs of the flock by themselves.

²⁹And Abimelech said unto Abraham, What *mean* these seven ewe lambs which thou hast set by themselves?

³⁰And he said, For *these* seven ewe lambs shalt thou take of my hand, that they may be a witness unto me, that I have digged this well.

³¹Wherefore he called that place Beer-sheba; because there they sware both of them.

³²Thus they made a covenant at Beer-sheba: then Abimelech rose up, and Phichol the chief captain of his host, and they returned into the land of the Philistines.

³³And *Abraham* planted a grove in Beer-sheba, and called there on the name of the LORD, the everlasting God.

³⁴And Abraham sojourned in the Philistines' land many days.

22 And it came to pass after these things, that God did tempt Abraham, and said unto him, Abraham: and he said, Behold, *here* I *am*.

²And he said, Take now thy son, thine only *son* Isaac, whom thou lovest, and get thee into the land of Moriah; and offer him there for a burnt offering upon one of the mountains which I will tell thee of.

³And Abraham rose up early in the morning, and saddled his ass, and took two of his young men with him, and Isaac his son, and clave the wood for the burnt offering, and rose up, and went unto the place of which God had told him.

⁴Then on the third day Abraham lift up his eyes, and saw the place afar off.

⁵And Abraham said unto his young men, Abide you here with the ass; and I and the lad

Amplified Bible

²¹He dwelt in the Wilderness of Paran; and his mother took a wife for him out of the land of Egypt.

²²At that time Abimelech and Phicol the commander of his army said to Abraham, God is with you in everything you do.

²³So now, swear to me here by God that you will not deal falsely with me or with my son or with my posterity; but as I have dealt with you kindly, you will do the same with me and with the land in which you have sojourned.

²⁴And Abraham said, I will swear.

²⁵When Abraham complained to *and* reasoned with Abimelech about a well of water [Abimelech's] servants had violently seized,

²⁶Abimelech said, I know not who did this thing; you did not tell me, and I did not hear of it until today.

²⁷So Abraham took sheep and oxen and gave them to Abimelech, and the two men made a league *or* covenant.

²⁸Abraham set apart seven ewe lambs of the flock,

²⁹And Abimelech said to Abraham, What do these seven ewe lambs which you have set apart mean?

³⁰He said, You are to accept these seven ewe lambs from me as a witness for me that I dug this well.

³¹Therefore that place was called Beersheba [well of the oath], because there both parties swore an oath.

³²Thus they made a covenant at Beersheba; then Abimelech and Phicol the commander of his army returned to the land of the Philistines.

³³Abraham planted a tamarisk tree in Beersheba and called there on the name of the Lord, the Eternal God.

³⁴And Abraham sojourned in Philistia many days.

22 AFTER THESE events, God tested *and* proved Abraham and said to him, Abraham! And he said, Here I am.

²[God] said, Take now your son, your only son Isaac, whom you love, and go to the region of Moriah; and offer him there as a burnt offering upon one of the mountains of which I will tell you.

³So Abraham rose early in the morning, saddled his donkey, and took two of his young men with him and his son Isaac; and he split the wood for the burnt offering, and then began the trip to the place of which God had told him.

⁴On the third day Abraham looked up and saw the place in the distance.

⁵And Abraham said to his servants, Settle down *and* stay here with the donkey, and I and

King James Version

will go yonder and worship, and come again to you.

⁶And Abraham took the wood of the burnt offering, and laid *it* upon Isaac his son; and he took the fire in his hand, and a knife; and they went both of them together.

⁷And Isaac spake unto Abraham his father, and said, My father: and he said, Here *am* I, my son. And he said, Behold the fire and the wood: but where *is* the lamb for a burnt offering?

⁸And Abraham said, My son, God will provide himself a lamb for a burnt offering: so they went both of them together.

⁹And they came to the place which God had told him of; and Abraham built an altar there, and laid the wood in order, and bound Isaac his son, and laid him on the altar upon the wood.

¹⁰And Abraham stretched forth his hand, and took the knife to slay his son.

¹¹And the angel of the LORD called unto him out of heaven, and said, Abraham, Abraham: and he said, Here *am* I.

¹²And he said, Lay not thine hand upon the lad, neither do thou any thing unto him: for now I know that thou fearest God, seeing thou hast not withheld thy son, thine only *son* from me.

¹³And Abraham lifted up his eyes, and looked, and behold behind *him* a ram caught in a thicket by his horns: and Abraham went and took the ram, and offered him up for a burnt offering in the stead of his son.

¹⁴And Abraham called the name of that place Jehovah-jireh: as it is said *to this* day, In the mount of the LORD it shall be seen.

¹⁵And the angel of the LORD called unto Abraham out of heaven the second time,

¹⁶And said, By myself have I sworn, saith the LORD, for because thou hast done this thing, and hast not withheld thy son, thine only *son:*

¹⁷That in blessing I will bless thee, and in multiplying I will multiply thy seed as the stars of the heaven, and as the sand which *is* upon the sea shore; and thy seed shall possess the gate of his enemies;

¹⁸And in thy seed shall all the nations of the

Amplified Bible

the young man will go yonder and worship and ᵃcome again to you.

⁶Then Abraham took the wood for the burnt offering and laid it on [the shoulders of] Isaac his son, and he took the fire (the firepot) in his own hand, and a knife; and the two of them went on together.

⁷And Isaac said to Abraham, My father! And he said, Here I am, my son. [Isaac] said, See, here are the fire and the wood, but where is the lamb for the burnt sacrifice?

⁸Abraham said, My son, ᵇGod Himself will provide a lamb for the burnt offering. So the two went on together.

⁹When they came to the place of which God had told him, Abraham built an altar there; then he laid the wood in order and ᶜbound Isaac his son and laid him on the altar on the wood.

¹⁰And Abraham stretched forth his hand and took hold of the knife to slay his son.

¹¹But the ᵈAngel of the Lord called to him from heaven and said, Abraham, Abraham! He answered, Here I am.

¹²And He said, Do not lay your hand on the lad or do anything to him; for now I know that you fear *and* revere God, since you have not held back from Me *or* begrudged giving Me your son, your only son.

¹³Then Abraham looked up *and* glanced around, and behold, behind him was a ram caught in a thicket by his horns. And Abraham went and took the ram and offered it up for a burnt offering *and* an ascending sacrifice instead of his son!

¹⁴So Abraham called the name of that place The Lord Will Provide. And it is said to this day, On the mount of the Lord it will be provided.

¹⁵The Angel of the Lord called to Abraham from heaven a second time

¹⁶And said, I have sworn by Myself, says the Lord, that since you have done this and have not withheld [from Me] *or* begrudged [giving Me] your son, your only son,

¹⁷In blessing I will bless you and in multiplying I will multiply your descendants like the stars of the heavens and like the sand on the seashore. And your Seed (Heir) will possess the gate of His enemies,

¹⁸And in your Seed [ᵉChrist] shall all the nations of the earth be blessed *and* [by Him] bless

AMP notes: ᵃ Abraham was not lying to his servants or trying to deceive them. He believed God, Who had promised him that this young man's posterity was to inherit the promises made to Abraham (Gen. 12:2, 3). ᵇ We must not suppose that this was the language merely of faith and obedience. Abraham spoke prophetically, and referred to that Lamb of God which He had provided for Himself, Who in the fullness of time would take away the sin of the world, and of Whom Isaac was a most expressive type (Adam Clarke, *The Holy Bible with A Commentary*). For Abraham was a prophet (Gen. 20:7). Jesus said Abraham hoped for "My day [My incarnation]; and he did see it and was delighted" (John 8:56). ᶜ Isaac, who was perhaps twenty-five years old (according to the ancient historian Josephus), shared his father's confidence in God's promise. Was not his very existence the result of God keeping His word? (Gen. 17:15-17.) ᵈ See footnote on Gen. 16:7. ᵉ We have the authority of the apostle Paul (Gal. 3:8, 16, 18) to restrict this promise to our blessed Lord, Who was the Seed through Whom alone all God's blessings of providence, mercy, grace, and glory should be conveyed to the nations of the earth (Adam Clarke, *The Holy Bible with A Commentary*).

King James Version

earth be blessed; because thou hast obeyed my voice.

¹⁹So Abraham returned unto his young men, and they rose up and went together to Beer-sheba; and Abraham dwelt at Beer-sheba.

²⁰ ¶ And it came to pass after these things, that it was told Abraham, saying, Behold, Milcah, she hath also born children unto thy brother Nahor;

²¹Huz his firstborn, and Buz his brother, and Kemuel the father of Aram,

²²And Chesed, and Hazo, and Pildash, and Jidlaph, and Bethuel.

²³And Bethuel begat Rebekah: these eight Milcah did bear to Nahor, Abraham's brother.

²⁴And his concubine, whose name *was* Reumah, she bare also Tebah, and Gaham, and Thahash, and Maachah.

23 And Sarah was an hundred and seven and twenty years old: *these were* the years of the life of Sarah.

²And Sarah died in Kirjath-arba; the same *is* Hebron in the land of Canaan: and Abraham came to mourn for Sarah, and to weep for her.

³And Abraham stood up from before his dead, and spake unto the sons of Heth, saying,

⁴I *am* a stranger and a sojourner with you: give me a possession of a buryingplace with you, that I may bury my dead out of my sight.

⁵And the children of Heth answered Abraham, saying unto him,

⁶Hear us, my lord: thou *art* a mighty prince among us: in the choice of our sepulchres bury thy dead; none of us shall withhold from thee his sepulchre, but that thou mayest bury thy dead.

⁷And Abraham stood up, and bowed himself to the people of the land, *even* to the children of Heth.

⁸And he communed with them, saying, If it be your mind that I should bury my dead out of my sight; hear me, and intreat for me to Ephron the son of Zohar,

⁹That he may give me the cave of Machpelah, which he hath, which *is* in the end of his field; for as much money as it is worth he shall give it me for a possession of a buryingplace amongst you.

¹⁰And Ephron dwelt amongst the children of Heth: and Ephron the Hittite answered Abraham in the audience of the children of Heth, *even* of all that went in at the gate of his city, saying,

¹¹Nay, my lord, hear me: the field give I thee,

Amplified Bible

themselves, because you have heard *and* obeyed My voice.

¹⁹So Abraham returned to his servants, and they rose up and went with him to Beersheba; there Abraham lived.

²⁰Now after these things, it was told Abraham, Milcah has also borne children to your brother Nahor:

²¹Uz the firstborn, Buz his brother, Kemuel the father of Aram,

²²Chesed, Hazo, Pildash, Jidlaph, and Bethuel.

²³Bethuel became the father of Rebekah. These eight Milcah bore to Nahor, Abraham's brother.

²⁴And his concubine, whose name was Reumah, bore Tebah, Gaham, Tahash, and Maacah.

23 SARAH LIVED 127 years; this was the length of the life of Sarah.

²And Sarah died in Kiriath-arba, *ᵃ*that is, Hebron, in the land of Canaan. And Abraham went to mourn for Sarah and to weep for her.

³And Abraham stood up from before his dead and said to the sons of Heth,

⁴I am a stranger and a sojourner with you; give me property for a burial place among you, that I may bury my dead out of my sight.

⁵And the Hittites replied to Abraham,

⁶Listen to us, my lord; you are a mighty prince among us. Bury your dead in any tomb *or* grave of ours that you choose; none of us will withhold from you his tomb or hinder you from burying your dead.

⁷And Abraham stood up and bowed himself to the people of the land, the Hittites.

⁸And he said to them, If you are willing to grant my dead a burial out of my sight, listen to me and ask Ephron son of Zohar for me,

⁹That he may give me the cave of Machpelah, which he owns—it is at the end of his field. For the full price let him give it to me here in your presence as a burial place to which I may hold fast among you.

¹⁰Now Ephron was present there among the sons of Heth; so, in the hearing of all who went in at the gate of his city, Ephron the Hittite answered Abraham, saying,

¹¹No, my lord, hear me; I give you the field,

AMP notes: ᵃ Surely this indicates that this detail was written at a very early date—before Israel had entered the land. No one in later times would need to be told where Hebron was. Not only was it conspicuous in Joshua's and Caleb's day, but it became a "city of refuge." Besides all this, David was king in Hebron for seven years. Obviously the Israelites had not yet entered Canaan and had to be told not only the name of the place where Abraham and Isaac had lived and were buried, but also its location (P. J. Wiseman, *New Discoveries in Babylonia About Genesis*).

King James Version

and the cave that *is* therein, I give it thee; in the presence of the sons of my people give I it thee: bury thy dead.

12And Abraham bowed down himself before the people of the land.

13And he spake unto Ephron in the audience of the people of the land, saying, But if thou *wilt give it,* I pray thee, hear me: I will give *thee* money for the field; take *it* of me, and I will bury my dead there.

14And Ephron answered Abraham, saying unto him,

15My lord, hearken unto me: the land *is worth* four hundred shekels of silver; what *is* that betwixt me and thee? bury therefore thy dead.

16And Abraham hearkened unto Ephron; and Abraham weighed to Ephron the silver, which he had named in the audience of the sons of Heth, four hundred shekels of silver, current *money* with the merchant.

17And the field of Ephron, which *was* in Machpelah, which *was* before Mamre, the field, and the cave which *was* therein, and all the trees that *were* in the field, that *were* in all the borders round about, were made sure

18Unto Abraham for a possession in the presence of the children of Heth, before all that went in *at* the gate of his city.

19And after this, Abraham buried Sarah his wife in the cave of the field of Machpelah before Mamre: the same *is* Hebron in the land of Canaan.

20And the field, and the cave that *is* therein, were made sure unto Abraham for a possession of a buryingplace by the sons of Heth.

24 And Abraham was old, *and* well stricken in age: and the LORD had blessed Abraham in all things.

2And Abraham said unto his eldest servant of his house that ruled over all that he had, Put, I pray thee, thy hand under my thigh:

3And I will make thee swear by the LORD, the God of heaven, and the God of the earth, that thou shalt not take a wife unto my son of the daughters of the Canaanites, amongst whom I dwell:

4But thou shalt go unto my country, and to my kindred, and take a wife unto my son Isaac.

5And the servant said unto him, Peradventure the woman will not be willing to follow me unto this land: must I needs bring thy son again unto the land from whence thou camest?

6And Abraham said unto him, Beware thou that thou bring not my son thither again.

Amplified Bible

and the cave that is in it I give you. In the presence of the sons of my people I give it to you. Bury your dead.

12Then Abraham bowed himself down before the people of the land.

13And he said to Ephron in the presence of the people of the land, But if you will give it, I beg of you, hear me. I will give you the price of the field; accept it from me, and I will bury my dead there.

14Ephron replied to Abraham, saying,

15My lord, listen to me. The land is worth 400 shekels of silver; what is that between you and me? So bury your dead.

16So Abraham listened to what Ephron said *and* acted upon it. He weighed to Ephron the silver which he had named in the hearing of the Hittites: 400 shekels of silver, according to the weights current among the merchants.

17So the field of Ephron in Machpelah, which was to the east of Mamre [Hebron]—the field and the cave which was in it, and all the trees that were in the field and in all its borders round about—was made over

18As a possession to Abraham in the presence of the Hittites, before all who went in at his city gate.

19After this, Abraham buried Sarah his wife in the cave of the field of *a*Machpelah to the east of Mamre, that is, Hebron, in the land of Canaan.

20The field and the cave in it were conveyed to Abraham for a permanent burial place by the sons of Heth.

24 NOW ABRAHAM was old, well advanced in years, and the Lord had blessed Abraham in all things.

2And Abraham said to the eldest servant of his house [Eliezer of Damascus], who ruled over all that he had, I beg of you, put your hand under my thigh;

3And you shall swear by the Lord, the God of heaven and earth, that you will not take a wife for my son from the daughters of the Canaanites, among whom I have settled,

4But you shall go to my country and to my relatives and take *b*a wife for my son Isaac.

5The servant said to him, But perhaps the woman will not be willing to come along after me to this country. Must I take your son to the country from which you came?

6Abraham said to him, See to it that you do not take my son back there.

AMP notes: *a* Here were buried Abraham and Sarah, Isaac and Rebekah, and Jacob and Leah (Gen. 49:31; 50:13).
b This chapter is highly illustrative of God the Father, Who sends forth His Holy Spirit to win the consent of the individual soul to become the bride of His Son. Keep these resemblances constantly in mind as you read and see how the story unfolds. First meet the Father and note His concern about His Son's bride. Then get acquainted with the Holy Spirit's great, selfless heart, Whose one purpose is to win the girl for His Master's Son. Then meet the Son and note His tenderness as He claims His bride. The longest chapter in Genesis is devoted to this important story.

King James Version

[7]The LORD God of heaven, which took me from my father's house, and from the land of my kindred, and which spake unto me, and that sware unto me, saying, Unto thy seed will I give this land; he shall send his angel before thee, and thou shalt take a wife unto my son from thence.

[8]And if the woman will not be willing to follow thee, then thou shalt be clear from this my oath: only bring not my son thither again.

[9]And the servant put his hand under the thigh of Abraham his master, and sware to him concerning that matter.

[10] ¶ And the servant took ten camels of the camels of his master, and departed; for all the goods of his master *were* in his hand: and he arose, and went to Mesopotamia, unto the city of Nahor.

[11]And he made *his* camels to kneel down without the city by a well of water at the time of the evening, *even* the time that *women* go out to draw *water*.

[12]And he said, O LORD God of my master Abraham, I pray thee, send me good speed *this* day, and shew kindness unto my master Abraham.

[13]Behold, I stand *here* by the well of water; and the daughters of the men of the city come out to draw water:

[14]And let it come to pass, *that* the damsel to whom I shall say, Let down thy pitcher, I pray thee, that I may drink; and she shall say, Drink, and I will give thy camels drink also: *let the same be* she *that* thou hast appointed for thy servant Isaac; and thereby shall I know that thou hast shewed kindness unto my master.

[15]And it came to pass, before he had done speaking, that behold, Rebekah came out, who was born to Bethuel, son of Milcah, the wife of Nahor, Abraham's brother, with her pitcher upon her shoulder.

[16]And the damsel *was* very fair to look upon, a virgin, neither had any man known her: and she went down to the well, and filled her pitcher, and came up.

[17]And the servant ran to meet her, and said, Let me, I pray thee, drink a little water of thy pitcher.

[18]And she said, Drink, my lord: and she hasted, and let down her pitcher upon her hand, and gave him drink.

[19]And when she had done giving him drink, she said, I will draw *water* for thy camels also, until they have done drinking.

[20]And she hasted, and emptied her pitcher into the trough, and ran again unto the well to draw *water*, and drew for all his camels.

Amplified Bible

[7]The Lord, the God of heaven, Who took me from my father's house, from the land of my family *and* my birth, Who spoke to me and swore to me, saying, To your offspring I will give this land—He will send His [a]Angel before you, and you will take a wife from there for my son.

[8]And if the woman should [b]not be willing to go along after you, then you will be clear from this oath; only you must not take my son back there.

[9]So the servant put his hand under the thigh of Abraham his master and swore to him concerning this matter.

[10]And the servant took ten of his master's camels and departed, taking some of all his master's treasures with him; thus he journeyed to Mesopotamia [between the Tigris and the Euphrates], to the city of Nahor [Abraham's brother].

[11]And he made his camels to kneel down outside the city by a well of water at the time of the evening when women go out to draw water.

[12]And he said, O Lord, God of my master Abraham, I pray You, cause me to meet with good success today, and show kindness to my master Abraham.

[13]See, I stand here by the well of water, and the daughters of the men of the city are coming to draw water.

[14]And let it so be that the girl to whom I say, I pray you, let down your jar that I may drink, and she replies, Drink, and I will give your camels drink also—let her be the one whom You have selected *and* appointed *and* indicated for Your servant Isaac [to be a wife to him]; and by it I shall know that You have shown kindness *and* faithfulness to my master.

[15]Before he had finished speaking, behold, out came Rebekah, who was the daughter of Bethuel son of Milcah, who was the wife of Nahor the brother of Abraham, with her water jar on her shoulder.

[16]And the girl was very beautiful *and* attractive, chaste *and* modest, and unmarried. And she went down to the well, filled her water jar, and came up.

[17]And the servant ran to meet her, and said, I pray you, let me drink a little water from your water jar.

[18]And she said, Drink, my lord; and she quickly let down her jar onto her hand and gave him a drink.

[19]When she had given him a drink, she said, I will draw water for your camels also, until they finish drinking.

[20]So she quickly emptied her jar into the trough and ran again to the well and drew water for all his camels.

AMP notes: [a] See footnote on Gen. 16:7.   [b] The Holy Spirit does not win unwilling souls, only "whosoever will."

King James Version

21And the man wondering at her held his peace, to wit whether the LORD had made his journey prosperous or not.

22And it came to pass, as the camels had done drinking, that the man took a golden earring of half a shekel weight, and two bracelets for her hands of ten *shekels* weight of gold;

23And said, Whose daughter *art* thou? tell me, I pray thee: is there room *in* thy father's house for us to lodge in?

24And she said unto him, I *am* the daughter of Bethuel the son of Milcah, which she bare unto Nahor.

25She said moreover unto him, We have both straw and provender enough, and room to lodge in.

26And the man bowed down his head, and worshipped the LORD.

27And he said, Blessed *be* the LORD God of my master Abraham, who hath not left destitute my master of his mercy and his truth: I *being* in the way, the LORD led me to the house of my master's brethren.

28And the damsel ran, and told *them of* her mother's house these things.

29And Rebekah had a brother, and his name *was* Laban: and Laban ran out unto the man, unto the well.

30And it came to pass, when he saw the earring and bracelets upon his sister's hands, and when he heard the words of Rebekah his sister, saying, Thus spake the man unto me; that he came unto the man; and behold, he stood by the camels at the well.

31And he said, Come in, thou blessed of the LORD; wherefore standest thou without? for I have prepared the house, and room for the camels.

32And the man came into the house: and he ungirded *his* camels, and gave straw and provender for the camels, and water to wash his feet, and the men's feet that *were* with him.

33And there was set *meat* before him to eat: but he said, I will not eat, until I have told mine errand. And he said, Speak on.

34And he said, I *am* Abraham's servant.

35And the LORD hath blessed my master greatly; and he is become great: and he hath given him flocks, and herds, and silver, and gold, and menservants, and maidservants, and camels, and asses.

36And Sarah my master's wife bare a son to my master when she was old: and unto him hath he given all that he hath.

37And my master made me swear, saying,

Amplified Bible

21The man stood gazing at her in silence, waiting to know if the Lord had made his trip prosperous.

22And when the camels had finished drinking, the man took a gold earring *or* nose ring of half a shekel in weight, and for her hands two bracelets of ten shekels in weight in gold,

23And said, Whose daughter are you? I pray you, tell me: Is there room in your father's house for us to lodge there?

24And she said to him, I am the daughter of Bethuel son of Milcah and [her husband] Nahor.

25She said also to him, We have both straw and provender (fodder) enough, and also room in which to lodge.

26The man bowed down his head and worshiped the Lord

27And said, Blessed be the Lord, the God of my master Abraham, Who has not left my master bereft *and* destitute of His loving-kindness and steadfastness. As for me, going on the way [of obedience and faith] the Lord led me to the house of my master's kinsmen.

28The girl related to her mother's household what had happened.

29Now Rebekah had a brother whose name was Laban, and Laban ran out to the man at the well.

30For when he saw the earring *or* nose ring, and the bracelets on his sister's arms, and when he heard Rebekah his sister saying, The man said this to me, he went to the man and found him standing by the camels at the well.

31He cried, Come in, you blessed of the Lord! Why do you stand outside? For I have made the house ready *and* have prepared a place for the camels.

32So the man came into the house; and [Laban] ungirded his camels and gave straw and provender for the camels and water to bathe his feet and the feet of the men who were with him.

33A meal was set before him, but he said, ^aI will not eat until I have told of my errand. And [Laban] said, Speak on.

34And he said, I am Abraham's servant.

35And the Lord has blessed my master mightily, and he has become great; and He has given him flocks, herds, silver, gold, menservants, maidservants, camels, and asses.

36And Sarah my master's wife bore a son to my master when she was old, and to him he has given all that he has.

37And my master made me swear, saying, You

AMP notes: ^a The characteristics of a model servant of God are pictured here: 1. He is dependable and trustworthy (Gen. 24:2); 2. He is a praying person (Gen. 24:12); 3. He is so in earnest that he refuses to eat before attending to his Master's business (Gen. 24:33); 4. He never speaks his own name but is always speaking about his Master (Gen. 24:35ff.); 5. He gives God all the glory (Gen. 24:48).

King James Version

Thou shalt not take a wife to my son of the daughters of the Canaanites, in whose land I dwell:

38 But thou shalt go unto my father's house, and to my kindred, and take a wife unto my son.

39 And I said unto my master, Peradventure the woman will not follow me.

40 And he said unto me, The LORD, before whom I walk, will send his angel with thee, and prosper thy way; and thou shalt take a wife for my son of my kindred, and of my father's house:

41 Then shalt thou be clear from *this* my oath, when thou comest to my kindred; and if they give not thee *one*, thou shalt be clear from my oath.

42 And I came this day unto the well, and said, O LORD God of my master Abraham, if now thou do prosper my way which I go:

43 Behold, I stand by the well of water; and it shall come to pass, *that when* the virgin cometh forth to draw *water,* and I say to her, Give me, I pray thee, a little water of thy pitcher to drink;

44 And she say to me, Both drink thou, and I will also draw for thy camels: *let* the same *be* the woman whom the LORD hath appointed out for my master's son.

45 And before I had done speaking in mine heart, behold, Rebekah came forth with her pitcher on her shoulder; and she went down unto the well, and drew *water:* and I said unto her, Let me drink, I pray thee.

46 And she made haste, and let down her pitcher from her *shoulder,* and said, Drink, and I will give thy camels drink also: so I drank, and she made the camels drink also.

47 And I asked her, and said, Whose daughter *art* thou? And she said, The daughter of Bethuel, Nahor's son, whom Milcah bare unto him: and I put the earring upon her face, and the bracelets upon her hands.

48 And I bowed down my head, and worshipped the LORD, and blessed the LORD God of my master Abraham, which had led me in the right way to take my master's brother's daughter unto his son.

49 And now if ye will deal kindly and truly with my master, tell me: and if not, tell me; that I may turn to the right hand, or to the left.

50 Then Laban and Bethuel answered and said, The thing proceedeth from the LORD: we cannot speak unto thee bad or good.✗

51 Behold, Rebekah *is* before thee, take *her,* and go, and let her be thy master's son's wife, as the LORD hath spoken.

52 And it came to pass, that, when Abraham's servant heard their words, he worshipped the LORD, *bowing himself* to the earth.

53 And the servant brought forth jewels of sil-

✗ *When a thing comes forth from God, you just accept it as a blessing from God*

Amplified Bible

must not take a wife for my son from the daughters of the Canaanites, in whose land I dwell,

38 But you shall go to my father's house and to my family and take a wife for my son.

39 And I said to my master, But suppose the woman will not follow me.

40 And he said to me, The Lord, in Whose presence I walk [habitually], will send His *a* Angel with you and prosper your way, and you will take a wife for my son from my kindred and from my father's house.

41 Then you shall be clear from my oath, when you come to my kindred; and if they do not give her to you, you shall be free *and* innocent of my oath.

42 I came today to the well and said, O Lord, God of my master Abraham, if You are now causing me to go on my way prosperously—

43 See, I am standing by the well of water; now let it be that when the maiden comes out to draw water and I say to her, I pray you, give me a little water from your [water] jar to drink,

44 And if she says to me, You drink, and I will draw water for your camels also, let that same woman be the one whom the Lord has selected *and* indicated for my master's son.

45 And before I had finished praying in my heart, behold, Rebekah came out with her [water] jar on her shoulder, and she went down to the well and drew water. And I said to her, I pray you, let me have a drink.

46 And she quickly let down her [water] jar from her shoulder and said, Drink, and I will water your camels also. So I drank, and she gave the camels drink also.

47 I asked her, Whose daughter are you? She said, The daughter of Bethuel, Nahor's son, whom Milcah bore to him. And I put the earring *or* nose ring on her face and the bracelets on her arms.

48 And I bowed down my head and worshiped the Lord and blessed the Lord, the God of my master Abraham, Who had led me in the right way to take my master's brother's daughter to his son.

49 And now if you will deal kindly and truly with my master [showing faithfulness to him], tell me; and if not, tell me, that I may turn to the right or to the left.

50 Then Laban and Bethuel answered, The thing comes forth from the Lord; we cannot speak bad or good to you.

51 Rebekah is before you; take her and go, and let her be the wife of your master's son, as the Lord has said.

52 And when Abraham's servant heard their words, he bowed himself to the ground before the Lord.

53 And the servant brought out jewels of sil-

AMP notes: *a* See footnote on Gen. 16:7.

King James Version

ver, and jewels of gold, and raiment, and gave *them* to Rebekah: he gave also to her brother and to her mother precious things.

⁵⁴And they did eat and drink, he and the men that *were* with him, and tarried all night; and they rose up in the morning, and he said, Send me away unto my master.

⁵⁵And her brother and her mother said, Let the damsel abide with us *a few* days, at the least ten; after *that* she shall go.

⁵⁶And he said unto them, Hinder me not, seeing the LORD hath prospered my way; send me away that I may go to my master.

⁵⁷And they said, We will call the damsel, and inquire at her mouth.

⁵⁸And they called Rebekah, and said unto her, Wilt thou go with this man? And she said, I will go.

⁵⁹And they sent away Rebekah their sister, and her nurse, and Abraham's servant, and his men.

⁶⁰And they blessed Rebekah, and said unto her, Thou *art* our sister, be thou *the mother* of thousands of millions, and let thy seed possess the gate of those which hate them.

⁶¹ ¶ And Rebekah arose, and her damsels, and they rode upon the camels, and followed the man: and the servant took Rebekah, and went his way.

⁶²And Isaac came from the way of the well Lahai-roi; for he dwelt in the south country.

⁶³And Isaac went out to meditate in the field at the eventide: and he lift up his eyes, and saw, and behold, the camels *were* coming.

⁶⁴And Rebekah lift up her eyes, and when she saw Isaac, she lighted off the camel.

⁶⁵For she had said unto the servant, What man *is* this that walketh in the field to meet us? And the servant had said, It *is* my master: therefore she took a vail, and covered herself.

⁶⁶And the servant told Isaac all things that he had done.

⁶⁷And Isaac brought her into his mother Sarah's tent, and took Rebekah, and she became his wife; and he loved her: and Isaac was comforted after his mother's *death*.

25 Then again Abraham took a wife, and her name *was* Keturah.

²And she bare him Zimran, and Jokshan, and Medan, and Midian, and Ishbak, and Shuah.

³And Jokshan begat Sheba, and Dedan. And the sons of Dedan were Asshurim, and Letushim, and Leummim.

⁴And the sons of Midian; Ephah, and Epher, and Hanoch, and Abidah, and Eldaah. All these *were* the children of Keturah.

⁵And Abraham gave all that he had unto Isaac.

Amplified Bible

ver, jewels of gold, and garments and gave them to Rebekah; he also gave precious things to her brother and her mother.

⁵⁴Then they ate and drank, he and the men who were with him, and stayed there all night. And in the morning they arose, and he said, Send me away to my master.

⁵⁵But [Rebekah's] brother and mother said, Let the girl stay with us a few days—at least ten; then she may go.

⁵⁶But [the servant] said to them, Do not hinder *and* delay me, seeing that the Lord has caused me to go prosperously on my way. Send me away, that I may go to my master.

⁵⁷And they said, We will call the girl and ask her [what is] her desire.

⁵⁸So they called Rebekah and said to her, Will you go with this man? And she said, I will go.

⁵⁹So they sent away Rebekah their sister and her nurse [Deborah] and Abraham's servant and his men.

⁶⁰And they blessed Rebekah and said to her, You are our sister; may you become the mother of thousands of ten thousands, and let your posterity possess the gate of their enemies.

⁶¹And Rebekah and her maids arose and followed the man upon their camels. Thus the servant took Rebekah and went on his way.

⁶²Now Isaac had returned from going to the well Beer-lahai-roi [A well to the Living One Who sees me], for he [now] dwelt in the South country (the Negeb).

⁶³And Isaac went out to meditate *and* bow down [in prayer] in the open country in the evening; and he looked up and saw that, behold, the camels were coming.

⁶⁴And Rebekah looked up, and when she saw Isaac, she dismounted from the camel.

⁶⁵For she [had] said to the servant, Who is that man walking across the field to meet us? And the servant [had] said, He is my master. So she took a veil and concealed herself with it.

⁶⁶And the servant told Isaac everything that he had done.

⁶⁷And Isaac brought her into his mother Sarah's tent, and he took Rebekah and she became his wife, and he loved her; thus Isaac was comforted after his mother's death.

25 ABRAHAM TOOK another wife, and her name was Keturah.

²And she bore him Zimran, Jokshan, Medan, Midian, Ishbak, and Shuah.

³Jokshan was the father of Sheba and Dedan. The sons of Dedan were Asshurim, Letushim, and Leummim.

⁴The sons of Midian were Ephah, Epher, Hanoch, Abida, and Eldaah. All these were the children of Keturah.

⁵And Abraham gave all that he had to Isaac.

King James Version

6But unto the sons of the concubines, which Abraham had, Abraham gave gifts, and sent them away from Isaac his son, while he yet lived, eastward, unto the east country.

7And these *are* the days of the years of Abraham's life which he lived, an hundred threescore and fifteen years.

8Then Abraham gave up the ghost, and died in a good old age, an old man, and full *of years;* and was gathered to his people.

9And his sons Isaac and Ishmael buried him in the cave of Machpelah, in the field of Ephron the son of Zohar the Hittite, which *is* before Mamre;

10The field which Abraham purchased of the sons of Heth: there was Abraham buried, and Sarah his wife.

11And it came to pass after the death of Abraham, that God blessed his son Isaac; and Isaac dwelt by the well Lahai-roi.

12 ¶ Now these *are* the generations of Ishmael, Abraham's son, whom Hagar the Egyptian, Sarah's handmaid, bare unto Abraham:

13And these *are* the names of the sons of Ishmael, by their names, according to their generations: the firstborn of Ishmael, Nebajoth; and Kedar, and Adbeel, and Mibsam,

14And Mishma, and Dumah, and Massa,

15Hadar, and Tema, Jetur, Naphish, and Kedemah:

16These *are* the sons of Ishmael, and these *are* their names, by their towns, and by their castles; twelve princes according to their nations.

17And these *are* the years of the life of Ishmael, an hundred and thirty and seven years: and he gave up the ghost and died; and was gathered unto his people.

18And they dwelt from Havilah unto Shur, that *is* before Egypt, as thou goest towards Assyria: *and* he died in the presence of all his brethren.

19 ¶ And these *are* the generations of Isaac, Abraham's son: Abraham begat Isaac:

20And Isaac was forty years old when he took Rebekah to wife, the daughter of Bethuel the Syrian of Padan-aram, the sister to Laban the Syrian.

21And Isaac intreated the LORD for his wife, because she *was* barren: and the LORD was intreated of him, and Rebekah his wife conceived.

22And the children struggled together within her; and she said, If *it be* so, why *am* I thus? And she went to inquire of the LORD.

23And the LORD said unto her, Two nations *are* in thy womb, and two manner of people shall be separated from thy bowels; and *the one* people

Amplified Bible

6But to the sons of his concubines [Hagar and Keturah] Abraham gave gifts, and while he was still living he sent them to the east country, away from Isaac his son [of promise].

7The days of Abraham's life were 175 years.

8Then Abraham's spirit was released, and he died at a good (ample, full) old age, an old man, satisfied *and* satiated, and *a*was gathered to his people.

9And his sons *b*Isaac and Ishmael buried him in the cave of Machpelah, in the field of Ephron the son of Zohar the Hittite, which is east of Mamre,

10The field which Abraham purchased from the Hittites. There Abraham was buried with Sarah his wife.

11After the death of Abraham, God blessed his son Isaac, and Isaac dwelt at Beer-lahai-roi [A well to the Living One Who sees me].

12Now this is the history of the descendants of Ishmael, Abraham's son, whom Hagar the Egyptian, Sarah's handmaid, bore to Abraham.

13These are the names of the sons of Ishmael, named in the order of their births: Nebaioth, the firstborn of Ishmael, and Kedar, Adbeel, Mibsam,

14Mishma, Dumah, Massa,

15Hadad, Tema, Jetur, Naphish, and Kedemah.

16These are the sons of Ishmael, and these are their names, by their villages and by their encampments (sheepfolds)—twelve princes according to their tribes. [Foretold in Gen. 17:20.]

17And Ishmael lived 137 years; then his spirit left him, and he died and was gathered to his kindred.

18And [Ishmael's sons] dwelt from Havilah to Shur, which is before Egypt in the direction of Assyria. [Ishmael] dwelt close [to the lands] of all his brethren.

19And this is the history of the descendants of Isaac, Abraham's son: Abraham was the father of Isaac.

20Isaac was forty years old when he married Rebekah, the daughter of Bethuel the Aramean of Padan-aram, the sister of Laban the Aramean.

21And Isaac prayed much to the Lord for his wife because she was unable to bear children; and the Lord granted his prayer, and Rebekah his wife became pregnant.

22[Two] children struggled together within her; and she said, If it is so [that the Lord has heard our prayer], why am I like this? And she went to inquire of the Lord.

23The Lord said to her, [The founders of] two nations are in your womb, and the separation of two peoples has begun in your body; the one

---

AMP notes: a This often repeated expression forms a remarkable testimony to the Old Testament belief in a life beyond the grave and to our recognition and fellowship with our loved ones there. *b* Isaac was seventy-five and Ishmael nearly ninety years of age when their father died. Jacob and Esau were fifteen, and may have been present.

King James Version

shall be stronger than *the other* people; and the elder shall serve the younger.

24 ¶ And when her days to be delivered were fulfilled, behold, *there were* twins in her womb.

25 And the first came out red, all over like a hairy garment; and they called his name Esau.

26 And after that came his brother out, and his hand took hold on Esau's heel; and his name was called Jacob: and Isaac *was* threescore years old when she bare them.

27 And the boys grew: and Esau was a cunning hunter, a man of the field; and Jacob *was* a plain man, dwelling in tents.

28 And Isaac loved Esau, because he did eat of *his* venison: but Rebekah loved Jacob.

29 ¶ And Jacob sod pottage: and Esau came from the field, and he *was* faint:

30 And Esau said to Jacob, Feed me, I pray thee, with that same red *pottage;* for I *am* faint: therefore was his name called Edom.

31 And Jacob said, Sell me *this* day thy birthright.

32 And Esau said, Behold, I *am* at the point to die: and what profit shall this birthright do to me?

33 And Jacob said, Swear to me *this* day; and he sware to him: and he sold his birthright unto Jacob.

34 Then Jacob gave Esau bread and pottage of lentiles; and he did eat and drink, and rose up, and went his way: thus Esau despised *his* birthright.

26 And there was a famine in the land, besides the first famine that was in the days of Abraham. And Isaac went unto Abimelech king of the Philistims unto Gerar.

2 And the LORD appeared unto him, and said, Go not down into Egypt; dwell in the land which I shall tell thee of:

3 Sojourn in this land, and I will be with thee, and will bless thee; for unto thee, and unto thy seed, I will give all these countries, and I will perform the oath which I sware unto Abraham thy father;

4 And I will make thy seed to multiply as the stars of heaven, and will give unto thy seed all these countries; and in thy seed shall all the nations of the earth be blessed;

5 Because that Abraham obeyed my voice, and kept my charge, my commandments, my statutes, and my laws.

6 And Isaac dwelt in Gerar:

7 And the men of the place asked *him* of his wife; and he said, She *is* my sister: for he feared to say, *She is* my wife; lest, *said he,* the men of

Amplified Bible

people shall be stronger than the other, and the elder shall serve the younger.

24 When her days to be delivered were fulfilled, behold, there were twins in her womb.

25 The first came out red all over like a hairy garment, and they named him Esau [hairy].

26 Afterward his brother came forth, and his hand grasped Esau's heel; so he was named Jacob [supplanter]. Isaac was sixty years old when she gave birth to them.

27 When the boys grew up, Esau was a cunning *and* skilled hunter, a man of the outdoors; but Jacob was a plain *and* quiet man, dwelling in tents.

28 And Isaac loved [and was partial to] Esau, because he ate of Esau's game; but Rebekah loved Jacob.

29 Jacob was boiling pottage (lentil stew) one day, when Esau came from the field and was faint [with hunger].

30 And Esau said to Jacob, I beg of you, let me have some of that red lentil stew to eat, for I am faint *and* famished! That is why his name was called Edom [red].

31 Jacob answered, Then sell me today your birthright (the rights of a firstborn).

32 Esau said, See here, I am at the point of death; what good can this birthright do me?

33 Jacob said, Swear to me today [that you are selling it to me]; and he swore to [Jacob] and sold him his birthright.

34 Then Jacob gave Esau bread and stew of lentils, and he ate and drank and rose up and went his way. Thus Esau scorned his birthright as beneath his notice.

26 AND THERE was a famine in the land, other than the former famine that was in the days of Abraham. And Isaac went to Gerar, to Abimelech king of the Philistines.

2 And the Lord appeared to him and said, Do not go down to Egypt; live in the land of which I will tell you.

3 Dwell temporarily in this land, and I will be with you and will favor you with blessings; for to you and to your descendants I will give all these lands, and I will perform the oath which I swore to Abraham your father.

4 And I will make your descendants to multiply as the stars of the heavens, and will give to your posterity all these lands (kingdoms); and by your Offspring shall all the nations of the earth be blessed, *or* by Him bless themselves,

5 For Abraham listened to *and* obeyed My voice and kept My charge, My commands, My statutes, and My laws.

6 So Isaac stayed in Gerar.

7 And the men of the place asked him about his wife, and he said, She is my sister; for he was afraid to say, She is my wife—[thinking],

King James Version

the place should kill me for Rebekah; because she *was* fair to look upon.

⁸And it came to pass, when he had been there a long time, that Abimelech king of the Philistims looked out at a window, and saw, and behold, Isaac *was* sporting with Rebekah his wife.

⁹And Abimelech called Isaac, and said, Behold, of a surety she *is* thy wife: and how saidst thou, She *is* my sister? And Isaac said unto him, Because I said, Lest I die for her.

¹⁰And Abimelech said, What *is* this thou hast done unto us? one of the people might lightly have lien with thy wife, and thou shouldest have brought guiltiness upon us.

¹¹And Abimelech charged all *his* people, saying, He that toucheth this man or his wife shall surely be put to death.

¹²Then Isaac sowed in that land, and received in the same year an hundredfold: and the Lord blessed him.

¹³And the man waxed great, and went forward, and grew until he became very great:

¹⁴For he had possession of flocks, and possession of herds, and great store of servants: and the Philistims envied him.

¹⁵For all the wells which his father's servants had digged in the days of Abraham his father, the Philistims had stopped them, and filled them *with* earth.

¹⁶And Abimelech said unto Isaac, Go from us; for thou art much mightier than we.

¹⁷ ¶ And Isaac departed thence, and pitched his tent in the valley of Gerar, and dwelt there.

¹⁸And Isaac digged again the wells of water, which they had digged in the days of Abraham his father; for the Philistims had stopped them after the death of Abraham: and he called their names after the names by which his father had called them.

¹⁹And Isaac's servants digged in the valley, and found there a well of springing water.

²⁰And the herdmen of Gerar did strive with Isaac's herdmen, saying, The water *is* ours: and he called the name of the well Esek; because they strove with him.

²¹And they digged another well, and strove for that also: and he called the name of it Sitnah.

²²And he removed from thence, and digged another well; and for that they strove not: and he called the name of it Rehoboth; and he said, For now the Lord hath made room for us, and we shall be fruitful in the land.

²³And he went up from thence to Beer-sheba.

²⁴And the Lord appeared unto him the same night, and said, I *am* the God of Abraham thy father: fear not, for I *am* with thee, and will bless thee, and multiply thy seed for my servant Abraham's sake.

Amplified Bible

Lest the men of the place should kill me for Rebekah, because she is attractive *and* is beautiful to look upon.

⁸When he had been there a long time, Abimelech king of the Philistines looked out of a window and saw Isaac caressing Rebekah his wife.

⁹And Abimelech called Isaac and said, See here, she is certainly your wife! How did you [dare] say to me, She is my sister? And Isaac said to him, Because I thought, Lest I die on account of her.

¹⁰And Abimelech said, What is this you have done to us? One of the men might easily have lain with your wife, and you would have brought guilt *and* sin upon us.

¹¹Then Abimelech charged all his people, He who touches this man or his wife shall surely be put to death.

¹²Then Isaac sowed seed in that land and received in the same year a hundred times as much as he had planted, and the Lord favored him with blessings.

¹³And the man became great and gained more and more until he became very wealthy *and* distinguished;

¹⁴He owned flocks, herds, and a great supply of servants, and the Philistines envied him.

¹⁵Now all the wells which his father's servants had dug in the days of Abraham his father, the Philistines had closed and filled with earth.

¹⁶And Abimelech said to Isaac, Go away from us, for you are much mightier than we are.

¹⁷So Isaac went away from there and pitched his tent in the Valley of Gerar, and dwelt there.

¹⁸And Isaac dug again the wells of water which had been dug in the days of Abraham his father, for the Philistines had stopped them after the death of Abraham; and he gave them the names by which his father had called them.

¹⁹Now Isaac's servants dug in the valley and found there a well of living [spring] water.

²⁰And the herdsmen of Gerar quarreled with Isaac's herdsmen, saying, The water is ours. And he named the well Esek [contention] because they quarreled with him.

²¹Then [his servants] dug another well, and they quarreled over that also; so he named it Sitnah [enmity].

²²And he moved away from there and dug another well, and for that one they did not quarrel. He named it Rehoboth [room], saying, For now the Lord has made room for us, and we shall be fruitful in the land.

²³Now he went up from there to Beersheba.

²⁴And the Lord appeared to him the same night and said, I am the God of Abraham your father. Fear not, for I am with you and will favor you with blessings and multiply your descendants for the sake of My servant Abraham.

King James Version

²⁵And he builded an altar there, and called upon the name of the LORD, and pitched his tent there: and there Isaac's servants digged a well.

²⁶Then Abimelech went to him from Gerar, and Ahuzzath *one* of his friends, and Phichol the chief captain of his army.

²⁷And Isaac said unto them, Wherefore come ye to me, seeing ye hate me, and have sent me away from you?

²⁸And they said, We saw certainly that the LORD was with thee: and we said, Let there be now an oath betwixt us, *even* betwixt us and thee, and let us make a covenant with thee;

²⁹That thou wilt do us no hurt, as we have not touched thee, and as we have done unto thee nothing but good, and have sent thee away in peace: thou *art* now the blessed of the LORD.

³⁰And he made them a feast, and they did eat and drink.

³¹And they rose up betimes in the morning, and sware one to another: and Isaac sent them away, and they departed from him in peace.

³²And it came to pass the same day, that Isaac's servants came, and told him concerning the well which they had digged, and said unto him, We have found water.

³³And he called it Shebah: therefore the name of the city *is* Beer-sheba unto this day.

³⁴And Esau was forty years old when he took to wife Judith the daughter of Beeri the Hittite, and Bashemath the daughter of Elon the Hittite:

³⁵Which were a grief of mind unto Isaac and to Rebekah.

27 And it came to pass, that when Isaac was old, and his eyes were dim, so that he could not see, he called Esau his eldest son, and said unto him, My son: and he said unto him, Behold, *here am* I.

²And he said, Behold now, I am old, I know not the day of my death:

³Now therefore take, I pray thee, thy weapons, thy quiver and thy bow, and go out to the field, and take me *some* venison;

⁴And make me savoury meat, such as I love, and bring *it* to me, that I may eat; that my soul may bless thee before I die.

⁵And Rebekah heard when Isaac spake to Esau his son. And Esau went to the field to hunt for venison, *and* to bring *it*.

⁶And Rebekah spake unto Jacob her son, saying, Behold, I heard thy father speak unto Esau thy brother, saying,

⁷Bring me venison, and make me savoury

Amplified Bible

²⁵And [Isaac] ᵃbuilt an altar there and called on the name of the Lord and pitched his tent there; and there Isaac's servants were digging a well.

²⁶Then Abimelech went to him from Gerar with Ahuzzah, one of his friends, and Phicol, his army's commander.

²⁷And Isaac said to them, Why have you come to me, seeing that you hate me and have sent me away from you?

²⁸They said, We saw that the Lord was certainly with you; so we said, Let there be now an oath between us [carrying a curse with it to befall the one who breaks it], even between you and us, and let us make a covenant with you

²⁹That you will do us no harm, inasmuch as we have not touched you and have done to you nothing but good and have sent you away in peace. You are now the blessed *or* favored of the Lord!

³⁰And he made them a [formal] dinner, and they ate and drank.

³¹And they rose up early in the morning and took oaths [with a curse] with one another; and Isaac sent them on their way and they departed from him in peace.

³²That same day Isaac's servants came and told him about the well they had dug, saying, We have found water!

³³And he named [the well] Shibah; therefore the name of the city is Beersheba [well of the oath] to this day.

³⁴Now Esau was 40 years old when he took as wife Judith the daughter of Beeri the Hittite, and Basemath the daughter of Elon the Hittite.

³⁵And they made life bitter *and* a grief of mind *and* spirit for Isaac and Rebekah [their parents-in-law].

27 WHEN ISAAC was old and his eyes were dim so that he could not see, he called Esau his elder son, and said to him, My son! And he answered him, Here I am.

²He said, See here now; I am old, I do not know when I may die.

³So now, I pray you, take your weapons, your [arrows in a] quiver and your bow, and go out into the open country and hunt game for me,

⁴And prepare me appetizing meat, such as I love, and bring it to me, that I may eat of it, [preparatory] to giving you my blessing [as my firstborn] before I die.

⁵But Rebekah heard what Isaac said to Esau his son; and when Esau had gone to the open country to hunt for game that he might bring it,

⁶Rebekah said to Jacob her younger son, See here, I heard your father say to Esau your brother,

⁷Bring me game and make me appetizing

AMP notes: ᵃ With Isaac God came first. Before doing anything else in the new place, he built an altar and then waited there to call upon the Lord. Second came his home; he pitched his tent. Third came his business; his servants dug a well.

King James Version

meat, that I may eat, and bless thee before the LORD before my death.

8 Now therefore, my son, obey my voice according to *that* which I command thee.

9 Go now to the flock, and fetch me from thence two good kids of the goats; and I will make them savoury meat for thy father, such as he loveth:

10 And thou shalt bring *it* to thy father, that he may eat, and that he may bless thee before his death.

11 And Jacob said to Rebekah his mother, Behold, Esau my brother *is* a hairy man, and I *am* a smooth man:

12 My father peradventure will feel me, and I shall seem to him as a deceiver; and I shall bring a curse upon me, and not a blessing.

13 And his mother said unto him, Upon me *be* thy curse, my son: only obey my voice, and go fetch me *them*.

14 And he went, and fetched, and brought *them* to his mother: and his mother made savoury meat, such as his father loved.

15 And Rebekah took goodly raiment of her eldest son Esau, which *were* with her in the house, and put them upon Jacob her younger son:

16 And she put the skins of the kids of the goats upon his hands, and upon the smooth of his neck:

17 And she gave the savoury meat and the bread, which she had prepared, into the hand of her son Jacob.

18 And he came unto his father, and said, My father: and he said, Here *am* I; who *art* thou, my son?

19 And Jacob said unto his father, I *am* Esau thy firstborn; I have done according as thou badest me: arise, I pray thee, sit and eat of my venison, that thy soul may bless me.

20 And Isaac said unto his son, How *is* it *that* thou hast found *it* so quickly, my son? And he said, Because the LORD thy God brought *it* to me.

21 And Isaac said unto Jacob, Come near, I pray thee, that I may feel thee, my son, whether thou *be* my very son Esau or not.

22 And Jacob went near unto Isaac his father; and he felt him, and said, The voice *is* Jacob's voice, but the hands *are* the hands of Esau.

23 And he discerned him not, because his hands were hairy, as his brother Esau's hands: so he blessed him.

24 And he said, *Art* thou my very son Esau? And he said, I *am*.

25 And he said, Bring *it* near to me, and I will eat of my son's venison, that my soul may bless thee. And he brought *it* near to him, and he did eat: and he brought him wine, and he drank.

26 And his father Isaac said unto him, Come near now, and kiss me, my son.

Amplified Bible

meat, so that I may eat and declare my blessing upon you before the Lord before my death.

8 So now, my son, do exactly as I command you.

9 Go now to the flock, and from it bring me two good *and* suitable kids; and I will make them into appetizing meat for your father, such as he loves.

10 And you shall bring it to your father, that he may eat and declare his blessing upon you before his death.

11 But Jacob said to Rebekah his mother, Listen, Esau my brother is a hairy man and I am a smooth man.

12 Suppose my father feels me; I will seem to him to be a cheat *and* an imposter, and I will bring [his] curse on me and not [his] blessing.

13 But his mother said to him, On me be your curse, my son; only obey my word and go, fetch them to me.

14 So [Jacob] went, got [the kids], and brought them to his mother; and his mother prepared appetizing meat with a delightful odor, such as his father loved.

15 Then Rebekah took her elder son Esau's best clothes which were with her in the house, and put them on Jacob her younger son.

16 And she put the skins of the kids on his hands and on the smooth part of his neck.

17 And she gave the savory meat and the bread which she had prepared into the hand of her son Jacob.

18 So he went to his father and said, My father. And he said, Here am I; who are you, my son?

19 And Jacob said to his father, I am Esau your firstborn; I have done what you told me to do. Now sit up and eat of my game, so that you may proceed to bless me.

20 And Isaac said to his son, How is it that you have found the game so quickly, my son? And he said, Because the Lord your God caused it to come to me.

21 But Isaac said to Jacob, Come close to me, I beg of you, that I may feel you, my son, *and* know whether you really are my son Esau or not.

22 So Jacob went near to Isaac, and his father felt him and said, The voice is Jacob's voice, but the hands are the hands of Esau.

23 He could not identify him, because his hands were hairy like his brother Esau's hands; so he blessed him.

24 But he said, Are you really my son Esau? He answered, I am.

25 Then [Isaac] said, Bring it to me and I will eat of my son's game, that I may bless you. He brought it to him and he ate; and he brought him wine and he drank.

26 Then his father Isaac said, Come near and kiss me, my son.

King James Version

27And he came near, and kissed him: and he smelled the smell of his raiment, and blessed him, and said, See, the smell of my son *is* as the smell of a field which the LORD hath blessed:

28Therefore God give thee of the dew of heaven, and the fatness of the earth, and plenty of corn and wine:

29Let people serve thee, and nations bow down to thee: be lord over thy brethren, and let thy mother's sons bow down to thee: cursed *be* every one that curseth thee, and blessed *be* he that blesseth thee.

30And it came to pass, as soon as Isaac had made an end of blessing Jacob, and Jacob was yet scarce gone out from the presence of Isaac his father, that Esau his brother came in from his hunting.

31And he also had made savoury meat, and brought *it* unto his father, and said unto his father, Let my father arise, and eat of his son's venison, that thy soul may bless me.

32And Isaac his father said unto him, Who *art* thou? And he said, I *am* thy son, thy firstborn Esau.

33And Isaac trembled very exceedingly, and said, Who? where *is* he that hath taken venison, and brought *it* me, and I have eaten of all before thou camest, and have blessed him? yea, *and* he shall be blessed.

34And when Esau heard the words of his father, he cried with a great and exceeding bitter cry, and said unto his father, Bless me, *even* me also, O my father.

35And he said, Thy brother came with subtilty, and hath taken away thy blessing.

36And he said, Is not he rightly named Jacob? for he hath supplanted me these two times: he took away my birthright; and behold, now he hath taken away my blessing. And he said, Hast thou not reserved a blessing for me?

37And Isaac answered and said unto Esau, Behold, I have made him thy lord, and all his brethren have I given to him for servants; and with corn and wine have I sustained him: and what shall I do now unto thee, my son?

38And Esau said unto his father, Hast thou but one blessing, my father? bless me, *even* me also, O my father. And Esau lift up his voice, and wept.

39And Isaac his father answered and said unto him, Behold, thy dwelling shall be the fatness of the earth, and of the dew of heaven from above;

40And by thy sword shalt thou live, and shalt serve thy brother; and it shall come to pass when thou shalt have the dominion, that thou shalt break his yoke from off thy neck.

41 ¶ And Esau hated Jacob because of the blessing wherewith his father blessed him: and Esau said in his heart, The days of mourning for

Amplified Bible

27So he came near and kissed him; and [Isaac] smelled his clothing and blessed him and said, The scent of my son is as the odor of a field which the Lord has blessed.

28And may God give you of the dew of the heavens and of the fatness of the earth and abundance of grain and [new] wine;

29Let peoples serve you and nations bow down to you; be master over your brothers, and let your mother's sons bow down to you. Let everyone be cursed who curses you and favored with blessings who blesses you.

30As soon as Isaac had finished blessing Jacob and Jacob was scarcely gone out from the presence of Isaac his father, Esau his brother came in from his hunting.

31Esau had also prepared savory food and brought it to his father and said to him, Let my father arise and eat of his son's game, that you may bless me.

32And Isaac his father said to him, Who are you? And he replied, I am your son, your first-born, Esau.

33Then Isaac trembled *and* shook violently, and he said, Who? Where is he who has hunted game and brought it to me, and I ate of it all before you came and I have blessed him? Yes, and he shall be blessed.

34When Esau heard the words of his father, he cried out with a great and bitter cry and said to his father, Bless me, even me also, O my father!

35[Isaac] said, Your brother came with crafty cunning *and* treacherous deceit and has taken your blessing.

36[Esau] replied, Is he not rightly named Jacob [the supplanter]? For he has supplanted me these two times: he took away my birthright, and now he has taken away my blessing! Have you not still a blessing reserved for me?

37And Isaac answered Esau, Behold, I have made [Jacob] your lord and master; I have given all his brethren to him for servants, and with corn and [new] wine have I sustained him. What then can I do for you, my son?

38Esau said to his father, Have you only one blessing, my father? Bless me, even me also, O my father! And Esau lifted up [could not control] his voice and wept aloud.

39Then Isaac his father answered, Your [blessing and] dwelling shall all come from the fruitfulness of the earth and from the dew of the heavens above;

40By your sword you shall live and serve your brother. But [the time shall come] when you will grow restive *and* break loose, and you shall tear his yoke from off your neck.

41And Esau hated Jacob because of the blessing with which his father blessed him; and Esau said in his heart, The days of mourning for my

King James Version

my father are at hand; then will I slay my brother Jacob.

⁴²And these words of Esau her elder son were told to Rebekah: and she sent and called Jacob her younger son, and said unto him, Behold, thy brother Esau, as touching thee, doth comfort himself, *purposing* to kill thee.

⁴³Now therefore, my son, obey my voice; and arise, flee thou to Laban my brother to Haran;

⁴⁴And tarry with him a few days, until thy brother's fury turn away;

⁴⁵Until thy brother's anger turn away from thee, and he forget *that* which thou hast done to him: then I will send, and fetch thee from thence: why should I be deprived also of you both *in* one day?

⁴⁶And Rebekah said to Isaac, I am weary of my life because of the daughters of Heth: if Jacob take a wife of the daughters of Heth, such as these *which are* of the daughters of the land, what good shall my life do me?

28 And Isaac called Jacob, and blessed him, and charged him, and said unto him, Thou shalt not take a wife of the daughters of Canaan.

²Arise, go to Padan-aram, to the house of Bethuel thy mother's father; and take thee a wife from thence of the daughters of Laban thy mother's brother.

³And God Almighty bless thee, and make thee fruitful, and multiply thee, that thou mayest be a multitude of people;

⁴And give thee the blessing of Abraham, to thee, and to thy seed with thee; that thou mayest inherit the land wherein thou art a stranger, which God gave unto Abraham.

⁵And Isaac sent away Jacob: and he went to Padan-aram unto Laban, son of Bethuel the Syrian, the brother of Rebekah, Jacob's and Esau's mother.

⁶When Esau saw that Isaac had blessed Jacob, and sent him away to Padan-aram, to take him a wife from thence; and that as he blessed him he gave him a charge, saying, Thou shalt not take a wife of the daughters of Canaan;

⁷And that Jacob obeyed his father and his mother, and was gone to Padan-aram;

⁸And Esau seeing that the daughters of Canaan pleased not Isaac his father;

⁹Then went Esau unto Ishmael, and took unto the wives which he had Mahalath the

Amplified Bible

father are very near. When [he is gone] I will ᵃkill my brother Jacob.

⁴²These words of Esau her elder son were repeated to Rebekah. She sent for Jacob her younger son and said to him, See here, your brother Esau comforts himself concerning you [by intending] to kill you.

⁴³So now, my son, do what I tell you; arise, flee to my brother Laban in Haran;

⁴⁴Linger and dwell with him for a while until your brother's fury is spent.

⁴⁵When your brother's anger is diverted from you, he will forget [the wrong] that you have done him. Then ᵇI will send and bring you back from there. Why should I be deprived of both of you in one day?

⁴⁶Then Rebekah said to Isaac, I am weary of my life because of the daughters of Heth [these wives of Esau]! If Jacob takes a wife of the daughters of Heth such as these Hittite girls around here, what good will my life be to me?

28 SO ISAAC called Jacob and blessed him and commanded him, You shall not marry one of the women of Canaan.

²Arise, go to Padan-aram, to the house of Bethuel your mother's father, and take from there as a wife one of the daughters of Laban your mother's brother.

³May God Almighty bless you and make you fruitful and multiply you until you become a group of peoples.

⁴May He give the blessing [He gave to] Abraham to you and your descendants with you, that you may inherit the land He gave to Abraham, in which you are a sojourner.

⁵Thus Isaac sent Jacob away. He went to Padan-aram, to Laban son of Bethuel the Aramean, the brother of Rebekah, Jacob and Esau's mother.

⁶Now Esau saw that Isaac had blessed Jacob and sent him to Padan-aram to take him a wife from there, and that as he blessed him, he gave him a charge, saying, You shall not take a wife of the daughters of Canaan;

⁷And that Jacob obeyed his father and his mother and had gone to Padan-aram.

⁸Also Esau saw that the daughters of Canaan did not please Isaac his father.

⁹So Esau went to Ishmael and took to be his wife, [in addition] to the wives he [already] had,

---

AMP notes: ᵃ Here began a feud that was to cost countless lives throughout succeeding centuries. Esau's descendants, the Amalekites, were the first enemies to obstruct the flight of Jacob's descendants from Egypt (Exod. 17:8); and the Edomites even refused to let their uncle Jacob's children pass through their land (Num. 20:17-20). Doeg, an Edomite, all but caused the death of Christ's chosen ancestor David (I Sam. 21, 22). Bloody battles were fought between the two nations in the centuries that followed. It was Herod, of Esau's race (Josephus, *Antiquities of the Jews* 14:1, Section 3), who had the male infants of Bethlehem slain in an effort to destroy the Christ Child (Matt. 2:16). Satan needs no better medium for his evil plans than a family feud, a "mere quarrel" between two brothers.
ᵇ But Rebekah never saw her son Jacob again. He was well over 40 and probably 57 years old when he fled from Esau to Haran, and he stayed there at least 20 years.

King James Version

daughter of Ishmael Abraham's son, the sister of Nebajoth, to be his wife.

¹⁰ ¶ And Jacob went out from Beer-sheba, and went toward Haran.

¹¹And he lighted upon a *certain* place, and tarried there all night, because the sun was set; and he took of the stones of *that* place, and put *them for* his pillows, and lay down in that place to sleep.

¹²And he dreamed, and behold a ladder set up on the earth, and the top of it reached to heaven: and behold the angels of God ascending and descending on it.

¹³And behold, the LORD stood above it, and said, I *am* the LORD God of Abraham thy father, and the God of Isaac: the land whereon thou liest, to thee will I give it, and to thy seed;

¹⁴And thy seed shall be as the dust of the earth, and thou shalt spread abroad to the west, and to the east, and to the north, and to the south: and in thee and in thy seed shall all the families of the earth be blessed. *Speaking of Christ.*

¹⁵And behold, I *am* with thee, and will keep thee in all *places* whither thou goest, and will bring thee again into this land; for I will not leave thee, until I have done *that* which I have spoken to thee of.

¹⁶And Jacob awaked out of his sleep, and he said, Surely the LORD is in this place; and I knew *it* not.

¹⁷And he was afraid, and said, How dreadful *is* this place! this *is* none other but the house of God, and this *is* the gate of heaven.

¹⁸And Jacob rose up early in the morning, and took the stone that he had put *for* his pillows, and set it up *for* a pillar, and poured oil upon the top of it. *House of God*

¹⁹And he called the name of that place Beth-el: but the name of *that* city *was called* Luz at the first.

²⁰And Jacob vowed a vow, saying, If God will be with me, and will keep me in this way that I go, and will give me bread to eat, and raiment to put on, *covenant Keeper*

²¹So that I come again to my father's house in peace; then shall the LORD be my God; *Strong One*

²²And this stone, which I have set *for* a pillar, shall be God's house: and of all that thou shalt give me I will surely give the tenth unto thee.

29 Then Jacob went on his journey, and came into the land of the people of the east.

²And he looked, and behold a well in the field,

Amplified Bible

Mahalath daughter of Ishmael, Abraham's son, the sister of Nebaioth.

¹⁰And Jacob left Beersheba and went toward Haran.

¹¹And he came to a certain place and stayed there overnight, because the sun was set. Taking one of the stones of the place, he put it under his head and lay down there to sleep.

¹²And he dreamed that there was a ladder set up on the earth, and the top of it reached to heaven; and the angels of God were ascending and descending on it!

¹³And behold, the Lord stood over *and* beside him and said, I am the Lord, the God of Abraham your father [forefather] and the God of Isaac; I will give to you and to your descendants the land on which you are lying.

¹⁴And your offspring shall be as [countless as] the dust *or* sand of the ground, and you shall spread abroad to the west and the east and the north and the south; and by you and your Offspring shall all the families of the earth be blessed *and* bless themselves.

¹⁵And behold, I am with you and will keep (watch over you with care, take notice of) you wherever you may go, and I will bring you back to this land; for I will not leave you until I have done all of which I have told you.

¹⁶And Jacob awoke from his sleep and he said, Surely the Lord is in this place and I did not know it.

¹⁷He was afraid and said, How to be feared *and* reverenced is this place! This is none other than the house of God, and ᵃthis is the gateway to heaven!

¹⁸And Jacob rose early in the morning and took the stone he had put under his head, and he set it up for a pillar (a monument to the vision in his dream), and he poured oil on its top [in dedication].

¹⁹And he named that place Bethel [the house of God]; but the name of that city was Luz at first.

²⁰Then Jacob made a vow, saying, If God will be with me and will keep me in this way that I go and will give me food to eat and clothing to wear,

²¹So that I may come again to my father's house in peace, then the Lord shall be my God;

²²And this stone which I have set up as a pillar (monument) shall be God's house [a sacred place to me], and of all [the increase of possessions] that You give me I will give the tenth to You.

29 THEN JACOB went [briskly and cheerfully] on his way [400 miles] and came to the land of the people of the East.

²As he looked, he saw a well in the field; and

AMP notes: ᵃ "There is an open way between heaven and earth for each of us. The movement of the tide and the circulation of the blood are not more regular than the intercommunication between heaven and earth. Jacob may have thought that God was local; now he found Him to be omnipresent. Every lonely spot was His house, filled with angels" (F. B. Meyer, *Through the Bible Day by Day*). When Jacob found God in his own heart, he found Him everywhere.

King James Version

and lo, there *were* three flocks of sheep lying by it; for out of that well they watered the flocks: and a great stone *was* upon the well's mouth.

³And thither were all the flocks gathered: and they rolled the stone from the well's mouth, and watered the sheep, and put the stone again upon the well's mouth in his place.

⁴And Jacob said unto them, My brethren, whence *be* ye? And they said, Of Haran *are* we.

⁵And he said unto them, Know ye Laban the son of Nahor? And they said, We know *him.*

⁶And he said unto them, *Is* he well? And they said, *He is* well: and behold, Rachel his daughter cometh with the sheep.

⁷And he said, Lo, *it is* yet high day, neither *is it* time that the cattle should be gathered together: water ye the sheep, and go *and* feed *them.*

⁸And they said, We cannot, until all the flocks be gathered together, and *till* they roll the stone from the well's mouth; then we water the sheep.

⁹And while he yet spake with them, Rachel came with her father's sheep: for she kept them.

¹⁰And it came to pass, when Jacob saw Rachel the daughter of Laban his mother's brother, and the sheep of Laban his mother's brother, that Jacob went near, and rolled the stone from the well's mouth, and watered the flock of Laban his mother's brother.

¹¹And Jacob kissed Rachel, and lifted up his voice, and wept.

¹²And Jacob told Rachel that he *was* her father's brother, and that he *was* Rebekah's son: and she ran and told her father.

¹³And it came to pass, when Laban heard the tidings of Jacob his sister's son, that he ran to meet him, and embraced him, and kissed him, and brought him to his house. And he told Laban all these things.

¹⁴And Laban said to him, Surely thou *art* my bone and my flesh. And he abode with him the space of a month.

¹⁵And Laban said unto Jacob, Because thou *art* my brother, shouldest thou therefore serve me for nought? tell me, what *shall* thy wages *be?*

¹⁶And Laban had two daughters: the name of the elder *was* Leah, and the name of the younger *was* Rachel.

¹⁷Leah *was* tender eyed; but Rachel was beautiful and well favoured.

¹⁸And Jacob loved Rachel; and said, I will serve thee seven years for Rachel thy younger daughter.

¹⁹And Laban said, *It is* better that I give her to thee, than that I should give her to another man: abide with me.

²⁰And Jacob served seven years for Rachel; and they seemed unto him *but* a few days, for the love he had to her.

Amplified Bible

behold, there were three flocks of sheep lying by it, for out of that well the flocks were watered. The stone on the well's mouth was a big one,

³And when all the flocks were gathered there, [the shepherds] would roll the stone from the well's mouth, water the sheep, and replace the stone on the well's mouth.

⁴And Jacob said to them, My brothers, where are you from? And they said, We are from Haran.

⁵[Jacob] said to them, Do you know Laban the grandson of Nahor? And they said, We know him.

⁶He said to them, Is it well with him? And they said, He is doing well; and behold, here comes his daughter Rachel with [his] sheep!

⁷He said, The sun is still high; it is a long time yet before the flocks need be gathered [in their folds]. [Why not] water the sheep and return them to their pasture?

⁸But they said, We cannot until all the flocks are gathered together; then [the shepherds] roll the stone from the well's mouth and we water the sheep.

⁹While he was still talking with them, Rachel came with her father's sheep, for she shepherded them.

¹⁰When Jacob saw Rachel daughter of Laban, his mother's brother, and the sheep of Laban his uncle, Jacob went near and rolled the stone from the well's mouth and watered the flock of his uncle Laban.

¹¹Then Jacob kissed Rachel and he wept aloud.

¹²Jacob told Rachel he was her father's relative, Rebekah's son; and she ran and told her father.

¹³When Laban heard of the arrival of Jacob his sister's son, he ran to meet him, and embraced and kissed him and brought him to his house. And [Jacob] told Laban all these things.

¹⁴Then Laban said to him, Surely you are my bone and my flesh. And [Jacob] stayed with him a month.

¹⁵Then Laban said to Jacob, Just because you are my relative, should you work for me for nothing? Tell me, what shall your wages be?

¹⁶Now Laban had two daughters; the name of the elder was Leah and the name of the younger was Rachel.

¹⁷Leah's eyes were weak *and* dull looking, but Rachel was beautiful and attractive.

¹⁸And Jacob loved Rachel; so he said, I will work for you for seven years for Rachel your younger daughter.

¹⁹And Laban said, It is better that I give her to you than to another man. Stay *and* live with me.

²⁰And Jacob served seven years for Rachel; and they seemed to him but a few days because of the love he had for her.

King James Version

21 ¶ And Jacob said unto Laban, Give *me* my wife, for my days are fulfilled, that I may go in unto her.

22 And Laban gathered together all the men of the place, and made a feast.

23 And it came to pass in the evening, that he took Leah his daughter, and brought her to him; and he went in unto her.

24 And Laban gave unto his daughter Leah Zilpah his maid *for* a handmaid.

25 And it came to pass, that in the morning, behold, it *was* Leah: and he said to Laban, What *is* this thou hast done unto me? did not I serve with thee for Rachel? wherefore then hast thou beguiled me?

26 And Laban said, It must not be so done in our country, to give the younger before the firstborn.

27 Fulfil her week, and we will give thee this also for the service which thou shalt serve with me yet seven other years.

28 And Jacob did so, and fulfilled her week: and he gave him Rachel his daughter to wife *also*.

29 And Laban gave to Rachel his daughter Bilhah his handmaid to be her maid.

30 And he went in also unto Rachel, and he loved also Rachel more than Leah, and served with him yet seven other years.

31 ¶ And when the LORD saw that Leah *was* hated, he opened her womb: but Rachel *was* barren.

32 And Leah conceived, and bare a son, and she called his name Reuben: for she said, Surely the LORD hath looked upon my affliction; now therefore my husband will love me.

33 And she conceived again, and bare a son; and said, Because the LORD hath heard that I *was* hated, he hath therefore given me this *son* also: and she called his name Simeon.

34 And she conceived again, and bare a son; and said, Now *this* time will my husband be joined unto me, because I have born him three sons: therefore was his name called Levi.

35 And she conceived again, and bare a son: and she said, Now will I praise the LORD: therefore she called his name Judah; and left bearing.

30 And when Rachel saw that she bare Jacob no *children,* Rachel envied her sister; and said unto Jacob, Give me children, or else I die.

2 And Jacob's anger was kindled against Rachel: and he said, *Am* I in God's stead, who hath withheld from thee the fruit of the womb?

3 And she said, Behold my maid Bilhah, go in unto her; and she shall bear upon my knees, that I may also have children by her.

Amplified Bible

21 Finally, Jacob said to Laban, Give me my wife, for my time is completed, so that I may take her to me.

22 And Laban gathered together all the men of the place and made a feast [with drinking].

23 But when night came, he took Leah his daughter and brought her to [Jacob], who had intercourse with her.

24 And Laban gave Zilpah his maid to his daughter Leah to be her maid.

25 But in the morning [Jacob saw his wife, and] behold, it was Leah! And he said to Laban, What is this you have done to me? Did I not work for you [all those seven years] for Rachel? Why then have you deceived *and* cheated *and* thrown me down [like this]?

26 And Laban said, It is not permitted in our country to give the younger [in marriage] before the elder.

27 Finish the [wedding feast] week [for Leah]; then we will give you [Rachel] also, and you shall work for me yet seven more years in return.

28 So Jacob complied and fulfilled [Leah's] week; then [Laban] gave him Rachel his daughter as his wife.

29 (And Laban gave Bilhah his maid to Rachel his daughter to be her maid.)

30 And Jacob lived with Rachel also as his wife, and he loved Rachel more than Leah and served [Laban] another seven years [for her].

31 And when the Lord saw that Leah was despised, He made her able to bear children, but Rachel was barren.

32 And Leah became pregnant and bore a son and named him Reuben [See, a son!]; for she said, Because the Lord has seen my humiliation *and* affliction; now my husband will love me.

33 [Leah] became pregnant again and bore a son and said, Because the Lord heard that I am despised, He has given me this son also; and she named him Simeon [God hears].

34 And she became pregnant again and bore a son and said, Now this time will my husband be a companion to me, for I have borne him three sons. Therefore he was named Levi [companion].

35 Again she conceived and bore a son, and she said, Now will I praise the Lord! So she called his name Judah [praise]; then [for a time] she ceased bearing.

30 WHEN RACHEL saw that she bore Jacob no children, she envied her sister, and said to Jacob, Give me children, or else I will die!

2 And Jacob became very angry with Rachel and he said, Am I in God's stead, Who has denied you children?

3 And she said, See here, take my maid Bilhah and have intercourse with her; and [when the baby comes] she shall deliver it upon my knees, that I by her may also have children.

King James Version

⁴And she gave him Bilhah her handmaid to wife: and Jacob went in unto her.

⁵And Bilhah conceived, and bare Jacob a son.

⁶And Rachel said, God hath judged me, and hath also heard my voice, and hath given me a son: therefore called she his name Dan.

⁷And Bilhah Rachel's maid conceived again, and bare Jacob a second son.

⁸And Rachel said, With great wrestlings have I wrestled with my sister, and I have prevailed: and she called his name Naphtali.

⁹When Leah saw that she had left bearing, she took Zilpah her maid, and gave her Jacob to wife.

¹⁰And Zilpah Leah's maid bare Jacob a son.

¹¹And Leah said, A troop cometh: and she called his name Gad.

¹²And Zilpah Leah's maid bare Jacob a second son.

¹³And Leah said, Happy am I, for the daughters will call me blessed: and she called his name Asher.

¹⁴And Reuben went in the days of wheat harvest, and found mandrakes in the field, and brought them unto his mother Leah. Then Rachel said to Leah, Give me, I pray thee, of thy son's mandrakes.

¹⁵And she said unto her, *Is it* a small matter that thou hast taken my husband? and wouldest thou take away my son's mandrakes also? And Rachel said, Therefore he shall lie with thee to night for thy son's mandrakes.

¹⁶And Jacob came out of the field in the evening, and Leah went out to meet him, and said, Thou must come in unto me; for surely I have hired thee with my son's mandrakes. And he lay with her that night.

¹⁷And God hearkened unto Leah, and she conceived, and bare Jacob the fifth son.

¹⁸And Leah said, God hath given *me* my hire, because I have given my maiden to my husband: and she called his name Issachar.

¹⁹And Leah conceived again, and bare Jacob the sixth son.

²⁰And Leah said, God hath endued me with a good dowry; now will my husband dwell with me, because I have born him six sons: and she called his name Zebulun.

²¹And afterwards she bare a daughter, and called her name Dinah.

²²And God remembered Rachel, and God hearkened to her, and opened her womb.

²³And she conceived, and bare a son; and said, God hath taken away my reproach:

Amplified Bible

⁴And she gave him Bilhah her maid as a [secondary] wife, and Jacob had intercourse with her.

⁵And Bilhah became pregnant and bore Jacob a son.

⁶And Rachel said, God has judged *and* vindicated me, and has heard my plea and has given me a son; so she named him Dan [judged].

⁷And Bilhah, Rachel's maid, conceived again and bore Jacob a second son.

⁸And Rachel said, With mighty wrestlings [in prayer to God] I have struggled with my sister and have prevailed; so she named him [this second son Bilhah bore] Naphtali [struggled].

⁹When Leah saw that she had ceased to bear, she gave Zilpah her maid to Jacob as a [secondary] wife.

¹⁰And Zilpah, Leah's maid, bore Jacob a son.

¹¹Then Leah said, Victory *and* good fortune have come; and she named him Gad [fortune].

¹²Zilpah, Leah's maid, bore Jacob [her] second son.

¹³And Leah said, I am happy, for women will call me blessed (happy, fortunate, to be envied); and she named him Asher [happy].

¹⁴Now Reuben went at the time of wheat harvest and found some mandrakes (love apples) in the field and brought them to his mother Leah. Then Rachel said to Leah, Give me, I pray you, some of your son's mandrakes.

¹⁵But [Leah] answered, Is it not enough that you have taken my husband without your taking away my son's *a* mandrakes also? And Rachel said, Jacob shall sleep with you tonight [in exchange] for your son's mandrakes.

¹⁶And Jacob came out of the field in the evening, and Leah went out to meet him and said, You must sleep with me [tonight], for I have certainly paid your hire with my son's mandrakes. So he slept with her that night.

¹⁷And God heeded Leah's [prayer], and she conceived and bore Jacob [her] fifth son.

¹⁸Leah said, God has given me my hire, because I have given my maid to my husband; and she called his name Issachar [hired].

¹⁹And Leah became pregnant again and bore Jacob [her] sixth son.

²⁰Then Leah said, God has endowed me with a good marriage gift [for my husband]; now will he dwell with me [and regard me as his wife in reality], because I have borne him six sons; and she named him Zebulun [dwelling].

²¹Afterwards she bore a daughter and called her Dinah.

²²Then God remembered Rachel and answered her pleading and made it possible for her to have children.

²³And [now for the first time] she became pregnant and bore a son; and she said, God has taken away my reproach, disgrace, *and* humiliation.

AMP notes: a Mandrakes were superstitiously supposed to excite and win love.

King James Version

²⁴And she called his name Joseph; and said, The LORD shall add to me another son.

²⁵ ¶ And it came to pass, when Rachel had born Joseph, that Jacob said unto Laban, Send me away, that I may go unto mine own place, and to my country.

²⁶Give *me* my wives and my children, for whom I have served thee, and let me go: for thou knowest my service which I have done thee.

²⁷And Laban said unto him, I pray thee, if I have found favour in thine eyes, *tarry: for* I have learned by experience that the LORD hath blessed me for thy sake.

²⁸And he said, Appoint me thy wages, and I will give *it.*

²⁹And he said unto him, Thou knowest how I have served thee, and how thy cattle was with me.

³⁰For *it was* little which thou hadst before I *came,* and it is *now* increased unto a multitude; and the LORD hath blessed thee since my coming: and now when shall I provide for mine own house also?

³¹And he said, What shall I give thee? And Jacob said, Thou shalt not give me any thing: if thou wilt do this thing for me, I will again feed *and* keep thy flock:

³²I will pass through all thy flock to day, removing from thence all the speckled and spotted cattle, and all the brown cattle among the sheep, and the spotted and speckled among the goats: and *of such* shall be my hire.

³³So shall my righteousness answer for me in time to come, when it shall come for my hire before thy face: every one that *is* not speckled and spotted amongst the goats, and brown amongst the sheep, that *shall be counted* stolen with me.

³⁴And Laban said, Behold, I would it might be according to thy word.

³⁵And he removed that day the he goats that were ringstraked and spotted, and all the she goats that were speckled and spotted, *and* every one that had *some* white in it, and all the brown amongst the sheep, and gave *them* into the hand of his sons.

³⁶And he set three days' journey betwixt himself and Jacob: and Jacob fed the rest of Laban's flocks.

³⁷ ¶ And Jacob took him rods of green poplar, and of the hazel and chesnut tree; and pilled white strakes in them, and made the white appear which *was* in the rods.

³⁸And he set the rods which he had pilled before the flocks in the gutters in the watering troughs when the flocks came to drink, that they should conceive when they came to drink.

³⁹And the flocks conceived before the rods, and brought forth cattle ringstraked, speckled, and spotted.

Amplified Bible

²⁴And she called his name Joseph [may he add] and said, May the Lord add to me another son.

²⁵When Rachel had borne Joseph, Jacob said to Laban, Send me away, that I may go to my own place and country.

²⁶Give me my wives and my children, for whom I have served you, and let me go; for you know the work which I have done for you.

²⁷And Laban said to him, If I have found favor in your sight, I pray you [do not go]; for I have learned by experience *and* from the omens in divination that the Lord has favored me with blessings on your account.

²⁸He said, State your salary and I will give it.

²⁹Jacob answered him, You know how I have served you, and how your possessions, your cattle *and* sheep *and* goats, have fared with me.

³⁰For you had little before I came, and it has increased *and* multiplied abundantly; and the Lord has favored you with blessings wherever I turned. But now, when shall I provide for my own house also?

³¹[Laban] said, What shall I give you? And Jacob said, You shall not give me anything, if you will do this one thing for me [of which I am about to tell you], and I will again feed *and* take care of your flock.

³²Let me pass through all your flock today, removing from it every speckled and spotted animal and every black one among the sheep, and the spotted and speckled among the goats; and such shall be my wages.

³³So later when the matter of my wages is brought before you, my fair dealing will be evident *and* answer for me. Every one that is not speckled and spotted among the goats and black among the sheep, if found with me, shall be counted as stolen.

³⁴And Laban said, Good; let it be done as you say.

³⁵But that same day [Laban] removed the he-goats that were streaked and spotted and all the she-goats that were speckled and spotted, every one that had white on it, and every black lamb, and put them in charge of his sons.

³⁶And he set [a distance of] three days' journey between himself and Jacob; and Jacob was then left in care of the rest of Laban's flock.

³⁷But Jacob took fresh rods of poplar and almond and plane trees and peeled white streaks in them, exposing the white in the rods.

³⁸Then he set the rods which he had peeled in front of the flocks in the watering troughs where the flocks came to drink. And since they bred *and* conceived when they came to drink,

³⁹The flocks bred *and* conceived in sight of the rods and brought forth lambs *and* kids streaked, speckled, and spotted.

King James Version

⁴⁰And Jacob did separate the lambs, and set the faces of the flocks toward the ringstraked, and all the brown in the flock of Laban; and he put his own flocks by themselves, and put them not unto Laban's cattle.

⁴¹And it came to pass, whensoever the stronger cattle did conceive, that Jacob laid the rods before the eyes of the cattle in the gutters, that they might conceive among the rods.

⁴²But when the cattle were feeble, he put *them* not in: so the feebler were Laban's, and the stronger Jacob's.

⁴³And the man increased exceedingly, and had much cattle, and maidservants, and menservants, and camels, and asses.

31 And he heard the words of Laban's sons, saying, Jacob hath taken away all that *was* our father's; and of *that* which *was* of our father's hath he gotten all this glory.

²And Jacob beheld the countenance of Laban, and behold, it *was* not toward him as before.

³And the LORD said unto Jacob, Return unto the land of thy fathers, and to thy kindred; and I will be with thee.

⁴And Jacob sent and called Rachel and Leah to the field unto his flock,

⁵And said unto them, I see your father's countenance, that it *is* not toward me as before; but the God of my father hath been with me.

⁶And ye know that with all my power I have served your father.

⁷And your father hath deceived me, and changed my wages ten times; but God suffered him not to hurt me.

⁸If he said thus, The speckled shall be thy wages; then all the cattle bare speckled: and if he said thus, The ringstraked shall be thy hire; then bare all the cattle ringstraked.

⁹Thus God hath taken away the cattle of your father, and given *them* to me.

¹⁰And it came to pass at the time that the cattle conceived, that I lifted up mine eyes, and saw in a dream, and behold, the rams which leaped upon the cattle *were* ringstraked, speckled, and grisled.

¹¹And the angel of God spake unto me in a dream, *saying*, Jacob: And I said, Here *am* I.

¹²And he said, Lift up now thine eyes, and see, all the rams which leap upon the cattle *are* ringstraked, speckled, and grisled: for I have seen all that Laban doeth unto thee.

¹³I *am* the God of Beth-el, where thou anointedst the pillar, *and* where thou vowedst a vow

Amplified Bible

⁴⁰Jacob separated the lambs, and [as he had done with the peeled rods] he also set the faces of the flocks toward the streaked and all the dark in the [new] flock of Laban; and he put his own droves by themselves and did not let them breed with Laban's flock.

⁴¹And whenever the stronger animals were breeding, Jacob laid the rods in the watering troughs before the eyes of the flock, that they might breed *and* conceive among the rods.

⁴²But when the sheep *and* goats were feeble, he omitted putting the rods there; so the feebler animals were Laban's and the stronger Jacob's.

⁴³Thus the man increased *and* became exceedingly rich, and had many sheep *and* goats, and maidservants, menservants, camels, and donkeys.

31 JACOB HEARD Laban's sons complaining, Jacob has taken away all that was our father's; he has acquired all this wealth *and* honor from what belonged to our father.

²And Jacob noticed that Laban looked at him less favorably than before.

³Then the Lord said to Jacob, Return to the land of your fathers and to your people, and I will be with you.

⁴So Jacob sent and called Rachel and Leah to the field to his flock,

⁵And he said to them, I see how your father looks at me, that he is not [friendly] toward me as before; but the God of my father has been with me.

⁶You know that I have served your father with all my might *and* power.

⁷But your father has deceived me and changed my wages ten times, but God did not allow him to hurt me.

⁸If he said, The speckled shall be your wages, then all the flock bore speckled; and if he said, The streaked shall be your hire, then all the flock bore streaked.

⁹Thus God has taken away the flocks of your father and given them to me.

¹⁰And I had a ᵃdream at the time the flock conceived. I looked up and saw that the rams which mated with the she-goats were streaked, speckled, and spotted.

¹¹And the ᵇAngel of God said to me in the dream, Jacob. And I said, Here am I.

¹²And He said, Look up and see, all the rams which mate with the flock are streaked, speckled, and mottled; for I have seen all that Laban does to you.

¹³I am the God of Bethel, where you anointed the pillar and where you vowed a vow to Me.

AMP notes: ᵃ We naturally wonder why we have not heard of this dream before and are tempted to question Jacob's truthfulness; but the Samaritan text removes all such doubt by recording the whole dream in the previous chapter (Gen. 30), right after Gen. 30:36 (Adam Clarke, *The Holy Bible with A Commentary*).   ᵇ See footnote on Gen. 16:7. Note especially Gen. 31:13, where the Angel says, "I am the God of Bethel."

King James Version

unto me: now arise, get thee out from this land, and return unto the land of thy kindred.

14And Rachel and Leah answered and said unto him, *Is there* yet any portion or inheritance for us in our father's house?

15Are we not counted of him strangers? for he hath sold us, and hath quite devoured also our money.

16For all the riches which God hath taken from our father, that *is* ours, and our children's: now then, whatsoever God hath said unto thee, do.

17 ¶ Then Jacob rose up, and set his sons and his wives upon camels;

18And he carried away all his cattle, and all his goods which he had gotten, the cattle of his getting, which he had gotten in Padan-aram, for to go to Isaac his father in the land of Canaan.

19And Laban went to shear his sheep: and Rachel had stolen the images that *were* her father's.

20And Jacob stale away unawares to Laban the Syrian, in that he told him not that he fled.

21So he fled with all that he had; and he rose up, and passed over the river, and set his face *toward* the mount Gilead.

22And it was told Laban on the third day that Jacob was fled.

23And he took his brethren with him, and pursued after him seven days' journey; and they overtook him in the mount Gilead.

24And God came to Laban the Syrian in a dream by night, and said unto him, Take heed that thou speak not to Jacob either good or bad.

25Then Laban overtook Jacob. Now Jacob had pitched his tent in the mount: and Laban with his brethren pitched in the mount of Gilead.

26And Laban said to Jacob, What hast thou done, that thou hast stolen away unawares to me, and carried away my daughters, as captives taken with the sword?

27Wherefore didst thou flee away secretly, and steal away from me; and didst not tell me, that I might have sent thee away with mirth, and with songs, with tabret, and with harp?

28And hast not suffered me to kiss my sons and my daughters? thou hast now done foolishly in *so* doing.

29It is in the power of my hand to do you hurt: but the God of your father spake unto me yesternight, saying, Take thou heed that thou speak not to Jacob either good or bad.

30And now, *though* thou wouldest needs be gone, because thou sore longedst after thy father's house, *yet* wherefore hast thou stolen my gods?

Amplified Bible

Now arise, get out from this land and return to your native land.

14And Rachel and Leah answered him, Is there any portion or inheritance for us in our father's house?

15Are we not counted by him as strangers? For he sold us and has also quite devoured our money [the price you paid for us].

16For all the riches which God has taken from our father are ours and our children's. Now then, whatever God has said to you, do it.

17Then Jacob rose up and set his sons and his wives upon the camels;

18And he drove away all his livestock and all his gain which he had gotten, the livestock he had obtained *and* accumulated in Padan-aram, to go to Isaac his father in the land of Canaan.

19Now Laban had gone to shear his sheep [possibly to the feast of sheepshearing], and Rachel stole her father's household gods.

20And Jacob outwitted Laban the Syrian [Aramean] in that he did not tell him that he [intended] to flee *and* slip away secretly.

21So he fled with all that he had, and arose and crossed the river [Euphrates] and set his face toward the hill country of Gilead.

22But on the third day Laban was told that Jacob had fled.

23So he took his kinsmen with him and pursued after [Jacob] for seven days, and they overtook him in the hill country of Gilead.

24But God came to Laban the Syrian [Aramean] in a dream by night and said to him, Be careful that you do not speak from good to bad to Jacob [peaceably, then violently].

25Then Laban overtook Jacob. Now Jacob had pitched his tent on the hill, and Laban coming with his kinsmen pitched [his tents] on the same hill of Gilead.

26And Laban said to Jacob, What do you mean stealing away *and* leaving like this without my knowing it, and carrying off my daughters as if captives of the sword?

27Why did you flee secretly and cheat me and did not tell me, so that I might have sent you away with joy *and* gladness and with singing, with tambourine and lyre?

28And why did you not permit me to kiss my sons [grandchildren] and my daughters good-bye? Now you have done foolishly [in behaving like this].

29It is in my power to do you harm; but the God of your father spoke to me last night, saying, Be careful that you do not speak from good to bad to Jacob [peaceably, then violently].

30And now you felt you must go because you were homesick for your father's house, but why did you steal my [household] *a*gods?

AMP notes: *a* Why was Laban making such a great commotion about some small idols? It had never been satisfactorily explained until the answer was found in the excavated Nuzi tablets (J. P. Free, *Archaeology Illuminates the Bible*),

King James Version

31And Jacob answered and said to Laban, Because I was afraid: for I said, Peradventure thou wouldest take by force thy daughters from me.

32With whomsoever thou findest thy gods, let him not live: before our brethren discern thou what *is* thine with me, and take *it* to thee. For Jacob knew not that Rachel had stolen them.

33And Laban went into Jacob's tent, and into Leah's tent, and into the two maidservants' tents; but he found *them* not. Then went he out of Leah's tent, and entered into Rachel's tent.

34Now Rachel had taken the images, and put them in the camel's furniture, and sat upon them. And Laban searched all the tent, but found *them* not.

35And she said to her father, Let it not displease my lord that I cannot rise up before thee; for the custom of women *is* upon me. And he searched, but found not the images.

36And Jacob was wroth, and chode with Laban: and Jacob answered and said to Laban, What *is* my trespass? what *is* my sin, that thou hast *so* hotly pursued after me?

37Whereas thou hast searched all my stuff, what hast thou found of all thy household stuff? set *it* here before my brethren and thy brethren, that they may judge betwixt us both.

38This twenty years *have* I *been* with thee; thy ewes and thy she goats have not cast their young, and the rams of thy flock have I not eaten.

39That which was torn *of beasts* I brought not unto thee; I bare the loss of it; of my hand didst thou require it, *whether* stolen by day, or stolen by night.

40*Thus* I was in the day, the drought consumed me, and the frost by night; and my sleep departed from mine eyes.

41Thus have I been twenty years in thy house; I served thee fourteen years for thy two daughters, and six years for thy cattle: and thou hast changed my wages ten times.

42Except the God of my father, the God of Abraham, and the fear of Isaac, had been with me, surely thou hadst sent me away now empty. God hath seen mine affliction and the labour of my hands, and rebuked *thee* yesternight.

43And Laban answered and said unto Jacob, *These* daughters *are* my daughters, and *these* children *are* my children, and *these* cattle *are* my cattle, and all that thou seest *is* mine: and what

Amplified Bible

31Jacob answered Laban, Because I was afraid; for I thought, Suppose you would take your daughters from me by force.

32The one with whom you find those gods of yours, let him not live. Here before our kinsmen [search my possessions and] take whatever you find that belongs to you. For Jacob did not know that Rachel had stolen [the images].

33So Laban went into Jacob's tent and into Leah's tent and the tent of the two maids, but he did not find them. Then he went from Leah's tent into Rachel's tent.

34Now Rachel had taken the images (gods) and put them in the camel's saddle and sat on them. Laban searched *and* felt through all the tent, but did not find them.

35And [Rachel] said to her father, Do not be displeased, my lord, that I cannot rise up before you, for the period of women is upon me *and* I am unwell. And he searched, but did not find the gods.

36Then Jacob became angry and reproached *and* argued with Laban. And Jacob said to Laban, What is my fault? What is my sin, that you so hotly pursued me?

37Although you have searched *and* felt through all my household possessions, what have you found of all your household goods? Put it here before my brethren and yours, that they may judge *and* decide between us.

38These twenty years I have been with you; your ewes and your she-goats have not lost their young, and the rams of your flock have not been eaten by me.

39I did not bring you [the carcasses of the animals] torn by wild beasts; I bore the loss of it; you required of me [to make good] all that was stolen, whether it occurred by day or by night.

40This was [my lot]; by day the heat consumed me and by night the cold, and I could not sleep.

41I have been twenty years in your house. I served you fourteen years for your two daughters and six years for your flocks; and you have changed my wages ten times.

42And if the God of my father, the God of Abraham and the Dread [lest he should fall] *and* Fear [lest he offend] of Isaac, had not been with me, surely you would have sent me away now empty-handed. God has seen my affliction *and* humiliation and the [wearying] labor of my hands and rebuked you last night.

43Laban answered Jacob, These daughters are my daughters, these children are my children, these flocks are my flocks, and all that you see is

AMP notes continued: which showed that possession of the father's household gods played an important role in inheritance (W. F. Albright, "Recent Discoveries in Bible Lands," in *Young's Analytical Concordance to the Bible*). One of the Nuzi tablets indicated that in the region where Laban lived, a son-in-law who possessed the family images could appear in court and make claim to the estate of his father-in-law (various authors cited by Allan A. MacRae, "The Relation of Archaeology to the Bible," in American Scientific Affiliation, *Modern Science and Christian Faith*). Since Jacob's possession of the images implied the right to inheritance of Laban's wealth, one can understand why Laban organized his hurried expedition to recover the images (J. P. Free, *Archaeology and Bible History*).

King James Version

can I do *this* day unto these my daughters, or unto their children which they have born?

44Now therefore come thou, let us make a covenant, I and thou; and let it be for a witness between me and thee.

45And Jacob took a stone, and set it up *for* a pillar.

46And Jacob said unto his brethren, Gather stones; and they took stones, and made a heap: and they did eat there upon the heap.

47And Laban called it Jegar-sahadutha: but Jacob called it Galeed.

48And Laban said, This heap *is* a witness between me and thee *this* day. Therefore was the name of it called Galeed;

49And Mizpah; for he said, The LORD watch between me and thee, when we are absent one from another.

50If thou shalt afflict my daughters, or if thou shalt take *other* wives beside my daughters, no man *is* with us; see, God *is* witness betwixt me and thee.

51And Laban said to Jacob, Behold this heap, and behold *this* pillar, which I have cast betwixt me and thee;

52This heap *be* witness, and *this* pillar *be* witness, that I will not pass over this heap to thee, and that thou shalt not pass over this heap and this pillar unto me, for harm.

53The God of Abraham, and the God of Nahor, the God of their father, judge betwixt us. And Jacob sware by the fear of his father Isaac.

54Then Jacob offered sacrifice upon the mount, and called his brethren to eat bread: and they did eat bread, and tarried all night in the mount.

55And early in the morning Laban rose up, and kissed his sons and his daughters, and blessed them: and Laban departed, and returned unto his place.

32 And Jacob went on his way, and the angels of God met him.

2And when Jacob saw them, he said, This *is* God's host: and he called the name of that place Mahanaim.

3And Jacob sent messengers before him to Esau his brother unto the land of Seir, the country of Edom.

4And he commanded them, saying, Thus shall ye speak unto my lord Esau; Thy servant Jacob saith thus, I have sojourned with Laban, and stayed *there* until now:

Amplified Bible

mine. But what can I do today to these my daughters or to their children whom they have borne?

44So come now, let us make a covenant *or* league, you and I, and let it be for a witness between you and me.

45So Jacob set up a stone for a pillar *or* monument.

46And Jacob said to his brethren, Gather stones; and they took stones and made a heap, and they ate [together] there upon the heap.

47Laban called it Jegar-sahadutha [witness heap, *in Aramaic*], but Jacob called it Galeed [*a* witness heap, *in Hebrew.*]

48Laban said, This heap is a witness today between you and me. Therefore it was named Galeed.

49And [the pillar or monument was called] Mizpah [watchpost], for he [Laban] said, May the Lord watch between you and me when we are absent *and* hidden one from another.

50If you should afflict, humiliate, *or* lower [divorce] my daughters, or if you should take other wives beside my daughters, although no man is with us [to witness], see (remember), God is witness between you and me.

51And Laban said to Jacob, See this heap and this pillar, which I have set up between you and me.

52This heap is a witness and this pillar is a witness, that I will not pass by this heap to you, and that you will not pass by this heap and this pillar to me, for harm.

53The God of Abraham and the God of Nahor, and the god [the object of worship] of their father [Terah, an idolator], judge between us. But Jacob swore [only] by [the one true God] the Dread *and* Fear of his father Isaac.

54Then Jacob offered a sacrifice on the mountain and called his brethren to eat food; and they ate food and lingered all night on the mountain.

55And early in the morning Laban rose up and kissed his grandchildren and his daughters and pronounced a blessing [asking God's favor] on them. Then Laban departed and returned to his home.

32 THEN JACOB went on his way, and God's angels met him.

2When Jacob saw them, he said, This is God's army! So he named that place Mahanaim [two armies].

3And Jacob sent messengers before him to Esau his brother in the land of Seir, the country of Edom.

4And he commanded them, Say this to my lord Esau: Your servant Jacob says this: I have been living temporarily with Laban and have stayed there till now.

AMP notes: a The Latin Vulgate adds, "Each according to the idiom of his own tongue"—i.e., Laban in Aramaic and Jacob in Hebrew.

King James Version

⁵And I have oxen, and asses, flocks, and menservants, and womenservants: and I have sent to tell my lord, that I may find grace in thy sight.

⁶And the messengers returned to Jacob, saying, We came to thy brother Esau, and also he cometh to meet thee, and four hundred men with him.

⁷Then Jacob was greatly afraid and distressed: and he divided the people that *was* with him, and the flocks, and herds, and the camels, into two bands;

⁸And said, If Esau come to the one company, and smite it, then the *other* company which is left shall escape.

⁹And Jacob said, O God of my father Abraham, and God of my father Isaac, the LORD which saidst unto me, Return unto thy country, and to thy kindred, and I will deal well with thee:

¹⁰I am not worthy of the least of all the mercies, and of all the truth, which thou hast shewed unto thy servant; for with my staff I passed over this Jordan; and now I am become two bands.

¹¹Deliver me, I pray thee, from the hand of my brother, from the hand of Esau: for I fear him, lest he will come and smite me, *and* the mother with the children.

¹²And thou saidst, I will surely do thee good, and make thy seed as the sand of the sea, which cannot be numbered for multitude.

¹³And he lodged there that *same* night; and took of that which came to his hand a present for Esau his brother;

¹⁴Two hundred she goats, and twenty he goats, two hundred ewes, and twenty rams,

¹⁵Thirty milch camels with their colts, forty kine, and ten bulls, twenty she asses, and ten foals.

¹⁶And he delivered *them* into the hand of his servants, every drove by themselves; and said unto his servants, Pass over before me, and put a space betwixt drove and drove.

¹⁷And he commanded the foremost, saying, When Esau my brother meeteth thee, and asketh thee, saying, Whose *art* thou? and whither goest thou? and whose *are* these before thee?

¹⁸Then thou shalt say, *They be* thy servant Jacob's; it *is* a present sent unto my lord Esau: and behold, also he *is* behind us.

¹⁹And so commanded he the second, and the third, and all that followed the droves, saying, On this manner shall ye speak unto Esau, when you find him.

²⁰And say ye moreover, Behold, thy servant Jacob *is* behind us. For he said, I will appease him with the present that goeth before me, and afterward I will see his face; peradventure he will accept of me.

Amplified Bible

⁵And I have oxen, donkeys, flocks, menservants, and women servants; and I have sent to tell my lord, that I may find mercy *and* kindness in your sight.

⁶And the messengers returned to Jacob, saying, We came to your brother Esau; and now he is [on the way] to meet you, and four hundred men are with him.

⁷Then Jacob was greatly afraid and distressed; and he divided the people who were with him, and the flocks and herds and camels, into two groups,

⁸Thinking, If Esau comes to the one group and smites it, then the other group which is left will escape.

⁹Jacob said, O God of my father Abraham and God of my father Isaac, the Lord Who said to me, Return to your country and to your people and I will do you good,

¹⁰I am not worthy of the least of all the mercy *and* loving-kindness and all the faithfulness which You have shown to Your servant, for with [only] my staff I passed over this Jordan [long ago], and now I have become two companies.

¹¹Deliver me, I pray You, from the hand of my brother, from the hand of Esau; for I fear him, lest he come and smite [us all], the mothers with the children.

¹²And You said, I will surely do you good and make your descendants as the sand of the sea, which cannot be numbered for multitude.

¹³And Jacob lodged there that night and took from what he had with him as a present for his brother Esau:

¹⁴Two hundred she-goats, 20 he-goats, 200 ewes, 20 rams,

¹⁵Thirty milk camels with their colts, 40 cows, 10 bulls, 20 she-donkeys, and 10 [donkey] colts.

¹⁶And he put them into the charge of his servants, every drove by itself, and said to his servants, Pass over before me and put a space between drove and drove.

¹⁷And he commanded the first, When Esau my brother meets you and asks to whom you belong, where you are going, and whose are the animals before you,

¹⁸Then you shall say, They are your servant Jacob's; it is a present sent to my lord Esau; and moreover, he is behind us.

¹⁹And so he commanded the second and the third and all that followed the droves, saying, This is what you are to say to Esau when you meet him.

²⁰And say, Moreover, your servant Jacob is behind us. For he said, I will appease him with the present that goes before me, and afterward I will see his face; perhaps he will accept me.

King James Version

²¹So went the present over before him: and himself lodged that night in the company.

²²And he rose up that night, and took his two wives, and his two womenservants, and his eleven sons, and passed over the ford Jabbok.

²³And he took them, and sent them over the brook, and sent over that he had.

²⁴ ¶ And Jacob was left alone; and there wrestled a man with him until the breaking of the day.

²⁵And when he saw that he prevailed not against him, he touched the hollow of his thigh; and the hollow of Jacob's thigh was out of joint, as he wrestled with him.

²⁶And he said, Let me go, for the day breaketh. And he said, I will not let thee go, except thou bless me.

²⁷And he said unto him, What is thy name? And he said, Jacob.

²⁸And he said, Thy name shall be called no more Jacob, but Israel: for as a prince hast thou power with God and with men, and hast prevailed.

²⁹And Jacob asked him, and said, Tell me, I pray thee, thy name. And he said, Wherefore is it that thou dost ask after my name? And he blessed him there.

³⁰And Jacob called the name of the place Peniel: for I have seen God face to face, and my life is preserved.

³¹And as he passed over Penuel the sun rose upon him, and he halted upon his thigh.

³²Therefore the children of Israel eat not of the sinew which shrank, which is upon the hollow of the thigh, unto this day: because he touched the hollow of Jacob's thigh in the sinew that shrank.

33 And Jacob lifted up his eyes, and looked, and behold, Esau came, and with him four hundred men. And he divided the children unto Leah, and unto Rachel, and unto the two handmaids.

²And he put the handmaids and their children foremost, and Leah and her children after, and Rachel and Joseph hindermost.

³And he passed over before them, and bowed himself to the ground seven times, until he came near to his brother.

⁴And Esau ran to meet him, and embraced him, and fell on his neck, and kissed him: and they wept.

⁵And he lift up his eyes, and saw the women and the children; and said, Who are those with

Amplified Bible

²¹So the present went on before him, and he himself lodged that night in the camp.

²²But he rose up that [same] night and took his two wives, his two women servants, and his eleven sons and passed over the ford [of the] Jabbok.

²³And he took them and sent them across the brook; also he sent over all that he had.

²⁴And Jacob was left alone, and a Man wrestled with him until daybreak.

²⁵And when [the ᵃMan] saw that He did not prevail against [Jacob], He touched the hollow of his thigh; and Jacob's thigh was put out of joint as he wrestled with Him.

²⁶Then He said, Let Me go, for day is breaking. But [Jacob] said, I will not let You go unless You declare a blessing upon me.

²⁷[The Man] asked him, What is your name? And [in shock of realization, whispering] he said, Jacob [supplanter, schemer, trickster, swindler]!

²⁸And He said, Your name shall be called no more Jacob [supplanter], but Israel [contender with God]; for you have contended and have power with God and with men and have prevailed.

²⁹Then Jacob asked Him, Tell me, I pray You, what [in contrast] is Your name? But He said, Why is it that you ask My name? And ᵃ[the Angel of God declared] a blessing on [Jacob] there.

³⁰And Jacob called the name of the place Peniel [the face of God], saying, For I have seen God face to face, and my life is spared and not snatched away.

³¹And as he passed Penuel [Peniel], the sun rose upon him, and he was limping because of his thigh.

³²That is why to this day the Israelites do not eat the sinew of the hip which is on the hollow of the thigh, because [the Angel of the Lord] touched the hollow of Jacob's thigh on the sinew of the hip.

33 AND JACOB raised his eyes and looked, and behold, Esau was coming and with him 400 men. So he divided the children to Leah and to Rachel and to the two maids.

²And he put the maids and their children in front, Leah and her children after them, and Rachel and Joseph last of all.

³Then Jacob went over [the stream] before them and bowed himself to the ground seven times, until he came near to his brother.

⁴But Esau ran to meet him, and embraced him and fell on his neck and kissed him, and they wept.

⁵[Esau] looked up and saw the women and the children and said, Who are these with you?

AMP notes: ᵃ This is God Himself (as Jacob eventually realizes in Gen. 32:30) in the form of an angel. See footnote on Gen. 16:7, as well as Hos. 12:3-4.

King James Version

thee? And he said, The children which God hath graciously given thy servant.

⁶Then the handmaidens came near, they and their children, and they bowed themselves.

⁷And Leah also with her children came near, and bowed themselves: and after came Joseph near and Rachel, and they bowed themselves.

⁸And he said, What meanest thou by all this drove which I met? And he said, *These are* to find grace in the sight of my lord.

⁹And Esau said, I have enough, my brother; keep that thou hast unto thyself.

¹⁰And Jacob said, Nay, I pray thee, if now I have found grace in thy sight, then receive my present at my hand: for therefore I have seen thy face, as though I had seen the face of God, and thou wast pleased with me.

¹¹Take, I pray thee, my blessing that is brought to thee; because God hath dealt graciously with me, and because I have enough. And he urged him, and he took *it*.

¹²And he said, Let us take our journey, and let us go, and I will go before thee.

¹³And he said unto him, My lord knoweth that the children *are* tender, and the flocks and herds with young *are* with me: and if *men* should overdrive them one day, all the flock will die.

¹⁴Let my lord, I pray thee, pass over before his servant: and I will lead on softly, according as the cattle that goeth before me and the children be able to endure, until I come unto my lord unto Seir.

¹⁵And Esau said, Let me now leave with thee *some* of the folk that *are* with me. And he said, What needeth it? let me find grace in the sight of my lord.

¹⁶So Esau returned that day on his way unto Seir.

¹⁷And Jacob journeyed to Succoth, and built him a house, and made booths for his cattle: therefore the name of the place is called Succoth.

¹⁸And Jacob came to Shalem, a city of Shechem, which *is* in the land of Canaan, when he came from Padan-aram; and pitched his tent before the city.

¹⁹And he bought a parcel of a field, where he had spread his tent, at the hand of the children of Hamor, Shechem's father, for an hundred pieces of money.

²⁰And he erected there an altar, and called it El-Elohe-Israel.

34 And Dinah the daughter of Leah, which she bare unto Jacob, went out to see the daughters of the land.

Amplified Bible

And [Jacob] replied, They are the children whom God has graciously given your servant.

⁶Then the maids came near, they and their children, and they bowed themselves.

⁷And Leah also with her children came near, and they bowed themselves. After them Joseph and Rachel came near, and they bowed themselves.

⁸Esau said, What do you mean by all this company which I met? And he said, These are that I might find favor in the sight of my lord.

⁹And Esau said, I have plenty, my brother; keep what you have for yourself.

¹⁰But Jacob replied, No, I beg of you, if now I have found favor in your sight, receive my gift that I am presenting; for truly to see your face is to me as if I had seen the face of God, and you have received me favorably.

¹¹Accept, I beg of you, my blessing *and* gift that I have brought to you; for God has dealt graciously with me and I have everything. And he kept urging him and he accepted it.

¹²Then [Esau] said, Let us get started on our journey, and I will go before you.

¹³But Jacob replied, You know, my lord, that the children are tender *and* delicate *and* need gentle care, and the flocks and herds with young are of concern to me; for if the men should overdrive them for a single day, the whole of the flocks would die.

¹⁴Let my lord, I pray you, pass over before his servant; and I will lead on slowly, governed by [consideration for] the livestock that set the pace before me and the endurance of the children, ᵃuntil I come to my lord in Seir.

¹⁵Then Esau said, Let me now leave with you some of the people who are with me. But [Jacob] said, What need is there for it? Let me find favor in the sight of my lord.

¹⁶So Esau turned back that day on his way to Seir.

¹⁷But Jacob journeyed to Succoth and built himself a house and made booths *or* places of shelter for his livestock; so the name of the place is called Succoth [booths].

¹⁸When Jacob came from Padan-aram, he arrived safely *and* in peace at the town of Shechem, in the land of Canaan, and pitched his tents before the [enclosed] town.

¹⁹Then he bought the piece of land on which he had encamped from the sons of Hamor, Shechem's father, for a hundred pieces of money.

²⁰There he erected an altar and called it El-Elohe-Israel [God, the God of Israel].

34 NOW DINAH daughter of Leah, whom she bore to Jacob, went out [unattended] to see the girls of the place.

AMP notes: ᵃ Ever the deceiver, Jacob had no intention of following Esau to Seir. In fact, he heads in the opposite direction.

King James Version

²And when Shechem the son of Hamor the Hivite, prince of the country, saw her, he took her, and lay with her, and defiled her.

³And his soul clave unto Dinah the daughter of Jacob, and he loved the damsel, and spake kindly unto the damsel.

⁴And Shechem spake unto his father Hamor, saying, Get me this damsel to wife.

⁵And Jacob heard that he had defiled Dinah his daughter: now his sons were with his cattle in the field: and Jacob held his peace until they were come.

⁶And Hamor the father of Shechem went out unto Jacob to commune with him.

⁷And the sons of Jacob came out of the field when they heard *it:* and the men were grieved, and they were very wroth, because he had wrought folly in Israel in lying with Jacob's daughter; which thing ought not to be done.

⁸And Hamor communed with them, saying, The soul of my son Shechem longeth for your daughter: I pray you give her him to wife.

⁹And make ye marriages with us, *and* give your daughters unto us, and take our daughters unto you.

¹⁰And ye shall dwell with us: and the land shall be before you; dwell and trade you therein, and get you possessions therein.

¹¹And Shechem said unto her father and unto her brethren, Let me find grace in your eyes, and what ye shall say unto me I will give.

¹²Ask me never so much dowry and gift, and I will give according as ye shall say unto me: but give me the damsel to wife.

¹³And the sons of Jacob answered Shechem and Hamor his father deceitfully, and said, because he had defiled Dinah their sister:

¹⁴And they said unto them, We cannot do this thing, to give our sister to one that is uncircumcised; for that *were* a reproach unto us:

¹⁵But in this will we consent unto you: If ye will be as we *be,* that every male of you be circumcised;

¹⁶Then will we give our daughters unto you, and we will take your daughters to us, and we will dwell with you, and we will become one people.

¹⁷But if ye will not hearken unto us, to be circumcised; then will we take our daughter, and we will be gone.

¹⁸And their words pleased Hamor, and Shechem Hamor's son.

¹⁹And the young man deferred not to do the thing, because he had delight in Jacob's daughter: and he *was* more honourable than all the house of his father.

Amplified Bible

²And when Shechem son of Hamor the Hivite, prince of the country, saw her, he seized her, lay with her, and humbled, defiled, *and* disgraced her.

³But his soul longed for *and* clung to Dinah daughter of Jacob, and he loved the girl and spoke comfortingly to her young heart's wishes.

⁴And Shechem said to his father Hamor, Get me this girl to be my wife.

⁵Jacob heard that [Shechem] had defiled Dinah his daughter. Now his sons were with his livestock in the field. So Jacob held his peace until they came.

⁶But Hamor father of Shechem went out to Jacob to have a talk with him.

⁷When Jacob's sons heard it, they came from the field; and they were distressed and grieved and very angry, for [Shechem] had done a vile thing to Israel in lying with Jacob's daughter, which ought not to be done.

⁸And Hamor conferred with them, saying, The soul of my son Shechem craves your daughter [and sister]. I beg of you give her to him to be his wife.

⁹And make marriages with us and give your daughters to us and take our daughters to you.

¹⁰You shall dwell with us; the country will be open to you; live and trade and get your possessions in it.

¹¹And Shechem said to [Dinah's] father and to her brothers, Let me find favor in your eyes, and I will give you whatever you ask of me.

¹²Ask me ever so much dowry and [marriage] gift, and I will give according to what you tell me; only give me the girl to be my wife.

¹³The sons of Jacob answered Shechem and Hamor his father deceitfully, [justifying their intended action by saying, in effect, we are going to do this] because Shechem had defiled *and* disgraced their sister Dinah.

¹⁴They said to them, We cannot do this thing *and* give our sister to one who is not circumcised, for that would be a reproach *and* disgrace to us.

¹⁵But we do consent to do this: if you will become as we are and every male among you be circumcised,

¹⁶Then we will give our daughters to you and we will take your daughters to us, and we will dwell with you and become one people.

¹⁷But if you will not listen to us and consent to be circumcised, then we will take our daughter and go.

¹⁸Their words pleased Hamor and his son Shechem.

¹⁹And the young man did not delay to do the thing, for he delighted in Jacob's daughter. He was honored above all his family [so, ranking first, he acted first].

King James Version

20 And Hamor and Shechem his son came unto the gate of their city, and communed with the men of their city, saying,

21 These men *are* peaceable with us; therefore let them dwell in the land, and trade therein; for the land, behold, *it is* large enough for them; let us take their daughters to us for wives, and let us give them our daughters.

22 Only herein will the men consent unto us for to dwell with us, to be one people, if every male among us be circumcised, as they *are* circumcised.

23 *Shall* not their cattle and their substance and every beast of theirs *be* ours? only let us consent unto them, and they will dwell with us.

24 And unto Hamor and unto Shechem his son hearkened all that went out of the gate of his city; and every male was circumcised, all that went out of the gate of his city.

25 And it came to pass on the third day, when they were sore, that two of the sons of Jacob, Simeon and Levi, Dinah's brethren, took each man his sword, and came upon the city boldly, and slew all the males.

26 And they slew Hamor and Shechem his son with the edge of the sword, and took Dinah out of Shechem's house, and went out.

27 The sons of Jacob came upon the slain, and spoiled the city, because they had defiled their sister.

28 They took their sheep, and their oxen, and their asses, and that which *was* in the city, and that which *was* in the field,

29 And all their wealth, and all their little ones, and their wives took they captive, and spoiled even all that *was* in the house.

30 And Jacob said to Simeon and Levi, Ye have troubled me to make me to stink among the inhabitants of the land, amongst the Canaanites and the Perizzites: and I *being* few in number, they shall gather themselves together against me, and slay me; and I shall be destroyed, I and my house.

31 And they said, Should he deal with our sister as with a harlot?

35 And God said unto Jacob, Arise, go up to Beth-el, and dwell there: and make there an altar unto God, that appeared unto thee when thou fleddest from the face of Esau thy brother.

2 Then Jacob said unto his household, and to all that *were* with him, Put away the strange gods that *are* among you, and be clean, and change your garments:

3 And let us arise, and go up to Beth-el; and I will make there an altar unto God, who answered me in the day of my distress, and was with me in the way which I went.

Amplified Bible

20 Then Hamor and Shechem his son came to the gate of their [enclosed] town and discussed the matter with the citizens, saying,

21 These men are peaceable with us; so let them dwell in the land and trade in it; for the land is large enough [for us and] for them; let us take their daughters for wives and let us give them our daughters.

22 But the men will consent to our request that they live among us and be one people only on condition that every male among us be circumcised, as they are.

23 Shall not their cattle and their possessions and all their beasts be ours? Only let us consent to them, and they will dwell here with us.

24 And all the people who went out of the town gate listened *and* heeded what Hamor and Shechem said; and every male was circumcised who was a resident of that town.

25 But on the third day [after the circumcision] when [all the men] were sore, two of the sons of Jacob, Simeon and Levi, Dinah's [full] brothers, took their swords, boldly entered the city [without danger], and slew all the males.

26 And they killed Hamor and Shechem his son with the edge of the sword and took Dinah out of Shechem's house [where she had been all this time] and departed.

27 [Then the rest of] Jacob's [eleven] sons came upon the slain and plundered the town, because their sister had been defiled *and* disgraced.

28 They took their flocks, their herds, their donkeys, and whatever was in the town and in the field;

29 All their wealth and all their little ones and their wives they took captive, making spoil even of all [they found] in the houses.

30 And Jacob said to Simeon and Levi, You have ruined me, making me infamous *and* embroiling me with the inhabitants of the land, the Canaanites and the Perizzites! And we are few in number, and they will gather together against me and attack me; and I shall be destroyed, I and my household.

31 And they said, Should he [be permitted to] deal with our sister as with a harlot?

35 AND GOD said to Jacob, Arise, go up to Bethel and dwell there. And make there an altar to God Who appeared to you [in a distinct manifestation] when you fled from the presence of Esau your brother.

2 Then Jacob said to his household and to all who were with him, Put away the [images of] strange gods that are among you, and purify yourselves and change [into fresh] garments;

3 Then let us arise and go up to Bethel, and I will make there an altar to God Who answered me in the day of my distress and was with me wherever I went.

King James Version

⁴And they gave unto Jacob all the strange gods which *were* in their hand, and *all their* earrings which *were* in their ears; and Jacob hid them under the oak which *was* by Shechem.

⁵And they journeyed: and the terror of God was upon the cities that *were* round about them, and they did not pursue after the sons of Jacob.

⁶So Jacob came to Luz, which *is* in the land of Canaan, that *is*, Beth-el, he and all the people that *were* with him.

⁷And he built there an altar, and called the place El-beth-el: because there God appeared unto him, when he fled from the face of his brother.

⁸But Deborah Rebekah's nurse died, and she was buried beneath Beth-el under an oak: and the name of it was called Allon-bachuth.

⁹And God appeared unto Jacob again, when he came out of Padan-aram, and blessed him.

¹⁰And God said unto him, Thy name *is* Jacob: thy name shall not be called any more Jacob, but Israel shall be thy name: and he called his name Israel.

¹¹And God said unto him, I *am* God Almighty: be fruitful and multiply; a nation and a company of nations shall be of thee, and kings shall come out of thy loins;

¹²And the land which I gave Abraham and Isaac, to thee I will give it, and to thy seed after thee will I give the land.

¹³And God went up from him in the place where he talked with him.

¹⁴And Jacob set up a pillar in the place where he talked with him, *even* a pillar of stone: and he poured a drink offering thereon, and he poured oil thereon.

¹⁵And Jacob called the name of the place where God spake with him, Beth-el.

¹⁶¶ And they journeyed from Beth-el; and there was but a little way to come to Ephrath: and Rachel travailed, and she had hard labour.

¹⁷And it came to pass, when she was in hard labour, that the midwife said unto her, Fear not; thou shalt have this son also.

¹⁸And it came to pass, as her soul was in departing (for she died) that she called his name Ben-oni: but his father called him Benjamin.

¹⁹And Rachel died, and was buried in the way to Ephrath, which *is* Beth-lehem.

²⁰And Jacob set a pillar upon her grave: that *is* the pillar of Rachel's grave unto *this* day.

²¹And Israel journeyed, and spread his tent beyond the tower of Edar.

Amplified Bible

⁴So they [both young men and women] gave to Jacob all the strange gods they had and their earrings which were [worn as charms against evil] in their ears; and Jacob buried *and* hid them under the oak near Shechem.

⁵And they journeyed and a terror from God fell on the towns round about them, and they did not pursue the sons of Jacob.

⁶So Jacob came to Luz, that is, Bethel, which is in the land of Canaan, he and all the people with him.

⁷There he built an altar, and called the place El-bethel [God of Bethel], for there God revealed Himself to him when he fled from the presence of his brother.

⁸But Deborah, Rebekah's nurse, died and was buried below Bethel under an oak; and the name of it was called Allon-bacuth [oak of weeping].

⁹And God [in a distinctly visible manifestation] appeared to Jacob again when he came out of Padan-aram, and declared a blessing on him.

¹⁰Again God said to him, Your name is Jacob [supplanter]; you shall not be called Jacob any longer, but Israel shall be your name. So He called him Israel [contender with God].

¹¹And God said to him, I am God Almighty. Be fruitful and multiply; a nation and a company of nations shall come from you and kings shall be born of your stock;

¹²The land which I gave Abraham and Isaac I will give to you, and to your descendants after you I will give the land.

¹³Then God ascended from him in the place where He talked with him.

¹⁴And Jacob set up a pillar (monument) in the place where he talked with [God], a pillar of stone; and he poured a drink offering on it and he poured oil on it.

¹⁵And Jacob called the name of the place where God had talked with him Bethel [house of God].

¹⁶And they journeyed from Bethel and had but a little way to go to Ephrath [Bethlehem] when Rachel suffered the pangs of childbirth and had hard labor.

¹⁷When she was in hard labor, the midwife said to her, Do not be afraid; you shall have this son also.

¹⁸And as her soul was departing, for she died, she called his name Ben-oni [son of my sorrow]; but his father called him Benjamin [son of the right hand].

¹⁹So Rachel died and was buried on the way to Ephrath, that is, Bethlehem.

²⁰And Jacob set a pillar (monument) on her grave; that is the pillar of Rachel's grave to this day.

²¹Then Israel journeyed on and spread his tent on the other side of the tower of Edar.

King James Version

22And it came to pass, when Israel dwelt in that land, that Reuben went and lay with Bilhah his father's concubine: and Israel heard *it*. Now the sons of Jacob were twelve:

23The sons of Leah; Reuben, Jacob's firstborn, and Simeon, and Levi, and Judah, and Issachar, and Zebulun:

24The sons of Rachel; Joseph, and Benjamin:

25And the sons of Bilhah, Rachel's handmaid; Dan, and Naphtali:

26And the sons of Zilpah, Leah's handmaid; Gad, and Asher: these *are* the sons of Jacob, which were born to him in Padan-aram.

27And Jacob came unto Isaac his father unto Mamre, unto the city of Arbah, which *is* Hebron, where Abraham and Isaac sojourned.

28And the days of Isaac were an hundred and fourscore years.

29And Isaac gave up the ghost, and died, and was gathered unto his people, *being* old and full of days: and his sons Esau and Jacob buried him.

36 Now these *are* the generations of Esau, who *is* Edom.

2Esau took his wives of the daughters of Canaan; Adah the daughter of Elon the Hittite, and Aholibamah the daughter of Anah the daughter of Zibeon the Hivite;

3And Bashemath Ishmael's daughter, sister of Nebajoth.

4And Adah bare to Esau Eliphaz; and Bashemath bare Reuel;

5And Aholibamah bare Jeush, and Jaalam, and Korah: these *are* the sons of Esau, which were born unto him in the land of Canaan.

6And Esau took his wives, and his sons, and his daughters, and all the persons of his house, and his cattle, and all his beasts, and all his substance, which he had got in the land of Canaan; and went into the country from the face of his brother Jacob.

7For their riches were more than that they might dwell together; and the land wherein they were strangers could not bear them because of their cattle.

8Thus dwelt Esau in mount Seir: Esau *is* Edom.

9 ¶ And these *are* the generations of Esau the father of the Edomites in mount Seir:

10These *are* the names of Esau's sons; Eliphaz the son of Adah the wife of Esau, Reuel the son of Bashemath the wife of Esau.

11And the sons of Eliphaz were Teman, Omar, Zepho, and Gatam, and Kenaz.

12And Timna was concubine to Eliphaz Esau's son; and she bare to Eliphaz Amalek: these *were* the sons of Adah Esau's wife.

13And these *are* the sons of Reuel; Nahath, and Zerah, Shammah, and Mizzah: these were the sons of Bashemath Esau's wife.

Amplified Bible

22When Israel dwelt there, Reuben [his eldest son] went and lay with Bilhah his father's concubine; and Israel heard about it. Now Jacob's sons were twelve.

23The sons of Leah: Reuben, Jacob's firstborn, Simeon, Levi, Judah, Issachar, and Zebulun.

24The sons of Rachel: Joseph and Benjamin.

25The sons of Bilhah, Rachel's maid: Dan and Naphtali.

26And the sons of Zilpah, Leah's maid: Gad and Asher. These are the sons of Jacob born to him in Padan-aram.

27And Jacob came to Isaac his father at Mamre or Kiriath-arba, that is, Hebron, where Abraham and Isaac had sojourned.

28Now the days of Isaac were 180 years.

29And Isaac's spirit departed; he died and was gathered to his people, being an old man, satisfied *and* satiated with days; his sons Esau and Jacob buried him.

36 NOW THIS is the history of the descendants of Esau, that is, Edom.

2Esau took his wives from the women of Canaan: Adah daughter of Elon the Hittite, and Oholibamah daughter of Anah, the son of Zibeon the Hivite,

3And Basemath, Ishmael's daughter, sister of Nebaioth.

4Adah bore to Esau, Eliphaz; Basemath bore Reuel;

5And Oholibamah bore Jeush, Jalam, and Korah. These are the sons of Esau born to him in Canaan.

6Now Esau took his wives, his sons, his daughters, and all the members of his household, his cattle, all his beasts, and all his possessions which he had obtained in the land of Canaan, and he went into a land away from his brother Jacob.

7For their great flocks *and* herds *and* possessions [which they had collected] made it impossible for them to dwell together; the land in which they were strangers could not support them because of their livestock.

8So Esau dwelt in the hill country of Seir; Esau is Edom.

9And this is the history of the descendants of Esau the father of the Edomites in the hill country of Seir.

10These are the names of Esau's sons: Eliphaz, the son of Adah, Esau's wife, and Reuel, the son of Basemath, Esau's wife.

11And the sons of Eliphaz were Teman, Omar, Zepho, Gatam, and Kenaz.

12And Timna was a concubine of Eliphaz, Esau's son; and she bore Amalek to Eliphaz. These are the sons of Adah, Esau's wife.

13These are the sons of Reuel: Nahath, Zerah, Shammah, and Mizzah. These are the sons of Basemath, Esau's wife.

King James Version

14And these were the sons of Aholibamah, the daughter of Anah, daughter of Zibeon, Esau's wife: and she bare to Esau Jeush, and Jaalam, and Korah.

15These *were* dukes of the sons of Esau: the sons of Eliphaz the firstborn *son* of Esau; duke Teman, duke Omar, duke Zepho, duke Kenaz,

16Duke Korah, duke Gatam, *and* duke Amalek: these *are* the dukes *that came* of Eliphaz in the land of Edom; these *were* the sons of Adah.

17And these *are* the sons of Reuel Esau's son; duke Nahath, duke Zerah, duke Shammah, duke Mizzah: these *are* the dukes *that came* of Reuel in the land of Edom; these *are* the sons of Bashemath Esau's wife.

18And these *are* the sons of Aholibamah Esau's wife; duke Jeush, duke Jaalam, duke Korah: these *were* the dukes *that came* of Aholibamah the daughter of Anah, Esau's wife.

19These *are* the sons of Esau, who *is* Edom, and these *are* their dukes.

20 ¶ These *are* the sons of Seir the Horite, who inhabited the land; Lotan, and Shobal, and Zibeon, and Anah,

21And Dishon, and Ezer, and Dishan: these *are* the dukes of the Horites, the children of Seir in the land of Edom.

22And the children of Lotan were Hori and Hemam; and Lotan's sister *was* Timna.

23And the children of Shobal *were* these; Alvan, and Manahath, and Ebal, Shepho, and Onam.

24And these *are* the children of Zibeon; both Aiah, and Anah: this *was that* Anah that found the mules in the wilderness, as he fed the asses of Zibeon his father.

25And the children of Anah *were* these; Dishon, and Aholibamah the daughter of Anah.

26And these *are* the children of Dishon; Hemdan, and Eshban, and Ithran, and Cheran.

27The children of Ezer *are* these; Bilhan, and Zaavan, and Akan.

28The children of Dishan *are* these; Uz, and Aran.

29These *are* the dukes *that came* of the Horites; duke Lotan, duke Shobal, duke Zibeon, duke Anah,

30Duke Dishon, duke Ezer, duke Dishan: these *are* the dukes *that came* of Hori, among their dukes in the land of Seir.

31 ¶ And these *are* the kings that reigned in the land of Edom, before there reigned *any* king over the children of Israel.

Amplified Bible

14And these are the sons of Oholibamah daughter of Anah, the son of Zibeon, Esau's wife. She bore to Esau: Jeush, Jalam, and Korah.

15These are the chiefs of the sons of Esau: The sons of Eliphaz the firstborn of Esau: Chiefs Teman, Omar, Zepho, Kenaz,

16Korah, Gatam, and Amalek. These are the chiefs of Eliphaz in the land of Edom; they are the sons of Adah.

17These are the sons of Reuel, Esau's son: Chiefs Nahath, Zerah, Shammah, Mizzah. These are the chiefs of Reuel in the land of Edom; they are the sons of Basemath, Esau's wife.

18These are the sons of Oholibamah, Esau's wife: Chiefs Jeush, Jalam, and Korah. These are the chiefs born of Oholibamah daughter of Anah, Esau's wife.

19These are the sons of Esau, that is, Edom, and these are their chiefs.

20These are the sons of Seir the Horite, the inhabitants of the land: Lotan, Shobal, Zibeon, Anah,

21Dishon, Ezer, and Dishan. These are the chiefs of the ^aHorites, the sons of Seir in the land of Edom.

22The sons of Lotan are Hori and Hemam; and Lotan's sister is Timna.

23The sons of Shobal are these: Alvan, Manahath, Ebal, Shepho, and Onam.

24These are the sons of Zibeon: Aiah and Anah. This is the Anah who found the hot springs in the wilderness as he pastured the donkeys of Zibeon his father.

25The children of Anah are these: Dishon and Oholibamah daughter of Anah [Esau's wife].

26These are the sons of Dishon: Hemdan, Eshban, Ithran, and Cheran.

27Ezer's sons are these: Bilhan, Zaavan, and Akan.

28The sons of Dishan are these: Uz and Aran.

29The Horite chiefs are these: Lotan, Shobal, Zibeon, Anah,

30Dishon, Ezer, Dishan. These are the Horite chiefs, according to their clans, in the land of Seir.

31And these are the kings who reigned in Edom before any king reigned over the Israelites:

AMP notes: ^a Because of the similarity of the word 'Horites' to a Hebrew word for "cave," the term Horite was formerly interpreted as "cave dweller." But later archaeological discoveries have shown that the Horites are not to be explained as cave dwellers, but are to be identified with an important group in the Near East in patriarchal times (J. P. Free, *Archaeology and Bible History*). In fact, neither the Bible nor archaeology has any proof of aboriginal "cavemen." Cities of great antiquity have been unearthed with ever-increasing evidence that "when civilization appears it is already fully grown," and "pre-Semitic culture springs into view ready-made" (Hall, *History of the Near East*).

King James Version

32And Bela the son of Beor reigned in Edom: and the name of his city *was* Dinhabah.

33And Bela died, and Jobab the son of Zerah of Bozrah reigned in his stead.

34And Jobab died, and Husham of the land of Temani reigned in his stead.

35And Husham died, and Hadad the son of Bedad, who smote Midian in the field of Moab, reigned in his stead: and the name of his city *was* Avith.

36And Hadad died, and Samlah of Masrekah reigned in his stead.

37And Samlah died, and Saul of Rehoboth *by* the river reigned in his stead.

38And Saul died, and Baal-hanan the son of Achbor reigned in his stead.

39And Baal-hanan the son of Achbor died, and Hadar reigned in his stead: and the name of his city *was* Pau; and his wife's name *was* Mehetabel, the daughter of Matred, the daughter of Mezahab.

40And these *are* the names of the dukes *that came* of Esau, according to their families, after their places, by their names; duke Timnah, duke Alvah, duke Jetheth,

41Duke Aholibamah, duke Elah, duke Pinon,

42Duke Kenaz, duke Teman, duke Mibzar,

43Duke Magdiel, duke Iram: these *be* the dukes of Edom, according to their habitations in the land of their possession: he *is* Esau the father of the Edomites.

37 And Jacob dwelt in the land wherein his father was a stranger, in the land of Canaan.

2These *are* the generations of Jacob. Joseph, *being* seventeen years old, was feeding the flock with his brethren; and the lad *was* with the sons of Bilhah, and with the sons of Zilpah, his father's wives: and Joseph brought unto his father their evil report.

3Now Israel loved Joseph more than all his children, because he *was* the son of his old age: and he made him a coat of many colours.

4And when his brethren saw that their father loved him more than all his brethren, they hated him, and could not speak peaceably unto him.

5And Joseph dreamed a dream, and he told *it* his brethren: and they hated him yet the more.

6And he said unto them, Hear, I pray you, this dream which I have dreamed:

7For, behold, we *were* binding sheaves in the field, and lo, my sheaf arose, and also stood upright; and behold, your sheaves stood round about, and made obeisance to my sheaf.

8And his brethren said to him, Shalt thou indeed reign over us? or shalt thou indeed have

Amplified Bible

32Bela son of Beor reigned in Edom. And the name of his city was Dinhabah.

33Now Bela died, and Jobab son of Zerah of Bozrah reigned in his stead.

34Then Jobab died, and Husham of the land of the Temanites reigned in his stead.

35And Husham died, and Hadad son of Bedad, who defeated Midian in the country of Moab, reigned in his stead. The name of his [enclosed] city was Avith.

36Hadad died, and Samlah of Masrekah succeeded him.

37Then Samlah died, and Shaul of Rehoboth on the river [Euphrates] reigned in his stead.

38And Shaul died, and Baal-hanan son of Achbor reigned in his stead.

39Baal-hanan son of Achbor died, and then Hadar reigned. His [enclosed] city was Pau; his wife's name was Mehetabel daughter of Matred, the daughter of Mezahab.

40And these are the names of the chiefs of Esau, according to their families and places of residence, by their names: Chiefs Timna, Alvah, Jetheth,

41Oholibamah, Elah, Pinon,

42Kenaz, Teman, Mibzar,

43Magdiel, and Iram. These are the chiefs of Edom [that is, of Esau the father of the Edomites], according to their dwelling places in their land.

37 SO JACOB dwelt in the land in which his father had been a stranger *and* sojourner, in the land of Canaan.

2This is the history of the descendants of Jacob *and* this is Jacob's line. Joseph, when he was seventeen years old, was shepherding the flock with his brothers; the lad was with the sons of Bilhah and Zilpah, his father's [secondary] wives; and Joseph brought to his father a bad report of them.

3Now Israel loved Joseph more than all his children because he was the son of his old age, and he made him a [distinctive] long tunic with sleeves.

4But when his brothers saw that their father loved [Joseph] more than all of his brothers, they hated him and could not say, Peace [in friendly greeting] to him *or* speak peaceably to him.

5Now Joseph had a dream and he told it to his brothers, and they hated him still more.

6And he said to them, Listen now *and* hear, I pray you, this dream that I have dreamed:

7We [brothers] were binding sheaves in the field, and behold, my sheaf arose and stood upright, and behold, your sheaves stood round about my sheaf and bowed down!

8His brothers said to him, Shall you indeed reign over us? Or are you going to have us as

King James Version

dominion over us? And they hated him yet the more for his dreams, and for his words.

⁹And he dreamed yet another dream, and told it to his brethren, and said, Behold, I have dreamed a dream more; and behold, the sun and the moon and the eleven stars made obeisance to me.

¹⁰And he told it to his father, and to his brethren: and his father rebuked him, and said unto him, What is this dream that thou hast dreamed? Shall I and thy mother and thy brethren indeed come to bow down ourselves to thee to the earth?

¹¹And his brethren envied him; but his father observed the saying.

¹² ¶ And his brethren went to feed their father's flock in Shechem.

¹³And Israel said unto Joseph, Do not thy brethren feed *the flock* in Shechem? come, and I will send thee unto them. And he said to him, Here *am* I.

¹⁴And he said to him, Go, I pray thee, see whether it be well with thy brethren, and well with the flocks; and bring me word again. So he sent him out of the vale of Hebron, and he came to Shechem.

¹⁵And a *certain* man found him, and behold, *he was* wandering in the field: and the man asked him, saying, What seekest thou?

¹⁶And he said, I seek my brethren: tell me, I pray thee, where they feed *their flocks*.

¹⁷And the man said, They are departed hence; for I heard *them* say, Let us go to Dothan. And Joseph went after his brethren, and found them in Dothan.

¹⁸And when they saw him afar off, even before he came near unto them, they conspired against him to slay him.

¹⁹And they said one to another, Behold, this dreamer cometh.

²⁰Come now therefore, and let us slay him, and cast him into some pit, and we will say, *Some* evil beast hath devoured him: and we shall see what will become of his dreams.

²¹And Reuben heard *it*, and he delivered him out of their hands; and said, Let us not kill him.

²²And Reuben said unto them, Shed no blood, *but* cast him into this pit that *is* in the wilderness, and lay no hand upon him, that he might rid him out of their hands, to deliver him to his father again.

²³And it came to pass, when Joseph was come unto his brethren, that they stript Joseph out of his coat, *his* coat of many colours that *was* on him;

Amplified Bible

your subjects *and* dominate us? And they hated him all the more for his dreams and for what he said.

⁹But Joseph dreamed yet another dream and told it to his brothers [also]. He said, See here, I have dreamed again, and behold, [this time not only] eleven stars [but also] the sun and the moon bowed down *and* did reverence to me!

¹⁰And he told it to his father [as well as] his brethren. But his father rebuked him and said to him, What is the meaning of this dream that you have dreamed? Shall I and your mother and your brothers actually come to bow down ourselves to the earth *and* do homage to you?

¹¹Joseph's brothers envied him *and* were jealous of him, but his father observed the saying *and* pondered over it.

¹²Joseph's brothers went to shepherd *and* feed their father's flock near Shechem.

¹³[One day] Israel said to Joseph, Do not your brothers shepherd my flock at Shechem? Come, and I will send you to them. And he said, Here I am.

¹⁴And [Jacob] said to him, Go, I pray you, see whether everything is all right with your brothers and with the flock; then come back and bring me word. So he sent him out of the Hebron Valley, and he came to Shechem.

¹⁵And a certain man found him, and behold, he had lost his way *and* was wandering in the open country. The man asked him, What are you trying to find?

¹⁶And he said, I am looking for my brothers. Tell me, I pray you, where they are pasturing our flocks.

¹⁷But the man said, [They were here, but] they have gone. I heard them say, Let us go to Dothan. And Joseph went after his brothers and found them at Dothan.

¹⁸And when they saw him far off, even before he came near to them, they conspired to kill him.

¹⁹And they said one to another, See, here comes this dreamer *and* master of dreams.

²⁰So come on now, let us kill him and throw his body into some pit; then we will say [to our father], Some wild *and* ferocious animal has devoured him; and we shall see what will become of his dreams!

²¹Now Reuben heard it and he delivered him out of their hands by saying, Let us not kill him.

²²And Reuben said to them, Shed no blood, but cast him into this pit *or* well that is out here in the wilderness and lay no hand on him. He was trying to get Joseph out of their hands in order to rescue him *and* deliver him again to his father.

²³When Joseph had come to his brothers, they stripped him of his [distinctive] long garment which he was wearing;

King James Version

24And they took him, and cast him into a pit: and the pit *was* empty, *there was* no water in it.

25And they sat down to eat bread: and they lift up their eyes and looked, and behold, a company of Ishmeelites came from Gilead with their camels bearing spicery and balm and myrrh, going to carry *it* down to Egypt.

26And Judah said unto his brethren, What profit *is it* if we slay our brother, and conceal his blood?

27Come, and let us sell him to the Ishmeelites, and let not our hand be upon him; for he *is* our brother *and* our flesh. And his brethren were content.

28Then there passed by Midianites merchantmen; and they drew and lift up Joseph out of the pit, and sold Joseph to the Ishmeelites for twenty *pieces* of silver: and they brought Joseph into Egypt.

29And Reuben returned unto the pit; and behold, Joseph *was* not in the pit; and he rent his clothes.

30And he returned unto his brethren, and said, The child *is* not; and I, whither shall I go?

31And they took Joseph's coat, and killed a kid of the goats, and dipped the coat in the blood;

32And they sent the coat of many colours, and they brought *it* to their father; and said, This have we found: know now whether it *be* thy son's coat or no.

33And he knew it, and said, *It is* my son's coat; an evil beast hath devoured him; Joseph is without doubt rent in pieces.

34And Jacob rent his clothes, and put sackcloth upon his loins, and mourned for his son many days.

35And all his sons and all his daughters rose up to comfort him; but he refused to be comforted; and he said, For I will go down into the grave unto my son mourning. Thus his father wept for him.

36And the Medanites sold him into Egypt unto Potiphar, an officer of Pharaoh's, *and* captain of the guard.

38 And it came to pass at that time, that Judah went down from his brethren, and turned in to a certain Adullamite, whose name *was* Hirah.

2And Judah saw there a daughter of a certain Canaanite, whose name *was* Shuah; and he took her, and went in unto her.

3And she conceived, and bare a son; and he called his name Er.

4And she conceived again, and bare a son; and she called his name Onan.

5And she yet again conceived, and bare a son;

Amplified Bible

24Then they took him and cast him into the [well-like] pit which was empty; there was no water in it.

25Then they sat down to eat their lunch. When they looked up, behold, they saw a caravan of Ishmaelites [mixed Arabians] coming from Gilead, with their camels bearing gum [of the styrax tree], balm (balsam), and myrrh *or* ladanum, going on their way to carry them down to Egypt.

26And Judah said to his brothers, What do we gain if we slay our brother and conceal his blood?

27Come, let us sell him to the Ishmaelites [and Midianites, these mixed Arabians who are approaching], and let not our hand be upon him, for he is our brother and our flesh. And his brothers consented.

28Then as the Midianite [and Ishmaelite] merchants were passing by, the brothers pulled Joseph up and lifted him out of the well. And they sold him for twenty pieces of silver to the Ishmaelites, who took Joseph [captive] into Egypt.

29Then Reuben [who had not been there when the brothers plotted to sell the lad] returned to the pit; and behold, Joseph was not in the pit, and he rent his clothes.

30He rejoined his brothers and said, The boy is not there! And I, where shall I go [to hide from my father]?

31Then they took Joseph's [distinctive] long garment, killed a young goat, and dipped the garment in the blood;

32And they sent the garment to their father, saying, We have found this! Examine *and* decide whether it is your son's tunic or not.

33He said, My son's long garment! An evil [wild] beast has devoured him; Joseph is without doubt rent in pieces.

34And Jacob tore his clothes, put on sackcloth, and mourned many days for his son.

35And all his sons and daughters attempted to console him, but he refused to be comforted and said, I will go down to Sheol (the place of the dead) to my son mourning. And his father wept for him.

36And the Midianites [and Ishmaelites] sold [Joseph] in Egypt to Potiphar, an officer of Pharaoh and the captain *and* chief executioner of the [royal] guard.

38 AT THAT time Judah withdrew from his brothers and went to [lodge with] a certain Adullamite named Hirah.

2There Judah saw *and* met a daughter of Shuah, a Canaanite; he took her as wife and lived with her.

3And she became pregnant and bore a son, and he called him Er.

4And she conceived again and bore a son and named him Onan.

5Again she conceived and bore a son and

King James Version

and called his name Shelah: and he was at Chezib, when she bare him.

⁶And Judah took a wife for Er his firstborn, whose name *was* Tamar.

⁷And Er, Judah's firstborn, was wicked in the sight of the LORD; and the LORD slew him.

⁸And Judah said unto Onan, Go in unto thy brother's wife, and marry her, and raise up seed to thy brother.

⁹And Onan knew that the seed should not be his; and it came to pass, when he went in unto his brother's wife, that he spilled *it* on the ground, lest that he should give seed to his brother.

¹⁰And *the thing* which he did displeased the LORD: wherefore he slew him also.

¹¹Then said Judah to Tamar his daughter in law, Remain a widow *at* thy father's house, till Shelah my son be grown: for he said, Lest peradventure he die also, as his brethren *did*. And Tamar went and dwelt *in* her father's house.

¹²And in process of time the daughter of Shuah Judah's wife died; and Judah was comforted, and went up unto his sheepshearers to Timnath, he and his friend Hirah the Adullamite.

¹³And it was told Tamar, saying, Behold thy father in law goeth up to Timnath to shear his sheep.

¹⁴And she put her widow's garments off from her, and covered her with a vail, and wrapped herself, and sat in an open place, which *is* by the way to Timnath; for she saw that Shelah was grown, and she was not given unto him to wife.

¹⁵When Judah saw her, he thought her to be a harlot; because she had covered her face.

¹⁶And he turned unto her by the way, and said, Go to, I pray thee, let me come in unto thee; (for he knew not that she *was* his daughter in law:) and she said, What wilt thou give me, that thou mayest come in unto me?

¹⁷And he said, I will send *thee* a kid from the flock. And she said, Wilt thou give *me* a pledge, till thou send *it?*

¹⁸And he said, What pledge shall I give thee? And she said, Thy signet, and thy bracelets, and thy staff that *is* in thine hand. And he gave *it* her, and came in unto her, and she conceived by him.

¹⁹And she arose, and went away, and laid by her vail from her, and put on the garments of her widowhood.

²⁰And Judah sent the kid by the hand of his friend the Adullamite, to receive *his* pledge from the woman's hand: but he found her not.

²¹Then he asked the men of that place, saying, Where *is* the harlot, that *was* openly by the way side? And they said, There was no harlot in this *place.*

Amplified Bible

named him Shelah. [They were living] at Chezib when she bore him.

⁶Now Judah took a wife for Er, his firstborn; her name was Tamar.

⁷And Er, Judah's firstborn, was wicked in the sight of the Lord, and the Lord slew him.

⁸Then Judah told Onan, Marry your brother's widow; live with her and raise offspring for your brother.

⁹But Onan knew that the family would not be his, so when he cohabited with his brother's widow, he prevented conception, lest he should raise up a child for his brother.

¹⁰And the thing which he did displeased the Lord; therefore He slew him also.

¹¹Then Judah said to Tamar, his daughter-in-law, Remain a widow at your father's house till Shelah my [youngest] son is grown; for he thought, Lest perhaps [if Shelah should marry her] he would die also, as his brothers did. So Tamar went and lived in her father's house.

¹²But later Judah's wife, the daughter of Shuah, died; and when Judah was comforted, he went up to his sheepshearers at Timnath with his friend Hirah the Adullamite.

¹³Then it was told Tamar, Listen, your father-in-law is going up to Timnath to shear his sheep.

¹⁴So she put off her widow's garments and covered herself with a veil, wrapped herself up [in disguise], and sat in the entrance of Enaim, which is by the road to Timnath; for she saw that Shelah was grown and she was not given to him as his wife.

¹⁵When Judah saw her, he thought she was a harlot *or* devoted prostitute [under a vow to her goddess], for she had covered her face [as such women did].

¹⁶He turned to her by the road and said, Come, let me have intercourse with you; for he did not know that she was his daughter-in-law. And she said, What will you give me that you may have intercourse with me?

¹⁷He answered, I will send you a kid from the flock. And she said, Will you give me a pledge (deposit) until you send it?

¹⁸And he said, What pledge shall I give you? She said, Your signet [seal], your [signet] cord, and your staff that is in your hand. And he gave them to her and came in to her, and she became pregnant by him.

¹⁹And she arose and went away and laid aside her veil and put on the garments of her widowhood.

²⁰And Judah sent the kid by the hand of his friend the Adullamite, to receive his pledge from the woman's hand; but he was unable to find her.

²¹He asked the men of that place, Where is the harlot *or* cult prostitute who was openly by the roadside? They said, There was no harlot *or* temple prostitute here.

King James Version

22And he returned to Judah, and said, I cannot find her; and also the men of the place said, *that* there was no harlot in this *place.*

23And Judah said, Let her take *it* to her, lest we be shamed: behold, I sent this kid, and thou hast not found her.

24And it came to pass about three months after, that it was told Judah, saying, Tamar thy daughter in law hath played the harlot; and also, behold, she *is* with child by whoredom. And Judah said, Bring her forth, and let her be burnt.

25When she *was* brought forth, she sent to her father in law, saying, By the man, whose these *are, am* I with child: and she said, Discern, I pray thee, whose *are* these, the signet, and bracelets, and staff.

26And Judah acknowledged *them,* and said, She hath been more righteous than I; because that I gave her not to Shelah my son. And he knew her again no more.

27And it came to pass in the time of her travail, that, behold, twins *were* in her womb.

28And it came to pass, when she travailed, that *the one* put out *his* hand: and the midwife took and bound upon his hand a scarlet thread, saying, This came out first.

29And it came to pass, as he drew back his hand, that, behold, his brother came out: and she said, How hast thou broken forth? *this* breach *be* upon thee: therefore his name was called Pharez.

30And afterward came out his brother, that had the scarlet thread upon his hand: and his name was called Zarah.

39 And Joseph was brought down to Egypt; and Potiphar, an officer of Pharaoh, captain of the guard, an Egyptian, bought him of the hand of the Ishmeelites, which had brought him down thither.

2And the LORD was with Joseph, and he was a prosperous man; and he was in the house of his master the Egyptian.

3And his master saw that the LORD *was* with him, and *that* the LORD made all that he did to prosper in his hand.

4And Joseph found grace in his sight, and he served him: and he made him overseer over his house, and all *that* he had he put into his hand.

5And it came to pass from the time *that* he had made him overseer in his house, and over all that he had, that the LORD blessed the Egyptian's house for Joseph's sake; and the blessing of the LORD was upon all that he had in the house, and in the field.

6And he left all that he had in Joseph's hand; and he knew not ought he had, save the bread

Amplified Bible

22So he returned to Judah and said, I cannot find her; and also the local men said, There was no harlot *or* temple prostitute around here.

23And Judah said, Let her keep [the pledge articles] for herself, lest we be made ashamed. I sent this kid, but you have not found her.

24But about three months later Judah was told, Tamar your daughter-in-law has played the harlot, and also she is with child by her lewdness. And Judah said, Bring her forth and let her be burned!

25When she was brought forth, she [took the things he had given her in pledge and] sent [them] to her father-in-law, saying, I am with child by the man to whom these articles belong. Then she added, Make out clearly, I pray you, to whom these belong, the signet [seal], [signet] cord, and staff.

26And Judah acknowledged them and said, She has been more righteous *and* just than I, because I did not give her to Shelah my son. And he did not cohabit with her again.

27Now when the time came for her to be delivered, behold, there were twins in her womb.

28And when she was in labor, one baby put out his hand; and the midwife took his hand and bound upon it a scarlet thread, saying, This baby was born first.

29But he drew back his hand, and behold, his brother was born first. And she said, What a breaking forth you have made for yourself! Therefore his name was called Perez [breaking forth].

30And afterward his brother who had the scarlet thread on his hand was born and was named Zerah [scarlet].

39 AND JOSEPH was brought down to Egypt; and Potiphar, an officer of Pharaoh, the captain *and* chief executioner of the [royal] guard, an Egyptian, bought him from the Ishmaelites who had brought him down there.

2But the Lord was with Joseph, and he [though a slave] was a successful *and* prosperous man; and he was in the house of his master the Egyptian.

3And his master saw that the Lord was with him and that the Lord made all that he did to flourish *and* succeed in his hand.

4So Joseph pleased [Potiphar] *and* found favor in his sight, and he served him. And [his master] made him supervisor over his house and he put all that he had in his charge.

5From the time that he made him supervisor in his house and over all that he had, the Lord blessed the Egyptian's house for Joseph's sake; and the Lord's blessing was on all that he had in the house and in the field.

6And [Potiphar] left all that he had in Joseph's charge and paid no attention to anything he had

King James Version

which he did eat. And Joseph was *a* goodly *person,* and well favoured.

7And it came to pass after these things, that his master's wife cast her eyes upon Joseph; and she said, Lie with me.

8But he refused, and said unto his master's wife, Behold, my master wotteth not what *is* with me in the house, and he hath committed all that he hath to my hand;

9*There is* none greater in this house than I; neither hath he kept back any thing from me but thee, because thou *art* his wife: how then can I do this great wickedness, and sin against God?

10And it came to pass, as she spake to Joseph day by day, that he hearkened not unto her, to lie by her, *or* to be with her.

11And it came to pass about this time, that *Joseph* went into the house to do his business; and *there was* none of the men of the house there within.

12And she caught him by his garment, saying, Lie with me: and he left his garment in her hand, and fled, and got him out.

13And it came to pass, when she saw that he had left his garment in her hand, and was fled forth,

14That she called unto the men of her house, and spake unto them, saying, See, he hath brought in a Hebrew unto us to mock us; he came in unto me to lie with me, and I cried with a loud voice:

15And it came to pass, when he heard that I lifted up my voice and cried, that he left his garment with me, and fled, and got him out.

16And she laid up his garment by her, until his lord came home.

17And she spake unto him according to these words, saying, The Hebrew servant, which thou hast brought unto us, came in unto me to mock me:

18And it came to pass, as I lift up my voice and cried, that he left his garment with me, and fled out.

19And it came to pass, when his master heard the words of his wife, which she spake unto him, saying, After this manner did thy servant to me; that his wrath was kindled.

20And Joseph's master took him, and put him into the prison, a place where the king's prisoners *were* bound: and he was there in the prison.

21But the LORD was with Joseph, and shewed him mercy, and gave him favour in the sight of the keeper of the prison.

22And the keeper of the prison committed to Joseph's hand all the prisoners that *were* in prison; and whatsoever they did there, he was the doer *of it.*

23The keeper of the prison looked not to any thing *that was* under his hand; because the LORD *was* with him, and *that* which he did, the LORD made *it* to prosper.

Amplified Bible

except the food he ate. Now Joseph was an attractive person and fine-looking.

7Then after a time his master's wife cast her eyes upon Joseph, and she said, Lie with me.

8But he refused and said to his master's wife, See here, with me in the house my master has concern about nothing; he has put all that he has in my care.

9He is not greater in this house than I am; nor has he kept anything from me except you, for you are his wife. How then can I do this great evil and sin against God?

10She spoke to Joseph day after day, but he did not listen to her, to lie with her or to be with her.

11Then it happened about this time that Joseph went into the house to attend to his duties, and none of the men of the house were indoors.

12And she caught him by his garment, saying, Lie with me! But he left his garment in her hand and fled and got out [of the house].

13And when she saw that he had left his garment in her hand and had fled away,

14She called to the men of her household and said to them, Behold, he [your master] has brought in a Hebrew to us to mock *and* insult us; he came in where I was to lie with me, and I screamed at the top of my voice.

15And when he heard me screaming and crying, he left his garment with me and fled and got out of the house.

16And she laid up his garment by her until his master came home.

17Then she told him the same story, saying, The Hebrew servant whom you brought among us came to me to mock *and* insult me.

18And when I screamed and cried, he left his garment with me and fled out [of the house].

19And when [Joseph's] master heard the words of his wife, saying to him, This is the way your servant treated me, his wrath was kindled.

20And Joseph's master took him and put him in the prison, a place where the state prisoners were confined; so he was there in the prison.

21But the Lord was with Joseph, and showed him mercy *and* loving-kindness and gave him favor in the sight of the warden of the prison.

22And the warden of the prison committed to Joseph's care all the prisoners who were in prison; and whatsoever was done there, he was in charge of it.

23The prison warden paid no attention to anything that was in [Joseph's] charge, for the Lord was with him and made whatever he did to prosper.

King James Version

40 And it came to pass after these things, *that* the butler of the king of Egypt and *his* baker had offended their lord the king of Egypt.

² And Pharaoh was wroth against two *of* his officers, against the chief of the butlers, and against the chief of the bakers.

³ And he put them in ward *in* the house of the captain of the guard, into the prison, the place where Joseph *was* bound.

⁴ And the captain of the guard charged Joseph with them, and he served them: and they continued a season in ward.

⁵ And they dreamed a dream both of them, each man his dream in one night, each man according to the interpretation of his dream, the butler and the baker of the king of Egypt, which *were* bound in the prison.

⁶ And Joseph came in unto them in the morning, and looked upon them, and behold, they *were* sad.

⁷ And he asked Pharaoh's officers that *were* with him in the ward of his lord's house, saying, Wherefore look ye *so* sadly to day?

⁸ And they said unto him, We have dreamed a dream, and *there is* no interpreter of it. And Joseph said unto them, *Do* not interpretations *belong* to God? tell me *them,* I pray you.

⁹ And the chief butler told his dream to Joseph, and said to him, In my dream, behold, a vine *was* before me;

¹⁰ And in the vine *were* three branches: and it *was* as though it budded, *and* her blossoms shot forth; *and* the clusters thereof brought forth ripe grapes:

¹¹ And Pharaoh's cup *was* in my hand: and I took the grapes, and pressed them into Pharaoh's cup, and I gave the cup into Pharaoh's hand.

¹² And Joseph said unto him, This *is* the interpretation of it: The three branches *are* three days:

¹³ Yet within three days shall Pharaoh lift up thine head, and restore thee unto thy place: and thou shalt deliver Pharaoh's cup into his hand, after the former manner when thou wast his butler.

¹⁴ But think on me when it shall be well with thee, and shew kindness, I pray thee, unto me, and make mention of me unto Pharaoh, and bring me out of this house:

¹⁵ For indeed I was stolen away out of the land of the Hebrews: and here also have I done nothing that they should put me into the dungeon.

¹⁶ When the chief baker saw that the interpretation was good, he said unto Joseph, I also *was* in my dream, and, behold, *I had* three white baskets on my head:

¹⁷ And in the uppermost basket *there was* of all

Amplified Bible

40 NOW SOME time later the butler and the baker of the king of Egypt offended their lord, Egypt's king.

² And Pharaoh was angry with his officers, the chief of the butlers and the chief of the bakers.

³ He put them in custody in the house of the captain of the guard, in the prison where Joseph was confined.

⁴ And the captain of the guard put them in Joseph's charge, and he served them; and they continued in custody for some time.

⁵ And they both dreamed a dream in the same night, each man according to [the personal significance of] the interpretation of his dream—the butler and the baker of the king of Egypt, who were confined in the prison.

⁶ When Joseph came to them in the morning and looked at them, he saw that they were sad *and* depressed.

⁷ So he asked Pharaoh's officers who were in custody with him in his master's house, Why do you look so dejected *and* sad today?

⁸ And they said to him, We have dreamed dreams, and there is no one to interpret them. And Joseph said to them, Do not interpretations belong to God? Tell me [your dreams], I pray you.

⁹ And the chief butler told his dream to Joseph and said to him, In my dream I saw a vine before me,

¹⁰ And on the vine were three branches. Then it was as though it budded; its blossoms burst forth and the clusters of them brought forth ripe grapes [almost all at once].

¹¹ And Pharaoh's cup was in my hand, and I took the grapes and pressed them into Pharaoh's cup; then I gave the cup into Pharaoh's hand.

¹² And Joseph said to him, This is the interpretation of it: The three branches are three days.

¹³ Within three days Pharaoh will lift up your head and restore you to your position, and you will again put Pharaoh's cup into his hand, as when you were his butler.

¹⁴ But think of me when it shall be well with you and show kindness, I beg of you, to me, and mention me to Pharaoh and get me out of this house.

¹⁵ For truly I was carried away from the land of the Hebrews by unlawful force, and here too I have done nothing for which they should put me into the dungeon.

¹⁶ When the chief baker saw that the interpretation was good, he said to Joseph, I also dreamed, and behold, I had three cake baskets on my head.

¹⁷ And in the uppermost basket were some of

King James Version

manner of bakemeats for Pharaoh; and the birds did eat them out of the basket upon my head.

18And Joseph answered and said, This *is* the interpretation thereof: The three baskets *are* three days:

19Yet within three days shall Pharaoh lift up thy head from off thee, and shall hang thee on a tree; and the birds shall eat thy flesh from off thee.

20And it came to pass the third day, *which was* Pharaoh's birthday, that he made a feast unto all his servants: and he lifted up the head of the chief butler and of the chief baker among his servants.

21And he restored the chief butler unto his butlership again; and he gave the cup into Pharaoh's hand:

22But he hanged the chief baker: as Joseph had interpreted to them.

23Yet did not the chief butler remember Joseph, but forgat him.

41 And it came to pass at the end of two full years, that Pharaoh dreamed: and behold, he stood by the river.

2And behold, there came up out of the river seven well favoured kine and fatfleshed; and they fed in a meadow.

3And behold, seven other kine came up after them out of the river, ill favoured and leanfleshed; and stood by the *other* kine upon the brink of the river.

4And the ill favoured and leanfleshed kine did eat up the seven well favoured and fat kine. So Pharaoh awoke.

5And he slept and dreamed the second time: and behold, seven ears of corn came up upon one stalk, rank and good.

6And behold, seven thin ears and blasted with the east wind sprang up after them.

7And the seven thin ears devoured the seven rank and full ears. And Pharaoh awoke, and behold, *it was* a dream.

8And it came to pass in the morning that his spirit was troubled; and he sent and called for all the magicians of Egypt, and all the wise men thereof: and Pharaoh told them his dream; but *there was* none that could interpret them unto Pharaoh.

9Then spake the chief butler unto Pharaoh, saying, I do remember my faults *this* day:

10Pharaoh was wroth with his servants, and put me in ward *in* the captain of the guard's house, *both* me and the chief baker:

11And we dreamed a dream in one night, I and he; we dreamed each man according to the interpretation of his dream.

12And *there was* there with us a young man, a Hebrew, servant to the captain of the guard; and

Amplified Bible

all kinds of baked food for Pharaoh, but the birds [of prey] were eating out of the basket on my head.

18And Joseph answered, This is the interpretation of it: The three baskets are three days.

19Within three days Pharaoh will lift up your head but will have you beheaded and hung on a tree, and [you will not so much as be given burial, but] the birds will eat your flesh.

20And on the third day, Pharaoh's birthday, he made a feast for all his servants; and he lifted up the heads of the chief butler and the chief baker [by inviting them also] among his servants.

21And he restored the chief butler to his butlership, and the butler gave the cup into Pharaoh's hand;

22But [Pharaoh] hanged the chief baker, as Joseph had interpreted to them.

23But [even after all that] the chief butler gave no thought to Joseph, but forgot [all about] him.

41 AFTER TWO full years, Pharaoh dreamed that he stood by the river [Nile].

2And behold, there came up out of the river [Nile] seven well-favored cows, sleek *and* handsome and fat; and they grazed in the reed grass [in a marshy pasture].

3And behold, seven other cows came up after them out of the river [Nile], ill favored and gaunt *and* ugly, and stood by the fat cows on the bank of the river [Nile].

4And the ill-favored, gaunt, *and* ugly cows ate up the seven well-favored and fat cows. Then Pharaoh awoke.

5But he slept and dreamed the second time; and behold, seven ears of grain came out on one stalk, plump and good.

6And behold, after them seven ears [of grain] sprouted, thin *and* blighted by the east wind.

7And the seven thin ears [of grain] devoured the seven plump and full ears. And Pharaoh awoke, and behold, it was a dream.

8So when morning came his spirit was troubled, and he sent and called for all the magicians and all the wise men of Egypt. And Pharaoh told them his dreams, but not one could interpret them to [him].

9Then the chief butler said to Pharaoh, I remember my faults today.

10When Pharaoh was angry with his servants and put me in custody in the captain of the guard's house, both me and the chief baker,

11We dreamed a dream in the same night, he and I; we dreamed each of us according to [the significance of] the interpretation of his dream.

12And there was there with us a young man, a Hebrew, servant to the captain of the guard *and* chief executioner; and we told him our dreams,

King James Version

we told him, and he interpreted to us our dreams; to each man according to his dream he did interpret.

¹³And it came to pass, as he interpreted to us, so it was; me he restored unto mine office, and him he hanged.

¹⁴ ¶ Then Pharaoh sent and called Joseph, and they brought him hastily out of the dungeon: and he shaved *himself*, and changed his raiment, and came in unto Pharaoh.

¹⁵And Pharaoh said unto Joseph, I have dreamed a dream, and *there is* none that can interpret it: and I have heard say of thee, *that* thou canst understand a dream to interpret it.

¹⁶And Joseph answered Pharaoh, saying, *It is* not in me: God shall give Pharaoh an answer of peace.

¹⁷And Pharaoh said unto Joseph, In my dream, behold, I stood upon the bank of the river:

¹⁸And behold, there came up out of the river seven kine, fatfleshed and well favoured; and they fed in a meadow:

¹⁹And behold, seven other kine came up after them, poor and very ill favoured and leanfleshed, such as I never saw in all the land of Egypt for badness:

²⁰And the lean and the ill favoured kine did eat up the first seven fat kine:

²¹And when they had eaten them up, it could not be known that they had eaten them; but they *were still* ill favoured, as at the beginning. So I awoke.

²²And I saw in my dream, and behold, seven ears came up in one stalk, full and good:

²³And behold, seven ears, withered, thin, *and* blasted with the east wind, sprung up after them:

²⁴And the thin ears devoured the seven good ears: and I told *this* unto the magicians; but *there was* none that could declare *it* to me.

²⁵And Joseph said unto Pharaoh, The dream of Pharaoh *is* one: God hath shewed Pharaoh what he *is* about to do.

²⁶The seven good kine *are* seven years; and the seven good ears *are* seven years: the dream *is* one.

²⁷And the seven thin and ill favoured kine that came up after them *are* seven years; and the seven empty ears blasted with the east wind shall be seven years of famine.

²⁸This *is* the thing which I have spoken unto Pharaoh: What God *is* about to do he sheweth unto Pharaoh.

²⁹Behold, there come seven years of great plenty throughout all the land of Egypt:

³⁰And there shall arise after them seven

Amplified Bible

and he interpreted them to us, to each man according to the significance of his dream.

¹³And as he interpreted to us, so it came to pass; I was restored to my office [as chief butler], and the baker was hanged.

¹⁴Then Pharaoh sent and called Joseph, and they brought him hastily out of the dungeon. But Joseph [first] shaved himself, changed his clothes, *and* made himself presentable; then he came into Pharaoh's presence.

¹⁵And Pharaoh said to Joseph, I have dreamed a dream, and there is no one who can interpret it; and I have heard it said of you that you can understand a dream *and* interpret it.

¹⁶Joseph answered Pharaoh, It is not in me; God [not I] will give Pharaoh a [favorable] answer of peace.

¹⁷And Pharaoh said to Joseph, In my dream, behold, I stood on the bank of the river [Nile];

¹⁸And behold, there came up out of the river [Nile] seven fat, sleek, *and* handsome cows, and they grazed in the reed grass [of a marshy pasture].

¹⁹And behold, seven other cows came up after them, undernourished, gaunt, *and* ugly [just skin and bones; such emaciated animals] as I have never seen in all of Egypt.

²⁰And the lean and ill favored cows ate up the seven fat cows that had come first.

²¹And when they had eaten them up, it could not be detected *and* known that they had eaten them, for they were still as thin *and* emaciated as at the beginning. Then I awoke. [But again I fell asleep and dreamed.]

²²And I saw in my dream, and behold, seven ears [of grain] growing on one stalk, plump and good.

²³And behold, seven [other] ears, withered, thin, and blighted by the east wind, sprouted after them.

²⁴And the thin ears devoured the seven good ears. Now I told this to the magicians, but there was no one who could tell me what it meant.

²⁵Then Joseph said to Pharaoh, The [two] dreams are one; God has shown Pharaoh what He is about to do.

²⁶The seven good cows are seven years, and the seven good ears [of grain] are seven years; the [two] dreams are one [in their meaning].

²⁷And the seven thin and ill favored cows that came up after them are seven years, and also the seven empty ears [of grain], blighted *and* shriveled by the east wind; they are seven years of hunger *and* famine.

²⁸This is the message just as I have told Pharaoh: God has shown Pharaoh what He is about to do.

²⁹Take note! Seven years of great plenty throughout all the land of Egypt are coming.

³⁰Then there will come seven years of hunger *and* famine, and [there will be so much want

King James Version

years of famine; and all the plenty shall be forgotten in the land of Egypt; and the famine shall consume the land;

31And the plenty shall not be known in the land by reason of that famine following; for it *shall be* very grievous.

32And for that the dream was doubled unto Pharaoh twice; *it is* because the thing *is* established by God, and God will shortly bring it to pass.

33Now therefore let Pharaoh look out a man discreet and wise, and set him over the land of Egypt.

34Let Pharaoh do *this,* and let him appoint officers over the land, and take up the fifth *part* of the land of Egypt in the seven plenteous years.

35And let them gather all the food of those good years that come, and lay up corn under the hand of Pharaoh, and let them keep food in the cities.

36And *that* food shall be for store to the land against the seven years of famine, which shall be in the land of Egypt; that the land perish not through the famine.

37 ¶ And the thing was good in the eyes of Pharaoh, and in the eyes of all his servants.

38And Pharaoh said unto his servants, Can we find *such a one* as this *is,* a man in whom the spirit of God *is?*

39And Pharaoh said unto Joseph, Forasmuch as God hath shewed thee all this, *there is* none so discreet and wise as thou *art:*

40Thou shalt be over my house, and according unto thy word shall all my people be ruled: only *in* the throne will I be greater than thou.

41And Pharaoh said unto Joseph, See, I have set thee over all the land of Egypt.

42And Pharaoh took off his ring from his hand, and put it upon Joseph's hand, and arrayed him in vestures of fine linen, and put a gold chain about his neck;

43And he made him to ride in the second chariot which he had; and they cried before him, Bow the knee: and he made him *ruler* over all the land of Egypt.

44And Pharaoh said unto Joseph, I *am* Pharaoh, and without thee shall no man lift up his hand or foot in all the land of Egypt.

45And Pharaoh called Joseph's name Zaphnath-paaneah; and he gave him to wife Asenath the daughter of Poti-pherah priest of On. And Joseph went out over *all* the land of Egypt.

Amplified Bible

that] all the great abundance of the previous years will be forgotten in the land of Egypt; and hunger (destitution, starvation) will exhaust (consume, finish) the land.

31And the plenty will become quite unknown in the land because of that following famine, for it will be very woefully severe.

32That the dream was sent twice to Pharaoh *and* in two forms indicates that this thing which God will very soon bring to pass is fully prepared *and* established by God.

33So now let Pharaoh seek out *and* provide a man discreet, understanding, proficient, *and* wise and set him over the land of Egypt [as governor].

34Let Pharaoh do this; then let him select and appoint officers over the land, and take one-fifth [of the produce] of the [whole] land of Egypt in the seven plenteous years [year by year].

35And let them gather all the food of these good years that are coming and lay up grain under the direction *and* authority of Pharaoh, and let them retain food [in fortified granaries] in the cities.

36And that food shall be put in store for the country against the seven years of hunger *and* famine that are to come upon the land of Egypt, so that the land may not be ruined *and* cut off by the famine.

37And the plan seemed good in the eyes of Pharaoh and in the eyes of all his servants.

38And Pharaoh said to his servants, Can we find this man's equal, a man in whom is the spirit of God?

39And Pharaoh said to Joseph, Forasmuch as [your] God has shown you all this, there is nobody as intelligent *and* discreet *and* understanding and wise as you are.

40You shall have charge over my house, and all my people shall be governed according to your word [with reverence, submission, and obedience]. Only in matters of the throne will I be greater than you are.

41Then Pharaoh said to Joseph, See, I have set you over all the land of Egypt.

42And Pharaoh took off his [signet] ring from his hand and put it on Joseph's hand, and arrayed him in [official] vestments of fine linen and put a gold chain about his neck;

43He made him to ride in the second chariot which he had, and [officials] cried before him, Bow the knee! And he set him over all the land of Egypt.

44And Pharaoh said to Joseph, I am Pharaoh, and without you shall no man lift up his hand or foot in all the land of Egypt.

45And Pharaoh called Joseph's name Zaphenath-paaneah and he gave him Asenath daughter of Potiphera, priest of On, to be his wife. And Joseph made an [inspection] tour of all the land of Egypt.

King James Version

⁴⁶ ¶ And Joseph *was* thirty years old when he stood before Pharaoh king of Egypt. And Joseph went out from the presence of Pharaoh, and went throughout all the land of Egypt.

⁴⁷And in the seven plenteous years the earth brought forth by handfuls.

⁴⁸And he gathered up all the food of the seven years, which were in the land of Egypt, and laid up the food in the cities: the food of the field, which *was* round about every city, laid he up in the same.

⁴⁹And Joseph gathered corn as the sand of the sea, very much, until he left numbering; for *it was* without number.

⁵⁰And unto Joseph were born two sons before the years of famine came, which Asenath the daughter of Poti-pherah priest of On bare unto him.

⁵¹And Joseph called the name of the firstborn Manasseh: For God, *said he,* hath made me forget all my toil, and all my father's house.

⁵²And the name of the second called he Ephraim: For God hath caused me to be fruitful in the land of my affliction.

⁵³ ¶ And the seven years of plenteousness, that was in the land of Egypt, were ended.

⁵⁴And the seven years of dearth began to come, according as Joseph had said: and the dearth was in all lands; but in all the land of Egypt there was bread.

⁵⁵And when all the land of Egypt was famished, the people cried to Pharaoh for bread: and Pharaoh said unto all the Egyptians, Go unto Joseph; what he saith to you, do.

⁵⁶And the famine was over all the face of the earth: And Joseph opened all the storehouses, and sold unto the Egyptians; and the famine waxed sore in the land of Egypt.

⁵⁷And all countries came into Egypt to Joseph for to buy *corn;* because that the famine was *so* sore in all lands.

42 Now when Jacob saw that there was corn in Egypt, Jacob said unto his sons, Why do ye look one upon another?

²And he said, Behold, I have heard that there is corn in Egypt: get you down thither, and buy for us from thence; that we may live, and not die.

³And Joseph's ten brethren went down to buy corn in Egypt.

⁴But Benjamin, Joseph's brother, Jacob sent not with his brethren; for he said, Lest peradventure mischief befall him.

⁵And the sons of Israel came to buy *corn* among those that came: for the famine was in the land of Canaan.

⁶And Joseph *was* the governor over the land, *and* he *it was* that sold to all the people of the land: and Joseph's brethren came, and bowed

Amplified Bible

⁴⁶Joseph [who had been in Egypt thirteen years] was thirty years old when he stood before Pharaoh king of Egypt. Joseph went out from the presence of Pharaoh and went [about his duties] through all the land of Egypt.

⁴⁷In the seven abundant years the earth brought forth by handfuls [for each seed planted].

⁴⁸And he gathered up all the [surplus] food of the seven [good] years in the land of Egypt and stored up the food in the cities; he stored away in each city the food from the fields around it.

⁴⁹And Joseph gathered grain as the sand of the sea, very much, until he stopped counting, for it could not be measured.

⁵⁰Now to Joseph were born two sons before the years of famine came, whom Asenath daughter of Potiphera, the priest of On, bore to him.

⁵¹And Joseph called the firstborn Manasseh [making to forget], For God, said he, has made me forget all my toil *and* hardship and all my father's house.

⁵²And the second he called Ephraim [to be fruitful], For [he said] God has caused me to be fruitful in the land of my affliction.

⁵³When the seven years of plenty were ended in the land of Egypt,

⁵⁴The seven years of scarcity *and* famine began to come, as Joseph had said they would; the famine was in all [the surrounding] lands, but in all of Egypt there was food.

⁵⁵But when all the land of Egypt was weakened with hunger, the people [there] cried to Pharaoh for food; and Pharaoh said to [them] all, Go to Joseph; what he says to you, do.

⁵⁶When the famine was over all the land, Joseph opened all the storehouses and sold to the Egyptians; for the famine grew extremely distressing in the land of Egypt.

⁵⁷And all countries came to Egypt to Joseph to buy grain, because the famine was severe over all [the known] earth.

42 NOW WHEN Jacob learned that there was grain in Egypt, he said to his sons, Why do you look at one another?

²For, he said, I have heard that there is grain in Egypt; get down there and buy [grain] for us, that we may live and not die.

³So ten of Joseph's brethren went to buy grain in Egypt.

⁴But Benjamin, Joseph's [full] brother, Jacob did not send with his brothers; for he said, Lest perhaps some harm *or* injury should befall him.

⁵So the sons of Israel came to buy grain among those who came, for there was hunger *and* general lack of food in the land of Canaan.

⁶Now Joseph was the governor over the land, and he it was who sold to all the people of the land; and Joseph's [half] brothers came and

King James Version

down themselves before him *with* their faces to the earth.

⁷And Joseph saw his brethren, and he knew them, but made himself strange unto them, and spake roughly unto them; and he said unto them, Whence come ye? And they said, From the land of Canaan to buy food.

⁸And Joseph knew his brethren, but they knew not him.

⁹And Joseph remembered the dreams which he dreamed of them, and said unto them, Ye *are* spies; to see the nakedness of the land you are come.

¹⁰And they said unto him, Nay, my lord, but to buy food are thy servants come.

¹¹We *are* all one man's sons; we *are* true *men,* thy servants are no spies.

¹²And he said unto them, Nay, but to see the nakedness of the land you are come.

¹³And they said, Thy servants *are* twelve brethren, the sons of one man in the land of Canaan; and behold, the youngest *is this* day with our father, and one *is* not.

¹⁴And Joseph said unto them, That *is it* that I spake unto you, saying, Ye *are* spies:

¹⁵Hereby ye shall be proved: By the life of Pharaoh ye shall not go forth hence, except your youngest brother come hither.

¹⁶Send one of you, and let him fetch your brother, and ye shall be kept in prison, that your words may be proved, whether *there be any* truth in you: or else by the life of Pharaoh surely ye *are* spies.

¹⁷And he put them all together into ward three days.

¹⁸And Joseph said unto them the third day, This do, and live; *for* I fear God:

¹⁹If ye *be* true *men,* let one of your brethren be bound in the house of your prison: go ye, carry corn *for* the famine of your houses:

²⁰But bring your youngest brother unto me; so shall your words be verified, and ye shall not die. And they did so.

²¹And they said one to another, We *are* verily guilty concerning our brother, in that we saw the anguish of his soul, when he besought us, and we would not hear; therefore is this distress come upon us.

²²And Reuben answered them, saying, Spake I not unto you, saying, Do not sin against the child; and ye would not hear? therefore, behold, also his blood is required.

²³And they knew not that Joseph understood *them;* for he spake unto them by an interpreter.

²⁴And he turned himself about from them, and wept; and returned to them *again,* and communed with them, and took from them Simeon, and bound him before their eyes.

Amplified Bible

bowed themselves down before him with their faces to the ground.

⁷Joseph saw his brethren and he recognized them, but he treated them as if he were a stranger to them and spoke roughly to them. He said, Where do you come from? And they replied, From the land of Canaan to buy food.

⁸Joseph knew his brethren, but they did not know him.

⁹And Joseph remembered the dreams he had dreamed about them and said to them, You are spies *and* with unfriendly purpose you have come to observe [secretly] the nakedness of the land.

¹⁰But they said to him, No, my lord, but your servants have come [only] to buy food.

¹¹We are all one man's sons; we are true men; your servants are not spies.

¹²And he said to them, No, but you have come to see the nakedness of the land.

¹³But they said, Your servants are twelve brothers, the sons of one man in the land of Canaan; the youngest is today with our father, and one is not.

¹⁴And Joseph said to them, It is as I said to you, You are spies.

¹⁵You shall be proved by this test: by the life of Pharaoh, you shall not go away from here unless your youngest brother comes here.

¹⁶Send one of you and let him bring your brother, and you will be kept in prison, that your words may be proved whether there is any truth in you; or else by the life of Pharaoh you certainly are spies.

¹⁷Then he put them all in custody for three days.

¹⁸And Joseph said to them on the third day, Do this and live! I reverence *and* fear God.

¹⁹If you are true men, let one of your brothers be bound in your prison, but [the rest of] you go and carry grain for those weakened with hunger in your households.

²⁰But bring your youngest brother to me, so your words will be verified and you shall live. And they did so.

²¹And they said one to another, We are truly guilty about our brother, for we saw the distress *and* anguish of his soul when he begged us [to let him go], and we would not hear. So this distress *and* difficulty has come upon us.

²²Reuben answered them, Did I not tell you, Do not sin against the boy, and you would not hear? Therefore, behold, his blood is required [of us].

²³But they did not know that Joseph understood them, for he spoke to them through an interpreter.

²⁴And he turned away from them and wept; then he returned to them and talked with them, and took from them Simeon and bound him before their eyes.

King James Version

25Then Joseph commanded to fill their sacks *with* corn, and to restore every man's money into his sack, and to give them provision for the way: and thus did he unto them.

26 ¶ And they laded their asses with the corn, and departed thence.

27And as one *of them* opened his sack to give his ass provender in the inn, he espied his money; for behold, it *was* in his sack's mouth.

28And he said unto his brethren, My money is restored; and lo, *it is* even in my sack: and their heart failed *them,* and they were afraid, saying one to another, What *is* this *that* God hath done unto us?

29And they came unto Jacob their father unto the land of Canaan, and told him all that befell unto them; saying,

30The man, *who is* the lord of the land, spake roughly to us, and took us for spies of the country.

31And we said unto him, We *are* true *men;* we are no spies:

32We *be* twelve brethren, sons of our father; one *is* not, and the youngest *is this* day with our father in the land of Canaan.

33And the man, the lord of the country, said unto us, Hereby shall I know that ye *are* true *men;* leave one of your brethren *here* with me, and take *food for* the famine of your households, and be gone:

34And bring your youngest brother unto me: then shall I know that ye *are* no spies, but *that* ye *are* true *men: so* will I deliver you your brother, and ye shall traffick in the land.

35And it came to pass as they emptied their sacks, that behold, every man's bundle of money *was* in his sack: and when *both* they and their father saw the bundles of money, they were afraid.

36And Jacob their father said unto them, Me have ye bereaved of my children: Joseph *is* not, and Simeon *is* not, and ye will take Benjamin *away:* all these things are against me.

37And Reuben spake unto his father, saying, Slay my two sons, if I bring him not to thee: deliver him into my hand, and I will bring him to thee again.

38And he said, My son shall not go down with you; for his brother is dead, and he is left alone: if mischief befall him by the way in the which ye go, then shall ye bring down my gray hairs with sorrow to the grave.

43 And the famine *was* sore in the land. 2And it came to pass, when they had eaten up the corn which they had brought out of

Amplified Bible

25Then [privately] Joseph commanded that their sacks be filled with grain, every man's money be restored to his sack, and provisions be given to them for the journey. And this was done for them.

26They loaded their donkeys with grain and left.

27And as one of them opened his sack to give his donkey fodder at the lodging place, he caught sight of his money; for behold, it was in his sack's mouth.

28And he said to his brothers, My money is restored! Here it is in my sack! And their hearts failed them and they were afraid *and* turned trembling one to another, saying, What is this that God has done to us?

29When they came to Jacob their father in Canaan, they told him all that had befallen them, saying,

30The man who is the lord of the land spoke roughly to us and took us for spies of the country.

31And we said to him, We are true men, not spies.

32We are twelve brothers with the same father; one is no more, and the youngest is today with our father in the land of Canaan.

33And the man, the lord of the country, said to us, By this test I will know whether or not you are honest men: leave one of your brothers here with me and take grain for your famishing households and be gone.

34Bring your youngest brother to me; then I will know that you are not spies, but that you are honest men. And I will deliver to you your brother [whom I have kept bound in prison], and you may do business in the land.

35When they emptied their sacks, behold, every man's parcel of money was in his sack! When both they and their father saw the bundles of money, they were afraid.

36And Jacob their father said to them, You have bereaved me! Joseph is not, and Simeon is not, and you would take Benjamin from me. All these things are against me!

37And Reuben said to his father, Slay my two sons if I do not bring [Benjamin] back to you. Deliver him into my keeping, and I will bring him back to you.

38But [Jacob] said, My son shall not go down with you, for his brother is dead and he alone is left [of his mother's children]; if harm *or* accident should befall him on the journey you are to take, you would bring my hoary head down to Sheol (the place of the dead) with grief.

43 BUT THE hunger *and* destitution *and* starvation were very severe *and* extremely distressing in the land [Canaan].

2And when [the families of Jacob's sons] had eaten up the grain which the men had brought

King James Version

Egypt, their father said unto them, Go again, buy us a little food.

3And Judah spake unto him, saying, The man did solemnly protest unto us, saying, Ye shall not see my face, except your brother *be* with you.

4If thou wilt send our brother with us, we will go down and buy thee food:

5But if thou wilt not send *him,* we will not go down: for the man said unto us, Ye shall not see my face, except your brother *be* with you.

6And Israel said, Wherefore dealt ye *so* ill with me, *as* to tell the man whether ye had yet a brother?

7And they said, The man asked us straitly of our state, and of our kindred, saying, *Is* your father yet alive? have ye *another* brother? and we told him according to the tenor of these words: could we certainly know that he would say, Bring your brother down?

8And Judah said unto Israel his father, Send the lad with me, and we will arise and go; that we may live, and not die, both we, and thou, *and* also our little ones.

9I will be surety for him; of my hand shalt thou require him: if I bring him not unto thee, and set him before thee, then let me bear the blame for ever:

10For except we had lingered, surely now we had returned this second time.

11And their father Israel said unto them, If *it must be* so now, do this; take of the best fruits in the land in your vessels, and carry down the man a present, a little balm, and a little honey, spices, and myrrh, nuts, and almonds:

12And take double money in your hand; and the money that was brought again in the mouth of your sacks, carry *it* again in your hand; peradventure it *was* an oversight:

13Take also your brother, and arise, go again unto the man:

14And God Almighty give you mercy before the man, that he may send away your other brother, and Benjamin. If I be bereaved of my children, I am bereaved.

15 ¶ And the men took that present, and they took double money in their hand, and Benjamin; and rose up, and went down *to* Egypt, and stood before Joseph.

16And when Joseph saw Benjamin with them, he said to the ruler of his house, Bring *these* men home, and slay, and make ready; for *these* men shall dine with me at noon.

17And the man did as Joseph bade; and the man brought the men into Joseph's house.

18And the men were afraid, because they were brought into Joseph's house; and they said, Because of the money that was returned in our sacks at the first time *are* we brought

Amplified Bible

from Egypt, their father said to them, Go again; buy us a little food.

3But Judah said to him, The man solemnly *and* sternly warned us, saying, You shall not see my face again unless your brother is with you.

4If you will send our brother with us, we will go down [to Egypt] and buy you food;

5But if you will not send him, we will not go down; for the man said to us, You shall not see my face unless your brother is with you.

6And Israel said, Why did you do me such a wrong *and* suffer this evil to come upon me by telling the man that you had another brother?

7And they said, The man asked us straightforward questions about ourselves and our relatives. He said, Is your father still alive? Have you another brother? And we answered him accordingly. How could we know that he would say, Bring your brother down here?

8And Judah said to Israel his father, Send the lad with me and we will arise and go, that we may live and not die, both we and you and also our little ones.

9I will be security for him; you shall require him of me [personally]; if I do not bring him back to you and put him before you, then let me bear the blame forever.

10For if we had not lingered like this, surely by now we would have returned the second time.

11And their father Israel said to them, If it must be so, now do this; take of the choicest products in the land in your sacks and carry down a present to the man, a little balm (balsam) and a little honey, aromatic spices and gum (of rock rose) *or* ladanum, pistachio nuts, and almonds.

12And take double the [grain] money with you; and the money that was put back in the mouth of your sacks, carry it again with you; there is a possibility that [its being in your sacks] was an oversight.

13Take your brother and arise and return to the man;

14May God Almighty give you mercy *and* favor before the man, that he may release to you your other brother and Benjamin. If I am bereaved [of my sons], I am bereaved.

15Then the men took the present, and they took double the [grain] money with them, and Benjamin; and they arose and went down to Egypt and stood before Joseph.

16And when Joseph saw Benjamin with them, he said to the steward of his house, Bring the men into the house and kill an animal and make ready, for the men will dine with me at noon.

17And the man did as Joseph ordered and brought the men to Joseph's house.

18The men were afraid because they were brought to Joseph's house; and they said, We are brought in because of the money that was returned in our sacks the first time we came, so

King James Version

in; that he may seek occasion against us, and fall upon us, and take us for bondmen, and our asses.

¹⁹And they came near to the steward of Joseph's house, and they communed with him *at* the door of the house,

²⁰And said, O sir, we came indeed down at the first time to buy food:

²¹And it came to pass, when we came to the inn, that we opened our sacks, and behold, every man's money *was* in the mouth of his sack, our money in full weight: and we have brought it again in our hand.

²²And other money have we brought down in our hands to buy food: we cannot tell who put our money in our sacks.

²³And he said, Peace *be* to you, fear not: your God, and the God of your father, hath given you treasure in your sacks: I had your money. And he brought Simeon out unto them.

²⁴And the man brought the men into Joseph's house, and gave *them* water, and they washed their feet; and he gave their asses provender.

²⁵And they made ready the present against Joseph came at noon: for they heard that they should eat bread there.

²⁶And when Joseph came home, they brought him the present which *was* in their hand into the house, and bowed themselves to him to the earth.

²⁷And he asked them of *their* welfare, and said, *Is* your father well, the old man of whom ye spake? *Is* he yet alive?

²⁸And they answered, Thy servant our father *is* in good health, he *is* yet alive. And they bowed down their heads, and made obeisance.

²⁹And he lift up his eyes, and saw his brother Benjamin, his mother's son, and said, *Is* this your younger brother, of whom ye spake unto me? And he said, God be gracious unto thee, my son.

³⁰And Joseph made haste; for his bowels did yern upon his brother: and he sought *where* to weep; and he entered into *his* chamber, and wept there.

³¹And he washed his face, and went out, and refrained himself, and said, Set on bread.

³²And they set on for him by himself, and for them by themselves, and for the Egyptians, which did eat with him, by themselves: because the Egyptians might not eat bread with the Hebrews; for that *is* an abomination unto the Egyptians.

³³And they sat before him, the firstborn according to his birthright, and the youngest according to his youth: and the men marvelled one at another.

³⁴And he took *and sent* messes unto them from before him: but Benjamin's mess was five times so much as any of theirs. And they drunk, and were merry with him.

Amplified Bible

that he may find occasion to accuse and assail us, take us for slaves, and seize our donkeys.

¹⁹So they came near to the steward of Joseph's house and talked with him at the door of the house,

²⁰And said, O sir, we came down truly the first time to buy food;

²¹And when we came to the inn, we opened our sacks and there was each man's money, full weight, returned in the mouth of his sack. Now we have brought it back again.

²²And we have brought down with us other money to buy food; we do not know who put our money in our sacks.

²³But [the steward] said, Peace be to you, fear not; your God and the God of your father has given you treasure in your sacks. I received your money. And he brought Simeon out to them.

²⁴And the man brought the men into Joseph's house and gave them water, and they washed their feet; and he gave their donkeys provender.

²⁵And they made ready the present they had brought for Joseph before his coming at noon, for they heard that they were to dine there.

²⁶And when Joseph came home, they brought into the house to him the present which they had with them, and bowed themselves to him to the ground.

²⁷He asked them of their welfare and said, Is your old father well, of whom you spoke? Is he still alive?

²⁸And they answered, Your servant our father is in good health; he is still alive. And they bowed down their heads and made obeisance.

²⁹And he looked up and saw his [full] brother Benjamin, his mother's [only other] son, and said, Is this your youngest brother, of whom you spoke to me? And he said, God be gracious to you, my son!

³⁰And Joseph hurried from the room, for his heart yearned for his brother, and he sought privacy to weep; so he entered his chamber and wept there.

³¹And he washed his face and went out, and, restraining himself, said, Let dinner be served.

³²And [the servants] set out [the food] for [Joseph] by himself, and for [his brothers] by themselves, and for those Egyptians who ate with him by themselves, according to the Egyptian custom not to eat food with the Hebrews; for that is an abomination to the Egyptians.

³³And [Joseph's brothers] were given seats before him—the eldest according to his birthright and the youngest according to his youth; and the men looked at one another amazed [that so much was known about them].

³⁴[Joseph] took and sent helpings to them from before him, but Benjamin's portion was five times as much as any of theirs. And they drank freely and were merry with him.

King James Version

44 And he commanded the steward of his house, saying, Fill the men's sacks *with* food, as much as they can carry, and put every man's money in his sack's mouth.

2 And put my cup, the silver cup, in the sack's mouth of the youngest, and his corn money. And he did according to the word that Joseph had spoken.

3 As soon as the morning was light, the men were sent away, they and their asses.

4 *And* when they were gone out of the city, *and* not *yet* far off, Joseph said unto his steward, Up, follow after the men; and when thou dost overtake them, say unto them, Wherefore have ye rewarded evil for good?

5 *Is* not this *it* in which my lord drinketh, and whereby indeed he divineth? ye have done evil in *so* doing.

6 And he overtook them, and he spake unto them these *same* words.

7 And they said unto him, Wherefore saith my lord these words? God forbid that thy servants should do according to this thing:

8 Behold, the money, which we found in our sacks' mouths, we brought again unto thee out of the land of Canaan: how then should we steal out of thy lord's house silver or gold?

9 With whom*soever* of thy servants it be found, both let him die, and we also will be my lord's bondmen.

10 And he said, Now also *let* it *be* according unto your words: he with whom it is found shall be my servant; and ye shall be blameless.

11 Then they speedily took down every man his sack to the ground, and opened every man his sack.

12 And he searched, *and* began at the eldest, and left at the youngest: and the cup was found in Benjamin's sack.

13 Then they rent their clothes, and laded every man his ass, and returned to the city.

14 ¶ And Judah and his brethren came to Joseph's house; for he *was* yet there: and they fell before him on the ground.

15 And Joseph said unto them, What deed *is* this that ye have done? wot ye not that such a man as I can certainly divine?

16 And Judah said, What shall we say unto my lord? what shall we speak? or how shall we clear ourselves? God hath found out the iniquity of thy servants: behold, we *are* my lord's servants, both we, and *he* also with whom the cup is found.

17 And he said, God forbid that I should do so: *but* the man in whose hand the cup is found, he shall be my servant; and as for you, get you up in peace unto your father.

Amplified Bible

44 AND HE commanded the steward of his house, saying, Fill the men's sacks with food, as much as they can carry, and put every man's money in his sack's mouth.

2 And put my cup, the silver cup, in the sack's mouth of the youngest, with his grain money. And [the steward] did according to what Joseph had said.

3 As soon as the morning was light, the men were sent away, they and their donkeys.

4 When they had left the city and were not yet far away, Joseph said to his steward, Up, follow after the men; and when you overtake them, say to them, Why have you rewarded evil for good? [Why have you stolen the silver cup?]

5 Is it not my master's drinking cup with which he divines [the future]? You have done wrong in doing this.

6 And the steward overtook them, and he said to them these same words.

7 They said to him, Why does my lord say these things? Far be it from your servants to do such a thing!

8 Note that the money which we found in the mouths of our sacks we brought back to you from the land of Canaan. Is it likely then that we would steal from your master's house silver or gold?

9 With whomever of your servants [your master's cup] is found, not only let that one die, but the rest of us will be my lord's slaves.

10 And the steward said, Now let it be as you say: he with whom [the cup] is found shall be my slave, but [the rest of] you shall be blameless.

11 Then quickly every man lowered his sack to the ground and every man opened his sack.

12 And [the steward] searched, beginning with the eldest and stopping with the youngest; and the cup was found in Benjamin's sack.

13 Then they rent their clothes; and after each man had loaded his donkey again, they returned to the city.

14 Judah and his brethren came to Joseph's house, for he was still there; and they fell prostrate before him.

15 Joseph said to them, What is this thing that you have done? Do you not realize that such a man as I can certainly detect *and* know by divination [everything you do without other knowledge of it]?

16 And Judah said, What shall we say to my lord? What shall we reply? Or how shall we clear ourselves, since God has found out *and* exposed the iniquity of your servants? Behold, we are my lord's slaves, the rest of us as well as he with whom the cup is found.

17 But [Joseph] said, God forbid that I should do that; but the man in whose hand the cup is found, he shall be my servant; and as for [the rest of] you, arise *and* go in peace to your father.

King James Version

18Then Judah came near unto him, and said, O my lord, let thy servant, I pray thee, speak a word in my lord's ears, and let not thine anger burn against thy servant: for thou *art* even as Pharaoh.

19My lord asked his servants, saying, Have ye a father, or a brother?

20And we said unto my lord, We have a father, an old man, and a child of *his* old age, a little one; and his brother is dead, and he alone is left of his mother, and his father loveth him.

21And thou saidst unto thy servants, Bring him down unto me, that I may set mine eyes upon him.

22And we said unto my lord, The lad cannot leave his father: for *if* he should leave his father, *his father* would die.

23And thou saidst unto thy servants, Except your youngest brother come down with you, ye shall see my face no more.

24And it came to pass when we came up unto thy servant my father, we told him the words of my lord.

25And our father said, Go again, *and* buy us a little food.

26And we said, We cannot go down: if our youngest brother be with us, then will we go down: for we may not see the man's face, except our youngest brother *be* with us.

27And thy servant my father said unto us, Ye know that my wife bare me two *sons:*

28And the one went out from me, and I said, Surely he is torn in pieces; and I saw him not since:

29And if ye take this also from me, and mischief befall him, ye shall bring down my gray hairs with sorrow to the grave.

30Now therefore when I come to thy servant my father, and the lad *be* not with us; seeing that his life *is* bound up in *the lad's* life;

31It shall come to pass, when he seeth that the lad *is* not *with us,* that he will die: and thy servants shall bring down the gray hairs of thy servant our father with sorrow to the grave.

32For thy servant became surety for the lad unto my father, saying, If I bring him not unto thee, then I shall bear the blame to my father for ever.

33Now therefore, I pray thee, let thy servant abide instead of the lad a bondman to my lord; and let the lad go up with his brethren.

34For how shall I go up to my father, and the lad *be* not with me? lest peradventure I see the evil that shall come on my father.

45 Then Joseph could not refrain himself before all them that stood by him; and he cried, Cause every man to go out from me. And

Amplified Bible

18Then Judah came close to [Joseph] and said, O my lord, let your servant, I pray you, speak a word to you in private, and let not your anger blaze against your servant, for you are as Pharaoh [so I will speak as if directly to him].

19My lord asked his servants, saying, Have you a father or a brother?

20And we said to my lord, We have a father— an old man—and a young [brother, the] child of his old age; and his brother is dead, and he alone is left of his mother's [offspring], and his father loves him.

21And you said to your servants, Bring him down to me, that I may set my eyes on him.

22And we said to my lord, The lad cannot leave his father; for if he should do so, his father would die.

23And you told your servants, Unless your youngest brother comes with you, you shall not see my face again.

24And when we went back to your servant my father, we told him what my lord had said.

25And our father said, Go again and buy us a little food.

26But we said, We cannot go down. If our youngest brother is with us, then we will go down; for we may not see the man's face except our youngest brother is with us.

27And your servant my father said to us, You know that [Rachel] my wife bore me two sons:

28And the one went out from me, and I said, Surely he is torn to pieces, and I have never seen him since.

29And if you take this son also from me, and harm *or* accident should befall him, you will bring down my gray hairs with sorrow *and* evil to Sheol (the place of the dead).

30Now therefore, when I come to your servant my father and the lad is not with us, since his life is bound up in the lad's life *and* his soul knit with the lad's soul,

31When he sees that the lad is not with us, he will die; and your servants will be responsible for his death *and* will bring down the gray hairs of your servant our father with sorrow to Sheol.

32For your servant became security for the lad to my father, saying, If I do not bring him to you, then I will bear the blame to my father forever.

33Now therefore, I pray you, let your servant remain instead of the youth [to be] a slave to my lord, and let the young man go home with his [half] brothers.

34For how can I go up to my father if the lad is not with me?—lest I witness the woe *and* the evil that will come upon my father.

45 THEN JOSEPH could not restrain himself [any longer] before all those who stood by him, and he called out, Cause every man to go out from me! So no one stood there

King James Version

there stood no man with him, while Joseph made himself known unto his brethren.

2And he wept aloud: and the Egyptians and the house of Pharaoh heard.

3And Joseph said unto his brethren, I *am* Joseph; doth my father yet live? And his brethren could not answer him; for they were troubled at his presence.

4And Joseph said unto his brethren, Come near to me, I pray you. And they came near. And he said, I *am* Joseph your brother, whom ye sold into Egypt.

5Now therefore be not grieved, nor angry with yourselves, that ye sold me hither: for God did send me before you to preserve life.

6For these two years *hath* the famine *been* in the land: and yet *there are* five years, *in* the which *there shall* neither *be* earing nor harvest.

7And God sent me before you to preserve you a posterity in the earth, and to save your lives by a great deliverance.

8So now *it was* not you *that* sent me hither, but God: and he hath made me a father to Pharaoh, and lord of all his house, and a ruler throughout all the land of Egypt.

9Haste you, and go up to my father, and say unto him, Thus saith thy son Joseph, God hath made me lord of all Egypt: come down unto me, tarry not:

10And thou shalt dwell in the land of Goshen, and thou shalt be near unto me, thou, and thy children, and thy children's children, and thy flocks, and thy herds, and all that thou hast:

11And there will I nourish thee; for yet *there are* five years of famine; lest thou, and thy household, and all that thou hast, come to poverty.

12And behold, your eyes see, and the eyes of my brother Benjamin, that *it is* my mouth that speaketh unto you.

13And you shall tell my father of all my glory in Egypt, and of all that you have seen; and ye shall haste and bring down my father hither.

14And he fell upon his brother Benjamin's neck, and wept; and Benjamin wept upon his neck.

15Moreover he kissed all his brethren, and wept upon them: and after that his brethren talked with him.

16 ¶ And the fame *thereof* was heard *in* Pharaoh's house, saying, Joseph's brethren are come: and it pleased Pharaoh well, and his servants.

17And Pharaoh said unto Joseph, Say unto thy brethren, This do ye; lade your beasts, and go, get you unto the land of Canaan;

18And take your father and your households, and come unto me: and I will give you the good

Amplified Bible

with Joseph while he made himself known to his brothers.

2And he wept *and* sobbed aloud, and the Egyptians [who had just left him] heard it, and the household of Pharaoh heard about it.

3And Joseph said to his brothers, I am Joseph! Is my father still alive? And his brothers could not reply, for they were distressingly disturbed *and* dismayed at [the startling realization that they were in] his presence.

4And Joseph said to his brothers, Come near to me, I pray you. And they did so. And he said, I am Joseph your brother, whom you sold into Egypt!

5But now, do not be distressed *and* disheartened or vexed *and* angry with yourselves because you sold me here, for God sent me ahead of you to preserve life.

6For these two years the famine has been in the land, and there are still five years more in which there will be neither plowing nor harvest.

7God sent me before you to preserve for you a posterity *and* to continue a remnant on the earth, to save your lives by a great escape *and* save for you many survivors.

8So now it was not you who sent me here, but God; and He has made me a father to Pharaoh and lord of all his house and ruler over all the land of Egypt.

9Hurry and go up to my father and tell him, Your son Joseph says this to you: God has put me in charge of all Egypt. Come down to me; do not delay.

10You will live in the land of Goshen, and you will be close to me—you and your children and your grandchildren, your flocks, your herds, and all you have.

11And there I will sustain *and* provide for you, so that you and your household and all that are yours may not come to poverty *and* want, for there are yet five [more] years of [the scarcity, hunger, and starvation of] famine.

12Now notice! Your own eyes and the eyes of my brother Benjamin can see that I am talking to you personally [in your language and not through an interpreter].

13And you shall tell my father of all my glory in Egypt and of all that you have seen; and you shall hurry and bring my father down here.

14And he fell on his brother Benjamin's neck and wept, and Benjamin wept on his neck.

15Moreover, he kissed all his brothers and wept upon them; and after that his brothers conversed with him.

16When the report was heard in Pharaoh's house that Joseph's brothers had come, it pleased Pharaoh and his servants well.

17And Pharaoh said to Joseph, Tell your brothers this: Load your animals and return to the land of Canaan,

18And get your father and your households and come to me. And I will give you the best in

King James Version

of the land of Egypt, and ye shall eat the fat of the land.

¹⁹Now thou art commanded, this do ye; take you wagons out of the land of Egypt for your little ones, and for your wives, and bring your father, and come.

²⁰Also regard not your stuff; for the good of all the land of Egypt *is* yours.

²¹And the children of Israel did so: and Joseph gave them wagons, according to the commandment of Pharaoh, and gave them provision for the way.

²²To all of them he gave each man changes of raiment; but to Benjamin he gave three hundred *pieces* of silver, and five changes of raiment.

²³And to his father he sent after this manner; ten asses laden with the good things of Egypt, and ten she asses laden with corn and bread and meat for his father by the way.

²⁴So he sent his brethren away, and they departed: and he said unto them, See that ye fall not out by the way.

²⁵And they went up out of Egypt, and came *into* the land of Canaan unto Jacob their father,

²⁶And told him, saying, Joseph *is* yet alive, and he *is* governor over all the land of Egypt. And *Jacob's* heart fainted, for he believed them not.

²⁷And they told him all the words of Joseph, which he had said unto them: and when he saw the wagons which Joseph had sent to carry him, the spirit of Jacob their father revived:

²⁸And Israel said, *It is* enough; Joseph my son *is* yet alive: I will go and see him before I die.

46 And Israel took his journey with all that he had, and came to Beer-sheba, and offered sacrifices unto the God of his father Isaac.

²And God spake unto Israel in the visions of the night, and said, Jacob, Jacob. And he said, Here *am* I.

³And he said, I *am* God, the God of thy father: fear not to go down into Egypt; for I will there make of thee a great nation.

⁴I will go down with thee into Egypt; and I will also surely bring thee up *again:* and Joseph shall put his hand upon thine eyes.

⁵And Jacob rose up from Beer-sheba: and the sons of Israel carried Jacob their father, and their little ones, and their wives, in the wagons which Pharaoh had sent to carry him.

⁶And they took their cattle, and their goods, which they had gotten in the land of Canaan, and came into Egypt, Jacob, and all his seed with him:

⁷His sons, and his sons' sons with him, his daughters, and his sons' daughters, and all his seed brought he with him into Egypt.

Amplified Bible

the land of Egypt and you will live on the fat of the land.

¹⁹You therefore command them, saying, You do this: take wagons from the land of Egypt for your little ones and for your wives, and bring your father and come.

²⁰Also do not look with regret *or* concern upon your goods, for the best of all the land of Egypt is yours.

²¹And the sons of Israel did so; and Joseph gave them wagons, as the order of Pharaoh permitted, and gave them provisions for the journey.

²²To each of them he gave changes of raiment, but to Benjamin he gave 300 pieces of silver and five changes of raiment.

²³And to his father he sent as follows: ten donkeys loaded with the good things of Egypt, and ten she-donkeys laden with grain, bread, and nourishing food *and* provision for his father [to supply all who were with him] on the way.

²⁴So he sent his brothers away, and they departed, and he said to them, See that you do not disagree (get excited, quarrel) along the road.

²⁵So they went up out of Egypt and came into the land of Canaan to Jacob their father,

²⁶And they said to him, Joseph is still alive! And he is governor over all the land of Egypt! And Jacob's heart began to stop beating *and* [he almost] fainted, for he did not believe them.

²⁷But when they told him all the words of Joseph which he had said to them, and when he saw the wagons which Joseph had sent to carry him, the spirit of Jacob their father revived [and warmth and life returned].

²⁸And Israel said, It is enough! Joseph my son is still alive. I will go and see him before I die.

46 SO ISRAEL made his journey with all that he had and came to Beersheba [a place hallowed by sacred memories] and offered sacrifices to the God of his father Isaac.

²And God spoke to Israel in visions of the night, and said, Jacob! Jacob! And he said, Here am I.

³And He said, I am God, the God of your father; do not be afraid to go down to Egypt, for I will there make of you a great nation.

⁴I will go down with you to Egypt, and I will also surely bring you [your people Israel] up again; and Joseph will put his hand upon your eyes [when they are about to close in death].

⁵So Jacob arose *and* set out from Beersheba, and Israel's sons conveyed their father, their little ones, and their wives in the wagons that Pharaoh had sent to carry him.

⁶And they took their cattle and the gains which they had acquired in the land of Canaan and came into Egypt, Jacob and all his offspring with him:

⁷His sons and his sons' sons with him, his daughters and his sons' daughters—all his offspring he brought with him into Egypt.

King James Version

⁸ ¶ And these *are* the names of the children of Israel, which came into Egypt, Jacob and his sons: Reuben, Jacob's firstborn.

⁹And the sons of Reuben; Hanoch, and Phallu, and Hezron, and Carmi.

¹⁰And the sons of Simeon; Jemuel, and Jamin, and Ohad, and Jachin, and Zohar, and Shaul the son of a Canaanitish woman.

¹¹And the sons of Levi; Gershon, Kohath, and Merari.

¹²And the sons of Judah; Er, and Onan, and Shelah, and Pharez, and Zerah: but Er and Onan died in the land of Canaan. And the sons of Pharez were Hezron and Hamul.

¹³And the sons of Issachar; Tola, and Phuvah, and Job, and Shimron.

¹⁴And the sons of Zebulun; Sered, and Elon, and Jahleel.

¹⁵These *be* the sons of Leah, which she bare unto Jacob in Padan-aram, with his daughter Dinah: all the souls of his sons and his daughters *were* thirty and three.

¹⁶And the sons of Gad; Ziphion, and Haggi, Shuni, and Ezbon, Eri, and Arodi, and Areli.

¹⁷And the sons of Asher; Jimnah, and Ishuah, and Ishui, and Beriah, and Serah their sister: and the sons of Beriah; Heber, and Malchiel.

¹⁸These *are* the sons of Zilpah, whom Laban gave to Leah his daughter, and these she bare unto Jacob, *even* sixteen souls.

¹⁹The sons of Rachel Jacob's wife; Joseph, and Benjamin.

²⁰And unto Joseph in the land of Egypt were born Manasseh and Ephraim, which Asenath the daughter of Poti-pherah priest of On bare unto him.

²¹And the sons of Benjamin *were* Belah, and Becher, and Ashbel, Gera, and Naaman, Ehi, and Rosh, Muppim, and Huppim, and Ard.

²²These *are* the sons of Rachel, which were born to Jacob: all the souls *were* fourteen.

²³And the sons of Dan; Hushim.

²⁴And the sons of Naphtali; Jahzeel, and Guni, and Jezer, and Shillem.

²⁵These *are* the sons of Bilhah, which Laban gave unto Rachel his daughter, and she bare these unto Jacob: all the souls *were* seven.

²⁶All the souls that came with Jacob into Egypt, which came out of his loins, besides Jacob's sons' wives, all the souls *were* threescore and six;

²⁷And the sons of Joseph, which were born him in Egypt, *were* two souls: all the souls of the house of Jacob, which came into Egypt, *were* threescore and ten.

²⁸ ¶ And he sent Judah before him unto Jo-

Amplified Bible

⁸And these are the names of the descendants of Israel who came into Egypt, Jacob and his sons: Reuben, Jacob's firstborn.

⁹And the sons of Reuben: Hanoch, Pallu, Hezron, and Carmi.

¹⁰The sons of Simeon: Jemuel, Jamin, Ohad, Jachin, Zohar, and Shaul the son of a Canaanite woman.

¹¹The sons of Levi: Gershon, Kohath, and Merari.

¹²The sons of Judah: Er, Onan, Shelah, Perez, and Zerah; but Er and Onan died in the land of Canaan. And the sons of Perez were Hezron and Hamul.

¹³The sons of Issachar: Tola, Puvah, Iob, and Shimron.

¹⁴The sons of Zebulun: Sered, Elon, and Jahleel.

¹⁵These are the sons of Leah, whom she bore to Jacob in Padan-aram, together with his daughter Dinah. All of his sons and his daughters numbered thirty-three.

¹⁶The sons of Gad: Ziphion, Haggi, Shuni, Ezbon, Eri, Arodi, and Areli.

¹⁷The sons of Asher: Imnah, Ishvah, Ishvi, Beriah, and Serah their sister. And the sons of Beriah: Heber and Malchiel.

¹⁸These are the sons of Zilpah, [the maid] whom Laban gave to Leah his daughter. And these she bore to Jacob—sixteen persons all told.

¹⁹The sons of Rachel, Jacob's wife: Joseph and Benjamin.

²⁰And to Joseph in the land of Egypt were born Manasseh and Ephraim, whom Asenath daughter of Potiphera, priest of On, bore to him.

²¹And the sons of ᵃBenjamin: Bela, Becher, Ashbel, Gera, Naaman, Ehi, Rosh, Muppim, Huppim, and Ard.

²²These are the sons of Rachel, who were born to Jacob—fourteen persons in all.

²³The son of Dan: Hushim.

²⁴The sons of Naphtali: Jahzeel, Guni, Jezer, and Shillem.

²⁵These are the sons of Bilhah, [the maid] whom Laban gave to Rachel his daughter. And she bore these to Jacob—seven persons in all.

²⁶All the persons who came with Jacob into Egypt—who were his own offspring, not counting the wives of Jacob's sons—were sixty-six persons all told.

²⁷And the sons of Joseph, who were born to him in Egypt, were two persons. All the persons of the house of Jacob [including Joseph and Jacob himself], who came into Egypt, were seventy.

²⁸And he sent Judah before him to Joseph, to

AMP notes: ᵃ Benjamin, whom uninformed artists have frequently pictured as a mere youth when he met Joseph in Egypt, was in fact the father of 10 sons at this time. Joseph was 17 when his brothers sold him; he was in prison 13 years; he had been governor of Egypt during the 7 good years and through 2 years of the famine. So Joseph was 39 years of age at this time, and Benjamin was only a few years younger.

King James Version

seph, to direct his face unto Goshen; and they came into the land of Goshen.

²⁹And Joseph made ready his chariot, and went up to meet Israel his father, to Goshen, and presented himself unto him; and he fell on his neck, and wept on his neck a good while.

³⁰And Israel said unto Joseph, Now let me die, since I have seen thy face, because thou *art* yet alive.

³¹And Joseph said unto his brethren, and unto his father's house, I will go up, and shew Pharaoh, and say unto him, My brethren, and my father's house, which *were* in the land of Canaan, are come unto me;

³²And the men *are* shepherds, for their trade hath been to feed cattle; and they have brought their flocks, and their herds, and all that they have.

³³And it shall come to pass, when Pharaoh shall call you, and shall say, What *is* your occupation?

³⁴That ye shall say, Thy servants' trade hath been about cattle from our youth even until now, both we, *and* also our fathers: that ye may dwell in the land of Goshen; for every shepherd *is* an abomination unto the Egyptians.

47 Then Joseph came and told Pharaoh, and said, My father and my brethren, and their flocks, and their herds, and all that they have, are come out of the land of Canaan; and behold, they *are* in the land of Goshen.

²And he took some of his brethren, *even* five men, and presented them unto Pharaoh.

³And Pharaoh said unto his brethren, What *is* your occupation? And they said unto Pharaoh, Thy servants *are* shepherds, both we, *and* also our fathers.

⁴They said moreover unto Pharaoh, For to sojourn in the land are we come; for thy servants have no pasture for their flocks; for the famine *is* sore in the land of Canaan: now therefore, we pray thee, let thy servants dwell in the land of Goshen.

⁵And Pharaoh spake unto Joseph, saying, Thy father and thy brethren are come unto thee:

⁶The land of Egypt *is* before thee; in the best of the land make thy father and brethren to dwell; in the land of Goshen let them dwell: and if thou knowest *any* man of activity amongst them, then make them rulers over my cattle.

⁷And Joseph brought in Jacob his father, and set him before Pharaoh: and Jacob blessed Pharaoh.

⁸And Pharaoh said unto Jacob, How old *art* thou?

⁹And Jacob said unto Pharaoh, The days of the years of my pilgrimage *are* an hundred and

Amplified Bible

direct him to Goshen *and* meet him there; and they came into the land of Goshen.

²⁹Then Joseph made ready his chariot and went up to meet Israel his father in Goshen; and he presented himself *and* gave distinct evidence of himself to him [that he was Joseph], and [each] fell on the [other's] neck and wept on his neck a good while.

³⁰And Israel said to Joseph, Now let me die, since I have seen your face [and know] that you are still alive.

³¹Joseph said to his brothers and to his father's household, I will go up and tell Pharaoh and say to him, My brothers and my father's household, who were in the land of Canaan, have come to me.

³²And the men are shepherds, for their occupation has been keeping livestock, and they have brought their flocks and their herds and all that they have.

³³When Pharaoh calls you and says, What is your occupation?

³⁴You shall say, Your servants' occupation has been as keepers of livestock from our youth until now, both we and our fathers before us—in order that you may live in the land of Goshen, for every shepherd is an abomination to the Egyptians.

47 THEN JOSEPH came and told Pharaoh, My father and my brothers, with their flocks and their herds and all that they own, have come from the land of Canaan, and they are in the land of Goshen.

²And from among his brothers he took five men and presented them to Pharaoh.

³And Pharaoh said to his brothers, What is your occupation? And they said to Pharaoh, Your servants are shepherds, both we and our fathers before us.

⁴Moreover, they said to Pharaoh, We have come to sojourn in the land, for your servants have no pasture for our flocks, for the famine is very severe in Canaan. So now, we pray you, let your servants dwell in the land of Goshen.

⁵And Pharaoh spoke to Joseph, saying, Your father and your brothers have come to you.

⁶The land of Egypt is before you; make your father and your brothers dwell in the best of the land. Let them live in the land of Goshen. And if you know of any men of ability among them, put them in charge of my cattle.

⁷Then Joseph brought in Jacob his father and presented him before Pharaoh; and Jacob blessed Pharaoh.

⁸And Pharaoh asked Jacob, How old are you?

⁹Jacob said to Pharaoh, The days of the years of my pilgrimage are 130 years; few and evil

King James Version

thirty years: few and evil have the days of the years of my life been, and have not attained unto the days of the years of the life of my fathers in the days of their pilgrimage.

¹⁰And Jacob blessed Pharaoh, and went out from before Pharaoh.

¹¹And Joseph placed his father and his brethren, and gave them a possession in the land of Egypt, in the best of the land, in the land of Rameses, as Pharaoh had commanded.

¹²And Joseph nourished his father, and his brethren, and all his father's household, *with* bread, according to *their* families.

¹³ ¶ And *there was* no bread in all the land; for the famine *was* very sore, so that the land of Egypt and *all* the land of Canaan fainted by reason of the famine.

¹⁴And Joseph gathered up all the money that was found in the land of Egypt, and in the land of Canaan, for the corn which they bought: and Joseph brought the money into Pharaoh's house.

¹⁵And when money failed in the land of Egypt, and in the land of Canaan, all the Egyptians came unto Joseph, and said, Give us bread: for why should we die in thy presence? for the money faileth.

¹⁶And Joseph said, Give your cattle; and I will give you for your cattle, if money fail.

¹⁷And they brought their cattle unto Joseph: and Joseph gave them bread *in exchange* for horses, and for the flocks, and for the cattle of the herds, and for the asses: and he fed them with bread for all their cattle for that year.

¹⁸When that year was ended, they came unto him the second year, and said unto him, We will not hide *it* from my lord, how that our money is spent; my lord also had our herds of cattle; there is not ought left in the sight of my lord, but our bodies, and our lands:

¹⁹Wherefore shall we die before thine eyes, both we and our land? buy us and our land for bread, and we and our land will be servants unto Pharaoh: and give *us* seed, that we may live, and not die, that the land be not desolate.

²⁰And Joseph bought all the land of Egypt for Pharaoh; for the Egyptians sold every man his field, because the famine prevailed over them: so the land became Pharaoh's.

²¹And as for the people, he removed them to cities from *one* end of the borders of Egypt even to the *other* end thereof.

²²Only the land of the priests bought he not;

Amplified Bible

have the days of the years of my life been, and they have *a*not attained to those of the life of my fathers in their pilgrimage.

¹⁰And Jacob blessed Pharaoh and went out from his presence.

¹¹Joseph settled his father and brethren and gave them a possession in Egypt in the best of the land, in the land of Rameses (Goshen), as Pharaoh commanded.

¹²And Joseph supplied his father and his brethren and all his father's household with food, according to [the needs of] their families.

¹³[In the course of time] there was no food in all the land, for the famine was distressingly severe, so that the land of Egypt and all the land of Canaan hung in doubt and wavered by reason of the hunger (destitution, starvation) of the famine.

¹⁴And Joseph gathered up all the money that was found in the land of Egypt and in the land of Canaan [in payment] for the grain which they bought, and Joseph brought the money into Pharaoh's house.

¹⁵And when the money was exhausted in the land of Egypt and in the land of Canaan, all the Egyptians came to Joseph and said, Give us food! Why should we die before your very eyes? For we have no money left.

¹⁶Joseph said, Give up your livestock, and I will give you food in exchange for [them] if your money is gone.

¹⁷So they brought their livestock to Joseph, and [he] gave them food in exchange for the horses, flocks, cattle of the herds, and the donkeys; and he supplied them with food in exchange for all their livestock that year.

¹⁸When that year was ended, they came to [Joseph] the second year and said to him, We will not hide from my lord [the fact] that our money is spent; my lord also has our herds of livestock; there is nothing left in the sight of my lord but our bodies and our lands.

¹⁹Why should we perish before your eyes, both we and our land? Buy us and our land in exchange for food, and we and our land will be servants to Pharaoh. And give us seed [to plant], that we may live and not die, and that the land may not be desolate.

²⁰And Joseph bought all the land of Egypt for Pharaoh; for the Egyptians sold every man his field because of the overwhelming severity of the famine upon them. The land became Pharaoh's,

²¹And as for the people, he removed them to cities *and* practically made slaves of them [at their own request], from one end of the borders of Egypt to the other.

²²Only the priests' land he did not buy, for the

AMP notes: *a* Abraham, Jacob's grandfather, had lived to be 175 years old; Isaac, his father, lived to be 180. Jacob lived seventeen years after making this statement to Pharaoh, in which time he had an opportunity to get a much more optimistic view of God's treatment of him. He died at 147, having said, "The redeeming Angel . . . has redeemed me continually from every evil" (Gen. 48:16).

King James Version

for the priests had a portion assigned them of Pharaoh, and did eat their portion which Pharaoh gave them: wherefore they sold not their lands.

23Then Joseph said unto the people, Behold, I have bought you *this* day and your land for Pharaoh: lo, *here is* seed for you, and ye shall sow the land.

24And it shall come to pass in the increase, that you shall give the fifth *part* unto Pharaoh, and four parts shall be your own, for seed of the field, and for your food, and for them of your households, and for food for your little ones.

25And they said, Thou hast saved our lives: let us find grace in the sight of my lord, and we will be Pharaoh's servants.

26And Joseph made it a law over the land of Egypt unto this day, *that* Pharaoh should have the fifth *part;* except the land of the priests only, *which* became not Pharaoh's.

27 ¶ And Israel dwelt in the land of Egypt, in the country of Goshen; and they had possession therein, and grew, and multiplied exceedingly.

28And Jacob lived in the land of Egypt seventeen years: so the whole age of Jacob was an hundred forty and seven years.

29And the time drew nigh that Israel must die: and he called his son Joseph, and said unto him, If now I have found grace in thy sight, put, I pray thee, thy hand under my thigh, and deal kindly and truly with me; bury me not, I pray thee, in Egypt:

30But I will lie with my fathers, and thou shalt carry me out of Egypt, and bury me in their buryingplace. And he said, I will do as thou hast said.

31And he said, Swear unto me. And he sware unto him. And Israel bowed himself upon the bed's head.

48 And it came to pass after these things, that *one* told Joseph, Behold, thy father *is* sick: and he took with him his two sons, Manasseh and Ephraim.

2And *one* told Jacob, and said, Behold, thy son Joseph cometh unto thee: and Israel strengthened himself, and sat upon the bed.

3And Jacob said unto Joseph, God Almighty appeared unto me at Luz in the land of Canaan, and blessed me,

4And said unto me, Behold, I will make thee fruitful, and multiply thee, and I will make of thee a multitude of people; and will give this land to thy seed after thee *for* an everlasting possession.

Amplified Bible

priests had a fixed pension from Pharaoh and lived on the amount Pharaoh gave them. So they did not sell their land.

23Then Joseph said to the people, Behold, I have today bought you and your land for Pharaoh. Now here is seed for you, and you shall sow the land.

24At [harvest time when you reap] the increase, you shall give one-fifth of it to Pharaoh, and four-fifths shall be your own to use for seed for the field and as food for you and those of your households and for your little ones.

25And they said, You have saved our lives! Let us find favor in the sight of my lord; and we will be Pharaoh's servants.

26And Joseph made it a law over the land of Egypt—to this day—that Pharaoh should have the fifth part [of the crops]; it was the priests' land only which did not become Pharaoh's.

27And Israel dwelt in the land of Egypt, in the country of Goshen; and they gained possessions there and grew and multiplied exceedingly.

28And Jacob lived in the land of Egypt seventeen years; so Jacob reached the age of 147 years.

29When the time drew near that Israel must die, he called his son Joseph and said to him, If now I have found favor in your sight, *a*put your hand under my thigh and [promise to] deal loyally and faithfully with me. Do not bury me, I beg of you, in Egypt,

30But let me lie with my fathers; you shall carry me out of Egypt and bury me in their burying place. And [Joseph] said, I will do as you have directed.

31Then Jacob said, Swear to me [that you will do it]. And he swore to him. And Israel bowed himself upon the head of the bed.

48 SOME TIME after these things occurred, someone told Joseph, Behold, your father is sick. And he took with him his two sons, Manasseh and Ephraim [and went to Goshen].

2When Jacob was told, Your son Joseph has come to you, Israel collected his strength and sat up on the bed.

3And Jacob said to Joseph, God Almighty appeared to me at Luz [Bethel] in the land of Canaan and blessed me

4And said to me, Behold, I will make you fruitful and multiply you, and I will make you a multitude of people and will give this land to your descendants after you as an everlasting possession.

AMP notes: *a* This was a customary manner of taking a solemn oath. The gesture was a reference to the mark of circumcision, the sign of God's covenant, which is equivalent to our laying our hand upon the Bible. (Adam Clarke, *The Holy Bible with A Commentary*).

King James Version

⁵And now thy two sons, Ephraim and Manasseh, which were born unto thee in the land of Egypt before I came unto thee into Egypt, *are* mine; as Reuben and Simeon, they shall be mine.

⁶And thy issue, which thou begettest after them, shall be thine, *and* shall be called after the name of their brethren in their inheritance.

⁷And as for me, when I came from Padan, Rachel died by me in the land of Canaan in the way, when yet *there was* but a little way to come unto Ephrath: and I buried her there in the way of Ephrath; the same *is* Beth-lehem.

⁸And Israel beheld Joseph's sons, and said, Who *are* these?

⁹And Joseph said unto his father, They *are* my sons, whom God hath given me in this *place*. And he said, Bring them, I pray thee, unto me, and I will bless them.

¹⁰Now the eyes of Israel were dim for age, *so that* he could not see. And he brought them near unto him; and he kissed them, and embraced them.

¹¹And Israel said unto Joseph, I had not thought to see thy face: and lo, God hath shewed me also thy seed.

¹²And Joseph brought them out from between his knees, and he bowed himself with his face to the earth.

¹³And Joseph took them both, Ephraim in his right hand toward Israel's left hand, and Manasseh in his left hand towards Israel's right hand, and brought *them* near unto him.

¹⁴And Israel stretched out his right hand, and laid *it* upon Ephraim's head, who *was* the younger, and his left hand upon Manasseh's head, guiding his hands wittingly; for Manasseh *was* the firstborn.

¹⁵And he blessed Joseph, and said, God, before whom my fathers Abraham and Isaac did walk, the God which fed me all my life long unto this day,

¹⁶The Angel which redeemed me from all evil, bless the lads; and let my name be named on them, and the name of my fathers Abraham and Isaac; and let them grow into a multitude in the midst of the earth.

¹⁷And when Joseph saw that his father laid his right hand upon the head of Ephraim, it dis-

Amplified Bible

⁵And now your two sons, [Ephraim and Manasseh], who were born to you in the land of Egypt before I came to you in Egypt, are mine. [I am adopting them, and now] as Reuben and Simeon, [they] shall be mine.

⁶But other sons who may be born after them shall be your own; and they shall be called after the names of these [two] brothers *and* reckoned as belonging to them [when they come] into their inheritance.

⁷And as for me, when I came from Padan, Rachel died at my side in the land of Canaan on the way, when yet there was but a little way to come to Ephrath; and I buried her there on the way to Ephrath, that is, Bethlehem.

⁸When Israel [almost blind] saw Joseph's sons, he said, Who are these?

⁹And Joseph said to his father, They are my sons, whom God has given me in this place. And he said, Bring them to me, I pray you, that I may bless them.

¹⁰Now Israel's eyes were dim from age, so that he could not see. And Joseph brought them near to him, and he kissed and embraced them.

¹¹Israel said to Joseph, I had not thought that I would see your face, but see, God has shown me your offspring also.

¹²Then Joseph took [the boys] from [his father's embrace] and he bowed [before him] with his face to the earth.

¹³Then Joseph took both [boys], Ephraim with his right hand toward Israel's left, and Manasseh with his left hand toward Israel's right, and brought them close to him.

¹⁴And Israel reached out his right hand and laid it on the head of Ephraim, who was the younger, and his left hand on Manasseh's head, *ᵃ*crossing his hands intentionally, for Manasseh was the firstborn.

¹⁵Then [Jacob] blessed Joseph and said, God [Himself], before Whom my fathers Abraham and Isaac lived *and* walked habitually, God [Himself], Who has [been my Shepherd and has led and] fed me from the time I came into being until this day,

¹⁶The *ᵇ*redeeming Angel [that is, the Angel the Redeemer—not a created being but the Lord Himself] Who has redeemed me continually from every evil, bless the lads! And let my name be perpetuated in them [may they be worthy of having their names coupled with mine], and the names of my fathers Abraham and Isaac; and let them become a multitude in the midst of the earth.

¹⁷When Joseph saw that his father laid his right hand on Ephraim's head, it displeased him;

AMP notes: *ᵃ* God acts independently of the claims of priority based on time of birth when He chooses men. He too "crossed His hands" in the case of Seth whom He chose over Cain; of Shem over Japheth; of Isaac over Ishmael; of Jacob over Esau; of Judah and Joseph over Reuben; of Moses over Aaron; of David over all his brothers; and of Mary over Martha. *ᵇ* The "Angel of the Lord" is here identified as Christ Himself. See also the footnote on Gen. 16:7.

King James Version

pleased him: and he held up his father's hand, to remove it from Ephraim's head unto Manasseh's head.

18And Joseph said unto his father, Not so, my father: for this *is* the firstborn; put thy right hand upon his head.

19And his father refused, and said, I know *it,* my son, I know *it:* he also shall become a people, and he also shall be great: but truly his younger brother shall be greater than he, and his seed shall become a multitude of nations.

20And he blessed them that day, saying, In thee shall Israel bless, saying, God make thee as Ephraim and as Manasseh: and he set Ephraim before Manasseh.

21And Israel said unto Joseph, Behold, I die: but God shall be with you, and bring you again unto the land of your fathers.

22Moreover I have given to thee one portion above thy brethren, which I took out of the hand of the Amorite with my sword and with my bow.

49 And Jacob called unto his sons, and said, Gather yourselves together, that I may tell you *that* which shall befall you in the last days.

2Gather yourselves together, and hear, ye sons of Jacob; and hearken unto Israel your father.

3Reuben, thou *art* my firstborn, my might, and the beginning of my strength, the excellency of dignity, and the excellency of power:

4Unstable as water, thou shalt not excel; because thou wentest up to thy father's bed; then defiledst thou *it:* he went up to my couch.

5Simeon and Levi *are* brethren; instruments of cruelty *are in* their habitations.

6O my soul, come not thou into their secret; unto their assembly, mine honour, be not thou united: for in their anger they slew a man, and in their selfwill they digged down a wall.

Amplified Bible

and he held up his father's hand to move it to Manasseh's head.

18And Joseph said, Not so, my father, for this is the firstborn; put your right hand upon his head.

19But his father refused and said, I know, my son, I know. He also shall become a people and shall be great; but his younger brother shall be *a*greater than he, and his offspring shall become a multitude of nations.

20And he blessed them that day, saying, By you shall Israel bless [one another], saying, May God make you like Ephraim and like Manasseh. And he set Ephraim before Manasseh.

21And Israel said to Joseph, Behold, I [am about to] die, but God will be with you and bring you again to the land of your fathers.

22Moreover, I have given to you [Joseph] one portion [Shechem, one mountain slope] more than any of your brethren, which I took [reclaiming it] out of the hand of the Amorites with my sword and with my bow.

49 AND JACOB called for his sons and said, Gather yourselves together [around me], that I may tell you what shall befall you *b*in the latter *or* last days.

2Gather yourselves together and hear, you sons of Jacob; and hearken to Israel your father.

3Reuben, you are my *c*firstborn, my might, the beginning (the firstfruits) of my manly strength *and* vigor; [your birthright gave you] the preeminence in dignity and the preeminence in power.

4But unstable *and* boiling over like water, you shall *d*not excel *and* have the preeminence [of the firstborn], because you went to your father's bed; you defiled it—he went to my couch!

5Simeon and Levi are brothers [equally headstrong, deceitful, vindictive, and cruel]; their swords are weapons of violence.

6O my soul, come not into their secret council; unto their assembly let not my honor be united [for I knew nothing of their plot], because in their anger they slew men [an honored man, Shechem, and the Shechemites], and in their self-will they disabled oxen.

AMP notes: *a* This prophecy begins to be fulfilled "from the days of the judges onward, as the tribe of Ephraim in power and compass so increased that it became the head of the northern ten tribes, and its name became of like significance with that of Israel; although, in the time of Moses, Manasseh still outnumbered Ephraim by 20,000" (Karl F. Keil and F. Delitzsch, *Biblical Commentary on the Old Testament*). Joshua, whom Israel so long regarded as their ruler, was an Ephraimite. The ark of the covenant was placed in Shiloh in the territory of Ephraim, which increased the tribe's prestige. How could Jacob have prophesied Ephraim's supremacy so positively except by divine inspiration?   *b* See Deut. 33, where Moses blesses the same tribes in a similar prophetic way.   *c* Reuben was the eldest of Jacob's twelve sons and therefore entitled to the birthright, which would make him successor to his father as head of the family or tribe and inheritor of a double portion of his father's estate. But Reuben forfeited all this by his conduct with Bilhah, his father's concubine (Gen. 35:22). By adopting Joseph's two sons, Ephraim and Manasseh, and giving each of them a portion of the inheritance, Jacob virtually gave Joseph Reuben's extra portion of the land. And Judah became the tribal leader in Reuben's place (Gen. 49:8-10).   *d* The whole fertile territory once occupied by the tribe of Reuben has long since been deserted by its settled inhabitants and given up to the nomad tribes of the desert. Reuben did "not excel," and even before Jacob's death he had lost his "preeminence of the firstborn" (John D. Davis, *A Dictionary of the Bible*).

King James Version

⁷Cursed *be* their anger, for *it was* fierce; and their wrath, for it was cruel: I will divide them in Jacob, and scatter them in Israel.

⁸Judah, thou *art he* whom thy brethren shall praise: thy hand *shall be* in the neck of thine enemies; thy father's children shall bow down before thee.

⁹Judah *is* a lion's whelp: from the prey, my son, thou art gone up: he stooped down, he couched as a lion, and as an old lion; who shall rouse him up?

¹⁰The sceptre shall not depart from Judah, nor a lawgiver from between his feet, until Shiloh come; and unto him *shall* the gathering of the people *be.*

¹¹Binding his foal unto the vine, and his ass's colt unto the choice vine; he washed his garments in wine, and his clothes in the blood of grapes:

¹²*His* eyes *shall be* red with wine, and *his* teeth white with milk.

¹³Zebulun shall dwell at the haven of the sea; and he *shall be* for a haven of ships; and his border *shall be* unto Zidon.

¹⁴Issachar *is* a strong ass couching down between two burdens:

¹⁵And he saw that rest *was* good, and the land that *it was* pleasant; and bowed his shoulder to bear, and became a servant unto tribute.

¹⁶Dan shall judge his people, as one of the tribes of Israel.

¹⁷Dan shall be a serpent by the way, an adder in the path, that biteth the horse heels, so that his rider shall fall backward.

¹⁸I have waited for thy salvation, O LORD.

¹⁹Gad, a troop shall overcome him: but he shall overcome at the last.

²⁰Out of Asher his bread *shall be* fat, and he shall yield royal dainties.

²¹Naphtali *is* a hind let loose: he giveth goodly words.

²²Joseph *is* a fruitful bough, *even* a fruitful bough by a well; *whose* branches run over the wall.

²³The archers have sorely grieved him, and shot *at him,* and hated him:

²⁴But his bow abode in strength, and the arms of his hands were made strong by the hands of the mighty *God* of Jacob; (from thence *is* the shepherd, the stone of Israel:)

²⁵*Even* by the God of thy father, who shall

Amplified Bible

⁷Cursed be their anger, for it was fierce, and their wrath, for it was cruel. I will divide them in Jacob and ᵃscatter them in Israel.

⁸Judah, you are the one whom your brothers shall praise; your hand shall be on the neck of your enemies; your father's sons shall bow down to you.

⁹Judah, a lion's cub! With the prey, my son, you have gone high up [the mountain]. He stooped down, he crouched like a lion, and like a lioness—who dares provoke *and* rouse him?

¹⁰The scepter *or* leadership shall not depart from Judah, nor the ruler's staff from between his feet, until Shiloh [the Messiah, the Peaceful One] comes to Whom it belongs, and to Him shall be the obedience of the people.

¹¹Binding His foal to the vine and His donkey's colt to the choice vine, He washes His garments in wine and His clothes in the blood of grapes.

¹²His eyes are darker *and* more sparkling than wine, and His teeth whiter than milk.

¹³Zebulun shall live toward the seashore, and he shall be a haven *and* a landing place for ships; and his border shall be toward Sidon.

¹⁴Issachar is a strong-boned donkey crouching down between the sheepfolds.

¹⁵And he saw that rest was good and that the land was pleasant; and he bowed his shoulder to bear [his burdens] and became a servant to tribute [subjected to forced labor].

¹⁶Dan shall judge his people as one of the tribes of Israel.

¹⁷Dan shall be a serpent by the way, a horned snake in the path, that bites at the horse's heels, so that his rider falls backward.

¹⁸I wait for Your salvation, O Lord.

¹⁹Gad—a raiding troop shall raid him, but he shall raid at their heels *and* assault them [victoriously].

²⁰Asher's food [supply] shall be rich *and* fat, and he shall yield *and* deliver royal delights.

²¹Naphtali is a hind let loose which yields lovely fawns.

²²Joseph is a fruitful bough, a fruitful bough by a well (spring or fountain), whose branches run over the wall.

²³Skilled archers have bitterly attacked *and* sorely worried him; they have shot at him and persecuted him.

²⁴But his bow remained strong *and* steady *and* rested in the Strength that does not fail him, for the arms of his hands were made strong *and* active by the hands of the Mighty God of Jacob, by the name of the Shepherd, the Rock of Israel,

²⁵By the God of your father, Who will help

AMP notes: ᵃ This was literally fulfilled. Levi got no inheritance except 48 towns scattered throughout different parts of Canaan. As to Simeon, they were originally given only a few towns and villages in Judah's lot (Josh. 19:1). Afterward, needing more room, they formed colonies in districts which they conquered from the Idumeans and the Amalekites [I Chron. 4:39, 40]. (Adam Clarke, *The Holy Bible with A Commentary*).

King James Version

help thee; and *by* the Almighty, who shall bless thee *with* blessings of heaven above, blessings of the deep that lieth under, blessings of the breasts, and of the womb:

²⁶The blessings of thy father have prevailed above the blessings of my progenitors unto the utmost bound of the everlasting hills: they shall be on the head of Joseph, and on the crown of the head of him *that was* separate from his brethren.

²⁷Benjamin shall ravin *as* a wolf: in the morning he shall devour the prey, and at night he shall divide the spoil.

²⁸ ¶ All these *are* the twelve tribes of Israel: and this *is it* that their father spake unto them, and blessed them; every one according to his blessing he blessed them.

²⁹And he charged them, and said unto them, I *am to be* gathered unto my people: bury me with my fathers in the cave that *is* in the field of Ephron the Hittite,

³⁰In the cave that *is* in the field of Machpelah, which *is* before Mamre, in the land of Canaan, which Abraham bought with the field of Ephron the Hittite for a possession of a buryingplace.

³¹There they buried Abraham and Sarah his wife; there they buried Isaac and Rebekah his wife; and there I buried Leah.

³²The purchase of the field and of the cave that *is* therein *was* from the children of Heth.

³³And when Jacob had made an end of commanding his sons, he gathered up his feet into the bed, and yielded up the ghost, and was gathered unto his people.

50 And Joseph fell upon his father's face, and wept upon him, and kissed him.

²And Joseph commanded his servants the physicians to embalm his father: and the physicians embalmed Israel.

³And forty days were fulfilled for him; for so are fulfilled the days of those which are embalmed: and the Egyptians mourned for him threescore and ten days.

⁴And when the days of his mourning were past, Joseph spake unto the house of Pharaoh, saying, If now I have found grace in your eyes, speak, I pray you, in the ears of Pharaoh, saying,

⁵My father made me swear, saying, Lo, I die: in my grave which I have digged for me in the

Amplified Bible

you, and by the Almighty, Who will bless you with blessings of the heavens above, blessings lying in the deep beneath, blessings of the breasts and of the womb.

²⁶The blessings of your father [on you] are greater than the blessings of my forefathers [Abraham and Isaac on me] *and* are as lasting as the bounties of the eternal hills; they shall be on the head of Joseph, and on the crown of the head of him who was the consecrated one *and* the one separated from his brethren *and* [the one who] is prince among them.

²⁷Benjamin is a ᵃravenous wolf, in the morning devouring the prey and at night dividing the spoil.

²⁸All these are the twelve tribes of Israel, and this is what their father said to them as he blessed them, blessing each one according to the blessing suited to him.

²⁹He charged them and said to them, I am to be gathered to my [departed] people; bury me with my fathers in the cave that is in the field of Ephron the Hittite,

³⁰In the cave in the field at Machpelah, east of Mamre in the land of Canaan, that Abraham bought, along with the field of Ephron the Hittite, to possess as a cemetery.

³¹There they buried Abraham and Sarah his wife, there they buried Isaac and Rebekah his wife, and there I buried Leah.

³²The purchase of the field and the cave that is in it was from the sons of Heth.

³³When Jacob had finished commanding his sons, he drew his feet up into the bed and breathed his last and was gathered to his [departed] people.

50 THEN JOSEPH fell upon his father's face and wept over him and kissed him.

²And Joseph ordered his servants the physicians to embalm his father. So the physicians embalmed Israel.

³Then forty days were devoted [to this purpose] for him, for that is the customary number of days required for those who are embalmed. And the Egyptians wept and bemoaned him [as they would for royalty] for seventy days.

⁴And when the days of his weeping *and* deep grief were past, Joseph said to [the nobles of] the house of Pharaoh, If now I have found grace in your eyes, speak, I pray you, to Pharaoh [for Joseph was dressed in mourning and could not do so himself], saying,

⁵My father made me swear, saying, I am about to die; in my tomb which I hewed out for

---

AMP notes: ᵃ The tribe of Benjamin is fitly compared to a ravenous wolf because of the rude courage and ferocity which they invariably displayed, particularly in their war with the other tribes, in which they killed more men than all of their own numbers combined (Adam Clarke, *The Holy Bible with A Commentary*). The tribe was absorbed by the tribe of Judah and is not mentioned after the return from the Babylonian captivity, except in connection with its former land or as the source of some individual person. Ehud, Saul, Jonathan, and the apostle Paul were Benjamites.

King James Version

land of Canaan, there shalt thou bury me. Now therefore let me go up, I pray thee, and bury my father, and I will come again.

⁶And Pharaoh said, Go up, and bury thy father, according as he made thee swear.

⁷And Joseph went up to bury his father: and with him went up all the servants of Pharaoh, the elders of his house, and all the elders of the land of Egypt,

⁸And all the house of Joseph, and his brethren, and his father's house: only their little ones, and their flocks, and their herds, they left in the land of Goshen.

⁹And there went up with him both chariots and horsemen: and it was a very great company.

¹⁰And they came to the threshingfloor of Atad, which *is* beyond Jordan, and there they mourned with a great and very sore lamentation: and he made a mourning for his father seven days.

¹¹And when the inhabitants of the land, the Canaanites, saw the mourning in the floor of Atad, they said, This *is* a grievous mourning to the Egyptians: wherefore the name of it was called Abel-mizraim, which *is* beyond Jordan.

¹²And his sons did unto him according as he commanded them:

¹³For his sons carried him into the land of Canaan, and buried him in the cave of the field of Machpelah, which Abraham bought with the field for a possession of a buryingplace of Ephron the Hittite, before Mamre.

¹⁴And Joseph returned into Egypt, he, and his brethren, and all that went up with him to bury his father, after he had buried his father.

¹⁵ ¶ And when Joseph's brethren saw that their father was dead, they said, Joseph will peradventure hate us, and will certainly requite us all the evil which we did unto him.

¹⁶And they sent a messenger unto Joseph, saying, Thy father did command before he died, saying,

¹⁷So shall ye say unto Joseph, Forgive, I pray thee now, the trespass of thy brethren, and their sin; for they did unto thee evil: and now, we pray thee, forgive the trespass of the servants of the God of thy father. And Joseph wept when they spake unto him.

¹⁸And his brethren also went and fell down before his face; and they said, Behold, we *be* thy servants.

¹⁹And Joseph said unto them, Fear not: for *am* I in the place of God?

²⁰But as for you, ye thought evil against me; *but* God meant it unto good, to bring to pass, as *it is* this day, to save much people alive.

Amplified Bible

myself in the land of Canaan, there you shall bury me. So now let me go up, I pray you, and bury my father, and I will come again.

⁶And Pharaoh said, Go up and bury your father, as he made you swear.

⁷And Joseph went up [to Canaan] to bury his father; and with him went all the officials of Pharaoh—the nobles of his court, *and* the elders of his house and all the nobles *and* elders of the land of Egypt—

⁸And all the household of Joseph and his brethren and his father's household. Only their little ones and their flocks and herds they left in the land of Goshen.

⁹And there went with [Joseph] both chariots and horsemen; and it was a very great company.

¹⁰And they came to the threshing floor of Atad, which is beyond [west of] the Jordan, and there they mourned with a great lamentation and extreme demonstrations of sorrow [according to Egyptian custom]; and [Joseph] made a mourning for his father seven days.

¹¹When the inhabitants of the land, the Canaanites, saw the mourning at the floor of Atad, they said, This is a grievous mourning for the Egyptians. Therefore the place was called Abel-mizraim [mourning of Egypt]; it is west of the Jordan.

¹²Thus [Jacob's] sons did for him as he had commanded them.

¹³For his sons carried him to the land of Canaan and buried him in the cave of the field of Machpelah, east of Mamre, which Abraham bought, along with the field, for a possession as a burying place from Ephron the Hittite.

¹⁴After he had buried his father, Joseph returned to Egypt, he and his brethren and all who had gone up with him.

¹⁵When Joseph's brethren saw that their father was dead, they said, Perhaps now Joseph will hate us and will pay us back for all the evil we did to him.

¹⁶And they sent a messenger to Joseph, saying, Your father commanded before he died, saying,

¹⁷So shall you say to Joseph: Forgive (take up and away all resentment and all claim to requital concerning), I pray you now, the trespass of your brothers and their sin, for they did evil to you. Now, we pray you, forgive the trespass of the servants of your father's God. And Joseph wept when they spoke thus to him.

¹⁸Then his brothers went and fell down before him, saying, See, we are your servants (your slaves)!

¹⁹And Joseph said to them, Fear not; for am I in the place of God? [Vengeance is His, not mine.]

²⁰As for you, you thought evil against me, but God meant it for good, to bring about that many people should be kept alive, as they are this day.

King James Version

21Now therefore fear ye not: I will nourish you and your little ones. And he comforted them, and spake kindly unto them.

22 ¶ And Joseph dwelt in Egypt, he, and his father's house: and Joseph lived an hundred and ten years.

23And Joseph saw Ephraim's children of the third *generation:* the children also of Machir the son of Manasseh were brought up upon Joseph's knees.

24And Joseph said unto his brethren, I die: and God will surely visit you, and bring you out of this land unto the land which he sware to Abraham, to Isaac, and to Jacob.

25And Joseph took an oath of the children of Israel, saying, God will surely visit you, and ye shall carry up my bones from hence.

26So Joseph died, *being* an hundred and ten years old: and they embalmed him, and he was put in a coffin in Egypt.

Amplified Bible

21Now therefore, do not be afraid. I will provide for *and* support you and your little ones. And he comforted them [imparting cheer, hope, strength] and spoke to their hearts [kindly].

22Joseph dwelt in Egypt, he and his father's household. And Joseph lived 110 years.

23And Joseph saw Ephraim's children of the third generation; the children also of Machir son of Manasseh were brought up on Joseph's knees.

24And Joseph said to his brethren, I am going to die. But God will surely visit you and bring you out of this land to the land He swore to Abraham, to Isaac, and to Jacob [to give you].

25And Joseph took an oath from the sons of Israel, saying, God will surely visit you, and you will carry up my bones from here.

26So Joseph died, being 110 years old; and they embalmed him, and he was put *a*in a coffin in Egypt.

AMP notes: *a* Joseph's body remained in Egypt until the exodus to the promised land of Canaan about 200 years later. Its final resting-place was Shechem, near Samaria, "in the parcel of ground which Jacob bought from the sons of Hamor, the father of Shechem" (Josh. 24:32). Here each of his brothers was also buried (Acts 7:15, 16).

King James Version

THE SECOND BOOK OF MOSES, CALLED

Exodus

1 Now these *are* the names of the children of Israel, which came into Egypt; every man and his household came with Jacob.
² Reuben, Simeon, Levi, and Judah,
³ Issachar, Zebulun, and Benjamin,
⁴ Dan, and Naphtali, Gad, and Asher.
⁵ And all the souls that came *out of* the loins of Jacob were seventy souls: for Joseph was in Egypt *already.*
⁶ And Joseph died, and all his brethren, and all that generation.
⁷ ¶ And the children of Israel were fruitful, and increased abundantly, and multiplied, and waxed exceeding mighty; and the land was filled with them.
⁸ Now there arose up a new king over Egypt, which knew not Joseph.
⁹ And he said unto his people, Behold, the people of the children of Israel *are* more and mightier than we:
¹⁰ Come on, let us deal wisely with them; lest they multiply, and it come to pass, that, when there falleth out any war, they join also unto our enemies, and fight against us, and *so* get them up out of the land.
¹¹ Therefore they did set over them taskmasters to afflict them with their burdens. And they built for Pharaoh treasure cities, Pithom and Raamses.
¹² But the more they afflicted them, the more they multiplied and grew. And they were grieved because of the children of Israel.
¹³ And the Egyptians made the children of Israel to serve with rigour:
¹⁴ And they made their lives bitter with hard bondage, in morter, and in brick, and in all manner of service in the field: all their service, wherein they made them serve, *was* with rigour.
¹⁵ ¶ And the king of Egypt spake to the Hebrew midwives, of which the name of the one *was* Shiphrah, and the name of the other Puah:
¹⁶ And he said, When ye do the office of a midwife to the Hebrew women, and see *them* upon the stools; if it *be* a son, then ye shall kill him: but if it *be* a daughter, then she shall live.

Amplified Bible

THE SECOND BOOK OF MOSES, COMMONLY CALLED

Exodus

1 THESE ARE the names of the sons of Israel who came into Egypt with Jacob, each with his household:
² Reuben, Simeon, Levi, and Judah,
³ Issachar, Zebulun, and Benjamin,
⁴ Dan and Naphtali, Gad and Asher.
⁵ All the offspring of Jacob were seventy persons; Joseph was already in Egypt.
⁶ Then Joseph died, and all his brothers and all that generation.
⁷ But the descendants of Israel were fruitful and increased abundantly; they multiplied and grew exceedingly strong, and the land was full of them.
⁸ Now a new king arose over Egypt who did not know Joseph.
⁹ He said to his people, Behold, the Israelites are too many and too mighty for us [and they ᵃoutnumber us both in people and in strength].
¹⁰ Come, let us deal shrewdly with them, lest they multiply more and, should war befall us, they join our enemies, fight against us, and escape out of the land.
¹¹ So they set over [the Israelites] taskmasters to afflict *and* oppress them with [increased] burdens. And [the Israelites] built Pithom and Rameses as store cities for Pharaoh.
¹² But the more [the Egyptians] oppressed them, the more they multiplied and expanded, so that [the Egyptians] were vexed *and* alarmed because of the Israelites.
¹³ And the Egyptians reduced the Israelites to severe slavery.
¹⁴ They made their lives bitter with hard service in mortar, brick, and all kinds of work in the field. All their service was with harshness *and* severity.
¹⁵ Then the king of Egypt said to the Hebrew midwives, of whom one was named Shiprah and the other Puah,
¹⁶ When you act as midwives to the Hebrew women and see them on the birthstool, if it is a son, you shall kill him; but if it is a daughter, she shall live.

AMP notes: ᵃ Is there in all human history a more amazing spectacle than the exodus? A family of 70 immigrants grows into a people of slavery. Suddenly, according to God's detailed and preannounced plan, they are seen flinging away the shackles of generations of slavery and emigrating to a new country and a new life, with miraculous deliverances rescuing them from destruction again and again. The marvel of the exodus grows in wonder when, after more than 3,000 years, we see that same race, often persecuted almost to extinction, carrying out in startling detail God's predictions for their amazing national revitalization and prominence "in the last days" (adapted from many historians).

King James Version

[17]But the midwives feared God, and did not as the king of Egypt commanded them, but saved the men children alive.

[18]And the king of Egypt called for the midwives, and said unto them, Why have ye done this thing, and have saved the men children alive?

[19]And the midwives said unto Pharaoh, Because the Hebrew women *are* not as the Egyptian women; for they *are* lively, and are delivered ere the midwives come in unto them.

[20]Therefore God dealt well with the midwives: and the people multiplied, and waxed very mighty.

[21]And it came to pass, because the midwives feared God, that he made them houses.

[22]And Pharaoh charged all his people, saying, Every son that is born ye shall cast into the river, and every daughter ye shall save alive.

2 And there went a man of the house of Levi, and took *to wife* a daughter of Levi.

[2]And the woman conceived, and bare a son: and when she saw him that he *was a* goodly *child,* she hid him three months.

[3]And when she could not longer hide him, she took for him an ark of bulrushes, and daubed it with slime and with pitch, and put the child therein; and she laid *it* in the flags by the river's brink.

[4]And his sister stood afar off, to wit what would be done to him.

[5]And the daughter of Pharaoh came down to wash *herself* at the river; and her maidens walked along by the river's side; and when she saw the ark among the flags, she sent her maid to fetch it.

[6]And when she had opened *it,* she saw the child: and behold, the babe wept. And she had compassion on him, and said, This *is one* of the Hebrews' children.

[7]Then said his sister to Pharaoh's daughter, Shall I go and call to thee a nurse of the Hebrew women, that she may nurse the child for thee?

[8]And Pharaoh's daughter said to her, Go. And the maid went and called the child's mother.

[9]And Pharaoh's daughter said unto her, Take this child away, and nurse it for me, and I will give *thee* thy wages. And the woman took the child, and nursed it.

[10]And the child grew, and she brought him unto Pharaoh's daughter, and he became her son. And she called his name Moses: and she said, Because I drew him out of the water.

Amplified Bible

[17]But the midwives feared God and did not do as the king of Egypt commanded, but let the male babies live.

[18]So the king of Egypt called for the midwives and said to them, Why have you done this thing and allowed the male children to live?

[19]The midwives answered Pharaoh, Because the Hebrew women are not like the Egyptian women; they are vigorous and quickly delivered; their babies are born before the midwife comes to them.

[20]So God dealt well with the midwives and the people multiplied and became very strong.

[21]And because the midwives revered *and* feared God, He made them households [of their own].

[22]Then Pharaoh charged all his people, saying, Every son born [to the Hebrews] you shall cast into the river [Nile], but every daughter you shall allow to live.

2 NOW [Amram] a man of the house of Levi [the priestly tribe] went and took as his wife [Jochebed] a daughter of Levi.

[2]And the woman became pregnant and bore a son; and when she saw that he was [exceedingly] beautiful, she hid him three months.

[3]And when she could no longer hide him, she took for him an ark *or* basket made of bulrushes *or* papyrus [making it watertight by] daubing it with bitumen and pitch. Then she put the child in it and laid it among the rushes by the brink of the river [Nile].

[4]And his sister [Miriam] stood some distance away to [a]learn what would be done to him.

[5]Now the daughter of Pharaoh came down to bathe at the river, and her maidens walked along the bank; she saw the ark among the rushes and sent her maid to fetch it.

[6]When she opened it, she saw the child; and behold, the baby cried. And she took pity on him and said, This is one of the Hebrews' children!

[7]Then his sister said to Pharaoh's daughter, Shall I go and call a nurse of the Hebrew women to nurse the child for you?

[8]Pharaoh's daughter said to her, Go. And the girl went and called the child's mother.

[9]Then Pharaoh's daughter said to her, Take this child away and nurse it for me, and I will give you your wages. So the woman took the child and nursed it.

[10]And the child grew, and she brought him to Pharaoh's daughter and he became her son. And she called him Moses, for she said, Because I drew him out of the water.

AMP notes: [a] They launched the ark not only on the Nile but on God's providence. He would be Captain, Steersman, and Convoy of the tiny ark. Miriam stood to watch. There was no fear of fatal consequences, only the quiet expectancy that God would do something worthy of Himself. They reckoned on God's faithfulness and they were amply rewarded when the daughter of their greatest foe became the babe's patroness (F. B. Meyer, *Through the Bible Day by Day*).

King James Version

11 ¶ And it came to pass in those days, when Moses was grown, that he went out unto his brethren, and looked on their burdens: and he spied an Egyptian smiting a Hebrew, *one* of his brethren.

12 And he looked this way and that way, and when he saw that *there was* no man, he slew the Egyptian, and hid him in the sand.

13 And when he went out the second day, behold, two men of the Hebrews strove together: and he said to him that did the wrong, Wherefore smitest thou thy fellow?

14 And he said, Who made thee a prince and a judge over us? intendest thou to kill me, as thou killedst the Egyptian? And Moses feared, and said, Surely *this* thing is known.

15 Now when Pharaoh heard this thing, he sought to slay Moses. But Moses fled from the face of Pharaoh, and dwelt in the land of Midian: and he sat down by a well.

16 Now the priest of Midian had seven daughters: and they came and drew water, and filled the troughs to water their father's flock.

17 And the shepherds came and drove them away: but Moses stood up and helped them, and watered their flock.

18 And when they came to Reuel their father, he said, How *is it that* you are come so soon to day?

19 And they said, An Egyptian delivered us out of the hand of the shepherds, and also drew water enough for us, and watered the flock.

20 And he said unto his daughters, And where *is* he? why *is it that* ye have left the man? call him, that he may eat bread.

21 And Moses was content to dwell with the man: and he gave Moses Zipporah his daughter.

22 And she bare *him* a son, and he called his name Gershom: for he said, I have been a stranger in a strange land.

23 ¶ And it came to pass in process of time, that the king of Egypt died: and the children of Israel sighed by reason of the bondage, and they cried, and their cry came up unto God by reason of the bondage.

24 And God heard their groaning, and God remembered his covenant with Abraham, with Isaac, and with Jacob.

25 And God looked upon the children of Israel, and God had respect unto *them.*

3 Now Moses kept the flock of Jethro his father in law, the priest of Midian: and he led

Amplified Bible

11 One day, after Moses was grown, it happened that he went out to his brethren and looked at their burdens; and he saw an Egyptian beating a Hebrew, one of [Moses'] brethren.

12 He looked this way and that way, and when he saw no one, he killed the Egyptian and hid him in the sand.

13 He went out the second day and saw two Hebrew men quarreling *and* fighting; and he said to the unjust aggressor, Why are you striking your comrade?

14 And the man said, Who made you a prince and a judge over us? Do you intend to kill me as you killed the Egyptian? Then Moses was afraid and thought, Surely this thing is known.

15 When Pharaoh heard of it, he sought to slay Moses. But Moses fled from Pharaoh's presence and *a* took refuge in the land of Midian, where he sat down by a well.

16 Now the priest of Midian had seven daughters, and they came and drew water and filled the troughs to water their father's flock.

17 The shepherds came and drove them away; but Moses stood up and helped them and watered their flock.

18 And when they came to Reuel [Jethro] their father, he said, How is it that you have come so soon today?

19 They said, An Egyptian delivered us from the shepherds; also he drew water for us and watered the flock.

20 He said to his daughters, Where is he? Why have you left the man? Call him, that he may eat bread.

21 And Moses was content to dwell with the man; and he gave Moses Zipporah his daughter.

22 And she bore a son, and he called his name Gershom [expulsion, or a stranger there]; for he said, I have been a stranger *and* a sojourner in a foreign land.

23 However, after a long time [nearly forty years] the king of Egypt died; and the Israelites were sighing *and* groaning because of the bondage. They kept crying, and their cry because of slavery ascended to God.

24 And God heard their sighing *and* groaning and [earnestly] remembered His covenant with Abraham, with Isaac, and with Jacob.

25 God saw the Israelites and took knowledge of them *and* concerned Himself about them [knowing all, understanding, remembering all].

3 NOW MOSES kept the flock of Jethro his father-in-law, the priest of Midian; and he

---

AMP notes: *a* "There was true heroism in the act, when Moses stepped down from Pharaoh's throne to share the lot of his brethren. But it would take many a long year of lonely waiting and trial before this strong and radiant nature could be broken down, shaped into a vessel meet for the Master's use, and prepared for every good work. . . . One blow struck when God's time is fulfilled is worth a thousand struck in premature eagerness" (F. B. Meyer, *Moses, the Servant of God*).

King James Version

the flock to the backside of the desert, and came to the mountain of God, *even* to Horeb.

²And the angel of the LORD appeared unto him in a flame of fire out of the midst of a bush: and he looked, and behold, the bush burned with fire, and the bush was not consumed.

³And Moses said, I will now turn aside, and see this great sight, why the bush is not burnt.

⁴And when the LORD saw that he turned aside to see, God called unto him out of the midst of the bush, and said, Moses, Moses. And he said, Here *am* I.

⁵And he said, Draw not nigh hither: put off thy shoes from off thy feet, for the place whereon thou standest *is* holy ground.

⁶Moreover he said, I *am* the God of thy father, the God of Abraham, the God of Isaac, and the God of Jacob. And Moses hid his face; for he was afraid to look upon God.

⁷And the LORD said, I have surely seen the affliction of my people which *are* in Egypt, and have heard their cry by reason of their taskmasters; for I know their sorrows;

⁸And I am come down to deliver them out of the hand of the Egyptians, and to bring them up out of that land unto a good land and a large, unto a land flowing with milk and honey; unto the place of the Canaanites, and the Hittites, and the Amorites, and the Perizzites, and the Hivites, and the Jebusites.

⁹Now therefore, behold, the cry of the children of Israel is come unto me: and I have also seen the oppression wherewith the Egyptians oppress them.

¹⁰Come now therefore, and I will send thee unto Pharaoh, that thou mayest bring forth my people the children of Israel out of Egypt.

¹¹And Moses said unto God, Who *am* I, that I should go unto Pharaoh, and that I should bring forth the children of Israel out of Egypt?

¹²And he said, Certainly I will be with thee; and this *shall be* a token unto thee, that I have sent thee: When thou hast brought forth the people of Egypt, ye shall serve God upon this mountain.

¹³And Moses said unto God, Behold, *when* I come unto the children of Israel, and shall say unto them, The God of your fathers hath sent me unto you; and they shall say to me, What *is* his name? what shall I say unto them?

¹⁴And God said unto Moses, I AM THAT I AM: and he said, Thus shalt thou say unto the children of Israel, I AM hath sent me unto you.

Amplified Bible

led the flock to the back *or* west side of the wilderness and came to Horeb *or* Sinai, the mountain of God.

²The *ᵃ*Angel of the Lord appeared to him in a flame of fire out of the midst of a bush; and he looked, and behold, the bush burned with fire, yet was not consumed.

³And Moses said, I will now turn aside and see this great sight, why the bush is not burned.

⁴And when the Lord saw that he turned aside to see, God called to him out of the midst of the bush and said, Moses, Moses! And he said, Here am I.

⁵God said, Do not come near; put your shoes off your feet, for the place on which you stand is holy ground.

⁶Also He said, I am the God of your father, the God of Abraham, the God of Isaac, and the God of Jacob. And Moses hid his face, for he was afraid to look at God.

⁷And the Lord said, I have surely seen the affliction of My people who are in Egypt, and have heard their cry because of their taskmasters *and* oppressors; for I know their sorrows *and* sufferings *and* trials.

⁸And I have come down to deliver them out of the hand *and* power of the Egyptians and to bring them up out of that land to a land good and large, a land flowing with milk and honey [a land of plenty]—to the place of the Canaanite, the Hittite, the Amorite, the Perizzite, the Hivite, and the Jebusite.

⁹Now behold, the cry of the Israelites has come to Me, and I have also seen how the Egyptians oppress them.

¹⁰Come now therefore, and I will send you to Pharaoh, that you may bring forth My people, the Israelites, out of Egypt.

¹¹And Moses said to God, *ᵇ*Who am I, that I should go to Pharaoh and bring the Israelites out of Egypt?

¹²God said, I will surely be with you; and this shall be the sign to you that I have sent you: when you have brought the people out of Egypt, you shall serve God on this mountain [Horeb, or Sinai].

¹³And Moses said to God, Behold, when I come to the Israelites and say to them, The God of your fathers has sent me to you, and they say to me, What is His name? What shall I say to them?

¹⁴And God said to Moses, I AM WHO I AM and WHAT I AM, *and* I WILL BE WHAT I WILL BE; and He said, You shall say this to the Israelites: I AM has sent me to you!

AMP notes: ᵃ In this report of Moses and the burning bush, "the Angel of the Lord" is identified as the Lord Himself. See especially Exod. 3:4, 6. See also the footnote on Gen. 16:7. *ᵇ* "There was something more than humility here; there was a tone of self-depreciation which was inconsistent with a true faith in God's selection and appointment. Surely it is God's business to choose His special instruments; and when we are persuaded that we are in the line of His purpose, we have no right to question the wisdom of His appointment. To do so is to depreciate His wisdom or to doubt His power and willingness to become **all that is necessary** to complete our need" (F. B. Meyer, *Moses, the Servant of God*).

King James Version

¹⁵And God said moreover unto Moses, Thus shalt thou say unto the children of Israel, The LORD God of your fathers, the God of Abraham, the God of Isaac, and the God of Jacob, hath sent me unto you: this *is* my name for ever, and this *is* my memorial unto all generations.

¹⁶Go, and gather the elders of Israel together, and say unto them, The LORD God of your fathers, the God of Abraham, of Isaac, and of Jacob, appeared unto me, saying, I have surely visited you, and *seen* that which is done to you in Egypt:

¹⁷And I have said, I will bring you out of the affliction of Egypt unto the land of the Canaanites, and the Hittites, and the Amorites, and the Perizzites, and the Hivites, and the Jebusites, unto a land flowing with milk and honey.

¹⁸And they shall hearken to thy voice: and thou shalt come, thou and the elders of Israel, unto the king of Egypt, and you shall say unto him, The LORD God of the Hebrews hath met with us: and now let us go, we beseech thee, three days' journey into the wilderness, that we may sacrifice to the LORD our God.

¹⁹And I am sure that the king of Egypt will not let you go, no, not by a mighty hand.

²⁰And I will stretch out my hand, and smite Egypt with all my wonders which I will do in the midst thereof: and after that he will let you go.

²¹And I will give this people favour in the sight of the Egyptians: and it shall come to pass, that, when ye go, ye shall not go empty:

²²But every woman shall borrow of her neighbour, and of her that sojourneth in her house, jewels of silver, and jewels of gold, and raiment: and ye shall put *them* upon your sons, and upon your daughters; and ye shall spoil the Egyptians.

4 And Moses answered and said, But behold, they will not believe me, nor hearken unto my voice: for they will say, The LORD hath not appeared unto thee.

²And the LORD said unto him, What *is* that in thine hand? And he said, A rod.

³And he said, Cast it on the ground. And he cast it on the ground, and it became a serpent; and Moses fled from before it.

⁴And the LORD said unto Moses, Put forth thine hand, and take it by the tail. And he put

Amplified Bible

¹⁵God said also to Moses, This shall you say to the Israelites: The Lord, the God of your fathers, of Abraham, of Isaac, and of Jacob, has sent me to you! This is My ᵃname forever, and by this name I am to be remembered to all generations.

¹⁶Go, gather the elders of Israel together [the mature teachers and tribal leaders], and say to them, The Lord God of your fathers, the God of Abraham, of Isaac, and of Jacob, appeared to me, saying, I have surely visited you and seen that which is done to you in Egypt;

¹⁷And I have declared that I will bring you up out of the affliction of Egypt to the land of the Canaanite, the Hittite, the Amorite, the Perizzite, the Hivite, and the Jebusite, to a land flowing with milk and honey.

¹⁸And [the elders] shall believe *and* obey your voice; and you shall go, you and the elders of Israel, to the king of Egypt and you shall say to him, The Lord, the God of the Hebrews, has met with us; and now let us go, we beseech you, three days' journey into the wilderness, that we may sacrifice to the Lord our God.

¹⁹And I know that the king of Egypt will not let you go [unless forced to do so], no, not by a mighty hand.

²⁰So I will stretch out My hand and smite Egypt with all My wonders which I will do in it; and after that he will let you go.

²¹And I will give this people favor *and* respect in the sight of the Egyptians; and it shall be that when you go, you shall not go empty-handed.

²²But every woman shall [insistently] solicit of her neighbor and of her that may be residing at her house jewels and articles of silver and gold, and garments, which you shall put on your sons and daughters; and you shall strip the Egyptians [of belongings due to you].

4 AND MOSES answered, ᵇBut behold, they will not believe me or listen to *and* obey my voice; for they will say, The Lord has not appeared to you.

²And the Lord said to him, What is that in your hand? And he said, A rod.

³And He said, Cast it on the ground. And he did so and it became a serpent [the symbol of royal and divine power worn on the crown of the Pharaohs]; and Moses fled from before it.

⁴And the Lord said to Moses, Put forth your hand and take it by the tail. And he stretched

---

AMP notes: ᵃ To know the **name** of God is to witness the manifestation of those attributes and apprehend that character which the name denotes (Exod. 6:3; I Kings 8:33ff.; Ps. 91:14; Isa. 52:6; 64:2; Jer. 16:21) (John D. Davis, *A Dictionary of the Bible*). God's name is His self-revelation (Charles Ellicott, *A Bible Commentary*). The name signifies the active presence of the person in the fullness of the revealed character (J. D. Douglas et al., eds., *The New Bible Dictionary*). ᵇ There need be no "buts" in our relationship to God's will. Nothing will take the Lord by surprise. The entire field has been surveyed and the preparations are complete. When the Lord says, "I will send thee," every provision has been made for the appointed task. "I will not fail thee." He who gives the command will also give the equipment (John Henry Jowett, *My Daily Meditation*).

King James Version

forth his hand, and caught it, and it became a rod in his hand:

⁵That they may believe that the LORD God of their fathers, the God of Abraham, the God of Isaac, and the God of Jacob, hath appeared unto thee.

⁶And the LORD said furthermore unto him, Put now thine hand into thy bosom. And he put his hand into his bosom: and when he took it out, behold, his hand *was* leprous as snow.

⁷And he said, Put thine hand into thy bosom again. And he put his hand into his bosom again; and plucked it out of his bosom, and behold, it was turned again as his *other* flesh.

⁸And it shall come to pass, if they will not believe thee, neither hearken to the voice of the first sign, that they will believe the voice of the latter sign.

⁹And it shall come to pass, if they will not believe also these two signs, neither hearken unto thy voice, that thou shalt take of the water of the river, and pour *it upon* the dry *land:* and the water which thou takest out of the river shall become blood upon the dry *land.*

¹⁰And Moses said unto the LORD, O my Lord, I *am* not eloquent, neither heretofore, nor since thou hast spoken unto thy servant: but I *am* slow of speech, and of a slow tongue.

¹¹And the LORD said unto him, Who hath made man's mouth? or who maketh the dumb, or deaf, or the seeing, or the blind? have not I the LORD?

¹²Now therefore go, and I will be with thy mouth, and teach thee what thou shalt say.

¹³And he said, O my Lord, send, I pray thee, by the hand *of him whom* thou wilt send.

¹⁴And the anger of the LORD was kindled against Moses, and he said, Is not Aaron the Levite thy brother? I know that he can speak well. And also, behold, he cometh forth to meet thee: and when he seeth thee, he will be glad in his heart.

¹⁵And thou shalt speak unto him, and put words in his mouth: and I will be with thy mouth, and with his mouth, and will teach you what ye shall do.

¹⁶And he shall be thy spokesman unto the people: and he shall be, *even* he shall be to thee instead of a mouth, and thou shalt be to him instead of God.

¹⁷And thou shalt take this rod in thine hand, wherewith thou shalt do signs.

¹⁸And Moses went and returned to Jethro his father in law, and said unto him, Let me go, I pray thee, and return unto my brethren which *are* in Egypt, and see whether they be yet alive. And Jethro said to Moses, Go in peace.

¹⁹And the LORD said unto Moses in Midian, Go, return *into* Egypt: for all the men are dead which sought thy life.

²⁰And Moses took his wife and his sons, and

Amplified Bible

out his hand and caught it, and it became a rod in his hand,

⁵[This you shall do, said the Lord] that the elders may believe that the Lord, the God of their fathers, of Abraham, of Isaac, and of Jacob, has indeed appeared to you.

⁶The Lord said also to him, Put your hand into your bosom. He put his hand into his bosom, and when he took it out, behold, his hand was leprous, as white as snow.

⁷[God] said, Put your hand into your bosom again. So he put his hand back into his bosom, and when he took it out, behold, it was restored as the rest of his flesh.

⁸[Then God said] If they will not believe you or heed the voice *or* the testimony of the first sign, they may believe the voice *or* the witness of the second sign.

⁹But if they will also not believe these two signs or heed your voice, you shall take some water of the river [Nile] and pour it upon the dry land; and the water which you take out of the river [Nile] shall become blood on the dry land.

¹⁰And Moses said to the Lord, O Lord, I am not eloquent *or* a man of words, neither before nor since You have spoken to Your servant; for I am slow of speech and have a heavy *and* awkward tongue.

¹¹And the Lord said to him, Who has made man's mouth? Or who makes the dumb, or the deaf, or the seeing, or the blind? Is it not I, the Lord?

¹²Now therefore go, and I will be with your mouth and will teach you what you shall say.

¹³And he said, Oh, my Lord, I pray You, send by the hand of [some other] whom You will [send].

¹⁴Then the anger of the Lord blazed against Moses; He said, Is there not Aaron your brother, the Levite? I know he can speak well. Also, he is coming out to meet you, and when he sees you, he will be overjoyed.

¹⁵You must speak to him and put the words in his mouth; and I will be with your mouth and with his mouth and will teach you what you shall do.

¹⁶He shall speak for you to the people, acting as a mouthpiece for you, and you shall be as God to him.

¹⁷And you shall take this rod in your hand with which you shall work the signs [that prove I sent you].

¹⁸And Moses went away and, returning to Jethro his father-in-law, said to him, Let me go back, I pray you, to my relatives in Egypt to see whether they are still alive. And Jethro said to Moses, Go in peace.

¹⁹The Lord said to Moses in Midian, Go back to Egypt; for all the men who were seeking your life [for killing the Egyptian] are dead.

²⁰And Moses took his wife and his sons and set

King James Version

set them upon an ass, and he returned to the land of Egypt: and Moses took the rod of God in his hand.

²¹And the LORD said unto Moses, When thou goest to return into Egypt, see that thou do all *those* wonders before Pharaoh, which I have put in thine hand: but I will harden his heart, that he shall not let the people go.

²²And thou shalt say unto Pharaoh, Thus saith the LORD, Israel *is* my son, *even* my first-born:

²³And I say unto thee, Let my son go, that he may serve me: and *if* thou refuse to let him go, behold, I will slay thy son, *even* thy firstborn.

²⁴ ¶ And it came to pass by the way in the inn, that the LORD met him, and sought to kill him.

²⁵Then Zipporah took a sharp stone, and cut off the foreskin of her son, and cast *it* at his feet, and said, Surely a bloody husband *art* thou to me.

²⁶So he let him go: then she said, A bloody husband *thou art*, because of the circumcision.

²⁷And the LORD said to Aaron, Go into the wilderness to meet Moses. And he went, and met him in the mount of God, and kissed him.

²⁸And Moses told Aaron all the words of the LORD who had sent him, and all the signs which he had commanded him.

²⁹And Moses and Aaron went and gathered together all the elders of the children of Israel:

³⁰And Aaron spake all the words which the LORD had spoken unto Moses, and did the signs in the sight of the people.

³¹And the people believed: and when they heard that the LORD had visited the children of Israel, and that he had looked upon their affliction, then they bowed their heads and worshipped.

5 And afterward Moses and Aaron went in, and told Pharaoh, Thus saith the LORD God of Israel, Let my people go, that they may hold a feast unto me in the wilderness.

²And Pharaoh said, Who *is* the LORD, that I should obey his voice to let Israel go? I know not the LORD, neither will I let Israel go.

³And they said, The God of the Hebrews hath met with us: let us go, we pray thee, three days' journey into the desert, and sacrifice unto the LORD our God; lest he fall upon us with pestilence, or with the sword.

⁴And the king of Egypt said unto them,

Amplified Bible

them on donkeys, and he returned to the land of Egypt; and Moses took the rod of God in his hand.

²¹And the Lord said to Moses, When you return into Egypt, see that you do before Pharaoh all those miracles *and* wonders which I have put in your hand; but I will make him stubborn *and* harden his heart, so that he will not let the people go.

²²And you shall say to Pharaoh, Thus says the Lord, Israel is My son, even My firstborn.

²³And I say to you, Let My son go, that he may serve Me; and if you refuse to let him go, behold, I will slay your son, your firstborn.

²⁴Along the way at a [resting-] place, the Lord met [Moses] and sought to kill him [made him acutely and almost fatally ill].

²⁵[Now apparently he had ªfailed to circumcise one of his sons, his wife being opposed to it; but seeing his life in such danger] Zipporah took a flint knife and cut off the foreskin of her son and cast it to touch [Moses'] feet, and said, Surely a husband of blood you are to me!

²⁶When He let [Moses] alone [to recover], Zipporah said, A husband of blood are you because of the circumcision.

²⁷The Lord said to Aaron, Go into the wilderness to meet Moses. And he went, and met him in the mountain of God [Horeb, or Sinai] and kissed him.

²⁸Moses told Aaron all the words of the Lord with which He had sent him, and all the signs with which He had charged him.

²⁹Moses and Aaron went and gathered together [in Egypt] all the elders of the Israelites.

³⁰Aaron spoke all the words which the Lord had spoken to Moses, and did the signs in the sight of the people.

³¹And the people believed; and when they heard that the Lord had visited the Israelites, and that He had looked [in compassion] upon their affliction, they bowed their heads and worshiped.

5 AFTERWARD MOSES and Aaron went in and told Pharaoh, Thus says the Lord, the God of Israel, Let My people go, that they may hold a feast to Me in the wilderness.

²But Pharaoh said, Who is the Lord, that I should obey His voice to let Israel go? I know not the Lord, neither will I let Israel go.

³And they said, The God of the Hebrews has met with us; let us go, we pray you, three days' journey into the desert and sacrifice to the Lord our God, lest He fall upon us with pestilence or with the sword.

⁴The king of Egypt said to Moses and Aaron,

AMP notes: ª He who is on his way to liberate the people of the circumcision has in Midian even neglected to circumcise his second son Eliezer (J. P. Lange, *A Commentary*). It was necessary that at this stage of Moses' experience he should learn that God is in earnest when He speaks, and will assuredly perform all that He has threatened (J. G. Murphy, *A Commentary on the Book of Exodus*).

King James Version

Wherefore do ye, Moses and Aaron, let the people from their works? get you unto your burdens.

⁵And Pharaoh said, Behold, the people of the land now *are* many, and you make them rest from their burdens.

⁶And Pharaoh commanded the same day the taskmasters of the people, and their officers, saying,

⁷Ye shall no more give the people straw to make brick, as heretofore: let them go and gather straw for themselves.

⁸And the tale of the bricks, which they did make heretofore, you shall lay upon them; you shall not diminish *ought* thereof: for they *be* idle; therefore they cry, saying, Let us go *and* sacrifice to our God.

⁹Let there more work be laid upon the men, that they may labour therein; and let them not regard vain words.

¹⁰And the taskmasters of the people went out, and their officers, and they spake to the people, saying, Thus saith Pharaoh, I will not give you straw.

¹¹Go ye, get you straw where you can find *it:* yet not ought of your work *shall be* diminished.

¹²So the people were scattered abroad throughout all the land of Egypt to gather stubble instead of straw.

¹³And the taskmasters hasted *them,* saying, Fulfil your works, *your* daily tasks, as when there was straw.

¹⁴And the officers of the children of Israel, which Pharaoh's taskmasters had set over them, were beaten, *and* demanded, Wherefore have ye not fulfilled your task in making brick both yesterday and to day, as heretofore?

¹⁵Then the officers of the children of Israel came and cried unto Pharaoh, saying, Wherefore dealest thou thus with thy servants?

¹⁶*There is* no straw given unto thy servants, and they say to us, Make brick: and behold, thy servants *are* beaten; but the fault *is* in thine own people.

¹⁷But he said, Ye *are* idle, *ye are* idle: therefore ye say, Let us go *and* do sacrifice to the LORD.

¹⁸Go therefore now, *and* work; for there shall no straw be given you, yet shall ye deliver the tale of bricks.

¹⁹And the officers of the children of Israel did see *that* they *were* in evil *case,* after it was said, Ye shall not minish *ought* from your bricks of *your* daily task.

Amplified Bible

Why do you take the people from their jobs? Get to your burdens!

⁵Pharaoh said, Behold, the people of the land now are many, and you make them rest from their burdens!

⁶The very same day Pharaoh commanded the taskmasters of the people and their officers,

⁷You shall no more give the people straw to make brick; let them go and gather straw for themselves.

⁸But the number of the bricks which they made before you shall still require of them; you shall not diminish it in the least. For they are idle; that is why they cry, Let us go and sacrifice to our God.

⁹Let heavier work be laid upon the men that they may labor at it and pay no attention to lying words.

¹⁰The taskmasters of the people went out, and their officers, and they said to the people, Thus says Pharaoh, I will not give you straw.

¹¹Go, get *ᵃ*straw where you can find it; but your work shall not be diminished in the least.

¹²So the people were scattered through all the land of Egypt to gather the short stubble instead of straw.

¹³And the taskmasters were urgent, saying, Finish your work, your daily quotas, as when there was straw.

¹⁴And the Hebrew foremen, whom Pharaoh's taskmasters had set over them, were beaten and were asked, Why have you not fulfilled all your quota of making bricks yesterday and today, as before?

¹⁵Then the Hebrew foremen came to Pharaoh and cried, Why do you deal like this with your servants?

¹⁶No straw is given to your servants, yet they say to us, Make bricks! And behold, your servants are beaten, but the fault is in your own people.

¹⁷But [Pharaoh] said, You are idle, lazy *and* idle! That is why you say, Let us go and sacrifice to the Lord.

¹⁸Get out now and get to work; for no straw shall be given you, yet you shall deliver the full quota of bricks.

¹⁹And the Hebrew foremen saw that they were in an evil situation when it was said, You shall not diminish in the least your full daily quota of bricks.

AMP notes: *ᵃ* Archaeologists became interested early in examining Egyptian bricks of Moses' time to see if they contained straw. They found that, while many did contain straw, many also did not, leaving the impression that the Bible was wrong. But as usual in such cases, sooner or later it is shown that "the testimony of the Lord is sure, making wise the simple" (Ps. 19:7)—who know no better than to doubt the truth of God's Word. It is now known that oat straw boiled in water, when added to clay, makes the clay much easier to handle. Without the organic material obtained from the straw, the difficulty of making bricks was greatly increased. The fact that brickmakers of Egypt found the use of straw essential, whether visible evidence remains or not, is fully borne out, as various writers have asserted. (See Allan A. MacRae's, "The Relation of Archaeology to the Bible" in *Modern Science and Christian Faith*.)

King James Version

²⁰And they met Moses and Aaron, who stood in the way, as they came forth from Pharaoh:

²¹And they said unto them, The LORD look upon you, and judge; because you have made our savour to be abhorred in the eyes of Pharaoh, and in the eyes of his servants, to put a sword in their hand to slay us.

²² ¶ And Moses returned unto the LORD, and said, Lord, wherefore hast thou *so* evil entreated this people? why *is* it *that* thou hast sent me?

²³For since I came to Pharaoh to speak in thy name, he hath done evil to this people; neither hast thou delivered thy people at all.

6 Then the LORD said unto Moses, Now shalt thou see what I will do to Pharaoh: for with a strong hand shall he let them go, and with a strong hand shall he drive them out of his land.

²And God spake unto Moses, and said unto him, I *am* the LORD:

³And I appeared unto Abraham, unto Isaac, and unto Jacob, by *the name of* God Almighty, but *by* my name JEHOVAH was I not known to them.

⁴And I have also established my covenant with them, to give them the land of Canaan, the land of their pilgrimage, wherein they were strangers.

⁵And I have also heard the groaning of the children of Israel, whom the Egyptians keep in bondage; and I have remembered my covenant.

⁶Wherefore say unto the children of Israel, I *am* the LORD, and I will bring you out from under the burdens of the Egyptians, and I will rid you out of their bondage, and I will redeem you with a stretched out arm, and with great judgments:

⁷And I will take you to me for a people, and I will be to you a God: and ye shall know that I *am* the LORD your God, which bringeth you out from under the burdens of the Egyptians.

⁸And I will bring you in unto the land, *concerning* the which I did swear to give it to Abraham, to Isaac, and to Jacob; and I will give it you *for* an heritage: I *am* the LORD.

⁹And Moses spake so unto the children of Israel: but they hearkened not unto Moses for anguish of spirit, and for cruel bondage.

¹⁰ ¶ And the LORD spake unto Moses, saying,

¹¹Go in, speak unto Pharaoh king of Egypt, that he let the children of Israel go out of his land.

¹²And Moses spake before the LORD, saying, Behold, the children of Israel have not hear-

Amplified Bible

²⁰And the foremen met Moses and Aaron, who were standing in the way as they came forth from Pharaoh.

²¹And the foremen said to them, The Lord look upon you and judge, because you have made us a rotten stench to be detested by Pharaoh and his servants and have put a sword in their hand to slay us.

²²Then Moses turned again to the Lord and said, O Lord, why have You dealt evil to this people? Why did You ever send me?

²³For since I came to Pharaoh to speak in Your name, he has done evil to this people, neither have You delivered Your people at all.

6 THEN THE Lord said to Moses, Now you shall see what I will do to Pharaoh; for [compelled] by a strong hand he will [not only] let them go, but he will drive them out of his land with a strong hand.

²And God said to Moses, I am the Lord.

³I appeared to Abraham, to Isaac, and to Jacob as God Almighty [El-Shaddai], but by My ^aname the Lord [Yahweh—the redemptive name of God] I did not make Myself known to them [in acts and great miracles].

⁴I have also established My covenant with them to give them the land of Canaan, the land of their temporary residence in which they were strangers.

⁵I have also heard the groaning of the Israelites whom the Egyptians have enslaved; and I have [earnestly] remembered My covenant [with Abraham, Isaac, and Jacob].

⁶Accordingly, say to the Israelites, I am the Lord, and I will bring you out from under the burdens of the Egyptians, and I will free you from their bondage, and I will rescue you with an outstretched arm [with special and vigorous action] and by mighty acts of judgment.

⁷And I will take you to Me for a people, and I will be to you a God; and you shall know that it is I, the Lord your God, Who brings you out from under the burdens of the Egyptians.

⁸And I will bring you into the land concerning which I lifted up My hand *and* swore that I would give it to Abraham, Isaac, and Jacob; and I will give it to you for a heritage. I am the Lord [you have the pledge of My changeless omnipotence and faithfulness].

⁹Moses told this to the Israelites, but they refused to listen to Moses because of their impatience *and* anguish of spirit and because of their cruel bondage.

¹⁰The Lord said to Moses,

¹¹Go in, tell Pharaoh king of Egypt to let the Israelites go out of his land.

¹²But Moses said to the Lord, Behold, [my own people] the Israelites have not listened to

AMP notes: ^a See footnote on Exod. 3:15.

King James Version

kened unto me; how then shall Pharaoh hear me, who *am* of uncircumcised lips?

¹³And the LORD spake unto Moses and unto Aaron, and gave them a charge unto the children of Israel, and unto Pharaoh king of Egypt, to bring the children of Israel out of the land of Egypt.

¹⁴ ¶ These *be* the heads of their fathers' houses: The sons of Reuben the firstborn of Israel; Hanoch, and Pallu, Hezron, and Carmi: these *be* the families of Reuben.

¹⁵And the sons of Simeon; Jemuel, and Jamin, and Ohad, and Jachin, and Zohar, and Shaul the son of a Canaanitish woman: these *are* the families of Simeon.

¹⁶And these *are* the names of the sons of Levi according to their generations; Gershon, and Kohath, and Merari: and the years of the life of Levi *were* an hundred thirty and seven years.

¹⁷The sons of Gershon; Libni, and Shimi, according to their families.

¹⁸And the sons of Kohath; Amram, and Izhar, and Hebron, and Uzziel: and the years of the life of Kohath *were* an hundred thirty and three years.

¹⁹And the sons of Merari; Mahali and Mushi: these *are* the families of Levi according to their generations.

²⁰And Amram took him Jochebed his father's sister to wife; and she bare him Aaron and Moses: and the years of the life of Amram *were* an hundred and thirty and seven years.

²¹And the sons of Izhar; Korah, and Nepheg, and Zichri.

²²And the sons of Uzziel; Mishael, and Elzaphan, and Zithri.

²³And Aaron took him Elisheba, daughter of Amminadab, sister of Naashon, to wife; and she bare him Nadab, and Abihu, Eleazar, and Ithamar.

²⁴And the sons of Korah; Assir, and Elkanah, and Abiasaph: these *are* the families of the Korhites.

²⁵And Eleazar Aaron's son took him *one* of the daughters of Putiel to wife; and she bare him Phinehas: these *are* the heads of the fathers of the Levites according to their families.

²⁶*These are* that Aaron and Moses, to whom the LORD said, Bring out the children of Israel from the land of Egypt according to their armies.

²⁷*These are* they which spake to Pharaoh king of Egypt, to bring out the children of Israel from Egypt: *these are* that Moses and Aaron.

²⁸ ¶ And it came to pass on the day *when* the LORD spake unto Moses in the land of Egypt,

²⁹That the LORD spake unto Moses, saying, I *am* the LORD: speak thou unto Pharaoh king of Egypt all that I say unto thee.

³⁰And Moses said before the LORD, Behold, I

Amplified Bible

me; how then shall Pharaoh give heed to me, who am of deficient *and* impeded speech?

¹³But the Lord spoke to Moses and Aaron, and gave them a command for the Israelites and for Pharaoh king of Egypt, to bring the Israelites out of the land of Egypt.

¹⁴These are the heads of their clans. The sons of Reuben, Israel's firstborn: Hanoch, Pallu, Hezron, and Carmi; these are the families of Reuben.

¹⁵The sons of Simeon: Jemuel, Jamin, Ohad, Jachin, Zohar, and Shaul the son of a Canaanite woman; these are the families of Simeon.

¹⁶These are the names of the sons of Levi according to their births: Gershon, Kohath, and Merari; and Levi lived 137 years.

¹⁷The sons of Gershon: Libni and Shimi, by their families.

¹⁸The sons of Kohath: Amram, Izhar, Hebron, and Uzziel; and Kohath lived 133 years.

¹⁹The sons of Merari: Mahli and Mushi. These are the families of Levi according to their generations.

²⁰Amram took Jochebed his father's sister as wife, and she bore him Aaron and Moses; and Amram lived 137 years.

²¹The sons of Izhar: Korah, Nepheg, and Zichri.

²²The sons of Uzziel: Mishael, Elzaphan, and Sithri.

²³Aaron took Elisheba, daughter of Amminadab and sister of Nahshon, as wife; she bore him Nadab, Abihu, Eleazar, and Ithamar.

²⁴The sons of Korah: Assir, Elkanah, and Abiasaph. These are the families of the Korahites.

²⁵Eleazar, Aaron's son, took one of the daughters of Putiel as wife; and she bore him Phinehas. These are the heads of the fathers' houses of the Levites by their families.

²⁶These are the [same] Aaron and Moses to whom the Lord said, Bring out the Israelites from the land of Egypt by their hosts,

²⁷And who spoke to [the] Pharaoh king of Egypt about bringing the Israelites out of Egypt; these are that Moses and Aaron.

²⁸On the day when the Lord spoke to Moses in Egypt,

²⁹The Lord said to Moses, I am the Lord; tell Pharaoh king of Egypt all that I say to you.

³⁰But Moses said to the Lord, Behold, I am of

King James Version

am of uncircumcised lips, and how shall Pharaoh hearken unto me?

7 And the LORD said unto Moses, See, I have made thee a god to Pharaoh: and Aaron thy brother shall be thy prophet.

²Thou shalt speak all that I command thee: and Aaron thy brother shall speak unto Pharaoh, that he send the children of Israel out of his land.

³And I will harden Pharaoh's heart, and multiply my signs and my wonders in the land of Egypt.

⁴But Pharaoh shall not hearken unto you, that I may lay my hand upon Egypt, and bring forth mine armies, *and* my people the children of Israel, out of the land of Egypt by great judgments.

⁵And the Egyptians shall know that I *am* the LORD, when I stretch forth mine hand upon Egypt, and bring out the children of Israel from among them.

⁶And Moses and Aaron did as the LORD commanded them, so did they.

⁷And Moses *was* fourscore years old, and Aaron fourscore and three years old, when they spake unto Pharaoh.

⁸ ¶ And the LORD spake unto Moses and unto Aaron, saying,

⁹When Pharaoh shall speak unto you, saying, Shew a miracle for you: then thou shalt say unto Aaron, Take thy rod, and cast *it* before Pharaoh, *and* it shall become a serpent.

¹⁰And Moses and Aaron went in unto Pharaoh, and they did so as the LORD had commanded: and Aaron cast down his rod before Pharaoh, and before his servants, and it became a serpent.

¹¹Then Pharaoh also called the wise men and the sorcerers: now the magicians of Egypt, they also did in like manner with their enchantments.

¹²For they cast down every man his rod, and they became serpents: but Aaron's rod swallowed up their rods.

¹³And he hardened Pharaoh's heart, that he hearkened not unto them; as the LORD had said.

¹⁴ ¶ And the LORD said unto Moses, Pharaoh's heart *is* hardened, he refuseth to let the people go.

¹⁵Get thee unto Pharaoh in the morning; lo, he goeth out unto the water; and thou shalt stand by the river's brink against he come; and the rod which was turned to a serpent shalt thou take in thine hand.

¹⁶And thou shalt say unto him, The LORD God of the Hebrews hath sent me unto thee, saying, Let my people go, that they may serve me in the wilderness: and behold, hitherto thou wouldest not hear.

Amplified Bible

deficient *and* impeded speech; how then shall Pharaoh listen to me?

7 THE LORD said to Moses, Behold, I make you as God to Pharaoh [to declare My will and purpose to him]; and Aaron your brother shall be your prophet.

²You shall speak all that I command you, and Aaron your brother shall tell Pharaoh to let the Israelites go out of his land.

³And I will make Pharaoh's heart stubborn *and* hard, and multiply My signs, My wonders, *and* miracles in the land of Egypt.

⁴But Pharaoh will not listen to you, and I will lay My hand upon Egypt and bring forth My hosts, My people the Israelites, out of the land of Egypt by great acts of judgment.

⁵The Egyptians shall know that I am the Lord when I stretch forth My hand upon Egypt and bring out the Israelites from among them.

⁶And Moses and Aaron did so, as the Lord commanded them.

⁷Now Moses was 80 years old and Aaron 83 years old when they spoke to Pharaoh.

⁸And the Lord said to Moses and Aaron,

⁹When Pharaoh says to you, Prove [your authority] by a miracle, then tell Aaron, Throw your rod down before Pharaoh, that it may become a serpent.

¹⁰So Moses and Aaron went to Pharaoh and did as the Lord had commanded; Aaron threw down his rod before Pharaoh and his servants, and it became a serpent.

¹¹Then Pharaoh called for the wise men [skilled in magic and divination] and the sorcerers (wizards and jugglers). And they also, these magicians of Egypt, did similar things with their enchantments *and* secret arts.

¹²For they cast down every man his rod and they became serpents; but Aaron's rod swallowed up their rods.

¹³But Pharaoh's heart was hardened *and* stubborn and he would not listen to them, just as the Lord had said.

¹⁴Then the Lord said to Moses, Pharaoh's heart is hard *and* stubborn; he refuses to let the people go.

¹⁵Go to Pharaoh in the morning; he will be going out to the water; wait for him by the river's brink; and the rod which was turned to a serpent you shall take in your hand.

¹⁶And say to him, The Lord, the God of the Hebrews has sent me to you, saying, Let My people go, that they may serve Me in the wilderness; and behold, heretofore you have not listened.

King James Version

¹⁷Thus saith the LORD, In this thou shalt know that I *am* the LORD: behold, I will smite with the rod that *is* in mine hand upon the waters which *are* in the river, and they shall be turned to blood.

¹⁸And the fish that *is* in the river shall die, and the river shall stink; and the Egyptians shall lothe to drink of the water of the river.

¹⁹And the LORD spake unto Moses, Say unto Aaron, Take thy rod, and stretch out thine hand upon the waters of Egypt, upon their streams, upon their rivers, and upon their ponds, and upon all their pools of water, that they may become blood; and *that* there may be blood throughout all the land of Egypt, both in *vessels of* wood, and in *vessels of* stone.

²⁰And Moses and Aaron did so, as the LORD commanded; and he lift up the rod, and smote the waters that *were* in the river, in the sight of Pharaoh, and in the sight of his servants; and all the waters that *were* in the river were turned to blood.

²¹And the fish that *was* in the river died; and the river stunk, and the Egyptians could not drink of the water of the river; and there was blood throughout all the land of Egypt.

²²And the magicians of Egypt did so with their enchantments: and Pharaoh's heart was hardened, neither did he hearken unto them; as the LORD had said.

²³And Pharaoh turned and went into his house, neither did he set his heart to this also.

²⁴And all the Egyptians digged round about the river *for* water to drink; for they could not drink of the water of the river.

²⁵And seven days were fulfilled, after *that* the LORD had smitten the river.

8 And the LORD spake unto Moses, Go unto Pharaoh, and say unto him, Thus saith the LORD, Let my people go, that they may serve me.

²And if thou refuse to let *them* go, behold, I will smite all thy borders with frogs:

³And the river shall bring forth frogs abundantly, which shall go up and come into thine house, and into thy bedchamber, and upon thy bed, and into the house of thy servants, and upon thy people, and into thine ovens, and into thy kneadingtroughs:

⁴And the frogs shall come up *both* on thee, and upon thy people, and upon all thy servants.

⁵And the LORD spake unto Moses, Say unto Aaron, Stretch forth thine hand with thy rod over the streams, over the rivers, and over the ponds, and cause frogs to come up upon the land of Egypt.

⁶And Aaron stretched out his hand over the waters of Egypt; and the frogs came up, and covered the land of Egypt.

Amplified Bible

¹⁷Thus says the Lord, In this you shall know, recognize, *and* understand that I am the Lord: behold, I will smite with the rod in my hand the waters in the [Nile] River, and they shall be turned to blood.

¹⁸The fish in the river shall die, the river shall become foul smelling, and the Egyptians shall loathe to drink from it.

¹⁹And the Lord said to Moses, Say to Aaron, Take your rod and stretch out your hand over the waters of Egypt, over their streams, rivers, pools, and ponds of water, that they may become blood; and there shall be blood throughout all the land of Egypt, in containers both of wood and of stone.

²⁰Moses and Aaron did as the Lord commanded; [Aaron] lifted up the rod and smote the waters in the river in the sight of Pharaoh and his servants, and all the waters in the river were turned to blood.

²¹And the fish in the river died; and the river became foul smelling, and the Egyptians could not drink its water, and there was blood throughout all the land of Egypt.

²²But the magicians of Egypt did the same by their enchantments *and* secret arts; and Pharaoh's heart was made hard *and* obstinate, and he did not listen to Moses and Aaron, just as the Lord had said.

²³And Pharaoh turned and went into his house; neither did he take even this to heart.

²⁴And all the Egyptians dug round about the river for water to drink, for they could not drink the water of the [Nile].

²⁵Seven days passed after the Lord had smitten the river.

8 THEN THE Lord said to Moses, Go to Pharaoh and say to him, Thus says the Lord, Let My people go, that they may serve Me.

²And if you refuse to let them go, behold, I will smite your entire land with frogs;

³And the river shall swarm with frogs which shall go up and come into your house, into your bedchamber and on your bed, and into the houses of your servants and upon your people, and into your ovens, your kneading bowls, *and* your dough.

⁴And the frogs shall come up on you and on your people and all your servants.

⁵And the Lord said to Moses, Say to Aaron, Stretch out your hand with your rod over the rivers, the streams *and* canals, and over the pools, and cause frogs to come up on the land of Egypt.

⁶So Aaron stretched out his hand over the waters of Egypt, and the frogs came up and covered the land.

King James Version

⁷And the magicians did so with their enchantments, and brought up frogs upon the land of Egypt.

⁸Then Pharaoh called for Moses and Aaron, and said, Intreat the LORD, that he may take away the frogs from me, and from my people; and I will let the people go, that they may do sacrifice unto the LORD.

⁹And Moses said unto Pharaoh, Glory over me: when shall I intreat for thee, and for thy servants, and for thy people, to destroy the frogs from thee and thy houses, *that* they may remain in the river only?

¹⁰And he said, To morrow. And he said, *Be it* according to thy word: that thou mayest know that *there is* none like unto the LORD our God.

¹¹And the frogs shall depart from thee, and from thy houses, and from thy servants, and from thy people; they shall remain in the river only.

¹²And Moses and Aaron went out from Pharaoh: and Moses cried unto the LORD because of the frogs which he had brought against Pharaoh.

¹³And the LORD did according to the word of Moses; and the frogs died out of the houses, out of the villages, and out of the fields.

¹⁴And they gathered them together upon heaps: and the land stank.

¹⁵But when Pharaoh saw that there was respite, he hardened his heart, and hearkened not unto them; as the LORD had said.

¹⁶ ¶ And the LORD said unto Moses, Say unto Aaron, Stretch out thy rod, and smite the dust of the land, that it may become lice throughout all the land of Egypt.

¹⁷And they did so; for Aaron stretched out his hand with his rod, and smote the dust of the earth, and it became lice in man, and in beast; all the dust of the land became lice throughout all the land of Egypt.

¹⁸And the magicians did so with their enchantments to bring forth lice, but they could not: so there were lice upon man, and upon beast.

¹⁹Then the magicians said unto Pharaoh, This *is* the finger of God: and Pharaoh's heart was hardened, and he hearkened not unto them; as the LORD had said.

²⁰ ¶ And the LORD said unto Moses, Rise up early in the morning, and stand before Pharaoh; lo, he cometh forth to the water; and say unto him, Thus saith the LORD, Let my people go, that they may serve me.

²¹Else, if thou wilt not let my people go, behold, I will send swarms *of flies* upon thee, and upon thy servants, and upon thy people, and into thy houses: and the houses of the Egyptians shall be full of swarms *of flies*, and also the ground whereon they *are*.

Amplified Bible

⁷But the magicians did the same thing with their enchantments *and* secret arts, and brought up [more] frogs upon the land of Egypt.

⁸Then Pharaoh called for Moses and Aaron, and said, Entreat the Lord, that He may take away the frogs from me and my people; and I will let the people go that they may sacrifice to the Lord.

⁹Moses said to Pharaoh, Glory over me in this: dictate when I shall pray [to the Lord] for you, your servants, and your people, that the frogs may be destroyed from you and your houses and remain only in the river.

¹⁰And [Pharaoh] said, Tomorrow. [Moses] said, Let it be as you say, that you may know that there is no one like the Lord our God.

¹¹And the frogs shall depart from you and your houses and from your servants and your people; they shall remain in the river only.

¹²So Moses and Aaron went out from Pharaoh, and Moses cried to the Lord [as he had agreed with Pharaoh] concerning the frogs which He had brought against him.

¹³And the Lord did according to the word of Moses, and the frogs died out of the houses, out of the courtyards *and* villages, and out of the fields.

¹⁴[The people] gathered them together in heaps, and the land was loathsome *and* stank.

¹⁵But when Pharaoh saw that there was temporary relief, he made his heart stubborn *and* hard and would not listen *or* heed them, just as the Lord had said.

¹⁶Then the Lord said to Moses, Say to Aaron, Stretch out your rod and strike the dust of the ground, that it may become biting gnats *or* mosquitoes throughout all the land of Egypt.

¹⁷And they did so; Aaron stretched out his hand with his rod and struck the dust of the earth, and there came biting gnats *or* mosquitoes on man and beast; all the dust of the land became biting gnats *or* mosquitoes throughout all the land of Egypt.

¹⁸The magicians tried by their enchantments *and* secret arts to bring forth gnats *or* mosquitoes, but they could not; and there were gnats *or* mosquitoes on man and beast.

¹⁹Then the magicians said to Pharaoh, This is the finger of God! But Pharaoh's heart was hardened *and* strong and he would not listen to them, just as the Lord had said.

²⁰Then the Lord said to Moses, Rise up early in the morning and stand before Pharaoh as he comes forth to the water; and say to him, Thus says the Lord, Let My people go, that they may serve Me.

²¹Else, if you will not let My people go, behold, I will send swarms [of bloodsucking gadflies] upon you, your servants, and your people, and into your houses; and the houses of the Egyptians shall be full of swarms [of bloodsucking gadflies], and also the ground on which they stand.

King James Version

22And I will sever in that day the land of Goshen, in which my people dwell, that no swarms *of flies* shall be there; to the end thou mayest know that I *am* the LORD in the midst of the earth.

23And I will put a division between my people and thy people: to morrow shall this sign be.

24And the LORD did so; and there came a grievous swarm *of flies* into the house of Pharaoh, and *into* his servants' houses, and into all the land of Egypt: the land was corrupted by reason of the swarm *of flies.*

25And Pharaoh called for Moses and for Aaron, and said, Go ye, sacrifice to your God in the land.

26And Moses said, It is not meet so to do; for we shall sacrifice the abomination of the Egyptians to the LORD our God: lo, shall we sacrifice the abomination of the Egyptians before their eyes, and will they not stone us?

27We will go three days' journey into the wilderness, and sacrifice to the LORD our God, as he shall command us.

28And Pharaoh said, I will let you go, that ye may sacrifice to the LORD your God in the wilderness; only you shall not go very far away: intreat for me.

29And Moses said, Behold, I go out from thee, and I will intreat the LORD that the swarms *of flies* may depart from Pharaoh, from his servants, and from his people, to morrow: but let not Pharaoh deal deceitfully any more in not letting the people go to sacrifice to the LORD.

30And Moses went out from Pharaoh, and intreated the LORD.

31And the LORD did according to the word of Moses; and he removed the swarms *of flies* from Pharaoh, from his servants, and from his people; there remained not one.

32And Pharaoh hardened his heart at this time also, neither would he let the people go.

9 Then the LORD said unto Moses, Go in unto Pharaoh, and tell him, Thus saith the LORD God of the Hebrews, Let my people go, that they may serve me.

2For if thou refuse to let *them* go, and wilt hold them still,

3Behold, the hand of the LORD is upon thy cattle which *is* in the field, upon the horses, upon the asses, upon the camels, upon the oxen, and upon the sheep: *there shall be* a very grievous murrain.

4And the LORD shall sever between the cattle of Israel and the cattle of Egypt: and there shall nothing die of all *that is* the children's of Israel.

Amplified Bible

22But on that day I will sever *and* set apart the land of Goshen in which My people dwell, that no swarms [of gadflies] shall be there, so that you may know that I am the Lord in the midst of the earth.

23And I will put a division *and* a sign of deliverance between My people and your people. By tomorrow shall this sign be in evidence.

24And the Lord did so; and there came heavy *and* oppressive swarms [of bloodsucking gadflies] into the house of Pharaoh and his servants' houses; and in all of Egypt the land was corrupted *and* ruined by reason of the great invasion [of gadflies].

25And Pharaoh called for Moses and Aaron, and said, Go, sacrifice to your God [here] in the land [of Egypt].

26And Moses said, It is not suitable *or* right to do that; for the animals the Egyptians hold sacred and will not permit to be slain are those which we are accustomed to sacrifice to the Lord our God; if we did this before the eyes of the Egyptians, would they not stone us?

27We will go a three days' journey into the wilderness and sacrifice to the Lord our God, as He will command us.

28So Pharaoh said, I will let you go, that you may sacrifice to the Lord your God in the wilderness; only you shall not go very far away. Entreat [your God] for me.

29Moses said, I go out from you, and I will entreat the Lord that the swarms [of bloodsucking gadflies] may depart from Pharaoh, his servants, and his people tomorrow; only let not Pharaoh deal deceitfully any more in not letting the people go to sacrifice to the Lord.

30So Moses went out from Pharaoh and entreated the Lord.

31And the Lord did as Moses had spoken: He removed the swarms [of attacking gadflies] from Pharaoh, from his servants, and his people; there remained not one.

32But Pharaoh hardened his heart *and* made it stubborn this time also, nor would he let the people go.

9 THEN THE Lord said to Moses, Go to Pharaoh and tell him, Thus says the Lord God of the Hebrews: Let My people go, that they may serve Me.

2If you refuse to let them go and still hold them,

3Behold, the hand of the Lord [will fall] upon your livestock which are out in the field, upon the horses, the donkeys, the camels, the herds and the flocks; there shall be a very severe plague.

4But the Lord shall make a distinction between the livestock of Israel and the livestock of Egypt, and nothing shall die of all that belongs to the Israelites.

King James Version

⁵And the LORD appointed a set time, saying, To morrow the LORD shall do this thing in the land.

⁶And the LORD did that thing on the morrow, and all the cattle of Egypt died: but of the cattle of the children of Israel died not one.

⁷And Pharaoh sent, and behold, there was not one of the cattle of the Israelites dead. And the heart of Pharaoh was hardened, and he did not let the people go.

⁸ ¶ And the LORD said unto Moses and unto Aaron, Take to you handfuls of ashes of the furnace, and let Moses sprinkle it towards the heaven in the sight of Pharaoh.

⁹And it shall become small dust in all the land of Egypt, and shall be a boil breaking forth *with* blains upon man, and upon beast, throughout all the land of Egypt.

¹⁰And they took ashes of the furnace, and stood before Pharaoh; and Moses sprinkled it *up* toward heaven; and it became a boil breaking forth *with* blains upon man, and upon beast.

¹¹And the magicians could not stand before Moses because of the boils; for the boil was upon the magicians, and upon all the Egyptians.

¹²And the LORD hardened the heart of Pharaoh, and he hearkened not unto them; as the LORD had spoken unto Moses.

¹³ ¶ And the LORD said unto Moses, Rise up early in the morning, and stand before Pharaoh, and say unto him, Thus saith the LORD God of the Hebrews, Let my people go, that they may serve me.

¹⁴For I will at this time send all my plagues upon thine heart, and upon thy servants, and upon thy people; that thou mayest know that *there is* none like me in all the earth.

¹⁵For now I will stretch out my hand, that I may smite thee and thy people with pestilence; and thou shalt be cut off from the earth.

¹⁶And in very deed for this cause have I raised thee up, for to shew *in* thee my power; and that my name may be declared throughout all the earth.

¹⁷As yet exaltest thou thyself against my people, that *thou* wilt not let them go?

¹⁸Behold, to morrow about *this* time I will cause it to rain a very grievous hail, such as hath not been in Egypt since the foundation thereof even until now.

¹⁹Send therefore now, *and* gather thy cattle, and all that thou hast in the field; *for upon* every man and beast which shall be found in the field, and shall not be brought home, the hail shall come down upon them, and they shall die.

²⁰He that feared the word of the LORD amongst the servants of Pharaoh made his servants and his cattle flee into the houses:

Amplified Bible

⁵And the Lord set a time, saying, Tomorrow the Lord will do this thing in the land.

⁶And the Lord did that the next day, and all [kinds of] the livestock of Egypt died; but of the livestock of the Israelites not one died.

⁷Pharaoh sent to find out, and behold, there was not one of the cattle of the Israelites dead. But the heart of Pharaoh was hardened [his mind was set] and he did not let the people go.

⁸The Lord said to Moses and Aaron, Take handfuls of ashes *or* soot from the brickkiln and let Moses sprinkle them toward the heavens in the sight of Pharaoh.

⁹And it shall become small dust over all the land of Egypt, and become boils breaking out in sores on man and beast in all the land [occupied by the Egyptians].

¹⁰So they took ashes *or* soot of the kiln and stood before Pharaoh; and Moses threw them toward the sky, and it became boils erupting in sores on man and beast.

¹¹And the magicians could not stand before Moses because of their boils; for the boils were on the magicians and all the Egyptians.

¹²But the Lord hardened the heart of Pharaoh, making it strong *and* obstinate, and he did not listen to them or heed them, just as the Lord had told Moses.

¹³Then the Lord said to Moses, Rise up early in the morning and stand before Pharaoh and say to him, Thus says the Lord, the God of the Hebrews, Let My people go, that they may serve Me.

¹⁴For this time I will send all My plagues upon your heart and upon your servants and your people, that you may recognize *and* know that there is none like Me in all the earth.

¹⁵For by now I could have put forth My hand and have struck you and your people with pestilence, and you would have been cut off from the earth.

¹⁶But for this very purpose have I let you live, that I might show you My power, and that My name may be declared throughout all the earth.

¹⁷Since you are still exalting yourself [in haughty defiance] against My people by not letting them go,

¹⁸Behold, tomorrow about this time I will cause it to rain a very heavy *and* dreadful fall of hail, such as has not been in Egypt from its founding until now.

¹⁹Send therefore now and gather your cattle in hastily, and all that you have in the field; for every man and beast that is in the field and is not brought home shall be struck by the hail and shall die.

²⁰Then he who feared the word of the Lord among the servants of Pharaoh made his servants and his livestock flee into the houses *and* shelters.

King James Version

21And he that regarded not the word of the LORD left his servants and his cattle in the field.

22And the LORD said unto Moses, Stretch forth thine hand toward heaven, that there may be hail in all the land of Egypt, upon man, and upon beast, and upon every herb of the field, throughout the land of Egypt.

23And Moses stretched forth his rod toward heaven: and the LORD sent thunder and hail, and the fire ran along upon the ground; and the LORD rained hail upon the land of Egypt.

24So there was hail, and fire mingled with the hail, very grievous, such as there was none like it in all the land of Egypt since it became a nation.

25And the hail smote throughout all the land of Egypt all that *was* in the field, both man and beast; and the hail smote every herb of the field, and brake every tree of the field.

26Only in the land of Goshen, where the children of Israel *were,* was there no hail.

27And Pharaoh sent, and called for Moses and Aaron, and said unto them, I have sinned *this* time: the LORD *is* righteous, and I and my people *are* wicked.

28Intreat the LORD (for *it is* enough) that there be no *more* mighty thunderings and hail; and I will let you go, and ye shall stay no longer.

29And Moses said unto him, As soon as I am gone out of the city, I will spread abroad my hands unto the LORD; *and* the thunder shall cease, neither shall there be any more hail; that thou mayest know how that the earth *is* the LORD'S.

30But as for thee and thy servants, I know that ye will not yet fear the LORD God.

31And the flax and the barley was smitten: for the barley *was* in the ear, and the flax *was* bolled.

32But the wheat and the rye were not smitten: for they *were* not grown up.

33And Moses went out of the city from Pharaoh, and spread abroad his hands unto the LORD: and the thunders and hail ceased, and the rain was not poured upon the earth.

34And when Pharaoh saw that the rain and the hail and the thunders were ceased, he sinned yet more, and hardened his heart, he and his servants.

35And the heart of Pharaoh was hardened, neither would he let the children of Israel go; as the LORD had spoken by Moses.

10 And the LORD said unto Moses, Go in unto Pharaoh: for I have hardened his heart, and the heart of his servants, that I might shew these my signs before him:

2And that thou mayest tell in the ears of thy

Amplified Bible

21And he who ignored the word of the Lord left his servants and his livestock in the field.

22The Lord said to Moses, Stretch forth your hand toward the heavens, that there may be hail in all the land of Egypt, upon man and beast, and upon all the vegetation of the field, throughout the land of Egypt.

23Then Moses stretched forth his rod toward the heavens, and the Lord sent thunder and hail, and fire (lightning) ran down to *and* along the ground, and the Lord rained hail upon the land of Egypt.

24So there was hail and fire flashing continually in the midst of the weighty hail, such as had not been in all the land of Egypt since it became a nation.

25The hail struck down throughout all the land of Egypt everything that was in the field, both man and beast; and the hail beat down all the vegetation of the field and shattered every tree of the field.

26Only in the land of Goshen, where the Israelites were, was there no hail.

27And Pharaoh sent for Moses and Aaron, and said to them, I have sinned this time; the Lord is in the right and I and my people are in the wrong.

28Entreat the Lord, for there has been enough of these mighty thunderings and hail [these voices of God]; I will let you go; you shall stay here no longer.

29Moses said to him, As soon as I leave the city, I will stretch out my hands to the Lord; the thunder shall cease, neither shall there be any more hail, that you may know that the earth is the Lord's.

30But as for you and your servants, I know that you do not yet [reverently] fear the Lord God.

31The flax and the barley were smitten *and* ruined, for the barley was in the ear and the flax in bloom.

32But the wheat and spelt [another wheat] were not smitten, for they ripen late and were not grown up yet.

33So Moses left the city and Pharaoh, and stretched forth his hands to the Lord; and the thunder and hail ceased, and rain was no longer poured upon the earth.

34But when Pharaoh saw that the rain, the hail, and the thunder had ceased, he sinned yet more, and toughened *and* stiffened his hard heart, he and his servants.

35So Pharaoh's heart was strong *and* obstinate; he would not let the Israelites go, just as the Lord had said by Moses.

10 THE LORD said to Moses, Go to Pharaoh, for I have made his heart hard, and his servants' hearts, that I might show these My signs [of divine power] before him,

2And that you may recount in the ears of your

King James Version

son, and of thy son's son, what things I have wrought in Egypt, and my signs which I have done amongst them; that ye may know how that I *am* the LORD.

³And Moses and Aaron came in unto Pharaoh, and said unto him, Thus saith the LORD God of the Hebrews, How long wilt thou refuse to humble thyself before me? let my people go, that they may serve me.

⁴Else, if thou refuse to let my people go, behold, to morrow will I bring the locusts into thy coast:

⁵And they shall cover the face of the earth, that *one* cannot be able to see the earth: and they shall eat the residue of that which is escaped which remaineth unto you from the hail, and shall eat every tree which groweth for you out of the field:

⁶And they shall fill thy houses, and the houses of all thy servants, and the houses of all the Egyptians; which neither thy fathers, nor thy fathers' fathers have seen, since the day that they were upon the earth unto this day. And he turned himself, and went out from Pharaoh.

⁷And Pharaoh's servants said unto him, How long shall this *man* be a snare unto us? let the men go, that they may serve the LORD their God: knowest thou not yet that Egypt is destroyed?

⁸And Moses and Aaron were brought again unto Pharaoh: and he said unto them, Go, serve the LORD your God: *but* who *are* they that shall go?

⁹And Moses said, We will go with our young and with our old, with our sons and with our daughters, with our flocks and with our herds will we go; for we *must hold* a feast unto the LORD.

¹⁰And he said unto them, Let the LORD be so with you, as I will let you go, and your little ones: look *to it;* for evil *is* before you.

¹¹Not so: go now ye *that are* men, and serve the LORD; for that you did desire. And they were driven out from Pharaoh's presence.

¹²And the LORD said unto Moses, Stretch out thine hand over the land of Egypt for the locusts, that they may come up upon the land of Egypt, and eat every herb of the land, *even* all that the hail hath left.

¹³And Moses stretched forth his rod over the land of Egypt, and the LORD brought an east wind upon the land all that day, and all *that* night; *and* when it was morning, the east wind brought the locusts.

¹⁴And the locusts went up over all the land of Egypt, and rested in all the coasts of Egypt: very grievous *were they;* before them there were no such locusts as they, neither after them shall be such.

¹⁵For they covered the face of the whole earth, so that the land was darkened; and they

Amplified Bible

son and of your grandson what I have done in derision of the Egyptians *and* what things I have [repeatedly] done there—My signs [of divine power] done among them—that you may recognize *and* know that I am the Lord.

³So Moses and Aaron went to Pharaoh, and said to him, Thus says the Lord, the God of the Hebrews, How long will you refuse to humble yourself before Me? Let My people go, that they may serve Me.

⁴For if you refuse to let My people go, behold, tomorrow I will bring locusts into your country.

⁵And they shall cover the land so that one cannot see the ground; and they shall eat the remainder of what escaped and is left to you from the hail, and they shall eat every tree of yours that grows in the field;

⁶The locusts shall fill your houses and those of all your servants and of all the Egyptians, as neither your fathers nor your fathers' fathers have seen from their birth until this day. Then Moses departed from Pharaoh.

⁷And Pharaoh's servants said to him, How long shall this man be a snare to us? Let the men go, that they may serve the Lord their God; do you not yet understand *and* know that Egypt is destroyed?

⁸So Moses and Aaron were brought again to Pharaoh; and he said to them, Go, serve the Lord your God; but just who are to go?

⁹And Moses said, We will go with our young and our old, with our sons and our daughters, with our flocks and our herds [all of us and all we have], for we must hold a feast to the Lord.

¹⁰Pharaoh said to them, Let the Lord be with you, if I ever let you go with your little ones! See, you have some evil purpose in mind.

¹¹Not so! You that are men, [without your families] go and serve the Lord, for that is what you want. And [Moses and Aaron] were driven from Pharaoh's presence.

¹²Then the Lord said to Moses, Stretch out your hand over the land of Egypt for the locusts, that they may come up on the land of Egypt and eat all the vegetation of the land, all that the hail has left.

¹³And Moses stretched forth his rod over the land of Egypt, and the Lord brought an east wind upon the land all that day and all that night; when it was morning, the east wind brought the locusts.

¹⁴And the locusts came up over all the land of Egypt and settled down on the whole country of Egypt, a very dreadful mass of them; never before were there such locusts as these, nor will there ever be again.

¹⁵For they covered the whole land, so that the ground was darkened, and they ate every bit of

King James Version

did eat every herb of the land, and all the fruit of the trees which the hail had left: and there remained not any green thing in the trees, or in the herbs of the field, through all the land of Egypt.

16Then Pharaoh called for Moses and Aaron in haste; and he said, I have sinned against the LORD your God, and against you.

17Now therefore forgive, I pray thee, my sin only *this* once, and intreat the LORD your God, that he may take away from me this death only.

18And he went out from Pharaoh, and intreated the LORD.

19And the LORD turned a mighty strong west wind, which took away the locusts, and cast them into the Red sea; there remained not one locust in all the coasts of Egypt.

20But the LORD hardened Pharaoh's heart, so that he would not let the children of Israel go.

21 ¶ And the LORD said unto Moses, Stretch out thine hand toward heaven, that there may be darkness over the land of Egypt, even darkness *which* may be felt.

22And Moses stretched forth his hand toward heaven; and there was a thick darkness in all the land of Egypt three days:

23They saw not one another, neither rose any from his place for three days: but all the children of Israel had light in their dwellings.

24And Pharaoh called unto Moses, and said, Go ye, serve the LORD; only let your flocks and your herds be stayed: let your little ones also go with you.

25And Moses said, Thou must give us also sacrifices and burnt offerings, that we may sacrifice unto the LORD our God.

26Our cattle also shall go with us; there shall not a hoof be left behind; for thereof must we take to serve the LORD our God; and we know not with what we must serve the LORD, until we come thither.

27But the LORD hardened Pharaoh's heart, and he would not let them go.

28And Pharaoh said unto him, Get thee from me, take heed to thyself, see my face no more; for in *that* day thou seest my face thou shalt die.

29And Moses said, Thou hast spoken well, I will see thy face again no more.

11 (And the LORD said unto Moses, Yet will I bring one plague *more* upon Pharaoh, and upon Egypt; afterwards he will let you go hence: when he shall let *you* go, he shall surely thrust you out hence altogether.

2Speak now in the ears of the people, and let every man borrow of his neighbour, and every

Amplified Bible

vegetation of the land and all the fruit of the trees which the hail had left; there remained not a green thing of the trees or the plants of the field in all the land of Egypt.

16Then Pharaoh sent for Moses and Aaron in haste. He said, I have sinned against the Lord your God and you.

17Now therefore forgive my sin, I pray you, only this once, and entreat the Lord your God only that He may remove from me this [plague of] death.

18Then Moses left Pharaoh and entreated the Lord.

19And the Lord turned a violent west wind, which lifted the locusts and drove them into the Red Sea; not one locust remained in all the country of Egypt.

20But the Lord made Pharaoh's heart more strong *and* obstinate, and he would not let the Israelites go.

21And the Lord said to Moses, Stretch out your hand toward the heavens, that there may be darkness over the land of Egypt, a darkness which may be felt.

22So Moses stretched out his hand toward the sky, and for three days a thick darkness was all over the land of Egypt.

23The Egyptians could not see one another, nor did anyone rise from his place for three days; but all the Israelites had natural light in their dwellings.

24And Pharaoh called to Moses, and said, Go, serve the Lord; let your little ones also go with you; it is only your flocks and your herds that must not go.

25But Moses said, You must give into our hand also sacrifices and burnt offerings, that we may sacrifice to the Lord our God.

26Our livestock also shall go with us; there shall not a hoof be left behind; for of them must we take to serve the Lord our God, and we know not with what we must serve the Lord until we arrive there.

27But the Lord made Pharaoh's heart stronger *and* more stubborn, and he would not let them go.

28And Pharaoh said to Moses, Get away from me! See that you never enter my presence again, for the day you see my face again you shall die!

29And Moses said, You have spoken truly; I will never see your face again.

11 THEN THE Lord said to Moses, Yet will I bring one plague more on Pharaoh and on Egypt; afterwards he will let you go. When he lets you go from here, he will thrust you out altogether.

2Speak now in the hearing of the people, and let every man solicit *and* ask of his neighbor,

King James Version

woman of her neighbour, jewels of silver, and jewels of gold.

3And the LORD gave the people favour in the sight of the Egyptians. Moreover the man Moses *was* very great in the land of Egypt, in the sight of Pharaoh's servants, and in the sight of the people.)

4And Moses said, Thus saith the LORD, About midnight will I go out into the midst of Egypt:

5And all the firstborn in the land of Egypt shall die, from the firstborn of Pharaoh that sitteth upon his throne, *even* unto the firstborn of the maidservant that *is* behind the mill; and all the firstborn of beasts.

6And there shall be a great cry throughout all the land of Egypt, such as there was none like it, nor shall be like it any more.

7But against any of the children of Israel shall not a dog move his tongue, against man or beast: that ye may know how that the LORD doth put a difference between the Egyptians and Israel.

8And all these thy servants shall come down unto me, and bow down themselves unto me, saying, Get thee out, and all the people that follow thee: and after that I will go out. And he went out from Pharaoh in a great anger.

9And the LORD said unto Moses, Pharaoh shall not hearken unto you; that my wonders may be multiplied in the land of Egypt.

10And Moses and Aaron did all these wonders before Pharaoh: and the LORD hardened Pharaoh's heart, so that he would not let the children of Israel go out of his land.

12 And the LORD spake unto Moses and Aaron in the land of Egypt, saying,

2This month *shall be* unto you the beginning of months: it *shall be* the first month of the year to you.

3Speak ye unto all the congregation of Israel, saying, In the tenth *day* of this month they shall take to them every man a lamb, according to the house of *their* fathers, a lamb for a house:

4And if the household be too little for the lamb, let him and his neighbour next unto his house take *it* according to the number of the souls; every man according to his eating shall make your count for the lamb.

5Your lamb shall be without blemish, a male of the first year: ye shall take *it* out from the sheep, or from the goats:

6And ye shall keep it *up* until the fourteenth day of the same month: and the whole assembly of the congregation of Israel shall kill it in the evening.

7And they shall take of the blood, and strike *it* on the two side posts and on the upper door post of the houses, wherein they shall eat it.

Amplified Bible

and every woman of her neighbor, jewels of silver and jewels of gold.

3And the Lord gave the people favor in the sight of the Egyptians. Moreover, the man Moses was exceedingly great in the land of Egypt, in the sight of Pharaoh's servants and of the people.

4And Moses said, Thus says the Lord, About midnight I will go out into the midst of Egypt;

5And all the firstborn in the land [the pride, hope, and joy] of Egypt shall die, from the firstborn of Pharaoh, who sits on his throne, even to the firstborn of the maidservant who is behind the hand mill, and all the firstborn of beasts.

6There shall be a great cry in all the land of Egypt, such as has never been nor ever shall be again.

7But against any of the Israelites shall not so much as a dog move his tongue against man or beast, that you may know that the Lord makes a distinction between the Egyptians and Israel.

8And all these your servants shall come down to me and bow down to me, saying, Get out, and all the people who follow you! And after that I will go out. And he went out from Pharaoh in great anger.

9Then the Lord said to Moses, Pharaoh will not listen to you, that My wonders *and* miracles may be multiplied in the land of Egypt.

10Moses and Aaron did all these wonders *and* miracles before Pharaoh; and the Lord hardened Pharaoh's stubborn heart, and he did not let the Israelites go out of his land.

12 THE LORD said to Moses and Aaron in the land of Egypt,

2This month shall be to you the beginning of months, the first month of the year to you.

3Tell all the congregation of Israel, On the tenth day of this month they shall take every man a lamb *or* kid, according to [the size of] the family of which he is the father, a lamb *or* kid for each house.

4And if the household is too small to consume the lamb, let him and his next door neighbor take it according to the number of persons, every man according to what each can eat shall make your count for the lamb.

5Your lamb *or* kid shall be without blemish, a male of the first year; you shall take it from the sheep or the goats.

6And you shall keep it until the fourteenth day of the same month; and the whole assembly of the congregation of Israel shall [each] kill [his] lamb in the evening.

7They shall take of the blood and put it on the two side posts and on the lintel [above the door space] of the houses in which they shall eat [the Passover lamb].

King James Version

8And they shall eat the flesh in that night, roast with fire, and unleavened bread; *and* with bitter *herbs* they shall eat it.

9Eat not of it raw, nor sodden at all with water, but roast with fire; his head with his legs, and with the purtenance thereof.

10And ye shall let nothing of it remain until the morning; and that which remaineth of it until the morning ye shall burn with fire.

11And thus shall ye eat it; *with* your loins girded, your shoes on your feet, and your staff in your hand; and ye shall eat it in haste: it *is* the LORD'S passover.

12For I will pass through the land of Egypt this night, and will smite all the firstborn in the land of Egypt, both man and beast; and against all the gods of Egypt I will execute judgment: I *am* the LORD.

13And the blood shall be to you for a token upon the houses where you *are;* and when I see the blood, I will pass over you, and the plague shall not be upon you to destroy *you,* when I smite the land of Egypt.

14And this day shall be unto you for a memorial; and you shall keep it a feast to the LORD throughout your generations; you shall keep it a feast by an ordinance for ever.

15Seven days shall ye eat unleavened bread; even the first day ye shall put away leaven out of your houses: for whosoever eateth leavened bread from the first day until the seventh day, that soul shall be cut off from Israel.

16And in the first day *there shall be* a holy convocation, and in the seventh day there shall be a holy convocation to you; no *manner of* work shall be done in them, save *that* which every man must eat, that only may be done of you.

17And ye shall observe the *feast of* unleavened bread; for in this selfsame day have I brought your armies out of the land of Egypt: therefore shall ye observe this day in your generations by an ordinance for ever.

18In the first *month,* on the fourteenth day of the month at even, ye shall eat unleavened bread, until the one and twentieth day of the month at even.

19Seven days shall there be no leaven found in your houses: for whosoever eateth that which is leavened, even that soul shall be cut off from the congregation of Israel, whether he be a stranger, or born in the land.

20Ye shall eat nothing leavened; in all your habitations shall ye eat unleavened bread.

21 ¶ Then Moses called for all the elders of Israel, and said unto them, Draw out and take you a lamb according to your families, and kill the passover.

Amplified Bible

8They shall eat the flesh that night roasted; with unleavened bread and bitter herbs they shall eat it.

9Eat not of it raw nor boiled at all with water, but roasted—its head, its legs, and its inner parts.

10You shall let nothing of the meat remain until the morning; and the bones *and* unedible bits which remain of it until morning you shall burn with fire.

11And you shall eat it thus: [as fully prepared for a journey] your loins girded, your shoes on your feet, and your staff in your hand; and you shall eat it in haste. It is the Lord's Passover.

12For I will pass through the land of Egypt this night and will smite all the firstborn in the land of Egypt, both man and beast; and against all the gods of Egypt I will execute judgment [proving their helplessness]. I am the Lord.

13The blood shall be for a token *or* sign to you upon [the doorposts of] the houses where you are, [that] when I see the blood, I will pass over you, and no plague shall be upon you to destroy you when I smite the land of Egypt.

14And this day shall be to you for a memorial. You shall keep it as a feast to the Lord throughout your generations, keep it as an ordinance forever.

15[In celebration of the Passover in future years] seven days shall you eat unleavened bread; even the first day you shall put away leaven [symbolic of corruption] out of your houses; for whoever eats leavened bread from the first day until the seventh day, that person shall be cut off from Israel.

16On the first day you shall hold a solemn *and* holy assembly, and on the seventh day there shall be a solemn *and* holy assembly; no kind of work shall be done in them, save [preparation of] that which every person must eat—that only may be done by you.

17And you shall observe the Feast of Unleavened Bread, for on this very day have I brought your hosts out of the land of Egypt; therefore shall you observe this day throughout your generations as an ordinance forever.

18In the first month, on the fourteenth day of the month at evening, you shall eat unleavened bread [and continue] until the twenty-first day of the month at evening.

19Seven days no leaven [symbolic of corruption] shall be found in your houses; whoever eats what is leavened shall be excluded from the congregation of Israel, whether a stranger or native-born.

20You shall eat nothing leavened; in all your dwellings you shall eat unleavened bread [during that week].

21Then Moses called for all the elders of Israel, and said to them, Go forth, select and take a lamb according to your families and kill the Passover [lamb].

King James Version

22And ye shall take a bunch of hyssop, and dip *it* in the blood that *is* in the bason, and strike the lintel and the two side posts with the blood that *is* in the bason; and none of you shall go out at the door of his house until the morning.

23For the LORD will pass through to smite the Egyptians; and when he seeth the blood upon the lintel, and on the two side posts, the LORD will pass over the door, and will not suffer the destroyer to come in unto your houses to smite *you.*

24And ye shall observe this thing for an ordinance to thee and to thy sons for ever.

25And it shall come to pass, when ye be come to the land which the LORD will give you, according as he hath promised, that ye shall keep this service.

26And it shall come to pass, when your children shall say unto you, What mean you by this service?

27That ye shall say, It *is* the sacrifice of the LORD'S passover, who passed over the houses of the children of Israel in Egypt, when he smote the Egyptians, and delivered our houses. And the people bowed the head and worshipped.

28And the children of Israel went away, and did as the LORD had commanded Moses and Aaron, so did they.

29 ¶ And it came to pass, that at midnight the LORD smote all the firstborn in the land of Egypt, from the firstborn of Pharaoh that sat on his throne unto the firstborn of the captive that *was* in the dungeon; and all the firstborn of cattle.

30And Pharaoh rose up in the night, he, and all his servants, and all the Egyptians; and there was a great cry in Egypt; for *there was* not a house where *there was* not one dead.

31And he called for Moses and Aaron by night, and said, Rise up, *and* get you forth from amongst my people, both you and the children of Israel; and go, serve the LORD, as ye have said.

32Also take your flocks and your herds, as ye have said, and be gone; and bless me also.

33And the Egyptians were urgent upon the people, that they might send them out of the land in haste; for they said, We *be* all dead *men.*

34And the people took their dough before it was leavened, their kneadingtroughs being bound up in their clothes upon their shoulders.

35And the children of Israel did according to the word of Moses; and they borrowed of the Egyptians jewels of silver, and jewels of gold, and raiment:

36And the LORD gave the people favour in the sight of the Egyptians, so that they lent unto them *such things as they required.* And they spoiled the Egyptians.

37 ¶ And the children of Israel journeyed from

Amplified Bible

22And you shall take a bunch of hyssop, dip it in the blood in the basin, and touch the lintel above the door and the two side posts with the blood; and none of you shall go out of his house until morning.

23For the Lord will pass through to slay the Egyptians; and when He sees the blood upon the lintel and the two side posts, the Lord will pass over the door and will not allow the destroyer to come into your houses to slay you.

24You shall observe this rite for an ordinance to you and to your sons forever.

25When you come to the land which the Lord will give you, as He has promised, you shall keep this service.

26When your children shall say to you, What do you mean by this service?

27You shall say, It is the sacrifice of the Lord's Passover, for He passed over the houses of the Israelites in Egypt when He slew the Egyptians but spared our houses. And the people bowed their heads and worshiped.

28The Israelites went and, as the Lord had commanded Moses and Aaron, so they did.

29At midnight the Lord slew every firstborn in the land of Egypt, from the firstborn of Pharaoh who sat on his throne to the firstborn of the prisoner in the dungeon, and all the firstborn of the livestock.

30Pharaoh rose up in the night, he, all his servants, and all the Egyptians; and there was a great cry in Egypt, for there was not a house where there was not one dead.

31He called for Moses and Aaron by night, and said, Rise up, get out from among my people, both you and the Israelites; and go, serve the Lord, as you said.

32Also take your flocks and your herds, as you have said, and be gone! And [ask your God to] bless me also.

33The Egyptians were urgent with the people to depart, that they might send them out of the land in haste; for they said, We are all dead men.

34The people took their dough before it was leavened, their kneading bowls being bound up in their clothes on their shoulders.

35The Israelites did according to the word of Moses; and they [urgently] asked of the Egyptians jewels of silver and of gold, and clothing.

36The Lord gave the people favor in the sight of the Egyptians, so that they gave them what they asked. And they stripped the Egyptians [of those things].

37The Israelites journeyed from Rameses to

King James Version

Rameses to Succoth, about six hundred thousand on foot *that were* men, beside children.

³⁸And a mixed multitude went up also with them; and flocks, and herds, *even* very much cattle.

³⁹And they baked unleavened cakes of the dough which they brought forth out of Egypt, for it was not leavened; because they were thrust out of Egypt, and could not tarry, neither had they prepared for themselves *any* victual.

⁴⁰Now the sojourning of the children of Israel, who dwelt in Egypt, *was* four hundred and thirty years.

⁴¹And it came to pass at the end of the four hundred and thirty years, even the selfsame day it came to pass, *that* all the hosts of the LORD went out from the land of Egypt.

⁴²It *is* a night to be much observed unto the LORD for bringing them out from the land of Egypt: this *is* that night of the LORD to be observed of all the children of Israel in their generations.

⁴³ ¶ And the LORD said unto Moses and Aaron, This *is* the ordinance of the passover: There shall no stranger eat thereof:

⁴⁴But every man's servant that is bought for money, when thou hast circumcised him, then shall he eat thereof.

⁴⁵A foreigner and a hired servant shall not eat thereof.

⁴⁶In one house shall it be eaten; thou shalt not carry forth *ought* of the flesh abroad out of the house; neither shall ye break a bone thereof.

⁴⁷All the congregation of Israel shall keep it.

⁴⁸And when a stranger shall sojourn with thee, and will keep the passover to the LORD, let all his males be circumcised, and then let him come near and keep it; and he shall be as one that is born in the land: for no uncircumcised person shall eat thereof.

⁴⁹One law shall be to him that is homeborn, and unto the stranger that sojourneth among you.

⁵⁰Thus did all the children of Israel; as the LORD commanded Moses and Aaron, so did they.

⁵¹And it came to pass the selfsame day, *that* the LORD did bring the children of Israel out of the land of Egypt by their armies.

13 And the LORD spake unto Moses, saying, ²Sanctify unto me all the firstborn, whatsoever openeth the womb among the children of Israel, *both* of man and of beast: it *is* mine.

³And Moses said unto the people, Remember this day, *in* which ye came out from Egypt, out of the house of bondage; for by strength of hand the LORD brought you out from this *place:* there shall no leavened bread be eaten.

Amplified Bible

Succoth, about 600,000 men on foot, besides women and children.

³⁸And a mixed multitude went also with them, and very much livestock, both flocks and herds.

³⁹They baked unleavened cakes of the dough which they brought from Egypt; it was not leavened because they were driven from Egypt and could not delay, nor had they prepared for themselves any food.

⁴⁰Now the time the Israelites dwelt in Egypt was 430 years.

⁴¹At the end of the 430 years, even that very day, all the hosts of the Lord went out of Egypt.

⁴²It was a night of watching unto the Lord *and* to be much observed for bringing them out of Egypt; this same night of watching unto the Lord is to be observed by all the Israelites throughout their generations.

⁴³The Lord said to Moses and Aaron, This is the ordinance of the Passover: No foreigner shall eat of it;

⁴⁴But every man's servant who is bought for money, when you have circumcised him, then may he eat of it.

⁴⁵A foreigner or hired servant shall not eat of it.

⁴⁶In one house shall it be eaten [by one company]; you shall not carry any of the flesh outside the house; neither shall you break a bone of it.

⁴⁷All the congregation of Israel shall keep it.

⁴⁸When a stranger sojourning with you wishes to keep the Passover to the Lord, let all his males be circumcised, and then let him come near and keep it; and he shall be as one that is born in the land. But no uncircumcised person shall eat of it.

⁴⁹There shall be one law for the native-born and for the stranger or foreigner who sojourns among you.

⁵⁰Thus did all the Israelites; as the Lord commanded Moses and Aaron, so did they.

⁵¹And on that very day the Lord brought the Israelites out of the land of Egypt by their hosts.

13 THE LORD said to Moses, ²Sanctify (consecrate, set apart) to Me all the firstborn [males]; whatever is first to open the womb among the Israelites, both of man and of beast, is Mine.

³And Moses said to the people, [Earnestly] remember this day in which you came out from Egypt, out of the house of bondage *and* bondmen, for by strength of hand the Lord brought you out from this place; no leavened bread shall be eaten.

King James Version

⁴*This* day came ye out in the month Abib.

⁵And it shall be when the LORD shall bring thee into the land of the Canaanites, and the Hittites, and the Amorites, and the Hivites, and the Jebusites, which he sware unto thy fathers to give thee, a land flowing with milk and honey, that thou shalt keep this service in this month.

⁶Seven days thou shalt eat unleavened bread, and in the seventh day *shall be* a feast to the LORD.

⁷Unleavened bread shall be eaten seven days; and there shall no leavened bread be seen with thee, neither shall there be leaven seen with thee in all thy quarters.

⁸And thou shalt shew thy son in that day, saying, *This is done* because of that *which* the LORD did unto me when I came forth out of Egypt.

⁹And it shall be for a sign unto thee upon thine hand, and for a memorial between thine eyes, that the LORD'S law may be in thy mouth: for with a strong hand hath the LORD brought thee out of Egypt.

¹⁰Thou shalt therefore keep this ordinance in his season from year to year.

¹¹And it shall be when the LORD shall bring thee into the land of the Canaanites, as he sware unto thee and to thy fathers, and shall give it thee,

¹²That thou shalt set apart unto the LORD all that openeth the matrix, and every firstling that cometh of a beast which thou hast; the males *shall be* the LORD'S.

¹³And every firstling of an ass thou shalt redeem with a lamb; and if thou wilt not redeem *it*, then thou shalt break his neck: and all the firstborn of man amongst thy children shalt thou redeem.

¹⁴And it shall be when thy son asketh thee in time to come, saying, What *is* this? that thou shalt say unto him, By strength of hand the LORD brought us out from Egypt, from the house of bondage:

¹⁵And it came to pass, when Pharaoh would hardly let us go, that the LORD slew all the firstborn in the land of Egypt, both the firstborn of man, and the firstborn of beast: therefore I sacrifice to the LORD all that openeth the matrix, being males; but all the firstborn of my children I redeem.

¹⁶And it shall be for a token upon thine hand, and for frontlets between thine eyes: for by strength of hand the LORD brought us forth out of Egypt.

¹⁷ ¶ And it came to pass, when Pharaoh had let the people go, that God led them not *through* the way of the land of the Philistines, although that *was* near; for God said, Lest peradventure the people repent when they see war, and they return to Egypt:

¹⁸But God led the people about, *through* the way of the wilderness of the Red sea: and the

Amplified Bible

⁴This day you go forth in the month Abib.

⁵And when the Lord brings you into the land of the Canaanites, Hittites, Amorites, Hivites, and Jebusites, which He promised *and* swore to your fathers to give you, a land flowing with milk and honey [a land of plenty], you shall keep this service in this month.

⁶Seven days you shall eat unleavened bread and the seventh day shall be a feast to the Lord.

⁷Unleavened bread shall be eaten for seven days; no leavened bread shall be seen with you, neither shall there be leaven in all your territory.

⁸You shall explain to your son on that day, This is done because of what the Lord did for me when I came out of Egypt.

⁹It shall be as a sign to you upon your hand and as a memorial between your eyes, that the law of the Lord may be in your mouth; for with a strong hand the Lord has brought you out of Egypt.

¹⁰You shall therefore keep this ordinance at this time from year to year.

¹¹And when the Lord brings you into the land of the Canaanites, as He promised *and* swore to you and your fathers, and shall give it to you,

¹²You shall set apart to the Lord all that first opens the womb. All the firstlings of your livestock that are males shall be the Lord's.

¹³Every firstborn of a donkey you shall redeem by [substituting for it] a lamb, or if you will not redeem it, then you shall break its neck; and every firstborn among your sons shall you redeem.

¹⁴And when, in time to come, your son asks you, What does this mean? You shall say to him, By strength of hand the Lord brought us out from Egypt, from the house of bondage *and* bondmen.

¹⁵For when Pharaoh stubbornly refused to let us go, the Lord slew all the firstborn in the land of Egypt, both the firstborn of man and of livestock. Therefore I sacrifice to the Lord all the males that first open the womb; but all the firstborn of my sons I redeem.

¹⁶And it shall be as a reminder upon your hand or as frontlets between your eyes, for by a strong hand the Lord brought us out of Egypt.

¹⁷When Pharaoh let the people go, God led them not by way of the land of the Philistines, although that was nearer; for God said, Lest the people change their purpose when they see war and return to Egypt.

¹⁸But God led the people around by way of the wilderness toward the Red Sea. And the Is-

King James Version

children of Israel went up harnessed out of the land of Egypt.

¹⁹And Moses took the bones of Joseph with him: for he had straitly sworn the children of Israel, saying, God will surely visit you; and ye shall carry up my bones away hence with you.

²⁰And they took their journey from Succoth, and encamped in Etham, in the edge of the wilderness.

²¹And the LORD went before them by day in a pillar of a cloud, to lead them the way; and by night in a pillar of fire, to give them light; to go by day and night:

²²He took not away the pillar of the cloud by day, nor the pillar of fire by night, *from* before the people.

14 And the LORD spake unto Moses, saying, ²Speak unto the children of Israel, that they turn and encamp before Pi-hahiroth, between Migdol and the sea, over against Baal-zephon: before it shall ye encamp by the sea.

³For Pharaoh will say of the children of Israel, They *are* entangled in the land, the wilderness hath shut them in.

⁴And I will harden Pharaoh's heart, that he shall follow after them; and I will be honoured upon Pharaoh, and upon all his host; that the Egyptians may know that I *am* the LORD. And they did so.

⁵And it was told the king of Egypt that the people fled: and the heart of Pharaoh and of his servants was turned against the people, and they said, Why have we done this, that we have let Israel go from serving us?

⁶And he made ready his chariot, and took his people with him:

⁷And he took six hundred chosen chariots, and all the chariots of Egypt, and captains over every one of them.

⁸And the LORD hardened the heart of Pharaoh king of Egypt, and he pursued after the children of Israel: and the children of Israel went out with a high hand.

⁹But the Egyptians pursued after them (all the horses *and* chariots of Pharaoh, and his horsemen, and his army) and overtook them encamping by the sea, beside Pi-hahiroth, before Baal-zephon.

¹⁰ ¶ And when Pharaoh drew nigh, the children of Israel lift up their eyes, and behold, the Egyptians marched after them; and they were sore afraid: and the children of Israel cried out unto the LORD.

¹¹And they said unto Moses, Because *there were* no graves in Egypt, hast thou taken us

Amplified Bible

raelites went up marshaled [in ranks] out of the land of Egypt.

¹⁹And Moses took the bones of Joseph with him, for [Joseph] had strictly sworn the Israelites, saying, Surely God will be with you, and you must carry my bones away from here with you.

²⁰They journeyed from Succoth and encamped at Etham on the edge of the wilderness.

²¹The Lord went before them by day in a pillar of cloud to lead them along the way and by night in a pillar of fire to give them light, that they might travel by day and by night.

²²The pillar of cloud by day and the pillar of fire by night did not depart from before the people.

14 AND THE Lord said to Moses, ²Tell the Israelites to turn back and encamp before Pi-hahiroth, between Migdol and the [Red] Sea, before ᵃBaal-zephon. You shall encamp opposite it by the sea.

³For Pharaoh will say of the Israelites, They are entangled in the land; the wilderness has shut them in.

⁴I will harden (make stubborn, strong) Pharaoh's heart, that he will pursue them, and I will gain honor *and* glory over Pharaoh and all his host, and the Egyptians shall know that I am the Lord. And they did so.

⁵It was told the king of Egypt that the people had fled; and the heart of Pharaoh and of his servants was changed toward the people, and they said, What is this we have done? We have let Israel go from serving us!

⁶And he made ready his chariots and took his army,

⁷And took 600 chosen chariots and all the other chariots of Egypt, with officers over all of them.

⁸The Lord made hard *and* strong the heart of Pharaoh king of Egypt, and he pursued the Israelites, for [they] left proudly *and* defiantly.

⁹The Egyptians pursued them, all the horses and chariots of Pharaoh and his horsemen and his army, and overtook them encamped at the [Red] Sea by Pi-hahiroth, in front of Baal-zephon.

¹⁰When Pharaoh drew near, the Israelites looked up, and behold, the Egyptians were marching after them; and the Israelites were exceedingly frightened and cried out to the Lord.

¹¹And they said to Moses, Is it because there are no graves in Egypt that you have taken us

AMP notes: ᵃ Melvin Grove Kyle has said that travelers who follow the coast of the Red Sea along the line of the exodus need no other guidebook than the Bible. The whole topography corresponds to that mentioned in the Biblical account (Floyd E. Hamilton, *The Basis of Christian Faith*).

King James Version

away to die in the wilderness? wherefore hast thou dealt thus with us, to carry us forth out of Egypt?

¹²*Is* not this the word that we did tell thee in Egypt, saying, Let us alone, that we may serve the Egyptians? For *it had been* better for us to serve the Egyptians, than that we should die in the wilderness.

¹³And Moses said unto the people, Fear ye not, stand still, and see the salvation of the LORD, which he will shew to you to day: for the Egyptians whom ye have seen to day, ye shall see them again no more for ever.

¹⁴The LORD shall fight for you, and ye shall hold your peace.

¹⁵And the LORD said unto Moses, Wherefore criest thou unto me? speak unto the children of Israel, that they go forward:

¹⁶But lift thou up thy rod, and stretch out thine hand over the sea, and divide it: and the children of Israel shall go on dry *ground* through the midst of the sea.

¹⁷And I, behold, I will harden the hearts of the Egyptians, and they shall follow them: and I will get me honour upon Pharaoh, and upon all his host, upon his chariots, and upon his horsemen.

¹⁸And the Egyptians shall know that I *am* the LORD, when I have gotten me honour upon Pharaoh, upon his chariots, and upon his horsemen.

¹⁹And the angel of God, which went before the camp of Israel, removed and went behind them; and the pillar of the cloud went from before their face, and stood behind them:

²⁰And it came between the camp of the Egyptians and the camp of Israel; and it was a cloud and darkness *to them*, but it gave light by night *to these:* so that the one came not near the other all the night.

²¹ ¶ And Moses stretched out his hand over the sea; and the LORD caused the sea to go *back* by a strong east wind all *that* night, and made the sea dry *land*, and the waters were divided.

²²And the children of Israel went into the midst of the sea upon the dry *ground:* and the waters *were* a wall unto them on their right hand, and on their left.

²³And the Egyptians pursued, and went in after them to the midst of the sea, *even* all Pharaoh's horses, his chariots, and his horsemen.

²⁴And it came to pass, that in the morning watch the LORD looked unto the host of the Egyptians through the pillar of fire and of the cloud, and troubled the host of the Egyptians,

²⁵And took off their chariot wheels, that they drave them heavily: so that the Egyptians said, Let us flee from the face of Israel; for the LORD fighteth for them against the Egyptians.

²⁶And the LORD said unto Moses, Stretch out

Amplified Bible

away to die in the wilderness? Why have you treated us this way and brought us out of Egypt?

¹²Did we not tell you in Egypt, Let us alone; let us serve the Egyptians? For it would have been better for us to serve the Egyptians than to die in the wilderness.

¹³Moses told the people, Fear not; stand still (firm, confident, undismayed) and see the salvation of the Lord which He will work for you today. For the Egyptians you have seen today you shall never see again.

¹⁴The Lord will fight for you, and you shall hold your peace *and* remain at rest.

¹⁵The Lord said to Moses, Why do you cry to Me? Tell the people of Israel to go forward!

¹⁶Lift up your rod and stretch out your hand over the sea and divide it, and the Israelites shall go on dry ground through the midst of the sea.

¹⁷And I, behold, I will harden (make stubborn and strong) the hearts of the Egyptians, and they shall go [into the sea] after them; and I will gain honor over Pharaoh and all his host, his chariots, and horsemen.

¹⁸The Egyptians shall know *and* realize that I am the Lord when I have gained honor *and* glory over Pharaoh, his chariots, and his horsemen.

¹⁹And the ᵃAngel of God Who went before the host of Israel moved and went behind them; and the pillar of the cloud went from before them and stood behind them,

²⁰Coming between the host of Egypt and the host of Israel. It was a cloud and darkness to the Egyptians, but it gave light by night to the Israelites; and the one host did not come near the other all night.

²¹Then Moses stretched out his hand over the sea, and the Lord caused the sea to go back by a strong east wind all that night and made the sea dry land; and the waters were divided.

²²And the Israelites went into the midst of the sea on dry ground, the waters being a wall to them on their right hand and on their left.

²³The Egyptians pursued and went in after them into the midst of the sea, even all Pharaoh's horses, his chariots, and his horsemen.

²⁴And in the morning watch the Lord through the pillar of fire and cloud looked down on the host of the Egyptians and discomfited [them],

²⁵And bound (clogged, took off) their chariot wheels, making them drive heavily; and the Egyptians said, Let us flee from the face of Israel, for the Lord fights for them against the Egyptians!

²⁶Then the Lord said to Moses, Stretch out

AMP notes: ᵃ See footnote on Gen. 16:7; here the "Angel of God" is associated with the cloud (Exod. 13:21).

King James Version

thine hand over the sea, that the waters may come again upon the Egyptians, upon their chariots, and upon their horsemen.

²⁷And Moses stretched forth his hand over the sea, and the sea returned to his strength when the morning appeared; and the Egyptians fled against it; and the LORD overthrew the Egyptians in the midst of the sea.

²⁸And the waters returned, and covered the chariots, and the horsemen, and all the host of Pharaoh that came into the sea after them; there remained not so much as one of them.

²⁹But the children of Israel walked upon dry *land* in the midst of the sea; and the waters *were* a wall unto them on their right hand, and on their left.

³⁰Thus the LORD saved Israel that day out of the hand of the Egyptians; and Israel saw the Egyptians dead upon the sea shore.

³¹And Israel saw *that* great work which the LORD did upon the Egyptians: and the people feared the LORD, and believed the LORD, and his servant Moses.

15 Then sang Moses and the children of Israel this song unto the LORD, and spake, saying, I will sing unto the LORD, for he hath triumphed gloriously: the horse and his rider hath he thrown into the sea.

²The LORD *is* my strength and song, and he is become my salvation: he *is* my God, and I will prepare him a habitation; my father's God, and I will exalt him.

³The LORD *is* a man of war: the LORD *is* his name.

⁴Pharaoh's chariots and his host hath he cast into the sea: his chosen captains also are drowned in the Red sea.

⁵The depths have covered them: they sank into the bottom as a stone.

⁶Thy right hand, O LORD, is become glorious in power: thy right hand, O LORD, hath dashed in pieces the enemy.

⁷And in the greatness of thine excellency thou hast overthrown them that rose up against thee: thou sentest forth thy wrath, *which* consumed them as stubble.

⁸And with the blast of thy nostrils the waters were gathered together, the floods stood upright as a heap, *and* the depths were congealed in the heart of the sea.

⁹The enemy said, I will pursue, I will overtake, I will divide the spoil; my lust shall be satisfied upon them; I will draw my sword, my hand shall destroy them.

¹⁰Thou didst blow with thy wind, the sea covered them: they sank as lead in the mighty waters.

¹¹Who *is* like unto thee, O LORD, among the

Amplified Bible

your hand over the sea, that the waters may come again upon the Egyptians, upon their chariots and horsemen.

²⁷So Moses stretched forth his hand over the sea, and the sea returned to its strength *and* normal flow when the morning appeared; and the Egyptians fled into it [being met by it]; and the Lord overthrew the Egyptians *and* shook them off into the midst of the sea.

²⁸The waters returned and covered the chariots, the horsemen, and all the host of Pharaoh that pursued them; not even one of them remained.

²⁹But the Israelites walked on dry ground in the midst of the sea, the waters being a wall to them on their right hand and on their left.

³⁰Thus the Lord saved Israel that day from the hand of the Egyptians, and Israel saw the Egyptians dead upon the seashore.

³¹And Israel saw that great work which the Lord did against the Egyptians, and the people [reverently] feared the Lord and trusted in (relied on, remained steadfast to) the Lord and to His servant Moses.

15 THEN MOSES and the Israelites sang this song to the Lord, saying, I will sing to the Lord, for He has triumphed gloriously; the horse and his rider *or* its chariot has He thrown into the sea.

²The Lord is my Strength and my Song, and He has become my Salvation; this is my God, and I will praise Him, my father's God, and I will exalt Him.

³The Lord is a Man of War; the Lord is His name.

⁴Pharaoh's chariots and his host has He cast into the sea; his chosen captains also are sunk in the Red Sea.

⁵The floods cover them; they sank in the depths [clad in mail] like a stone.

⁶Your right hand, O Lord, is glorious in power; Your right hand, O Lord, shatters the enemy.

⁷In the greatness of Your majesty You overthrow those rising against You. You send forth Your fury; it consumes them like stubble.

⁸With the blast of Your nostrils the waters piled up, the floods stood fixed in a heap, the deeps congealed in the heart of the sea.

⁹The enemy said, I will pursue, I will overtake, I will divide the spoil; my desire shall be satisfied upon them; I will draw my sword, my hand shall destroy them.

¹⁰You [Lord] blew with Your wind, the sea covered them; [clad in mail] they sank as lead in the mighty waters.

¹¹Who is like You, O Lord, among the gods?

King James Version

gods? who *is* like thee, glorious in holiness, fearful *in* praises, doing wonders?

¹²Thou stretchedst out thy right hand, the earth swallowed them.

¹³Thou in thy mercy hast led forth the people *which* thou hast redeemed: thou hast guided *them* in thy strength unto thy holy habitation.

¹⁴The people shall hear, *and* be afraid: sorrow shall take hold on the inhabitants of Palestina.

¹⁵Then the dukes of Edom shall be amazed; the mighty men of Moab, trembling shall take hold upon them; all the inhabitants of Canaan shall melt away.

¹⁶Fear and dread shall fall upon them; by the greatness of thine arm they shall be *as* still as a stone; till thy people pass over, O LORD, till the people pass over, *which* thou hast purchased.

¹⁷Thou shalt bring them in, and plant them in the mountain of thine inheritance, *in* the place, O LORD, *which* thou hast made for thee to dwell in, *in* the Sanctuary, O Lord, *which* thy hands have established.

¹⁸The LORD shall reign for ever and ever.

¹⁹ ¶ For the horse of Pharaoh went in with his chariots and with his horsemen into the sea, and the LORD brought again the waters of the sea upon them; but the children of Israel went on dry *land* in the midst of the sea.

²⁰And Miriam the prophetess, the sister of Aaron, took a timbrel in her hand; and all the women went out after her with timbrels and with dances.

²¹And Miriam answered them, Sing ye to the LORD, for he hath triumphed gloriously; the horse and his rider hath he thrown into the sea.

²² ¶ So Moses brought Israel from the Red sea, and they went out into the wilderness of Shur; and they went three days in the wilderness, and found no water.

²³And when they came to Marah, they could not drink of the waters of Marah, for they *were* bitter: therefore the name of it was called Marah.

²⁴And the people murmured against Moses, saying, What shall we drink?

²⁵And he cried unto the LORD; and the LORD shewed him a tree, *which* when he had cast into the waters, the waters were made sweet: there he made for them a statute and an ordinance, and there he proved them,

²⁶And said, If thou wilt diligently hearken to the voice of the LORD thy God, and wilt do that which is right in his sight, and wilt give ear to his commandments, and keep all his statutes, I will put none of *these* diseases upon thee, which I have brought upon the Egyptians: for I *am* the LORD that healeth thee.

Amplified Bible

Who is like You, glorious in holiness, awesome in splendor, doing wonders?

¹²You stretched out Your right hand, the earth's [sea] swallowed them.

¹³You in Your mercy *and* loving-kindness have led forth the people whom You have redeemed; You have guided them in Your strength to Your holy habitation.

¹⁴The peoples have heard of it; they tremble; pangs have taken hold on the inhabitants of Philistia.

¹⁵Now the chiefs of Edom are dismayed; the mighty men of Moab [renowned for strength], trembling takes hold of them; all the inhabitants of Canaan have melted away—little by little.

¹⁶Terror and dread fall upon them; because of the greatness of Your arm they are as still as a stone—till Your people pass by *and* over [into Canaan], O Lord, till the people pass by whom You have purchased.

¹⁷You will bring them in [to the land] and plant them on Your own mountain, the place, O Lord, You have made for Your dwelling, the sanctuary, O Lord, which Your hands have established.

¹⁸The Lord will reign forever and ever.

¹⁹For the horses of Pharaoh went with his chariots and horsemen into the sea, and the Lord brought back the waters of the sea upon them, but the Israelites walked on dry ground in the midst of the sea.

²⁰Then Miriam the prophetess, the sister of Aaron, took a timbrel in her hand, and all the women went out after her with timbrels and dancing.

²¹And Miriam responded to them, Sing to the Lord, for He has triumphed gloriously *and* is highly exalted; the horse and his rider He has thrown into the sea.

²²Then Moses led Israel onward from the Red Sea and they went into the Wilderness of Shur; they went three days [thirty-three miles] in the wilderness and found no water.

²³When they came to Marah, they could not drink its waters for they were bitter; therefore it was named Marah [bitterness].

²⁴The people murmured against Moses, saying, What shall we drink?

²⁵And he cried to the Lord, and the Lord showed him a tree which he cast into the waters, and the waters were made sweet. There [the Lord] made for them a statute and an ordinance, and there He proved them,

²⁶Saying, If you will diligently hearken to the voice of the Lord your God and will do what is right in His sight, and will listen to *and* obey His commandments and keep all His statutes, I will put none of the diseases upon you which I brought upon the Egyptians, for I am the Lord Who heals you.

King James Version

27And they came to Elim, where *were* twelve wells of water, and threescore and ten palm trees: and they encamped there by the waters.

16 And they took their journey from Elim, and all the congregation of the children of Israel came unto the wilderness of Sin, which *is* between Elim and Sinai, on the fifteenth day of the second month after their departing out of the land of Egypt.

2And the whole congregation of the children of Israel murmured against Moses and Aaron in the wilderness:

3And the children of Israel said unto them, Would to God we had died by the hand of the LORD in the land of Egypt, when we sat by the flesh pots, *and* when we did eat bread to the full; for ye have brought us forth into this wilderness, to kill this whole assembly with hunger.

4Then said the LORD unto Moses, Behold, I will rain bread from heaven for you; and the people shall go out and gather a certain rate every day, that I may prove them, whether they will walk in my law, or no.

5And it shall come to pass, that on the sixth day they shall prepare *that* which they bring in; and it shall be twice as much as they gather daily.

6And Moses and Aaron said unto all the children of Israel, At even, then ye shall know that the LORD hath brought you out from the land of Egypt:

7And in the morning, then ye shall see the glory of the LORD; for that he heareth your murmurings against the LORD: and what *are* we, that ye murmur against us?

8And Moses said, *This shall be,* when the LORD shall give you in the evening flesh to eat, and in the morning bread to the full; for that the LORD heareth your murmurings which ye murmur against him: and what *are* we? your murmurings *are* not against us, but against the LORD.

9And Moses spake unto Aaron, Say unto all the congregation of the children of Israel, Come near before the LORD: for he hath heard your murmurings.

10And it came to pass, as Aaron spake unto the whole congregation of the children of Israel, that they looked toward the wilderness, and behold, the glory of the LORD appeared in the cloud.

11And the LORD spake unto Moses, saying,

12I have heard the murmurings of the children of Israel: speak unto them, saying, At even ye shall eat flesh, and in the morning ye shall be filled *with* bread; and ye shall know that I *am* the LORD your God.

13And it came to pass, that at even the quails came up, and covered the camp: and in the morning the dew lay round about the host.

Amplified Bible

27And they came to Elim, where there were twelve springs of water and seventy palm trees; and they encamped there by the waters.

16 THEY SET out from Elim, and all the congregation of Israel came to the Wilderness of Sin, which is between Elim and Sinai, on the fifteenth day of the second month after they left the land of Egypt.

2And the whole congregation of Israel murmured against Moses and Aaron in the wilderness,

3And said to them, Would that we had died by the hand of the Lord in the land of Egypt, when we sat by the fleshpots and ate bread to the full; for you have brought us out into this wilderness to kill this whole assembly with hunger.

4Then the Lord said to Moses, Behold, I will rain bread from the heavens for you; and the people shall go out and gather a day's portion every day, that I may prove them, whether they will walk in My law or not.

5On the sixth day they shall prepare to bring in twice as much as they gather daily.

6So Moses and Aaron said to all Israel, At evening you shall know that the Lord has brought you out from the land of Egypt,

7And in the morning you shall see the glory of the Lord, for He hears your murmurings against the Lord. For what are we, that you murmur against us?

8And Moses said, [This will happen] when the Lord gives you in the evening flesh to eat and in the morning bread to the full, because the Lord has heard your grumblings which you murmur against Him; what are we? Your murmurings are not against us, but against the Lord.

9And Moses said to Aaron, Say to all the congregation of Israel, Come near before the Lord, for He has heard your murmurings.

10And as Aaron spoke to the whole congregation of Israel, they looked toward the wilderness, and behold, the glory of the Lord appeared in the cloud!

11The Lord said to Moses,

12I have heard the murmurings of the Israelites; speak to them, saying, At twilight you shall eat meat, and between the two evenings you shall be filled with bread; and you shall know that I am the Lord your God.

13In the evening quails came up and covered the camp; and in the morning the dew lay round about the camp.

King James Version

¹⁴And when the dew that lay was gone up, behold, upon the face of the wilderness *there lay* a small round thing, *as* small as the hoar frost on the ground.

¹⁵And when the children of Israel saw *it*, they said one to another, It *is* manna: for they wist not what it *was*. And Moses said unto them, This *is* the bread which the LORD hath given you to eat.

¹⁶This *is* the thing which the LORD hath commanded, Gather of it every man according to his eating, an omer for every man, *according to* the number of your persons; take ye every man for *them* which *are* in his tents.

¹⁷And the children of Israel did so, and gathered, some more, some less.

¹⁸And when they did mete *it* with an omer, he that gathered much had nothing over, and he that gathered little had no lack; they gathered every man according to his eating.

¹⁹And Moses said, Let no man leave of it till the morning.

²⁰Notwithstanding they hearkened not unto Moses; but some of them left of it until the morning, and it bred worms, and stank: and Moses was wroth with them.

²¹And they gathered it every morning, every man according to his eating: and when the sun waxed hot, it melted.

²²And it came to pass, *that* on the sixth day they gathered twice as much bread, two omers for one *man:* and all the rulers of the congregation came and told Moses.

²³And he said unto them, This *is that* which the LORD hath said, To morrow *is* the rest of the holy sabbath unto the LORD: bake *that* which you will bake *to day,* and seethe that ye will seethe; and that which remaineth over lay up for you to be kept until the morning.

²⁴And they laid it up till the morning, as Moses bade: and it did not stink, neither was there any worm therein.

²⁵And Moses said, Eat that to day; for to day *is* a sabbath unto the LORD: to day ye shall not find it in the field.

²⁶Six days ye shall gather it; but on the seventh day, *which is* the sabbath, in it there shall be none.

²⁷And it came to pass, *that* there went out *some* of the people on the seventh day for to gather, and they found none.

²⁸And the LORD said unto Moses, How long refuse ye to keep my commandments and my laws?

²⁹See, for that the LORD hath given you the sabbath, therefore he giveth you on the sixth day the bread of two days; abide ye every man in his place, let no man go out of his place on the seventh day.

³⁰So the people rested on the seventh day.

Amplified Bible

¹⁴And when the dew had gone, behold, upon the face of the wilderness there lay a fine, round *and* flakelike thing, as fine as hoarfrost on the ground.

¹⁵When the Israelites saw it, they said one to another, Manna [What is it?]. For they did not know what it was. And Moses said to them, This is the bread which the Lord has given you to eat.

¹⁶This is what the Lord has commanded: Let every man gather of it as much as he will need, an omer for each person, according to the number of your persons; take it, every man for those in his tent.

¹⁷The [people] did so, and gathered, some more, some less.

¹⁸When they measured it with an omer, he who gathered much had nothing over, and he who gathered little had no lack; each gathered according to his need.

¹⁹Moses said, Let none of it be left until morning.

²⁰But they did not listen to Moses; some of them left of it until morning, and it bred worms, became foul, *and* stank; and Moses was angry with them.

²¹They gathered it every morning, each as much as he needed, for when the sun became hot it melted.

²²And on the sixth day they gathered twice as much bread, two omers for each person; and all the leaders of the congregation came and told Moses.

²³He said to them, The Lord has said, Tomorrow is a solemn rest, a holy Sabbath to the Lord; bake and boil what you will bake and boil today; and all that remains over put aside for you to keep until morning.

²⁴They laid it aside till morning, as Moses told them; and it did not become foul, neither was it wormy.

²⁵Moses said, Eat that today, for today is a Sabbath to the Lord. Today you shall find none in the field.

²⁶Six days you shall gather it, but on the seventh day, the Sabbath, there shall be none.

²⁷On the seventh day some of the people went out to gather, but they found none.

²⁸The Lord said to Moses, How long do you [people] refuse to keep My commandments and My laws?

²⁹See, the Lord has given you the Sabbath; therefore He gives you on the sixth day the bread for two days; let every man remain in his place; let no man leave his place on the seventh day.

³⁰So the people rested on the seventh day.

King James Version

31And the house of Israel called the name thereof Manna: and it *was* like coriander seed, white; and the taste of it *was* like wafers *made* with honey.

32And Moses said, This *is* the thing which the LORD commandeth, Fill an omer of it to be kept for your generations; that they may see the bread wherewith I have fed you in the wilderness, when I brought you forth from the land of Egypt.

33And Moses said unto Aaron, Take a pot, and put an omer full of manna therein, and lay it up before the LORD, to be kept for your generations.

34As the LORD commanded Moses, so Aaron laid it up before the Testimony, to be kept.

35And the children of Israel did eat manna forty years, until they came to a land inhabited; they did eat manna, until they came unto the borders of the land of Canaan.

36Now an omer *is* the tenth *part* of an ephah.

17 And all the congregation of the children of Israel journeyed from the wilderness of Sin, after their journeys, according to the commandment of the LORD, and pitched in Rephidim: and *there was* no water for the people to drink.

2Wherefore the people did chide with Moses, and said, Give us water that we may drink. And Moses said unto them, Why chide you with me? wherefore do ye tempt the LORD?

3And the people thirsted there for water; and the people murmured against Moses, and said, Wherefore *is* this *that* thou hast brought us up out of Egypt, to kill us and our children and our cattle with thirst?

4And Moses cried unto the LORD, saying, What shall I do unto this people? they be almost ready to stone me.

5And the LORD said unto Moses, Go on before the people, and take with thee of the elders of Israel; and thy rod, wherewith thou smotest the river, take in thine hand, and go.

6Behold, I will stand before thee there upon the rock in Horeb; and thou shalt smite the rock, and there shall come water out of it, that the people may drink. And Moses did so in the sight of the elders of Israel.

7And he called the name of the place Massah, and Meribah, because of the chiding of the children of Israel, and because they tempted the LORD, saying, Is the LORD amongst us, or not?

8 ¶ Then came Amalek, and fought with Israel in Rephidim.

9And Moses said unto Joshua, Choose us out men, and go out, fight with Amalek: to morrow I will stand on the top of the hill with the rod of God in mine hand.

10So Joshua did as Moses had said to him, and

Amplified Bible

31The house of Israel called the bread manna; it was like coriander seed, white, and it tasted like wafers made with honey.

32Moses said, This is what the Lord commands, Take an omer of it to be kept throughout your generations, that they may see the bread with which I fed you in the wilderness when I brought you out of the land of Egypt.

33And Moses said to Aaron, Take a pot and put an omer of manna in it, and lay it up before the Lord, to be kept throughout your generations.

34As the Lord commanded Moses, Aaron laid it up before the Testimony to be kept [in the ark].

35And the Israelites ate manna forty years, until they came to a habitable land; they ate the manna until they came to the border of the land of Canaan.

36(Now an omer is the tenth of an ephah.)

17 ALL THE congregation of the Israelites moved on from the Wilderness of Sin by stages, according to the commandment of the Lord, and encamped at Rephidim; but there was no water for the people to drink.

2Therefore, the people contended with Moses, and said, Give us water that we may drink. And Moses said to them, Why do you find fault with me? Why do you tempt the Lord *and* try His patience?

3But the people thirsted there for water, and the people murmured against Moses, and said, Why did you bring us up out of Egypt to kill us and our children and livestock with thirst?

4So Moses cried to the Lord, What shall I do with this people? They are almost ready to stone me.

5And the Lord said to Moses, Pass on before the people, and take with you some of the elders of Israel; and take in your hand the rod with which you smote the river [Nile], and go.

6Behold, I will stand before you there on the rock at [Mount] Horeb; and you shall strike the rock, and water shall come out of it, that the people may drink. And Moses did so in the sight of the elders of Israel.

7He called the place Massah [proof] and Meribah [contention] because of the faultfinding of the Israelites and because they tempted *and* tried the patience of the Lord, saying, Is the Lord among us or not?

8Then came Amalek [descendants of Esau] and fought with Israel at Rephidim.

9And Moses said to Joshua, Choose us out men and go out, fight with Amalek. Tomorrow I will stand on the top of the hill with the rod of God in my hand.

10So Joshua did as Moses said and fought with

King James Version

fought with Amalek: and Moses, Aaron, and Hur went up *to* the top of the hill.

¹¹And it came to pass, when Moses held up his hand, that Israel prevailed: and when he let down his hand, Amalek prevailed.

¹²But Moses' hands *were* heavy; and they took a stone, and put *it* under him, and he sat thereon; and Aaron and Hur stayed up his hands, the one on the one side, and the other on the other side; and his hands were steady until the going down of the sun.

¹³And Joshua discomfited Amalek and his people with the edge of the sword.

¹⁴And the LORD said unto Moses, Write this *for* a memorial in a book, and rehearse *it* in the ears of Joshua: for I will utterly put out the remembrance of Amalek from under heaven.

¹⁵And Moses built an altar, and called the name of it Jehovah-nissi:

¹⁶For he said, Because the LORD hath sworn *that* the LORD *will have* war with Amalek from generation *to* generation.

18 When Jethro, the priest of Midian, Moses' father in law, heard of all that God had done for Moses, and for Israel his people, *and* that the LORD had brought Israel out of Egypt;

²Then Jethro, Moses' father in law, took Zipporah, Moses' wife, after he had sent her *back,*

³And her two sons; of which the name of the one *was* Gershom; for he said, I have been an alien in a strange land:

⁴And the name of the other *was* Eliezer; for the God of my father, *said he, was* mine help, and delivered me from the sword of Pharaoh:

⁵And Jethro, Moses' father in law, came with his sons and his wife unto Moses into the wilderness, where he encamped *at* the mount of God:

⁶And he said unto Moses, I thy father in law Jethro am come unto thee, and thy wife, and her two sons with her.

⁷And Moses went out to meet his father in law, and did obeisance, and kissed him; and they asked each other of *their* welfare; and they came into the tent.

⁸And Moses told his father in law all that the LORD had done unto Pharaoh and to the Egyptians for Israel's sake, *and* all the travail that had come upon them by the way, and *how* the LORD delivered them.

⁹And Jethro rejoiced for all the goodness which the LORD had done to Israel, whom he had delivered out of the hand of the Egyptians.

¹⁰And Jethro said, Blessed *be* the LORD, who hath delivered you out of the hand of the Egyp-

Amplified Bible

Amalek; and Moses, Aaron, and Hur went up to the hilltop.

¹¹When Moses held up his hand, Israel prevailed; and when he lowered his hand, Amalek prevailed.

¹²But Moses' hands were heavy *and* grew weary. So [the other men] took a stone and put it under him and he sat on it. Then Aaron and Hur held up his hands, one on one side and one on the other side; so his hands were steady until the going down of the sun.

¹³And Joshua mowed down *and* disabled Amalek and his people with the sword.

¹⁴And the Lord said to Moses, Write this for a memorial in the book and rehearse it in the ears of Joshua, that I will utterly blot out the remembrance of Amalek from under the heavens.

¹⁵And Moses built an altar and called the name of it, The Lord is my Banner;

¹⁶And he said, Because [theirs] is a hand against the throne of the Lord, the Lord will have war with Amalek from generation to generation.

18 NOW JETHRO [Reuel], the priest of Midian, Moses' father-in-law, heard of all that God had done for Moses and for Israel His people, and that the Lord had brought Israel out of Egypt.

²Then Jethro, Moses' father-in-law, took Zipporah, Moses' wife, after Moses had sent her back [to her father],

³And her two sons, of whom the name of the one was Gershom [expulsion, or a stranger there], for Moses said, I have been an alien in a strange land;

⁴And the name of the other was Eliezer [God is help], for the God of my father, said Moses, was my help, and delivered me from the sword of Pharaoh.

⁵And Jethro, Moses' father-in-law, came with Moses' sons and his wife to the wilderness where he was encamped at the mount of God [Horeb, or Sinai].

⁶And he said [in a message] to Moses, I, your father-in-law Jethro, am come to you and your wife and her two sons with her.

⁷And Moses went out to meet his father-in-law and bowed in homage and kissed him; and each asked the other of his welfare and they came into the tent.

⁸Moses told his father-in-law all the Lord had done to Pharaoh and the Egyptians for Israel's sake and all the hardships that had come upon them by the way and how the Lord delivered them.

⁹Jethro rejoiced for all the goodness the Lord had done to Israel in that He had delivered them out of the hand of the Egyptians.

¹⁰Jethro said, Blessed be the Lord, Who has delivered you out of the hand of the Egyptians

King James Version

tians, and out of the hand of Pharaoh, who hath delivered the people from under the hand of the Egyptians.

¹¹Now I know that the LORD *is* greater than all gods: for in the thing wherein they dealt proudly *he was* above them.

¹²And Jethro, Moses' father in law, took a burnt offering and sacrifices for God: and Aaron came, and all the elders of Israel, to eat bread with Moses' father in law before God.

¹³ ¶ And it came to pass on the morrow, that Moses sat to judge the people: and the people stood by Moses from the morning unto the evening.

¹⁴And when Moses' father in law saw all that he did to the people, he said, What *is* this thing that thou doest to the people? why sittest thou thyself alone, and all the people stand by thee from morning unto even?

¹⁵And Moses said unto his father in law, Because the people come unto me to inquire of God:

¹⁶When they have a matter, they come unto me; and I judge between one and another, and I do make *them* know the statutes of God, and his laws.

¹⁷And Moses' father in law said unto him, The thing that thou doest *is* not good.

¹⁸Thou wilt surely wear away, both thou, and this people that *is* with thee: for *this* thing *is* too heavy for thee; thou art not able to perform it thyself alone.

¹⁹Hearken now unto my voice, I will give thee counsel, and God shall be with thee: be thou for the people to God-ward, that thou mayest bring the causes unto God:

²⁰And thou shalt teach them ordinances and laws, and shalt shew them the way *wherein* they must walk, and the work that they must do.

²¹Moreover thou shalt provide out of all the people able men, such as fear God, men of truth, hating covetousness; and place *such* over them, *to be* rulers of thousands, *and* rulers of hundreds, rulers of fifties, and rulers of tens:

²²And let them judge the people at all seasons: and it shall be, *that* every great matter they shall bring unto thee, but every small matter they shall judge: so shall it be easier for thyself, and they shall bear *the burden* with thee.

²³If thou shalt do this thing, and God command thee *so*, then thou shalt be able to endure, and all this people shall also go to their place in peace.

²⁴So Moses hearkened to the voice of his father in law, and did all that he had said.

²⁵And Moses chose able men out of all Israel, and made them heads over the people, rulers of thousands, rulers of hundreds, rulers of fifties, and rulers of tens.

²⁶And they judged the people at all seasons:

Amplified Bible

and out of the hand of Pharaoh, Who has delivered the people [Israel] from under the hand of the Egyptians.

¹¹Now I know that the Lord is greater than all gods. Yes, in the [very] thing in which they dealt proudly [He showed Himself infinitely superior to all their gods].

¹²And Jethro, Moses' father-in-law, took a burnt offering and sacrifices [to offer] to God, and Aaron came with all the elders of Israel to eat bread with Moses' father-in-law before God.

¹³Next day Moses sat to judge the people, and the people stood around Moses from morning till evening.

¹⁴When Moses' father-in-law saw all that he was doing for the people, he said, What is this that you do for the people? Why do you sit alone, and all the people stand around you from morning till evening?

¹⁵Moses said to his father-in-law, Because the people come to me to inquire of God.

¹⁶When they have a dispute they come to me, and I judge between a man and his neighbor, and I make them know the statutes of God and His laws.

¹⁷Moses' father-in-law said to him, The thing that you are doing is not good.

¹⁸You will surely wear out both yourself and this people with you, for the thing is too heavy for you; you are not able to perform it all by yourself.

¹⁹Listen now to [me]; I will counsel you, and God will be with you. You shall represent the people before God, bringing their cases *and* causes to Him,

²⁰Teaching them the decrees and laws, showing them the way they must walk and the work they must do.

²¹Moreover, you shall choose able men from all the people—God-fearing men of truth who hate unjust gain—and place them over thousands, hundreds, fifties, and tens, to be their rulers.

²²And let them judge the people at all times; every great matter they shall bring to you, but every small matter they shall judge. So it will be easier for you, and they will bear the burden with you.

²³If you will do this, and God so commands you, you will be able to endure [the strain], and all these people also will go to their [tents] in peace.

²⁴So Moses listened to *and* heeded the voice of his father-in-law and did all that he had said.

²⁵Moses chose able men out of all Israel and made them heads over the people, rulers of thousands, of hundreds, of fifties, and of tens.

²⁶And they judged the people at all times; the

King James Version

the hard causes they brought unto Moses, but every small matter they judged themselves.

²⁷And Moses let his father in law depart; and he went his way into his own land.

19 In the third month, when the children of Israel were gone forth out of the land of Egypt, the same day came they *into* the wilderness of Sinai.

²For they were departed from Rephidim, and were come *to* the desert of Sinai, and had pitched in the wilderness; and there Israel camped before the mount.

³And Moses went up unto God, and the LORD called unto him out of the mountain, saying, Thus shalt thou say to the house of Jacob, and tell the children of Israel;

⁴Ye have seen what I did unto the Egyptians, and *how* I bare you on eagles' wings, and brought you unto myself.

⁵Now therefore, if ye will obey my voice indeed, and keep my covenant, then ye shall be a peculiar treasure unto me above all people: for all the earth *is* mine:

⁶And ye shall be unto me a kingdom of priests, and a holy nation. These *are* the words which thou shalt speak unto the children of Israel.

⁷And Moses came and called for the elders of the people, and laid before their faces all these words which the LORD commanded him.

⁸And all the people answered together, and said, All that the LORD hath spoken we will do. And Moses returned the words of the people unto the LORD.

⁹And the LORD said unto Moses, Lo, I come unto thee in a thick cloud, that the people may hear when I speak with thee, and believe thee for ever. And Moses told the words of the people unto the LORD.

¹⁰ ¶ And the LORD said unto Moses, Go unto the people, and sanctify them to day and to morrow, and let them wash their clothes,

¹¹And be ready against the third day: for the third day the LORD will come down in the sight of all the people upon mount Sinai.

¹²And thou shalt set bounds unto the people round about, saying, Take heed to yourselves, *that ye* go *not* up into the mount, or touch the border of it: whosoever toucheth the mount shall be surely put to death:

¹³There shall not a hand touch it, but he shall surely be stoned, or shot through; whether *it be* beast or man, it shall not live: when the trumpet soundeth long, they shall come up to the mount.

¹⁴And Moses went down from the mount unto the people, and sanctified the people; and they washed their clothes.

¹⁵And he said unto the people, Be ready against the third day: come not at *your* wives.

¹⁶And it came to pass on the third day in the

Amplified Bible

hard cases they brought to Moses, but every small matter they decided themselves.

²⁷Then Moses let his father-in-law depart, and he went his way into his own land.

19 IN THE third month after the Israelites left the land of Egypt, the same day, they came into the Wilderness of Sinai.

²When they had departed from Rephidim and had come to the Wilderness of Sinai, they encamped there before the mountain.

³And Moses went up to God, and the Lord called to him out of the mountain, Say this to the house of Jacob and tell the Israelites:

⁴You have seen what I did to the Egyptians, and how I bore you on eagles' wings and brought you to Myself.

⁵Now therefore, if you will obey My voice in truth and keep My covenant, then you shall be My own peculiar possession *and* treasure from among *and* above all peoples; for all the earth is Mine.

⁶And you shall be to Me a kingdom of priests, a holy nation [consecrated, set apart to the worship of God]. These are the words you shall speak to the Israelites.

⁷So Moses called for the elders of the people and told them all these words which the Lord commanded him.

⁸And all the people answered together, and said, All that the Lord has spoken we will do. And Moses reported the words of the people to the Lord.

⁹And the Lord said to Moses, Behold, I come to you in a thick cloud, that the people may hear when I speak with you and believe you *and* remain steadfast forever. Then Moses told the words of the people to the Lord.

¹⁰And the Lord said to Moses, Go and sanctify the people [set them apart for God] today and tomorrow, and let them wash their clothes

¹¹And be ready by the third day, for the third day the Lord will come down upon Mount Sinai [in the cloud] in the sight of all the people.

¹²And you shall set bounds for the people round about, saying, Take heed that you go not up into the mountain or touch the border of it. Whoever touches the mountain shall surely be put to death.

¹³No hand shall touch it [or the offender], but he shall surely be stoned or shot [with arrows]; whether beast or man, he shall not live. When the trumpet sounds a long blast, they shall come up to the mountain.

¹⁴So Moses went down from the mountain to the people and sanctified them [set them apart for God], and they washed their clothes.

¹⁵And he said to the people, Be ready by the day after tomorrow; do not go near a woman.

¹⁶The third morning there were thunders and

King James Version

morning, that there were thunders and lightnings, and a thick cloud upon the mount, and the voice of the trumpet exceeding loud; so that all the people that *was* in the camp trembled.

17And Moses brought forth the people out of the camp to meet with God; and they stood at the nether part of the mount.

18And mount Sinai was altogether on a smoke, because the LORD descended upon it in fire: and the smoke thereof ascended as the smoke of a furnace, and the whole mount quaked greatly.

19And when the voice of the trumpet sounded long, and waxed louder and louder, Moses spake, and God answered him by a voice.

20And the LORD came down upon mount Sinai, on the top of the mount: and the LORD called Moses *up* to the top of the mount; and Moses went up.

21And the LORD said unto Moses, Go down, charge the people, lest they break through unto the LORD to gaze, and many of them perish.

22And let the priests also, which come near to the LORD, sanctify themselves, lest the LORD break forth upon them.

23And Moses said unto the LORD, The people cannot come up to mount Sinai: for thou chargedst us, saying, Set bounds about the mount, and sanctify it.

24And the LORD said unto him, Away, get thee down, and thou shalt come up, thou, and Aaron with thee: but let not the priests and the people break through to come up unto the LORD, lest he break forth upon them.

25So Moses went down unto the people, and spake unto them.

20 And God spake all these words, saying, 2I *am* the LORD thy God, which have brought thee out of the land of Egypt, out of the house of bondage.

3Thou shalt have no other gods before me.

4Thou shalt not make unto thee *any* graven image, or any likeness *of any thing* that *is* in heaven above, or that *is* in the earth beneath, or that *is* in the water under the earth:

5Thou shalt not bow down thyself to them, nor serve them: for I the LORD thy God *am* a jealous God, visiting the iniquity of the fathers upon the children unto the third and fourth *generation* of them that hate me;

6And shewing mercy unto thousands of them that love me, and keep my commandments.

7Thou shalt not take the name of the LORD thy God in vain; for the LORD will not hold him guiltless that taketh his name in vain.

Amplified Bible

lightnings, and a thick cloud upon the mountain, and a very loud trumpet blast, so that all the people in the camp trembled.

17Then Moses brought the people from the camp to meet God, and they stood at the foot of the mountain.

18Mount Sinai was wrapped in smoke, for the Lord descended upon it in fire; its smoke ascended like that of a furnace, and the whole mountain quaked greatly.

19As the trumpet blast grew louder and louder, Moses spoke and God answered him with a voice.

20The Lord came down upon Mount Sinai to the top of the mountain, and the Lord called Moses to the top of the mountain, and Moses went up.

21The Lord said to Moses, Go down and warn the people, lest they break through to the Lord to gaze and many of them perish.

22And also let the priests, who come near to the Lord, sanctify (set apart) themselves [for God], lest the Lord break forth against them.

23And Moses said to the Lord, The people cannot come up to Mount Sinai, for You Yourself charged us, saying, Set bounds about the mountain and sanctify it [set it apart for God].

24Then the Lord said to him, Go, get down and you shall come up, you and Aaron with you; but let not the priests and the people break through to come up to the Lord, lest He break forth against them.

25So Moses went down to the people and told them.

20 THEN GOD spoke all these words: 2I am the Lord your God, Who has brought you out of the land of Egypt, out of the house of bondage.

3You shall have no other gods before or besides Me.

4You shall not make yourself any graven image [to worship it] or any likeness of anything that is in the heavens above, or that is in the earth beneath, or that is in the water under the earth;

5You shall not bow down yourself to them or serve them; for I the Lord your God am a jealous God, visiting the iniquity of the fathers upon the children to the third and fourth generation of those who hate Me,

6But showing mercy *and* steadfast love to a thousand generations of those who love Me and keep My commandments.

7You shall not use *or* repeat the name of the Lord your God in vain [that is, lightly or frivolously, in false affirmations or profanely]; for the Lord will not hold him guiltless who takes His name in vain.

King James Version

8Remember the sabbath day, to keep it holy.

9Six days shalt thou labour, and do all thy work:

10But the seventh day *is* the sabbath of the LORD thy God: *in it* thou shalt not do any work, thou, nor thy son, nor thy daughter, nor thy manservant, nor thy maidservant, nor thy cattle, nor thy stranger that *is* within thy gates:

11For *in* six days the LORD made heaven and earth, the sea, and all that in them *is,* and rested the seventh day: wherefore the LORD blessed the sabbath day, and hallowed it.

12Honour thy father and thy mother: that thy days may be long upon the land which the LORD thy God giveth thee.

13Thou shalt not kill.

14Thou shalt not commit adultery.

15Thou shalt not steal.

16Thou shalt not bear false witness against thy neighbour.

17Thou shalt not covet thy neighbour's house, thou shalt not covet thy neighbour's wife, nor his manservant, nor his maidservant, nor his ox, nor his ass, nor any thing that *is* thy neighbour's.

18 ¶ And all the people saw the thunderings, and the lightnings, and the noise of the trumpet, and the mountain smoking: and when the people saw *it,* they removed, and stood afar off.

19And they said unto Moses, Speak thou with us, and we will hear: but let not God speak with us, lest we die.

20And Moses said unto the people, Fear not: for God is come to prove you, and that his fear may be before your faces, that ye sin not.

21And the people stood afar off, and Moses drew near unto the thick darkness where God *was.*

22And the LORD said unto Moses, Thus thou shalt say unto the children of Israel, Ye have seen that I have talked with you from heaven.

23Ye shall not make with me gods of silver, neither shall ye make unto you gods of gold.

24An altar of earth thou shalt make unto me, and shalt sacrifice thereon thy burnt offerings, and thy peace offerings, thy sheep, and thine oxen: in all places where I record my name I will come unto thee, and I will bless thee.

25And if thou wilt make me an altar of stone,

Amplified Bible

8[Earnestly] remember the Sabbath day, to keep it holy (withdrawn from common employment and dedicated to God).

9Six days you shall labor and do all your work,

10But the seventh day is a Sabbath to the Lord your God; in it you shall not do any work, you, or your son, your daughter, your manservant, your maidservant, your domestic animals, or the sojourner within your gates.

11For in six days the Lord made the heavens and the earth, the sea, and all that is in them, and rested the seventh day. That is why the Lord blessed the Sabbath day and hallowed it [set it apart for His purposes].

12Regard (treat with honor, due obedience, and courtesy) your father and mother, that your days may be long in the land the Lord your God gives you.

13You shall not commit murder.

14You shall not commit [a]adultery.

15You shall not steal.

16You shall not witness falsely against your neighbor.

17You shall not covet your neighbor's house, your neighbor's wife, or his manservant, or his maidservant, or his ox, or his donkey, or anything that is your neighbor's.

18Now all the people perceived the thunderings and the lightnings and the noise of the trumpet and the smoking mountain, and as [they] looked they trembled with fear *and* fell back and stood afar off.

19And they said to Moses, You speak to us and we will listen, but let not God speak to us, lest we die.

20And Moses said to the people, Fear not; for God has come to prove you, so that the [reverential] fear of Him may be before you, that you may not sin.

21And the people stood afar off, but Moses drew near to the thick darkness where God was.

22And the Lord said to Moses, Thus shall you say to the Israelites, You have seen for yourselves that I have talked with you from heaven.

23You shall not make [gods to share] with Me [My glory and your worship]; gods of silver or gods of gold you shall not make for yourselves.

24An altar of earth you shall make to Me and sacrifice on it your burnt offerings and your peace offerings, your sheep and your oxen. In every place where I record My name and cause it to be remembered I will come to you and bless you.

25And if you will make Me an altar of stone,

AMP notes: a Observe here the expansion of the meaning of the seventh commandment in many catechisms to include whoredom in all its forms, as well as unchastity [premarital relations, sexual impurity, and lustful desire under whatever name] (J. P. Lange, *A Commentary*). Not only is adultery forbidden here, but also fornication and all kinds of mental and sensual uncleanness. All impure books, songs, pictures, etc., which tend to inflame and debauch the mind are against this law (Adam Clarke, *The Holy Bible with A Commentary*).

King James Version

thou shalt not build it *of* hewn stone: for if thou lift up thy tool upon it, thou hast polluted it.

²⁶Neither shalt thou go up by steps unto mine altar, that thy nakedness be not discovered thereon.

21 Now these *are* the judgments which thou shalt set before them.

²If thou buy a Hebrew servant, six years he shall serve: and in the seventh he shall go out free for nothing.

³If he came in by himself, he shall go out by himself: if he *were* married, then his wife shall go out with him.

⁴If his master have given him a wife, and she have born him sons or daughters; the wife and her children shall be her master's, and he shall go out by himself.

⁵And if the servant shall plainly say, I love my master, my wife, and my children; I will not go out free:

⁶Then his master shall bring him unto the judges; he shall also bring him to the door, or unto the door post; and his master shall bore his ear through with an aul; and he shall serve him for ever.

⁷And if a man sell his daughter to be a maidservant, she shall not go out as the menservants do.

⁸If she please not her master, who hath betrothed her to himself, then shall he let her be redeemed: to sell her unto a strange nation he shall have no power, seeing he hath dealt deceitfully with her.

⁹And if he have betrothed her unto his son, he shall deal with her after the manner of daughters.

¹⁰If he take him another *wife;* her food, her raiment, and her duty of marriage, shall he not diminish.

¹¹And if he do not these three unto her, then shall she go out free without money.

¹² ¶ He that smiteth a man, so that he die, shall be surely put to death.

¹³And if a man lie not in wait, but God deliver *him* into his hand; then I will appoint thee a place whither he shall flee.

¹⁴But if a man come presumptuously upon his neighbour, to slay him with guile; thou shalt take him from mine altar, that he may die.

¹⁵And he that smiteth his father, or his mother, shall be surely put to death.

¹⁶And he that stealeth a man, and selleth him, or if he be found in his hand, he shall surely be put to death.

¹⁷And he that curseth his father, or his mother, shall surely be put to death.

¹⁸And if men strive together, and one smite another with a stone, or with *his* fist, and he die not, but keepeth *his* bed:

Amplified Bible

you shall not build it of hewn stone, for if you lift up a tool upon it you have polluted it.

²⁶Neither shall you go up by steps to My altar, that your nakedness be not exposed upon it.

21 NOW THESE are the ordinances you [Moses] shall set before [the Israelites].

²If you buy a Hebrew servant [as the result of debt or theft], he shall serve six years, and in the seventh he shall go out free, paying nothing.

³If he came [to you] by himself, he shall go out by himself; if he came married, then his wife shall go out with him.

⁴If his master has given him a wife and she has borne him sons or daughters, the wife and her children shall be her master's, and he shall go out [of your service] alone.

⁵But if the servant shall plainly say, I love my master, my wife, and my children; I will not go free,

⁶Then his master shall bring him to God [the judges as His agents]; he shall bring him to the door or doorpost and shall pierce his ear with an awl; and he shall serve him for life.

⁷If a man sells his daughter to be a maidservant *or* bondwoman, she shall not go out [in six years] as menservants do.

⁸If she does not please her master who has not espoused her to himself, he shall let her be redeemed. To sell her to a foreign people he shall have no power, for he has dealt faithlessly with her.

⁹And if he espouses her to his son, he shall deal with her as with a daughter.

¹⁰If he marries again, her food, clothing, and privilege as a wife shall he not diminish.

¹¹And if he does not do these three things for her, then shall she go out free, without payment of money.

¹²Whoever strikes a man so that he dies shall surely be put to death.

¹³But if he did not lie in wait for him, but God allowed him to fall into his hand, then I will appoint you a place to which he may flee [for protection until duly tried].

¹⁴But if a man comes willfully upon another to slay him craftily, you shall take him from My altar [to which he may have fled for protection], that he may die.

¹⁵Whoever strikes his father or his mother shall surely be put to death.

¹⁶Whoever kidnaps a man, whether he sells him or is found with him in his possession, shall surely be put to death.

¹⁷Whoever curses his father or his mother shall surely be put to death.

¹⁸If men quarrel and one strikes another with a stone or with his fist and he does not die but keeps his bed,

King James Version

¹⁹If he rise again, and walk abroad upon his staff, then shall he that smote *him* be quit: only he shall pay *for* the loss of his time, and shall cause *him* to be thoroughly healed.

²⁰And if a man smite his servant, or his maid, with a rod, and he die under his hand; he shall be surely punished.

²¹Notwithstanding, if he continue a day or two, he shall not be punished: for he *is* his money.

²²If men strive, and hurt a woman with child, so that her fruit depart *from her,* and yet no mischief follow: he shall be surely punished, according as the woman's husband will lay upon him; and he shall pay as the judges determine.

²³And if *any* mischief follow, then thou shalt give life for life,

²⁴Eye for eye, tooth for tooth, hand for hand, foot for foot,

²⁵Burning for burning, wound for wound, stripe for stripe.

²⁶And if a man smite the eye of his servant, or the eye of his maid, that it perish; he shall let him go free for his eye's sake.

²⁷And if he smite out his manservant's tooth, or his maidservant's tooth; he shall let him go free for his tooth's sake.

²⁸ ¶ If an ox gore a man or a woman, that they die: then the ox shall be surely stoned, and his flesh shall not be eaten; but the owner of the ox *shall be* quit.

²⁹But if the ox *were* wont to push with his horn in time past, and it hath been testified to his owner, and he hath not kept him in, but that he hath killed a man or a woman; the ox shall be stoned, and his owner also shall be put to death.

³⁰If there be laid on him a sum of money, then he shall give *for* the ransom of his life whatsoever is laid upon him.

³¹Whether he have gored a son, or have gored a daughter, according to this judgment shall it be done unto him.

³²If the ox shall push a manservant or a maidservant; he shall give unto their master thirty shekels *of* silver, and the ox shall be stoned.

³³And if a man shall open a pit, or if a man shall dig a pit, and not cover it, and an ox or an ass fall therein;

³⁴The owner of the pit shall make *it* good, *and* give money unto the owner of them; and the dead *beast* shall be his.

³⁵And if one man's ox hurt another's, that he die; then they shall sell the live ox, and divide the money of it; and the dead *ox* also they shall divide.

³⁶Or *if* it be known that the ox *hath* used to push in time past, and his owner hath not kept him in; he shall surely pay ox for ox; and the dead shall be his own.

Amplified Bible

¹⁹If he rises again and walks about leaning upon his staff, then he that struck him shall be clear, except he must pay for the loss of his time and shall cause him to be thoroughly healed.

²⁰And if a man strikes his servant or his maid with a rod and he [or she] dies under his hand, he shall surely be punished.

²¹But if the servant lives on for a day or two, the offender shall not be punished, for he [has injured] his own property.

²²If men contend with each other, and a pregnant woman [interfering] is hurt so that she has a miscarriage, yet no further damage follows, [the one who hurt her] shall surely be punished with a fine [paid] to the woman's husband, as much as the judges determine.

²³But if any damage follows, then you shall give life for life,

²⁴Eye for eye, tooth for tooth, hand for hand, foot for foot,

²⁵Burn for burn, wound for wound, and lash for lash.

²⁶And if a man hits the eye of his servant or the eye of his maid so that it is destroyed, he shall let him go free for his eye's sake.

²⁷And if he knocks out his manservant's tooth or his maidservant's tooth, he shall let him go free for his tooth's sake.

²⁸If an ox gores a man or a woman to death, then the ox shall surely be stoned, and its flesh shall not be eaten; but the owner of the ox shall be clear.

²⁹But if the ox has tried to gore before, and its owner has been warned but has not kept it closed in and it kills a man or a woman, the ox shall be stoned and its owner also put to death.

³⁰If a ransom is put on [the man's] life, then he shall give for the redemption of his life whatever is laid upon him.

³¹If the [man's ox] has gored another's son or daughter, he shall be dealt with according to this same rule.

³²If the ox gores a manservant or a maidservant, the owner shall give to their master thirty shekels of silver, and the ox shall be stoned.

³³If a man leaves a pit open or digs a pit and does not cover it and an ox or a donkey falls into it,

³⁴The owner of the pit shall make it good; he shall give money to the animal's owner, but the dead beast shall be his.

³⁵If one man's ox hurts another's so that it dies, they shall sell the live ox and divide the price of it; the dead ox also they shall divide between them.

³⁶Or if it is known that the ox has gored in the past, and its owner has not kept it closed in, he shall surely pay ox for ox, and the dead beast shall be his.

King James Version

22 If a man shall steal an ox, or a sheep, and kill it, or sell it; he shall restore five oxen for an ox, and four sheep for a sheep.

²If a thief be found breaking up, and be smitten that he die, *there shall* no blood *be shed* for him.

³If the sun be risen upon him, *there shall be* blood *shed* for him; *for* he should make full restitution; if he have nothing, then he shall be sold for his theft.

⁴If the theft be certainly found in his hand alive, whether it be ox, or ass, or sheep; he shall restore double.

⁵ ¶ If a man shall cause a field or vineyard to be eaten, and shall put in his beast, and shall feed in another man's field; of the best of his own field, and of the best of his own vineyard, shall he make restitution.

⁶If fire break out, and catch in thorns, so that the stacks of corn, or the standing corn, or the field, be consumed *therewith;* he that kindled the fire shall surely make restitution.

⁷If a man shall deliver unto his neighbour money or stuff to keep, and it be stolen out of the man's house; if the thief be found, let him pay double.

⁸If the thief be not found, then the master of the house shall be brought unto the judges, *to see* whether he have put his hand unto his neighbour's goods.

⁹For all manner of trespass, *whether it be* for ox, for ass, for sheep, for raiment, *or* for any manner of lost *thing,* which *another* challengeth to be his, the cause of both parties shall come before the judges; *and* whom the judges shall condemn, he shall pay double unto his neighbour.

¹⁰If a man deliver unto his neighbour an ass, or an ox, or a sheep, or any beast, to keep; and it die, or be hurt, or driven away, no man seeing *it:*

¹¹*Then* shall an oath of the LORD be between them both, that he hath not put his hand unto his neighbour's goods; and the owner of it shall accept *thereof,* and he shall not make *it* good.

¹²And if it be stolen from him, he shall make restitution unto the owner thereof.

¹³If it be torn in pieces, *then* let him bring it *for* witness, *and* he shall not make good that which was torn.

¹⁴And if a man borrow *ought* of his neighbour, and it be hurt, or die, the owner thereof *being* not with it, he shall surely make *it* good.

¹⁵*But* if the owner thereof *be* with it, he shall not make *it* good: if it *be* a hired *thing,* it came for his hire.

¹⁶ ¶ And if a man entice a maid that is not betrothed, and lie with her, he shall surely endow her to be his wife.

¹⁷If her father utterly refuse to give her unto

Amplified Bible

22 IF A man steals an ox or sheep and kills or sells it, he shall pay five oxen for an ox, or four sheep for a sheep.

²If a thief is found breaking in and is struck so that he dies, there shall be no blood shed for him.

³But if the sun has risen [so he can be seen], blood must be shed for slaying him. The thief [if he lives] must make full restitution; if he has nothing, then he shall be sold for his theft.

⁴If the beast which he stole is found in his possession alive, whether it is ox or ass or sheep, he shall restore double.

⁵If a man causes a field or vineyard to be grazed over or lets his beast loose and it feeds in another man's field, he shall make restitution of the best of his own field or his own vineyard.

⁶If fire breaks out and catches so that the stacked grain or standing grain or the field be consumed, he who kindled the fire shall make full restitution.

⁷If a man delivers to his neighbor money or goods to keep and it is stolen out of the neighbor's house, then, if the thief is found, he shall pay double.

⁸But if the thief is not found, the house owner shall appear before God [the judges as His agents] to find whether he stole his neighbor's goods.

⁹For every unlawful deed, whether it concerns ox, donkey, sheep, clothing, or any lost thing at all, which another identifies as his, the cause of both parties shall come before God [the judges]. Whomever [they] shall condemn shall pay his neighbor double.

¹⁰If a man delivers to his neighbor a donkey or an ox or a sheep or any beast to keep and it dies or is hurt or driven away, no man seeing it,

¹¹Then an oath before the Lord shall be required between the two that the man has not taken his neighbor's property; and the owner of it shall accept his word and not require him to make good the loss.

¹²But if it is stolen when in his care, he shall make restitution to its owner.

¹³If it be torn in pieces [by some wild beast or by accident], let him bring [the mangled carcass] for witness; he shall not make good what was torn.

¹⁴And if a man borrows anything of his neighbor and it gets hurt or dies without its owner being with it, the borrower shall make full restitution.

¹⁵But if the owner is with it [when the damage is done], the borrower shall not make it good. If it is a hired thing, the damage is included in its hire.

¹⁶If a man seduces a virgin not betrothed and lies with her, he shall surely pay a dowry for her to become his wife.

¹⁷If her father utterly refuses to give her to

King James Version

him, he shall pay money according to the dowry of virgins.

¹⁸Thou shalt not suffer a witch to live.

¹⁹Whosoever lieth with a beast shall surely be put to death.

²⁰He that sacrificeth unto *any* god, save unto the LORD only, he shall be utterly destroyed.

²¹ ¶ Thou shalt neither vex a stranger, nor oppress him: for ye were strangers in the land of Egypt.

²²Ye shall not afflict any widow, or fatherless child.

²³If thou afflict them in any wise, and they cry at all unto me, I will surely hear their cry;

²⁴And my wrath shall wax hot, and I will kill you with the sword; and your wives shall be widows, and your children fatherless.

²⁵ ¶ If thou lend money to *any of* my people *that is* poor by thee, thou shalt not be to him as an usurer, neither shalt thou lay upon him usury.

²⁶If thou at all take thy neighbour's raiment to pledge, thou shalt deliver it unto him by that the sun goeth down:

²⁷For that *is* his covering only, it *is* his raiment for his skin: wherein shall he sleep? and it shall come to pass, when he crieth unto me, that I will hear; for I *am* gracious.

²⁸ ¶ Thou shalt not revile the gods, nor curse the ruler of thy people.

²⁹Thou shalt not delay *to offer the first of* thy ripe fruits, and *of* thy liquors: the firstborn of thy sons shalt thou give unto me.

³⁰Likewise shalt thou do with thine oxen, *and* with thy sheep: seven days it shall be with his dam; on the eighth day thou shalt give it me.

³¹And ye shall be holy men unto me: neither shall ye eat *any* flesh *that is* torn *of beasts* in the field; ye shall cast it to the dogs.

23 Thou shalt not raise a false report: put not thine hand with the wicked to be an unrighteous witness.

²Thou shalt not follow a multitude to *do* evil; neither shalt thou speak in a cause to decline after many to wrest *judgment:*

³Neither shalt thou countenance a poor *man* in his cause.

⁴If thou meet thine enemy's ox or his ass going astray, thou shalt surely bring it back to him again.

⁵If thou see the ass of him that hateth thee lying under his burden, and wouldest forbear to help him, thou shalt surely help with him.

⁶Thou shalt not wrest the judgment of thy poor in his cause.

⁷Keep thee far from a false matter; and the in-

Amplified Bible

him, he shall pay money equivalent to the dowry of virgins.

¹⁸You shall not allow a woman to live who practices sorcery.

¹⁹Whoever lies carnally with a beast shall surely be put to death.

²⁰He who sacrifices to any god but the Lord only shall be utterly destroyed.

²¹You shall not wrong a stranger or oppress him; for you were strangers in the land of Egypt.

²²You shall not afflict any widow or fatherless child.

²³If you afflict them in any way and they cry at all to Me, I will surely hear their cry;

²⁴And My wrath shall burn; I will kill you with the sword, and your wives shall be widows and your children fatherless.

²⁵If you lend money to any of My people with you who is poor, you shall not be to him as a creditor, neither shall you require interest from him.

²⁶If you ever take your neighbor's garment in pledge, you shall give it back to him before the sun goes down;

²⁷For that is his only covering, his clothing for his body. In what shall he sleep? When he cries to Me, I will hear, for I am gracious *and* merciful.

²⁸You shall not revile God [the judges as His agents] or esteem lightly *or* curse a ruler of your people.

²⁹You shall not delay to bring to Me from the fullness [of your harvested grain] and the outflow [of your grape juice *and* olive oil]; give Me the firstborn of your sons [or redeem them].

³⁰Likewise shall you do with your oxen *and* your sheep. Seven days the firstborn [beast] shall be with its mother; on the eighth day you shall give it to Me.

³¹And you shall be holy men [consecrated] to Me; therefore you shall not eat any flesh that is torn by beasts in the field; you shall throw it to the dogs.

23 YOU SHALL not repeat *or* raise a false report; you shall not join with the wicked to be an unrighteous witness.

²You shall not follow a crowd to do evil; nor shall you bear witness at a trial so as to side with a multitude to pervert justice.

³Neither shall you be partial to a poor man in his trial [just because he is poor].

⁴If you meet your enemy's ox or his donkey going astray, you shall surely bring it back to him again.

⁵If you see the donkey of one who hates you lying [helpless] under his load, you shall refrain from leaving the man to cope with it alone; you shall help him to release the animal.

⁶You shall not pervert the justice due to your poor in his cause.

⁷Keep far from a false matter and [be very

King James Version

nocent and righteous slay thou not: for I will not justify the wicked.

8And thou shalt take no gift: for the gift blindeth the wise, and perverteth the words of the righteous.

9Also thou shalt not oppress a stranger: for ye know the heart of a stranger, seeing ye were strangers in the land of Egypt.

10 ¶ And six years thou shalt sow thy land, and shalt gather in the fruits thereof:

11But the seventh *year* thou shalt let it rest and lie still; that the poor of thy people may eat: and what they leave the beasts of the field shall eat. In like manner thou shalt deal with thy vineyard, *and* with thy oliveyard.

12Six days thou shalt do thy work, and on the seventh day thou shalt rest: that thine ox and thine ass may rest, and the son of thy handmaid, and the stranger, may be refreshed.

13And in all *things* that I have said unto you be circumspect: and make no mention of the name of other gods, neither let it be heard out of thy mouth.

14 ¶ Three times thou shalt keep a feast unto me in the year.

15Thou shalt keep the feast of unleavened bread: thou shalt eat unleavened bread seven days, as I commanded thee, in the time appointed of the month Abib; for in it thou camest out from Egypt: and none shall appear before me empty:

16And the feast of harvest, the firstfruits of thy labours, which thou hast sown in the field: and the feast of ingathering, *which is* in the end of the year, when thou hast gathered in thy labours out of the field.

17Three times in the year all thy males shall appear before the Lord GOD.

18Thou shalt not offer the blood of my sacrifice with leavened bread; neither shall the fat of my sacrifice remain until the morning.

19The first of the firstfruits of thy land thou shalt bring *into* the house of the LORD thy God. Thou shalt not seethe a kid in his mother's milk.

20 ¶ Behold, I send an Angel before thee, to keep thee in the way, and to bring thee into the place which I have prepared.

21Beware of him, and obey his voice, provoke him not; for he will not pardon your transgressions: for my name *is* in him.

Amplified Bible

careful] not to condemn to death the innocent and the righteous, for I will not justify *and* acquit the wicked.

8You shall take no bribe, for the bribe blinds those who have sight and perverts the testimony *and* the cause of the righteous.

9Also you shall not oppress a temporary resident, for you know the heart of a stranger *and* sojourner, seeing you were strangers *and* sojourners in Egypt.

10Six years you shall sow your land and reap its yield.

11But the seventh year you shall release it *and* let it rest and lie fallow, that the poor of your people may eat [what the land voluntarily yields], and what they leave the wild beasts shall eat. In like manner you shall deal with your vineyard and olive grove.

12Six days you shall do your work, but the seventh day you shall rest and keep Sabbath, that your ox and your donkey may rest, and the son of your bondwoman, and the alien, may be refreshed.

13In all I have said to you take heed; do not mention the name of other gods [either in blessing or cursing]; do not let such speech be heard from your mouth.

14Three times in the year you shall keep a feast to Me.

15You shall keep the Feast of Unleavened Bread; seven days you shall eat unleavened bread as I commanded you, at the time appointed in the month of Abib, for in it you came out of Egypt. None shall appear before Me empty-handed.

16Also you shall keep the Feast of Harvest [Pentecost], [acknowledging] the firstfruits of your toil, of what you sow in the field. And [third] you shall keep the Feast of Ingathering [Booths or Tabernacles] at the end of the year, when you gather in the fruit of your labors from the field.

17Three times in the year all your males shall appear before the Lord God.

18You shall not offer the blood of My sacrifice with leavened bread [but keep it unmixed], neither shall the fat of My feast remain all night until morning.

19The first of the firstfruits of your ground you shall bring into the house of the Lord your God. You shall not boil a kid in its mother's milk.

20Behold, I send an *a*Angel before you to keep *and* guard you on the way and to bring you to the place I have prepared.

21Give heed to Him, listen to *and* obey His voice; be not rebellious before Him *or* provoke Him, for He will not pardon your transgression; for My *b*Name is in Him.

AMP notes: a See footnote on Gen. 16:7. *b* Representing God's presence.

King James Version

²²But if thou shalt indeed obey his voice, and do all that I speak; then I will be an enemy unto thine enemies, and an adversary unto thine adversaries.

²³For mine Angel shall go before thee, and bring thee in unto the Amorites, and the Hittites, and the Perizzites, and the Canaanites, the Hivites, and the Jebusites: and I will cut them off.

²⁴Thou shalt not bow down to their gods, nor serve them, nor do after their works: but thou shalt utterly overthrow them, and quite break down their images.

²⁵And ye shall serve the LORD your God, and he shall bless thy bread, and thy water; and I will take sickness away from the midst of thee.

²⁶There shall nothing cast their young, nor be barren, in thy land: the number of thy days I will fulfil.

²⁷I will send my fear before thee, and will destroy all the people to whom thou shalt come, and I will make all thine enemies turn their backs unto thee.

²⁸And I will send hornets before thee, which shall drive out the Hivite, the Canaanite, and the Hittite, from before thee.

²⁹I will not drive them out from before thee in one year; lest the land become desolate, and the beast of the field multiply against thee.

³⁰By little and little I will drive them out from before thee, until thou be increased, and inherit the land.

³¹And I will set thy bounds from the Red sea even unto the sea of the Philistines, and from the desert unto the river: for I will deliver the inhabitants of the land into your hand; and thou shalt drive them out before thee.

³²Thou shalt make no covenant with them, nor with their gods.

³³They shall not dwell in thy land, lest they make thee sin against me: for if thou serve their gods, it will surely be a snare unto thee.

24 And he said unto Moses, Come up unto the LORD, thou, and Aaron, Nadab, and Abihu, and seventy of the elders of Israel; and worship ye afar off.

²And Moses alone shall come near the LORD: but they shall not come nigh; neither shall the people go up with him.

³And Moses came and told the people all the words of the LORD, and all the judgments: and all the people answered *with* one voice, and said, All the words which the LORD hath said will we do.

⁴And Moses wrote all the words of the LORD,

Amplified Bible

²²But if you will indeed listen to and obey His voice and all that I speak, then I will be an enemy to your enemies and an adversary to your adversaries.

²³When My Angel goes before you and brings you to the Amorites, the Hittites, the Perizzites, the Canaanites, the Hivites, and the Jebusites, and I reject them *and* blot them out,

²⁴You shall not bow down to their gods or serve them or do after their works; but you shall utterly overthrow them and break down their pillars *and* images.

²⁵You shall serve the Lord your God; He shall bless your bread and water, and I will take sickness from your midst.

²⁶None shall lose her young by miscarriage or be barren in your land; I will fulfill the number of your days.

²⁷I will send My terror before you and will throw into confusion all the people to whom you shall come, and I will make all your foes turn from you [in flight].

²⁸And I will send hornets before you which shall drive out the Hivite, Canaanite, and Hittite from before you.

²⁹I will not drive them out from before you in one year, lest the land become desolate [for lack of attention] and the wild beasts multiply against you.

³⁰Little by little I will drive them out from before you, until you have increased *and* are numerous enough to take possession of the land.

³¹I will set your borders from the Red Sea to the Sea of the Philistines, and from the wilderness to the river [Euphrates]; for I will deliver the inhabitants of the land into your hand and you shall drive them out before you.

³²You shall make no covenant with them or with their gods.

³³They shall not dwell in your land, lest they make you sin against Me; for if you serve their gods, it will surely be a snare to you.

24 GOD SAID to Moses, Come up to the Lord, you and Aaron, Nadab and Abihu [Aaron's sons], and seventy of Israel's elders, and worship at a distance.

²Moses alone shall come near the Lord; the others shall not come near, and neither shall the people come up with him.

³Moses came and told the people all that the Lord had said and all the ordinances; and all the people answered with one voice, All that the Lord has spoken we will do.

⁴Moses *a*wrote all the words of the Lord. He

AMP notes: a The contemporary evidence, supplied by archaeology, that writing had long been in common use before the time of Moses now makes conjectures about the contents of the earlier books of the Old Testament being handed down **orally** look absurd. Not only is much of the misleading criticism of the Bible now recognized as unjustified, it is out of harmony with the scientific outlook of the present day (Sir Charles Marston, *New Bible Evidence*).

King James Version

and rose up early in the morning, and builded an altar under the hill, and twelve pillars, according to the twelve tribes of Israel.

⁵And he sent young men of the children of Israel, which offered burnt offerings, and sacrificed peace offerings *of* oxen unto the LORD.

⁶And Moses took half of the blood, and put *it* in basons; and half of the blood he sprinkled on the altar.

⁷And he took the book of the covenant, and read in the audience of the people: and they said, All that the LORD hath said will we do, and be obedient.

⁸And Moses took the blood, and sprinkled *it* on the people, and said, Behold the blood of the covenant, which the LORD hath made with you concerning all these words.

⁹Then went up Moses, and Aaron, Nadab, and Abihu, and seventy of the elders of Israel:

¹⁰And they saw the God of Israel: and *there was* under his feet as it were a paved work of a sapphire stone, and as it were the body of heaven in *his* clearness.

¹¹And upon the nobles of the children of Israel he laid not his hand: also they saw God, and did eat and drink.

¹² ¶ And the LORD said unto Moses, Come up to me into the mount, and be there: and I will give thee tables of stone, and a law, and commandments which I have written; that thou mayest teach them.

¹³And Moses rose up, and his minister Joshua: and Moses went up into the mount of God.

¹⁴And he said unto the elders, Tarry ye here for us, until we come again unto you: and behold, Aaron and Hur *are* with you: if any man have any matters to do, let him come unto them.

¹⁵And Moses went up into the mount, and a cloud covered the mount.

¹⁶And the glory of the LORD abode upon mount Sinai, and the cloud covered it six days: and the seventh day he called unto Moses out of the midst of the cloud.

¹⁷And the sight of the glory of the LORD *was* like devouring fire on the top of the mount in the eyes of the children of Israel.

¹⁸And Moses went into the midst of the cloud, and gat him up into the mount: and Moses was in the mount forty days and forty nights.

25 And the LORD spake unto Moses, saying, ²Speak unto the children of Israel, that

Amplified Bible

rose up early in the morning and built an altar at the foot of the mountain and set up twelve pillars representing Israel's twelve tribes.

⁵And he sent young Israelite men, who offered burnt offerings and sacrificed peace offerings of oxen to the Lord.

⁶And Moses took half of the blood and put it in basins, and half of the blood he dashed against the altar.

⁷Then he took the Book of the Covenant and read in the hearing of the people; and they said, All that the Lord has said we will do, and we will be obedient.

⁸And Moses took the [remaining half of the] blood and sprinkled it on the people, and said, Behold the blood of the covenant which the Lord has made with you in accordance with all these words.

⁹Then Moses, Aaron, Nadab, and Abihu, and seventy of the elders of Israel went up [the mountainside].

¹⁰And they saw the God of Israel [that is, a convincing manifestation of His presence], and under His feet it was like pavement of bright sapphire stone, like the very heavens in clearness.

¹¹And upon the nobles of the Israelites He laid not His hand [to conceal Himself from them, to rebuke their daring, or to harm them]; but they saw [the manifestation of the presence of] God, and ate and drank.

¹²And the Lord said to Moses, Come up to Me into the mountain and be there, and I will give you tables of stone, with the law and the commandments which ᵃI have written that you may teach them.

¹³So Moses rose up with Joshua his attendant; and Moses went up into the mountain of God.

¹⁴And he said to the elders, Tarry here for us until we come back to you; remember, Aaron and Hur are with you; whoever has a cause, let him go to them.

¹⁵Then Moses went up into the mountain, and the cloud covered the mountain.

¹⁶The glory of the Lord rested on Mount Sinai, and the cloud covered it for six days. On the seventh day [God] called to Moses out of the midst of the cloud.

¹⁷And the glory of the Lord appeared to the Israelites like devouring fire on the top of the mountain.

¹⁸Moses entered into the midst of the cloud and went up the mountain, and Moses was on the mountain forty days and nights.

25 AND THE Lord said to Moses, ²Speak to the Israelites, that they take

AMP notes: ᵃ The two tables were "written with the finger of God" (Exod. 31:18), and "the tables were the work of God" (Exod. 32:16). A man may be said to write what a secretary writes at his dictation; but if he expressly states that certain things are written with his own hand, it is unreasonable to suppose that they were written by the hand of another (J. P. Lange, *A Commentary*).

King James Version

they bring me an offering: of every man that giveth it willingly with his heart ye shall take my offering.

³And this *is* the offering which ye shall take of them; gold, and silver, and brass,

⁴And blue, and purple, and scarlet, and fine linen, and goats' *hair,*

⁵And rams' skins dyed red, and badgers' skins, and shittim wood,

⁶Oil for the light, spices for anointing oil, and for sweet incense,

⁷Onyx stones, and stones to be set in the ephod, and in the breastplate.

⁸And let them make me a sanctuary; that I may dwell amongst them.

⁹According to all that I shew thee, *after* the pattern of the tabernacle, and the pattern of all the instruments thereof, even so shall ye make *it.*

¹⁰ ¶ And they shall make an ark of shittim wood: two cubits and a half *shall be* the length thereof, and a cubit and a half the breadth thereof, and a cubit and a half the height thereof.

¹¹And thou shalt overlay it with pure gold, within and without shalt thou overlay it, and shalt make upon it a crown *of* gold round about.

¹²And thou shalt cast four rings of gold for it, and put *them* in the four corners thereof; and two rings *shall be* in the one side of it, and two rings in the other side of it.

¹³And thou shalt make staves of shittim wood, and overlay them with gold.

¹⁴And thou shalt put the staves into the rings by the sides of the ark, that the ark may be borne with them.

¹⁵The staves shall be in the rings of the ark: they shall not be taken from it.

¹⁶And thou shalt put into the ark the Testimony which I shall give thee.

¹⁷And thou shalt make a mercy seat *of* pure gold: two cubits and a half *shall be* the length thereof, and a cubit and a half the breadth thereof.

¹⁸And thou shalt make two cherubims *of* gold, *of* beaten work shalt thou make them, in the two ends of the mercy seat.

¹⁹And make one cherub on the one end, and the other cherub on the other end: *even* of the mercy seat shall ye make the cherubims on the two ends thereof.

²⁰And the cherubims shall stretch forth *their* wings on high, covering the mercy seat with their wings, and their faces *shall look* one to another; toward the mercy seat shall the faces of the cherubims be.

²¹And thou shalt put the mercy seat above upon the ark; and in the ark thou shalt put the Testimony that I shall give thee.

²²And there I will meet with thee, and I will commune with thee from above the mercy seat, from between the two cherubims which *are*

Amplified Bible

for Me an offering. From every man who gives it willingly *and* ungrudgingly with his heart you shall take My offering.

³This is the offering you shall receive from them: gold, silver, and bronze,

⁴Blue, purple, and scarlet [stuff] and fine twined linen and goats' hair,

⁵Rams' skins tanned red, goatskins, dolphin *or* porpoise skins, acacia wood,

⁶Oil for the light, spices for anointing oil and for sweet incense,

⁷Onyx stones, and stones for setting in the ephod and in the breastplate.

⁸Let them make Me a sanctuary, that I may dwell among them.

⁹And you shall make it according to all that I show you, the pattern of the tabernacle *or* dwelling and the pattern of all the furniture of it.

¹⁰They shall make an ark of acacia wood: two and a half cubits long, a cubit and a half wide, and a cubit and a half high.

¹¹You shall overlay the ark with pure gold, inside and out, and make a gold crown, a rim *or* border, around its top.

¹²You shall cast four gold rings and attach them to the four lower corners of it, two rings on either side.

¹³You shall make poles of acacia wood and overlay them with gold,

¹⁴And put the poles through the rings on the ark's sides, by which to carry it.

¹⁵The poles shall remain in the rings of the ark; they shall not be removed from it [that the ark be not touched].

¹⁶And you shall put inside the ark the Testimony [the Ten Commandments] which I will give you.

¹⁷And you shall make a mercy seat (a covering) of pure gold, two cubits and a half long and a cubit and a half wide.

¹⁸And you shall make two cherubim (winged angelic figures) of [solid] hammered gold on the two ends of the mercy seat.

¹⁹Make one cherub on each end, making the cherubim of one piece with the mercy seat, on the two ends of it.

²⁰And the cherubim shall spread out their wings above, covering the mercy seat with their wings, facing each other and looking down toward the mercy seat.

²¹You shall put the mercy seat on the top of the ark, and in the ark you shall put the Testimony [the Ten Commandments] that I will give you.

²²There I will meet with you and, from above the mercy seat, from between the two cherubim

King James Version

upon the ark of the Testimony, of all *things* which I will give thee in commandment unto the children of Israel.

23 ¶ Thou shalt also make a table *of* shittim wood: two cubits *shall be* the length thereof, and a cubit the breadth thereof, and a cubit and a half the height thereof.

24 And thou shalt overlay it with pure gold, and make thereto a crown *of* gold round about.

25 And thou shalt make unto it a border of a handbreadth round about, and thou shalt make a golden crown to the border thereof round about.

26 And thou shalt make for it four rings of gold, and put the rings in the four corners that *are* on the four feet thereof.

27 Over against the border shall the rings be for places of the staves to bear the table.

28 And thou shalt make the staves *of* shittim wood, and overlay them with gold, that the table may be borne with them.

29 And thou shalt make the dishes thereof, and spoons thereof, and covers thereof, and bowls thereof, to cover withal: *of* pure gold shalt thou make them.

30 And thou shalt set upon the table shewbread before me alway.

31 ¶ And thou shalt make a candlestick of pure gold: *of* beaten work shall the candlestick be made: his shaft, and his branches, his bowls, his knops, and his flowers, shall be of the same.

32 And six branches shall come out of the sides of it; three branches of the candlestick out of the one side, and three branches of the candlestick out of the other side:

33 Three bowls made like unto almonds, *with* a knop and a flower in one branch; and three bowls made like almonds in the other branch, *with* a knop and a flower: so in the six branches that come out of the candlestick.

34 And in the candlestick *shall be* four bowls made like unto almonds, *with* their knops and their flowers.

35 And *there shall be* a knop under two branches of the same, and a knop under two branches of the same, and a knop under two branches of the same, according to the six branches that proceed out of the candlestick.

36 Their knops and their branches shall be of the same: all it *shall be* one beaten work *of* pure gold.

37 And thou shalt make the seven lamps thereof: and they shall light the lamps thereof, that they may give light over against it.

Amplified Bible

that are upon the ark of the Testimony, I will speak intimately with you of all which I will give you in commandment to the Israelites.

23 Also, make a table of acacia wood, two cubits long, one cubit wide, and a cubit and a half high [for the showbread].

24 You shall overlay it with pure gold and make a crown, a rim *or* molding, of gold around the top of it;

25 And make a frame of a handbreadth around *and* below the top of it and put around it a gold molding as a border.

26 You shall make for it four rings of gold and fasten them at the four corners that are on the table's four legs.

27 Close against the frame shall the rings be as places for the poles to pass to carry the table [of showbread].

28 You shall make the poles of acacia wood and overlay them with gold, that the table may be carried with them.

29 And you shall make its plates [for showbread] and cups [for incense], and its flagons and bowls [for liquids in sacrifice]; make them of pure gold.

30 And you shall set the showbread (the bread of the Presence) on the table before Me always.

31 You shall make a lampstand of pure gold. Of beaten *and* turned work shall the lampstand be made, both its base and its shaft; its cups, its knobs, and its flowers shall be of one piece with it.

32 Six branches shall come out of the sides of it; three branches of the lampstand out of the one side and three branches out of its other side;

33 Three cups made like almond blossoms, each with a knob and a flower on one branch, and three cups made like almond blossoms on the other branch with a knob and a flower; so for the six branches coming out of the lampstand;

34 And on the [center shaft] itself you shall [make] four cups like almond blossoms with their knobs and their flowers.

35 Also make a knob [on the shaft] under each pair of the six branches going out from the lampstand and one piece with it;

36 Their knobs and their branches shall be of one piece with it; the whole of it one beaten work of pure gold.

37 And you shall make the lamps of the [lampstand] to include a [a]seventh one [at the top of the shaft]. [The priests] shall set up the [seven] lamps of it so they may give light in front of it.

AMP notes: [a] Certain Biblical critics in the past doubted the existence of the tabernacle and asserted that the concept of a sevenfold lamp was unknown until hundreds of years later, in Babylonian times (600 B.C.). The first objective evidence to the contrary came to light in W. F. Albright's excavation of Tell Beit Mirsim, south of Jerusalem, where he found seven-sprouted lamps from about 1200 B.C. The seventh season at Dothan yielded three sevenfold lamps from the period 1200-1400 B.C., showing again that this was not a late idea (Joseph P. Free, *Near Eastern Archaeology*).

King James Version

38And the tongs thereof, and the snuffdishes thereof, *shall be of* pure gold.

39*Of* a talent of pure gold shall he make it, with all these vessels.

40And look that thou make *them* after their pattern, which was shewed thee in the mount.

26 Moreover thou shalt make the tabernacle *with* ten curtains *of* fine twined linen, and blue, and purple, and scarlet: *with* cherubims *of* cunning work shalt thou make them.

2The length of one curtain *shall be* eight and twenty cubits, and the breadth of one curtain four cubits: *and* every one of the curtains shall have one measure.

3The five curtains shall be coupled together one to another; and *other* five curtains *shall be* coupled one to another.

4And thou shalt make loops of blue upon the edge of the one curtain from the selvedge in the coupling; and likewise shalt thou make in the uttermost edge of *another* curtain, in the coupling of the second.

5Fifty loops shalt thou make in the one curtain, and fifty loops shalt thou make in the edge of the curtain that *is* in the coupling of the second; that the loops may take hold one of another.

6And thou shalt make fifty taches of gold, and couple the curtains together with the taches: and it shall be one tabernacle.

7 ¶ And thou shalt make curtains *of* goats' *hair* to be a covering upon the tabernacle: eleven curtains shalt thou make.

8The length of one curtain *shall be* thirty cubits, and the breadth of one curtain four cubits: *and* the eleven curtains *shall be* all of one measure.

9And thou shalt couple five curtains by themselves, and six curtains by themselves, and shalt double the sixth curtain in the forefront of the tabernacle.

10And thou shalt make fifty loops on the edge of the one curtain *that is* outmost in the coupling, and fifty loops in the edge of the curtain which coupleth the second.

11And thou shalt make fifty taches of brass, and put the taches into the loops, and couple the tent together, that it may be one.

12And the remnant that remaineth of the curtains of the tent, the half curtain that remaineth, shall hang over the backside of the tabernacle.

13And a cubit on the one side, and a cubit on the other side of that which remaineth in the length of the curtains of the tent, it shall hang over the sides of the tabernacle on this side and on that side, to cover it.

14And thou shalt make a covering for the tent *of* rams' skins dyed red, and a covering above of badgers' skins.

Amplified Bible

38Its snuffers and its ashtrays shall be of pure gold.

39Use a talent of pure gold for it, including all these utensils.

40And see to it that you copy [exactly] their pattern which was shown you on the mountain.

26 MOREOVER, YOU shall make the tabernacle with ten curtains; of fine twined linen, and blue and purple and scarlet [stuff], with cherubim skillfully embroidered shall you make them.

2The length of one curtain shall be twenty-eight cubits and the breadth of one curtain four cubits; each of the curtains shall measure the same.

3The five curtains shall be coupled to one another, and the other five curtains shall be coupled to one another.

4And you shall make loops of blue on the edge of the last curtain in the first set, and likewise in the second set.

5Fifty loops you shall make on the one curtain and fifty loops on the edge of the last curtain that is in the second coupling *or* set, so that the loops on one correspond to the loops on the other.

6And you shall make fifty clasps of gold and fasten the curtains together with the clasps; then the tabernacle shall be one whole.

7And make curtains of goats' hair to be a [second] covering over the tabernacle; eleven curtains shall you make.

8One curtain shall be thirty cubits long and four cubits wide; and the eleven curtains shall all measure the same.

9You shall join together five curtains by themselves and six curtains by themselves, and shall double over the sixth curtain in the front of the tabernacle [to make a closed door].

10And make fifty loops on the edge of the outmost curtain in the one set and fifty loops on the edge of the outmost curtain in the second set.

11You shall make fifty clasps of bronze and put the clasps into the loops and couple the tent together, that it may be one whole.

12The surplus that remains of the tent curtains, the half curtain that remains, shall hang over the back of the tabernacle.

13And the cubit on the one side and the cubit on the other side of what remains in the length of the curtains of the tent shall hang over the sides of the tabernacle, on this side and that side, to cover it.

14You shall make a [third] covering for the tent of rams' skins tanned red, and a [fourth] covering above that of dolphin *or* porpoise skins.

King James Version

15 ¶ And thou shalt make boards for the tabernacle *of* shittim wood standing up.

16 Ten cubits *shall be* the length of a board, and a cubit and a half *shall be* the breadth of one board.

17 Two tenons *shall there be* in one board, set in order one against another: thus shalt thou make for all the boards of the tabernacle.

18 And thou shalt make the boards for the tabernacle, twenty boards on the south side southward.

19 And thou shalt make forty sockets of silver under the twenty boards; two sockets under one board for his two tenons, and two sockets under another board for his two tenons.

20 And for the second side of the tabernacle on the north side *there shall be* twenty boards:

21 And their forty sockets *of* silver; two sockets under one board, and two sockets under another board.

22 And for the sides of the tabernacle westward thou shalt make six boards.

23 And two boards shalt thou make for the corners of the tabernacle in the two sides.

24 And they shall be coupled together beneath, and they shall be coupled together above the head of it unto one ring: thus shall it be for them both; they shall be for the two corners.

25 And they shall be eight boards, and their sockets *of* silver, sixteen sockets; two sockets under one board, and two sockets under another board.

26 And thou shalt make bars *of* shittim wood; five for the boards of the one side of the tabernacle,

27 And five bars for the boards of the other side of the tabernacle, and five bars for the boards of the side of the tabernacle, for the two sides westward.

28 And the middle bar in the midst of the boards shall reach from end to end.

29 And thou shalt overlay the boards with gold, and make their rings *of* gold *for* places for the bars: and thou shalt overlay the bars with gold.

30 And thou shalt rear up the tabernacle according to the fashion thereof which was shewed thee in the mount.

31 ¶ And thou shalt make a vail *of* blue, and purple, and scarlet, and fine twined linen *of* cunning work: *with* cherubims shall it be made:

32 And thou shalt hang it upon four pillars of shittim *wood* overlaid with gold: their hooks *shall be of* gold, upon the four sockets of silver.

33 And thou shalt hang up the vail under the taches, that thou mayest bring in thither within the vail the ark of the Testimony: and the vail shall divide unto you between the holy *place* and the most holy.

34 And thou shalt put the mercy seat upon the ark of the Testimony in the most holy *place.*

Amplified Bible

15 And you shall make the upright frame for the tabernacle of boards of acacia wood.

16 Ten cubits shall be the length of a board and a cubit and a half shall be the breadth of one board.

17 Make two tenons in each board for dovetailing *and* fitting together; so shall you do for all the tabernacle boards.

18 And make the boards for the tabernacle: twenty boards for the south side;

19 And you shall make forty silver sockets under the twenty boards, two sockets under each board for its two tenons.

20 And for the north side of the tabernacle there shall be twenty boards

21 And their forty silver sockets, two sockets under each board.

22 For the back or west side of the tabernacle you shall make six boards.

23 Make two boards for the corners of the tabernacle in the rear on both sides.

24 They shall be coupled down below and coupled together on top with one ring. Thus shall it be for both of them; they shall form the two corners.

25 And that will be eight boards and their sockets of silver, sixteen sockets, two sockets under each board.

26 And you shall make bars of acacia wood: five for the boards of one side,

27 And five bars for the boards of the other side of the tabernacle, and five bars for the boards of the rear end of the tabernacle, for the back wall to the west.

28 And the middle bar halfway up the boards shall pass through from end to end.

29 You shall overlay the boards with gold and make their rings of gold to hold the bars and overlay the bars with gold.

30 You shall erect the tabernacle after the plan of it shown you on the mountain.

31 And make a veil of blue, purple, and scarlet [stuff] and fine twined linen, skillfully worked with cherubim on it.

32 You shall hang it on four pillars of acacia wood overlaid with gold, with gold hooks, on four sockets of silver.

33 And you shall hang the veil from the clasps and bring the ark of the Testimony into place within the veil; and the veil shall separate for you the Holy Place from the Most Holy Place.

34 And you shall put the mercy seat on the ark of the Testimony in the Most Holy Place.

King James Version

³⁵And thou shalt set the table without the vail, and the candlestick over against the table on the side of the tabernacle toward the south: and thou shalt put the table on the north side.

³⁶And thou shalt make a hanging for the door of the tent, *of* blue, and purple, and scarlet, and fine twined linen, wrought with needlework.

³⁷And thou shalt make for the hanging five pillars of shittim *wood,* and overlay them with gold, *and* their hooks *shall be of* gold: and thou shalt cast five sockets of brass for them.

27 And thou shalt make an altar *of* shittim wood, five cubits long, and five cubits broad; the altar shall be foursquare: and the height thereof *shall be* three cubits.

²And thou shalt make the horns of it upon the four corners thereof: his horns shall be of the same: and thou shalt overlay it with brass.

³And thou shalt make his pans to receive his ashes, and his shovels, and his basons, and his fleshhooks, and his firepans: all the vessels thereof thou shalt make *of* brass.

⁴And thou shalt make for it a grate of network *of* brass; and upon the net shalt thou make four brasen rings in the four corners thereof.

⁵And thou shalt put it under the compass of the altar beneath, that the net may be even to the midst of the altar.

⁶And thou shalt make staves for the altar, staves of shittim wood, and overlay them with brass.

⁷And the staves shall be put into the rings, and the staves shall be upon the two sides of the altar, to bear it.

⁸Hollow with boards shalt thou make it: as it was shewed thee in the mount, so shall they make *it.*

⁹ ¶ And thou shalt make the court of the tabernacle: for the south side southward *there shall be* hangings for the court *of* fine twined linen of an hundred cubits long for one side:

¹⁰And the twenty pillars thereof and their twenty sockets *shall be of* brass; the hooks of the pillars and their fillets *shall be of* silver.

¹¹And likewise for the north side in length *there shall be* hangings of an hundred *cubits* long, and his twenty pillars and their twenty sockets *of* brass; the hooks of the pillars and their fillets *of* silver.

¹²And *for* the breadth of the court on the west side *shall be* hangings of fifty cubits: their pillars ten, and their sockets ten.

¹³And the breadth of the court on the east side eastward *shall be* fifty cubits.

¹⁴The hangings of *one* side *of the gate shall be* fifteen cubits: their pillars three, and their sockets three.

Amplified Bible

³⁵And you shall set the table [for the showbread] outside the veil [in the Holy Place] on the north side and the lampstand opposite the table on the south side of the tabernacle.

³⁶You shall make a hanging [to form a screen] for the door of the tent of blue, purple, and scarlet [stuff] and fine twined linen, embroidered.

³⁷You shall make five pillars of acacia wood to support the hanging curtain and overlay them with gold; their hooks shall be of gold, and you shall cast five [base] sockets of bronze for them.

27 AND MAKE the altar of acacia wood, five cubits square and three cubits high [within reach of all].

²Make horns for it on its four corners; they shall be of one piece with it, and you shall overlay it with bronze.

³You shall make pots to take away its ashes, and shovels, basins, forks, and firepans; make all its utensils of bronze.

⁴Also make for it a grate, a network of bronze; and on the net you shall make four bronze rings at its four corners.

⁵And you shall put it under the ledge of the altar, so that the net will extend halfway down the altar.

⁶And make poles for the altar, poles of acacia wood overlaid with bronze.

⁷The poles shall be put through the rings on the two sides of the altar, with which to carry it.

⁸You shall make [the altar] hollow with slabs *or* planks; as shown you on the mountain, so shall it be made.

⁹And you shall make the court of the tabernacle. On the south side the court shall have hangings of fine twined linen, a hundred cubits long for one side;

¹⁰Their pillars shall be twenty and their sockets twenty, of bronze, but the hooks of the pillars and their joinings shall be of silver;

¹¹Likewise for the north side hangings, a hundred cubits long, and their twenty pillars and their twenty sockets of bronze, but the hooks of the pillars and their joinings shall be of silver.

¹²And for the breadth of the court on the west side there shall be hangings of fifty cubits, with ten pillars and ten sockets.

¹³The breadth of the court to the front, the east side, shall be fifty cubits.

¹⁴The hangings for one side of the gate shall be fifteen cubits, with three pillars and three sockets.

King James Version

15And on the other side *shall be* hangings, fifteen *cubits:* their pillars three, and their sockets three.

16And for the gate of the court *shall be* a hanging of twenty cubits, *of* blue, and purple, and scarlet, and fine twined linen, wrought with needlework: *and* their pillars *shall be* four, and their sockets four.

17All the pillars round about the court *shall be* filleted *with* silver; their hooks *shall be of* silver, and their sockets *of* brass.

18The length of the court *shall be* an hundred cubits, and the breadth fifty every where, and the height five cubits *of* fine twined linen, and their sockets *of* brass.

19All the vessels of the tabernacle in all the service thereof, and all the pins thereof, and all the pins of the court, *shall be of* brass.

20 ¶ And thou shalt command the children of Israel, that they bring thee pure oil olive beaten for the light, to cause the lamp to burn always.

21In the tabernacle of the congregation without the vail, which *is* before the Testimony, Aaron and his sons shall order it from evening to morning before the LORD: *it shall be* a statute for ever unto their generations on the behalf of the children of Israel.

28 And take thou unto thee Aaron thy brother, and his sons with him, from among the children of Israel, that he may minister unto me in the priest's office, *even* Aaron, Nadab and Abihu, Eleazar and Ithamar, Aaron's sons.

2And thou shalt make holy garments for Aaron thy brother, for glory and for beauty.

3And thou shalt speak unto all *that are* wise hearted, whom I have filled with the spirit of wisdom, that they may make Aaron's garments to consecrate him, that he may minister unto me in the priest's office.

4And these *are* the garments which they shall make; a breastplate, and an ephod, and a robe, and a broidered coat, a mitre, and a girdle: and they shall make holy garments for Aaron thy brother, and his sons, that he may minister unto me in the priest's office.

5And they shall take gold, and blue, and purple, and scarlet, and fine linen.

6 ¶ And they shall make the ephod *of* gold, *of* blue, and *of* purple, *of* scarlet, and fine twined linen, *with* cunning work.

7It shall have the two shoulderpieces *thereof* joined at the two edges thereof; and *so* it shall be joined together.

8And the curious girdle of the ephod, which *is* upon it, shall be of the same, according to the work thereof; *even of* gold, *of* blue, and purple, and scarlet, and fine twined linen.

Amplified Bible

15On the other side the hangings shall be fifteen cubits, with three pillars and three sockets.

16And for the gate of the court there shall be a hanging [for a screen] twenty cubits long, of blue, purple, and scarlet [stuff] and fine twined linen, embroidered. It shall have four pillars and four sockets for them.

17All the pillars round about the court shall be joined together with silver rods; their hooks shall be of silver and their sockets of bronze.

18The length of the court shall be a hundred cubits and the breadth fifty and the height five cubits, [with hangings of] fine twined linen and sockets of bronze.

19All the tabernacle's utensils *and* instruments used in all its service, and all its pegs and all the pegs for the court, shall be of bronze.

20You shall command the Israelites to provide you with pure oil of crushed olives for the light, to cause it to burn continually [every night].

21In the Tent of Meeting [of God with His people], outside the veil which sets apart the Testimony, Aaron and his sons shall keep it burning from evening to morning before the Lord. It shall be a statute to be observed on behalf of the Israelites throughout their generations.

28 FROM AMONG the Israelites take your brother Aaron and his sons with him, that he may minister to Me in the priest's office, even Aaron, Nadab and Abihu, Eleazar and Ithamar, Aaron's sons.

2And you shall make for Aaron your brother sacred garments [appointed official dress set apart for special holy services] for honor and for beauty.

3Tell all who are expert, whom I have endowed with skill *and* good judgment, that they shall make Aaron's garments to sanctify him for My priesthood.

4They shall make these garments: a breastplate, an ephod [a distinctive vestment to which the breastplate was to be attached], a robe, long *and* sleeved tunic of checkerwork, a turban, and a sash *or* band. They shall make sacred garments for Aaron your brother and his sons to minister to Me in the priest's office.

5They shall receive [from the people] *and* use gold, and blue, purple, and scarlet [stuff], and fine linen.

6And they shall make the ephod of gold, of blue, purple, and scarlet [stuff], and fine twined linen, skillfully woven *and* worked.

7It shall have two shoulder straps to join the two [back and front] edges, that it may be held together.

8The skillfully woven girding band which is on the ephod shall be made of the same, of gold, blue, purple, and scarlet [stuff], and fine twined linen.

King James Version

⁹And thou shalt take two onyx stones, and grave on them the names of the children of Israel:

¹⁰Six of their names on one stone, and the *other* six names of the rest on the other stone, according to their birth.

¹¹*With* the work of an engraver in stone, *like* the engravings of a signet, shalt thou engrave the two stones with the names of the children of Israel: thou shalt make them to be set *in* ouches *of* gold.

¹²And thou shalt put the two stones upon the shoulders of the ephod *for* stones of memorial unto the children of Israel: and Aaron shall bear their names before the LORD upon his two shoulders for a memorial.

¹³And thou shalt make ouches *of* gold;

¹⁴And two chains *of* pure gold at the ends; *of* wreathen work shalt thou make them, and fasten the wreathen chains to the ouches.

¹⁵ ¶ And thou shalt make the breastplate of judgment *with* cunning work; after the work of the ephod thou shalt make it; *of* gold, *of* blue, and *of* purple, and *of* scarlet, and *of* fine twined linen, shalt thou make it.

¹⁶Foursquare it shall be *being* doubled; a span *shall be* the length thereof, and a span *shall be* the breadth thereof.

¹⁷And thou shalt set in it settings of stones, *even* four rows of stones: *the first* row *shall be* a sardius, a topaz, and a carbuncle: this *shall be* the first row.

¹⁸And the second row *shall be* an emerald, a sapphire, and a diamond.

¹⁹And the third row a ligure, an agate, and an amethyst.

²⁰And the fourth row a beryl, and an onyx, and a jasper: they shall be set in gold in their inclosings.

²¹And the stones shall be with the names of the children of Israel, twelve, according to their names, *like* the engravings of a signet; every one with his name shall they be according to the twelve tribes.

²²And thou shalt make upon the breastplate chains at the ends *of* wreathen work *of* pure gold.

²³And thou shalt make upon the breastplate two rings of gold, and shalt put the two rings on the two ends of the breastplate.

²⁴And thou shalt put the two wreathen *chains of* gold in the two rings *which are* on the ends of the breastplate.

²⁵And *the other* two ends of the two wreathen *chains* thou shalt fasten in the two ouches, and put *them* on the shoulderpieces of the ephod before it.

²⁶And thou shalt make two rings of gold, and thou shalt put them upon the two ends of the breastplate in the border thereof, which *is* in the side of the ephod inward.

Amplified Bible

⁹And you shall take two onyx *or* beryl stones and engrave on them the names of the twelve sons of Israel;

¹⁰Six of their names on one stone and the six names of the rest on the other stone, arranged in order of their birth.

¹¹With the work of a stone engraver, like the engravings of a signet, you shall engrave the two stones according to the names of the sons of Israel. You shall have them set in sockets *or* rosettes of gold.

¹²And you shall put the two stones upon the [two] shoulder straps of the ephod [of the high priest] as memorial stones for Israel; and Aaron shall bear their names upon his two shoulders as a memorial before the Lord.

¹³And you shall make sockets *or* rosettes of gold for settings,

¹⁴And two chains of pure gold, like cords shall you twist them, and fasten the corded chains to the settings.

¹⁵You shall make a breastplate of judgment, in skilled work; like the workmanship of the ephod shall you make it, of gold, blue, purple, and scarlet [stuff], and of fine twined linen.

¹⁶The breastplate shall be square *and* doubled; a span [nine inches] shall be its length and a span shall be its breadth.

¹⁷You shall set in it four rows of stones: a sardius, a topaz, and a carbuncle shall be the first row;

¹⁸The second row an emerald, a sapphire, and a diamond [so called at that time];

¹⁹The third row a jacinth, an agate, and an amethyst;

²⁰And the fourth row a beryl, an onyx, and a jasper; they shall be set in gold filigree.

²¹And the stones shall be twelve, according to the names of the sons of Israel, like the engravings of a signet, each with its name for the twelve tribes.

²²You shall make for the breastplate chains of pure gold twisted like cords.

²³You shall make on the breastplate two rings of gold and put [them] on the two edges of the breastplate.

²⁴And you shall put the two twisted, cordlike chains of gold in the two rings which are on the edges of the breastplate.

²⁵The other two ends of the two twisted, cordlike chains you shall fasten in the two sockets *or* rosettes in front, putting them on the shoulder straps of the ephod;

²⁶And make two rings of gold and put them at the two ends of the breastplate on its inside edge next to the ephod.

King James Version

27And two *other* rings of gold thou shalt make, and shalt put them on the two sides of the ephod underneath, towards the forepart thereof, over against *the other* coupling thereof, above the curious girdle of the ephod.

28And they shall bind the breastplate by the rings thereof unto the rings of the ephod with a lace of blue, that *it* may be above the curious girdle of the ephod, and that the breastplate be not loosed from the ephod.

29And Aaron shall bear the names of the children of Israel in the breastplate of judgment upon his heart, when he goeth in unto the holy *place,* for a memorial before the LORD continually.

30And thou shalt put in the breastplate of judgment the Urim and the Thummim; and they shall be upon Aaron's heart, when he goeth in before the LORD: and Aaron shall bear the judgment of the children of Israel upon his heart before the LORD continually.

31 ¶ And thou shalt make the robe of the ephod all of blue.

32And there shall be a hole in the top of it, in the midst thereof: it shall have a binding of woven work round about the hole of it, as it were the hole of an habergeon, *that* it be not rent.

33And *beneath* upon the hem of it thou shalt make pomegranates of blue, and of purple, and of scarlet, round about the hem thereof; and bells of gold between them round about:

34A golden bell and a pomegranate, a golden bell and a pomegranate, upon the hem of the robe round about.

35And it shall be upon Aaron to minister: and his sound shall be heard when he goeth in unto the holy *place* before the LORD, and when he cometh out, that he die not.

36And thou shalt make a plate *of* pure gold, and grave upon it, *like* the engravings of a signet, HOLINESS TO THE LORD.

37And thou shalt put it on a blue lace, that it may be upon the mitre; upon the forefront of the mitre it shall be.

38And it shall be upon Aaron's forehead, that Aaron may bear the iniquity of the holy *things,* which the children of Israel shall hallow in all their holy gifts; and it shall be always upon his forehead, that they may be accepted before the LORD.

39 ¶ And thou shalt embroider the coat of fine linen, and thou shalt make the mitre *of* fine linen, and thou shalt make the girdle *of* needlework.

40And for Aaron's sons thou shalt make coats, and thou shalt make for them girdles, and bonnets shalt thou make for them, for glory and for beauty.

41And thou shalt put them upon Aaron thy brother, and his sons with him; and shalt anoint them, and consecrate them, and sanctify them,

Amplified Bible

27Two gold rings you shall make and attach them to the lower part of the two shoulder pieces of the ephod in front, close by where they join, above the skillfully woven girdle *or* band of the ephod.

28And they shall bind the breastplate by its rings to the rings of the ephod with a lace of blue, that it may be above the skillfully woven girding band of the ephod, and that the breastplate may not become loose from the ephod.

29So Aaron shall bear the names of the sons of Israel in the breastplate of judgment upon his heart when he goes into the Holy Place, to bring them in continual remembrance before the Lord.

30In the breastplate of judgment you shall put the Urim and the Thummim [unspecified articles used when the high priest asked God's counsel for all Israel]; they shall be upon Aaron's heart when he goes in before the Lord, and Aaron shall bear the judgment (rights, judicial decisions) of the Israelites upon his heart before the Lord continually.

31Make the robe [to be worn beneath] the ephod all of blue.

32There shall be a hole in the center of it [to slip over the head], with a binding of woven work around the hole, like the opening in a coat of mail *or* a garment, that it may not fray *or* tear.

33And you shall make pomegranates of blue, purple, and scarlet [stuff] around about its skirts, with gold bells between them;

34A gold bell and a pomegranate, a gold bell and a pomegranate, round about on the skirts of the robe.

35Aaron shall wear the robe when he ministers, and its sound shall be heard when he goes [alone] into the Holy of Holies before the Lord and when he comes out, lest he die there.

36And you shall make a plate of pure gold and engrave on it, like the engravings of a signet, HOLY TO THE LORD.

37You shall fasten it on the front of the turban with a blue cord.

38It shall be upon Aaron's forehead, that Aaron may take upon himself *and* bear [any] iniquity [connected with] the holy things which the Israelites shall give *and* dedicate; and it shall always be upon his forehead, that they may be accepted before the Lord [in the priest's person].

39And you shall weave the long *and* sleeved tunic of checkerwork of fine linen *or* silk and make a turban of fine linen *or* silk; and you shall make a girdle, the work of the embroiderer.

40For Aaron's sons you shall make long *and* sleeved tunics and belts *or* sashes and caps, for glory *and* honor and beauty.

41And you shall put them on Aaron your brother and his sons with him, and shall anoint them and ordain and sanctify them [set them

King James Version

that they may minister unto me in the priest's office.

⁴²And thou shalt make them linen breeches to cover *their* nakedness; from the loins even unto the thighs they shall reach:

⁴³And they shall be upon Aaron, and upon his sons, when they come in unto the tabernacle of the congregation, or when they come near unto the altar to minister in the holy *place;* that they bear not iniquity, and die: *it shall be* a statute for ever unto him and his seed after him.

29 And this *is* the thing that thou shalt do unto them to hallow them, to minister unto me in the priest's office: Take one young bullock, and two rams without blemish,

²And unleavened bread, and cakes unleavened tempered with oil, and wafers unleavened anointed with oil: *of* wheaten flour shalt thou make them.

³And thou shalt put them into one basket, and bring them in the basket, with the bullock and the two rams.

⁴And Aaron and his sons thou shalt bring unto the door of the tabernacle of the congregation, and shalt wash them with water.

⁵And thou shalt take the garments, and put upon Aaron the coat, and the robe of the ephod, and the ephod, and the breastplate, and gird him with the curious girdle of the ephod:

⁶And thou shalt put the mitre upon his head, and put the holy crown upon the mitre.

⁷Then shalt thou take the anointing oil, and pour *it* upon his head, and anoint him.

⁸And thou shalt bring his sons, and put coats upon them.

⁹And thou shalt gird them *with* girdles, Aaron and his sons, and put the bonnets on them: and the priest's office shall be theirs for a perpetual statute: and thou shalt consecrate Aaron and his sons.

¹⁰And thou shalt cause a bullock to be brought before the tabernacle of the congregation: and Aaron and his sons shall put their hands upon the head of the bullock.

¹¹And thou shalt kill the bullock before the LORD, *by* the door of the tabernacle of the congregation.

¹²And thou shalt take of the blood of the bullock, and put *it* upon the horns of the altar with thy finger, and pour all the blood beside the bottom of the altar.

¹³And thou shalt take all the fat that covereth the inwards, and the caul *that is* above the liver, and the two kidneys, and the fat that *is* upon them, and burn *them* upon the altar.

¹⁴But the flesh of the bullock, and his skin, and his dung, shalt thou burn with fire without the camp: it *is* a sin offering.

¹⁵Thou shalt also take one ram; and Aaron

Amplified Bible

apart for God], that they may serve Me as priests.

⁴²You shall make for them [white] linen trunks to cover their naked flesh, reaching from the waist to the thighs.

⁴³And they shall be on Aaron and his sons when they go into the Tent of Meeting or when they come near to the altar to minister in the Holy Place, lest they bring iniquity upon themselves and die; it shall be a statute forever to Aaron and to his descendants after him.

29 THIS IS what you shall do to consecrate (set them apart) that they may serve Me as priests. Take one young bull and two rams, all without blemish,

²And unleavened bread and unleavened cakes mixed with oil and unleavened wafers spread with oil; of fine flour shall you make them.

³You shall put them in one basket and bring them in [it], and bring also the bull and the two rams;

⁴And bring Aaron and his sons to the door of the Tent of Meeting [out where the laver is] and wash them with water.

⁵Then take the garments and put on Aaron the long *and* sleeved tunic and the robe of the ephod and the ephod and the breastplate, and gird him with the skillfully woven girding band of the ephod.

⁶And you shall put the turban *or* miter upon his head and put the holy crown upon the turban.

⁷Then take the anointing oil and pour it on his head and anoint him.

⁸And bring his sons and put long *and* sleeved tunics on them.

⁹And you shall gird them with sashes *or* belts, Aaron and his sons, and bind caps on them; and the priest's office shall be theirs by a perpetual statute. Thus you shall ordain *and* consecrate Aaron and his sons.

¹⁰Then bring the bull before the Tent of Meeting, and Aaron and his sons shall lay their hands upon its head.

¹¹And you shall kill the bull before the Lord by the door of the Tent of Meeting.

¹²And you shall take of the blood of the bull and put it on the horns of the altar with your finger, and pour out all the blood at the base of the altar.

¹³And take all the fat that covers the entrails, and the appendage that is on the liver, and the two kidneys, and the fat that is on them, and burn them on the altar.

¹⁴But the flesh of the bull, its hide, and the contents of its entrails you shall burn with fire outside the camp; it is a sin offering.

¹⁵You shall also take one of the rams, and Aar-

King James Version

and his sons shall put their hands upon the head of the ram.

¹⁶And thou shalt slay the ram, and thou shalt take his blood, and sprinkle *it* round about upon the altar.

¹⁷And thou shalt cut the ram in pieces, and wash the inwards of him, and his legs, and put *them* unto his pieces, and unto his head.

¹⁸And thou shalt burn the whole ram upon the altar: it *is* a burnt offering unto the LORD: it *is* a sweet savour, an offering made by fire unto the LORD.

¹⁹And thou shalt take the other ram; and Aaron and his sons shall put their hands upon the head of the ram.

²⁰Then shalt thou kill the ram, and take of his blood, and put *it* upon the tip of the *right* ear of Aaron, and upon the tip of the right ear of his sons, and upon the thumb of their right hand, and upon the great toe of their right foot, and sprinkle the blood upon the altar round about.

²¹And thou shalt take of the blood that *is* upon the altar, and of the anointing oil, and sprinkle *it* upon Aaron, and upon his garments, and upon his sons, and upon the garments of his sons with him: and he shall be hallowed, and his garments, and his sons, and his sons' garments with him.

²²Also thou shalt take of the ram the fat and the rump, and the fat that covereth the inwards, and the caul *above* the liver, and the two kidneys, and the fat that *is* upon them, and the right shoulder; for it *is* a ram of consecration:

²³And one loaf of bread, and one cake of oiled bread, and one wafer out of the basket of the unleavened bread that *is* before the LORD:

²⁴And thou shalt put all in the hands of Aaron, and in the hands of his sons; and shalt wave them *for* a wave offering before the LORD.

²⁵And thou shalt receive them of their hands, and burn *them* upon the altar for a burnt offering, for a sweet savour before the LORD: it *is* an offering made by fire unto the LORD.

²⁶And thou shalt take the breast of the ram of Aaron's consecrations, and wave it *for* a wave offering before the LORD: and it shall be thy part.

²⁷And thou shalt sanctify the breast of the wave offering, and the shoulder of the heave offering, which is waved, and which is heaved up, of the ram of the consecration, *even* of *that* which *is* for Aaron, and of *that* which *is* for his sons:

²⁸And it shall be Aaron's and his sons' by a statute for ever from the children of Israel: for it *is* a heave offering: and it shall be a heave offering from the children of Israel of the sacrifice of their peace offerings, *even* their heave offering unto the LORD.

²⁹And the holy garments of Aaron shall be his

Amplified Bible

on and his sons shall lay their hands upon the head of the ram.

¹⁶And you shall kill the ram and you shall take its blood and throw it against the altar round about.

¹⁷And you shall cut the ram in pieces and wash its entrails and legs and put them with its pieces and its head,

¹⁸And you shall burn the whole ram upon the altar. It is a burnt offering to the Lord; it is a sweet *and* satisfying fragrance, an offering made by fire to the Lord.

¹⁹And you shall take the other ram, and Aaron and his sons shall lay their hands upon the head of the ram;

²⁰Then you shall kill the ram and take part of its blood and put it on the tip of the right ears of Aaron and his sons and on the thumb of their right hands and on the great toe of their right feet, and dash the rest of the blood against the altar round about.

²¹Then you shall take part of the blood that is on the altar, and of the anointing oil, and sprinkle it upon Aaron and his garments and on his sons and their garments; and he and his garments and his sons and their garments shall be sanctified *and* made holy.

²²Also you shall take the fat of the ram, the fat tail, the fat that covers the entrails, the appendage on the liver, the two kidneys with the fat that is on them, and the right thigh; for it is a ram of consecration *and* ordination.

²³Take also one loaf of bread, and one cake of oiled bread, and one wafer out of the basket of the unleavened bread that is before the Lord.

²⁴And put all these in the hands of Aaron and his sons and they shall wave them for a wave offering before the Lord.

²⁵Then you shall take them from their hands, add them to the burnt offering, and burn them on the altar for a sweet *and* satisfying fragrance before the Lord; it is an offering made by fire to the Lord.

²⁶And take the breast of the ram of Aaron's consecration *and* ordination and wave it for a wave offering before the Lord; and it shall be your portion [Moses].

²⁷And you shall sanctify (set apart for God) the waved breast of the ram used in the ordination and the waved thigh of the priests' portion, since it is for Aaron and his sons.

²⁸It shall be for Aaron and his sons as their due portion from the Israelites perpetually, an offering from the Israelites of their peace *and* thanksgiving sacrifices, their offering to the Lord.

²⁹The holy garments of Aaron shall pass to

King James Version

sons' after him, to be anointed therein, and to be consecrated in them.

³⁰*And* that son that is priest in his stead shall put them on seven days, when he cometh into the tabernacle of the congregation to minister in the holy *place*.

³¹And thou shalt take the ram of the consecration, and seethe his flesh in the holy place.

³²And Aaron and his sons shall eat the flesh of the ram, and the bread that *is* in the basket, *by* the door of the tabernacle of the congregation.

³³And they shall eat those *things* wherewith the atonement was made, to consecrate *and* to sanctify them: but a stranger shall not eat *thereof*, because they *are* holy.

³⁴And if *ought* of the flesh of the consecrations, or of the bread, remain unto the morning, then thou shalt burn the remainder with fire: it shall not be eaten, because it *is* holy.

³⁵And thus shalt thou do unto Aaron, and to his sons, according to all *things* which I have commanded thee: seven days shalt thou consecrate them.

³⁶ ¶ And thou shalt offer every day a bullock *for* a sin offering for atonement: and thou shalt cleanse the altar, when thou hast made an atonement for it, and thou shalt anoint it, to sanctify it.

³⁷Seven days thou shalt make an atonement for the altar, and sanctify it; and it shall be an altar most holy: whatsoever toucheth the altar shall be holy.

³⁸ ¶ Now this *is that* which thou shalt offer upon the altar; two lambs of the first year day by day continually.

³⁹The one lamb thou shalt offer in the morning; and the other lamb thou shalt offer at even:

⁴⁰And with the one lamb a tenth deal of flour mingled with the fourth part of a hin of beaten oil; and the fourth *part* of a hin of wine *for* a drink offering.

⁴¹And the other lamb thou shalt offer at even, *and* shalt do thereto according to the meat offering of the morning, and according to the drink offering thereof, for a sweet savour, an offering made by fire unto the LORD.

⁴²*This shall be* a continual burnt offering throughout your generations *at* the door of the tabernacle of the congregation before the LORD: where I will meet you, to speak there unto thee.

⁴³And there I will meet with the children of Israel, and *the tabernacle* shall be sanctified by my glory.

⁴⁴And I will sanctify the tabernacle of the congregation, and the altar: I will sanctify also both Aaron and his sons, to minister to me in the priest's office.

⁴⁵And I will dwell amongst the children of Israel, and will be their God.

Amplified Bible

his descendants who succeed him, to be anointed in them and to be consecrated *and* ordained in them.

³⁰And that son who is [high] priest in his stead shall put them on [each day for] seven days when he comes into the Tent of Meeting to minister in the Holy Place.

³¹You shall take the ram of the consecration *and* ordination and boil its flesh in a holy *and* set-apart place.

³²Aaron and his sons shall eat the flesh of the ram and the bread in the basket, at the door of the Tent of Meeting.

³³They shall eat those things with which atonement was made, to ordain and consecrate them; but a stranger (layman) shall not eat of them because they are holy (set apart to the worship of God).

³⁴And if any of the flesh or bread for the ordination remains until morning, you shall burn it with fire; it shall not be eaten, because it is holy (set apart to the worship of God).

³⁵Thus shall you do to Aaron and to his sons according to all I have commanded you; during seven days shall you ordain them.

³⁶You shall offer every day a bull as a sin offering for atonement. And you shall cleanse the altar by making atonement for it, and anoint it to consecrate it.

³⁷Seven days you shall make atonement for the altar and sanctify it [set it apart for God]; and the altar shall be most holy; whoever *or* whatever touches the altar must be holy (set apart for God's service).

³⁸Now this is what you shall offer on the altar: two lambs a year old shall be offered day by day continually.

³⁹One lamb you shall offer in the morning and the other lamb in the evening;

⁴⁰And with the one lamb a tenth measure of fine flour mixed with a fourth of a hin of beaten oil, and a fourth of a hin of wine for a drink offering [to be poured out].

⁴¹And the other lamb you shall offer at evening, and do with it as with the cereal offering of the morning and with the drink offering, for a sweet *and* satisfying fragrance, an offering made by fire to the Lord.

⁴²This shall be a continual burnt offering throughout your generations at the door of the Tent of Meeting before the Lord, where I will meet with you to speak there to you.

⁴³There I will meet with the Israelites, and the Tent of Meeting shall be sanctified by My glory [the Shekinah, God's visible presence].

⁴⁴And I will sanctify the Tent of Meeting and the altar; I will sanctify also both Aaron and his sons to minister to Me in the priest's office.

⁴⁵And I will dwell among the Israelites and be their God.

King James Version

46And they shall know that I *am* the LORD their God, that brought them forth out of the land of Egypt, that I may dwell amongst them: I *am* the LORD their God.

30 And thou shalt make an altar to burn incense upon: *of* shittim wood shalt thou make it.

2A cubit *shall be* the length thereof, and a cubit the breadth thereof; foursquare shall it be: and two cubits *shall be* the height thereof: the horns thereof *shall be* of the same.

3And thou shalt overlay it with pure gold, the top thereof, and the sides thereof round about, and the horns thereof; and thou shalt make unto it a crown *of* gold round about.

4And two golden rings shalt thou make to it under the crown of it, by the two corners thereof, upon the two sides of it shalt thou make *it;* and they shall be for places for the staves to bear it withal.

5And thou shalt make the staves *of* shittim wood, and overlay them with gold.

6And thou shalt put it before the vail that *is* by the ark of the Testimony, before the mercy seat that *is* over the Testimony, where I will meet with thee.

7And Aaron shall burn thereon sweet incense every morning: when he dresseth the lamps, he shall burn incense upon it.

8And when Aaron lighteth the lamps at even, he shall burn incense upon it, a perpetual incense before the LORD throughout your generations.

9Ye shall offer no strange incense thereon, nor burnt sacrifice, nor meat offering; neither shall ye pour drink offering thereon.

10And Aaron shall make an atonement upon the horns of it once in a year with the blood of the sin offering of atonements: once in the year shall he make atonement upon it throughout your generations: it *is* most holy unto the LORD.

11 ¶ And the LORD spake unto Moses, saying,

12When thou takest the sum of the children of Israel after their number, then shall they give every man a ransom for his soul unto the LORD, when *thou* numberest them; that there be no plague amongst them, when *thou* numberest them.

13This they shall give, every one that passeth among them that are numbered, half a shekel after the shekel of the sanctuary: (a shekel *is* twenty gerahs:) a half shekel *shall be* the offering of the LORD.

14Every one that passeth among them that are numbered, from twenty years old and above, shall give an offering unto the LORD.

15The rich shall not give more, and the poor shall not give less than half a shekel, when *they* give an offering unto the LORD, to make an atonement for your souls.

Amplified Bible

46And they shall know [from personal experience] that I am the Lord their God, Who brought them forth out of the land of Egypt that I might dwell among them; I am the Lord their God.

30 AND YOU shall make an altar to burn incense upon; of acacia wood you shall make it.

2A cubit shall be its length and a cubit its breadth; its top shall be square and it shall be two cubits high. Its horns shall be of one piece with it.

3And you shall overlay it with pure gold, its top and its sides round about and its horns, and you shall make a crown (a rim or molding) of gold around it.

4You shall make two golden rings under the rim of it, on the two ribs on the two opposite sides of it; and they shall be holders for the poles with which to carry it.

5And you shall make the poles of acacia wood, overlaid with gold.

6You shall put the altar [of incense] in front *and* outside of the veil that screens the ark of the Testimony, before the mercy seat that is over the Testimony (the Law, the tables of stone), where I will meet with you.

7And Aaron shall burn on it incense of sweet spices; every morning when he trims *and* fills the lamps he shall burn it.

8And when Aaron lights the lamps in the evening, he shall burn it, a perpetual incense before the Lord throughout your generations.

9You shall offer no unholy incense on the altar nor burnt sacrifice nor cereal offering; and you shall pour no libation (drink offering) on it.

10Aaron shall make atonement upon the horns of it once a year; with the blood of the sin offering of atonement once in the year shall he make atonement upon *and* for it throughout your generations. It is most holy to the Lord.

11And the Lord said to Moses,

12When you take the census of the Israelites, every man shall give a ransom for himself to the Lord when you number them, that no plague may fall upon them when you number them.

13This is what everyone shall give as he joins those already numbered: a half shekel, in terms of the sanctuary shekel, a shekel being twenty gerahs; a half shekel as an offering to the Lord.

14Everyone from twenty years old and upward, as he joins those already numbered, shall give this offering to the Lord.

15The rich shall not give more and the poor shall not give less than half a shekel when [you] give this offering to the Lord to make atonement for yourselves.

King James Version

¹⁶And thou shalt take the atonement money of the children of Israel, and shalt appoint it for the service of the tabernacle of the congregation; that it may be a memorial unto the children of Israel before the LORD, to make an atonement for your souls.

¹⁷¶ And the LORD spake unto Moses, saying,

¹⁸Thou shalt also make a laver *of* brass, and his foot *also of* brass, to wash *withal:* and thou shalt put it between the tabernacle of the congregation and the altar, and thou shalt put water therein.

¹⁹For Aaron and his sons shall wash their hands and their feet thereat:

²⁰When they go into the tabernacle of the congregation, they shall wash *with* water, that they die not; or when they come near to the altar to minister, to burn offering made by fire unto the LORD:

²¹So they shall wash their hands and their feet, that they die not: and it shall be a statute for ever to them, *even* to him and to his seed throughout their generations.

²²¶ Moreover the LORD spake unto Moses, saying,

²³Take thou also unto thee principal spices, of pure myrrh five hundred *shekels,* and of sweet cinnamon half so much, *even* two hundred and fifty *shekels,* and of sweet calamus two hundred and fifty *shekels,*

²⁴And of cassia five hundred *shekels,* after the shekel of the sanctuary, and of oil olive a hin:

²⁵And thou shalt make it an oil of holy ointment, an ointment compound *after* the art of the apothecary: it shall be a holy anointing oil.

²⁶And thou shalt anoint the tabernacle of the congregation therewith, and the ark of the Testimony,

²⁷And the table and all his vessels, and the candlestick and his vessels, and the altar of incense,

²⁸And the altar of burnt offering with all his vessels, and the laver and his foot.

²⁹And thou shalt sanctify them, that they may be most holy: whatsoever toucheth them shall be holy.

³⁰And thou shalt anoint Aaron and his sons, and consecrate them, that *they* may minister unto me in the priest's office.

³¹And thou shalt speak unto the children of Israel, saying, This shall be a holy anointing oil unto me throughout your generations.

³²Upon man's flesh shall it not be poured, neither shall ye make *any other* like it, after the composition of it: it *is* holy, *and* it shall be holy unto you.

³³Whosoever compoundeth *any* like it, or whosoever putteth *any* of it upon a stranger, shall even be cut off from his people.

³⁴¶ And the LORD said unto Moses, Take unto

Amplified Bible

¹⁶And you shall take the atonement money of the Israelites and use it [exclusively] for the service of the Tent of Meeting, that it may bring the Israelites to remembrance before the Lord, to make atonement for yourselves.

¹⁷And the Lord said to Moses,

¹⁸You shall also make a laver *or* large basin of bronze, and its base of bronze, for washing; and you shall put it [outside in the court] between the Tent of Meeting and the altar [of burnt offering], and you shall put water in it;

¹⁹There Aaron and his sons shall wash their hands and their feet.

²⁰When they go into the Tent of Meeting, they shall wash with water, that they die not; or when they come near to the altar to minister, to burn an offering made by fire to the Lord,

²¹So they shall wash their hands and their feet, lest they die; it shall be a perpetual statute for [Aaron] and his descendants throughout their generations.

²²Moreover, the Lord said to Moses,

²³Take the best spices: of liquid myrrh 500 shekels, of sweet-scented cinnamon half as much, 250 shekels, of fragrant calamus 250 shekels,

²⁴And of cassia 500 shekels, in terms of the sanctuary shekel, and of olive oil a hin.

²⁵And you shall make of these a holy anointing oil, a perfume compounded after the art of the perfumer; it shall be a sacred anointing oil.

²⁶And you shall anoint the Tent of Meeting with it, and the ark of the Testimony,

²⁷And the [showbread] table and all its utensils, and the lampstand and its utensils, and the altar of incense,

²⁸And the altar of burnt offering with all its utensils, and the laver [for cleansing] and its base.

²⁹You shall sanctify (separate) them, that they may be most holy; whoever *and* whatever touches them must be holy (set apart to God).

³⁰And you shall anoint Aaron and his sons and sanctify (separate) them, that they may minister to Me as priests.

³¹And say to the Israelites, This is a holy anointing oil [symbol of the Holy Spirit], sacred to Me alone throughout your generations.

³²It shall not be poured upon a layman's body, nor shall you make any other like it in composition; it is holy, and you shall hold it sacred.

³³Whoever compounds any like it or puts any of it upon an outsider shall be cut off from his people.

³⁴Then the Lord said to Moses, Take sweet

King James Version

thee sweet spices, stacte, and onycha, and galbanum; *these* sweet spices with pure frankincense: of each shall there be a like *weight:*

35And thou shalt make it a perfume, a confec-
tion *after* the art of the apothecary, tempered together, pure *and* holy:

36And thou shalt beat *some* of it very small,
and put of it before the Testimony in the tabernacle of the congregation, where I will meet
with thee: it shall be unto you most holy.

37And *as for* the perfume which thou shalt
make, you shall not make to yourselves according to the composition thereof: it shall be unto
thee holy for the LORD.

38Whosoever shall make like unto that, to
smell thereto, shall even be cut off from his people.

31 And the LORD spake unto Moses, saying,
2See, I have called by name Bezaleel the
son of Uri, the son of Hur, of the tribe of Judah:

3And I have filled him *with* the spirit of God,
in wisdom, and in understanding, and in knowledge, and in all *manner of* workmanship,

4To devise cunning works, to work in gold,
and in silver, and in brass,

5And in cutting of stones, to set *them,* and in
carving of timber, to work in all *manner of* workmanship.

6And I, behold, I have given with him Aholiab,
the son of Ahisamach, of the tribe of Dan: and in
the hearts of all that are wise hearted I have put
wisdom, that they may make all that I have commanded thee;

7The tabernacle of the congregation, and the
ark of the Testimony, and the mercy seat that *is*
thereupon, and all the furniture of the tabernacle,

8And the table and his furniture, and the pure
candlestick with all his furniture, and the altar
of incense,

9And the altar of burnt offering with all his
furniture, and the laver and his foot,

10And the clothes of service, and the holy garments for Aaron the priest, and the garments of
his sons, to minister in the priest's office,

11And the anointing oil, and sweet incense for
the holy *place:* according to all that I have commanded thee shall they do.

12 ¶ And the LORD spake unto Moses, saying,

13Speak thou also unto the children of Israel,
saying, Verily my sabbaths ye shall keep: for it
is a sign between me and you throughout your
generations; that *ye* may know that I *am* the
LORD that doth sanctify you.

14Ye shall keep the sabbath therefore; for it *is*
holy unto you: *every* one that defileth it shall
surely be put to death: for whosoever doeth *any*
work therein, that soul shall be cut off from
amongst his people.

Amplified Bible

spices—stacte, onycha, and galbanum, sweet
spices with pure frankincense, an equal amount
of each—

35And make of them incense, a perfume after
the perfumer's art, seasoned with salt *and*
mixed, pure and sacred.

36You shall beat some of it very small and put
some of it before the Testimony in the Tent of
Meeting, where I will meet with you; it shall be
to you most holy.

37And the incense which you shall make according to its composition you shall not make
for yourselves; it shall be to you holy to the
Lord.

38Whoever makes any like it for perfume shall
be cut off from his people.

31 AND THE Lord said to Moses,
2See, I have called by name Bezalel son
of Uri, the son of Hur, of the tribe of Judah.

3And I have filled him with the Spirit of God,
in wisdom *and* ability, in understanding *and* intelligence, and in knowledge, and in all kinds of
craftsmanship,

4To devise skillful works, to work in gold, and
in silver, and in bronze,

5And in cutting of stones for setting, and in
carving of wood, to work in all kinds of craftsmanship.

6And behold, I have appointed with him Aholiab son of Ahisamach, of the tribe of Dan; and to
all who are wisehearted I have given wisdom
and ability to make all that I have commanded
you:

7The Tent of Meeting, the ark of the Testimony, the mercy seat that is on it, all the furnishings of the tent—

8The table [of the showbread] and its utensils, the pure lampstand with all its utensils, the
altar of incense,

9The altar of burnt offering with all its utensils, the laver and its base—

10The finely worked garments, the holy garments for Aaron the [high] priest and for his
sons to minister as priests,

11And the anointing oil and incense of sweet
spices for the Holy Place. According to all that I
have commanded you shall they do.

12And the Lord said to Moses,

13Say to the Israelites, Truly you shall keep
My Sabbaths, for it is a sign between Me and
you throughout your generations, that you may
know that I, the Lord, sanctify you [set you
apart for Myself].

14You shall keep the Sabbath therefore, for it
is holy to you; everyone who profanes it shall
surely be put to death; for whoever does work
on the Sabbath shall be cut off from among his
people.

King James Version

¹⁵Six days may work be done; but in the seventh *is* the sabbath of rest, holy to the LORD: whosoever doeth *any* work in the sabbath day, he shall surely be put to death.

¹⁶Wherefore the children of Israel shall keep the sabbath, to observe the sabbath throughout their generations, *for* a perpetual covenant.

¹⁷It *is* a sign between me and the children of Israel for ever: for *in* six days the LORD made heaven and earth, and on the seventh day he rested, and was refreshed.

¹⁸And he gave unto Moses, when he had made an end of communing with him upon mount Sinai, two tables of Testimony, tables of stone, written with the finger of God.

32 And when the people saw that Moses delayed to come down out of the mount, the people gathered themselves together unto Aaron, and said unto him, Up, make us gods, which shall go before us; for *as for* this Moses, the man that brought us up out of the land of Egypt, we wot not what is become of him.

²And Aaron said unto them, Break off the golden earrings, which *are* in the ears of your wives, of your sons, and of your daughters, and bring *them* unto me.

³And all the people brake off the golden earrings which *were* in their ears, and brought *them* unto Aaron.

⁴And he received *them* at their hand, and fashioned it with a graving tool, after he had made it a molten calf: and they said, These *be* thy gods, O Israel, which brought thee up out of the land of Egypt.

⁵And when Aaron saw *it,* he built an altar before it; and Aaron made proclamation, and said, To morrow *is* a feast to the LORD.

⁶And they rose up early on the morrow, and offered burnt offerings, and brought peace offerings; and the people sat down to eat and to drink, and rose up to play.

⁷ ¶ And the LORD said unto Moses, Go, get thee down; for thy people, which thou broughtest out of the land of Egypt, have corrupted *themselves:*

⁸They have turned aside quickly out of the way which I commanded them: they have made them a molten calf, and have worshipped it, and have sacrificed thereunto, and said, These *be* thy gods, O Israel, which have brought thee up out of the land of Egypt.

⁹And the LORD said unto Moses, I have seen this people, and, behold, it *is* a stiffnecked people:

¹⁰Now therefore let me alone, that my wrath may wax hot against them, and that I may consume them: and I will make of thee a great nation.

¹¹And Moses besought the LORD his God, and said, LORD, why doth thy wrath wax hot against

Amplified Bible

¹⁵Six days may work be done, but the seventh is the Sabbath of rest, sacred to the Lord; whoever does work on the Sabbath day shall surely be put to death.

¹⁶Wherefore the Israelites shall keep the Sabbath to observe it throughout their generations, a perpetual covenant.

¹⁷It is a sign between Me and the Israelites forever; for in six days the Lord made the heavens and earth, and on the seventh day He ceased and was refreshed.

¹⁸And He gave to Moses, when He had ceased communing with him on Mount Sinai, the two tables of the Testimony, tables of stone, written with the finger of God.

32 WHEN THE people saw that Moses delayed to come down from the mountain, [they] gathered together to Aaron, and said to him, Up, make us gods to go before us; as for this Moses, the man who brought us up out of the land of Egypt, we do not know what has become of him.

²So Aaron replied, Take the gold rings from the ears of your wives, your sons, and daughters, and bring them to me.

³So all the people took the gold rings from their ears and brought them to Aaron.

⁴And he received the gold at their hand and fashioned it with a graving tool and made it a molten calf; and they said, These are your gods, O Israel, which brought you up out of the land of Egypt!

⁵And when Aaron saw the molten calf, he built an altar before it; and Aaron made proclamation, and said, Tomorrow shall be a feast to the Lord.

⁶And they rose up early the next day and offered burnt offerings and brought peace offerings; and the people sat down to eat and drink and rose up to play.

⁷The Lord said to Moses, Go down, for your people, whom you brought out of the land of Egypt, have corrupted themselves;

⁸They have turned aside quickly out of the way which I commanded them; they have made them a molten calf and have worshiped it and sacrificed to it, and said, These are your gods, O Israel, that brought you up out of the land of Egypt!

⁹And the Lord said to Moses, I have seen this people, and behold, it is a stiff-necked people;

¹⁰Now therefore let Me alone, that My wrath may burn hot against them and that I may destroy them; but I will make of you a great nation.

¹¹But Moses besought the Lord his God, and said, Lord, why does Your wrath blaze hot

King James Version

thy people, which thou hast brought forth out of the land of Egypt with great power, and with a mighty hand?

12Wherefore should the Egyptians speak, and say, For mischief did he bring them out, to slay them in the mountains, and to consume them from the face of the earth? Turn from thy fierce wrath, and repent of *this* evil against thy people.

13Remember Abraham, Isaac, and Israel, thy servants, to whom thou swarest by thine own self, and saidst unto them, I will multiply your seed as the stars of heaven, and all this land that I have spoken of will I give unto your seed, and they shall inherit *it* for ever.

14And the LORD repented of the evil which he thought to do unto his people.

15 ¶ And Moses turned, and went down from the mount, and the two tables of the Testimony *were* in his hand: the tables *were* written on both their sides; on the one side and on the other *were* they written.

16And the tables *were* the work of God, and the writing *was* the writing of God, graven upon the tables.

17And when Joshua heard the noise of the people as they shouted, he said unto Moses, *There is* a noise of war in the camp.

18And he said, *It is* not the voice of *them that* shout for mastery, neither *is it* the voice of *them that* cry for being overcome: *but* the noise of *them that* sing do I hear. *Moses knew right away that the singing was wicked & carnal*

19And it came to pass, as soon as he came nigh unto the camp, that he saw the calf, and the dancing: and Moses' anger waxed hot, and he cast the tables out of his hands, and brake them beneath the mount.

20And he took the calf which they had made, and burnt *it* in the fire, and ground *it* to powder, and strawed *it* upon the water, and made the children of Israel drink *of it.*

21And Moses said unto Aaron, What did this people unto thee, that thou hast brought *so* great a sin upon them?

22And Aaron said, Let not the anger of my lord wax hot: thou knowest the people, that they *are set* on mischief.

23For they said unto me, Make us gods, which shall go before us: for *as for* this Moses, the man that brought us up out of the land of Egypt, we wot not what is become of him.

24And I said unto them, Whosoever hath *any* gold, let them break *it* off. So they gave *it* me: then I cast it into the fire, and there came out this calf.

25And when Moses saw that the people *were* naked; (for Aaron had made them naked unto *their* shame amongst their enemies:)

26Then Moses stood in the gate of the camp, and said, Who *is* on the LORD's side? *let him come* unto me. And all the sons of Levi gathered themselves together unto him.

Amplified Bible

against Your people, whom You have brought forth out of the land of Egypt with great power and a mighty hand?

12Why should the Egyptians say, For evil He brought them forth, to slay them in the mountains and consume them from the face of the earth? Turn from Your fierce wrath, and change Your mind concerning this evil against Your people.

13[Earnestly] remember Abraham, Isaac, and Israel, Your servants, to whom You swore by Your own self and said to them, I will multiply your seed as the stars of the heavens, and all this land that I have spoken of will I give to your seed, and they shall inherit it forever.

14Then the Lord turned from the evil which He had thought to do to His people.

15And Moses turned and went down from the mountain with the two tables of the Testimony in his hand, tables *or* tablets that were written on both sides.

16The tables were the work of God; the writing was the writing of God, graven upon the tables.

17And when Joshua heard the noise of the people as they shouted, he said to Moses, There is a noise of war in the camp.

18But Moses said, It is not the sound of shouting for victory, neither is it the sound of the cry of the defeated, but the sound of singing that I hear.

19And as soon as he came near to the camp he saw the calf and the dancing. And Moses' anger blazed hot and he cast the tables out of his hands and broke them at the foot of the mountain.

20And he took the calf they had made and burned it in the fire, and ground it to powder and scattered it on the water and made the Israelites drink it.

21And Moses said to Aaron, What did this people do to you, that you have brought so great a sin upon them?

22And Aaron said, Let not the anger of my lord blaze hot; you know the people, that they are set on evil.

23For they said to me, Make us gods which shall go before us; as for this Moses, the man who brought us up out of the land of Egypt, we do not know what has become of him.

24I said to them, Those who have any gold, let them take it off. So they gave it to me; then I cast it into the fire, and there came out this calf.

25And when Moses saw that the people were unruly *and* unrestrained (for Aaron had let them get out of control, so that they were a derision *and* object of shame among their enemies),

26Then Moses stood in the gate of the camp, and said, Whoever is on the Lord's side, let him come to me. And all the Levites [the priestly tribe] gathered together to him.

King James Version

27And he said unto them, Thus saith the LORD God of Israel, Put every man his sword by his side, *and* go in and out from gate to gate throughout the camp, and slay every man his brother, and every man his companion, and every man his neighbour.

28And the children of Levi did according to the word of Moses: and there fell of the people that day about three thousand men.

29For Moses had said, Consecrate yourselves to day to the LORD, even every man upon his son, and upon his brother; that he may bestow upon you a blessing *this* day.

30 ¶ And it came to pass on the morrow, that Moses said unto the people, Ye have sinned a great sin: and now I will go up unto the LORD; peradventure I shall make an atonement for your sin.

31And Moses returned unto the LORD, and said, Oh, this people have sinned a great sin, and have made them gods of gold.

32Yet now, if thou wilt forgive their sin; and if not, blot me, I pray thee, out of thy book which thou hast written.

33And the LORD said unto Moses, Whosoever hath sinned against me, him will I blot out of my book.

34Therefore now go, lead the people unto *the place* of which I have spoken unto thee: behold, mine Angel shall go before thee: nevertheless in the day when I visit, I will visit their sin upon them.

35And the LORD plagued the people, because they made the calf, which Aaron made.

33 And the LORD said unto Moses, Depart, *and* go up hence, thou and the people which thou hast brought up out of the land of Egypt, unto the land which I sware unto Abraham, to Isaac, and to Jacob, saying, Unto thy seed will I give it:

2And I will send an angel before thee; and I will drive out the Canaanite, the Amorite, and the Hittite, and the Perizzite, the Hivite, and the Jebusite:

3Unto a land flowing with milk and honey: for I will not go up in the midst of thee; for thou *art* a stiffnecked people: lest I consume thee in the way.

4And when the people heard these evil tidings, they mourned: and no man did put on him his ornaments.

5For the LORD had said unto Moses, Say unto the children of Israel, Ye *are* a stiffnecked people: I will come up into the midst of thee in a moment, and consume thee: therefore now put

Amplified Bible

27And he said to them, Thus says the Lord God of Israel, Every man put his sword on his side and go in and out from gate to gate throughout the camp and slay every man his brother, and every man his companion, and every man his neighbor.

28And the sons of Levi did according to the word of Moses; and there fell of the people that day about 3000 men.

29And Moses said [to the Levites, By your obedience to God's command] you have consecrated yourselves today [as priests] to the Lord, each man [at the cost of being] against his own son and his own brother, that the Lord may restore *and* bestow His blessing upon *you* this day.

30The next day Moses said to the people, You have sinned a great sin. And now I will go up to the Lord; perhaps I can make atonement for your sin.

31So Moses returned to the Lord, and said, Oh, these people have sinned a great sin and have made themselves gods of gold!

32Yet now, if You will forgive their sin—and if not, blot me, I pray You, out of Your book which You have written!

33But the Lord said to Moses, Whoever has sinned against Me, I will blot him [not you] out of My book.

34But now go, lead the people to the place of which I have told you. Behold, My *a*Angel shall go before you. Nevertheless, in the day when I punish I will visit their sin upon them!

35And the Lord sent a plague upon the people because they made the calf which Aaron fashioned for them.

33 THE LORD said to Moses, Depart, go up from here, you and the people whom you have brought from the land of Egypt, to the land which I swore to Abraham, Isaac, and Jacob, saying, To your descendants I will give it.

2I will send an *a*Angel before you, and I will drive out the Canaanite, Amorite, Hittite, Perizzite, Hivite, and Jebusite.

3Go up to a land flowing with milk and honey; but I will not go up among you, for you are a stiff-necked people, lest I destroy you on the way.

4When the people heard these evil tidings, they mourned and no man put on his ornaments.

5For the Lord had said to Moses, Say to the Israelites, You are a stiff-necked people! If I should come among you for one moment, I would consume *and* destroy you. Now therefore

AMP notes: *a* See footnote on Gen. 16:7.

King James Version

off thy ornaments from thee, that I may know what to do unto thee.

6And the children of Israel stript themselves of their ornaments by the mount Horeb.

7 ¶ And Moses took the tabernacle, and pitched it without the camp, afar off from the camp, and called it the Tabernacle of the Congregation. And it came to pass, *that* every one which sought the LORD went out unto the Tabernacle of the Congregation, which *was* without the camp.

8And it came to pass, when Moses went out unto the tabernacle, *that* all the people rose up, and stood every man *at* his tent door, and looked after Moses, until he was gone into the tabernacle.

9And it came to pass, as Moses entered into the tabernacle, the cloudy pillar descended, and stood *at* the door of the tabernacle, and *the* LORD talked with Moses.

10And all the people saw the cloudy pillar stand *at* the tabernacle door: and all the people rose up and worshipped, every man *in* his tent door.

11And the LORD spake unto Moses face to face, as a man speaketh unto his friend. And he turned again into the camp: but his servant Joshua, the son of Nun, a young man, departed not out of the tabernacle.

12And Moses said unto the LORD, See, thou sayest unto me, Bring up this people: and thou hast not let me know whom thou wilt send with me. Yet thou hast said, I know thee by name, and thou hast also found grace in my sight.

13Now therefore, I pray thee, if I have found grace in thy sight, shew me now thy way, that I may know thee, that I may find grace in thy sight: and consider that this nation *is* thy people.

14And he said, My presence shall go *with thee,* and I will give thee rest.

15And he said unto him, If thy presence go not *with me,* carry us not up hence.

16For wherein shall it be known here that I and thy people have found grace in thy sight? *is it* not in that thou goest with us? so shall we be separated, I and thy people, from all the people that *are* upon the face of the earth.

17And the LORD said unto Moses, I will do this thing also that thou hast spoken: for thou hast found grace in my sight, and I know thee by name.

18And he said, I beseech thee, shew me thy glory.

19And he said, I will make all my goodness pass before thee, and I will proclaim the name of the LORD before thee; and will be gracious to whom I will be gracious, and will shew mercy on whom I will shew mercy.

Amplified Bible

[penitently] leave off your ornaments, that I may know what to do with you.

6And the Israelites left off all their ornaments, from Mount Horeb onward.

7Now Moses used to take [his own] tent and pitch it outside the camp, far off from the camp, and he called it the tent of meeting [of God with His own people]. And everyone who sought the Lord went out to [that temporary] tent of meeting which was outside the camp.

8When Moses went out to the tent of meeting, all the people rose and stood, every man at his tent door, and looked after Moses until he had gone into the tent.

9When Moses entered the tent, the pillar of cloud would descend and stand at the door of the tent, and the Lord would talk with Moses.

10And all the people saw the pillar of cloud stand at the tent door, and all the people rose up and worshiped, every man at his tent door.

11And the Lord spoke to Moses face to face, as a man speaks to his friend. Moses returned to the camp, but his minister Joshua son of Nun, a young man, did not depart from the [temporary prayer] tent.

12Moses said to the Lord, See, You say to me, Bring up this people, but You have not let me know whom You will send with me. Yet You said, I know you by name and you have also found favor in My sight.

13Now therefore, I pray You, if I have found favor in Your sight, show me now Your way, that I may know You [progressively become more deeply and intimately acquainted with You, perceiving and recognizing and understanding more strongly and clearly] and that I may find favor in Your sight. And [Lord, do] consider that this nation is Your people.

14And the Lord said, My Presence shall go with you, and I will give you rest.

15And Moses said to the Lord, If Your Presence does not go with me, do not carry us up from here!

16For by what shall it be known that I and Your people have found favor in Your sight? Is it not in Your going with us so that we are distinguished, I and Your people, from all the other people upon the face of the earth?

17And the Lord said to Moses, I will do this thing also that you have asked, for you have found favor, loving-kindness, *and* mercy in My sight and I know you personally *and* by name.

18And Moses said, I beseech You, show me Your glory.

19And God said, I will make all My goodness pass before you, and I will proclaim My name, THE LORD, before you; for I will be gracious to whom I will be gracious, and will show mercy *and* loving-kindness on whom I will show mercy *and* loving-kindness.

King James Version

20And he said, Thou canst not see my face: for there shall no man see me, and live.

21And the LORD said, Behold, *there is* a place by me, and thou shalt stand upon a rock:

22And it shall come to pass, while my glory passeth by, that I will put thee in a clift of the rock, and will cover thee with my hand while I pass by:

23And I will take away mine hand, and thou shalt see my back parts: but my face shall not be seen.

34 And the LORD said unto Moses, Hew thee two tables of stone like unto the first: and I will write upon *these* tables the words that were in the first tables, which thou brakest.

2And be ready in the morning, and come up in the morning unto mount Sinai, and present thyself there to me in the top of the mount.

3And no man shall come up with thee, neither let any man be seen throughout all the mount; neither let the flocks nor herds feed before that mount.

4And he hewed two tables of stone like unto the first; and Moses rose up early in the morning, and went up unto mount Sinai, as the LORD had commanded him, and took in his hand the two tables of stone.

5And the LORD descended in the cloud, and stood with him there, and proclaimed the name of the LORD.

6And the LORD passed by before him, and proclaimed, The LORD, The LORD God, merciful and gracious, longsuffering, and abundant in goodness and truth,

7Keeping mercy for thousands, forgiving iniquity and transgression and sin, and *that* will by no means clear *the guilty;* visiting the iniquity of the fathers upon the children, and upon the children's children, unto the third and to the fourth *generation.*

8And Moses made haste, and bowed his head toward the earth, and worshipped.

9And he said, If now I have found grace in thy sight, O Lord, let my Lord, I pray thee, go amongst us; for it *is* a stiffnecked people; and pardon our iniquity and our sin, and take us for thine inheritance.

10And he said, Behold, I make a covenant: before all thy people I will do marvels, such as have not been done in all the earth, nor in any nation: and all the people among which thou *art* shall see the work of the LORD: for it *is* a terrible thing that I will do with thee.

Amplified Bible

20But, He said, You can not see My face, for no man shall see Me and live.

21And the Lord said, Behold, there is a place beside Me, and you shall stand upon the rock,

22And while My glory passes by, I will put you in a cleft of the rock and cover you with My hand until I have passed by.

23Then I will take away My hand and you shall see My back; but My face shall not be seen.

34 THE LORD said to Moses, Cut two tables of stone like the first, and I will write upon these tables the words that were on the first tables, which you broke.

2Be ready and come up in the morning to Mount Sinai, and present yourself there to Me on the top of the mountain.

3And no man shall come up with you, neither let any man be seen throughout all the mountain; neither let flocks or herds feed before that mountain.

4So Moses cut two tables of stone like the first, and he rose up early in the morning and went up on Mount Sinai, as the Lord had commanded him, and took *a*in his hand two tables of stone.

5And the Lord descended in the cloud and stood with him there and proclaimed the name of the Lord.

6And the Lord passed by before him, and proclaimed, The Lord! the Lord! a God merciful and gracious, slow to anger, and abundant in loving-kindness and truth,

7Keeping mercy *and* loving-kindness for thousands, forgiving iniquity and transgression and sin, but Who will by no means clear the guilty, visiting the iniquity of the fathers upon the children and the children's children, to the third and fourth generation.

8And Moses made haste to bow his head toward the earth and worshiped.

9And he said, If now I have found favor *and* loving-kindness in Your sight, O Lord, let the Lord, I pray You, go in the midst of us, although it is a stiff-necked people, and pardon our iniquity and our sin, and take us for Your inheritance.

10And the Lord said, Behold, I lay down [afresh the terms of the mutual agreement between Israel and Me] a covenant. Before all your people I will do marvels (wonders, miracles) such as have not been wrought *or* created in all the earth or in any nation; and all the people among whom you are shall see the work of the Lord; for it is a terrible thing [fearful and full of awe] that I will do with you.

AMP notes: a The two tables of stone are believed to have been pocket-size, easily carried in one hand. The pictures of Moses carrying tombstone-size tables are the result of the misconception of artists, and are not supported by the Bible.

King James Version

¹¹Observe thou that which I command thee *this* day: behold, I drive out before thee the Amorite, and the Canaanite, and the Hittite, and the Perizzite, and the Hivite, and the Jebusite.

¹²Take heed to thyself, lest thou make a covenant with the inhabitants of the land whither thou goest, lest it be for a snare in the midst of thee:

¹³But ye shall destroy their altars, break their images, and cut down their groves:

¹⁴For thou shalt worship no other god: for the LORD, whose name *is* Jealous, *is* a jealous God:

¹⁵Lest thou make a covenant with the inhabitants of the land, and they go a whoring after their gods, and do sacrifice unto their gods, and *one* call thee, and thou eat of his sacrifice;

¹⁶And thou take of their daughters unto thy sons, and their daughters go a whoring after their gods, and make thy sons go a whoring after their gods.

¹⁷Thou shalt make thee no molten gods.

¹⁸The feast of unleavened bread shalt thou keep: seven days thou shalt eat unleavened bread, as I commanded thee, in the time of the month Abib: for in the month Abib thou camest out from Egypt.

¹⁹All that openeth the matrix *is* mine; and every firstling amongst thy cattle, *whether* ox or sheep, *that* is male.

²⁰But the firstling of an ass thou shalt redeem with a lamb: and if thou redeem *him* not, then shalt thou break his neck. All the firstborn of thy sons thou shalt redeem: and none shall appear before me empty.

²¹Six days thou shalt work, but on the seventh day thou shalt rest: in earing time and in harvest thou shalt rest.

²²And thou shalt observe the feast of weeks, of the firstfruits of wheat harvest, and the feast of ingathering *at* the year's end.

²³Thrice in the year shall all your men children appear before the Lord GOD, the God of Israel.

²⁴For I will cast out the nations before thee, and enlarge thy borders: neither shall any man desire thy land, when thou shalt go up to appear before the LORD thy God thrice in the year.

²⁵Thou shalt not offer the blood of my sacrifice with leaven; neither shall the sacrifice of the feast of the passover be left unto the morning.

²⁶The first of the firstfruits of thy land thou shalt bring *unto* the house of the LORD thy God. Thou shalt not seethe a kid in his mother's milk.

²⁷And the LORD said unto Moses, Write thou these words: for after the tenor of these words I have made a covenant with thee and with Israel.

Amplified Bible

¹¹Observe what I command you this day. Behold, I drive out before you the Amorite, Canaanite, Hittite, Perizzite, Hivite, and Jebusite.

¹²Take heed to yourself, lest you make a covenant *or* mutual agreement with the inhabitants of the land to which you go, lest it become a snare in the midst of you.

¹³But you shall destroy their altars, dash in pieces their pillars (obelisks, images), and cut down their Asherim [symbols of the goddess Asherah];

¹⁴For you shall worship no other god; for the Lord, Whose name is Jealous, is a jealous (impassioned) God,

¹⁵Lest you make a covenant with the inhabitants of the land, and when they play the harlot after their gods and sacrifice to their gods and one invites you, you eat of his food sacrificed to idols,

¹⁶And you take of their daughters for your sons, and their daughters play the harlot after their gods and make your sons play the harlot after their gods.

¹⁷You shall make for yourselves no molten gods.

¹⁸The Feast of Unleavened Bread you shall keep. Seven days you shall eat unleavened bread, as I commanded you, in the time of the month of Abib; for in the month of Abib you came out of Egypt.

¹⁹All the males that first open the womb among your livestock are Mine, whether ox or sheep.

²⁰But the firstling of a donkey [an unclean beast] you shall redeem with a lamb *or* kid, and if you do not redeem it, then you shall break its neck. All the firstborn of your sons you shall redeem. And none of you shall appear before Me empty-handed.

²¹Six days you shall work, but on the seventh day you shall rest; even in plowing time and in harvest you shall rest [on the Sabbath].

²²You shall observe the Feast of Weeks, the firstfruits of the wheat harvest, and the Feast of Ingathering at the year's end.

²³Three times in the year shall all your males appear before the Lord God, the God of Israel.

²⁴For I will cast out the nations before you and enlarge your borders; neither shall any man desire [and molest] your land when you go up to appear before the Lord your God three times in the year.

²⁵You shall not offer the blood of My sacrifice with leaven; neither shall the sacrifice of the Feast of the Passover be left until morning.

²⁶The first of the firstfruits of your ground you shall bring to the house of the Lord your God. You shall not boil a kid in his mother's milk.

²⁷And the Lord said to Moses, Write these words, for after the purpose *and* character of these words I have made a covenant with you and with Israel.

King James Version

28 And he was there with the LORD forty days and forty nights; he did neither eat bread, nor drink water. And he wrote upon the tables the words of the covenant, the ten commandments.

29 ¶ And it came to pass, when Moses came down from mount Sinai with the two tables of Testimony in Moses' hand, when he came down from the mount, that Moses wist not that the skin of his face shone while he talked with him.

30 And when Aaron and all the children of Israel saw Moses, behold, the skin of his face shone; and they were afraid to come nigh him.

31 And Moses called unto them; and Aaron and all the rulers of the congregation returned unto him: and Moses talked with them.

32 And afterward all the children of Israel came nigh: and he gave them in commandment all that the LORD had spoken with him in mount Sinai.

33 And till Moses had done speaking with them, he put a vail on his face.

34 But when Moses went in before the LORD to speak with him, he took the vail off, until he came out. And he came out, and spake unto the children of Israel that which he was commanded.

35 And the children of Israel saw the face of Moses, that the skin of Moses' face shone: and Moses put the vail upon his face again, until he went in to speak with him.

35 And Moses gathered all the congregation of the children of Israel together, and said unto them, These are the words which the LORD hath commanded, that ye should do them.

2 Six days shall work be done, but on the seventh day there shall be to you a holy day, a sabbath of rest to the LORD: whosoever doeth work therein shall be put to death.

3 Ye shall kindle no fire throughout your habitations upon the sabbath day.

4 And Moses spake unto all the congregation of the children of Israel, saying, This is the thing which the LORD commanded, saying,

5 Take ye from amongst you an offering unto the LORD: whosoever is of a willing heart, let him bring it, an offering of the LORD; gold, and silver, and brass,

6 And blue, and purple, and scarlet, and fine linen, and goats' hair,

7 And rams' skins dyed red, and badgers' skins, and shittim wood,

8 And oil for the light, and spices for anointing oil, and for the sweet incense,

Amplified Bible

28 Moses was there with the Lord forty days and forty nights; he ate no bread and drank no water. And he wrote upon the tables the words of the covenant, the Ten Commandments.

29 When Moses came down from Mount Sinai with the two tables of the Testimony in his hand, he did not know that the skin of his face shone and sent forth beams by reason of his speaking with the Lord.

30 When Aaron and all the Israelites saw Moses, behold, the skin of his face shone, and they feared to come near him.

31 But Moses called to them; and Aaron and all the leaders of the congregation returned to him, and [he] talked with them.

32 Afterward all the Israelites came near, and he gave them in commandment all the Lord had said to him in Mount Sinai.

33 And when Moses had finished speaking with them, he put a veil on his face.

34 But when Moses went in before the Lord to speak with Him, [a]he took the veil off until he came out. And he came out and told the Israelites what he was commanded.

35 The Israelites saw the face of Moses, how the skin of it shone; and Moses put the veil on his face again until he went in to speak with God.

35 MOSES GATHERED all the congregation of the Israelites together and said to them, These are the things which the Lord has commanded that you do:

2 Six days shall work be done, but the seventh day shall be to you a holy day, a Sabbath of rest to the Lord; whoever works [on that day] shall be put to death.

3 You shall kindle no fire in all your dwellings on the Sabbath day.

4 And Moses said to all the congregation of the Israelites, This is what the Lord commanded:

5 Take from among you an offering to the Lord. Whoever is of a willing and generous heart, let him bring the Lord's offering: gold, silver, and bronze;

6 Blue, purple, and scarlet [stuff], fine linen; goats' hair;

7 And rams' skins tanned red, and skins of dolphins or porpoises; and acacia wood;

8 And oil for the light; and spices for anointing oil and for fragrant incense;

AMP notes: a The apostle Paul expressly refers to this incident when he says that we all may, with unveiled faces, behold the glory of the Lord, and be transformed (II Cor. 3:13-18). That blessed vision, which of old was given only to the great leader of Israel, is now within reach of each individual believer. The Gospel has no fences to keep the crowd off the mount of vision; the lowliest and most unworthy of its children may pass upward where the shining glory is to be seen. "We all . . . are changed" (F. B. Meyer, Moses, the Servant of God).

King James Version

⁹And onyx stones, and stones to be set for the ephod, and for the breastplate.

¹⁰And every wise hearted among you shall come, and make all that the LORD hath commanded;

¹¹The tabernacle, his tent, and his covering, his taches, and his boards, his bars, his pillars, and his sockets,

¹²The ark, and the staves thereof, *with* the mercy seat, and the vail of the covering,

¹³The table, and his staves, and all his vessels, and the shewbread,

¹⁴The candlestick also for the light, and his furniture, and his lamps, with the oil for the light,

¹⁵And the incense altar and his staves, and the anointing oil, and the sweet incense, and the hanging for the door at the entering in of the tabernacle,

¹⁶The altar of burnt offering with his brasen grate, his staves, and all his vessels, the laver and his foot,

¹⁷The hangings of the court, his pillars, and their sockets, and the hanging for the door of the court,

¹⁸The pins of the tabernacle, and the pins of the court, and their cords,

¹⁹The clothes of service, to do service in the holy *place*, the holy garments for Aaron the priest, and the garments of his sons, to minister in the priest's office.

²⁰ ¶ And all the congregation of the children of Israel departed from the presence of Moses.

²¹And they came, every one whose heart stirred him up, and every one whom his spirit made willing, *and* they brought the LORD'S offering to the work of the tabernacle of the congregation, and for all his service, and for the holy garments.

²²And they came, both men and women, as many as were willing hearted, *and* brought bracelets, and earrings, and rings, and tablets, all jewels of gold: and every man that offered *offered* an offering of gold unto the LORD.

²³And every man, with whom was found blue, and purple, and scarlet, and fine linen, and goats' *hair,* and red skins of rams, and badgers' skins, brought *them.*

²⁴Every one that did offer an offering of silver and brass brought the LORD'S offering: and every man, with whom was found shittim wood for any work of the service, brought *it.*

²⁵And all the women that were wise hearted did spin with their hands, and brought that which they had spun, *both* of blue, and of purple, *and* of scarlet, and of fine linen.

²⁶And all the women whose heart stirred them up in wisdom spun goats' *hair.*

²⁷And the rulers brought onyx stones, and

Amplified Bible

⁹And onyx stones and other stones to be set for the ephod and the breastplate.

¹⁰And let every able *and* wisehearted man among you come and make all that the Lord has commanded:

¹¹The tabernacle, its tent and its covering, its hooks, its boards, its bars, its pillars, and its sockets *or* bases;

¹²The ark and its poles, with the mercy seat, and the veil of the screen;

¹³The table and its poles and all its utensils, and the showbread (the bread of the Presence);

¹⁴The lampstand also for the light, and its utensils and its lamps, and the oil for the light;

¹⁵And the incense altar and its poles, the anointing oil and the fragrant incense, the hanging *or* screen for the door at the entrance of the tabernacle;

¹⁶The altar of burnt offering, with its bronze grating, its poles and all its utensils, the laver and its base;

¹⁷The court's hangings, its pillars and their sockets *or* bases, and the hanging *or* screen for the gate of the court;

¹⁸The pegs of the tabernacle and of the court, and their cords,

¹⁹The finely wrought garments for ministering in the Holy Place, the holy garments for Aaron the [high] priest and for his sons to minister as priests.

²⁰Then all the congregation of the Israelites left Moses' presence.

²¹And they came, each one whose heart stirred him up and whose spirit made him willing, and brought the Lord's offering to be used for the [new] Tent of Meeting, for all its service, and the holy garments.

²²They came, both men and women, all who were willinghearted, and brought brooches, earrings *or* nose rings, signet rings, and armlets *or* necklaces, all jewels of gold, everyone bringing an offering of gold to the Lord.

²³And everyone with whom was found blue or purple or scarlet [stuff], or fine linen, or goats' hair, or rams' skins made red [in tanning], or dolphin *or* porpoise skins brought them.

²⁴Everyone who could make an offering of silver or bronze brought it as the Lord's offering, and every man with whom was found any acacia wood for any work of the service brought it.

²⁵All the women who had ability *and* were wisehearted spun with their hands and brought what they had spun of blue and purple and scarlet [stuff] and fine linen;

²⁶And all the women who had ability *and* whose hearts stirred them up in wisdom spun the goats' hair.

²⁷The leaders brought onyx stones and

King James Version

stones to be set, for the ephod, and for the breastplate;

28And spice, and oil for the light, and for the anointing oil, and for the sweet incense.

29The children of Israel brought a willing offering unto the LORD, every man and woman, whose heart made them willing to bring for all *manner of* work, which the LORD had commanded to be made by the hand of Moses.

30 ¶ And Moses said unto the children of Israel, See, the LORD hath called by name Bezaleel the son of Uri, the son of Hur, of the tribe of Judah;

31And he hath filled him *with* the spirit of God, in wisdom, in understanding, and in knowledge, and in all *manner of* workmanship;

32And to devise curious works, to work in gold, and in silver, and in brass,

33And in the cutting of stones, to set *them,* and in carving of wood, to make any *manner of* cunning work.

34And he hath put in his heart that *he* may teach, *both* he, and Aholiab, the son of Ahisamach, of the tribe of Dan.

35Them hath he filled *with* wisdom of heart, to work all *manner of* work, of the engraver, and of the cunning workman, and of the embroiderer, in blue, and in purple, in scarlet, and in fine linen, and of the weaver, *even* of them that do any work, and of those that devise cunning work.

36 Then wrought Bezaleel and Aholiab, and every wise hearted man, in whom the LORD put wisdom and understanding to know how to work all *manner of* work for the service of the sanctuary, according to all that the LORD had commanded.

2And Moses called Bezaleel and Aholiab, and every wise hearted man, in whose heart the LORD had put wisdom, *even* every one whose heart stirred him up to come unto the work to do it:

3And they received of Moses all the offering, which the children of Israel had brought for the work of the service of the sanctuary, to make it *withal.* And they brought yet unto him free offerings every morning.

4And all the wise *men,* that wrought all the work of the sanctuary, came every man from his work which they made;

5And they spake unto Moses, saying, The people bring much more than enough for the service of the work, which the LORD commanded to make.

6And Moses gave commandment, and they caused it to be proclaimed throughout the camp, saying, Let neither man nor woman make any more work for the offering of the sanctuary. So the people were restrained from bringing.

Amplified Bible

stones to be set for the ephod and for the breastplate,

28And spice, and oil for the light, and for the anointing oil and for the fragrant incense.

29The Israelites brought a freewill offering to the Lord, all men and women whose hearts made them willing *and* moved them to bring anything for any of the work which the Lord had commanded by Moses to be done.

30And Moses said to the Israelites, See, the Lord called by name Bezalel son of Uri, the son of Hur, of the tribe of Judah;

31And He has filled him with the Spirit of God, with ability *and* wisdom, with intelligence *and* understanding, and with knowledge and all craftsmanship,

32To devise artistic designs, to work in gold, silver, and bronze,

33In cutting of stones for setting, and in carving of wood, for work in every skilled craft.

34And God has put in Bezalel's heart that he may teach, both he and Aholiab son of Ahisamach, of the tribe of Dan.

35He has filled them with wisdom of heart *and* ability to do all manner of craftsmanship, of the engraver, of the skillful workman, of the embroiderer in blue, purple, and scarlet [stuff] and in fine linen, and of the weaver, even of those who do or design any skilled work.

36 BEZALEL AND Aholiab and every wisehearted man in whom the Lord has put wisdom and understanding to know how to do all the work for the service of the sanctuary shall work according to all that the Lord has commanded.

2And Moses called Bezalel and Aholiab and every able *and* wisehearted man in whose mind the Lord had put wisdom *and* ability, everyone whose heart stirred him up to come to do the work;

3And they received from Moses all the freewill offerings which the Israelites had brought for doing the work of the sanctuary, to prepare it for service. And they continued to bring him freewill offerings every morning.

4And all the wise *and* able men who were doing the work on the sanctuary came, every man from the work he was doing,

5And they said to Moses, The people bring much more than enough for doing the work which the Lord commanded to do.

6So Moses commanded and it was proclaimed in all the camp, Let no man or woman do anything more for the sanctuary offering. So the people were restrained from bringing,

King James Version

⁷For the stuff *they had* was sufficient for all the work to make it, and too much.

⁸ ¶ And every wise hearted *man* among them that wrought the work *of* the tabernacle made ten curtains *of* fine twined linen, and blue, and purple, and scarlet: *with* cherubims *of* cunning work made he them.

⁹The length of one curtain *was* twenty and eight cubits, and the breadth of one curtain four cubits: the curtains *were* all of one size.

¹⁰And he coupled the five curtains one unto another: and *the other* five curtains he coupled one unto another.

¹¹And he made loops of blue on the edge of one curtain from the selvedge in the coupling: likewise he made in the uttermost side of *another* curtain, in the coupling of the second.

¹²Fifty loops made he in one curtain, and fifty loops made he in the edge of the curtain which *was* in the coupling of the second: the loops held one *curtain* to another.

¹³And he made fifty taches of gold, and coupled the curtains one unto another with the taches: so it became one tabernacle.

¹⁴And he made curtains *of* goats' *hair* for the tent over the tabernacle: eleven curtains he made them.

¹⁵The length of one curtain *was* thirty cubits, and four cubits *was* the breadth of one curtain: the eleven curtains *were* of one size.

¹⁶And he coupled five curtains by themselves, and six curtains by themselves.

¹⁷And he made fifty loops upon the uttermost edge of the curtain in the coupling, and fifty loops made he upon the edge of the curtain which coupleth the second.

¹⁸And he made fifty taches of brass to couple the tent together, that *it* might be one.

¹⁹And he made a covering for the tent *of* rams' skins dyed red, and a covering of badgers' skins above *that*.

²⁰And he made boards for the tabernacle *of* shittim wood, standing up.

²¹The length of a board *was* ten cubits, and the breadth of a board one cubit and a half.

²²One board had two tenons, equally distant one from another: thus did he make for all the boards of the tabernacle.

²³And he made boards for the tabernacle; twenty boards for the south side southward:

²⁴And forty sockets of silver he made under the twenty boards; two sockets under one board for his two tenons, and two sockets under another board for his two tenons.

Amplified Bible

⁷For the stuff they had was sufficient to do all the work and more.

⁸And all the able *and* wisehearted men among them who did the work on the tabernacle made ten curtains of fine twined linen and blue, purple, and scarlet [stuff], with cherubim skillfully worked on them.

⁹The length of each curtain was twenty-eight cubits and its breadth four cubits; all the curtains were one size.

¹⁰[Bezalel] coupled five curtains one to another and the other five curtains he coupled one to another.

¹¹And he made loops of blue on the outer edge of the last curtain in the first set; this he did also on the inner edge of the first curtain in the second set.

¹²Fifty loops he made in the one curtain and fifty loops in the edge of the curtain which was the second set; the loops were opposite one another.

¹³And he made fifty clasps of gold and coupled the curtains together with the clasps so that the tabernacle became one unit.

¹⁴And he made eleven curtains of goats' hair for a tent over the tabernacle.

¹⁵The length of one curtain was thirty cubits and four cubits was the breadth; the eleven curtains were of equal size.

¹⁶And he coupled five curtains by themselves and the other six curtains by themselves.

¹⁷And he made fifty loops on the outmost edge of the curtain to be coupled and fifty loops he made on the inner edge of the second curtain to be coupled.

¹⁸He made fifty clasps of bronze to couple the tent together into one whole.

¹⁹He made a covering for the tent of ᵃrams' skins tanned red, and above it a covering of dolphin *or* porpoise skins.

²⁰He made boards of acacia wood for the upright framework of the tabernacle.

²¹The length of a board was ten cubits and the breadth one cubit and a half.

²²Each board had two tenons (projections) to fit into a mortise to form a clutch; he did this for all the boards of the tabernacle.

²³And he made thus the boards [for frames] for the tabernacle: twenty boards for the south side,

²⁴And he made under the twenty boards forty sockets *or* bases of silver, two sockets under one board for its two tenons *or* hands, and two sockets under another board for its two tenons.

AMP notes: ᵃ The final coverings of the tabernacle tent are not to be confused with the second one of goats' hair (Exod. 36:14). There were **four distinct coverings** of the tabernacle tent: 1. A covering of fine twined linen woven with blue, purple, and scarlet, with figures of cherubim upon it. It was made of two long pieces, one running from north to south, the other from east to west [and overlapping for the ceiling] (Exod. 26:1, 6; 36:8ff.). 2. Over this a covering of woven goats' hair was thrown (Exod. 26:7; 36:14). 3. A third covering of rams' skins made red (Exod. 26:14; 36:19). 4. And "above it" another covering of dolphin or porpoise skins, weighing the others down and giving perfect protection from the weather (Exod. 26:14; 36:19).

King James Version

25And for the other side of the tabernacle, *which is* toward the north corner, he made twenty boards,

26And their forty sockets *of* silver; two sockets under one board, and two sockets under another board.

27And for the sides of the tabernacle westward he made six boards.

28And two boards made he for the corners of the tabernacle in the two sides.

29And they were coupled beneath, and coupled together at the head thereof, to one ring: thus he did to both of them in both the corners.

30And there were eight boards; and their sockets *were* sixteen sockets *of* silver, under every board two sockets.

31And he made bars of shittim wood; five for the boards of the one side of the tabernacle,

32And five bars for the boards of the other side of the tabernacle, and five bars for the boards of the tabernacle for the sides westward.

33And he made the middle bar to shoot through the boards from the one end to the other.

34And he overlaid the boards with gold, and made their rings *of* gold *to be* places for the bars, and overlaid the bars with gold.

35 ¶ And he made a vail *of* blue, and purple, and scarlet, and fine twined linen: *with* cherubims made he it *of* cunning work.

36And he made thereunto four pillars of shittim *wood,* and overlaid them with gold: their hooks *were of* gold; and he cast for them four sockets of silver.

37And he made a hanging for the tabernacle door *of* blue, and purple, and scarlet, and fine twined linen, *of* needlework;

38And the five pillars of it with their hooks: and he overlaid their chapiters and their fillets with gold: but their five sockets *were of* brass.

37 And Bezaleel made the ark *of* shittim wood: two cubits and a half *was* the length of it, and a cubit and a half the breadth of it, and a cubit and a half the height of it:

2And he overlaid it with pure gold within and without, and made a crown *of* gold to it round about.

3And he cast for it four rings of gold, *to be set* by the four corners of it; even two rings upon the one side of it, and two rings upon the other side of it.

4And he made staves of shittim wood, and overlaid them with gold.

5And he put the staves into the rings by the sides of the ark, to bear the ark.

6And he made the mercy seat *of* pure gold: two cubits and a half *was* the length thereof, and one cubit and a half the breadth thereof.

7And he made two cherubims *of* gold, beaten

Amplified Bible

25For the other side of the tabernacle, the north side, he made twenty boards

26And their forty sockets *or* bases of silver, two sockets under [the end of] each board.

27And for the rear or west side of the tabernacle he made six [frame] boards.

28And two boards he made for each corner of the tabernacle in the rear.

29They were separate below but linked together at the top with one ring; thus he made both of them in both corners.

30There were eight boards with sixteen sockets *or* bases of silver, and under [the end of] each board two sockets.

31He made bars of acacia wood, five for the [frame] boards of the one side of the tabernacle,

32And five bars for the boards of its other side, and five bars for the boards at the rear or west side.

33And he made the middle bar pass through halfway up the boards from one end to the other.

34He overlaid the boards and the bars with gold and made their rings of gold as places for the bars.

35And he made the veil of blue, purple, and scarlet [stuff] and fine twined linen, with cherubim skillfully worked.

36For [the veil] he made four pillars of acacia [wood] and overlaid them with gold; their hooks were of gold, and he cast for them four sockets *or* bases of silver.

37And he made a screen for the tent door of blue, purple, and scarlet [stuff] and fine twined linen, embroidered,

38And he made the five pillars of it with their hooks, and overlaid their ornamental tops and joinings with gold, but their five sockets were of bronze.

37 BEZALEL MADE the ark of acacia wood—two cubits and a half was the length of it, a cubit and a half the breadth of it, and a cubit and a half the height of it.

2He overlaid it with pure gold within and without and made a molding *or* crown of gold to go around the top of it.

3He cast four rings of gold for its four corners, two rings on either side.

4He made poles of acacia wood and overlaid them with gold.

5He put the poles through the rings at the sides of the ark to carry it.

6[Bezalel] made the mercy seat of pure gold, two cubits and a half its length and one cubit and a half its breadth.

7And he made two cherubim of beaten gold;

King James Version

out of one piece made he them, on the two ends of the mercy seat;

8One cherub on the end on this side, and another cherub on the *other* end on that side: out of the mercy seat made he the cherubims on the two ends thereof.

9And the cherubims spread out *their* wings on high, *and* covered with their wings over the mercy seat, with their faces one to another; *even* to the mercy seatward were the faces of the cherubims.

10 ¶ And he made the table *of* shittim wood: two cubits *was* the length thereof, and a cubit the breadth thereof, and a cubit and a half the height thereof:

11And he overlaid it with pure gold, and made thereunto a crown *of* gold round about.

12Also he made thereunto a border of a handbreadth round about; and made a crown of gold for the border thereof round about.

13And he cast for it four rings of gold, and put the rings upon the four corners that *were* in the four feet thereof.

14Over against the border were the rings, the places for the staves to bear the table.

15And he made the staves *of* shittim wood, and overlaid them with gold, to bear the table.

16And he made the vessels which *were* upon the table, his dishes, and his spoons, and his bowls, and *his* covers to cover withal, *of* pure gold.

17 ¶ And he made the candlestick *of* pure gold: *of* beaten work made he the candlestick; his shaft, and his branch, his bowls, his knops, and his flowers, were of the same:

18And six branches going out of the sides thereof; three branches of the candlestick out of the one side thereof, and three branches of the candlestick out of the other side thereof:

19Three bowls made after the fashion of almonds in one branch, a knop and a flower; and three bowls made like almonds in another branch, a knop and a flower: so throughout the six branches going out of the candlestick.

20And in the candlestick *were* four bowls made like almonds, his knops, and his flowers:

21And a knop under two branches of the same, and a knop under two branches of the same, and a knop under two branches of the same, according to the six branches going out of it.

22Their knops and their branches were of the same: all of it *was* one beaten work *of* pure gold.

23And he made his seven lamps, and his snuffers, and his snuffdishes, *of* pure gold.

24*Of* a talent *of* pure gold made he it, and all the vessels thereof.

25 ¶ And he made the incense altar *of* shittim wood: the length of it *was* a cubit, and the breadth of it a cubit; *it was* foursquare; and two cubits *was* the height of it; the horns thereof were of the same.

Amplified Bible

on the two ends of the mercy seat he made them,

8One cherub at one end and one at the other end; of one piece with the mercy seat he made the cherubim at its two ends.

9And the cherubim spread out their wings on high, covering the mercy seat with their wings, with their faces to each other, looking down to the mercy seat.

10Bezalel made the [showbread] table of acacia wood; it was two cubits long, a cubit wide, and a cubit and a half high.

11He overlaid it with pure gold and made a molding of gold around its top.

12And he made a border around it [just under the top] a handbreadth wide, and a molding of gold around the border.

13And he cast for it four rings of gold and fastened the rings on the four corners that were at its four legs.

14Close to the border were the rings, the places for the poles to pass through to carry the [showbread] table.

15[Bezalel] made the poles of acacia wood to carry the [showbread] table and overlaid them with gold.

16He made of pure gold the vessels which were to be on the table, its plates and dishes [for bread], its bowls and flagons for pouring [liquid sacrifices].

17And he made the lampstand of pure gold; its base and shaft were made of hammered work; its cups, its knobs, and its flowers were of one piece with it.

18There were six branches going out of the sides of the lampstand, three branches out of one side of it and three branches out of the other side of it;

19Three cups made like almond blossoms in one branch, each with a [calyx] knob and a flower, and three cups made like almond blossoms in the [opposite] branch, each with a [calyx] knob and a flower; and so for the six branches going out of the lampstand.

20On [the shaft of] the lampstand were four cups made like almond blossoms, with knobs and flowers [one at the top].

21And a knob under each pair of branches, of one piece with the lampstand, for the six branches going out of it.

22Their knobs and their branches were of one piece with it, all of it hammered work of pure gold.

23And he made of pure gold its seven lamps, its snuffers, and its ashtrays.

24Of a talent of pure gold he made the lampstand and all its utensils.

25And [Bezalel] made the incense altar of acacia wood; its top was a cubit square and it was two cubits high; the horns were one piece with it.

King James Version

26And he overlaid it with pure gold, *both* the top of it, and the sides thereof round about, and the horns of it: also he made unto it a crown *of* gold round about.

27And he made two rings of gold for it under the crown thereof, by the two corners of it, upon the two sides thereof, to be places for the staves to bear it withal.

28And he made the staves *of* shittim wood, and overlaid them with gold.

29¶ And he made the holy anointing oil, and the pure incense of sweet spices, *according to* the work of the apothecary.

38 And he made the altar of burnt offering *of* shittim wood: five cubits *was* the length thereof, and five cubits the breadth thereof; *it was* foursquare; and three cubits the height thereof.

2And he made the horns thereof on the four corners of it; the horns thereof were of the same: and he overlaid it with brass.

3And he made all the vessels of the altar, the pots, and the shovels, and the basons, *and* the fleshhooks, and the firepans: all the vessels thereof made he *of* brass.

4And he made for the altar a brasen grate of network under the compass thereof beneath unto the midst of it.

5And he cast four rings for the four ends of the grate of brass, *to be* places for the staves.

6And he made the staves *of* shittim wood, and overlaid them with brass.

7And he put the staves into the rings on the sides of the altar, to bear it withal; he made the *altar* hollow with boards.

8And he made the laver *of* brass, and the foot of it *of* brass, of the looking-glasses of *the women* assembling, which assembled *at* the door of the tabernacle of the congregation.

9¶ And he made the court: on the south side southward the hangings of the court *were of* fine twined linen, an hundred cubits:

10Their pillars *were* twenty, and their brasen sockets twenty; the hooks of the pillars and their fillets *were of* silver.

11And for the north side *the hangings were* an hundred cubits, their pillars *were* twenty, and their sockets *of* brass twenty; the hooks of the pillars and their fillets *of* silver.

12And for the west side *were* hangings of fifty cubits, their pillars ten, and their sockets ten; the hooks of the pillars and their fillets *of* silver.

13And for the east side eastward fifty cubits.

14The hangings of the *one* side *of the gate were* fifteen cubits; their pillars three, and their sockets three.

15And for the other side of the court gate, on this hand and that hand, *were* hangings of fifteen cubits; their pillars three, and their sockets three.

Amplified Bible

26He overlaid it with pure gold, its top, its sides round about, and its horns; also he made a rim around it of gold.

27And he made two rings of gold for it under its rim, on its two opposite sides, as places for the poles [to pass through] to carry it.

28And he made the poles of acacia wood and overlaid them with gold.

29He also made the holy anointing oil [symbol of the Holy Spirit] and the pure, fragrant incense, after the perfumer's art.

38 BEZALEL MADE the burnt offering altar of acacia wood; its top was five cubits square and it was three cubits high.

2He made its horns on the four corners of it; the horns were of one piece with it, and he overlaid it with bronze.

3He made all the utensils *and* vessels of the altar, the pots, shovels, basins, forks *or* fleshhooks, and firepans; all its utensils *and* vessels he made of bronze.

4And he made for the altar a bronze grate of network under its ledge, extending halfway down it.

5He cast four rings for the four corners of the bronze grating to be places for the poles [with which to carry it].

6And he made the poles of acacia wood and overlaid them with bronze.

7And he put the poles through the rings on the altar's sides with which to carry it; he made it hollow with planks.

8He made the laver and its base of bronze from the mirrors of the women who ministered at the door of the Tent of Meeting.

9And he made the court: for the south side the hangings of the court were of fine twined linen, a hundred cubits;

10Their pillars and their bronze sockets *or* bases were twenty; the hooks of the pillars and their joinings were silver.

11And for the north side the hangings were [also] a hundred cubits; their pillars and their sockets *or* bases of bronze were twenty; the hooks of the pillars and their joinings were of silver.

12But for the west side were hangings of fifty cubits; their pillars and their sockets *or* bases were ten; the hooks of the pillars and their joinings were of silver.

13And for the front, the east side, fifty cubits.

14The hangings for one side of the gate were fifteen cubits; their pillars three and their sockets *or* bases three.

15Also for the other side of the court gate, left and right, were hangings of fifteen cubits; their pillars three and their sockets *or* bases three.

King James Version

16All the hangings of the court round about *were of* fine twined linen.

17And the sockets for the pillars *were of* brass; the hooks of the pillars and their fillets *of* silver; and the overlaying of their chapiters *of* silver; and all the pillars of the court *were* filleted *with* silver.

18And the hanging for the gate of the court *was* needlework, *of* blue, and purple, and scarlet, and fine twined linen: and twenty cubits *was* the length, and the height in the breadth *was* five cubits, answerable to the hangings of the court.

19And their pillars *were* four, and their sockets *of* brass four; their hooks *of* silver, and the overlaying of their chapiters and their fillets *of* silver.

20And all the pins of the tabernacle, and of the court round about, *were of* brass.

21 ¶ This is the sum of the tabernacle, *even* of the tabernacle of Testimony, as it was counted, according to the commandment of Moses, *for* the service of the Levites, by the hand of Ithamar, son to Aaron the priest.

22And Bezaleel the son of Uri, the son of Hur, of the tribe of Judah, made all that the LORD commanded Moses.

23And with him *was* Aholiab, son of Ahisamach, of the tribe of Dan, an engraver, and a cunning workman, and an embroiderer in blue, and in purple, and in scarlet, and fine linen.

24All the gold that was occupied for the work in all the work of the holy *place,* even the gold of the offering, was twenty and nine talents, and seven hundred and thirty shekels, after the shekel of the sanctuary.

25And the silver of them that were numbered of the congregation *was* an hundred talents, and a thousand seven hundred and threescore and fifteen shekels, after the shekel of the sanctuary:

26A bekah for every man, *that is,* half a shekel, after the shekel of the sanctuary, for every one that went to be numbered, from twenty years old and upward, for six hundred thousand and three thousand and five hundred and fifty *men.*

27And of the hundred talents of silver were cast the sockets of the sanctuary, and the sockets of the vail; an hundred sockets of the hundred talents, a talent for a socket.

28And of the thousand seven hundred seventy and five *shekels* he made hooks for the pillars, and overlaid their chapiters, and filleted them.

29And the brass of the offering *was* seventy talents, and two thousand and four hundred shekels.

30And therewith he made the sockets to the door of the tabernacle of the congregation, and the brasen altar, and the brasen grate for it, and all the vessels of the altar,

31And the sockets of the court round about,

Amplified Bible

16All the hangings around the court were of fine twined linen.

17The sockets for the pillars were of bronze, the hooks of the pillars and their joinings of silver, the overlaying of their tops of silver, and all the pillars of the court were joined with silver.

18The hanging *or* screen for the gate of the court was embroidered in blue, purple, and scarlet [stuff], and fine twined linen; the length was twenty cubits and the height in the breadth was five cubits, corresponding to the hangings of the court.

19Their pillars were four and their sockets of bronze four; their hooks were of silver, and the overlaying of their tops and their joinings were of silver.

20All the pegs for the tabernacle and around the court were of bronze.

21This is the sum of the things for the tabernacle of the Testimony, as counted at the command of Moses, for the work of the Levites under the direction of Ithamar son of Aaron, the [high] priest.

22Bezalel son of Uri, the son of Hur, of the tribe of Judah, made all that the Lord commanded Moses.

23With him was Aholiab son of Ahisamach, of the tribe of Dan, an engraver, a skillful craftsman, and embroiderer in blue, purple, and scarlet [stuff], and in fine linen.

24All the gold that was used for the work in all the building *and* furnishing of the sanctuary, the gold from the offering, was 29 talents and 730 shekels, by the shekel of the sanctuary.

25And the silver from those numbered of the congregation was 100 talents and 1,775 shekels, by sanctuary standards:

26A beka for each man, that is, half a shekel, by the sanctuary shekel, for everyone who was counted, from twenty years old and upward, for 603,550 men.

27The 100 talents of silver were for casting the sockets *or* bases of the sanctuary and of the veil; 100 sockets for the 100 talents, a talent for a socket.

28Of the 1,775 shekels he made hooks for the pillars, and overlaid their tops, and made joinings for them.

29The bronze of the offering was 70 talents and 2,400 shekels.

30With it Bezalel made the sockets for the door of the Tent of Meeting, and the bronze altar and the bronze grate for it, and all the utensils of the altar,

31The sockets of the court round about and of

King James Version

and the sockets of the court gate, and all the pins of the tabernacle, and all the pins of the court round about.

39 And of the blue, and purple, and scarlet, they made clothes of service, to do service in the holy *place*, and made the holy garments for Aaron; as the LORD commanded Moses.

2And he made the ephod *of* gold, blue, and purple, and scarlet, and fine twined linen.

3And they did beat the gold into thin plates, and cut *it into* wires, to work *it* in the blue, and in the purple, and in the scarlet, and in the fine linen, *with* cunning work.

4They made shoulderpieces for it, to couple *it* together: by the two edges was it coupled together.

5And the curious girdle of his ephod, that *was* upon it, *was* of the same, according to the work thereof; *of* gold, blue, and purple, and scarlet, and fine twined linen; as the LORD commanded Moses.

6And they wrought onyx stones inclosed *in* ouches *of* gold, graven *as* signets are graven, with the names of the children of Israel.

7And he put them on the shoulders of the ephod, *that they should be* stones for a memorial to the children of Israel; as the LORD commanded Moses.

8And he made the breastplate *of* cunning work, like the work of the ephod; *of* gold, blue, and purple, and scarlet, and fine twined linen.

9It was foursquare; they made the breastplate double: a span *was* the length thereof, and a span the breadth thereof, *being* doubled.

10And they set in it four rows of stones: *the first* row *was* a sardius, a topaz, and a carbuncle: *this was* the first row.

11And the second row, an emerald, a sapphire, and a diamond.

12And the third row, a ligure, an agate, and an amethyst.

13And the fourth row, a beryl, an onyx, and a jasper: *they were* inclosed *in* ouches *of* gold in their inclosings.

14And the stones *were* according to the names of the children of Israel, twelve, according to their names, *like* the engravings of a signet, every one with his name, according to the twelve tribes.

15And they made upon the breastplate chains at the ends, *of* wreathen work *of* pure gold.

16And they made two ouches *of* gold, and two gold rings; and put the two rings in the two ends of the breastplate.

17And they put the two wreathen *chains of* gold in the two rings on the ends of the breastplate.

18And the two ends of the two wreathen

Amplified Bible

the court gate, and all the pegs of the tabernacle and around the court.

39 AND OF the blue and purple and scarlet [stuff] they made finely wrought garments for serving in the Holy Place; they made the holy garments for Aaron, as the Lord had commanded Moses.

2And Bezalel made the ephod of gold, blue, purple, and scarlet [stuff], and fine twined linen.

3And they beat the gold into thin sheets and cut it into wires to work into the blue, purple, and scarlet [stuff] and the fine linen, in skilled design.

4They made shoulder pieces for the ephod, joined to it at its two edges.

5And the skillfully woven band on it, to gird it on, was of the same piece and workmanship with it, of gold, blue, purple, and scarlet [stuff], and fine twined linen, as the Lord had commanded Moses.

6And they prepared the onyx stones enclosed in settings of gold filigree and engraved as signets are engraved with the names of the sons of Israel.

7And he put them on the shoulder pieces of the ephod to be stones of memorial *or* remembrance for the Israelites, as the Lord had commanded Moses.

8And [Bezalel] made the breastplate skillfully, like the work of the ephod, of gold, blue, purple, and scarlet [stuff], and fine twined linen.

9The breastplate was a [hand's] span square when doubled over.

10And they set in it four rows of stones; a sardius, a topaz, and a carbuncle made the first row;

11The second row an emerald, a sapphire, and a diamond;

12The third row a jacinth, an agate, and an amethyst;

13And the fourth row a beryl, an onyx, and a jasper; they were enclosed in settings of gold filigree.

14There were twelve stones with their names according to those of the sons of Israel, engraved like a signet, each with its name, according to the twelve tribes.

15And they made [at the ends] of the breastplate twisted chains like cords, of pure gold.

16And they made two settings of gold filigree and two gold rings which they put on the two ends of the breastplate.

17And they put the two twisted cords *or* woven chains of gold in the two rings on the end edges of the breastplate.

18And the other two ends of the twisted cords

King James Version

chains they fastened in the two ouches, and put them on the shoulderpieces of the ephod, before it.

19 And they made two rings of gold, and put *them* on the two ends of the breastplate, upon the border of it, which *was* on the side of the ephod inward.

20 And they made two *other* golden rings, and put them on the two sides of the ephod underneath, toward the forepart of it, over against the *other* coupling thereof, above the curious girdle of the ephod.

21 And they did bind the breastplate by his rings unto the rings of the ephod with a lace of blue, that *it* might be above the curious girdle of the ephod, and that the breastplate might not be loosed from the ephod; as the LORD commanded Moses.

22 And he made the robe of the ephod *of* woven work, all of blue.

23 And *there was* a hole in the midst of the robe, as the hole of an habergeon, *with* a band round about the hole, *that* it should not rend.

24 And they made upon the hems of the robe pomegranates of blue, and purple, and scarlet, *and* twined *linen*.

25 And they made bells of pure gold, and put the bells between the pomegranates upon the hem of the robe, round about between the pomegranates;

26 A bell and a pomegranate, a bell and a pomegranate, round about the hem of the robe to minister *in;* as the LORD commanded Moses.

27 And they made coats of fine linen *of* woven work for Aaron, and for his sons,

28 And a mitre *of* fine linen, and goodly bonnets *of* fine linen, and linen breeches *of* fine twined linen,

29 And a girdle *of* fine twined linen, and blue, and purple, and scarlet, *of* needlework; as the LORD commanded Moses.

30 And they made the plate of the holy crown *of* pure gold, and wrote upon it a writing, *like to* the engravings of a signet, HOLINESS TO THE LORD.

31 And they tied unto it a lace of blue, to fasten *it* on high upon the mitre; as the LORD commanded Moses.

32 ¶ Thus was all the work of the tabernacle of the tent of the congregation finished: and the children of Israel did according to all that the LORD commanded Moses, so did they.

33 And they brought the tabernacle unto Moses, the tent, and all his furniture, his taches, his boards, his bars, and his pillars, and his sockets,

34 And the covering of rams' skins dyed red, and the covering of badgers' skins, and the vail of the covering,

35 The ark of the Testimony, and the staves thereof, and the mercy seat,

Amplified Bible

or chains of gold they put on the two settings and put them on the shoulder pieces of the ephod, in front.

19 They made two rings of gold and put them on the two ends of the breastplate, on the inside edge of it next to the ephod.

20 And they made two [other] gold rings and attached them to the two shoulder pieces of the ephod underneath, in front, at its joining above the skillfully woven band of the ephod.

21 They bound the breastplate by its rings to those of the ephod with a blue lace, that it might lie upon the skillfully woven band of the ephod and that the breastplate might not be loosed from the ephod, as the Lord commanded Moses.

22 And he made the robe of the ephod of woven work all of blue.

23 And there was an opening [for the head] in the middle of the robe like the hole in a coat of mail, with a binding around it, that it should not be torn.

24 On the skirts of the robe they made pomegranates of blue and purple and scarlet [stuff] and twined linen.

25 And they made bells of pure gold and put [them] between the pomegranates around the skirts of the robe;

26 A bell and a pomegranate, a bell and a pomegranate, round about on the skirts of the robe for ministering, as the Lord commanded Moses.

27 And they made the long and sleeved tunics woven of fine linen for Aaron and his sons,

28 And the turban, and the ornamental caps of fine linen, and the breeches of fine twined linen,

29 The girdle or sash of fine twined linen, and blue, purple, and scarlet embroidery, as the Lord commanded Moses.

30 And they made the plate of the holy crown of pure gold and wrote upon it an inscription, like the engravings of a signet, HOLY TO THE LORD.

31 They tied to it a lace of blue to fasten it on the turban above, as the Lord commanded Moses.

32 Thus all the work of the tabernacle of the Tent of Meeting was finished; according to all that the Lord commanded Moses, so the Israelites had done.

33 And they brought the tabernacle to Moses: the tent and all its furnishings, its clasps, its [frame] boards, its bars, its pillars, its sockets or bases;

34 And the covering of rams' skins made red, and the covering of dolphin or porpoise skins, and the veil of the screen;

35 The ark of the Testimony, its poles, and the mercy seat;

King James Version

36The table, *and* all the vessels thereof, and the shewbread,

37The pure candlestick, *with* the lamps thereof, *even with* the lamps to be set in order, and all the vessels thereof, and the oil for light,

38And the golden altar, and the anointing oil, and the sweet incense, and the hanging for the tabernacle door,

39The brasen altar, and his grate of brass, his staves, and all his vessels, the laver and his foot,

40The hangings of the court, his pillars, and his sockets, and the hanging for the court gate, his cords, and his pins, and all the vessels of the service of the tabernacle, for the tent of the congregation,

41The clothes of service to do service in the holy *place*, and the holy garments for Aaron the priest, and his sons' garments, to minister in the priest's office.

42According to all that the LORD commanded Moses, so the children of Israel made all the work.

43And Moses did look upon all the work, and behold, they had done it as the LORD had commanded, *even* so had they done it: and Moses blessed them.

40 And the LORD spake unto Moses, saying, 2On the first day of the first month shalt thou set up the tabernacle of the tent of the congregation.

3And thou shalt put therein the ark of the Testimony, and cover the ark with the vail.

4And thou shalt bring in the table, and set in order the things that are to be set in order upon it; and thou shalt bring in the candlestick, and light the lamps thereof.

5And thou shalt set the altar of gold for the incense before the ark of the Testimony, and put the hanging of the door to the tabernacle.

6And thou shalt set the altar of the burnt offering before the door of the tabernacle of the tent of the congregation.

7And thou shalt set the laver between the tent of the congregation and the altar, and shalt put water therein.

8And thou shalt set up the court round about, and hang up the hanging at the court gate.

9And thou shalt take the anointing oil, and

Amplified Bible

36The table and all its utensils, and the showbread (bread of the Presence);

37The pure [gold] lampstand and its lamps, with the lamps set in order, all its utensils, and the oil for the light;

38The golden altar, the anointing oil, the fragrant incense, and the hanging for the door of the tent;

39The bronze altar and its grate of bronze, its poles and all its utensils; the laver and its base;

40The hangings of the court, its pillars and sockets *or* bases, and the screen for the court gate, its cords, and pegs, and all the utensils for the service of the tabernacle, for the Tent of Meeting [of God with His people];

41The finely worked vestments for ministering in the Holy Place, the holy garments for Aaron the priest, and the garments of his sons to minister as priests.

42According to all that the Lord had commanded Moses, so the Israelites had done all the work.

43And Moses inspected all the work, and behold, they had done it; as the Lord had commanded, so had they done it. And Moses blessed them.

40 AND THE Lord said to Moses, 2On the first day of the first month you shall set up the tabernacle of the Tent of Meeting [of God with you].

3And you shall put in it the ark of the Testimony and screen the ark [of God's Presence] with the veil.

4You shall bring in the [showbread] table and set in order the things that are to be upon it; and you shall bring in the lampstand and set up *and* light its lamps.

5You shall set the golden altar for the incense before the ark of the Testimony [outside the veil] and put the hanging *or* screen at the tabernacle door.

6You shall set the altar of the burnt offering before the door of the tabernacle of the Tent of Meeting.

7And you shall *a*set the laver between the Tent of Meeting and the altar and put water in it.

8And you shall set up the court [curtains] round about and hang up the hanging *or* screen at the court gate.

9You shall take the anointing oil and anoint the

AMP notes: *a* Why was it necessary for one exact position for the laver to be demanded of Moses by God? Those who have published charts of the tabernacle furniture arrangement, with the laver off to one side or the other of the door into the sanctuary, have missed a point here. The laver was to be placed directly "between [the doors of] the Tent of Meeting and the altar [of burnt offering]," thus completing the "cross" made by the arrangement of the furniture, from the ark to the altar. It could have no significance to the Jews of that time, but the One Who planned it had those in mind to whom Christ would one day say, "And these [very Scriptures] testify about Me!" (John 5:39.) How fitting that at the foot of that "cross" there should be the altar, picturing our complete surrender, and then the laver, picturing our cleansing, that we may enter in through Him Who alone is "the Door" to the eternal Holy of Holies (John 10:1-9).

King James Version

anoint the tabernacle, and all that *is* therein, and shalt hallow it, and all the vessels thereof: and it shall be holy.

¹⁰And thou shalt anoint the altar of the burnt offering, and all his vessels, and sanctify the altar: and it shall be an altar most holy.

¹¹And thou shalt anoint the laver and his foot, and sanctify it.

¹²And thou shalt bring Aaron and his sons unto the door of the tabernacle of the congregation, and wash them with water.

¹³And thou shalt put upon Aaron the holy garments, and anoint him, and sanctify him; that he may minister unto me in the priest's office.

¹⁴And thou shalt bring his sons, and clothe them with coats:

¹⁵And thou shalt anoint them, as thou didst anoint their father, that they may minister unto me in the priest's office: for their anointing shall surely be an everlasting priesthood throughout their generations.

¹⁶Thus did Moses: according to all that the LORD commanded him, so did he.

¹⁷ ¶ And it came to pass in the first month in the second year, on the first *day* of the month, *that* the tabernacle was reared up.

¹⁸And Moses reared up the tabernacle, and fastened his sockets, and set up the boards thereof, and put in the bars thereof, and reared up his pillars.

¹⁹And he spread abroad the tent over the tabernacle, and put the covering of the tent above upon it; as the LORD commanded Moses.

²⁰And he took and put the Testimony into the ark, and set the staves on the ark, and put the mercy seat above upon the ark:

²¹And he brought the ark into the tabernacle, and set up the vail of the covering, and covered the ark of the Testimony; as the LORD commanded Moses.

²²And he put the table in the tent of the congregation, upon the side of the tabernacle northward, without the vail.

²³And he set the bread in order upon it before the LORD; as the LORD had commanded Moses.

²⁴And he put the candlestick in the tent of the congregation, over against the table, on the side of the tabernacle southward.

²⁵And he lighted the lamps before the LORD; as the LORD commanded Moses.

²⁶And he put the golden altar in the tent of the congregation before the vail:

²⁷And he burnt sweet incense thereon; as the LORD commanded Moses.

²⁸And he set up the hanging at the door of the tabernacle.

²⁹And he put the altar of burnt offering *by* the door of the tabernacle of the tent of the congregation, and offered upon it the burnt offering and the meat offering; as the LORD commanded Moses.

Amplified Bible

tabernacle and all that is in it, and shall consecrate it and all its furniture, and it shall be holy.

¹⁰You shall anoint the altar of burnt offering and all its utensils; and consecrate (set apart for God) the altar, and the altar shall be most holy.

¹¹And you shall anoint the laver and its base and consecrate it.

¹²You shall bring Aaron and his sons to the door of the Tent of Meeting and wash them with water.

¹³You shall put on Aaron the holy garments, and anoint and consecrate him, so he may serve Me as priest.

¹⁴And you shall bring his sons and put long *and* sleeved tunics on them,

¹⁵And you shall anoint them as you anointed their father, that they may minister to Me as priests; for their anointing shall be to them for an everlasting priesthood throughout their generations.

¹⁶Thus did Moses; according to all that the Lord commanded him, so he did.

¹⁷And on the first day of the first month in the second year the tabernacle was erected.

¹⁸Moses set up the tabernacle, laid its sockets, set up its boards, put in its bars, and erected its pillars.

¹⁹[Moses] spread the tent over the tabernacle and put the covering of the tent over it, as the Lord had commanded him.

²⁰He took the Testimony [the Ten Commandments] and put it into the ark, and set the poles [in the rings] on the ark, and put the mercy seat on top of the ark.

²¹[Moses] brought the ark into the tabernacle and set up the veil of the screen and screened the ark of the Testimony, as the Lord had commanded him.

²²Moses put the table [of showbread] in the Tent of Meeting on the north side of the tabernacle outside the veil;

²³He set the bread [of the Presence] in order on it before the Lord, as the Lord had commanded him.

²⁴And he put the lampstand in the Tent of Meeting opposite the table on the south side of the tabernacle.

²⁵Moses set up *and* lighted the lamps before the Lord, as the Lord commanded him.

²⁶He put the golden altar [of incense] in the Tent of Meeting before the veil;

²⁷He burned sweet incense [symbol of prayer] upon it, as the Lord commanded him.

²⁸And he set up the hanging *or* screen at the door of the tabernacle.

²⁹[Moses] put the altar of burnt offering at the door of the tabernacle of the Tent of Meeting and offered on it the burnt offering and the cereal offering, as the Lord commanded him.

King James Version

30And he set the laver between the tent of the congregation and the altar, and put water there, to wash *withal*.

31And Moses and Aaron and his sons washed their hands and their feet thereat:

32When they went into the tent of the congregation, and when they came near unto the altar, they washed; as the LORD commanded Moses.

33And he reared up the court round about the tabernacle and the altar, and set up the hanging of the court gate. So Moses finished the work.

34 ¶ Then a cloud covered the tent of the congregation, and the glory of the LORD filled the tabernacle.

35And Moses was not able to enter into the tent of the congregation, because the cloud abode thereon, and the glory of the LORD filled the tabernacle.

36And when the cloud was taken up from over the tabernacle, the children of Israel went onward in all their journeys:

37But if the cloud were not taken up, then they journeyed not till the day that it was taken up.

38For the cloud of the LORD *was* upon the tabernacle by day, and fire was on it by night, in the sight of all the house of Israel, throughout all their journeys.

Amplified Bible

30And Moses set the laver between the Tent of Meeting and the altar and put water in it for washing.

31And Moses and Aaron and his sons washed their hands and their feet there.

32When they went into the Tent of Meeting or came near the altar, they washed, as the Lord commanded Moses.

33And he erected the court round about the tabernacle and the altar and set up the hanging *or* screen at the court gate. So Moses finished the work.

34Then the cloud [the Shekinah, God's visible presence] covered the Tent of Meeting, and the glory of the Lord filled the tabernacle!

35And Moses was not able to enter the Tent of Meeting because the cloud remained upon it, and the glory of the Lord filled the tabernacle.

36In all their journeys, whenever the cloud was taken up from over the tabernacle, the Israelites went onward;

37But if the cloud was not taken up, they did not journey on till the day that it was taken up.

38For throughout all their journeys the cloud of the Lord was upon the tabernacle by day, and fire was in it by night, in the sight of all the house of Israel.

King James Version	Amplified Bible

THE THIRD BOOK OF MOSES, CALLED

Leviticus

THE THIRD BOOK OF MOSES, CALLED

Leviticus

1 And the LORD called unto Moses, and spake unto him out of the tabernacle of the congregation, saying,

2 Speak unto the children of Israel, and say unto them, If *any* man of you bring an offering unto the LORD, ye shall bring your offering of the cattle, *even* of the herd, and of the flock.

3 If his offering *be* a burnt sacrifice of the herd, let him offer a male without blemish: he shall offer it of his own voluntary will at the door of the tabernacle of the congregation before the LORD.

4 And he shall put his hand upon the head of the burnt offering; and it shall be accepted for him to make atonement for him.

5 And he shall kill the bullock before the LORD: and the priests, Aaron's sons, shall bring the blood, and sprinkle the blood round about upon the altar that *is by* the door of the tabernacle of the congregation.

6 And he shall flay the burnt offering, and cut it into his pieces.

7 And the sons of Aaron the priest shall put fire upon the altar, and lay the wood in order upon the fire:

8 And the priests, Aaron's sons, shall lay the parts, the head, and the fat, in order upon the wood that *is* on the fire which *is* upon the altar:

9 But his inwards and his legs shall he wash in water: and the priest shall burn all on the altar, *to be* a burnt sacrifice, an offering made by fire, of a sweet savour unto the LORD.

10 And if his offering *be* of the flocks, *namely,* of the sheep, or of the goats, for a burnt sacrifice; he shall bring it a male without blemish.

11 And he shall kill it on the side of the altar northward before the LORD: and the priests, Aaron's sons, shall sprinkle his blood round about upon the altar.

12 And he shall cut it into his pieces, with his head and his fat: and the priest shall lay them in order on the wood that *is* on the fire which *is* upon the altar:

1 THE LORD [a]called to Moses out of the Tent of Meeting, and said to him,

2 Say to the Israelites, When any man of you brings an offering to the Lord, you shall bring your offering of [domestic] animals from the herd or from the flock.

3 If his offering is a burnt offering from the herd, he shall offer a male without blemish; he shall offer it at the door of the Tent of Meeting, that he may be accepted before the Lord.

4 And he shall lay [both] his hands upon the head of the burnt offering [transferring symbolically his guilt to the victim], and it shall be [b]an acceptable atonement for him.

5 The man shall kill the young bull before the Lord, and the priests, Aaron's sons, shall present the blood and dash [it] round about upon the altar that is at the door of the Tent of Meeting.

6 And he shall skin the burnt offering and cut it into pieces.

7 And the sons of Aaron the priest shall put fire on the altar and lay wood in order on the fire;

8 And Aaron's sons the priests shall lay the pieces, the head and the fat, in order on the wood on the fire on the altar.

9 But its entrails and its legs he shall wash with water. And the priest shall burn all of it on the altar for a burnt offering, an offering by fire, a sweet *and* satisfying odor to the Lord.

10 And if the man's offering is of the flock, from the sheep or the goats, for a burnt offering, he shall offer a male without blemish.

11 And he shall kill it on the north side of the altar before the Lord, and Aaron's sons the priests shall dash its blood round about against the altar.

12 And [the man] shall cut it into pieces, with its head and its fat, and the priest shall lay them in order on the wood that is on the fire on the altar.

AMP notes: a The first step toward understanding the message of Leviticus is to appreciate its viewpoint indicated here—"The Lord called to Moses out of the Tent of Meeting," and talked to him. Before this a forbidding God had spoken from the burning mountain. But now the tabernacle is erected according to the God-given pattern, and the God Who dwells among His people in fellowship with them talks with His servant Moses "out of the Tent of Meeting." The people, therefore, are not treated as sinners alienated from God, "but as being already brought into a new relationship, even that of fellowship, on the ground of a blood-sealed covenant" (J. Sidlow Baxter, *Explore the Book*). b To render the self-sacrifice perfect, it was necessary that the offerer should spiritually die, sinking it as it were into the death of the sacrifice that had died for him, so that through the mediator of his salvation he should put his soul into a living fellowship with the Lord and bring his bodily members within the operations of the gracious Spirit of God. Thereby he would be renewed and sanctified [separated for holy use], both body and soul, and enter into union with God (Karl Keil and F. Delitzsch, *Biblical Commentary on the Old Testament*).

King James Version

¹³But he shall wash the inwards and the legs with water: and the priest shall bring *it* all, and burn *it* upon the altar: it *is* a burnt sacrifice, an offering made by fire, of a sweet savour unto the LORD.

¹⁴And if the burnt sacrifice for his offering to the LORD *be* of fowls, then he shall bring his offering of turtledoves, or of young pigeons.

¹⁵And the priest shall bring it unto the altar, and wring off his head, and burn *it* on the altar; and the blood thereof shall be wrung out at the side of the altar:

¹⁶And he shall pluck away his crop with his feathers, and cast it beside the altar on the east part, by the place of the ashes:

¹⁷And he shall cleave it with the wings thereof, *but* shall not divide *it* asunder: and the priest shall burn it upon the altar, upon the wood that *is* upon the fire: it *is* a burnt sacrifice, an offering made by fire, of a sweet savour unto the LORD.

2 And when any will offer a meat offering unto the LORD, his offering shall be *of* fine flour; and he shall pour oil upon it, and put frankincense thereon:

²And he shall bring it to Aaron's sons the priests: and he shall take thereout his handful of the flour thereof, and of the oil thereof, with all the frankincense thereof; and the priest shall burn the memorial of it upon the altar, *to be* an offering made by fire, of a sweet savour unto the LORD:

³And the remnant of the meat offering *shall be* Aaron's and his sons': *it is a thing* most holy of the offerings of the LORD made by fire.

⁴And if thou bring an oblation of a meat offering baken in the oven, *it shall be* unleavened cakes of fine flour mingled with oil, or unleavened wafers anointed with oil.

⁵And if thy oblation *be* a meat offering *baken* in a pan, it shall be *of* fine flour unleavened, mingled with oil.

⁶Thou shalt part it in pieces, and pour oil thereon: it *is* a meat offering.

⁷And if thy oblation *be* a meat offering *baken* in the fryingpan, it shall be made *of* fine flour with oil.

⁸And thou shalt bring the meat offering that is made of these *things* unto the LORD: and when it is presented unto the priest, he shall bring it unto the altar.

⁹And the priest shall take from the meat offering a memorial thereof, and shall burn *it* upon the altar: *it is* an offering made by fire, of a sweet savour unto the LORD.

¹⁰And that which is left of the meat offering *shall be* Aaron's and his sons': *it is* a thing most holy of the offerings of the LORD made by fire.

¹¹No meat offering, which ye shall bring unto the LORD, shall be made *with* leaven: for ye shall

Amplified Bible

¹³But he shall wash the entrails and legs with water. The priest shall offer all of it and burn it on the altar; it is a burnt offering, an offering made by fire, a sweet *and* satisfying fragrance to the Lord.

¹⁴And if the offering to the Lord is a burnt offering of birds, then [the man] shall bring turtledoves or young pigeons.

¹⁵And the priest shall bring it to the altar, and wring off its head, and burn it on the altar; and its blood shall be drained out on the side of the altar.

¹⁶And he shall take away its crop with its feathers and cast it beside the altar on the east side, in the place for ashes.

¹⁷And he shall split it open [holding it] by its wings, but shall not cut it in two. And the priest shall burn it on the altar, on the wood that is on the fire; it is a burnt offering, an offering made by fire, a sweet *and* satisfying odor to the Lord.

2 WHEN ANYONE offers a cereal offering to the Lord, it shall be of fine flour; and he shall pour oil over it and lay frankincense on it.

²And he shall bring it to Aaron's sons the priests. Out of it he shall take a handful of the fine flour and oil, with all its frankincense, and the priest shall burn this on the altar as the memorial portion of it, an offering made by fire, of a sweet *and* satisfying fragrance to the Lord.

³What is left of the cereal offering shall be Aaron's and his sons'; it is a most holy part of the offerings made to the Lord by fire.

⁴When you bring as an offering cereal baked in the oven, it shall be unleavened cakes of fine flour mixed with oil, or unleavened wafers spread with oil.

⁵If your offering is cereal baked on a griddle, it shall be of fine flour unleavened, mixed with oil.

⁶You shall break it in pieces and pour oil on it; it is a cereal offering.

⁷And if your offering is cereal cooked in the frying pan, it shall be made of fine flour with oil.

⁸And you shall bring the cereal offering that is made of these things to the Lord; it shall be presented to the priest, and he shall bring it to the [bronze] altar.

⁹The priest shall take from the cereal offering its memorial portion and burn it on the altar, an offering made by fire, a sweet *and* satisfying fragrance to the Lord.

¹⁰What is left of the cereal offering shall be Aaron's and his sons'; it is a most holy part of the offerings made to the Lord by fire.

¹¹No cereal offering that you bring to the Lord shall be made with leaven, for you shall burn no

King James Version

burn no leaven, nor any honey, *in* any offering of the LORD made by fire.

¹²*As for* the oblation of the firstfruits, ye shall offer them unto the LORD: but they shall not be burnt on the altar for a sweet savour.

¹³And every oblation of thy meat offering shalt thou season with salt; neither shalt thou suffer the salt of the covenant of thy God to be lacking from thy meat offering: with all thine offerings thou shalt offer salt.

¹⁴And if thou offer a meat offering of *thy* firstfruits unto the LORD, thou shalt offer for the meat offering of thy firstfruits green ears of corn dried by the fire, *even* corn beaten out of full ears.

¹⁵And thou shalt put oil upon it, and lay frankincense thereon: it *is* a meat offering.

¹⁶And the priest shall burn the memorial of it, *part* of the beaten corn thereof, and *part* of the oil thereof, with all the frankincense thereof: *it is* an offering made by fire unto the LORD.

3 And if his oblation *be* a sacrifice of peace offering, if he offer *it* of the herd; whether *it be* a male or female, he shall offer it without blemish before the LORD.

²And he shall lay his hand upon the head of his offering, and kill it *at* the door of the tabernacle of the congregation: and Aaron's sons the priests shall sprinkle the blood upon the altar round about.

³And he shall offer of the sacrifice of the peace offering an offering made by fire unto the LORD; the fat that covereth the inwards, and all the fat that *is* upon the inwards,

⁴And the two kidneys, and the fat that *is* on them, which *is* by the flanks, and the caul above the liver, with the kidneys, it shall he take away.

⁵And Aaron's sons shall burn it on the altar upon the burnt sacrifice, which *is* upon the wood that *is* on the fire: *it is* an offering made by fire, of a sweet savour unto the LORD.

⁶And if his offering for a sacrifice of peace offering unto the LORD *be* of the flock, male or female, he shall offer it without blemish.

⁷If he offer a lamb for his offering, then shall he offer it before the LORD.

⁸And he shall lay his hand upon the head of his offering, and kill it before the tabernacle of the congregation: and Aaron's sons shall sprinkle the blood thereof round about upon the altar.

⁹And he shall offer of the sacrifice of the peace offering an offering made by fire unto the LORD; the fat thereof, *and* the whole rump, it shall he take off hard by the back bone; and the

Amplified Bible

leaven or honey in any offering made by fire to the Lord.

¹²As an offering of firstfruits you may offer leaven and honey to the Lord, but ᵃthey shall not be burned on the altar for a sweet odor [to the Lord, for their aid to fermentation is symbolic of corruption in the human heart].

¹³Every cereal offering you shall season with salt [symbol of preservation]; neither shall you allow the salt of the covenant of your God to be lacking from your cereal offering; with all your offerings you shall offer salt.

¹⁴If you offer a cereal offering of your firstfruits to the Lord, you shall offer for it of your firstfruits grain in the ear parched with fire, bruised *and* crushed grain out of the fresh *and* fruitful ear.

¹⁵And you shall put oil on it and lay frankincense on it; it is a cereal offering.

¹⁶The priest shall burn as its memorial portion part of the bruised *and* crushed grain of it and part of the oil of it, with all its frankincense; it is an offering made by fire to the Lord.

3 IF A man's offering is a sacrifice of peace offering, if he offers an animal from the herd, whether male or female, he shall offer it without blemish before the Lord.

²He shall lay [both] his ᵇhands upon the head of his offering and kill it at the door of the Tent of Meeting; and Aaron's sons the priests shall throw the blood against the altar round about.

³And from the sacrifice of the peace offering, an offering made by fire to the Lord, he shall offer the fat that covers and is upon the entrails,

⁴And the two kidneys with the fat that is on them at the loins, and the appendage of the liver which he shall take away with the kidneys.

⁵Aaron's sons shall burn it all on the altar upon the burnt offering which is on the wood on the fire, an offering made by fire, of a sweet *and* satisfying odor to the Lord.

⁶If his peace offering to the Lord is an animal from the flock, male or female, he shall offer it without blemish.

⁷If he offers a lamb, then he shall offer it before the Lord.

⁸He shall lay [both] his hands on the head of his offering and kill it before the Tent of Meeting; and Aaron's sons shall throw its blood around against the altar.

⁹And he shall offer from the peace offering as an offering made by fire to the Lord: the fat of it, the fat tail as a whole, taking it off close to the

AMP notes: ᵃ There is to be no division between one's spiritual life and one's secular life, but the whole of one's life is to be of the nature of a sacrament (Col. 3:23, 24).   ᵇ *The Septuagint* (Greek translation of the Old Testament) so reads.

King James Version

fat that covereth the inwards, and all the fat that *is* upon the inwards,

10And the two kidneys, and the fat that *is* upon them, which *is* by the flanks, and the caul above the liver, with the kidneys, it shall he take away.

11And the priest shall burn it upon the altar: *it is* the food of the offering made by fire unto the LORD.

12And if his offering *be* a goat, then he shall offer it before the LORD.

13And he shall lay his hand upon the head of it, and kill it before the tabernacle of the congregation: and the sons of Aaron shall sprinkle the blood thereof upon the altar round about.

14And he shall offer thereof his offering, *even* an offering made by fire unto the LORD; the fat that covereth the inwards, and all the fat that *is* upon the inwards,

15And the two kidneys, and the fat that *is* upon them, which *is* by the flanks, and the caul above the liver, with the kidneys, it shall he take away.

16And the priest shall burn them upon the altar: *it is* the food of the offering made by fire for a sweet savour: all the fat *is* the LORD'S.

17*It shall be* a perpetual statute for your generations throughout all your dwellings, *that* ye eat neither fat nor blood.

4 And the LORD spake unto Moses, saying, 2Speak unto the children of Israel, saying, If a soul shall sin through ignorance against any of the commandments of the LORD (*concerning things* which ought not to be done), and shall do against any of them:

3If the priest that is anointed do sin according to the sin of the people; then let him bring for his sin, which he hath sinned, a young bullock without blemish unto the LORD for a sin offering.

4And he shall bring the bullock unto the door of the tabernacle of the congregation before the LORD; and shall lay his hand upon the bullock's head, and kill the bullock before the LORD.

5And the priest that is anointed shall take of the bullock's blood, and bring it to the tabernacle of the congregation:

6And the priest shall dip his finger in the blood, and sprinkle of the blood seven times before the LORD, before the vail of the sanctuary.

7And the priest shall put *some* of the blood upon the horns of the altar of sweet incense before the LORD, which *is* in the tabernacle of the congregation; and shall pour all the blood of the bullock at the bottom of the altar of the burnt offering, which *is at* the door of the tabernacle of the congregation.

8And he shall take off from it all the fat of the

Amplified Bible

backbone, and the fat that covers and is upon the entrails,

10And the two kidneys, and the fat on them at the loins, and the appendage of the liver, which he shall take away with the kidneys.

11The priest shall burn it upon the altar, a food offering made by fire to the Lord.

12If [a man's] offering is a goat, he shall offer it before the Lord,

13And lay his hands upon its head, and kill it before the Tent of Meeting; and the sons of Aaron shall throw its blood against the altar round about.

14Then he shall offer from it as his offering made by fire to the Lord: the fat that covers and is on the entrails,

15And the two kidneys and the fat that is on them at the loins, and the appendage of the liver which he shall take away with the kidneys.

16The priest shall burn them on the altar as food, offered by fire, for a sweet *and* satisfying fragrance. All the fat is the Lord's.

17It shall be a perpetual statute for your generations in all your dwelling places, that you eat neither fat nor blood.

4 AND THE Lord said to Moses, 2Say to the Israelites, If anyone shall sin through error *or* unwittingly in any of the things which the Lord has commanded not to be done, and shall do any one of them—

3If it is the anointed priest who sins, thus bringing guilt on the people, then let him offer for his sin which he has committed a young bull without blemish to the Lord as a sin offering.

4He shall bring the bull to the door of the Tent of Meeting before the Lord, and shall lay [both] his hands on the bull's head and kill [it] before the Lord.

5And the anointed priest shall take some of the bull's blood and bring it into the Tent of Meeting;

6And the priest shall dip his finger in the blood and sprinkle some of [it] seven times before the Lord before the veil of the sanctuary.

7And the priest shall put some of the blood on the horns of the altar of sweet incense before the Lord which is in the Tent of Meeting; and all the rest of the blood of the bull shall he pour out at the base of the altar of the burnt offering at the door of the Tent of Meeting.

8And all the fat of the bull for the sin offering

King James Version

bullock *for* the sin offering; the fat that covereth the inwards, and all the fat that *is* upon the inwards,

⁹And the two kidneys, and the fat that *is* upon them, which *is* by the flanks, and the caul above the liver, with the kidneys, it shall he take away,

¹⁰As it was taken off from the bullock of the sacrifice of peace offerings: and the priest shall burn them upon the altar of the burnt offering.

¹¹And the skin of the bullock, and all his flesh, with his head, and with his legs, and his inwards, and his dung,

¹²Even the whole bullock shall he carry forth without the camp unto a clean place, where the ashes are poured out, and burn him on the wood with fire: where the ashes are poured out shall he be burnt.

¹³ ¶ And if the whole congregation of Israel sin through ignorance, and the thing be hid from the eyes of the assembly, and they have done somewhat against any of the commandments of the LORD *concerning things* which should not be done, and are guilty;

¹⁴When the sin, which they have sinned against it, is known, then the congregation shall offer a young bullock for the sin, and bring him before the tabernacle of the congregation.

¹⁵And the elders of the congregation shall lay their hands upon the head of the bullock before the LORD: and the bullock shall be killed before the LORD.

¹⁶And the priest that is anointed shall bring of the bullock's blood to the tabernacle of the congregation:

¹⁷And the priest shall dip his finger *in some* of the blood, and sprinkle *it* seven times before the LORD, *even* before the vail.

¹⁸And he shall put *some* of the blood upon the horns of the altar which *is* before the LORD, that *is* in the tabernacle of the congregation, and shall pour out all the blood at the bottom of the altar of the burnt offering, which *is at* the door of the tabernacle of the congregation.

¹⁹And he shall take all his fat from him, and burn *it* upon the altar.

²⁰And he shall do with the bullock as he did with the bullock for a sin offering, so shall he do with this: and the priest shall make an atonement for them, and it shall be forgiven them.

²¹And he shall carry forth the bullock without the camp, and burn him as he burned the first bullock: it *is* a sin offering for the congregation.

²² ¶ When a ruler hath sinned, and done somewhat through ignorance against any of the commandments of the LORD his God *concerning things* which should not be done, and is guilty;

²³Or if his sin, wherein he hath sinned, come to his knowledge, he shall bring his offering, a kid of the goats, a male without blemish;

²⁴And he shall lay his hand upon the head of

Amplified Bible

he shall take off of it—the fat that covers and is on the entrails,

⁹And the two kidneys and the fat that is on them at the loins, and the appendage of the liver, which he shall take away with the kidneys—

¹⁰Just as these are taken off of the bull of the sacrifice of the peace offerings; and the priest shall burn them on the altar of burnt offering.

¹¹But the hide of the bull and all its flesh, its head, its legs, its entrails, and its dung,

¹²Even the whole bull shall he carry forth without the camp to a clean place, where the ashes are poured out, and burn it on a fire of wood, there where the ashes are poured out.

¹³If the whole congregation of Israel sins unintentionally, and it be hidden from the eyes of the assembly, and they have done what the Lord has commanded not to be done and are guilty,

¹⁴When the sin which they have committed becomes known, then the congregation shall offer a young bull for a sin offering and bring it before the Tent of Meeting.

¹⁵The elders of the congregation shall lay their hands upon the head of the bull before the Lord, and the bull shall be killed before the Lord.

¹⁶The anointed priest shall bring some of the bull's blood to the Tent of Meeting,

¹⁷And shall dip his finger in the blood, and sprinkle it seven times before the Lord, before the veil [which screens the ark of the covenant].

¹⁸He shall put some of the blood on the horns of the altar [of incense] which is before the Lord in the Tent of Meeting, and he shall pour out all the blood at the base of the altar of burnt offering near the door of the Tent of Meeting.

¹⁹And he shall take all its fat from the bull and burn it on the altar.

²⁰Thus shall he do with the bull; as he did with the bull for a sin offering, so shall he do with this; and the priest shall make atonement for [the people], and they shall be forgiven.

²¹And he shall carry forth the bull outside the camp and burn it as he burned the first bull; it is the sin offering for the congregation.

²²When a ruler *or* leader sins and unwittingly does any one of the things the Lord his God has forbidden, and is guilty,

²³If his sin which he has committed be known to him, he shall bring as his offering a goat, a male without blemish.

²⁴He shall lay his hand on the head of the goat

King James Version

the goat, and kill it in the place where they kill the burnt offering before the LORD: it *is* a sin offering.

25And the priest shall take of the blood of the sin offering with his finger, and put *it* upon the horns of the altar of burnt offering, and shall pour out his blood at the bottom of the altar of burnt offering.

26And he shall burn all his fat upon the altar, as the fat of the sacrifice of peace offerings: and the priest shall make an atonement for him as concerning his sin, and it shall be forgiven him.

27 ¶ And if any one of the common people sin through ignorance, while he doeth somewhat against *any of* the commandments of the LORD *concerning things* which ought not to be done, and be guilty;

28Or if his sin, which he hath sinned, come to his knowledge, then he shall bring his offering, a kid of the goats, a female without blemish, for his sin which he hath sinned.

29And he shall lay his hand upon the head of the sin offering, and slay the sin offering in the place of the burnt offering.

30And the priest shall take of the blood thereof with his finger, and put *it* upon the horns of the altar of burnt offering, and shall pour out all the blood thereof at the bottom of the altar.

31And he shall take away all the fat thereof, as the fat is taken away from off the sacrifice of peace offerings; and the priest shall burn *it* upon the altar for a sweet savour unto the LORD; and the priest shall make an atonement for him, and it shall be forgiven him.

32And if he bring a lamb for a sin offering, he shall bring it a female without blemish.

33And he shall lay his hand upon the head of the sin offering, and slay it for a sin offering in the place where they kill the burnt offering.

34And the priest shall take of the blood of the sin offering with his finger, and put *it* upon the horns of the altar of burnt offering, and shall pour out all the blood thereof at the bottom of the altar;

35And he shall take away all the fat thereof, as the fat of the lamb is taken away from the sacrifice of the peace offerings; and the priest shall burn them upon the altar, according to the offerings made by fire unto the LORD; and the priest shall make an atonement for his sin that he hath committed, and it shall be forgiven him.

5 And if a soul sin, and hear the voice of swearing, and *is* a witness, whether he hath seen or known *of it;* if he do not utter *it,* then he shall bear his iniquity.

2Or if a soul touch any unclean thing, whether *it be* a carcase of an unclean beast, or a carcase of unclean cattle, or the carcase of unclean

Amplified Bible

and kill it in the place where they kill the burnt offering before the Lord; it is a sin offering.

25The priest shall take some of the blood of the sin offering with his finger and put it on the horns of the altar of burnt offering and pour the rest of its blood at the base of the altar of burnt offering.

26And he shall burn all its fat upon the altar like the fat of the sacrifice of peace offerings; so the priest shall make atonement for him for his sin, and it shall be forgiven him.

27If any one of the common people sins unwittingly in doing anything the Lord has commanded not to be done, and is guilty,

28When the sin which he has committed is made known to him, he shall bring for his offering a goat, a female without blemish, for his sin which he has committed.

29The offender shall lay his hand on the head of the sin offering and kill [it] at the place of the burnt offering.

30And the priest shall take some of its blood with his finger and put it on the horns of the altar of burnt offering and shall pour out the rest of its blood at the base of the altar.

31And all the fat of it he shall take away, as the fat is taken away from off the sacrifice of peace offerings; and the priest shall burn it on the altar for a sweet *and* satisfying fragrance to the Lord; and the priest shall make atonement for [the man], and he shall be forgiven.

32If he brings a lamb as his sin offering, he shall bring a female without blemish.

33He shall lay his hand upon the head of the sin offering and kill it in the place where they kill the burnt offering.

34And the priest shall take some of the blood of the sin offering with his finger and put it on the horns of the altar of burnt offering and all the rest of the blood of the lamb he shall pour out at the base of the altar.

35And he shall take away all the fat of it, just as the fat of the lamb is removed from the sacrifice of the peace offerings; and the priest shall burn it on the altar upon the offerings made by fire to the Lord; and the priest shall make atonement for the sin which the man has committed, and he shall be forgiven.

5 IF ANYONE sins in that he is sworn to testify and has knowledge of the matter, either by seeing or hearing of it, but fails to report it, then he shall bear his iniquity *and* willfulness.

2Or if anyone touches an unclean thing, whether the carcass of an unclean wild beast or of an unclean domestic animal or of unclean

King James Version

creeping things, and *if* it be hidden from him; he also shall be unclean, and guilty.

³Or if he touch the uncleanness of man, whatsoever uncleanness *it be* that a man shall be defiled withal, and it be hid from him; when he knoweth *of it,* then he shall be guilty.

⁴Or if a soul swear, pronouncing with *his* lips to do evil, or to do good, whatsoever *it be* that a man shall pronounce with an oath, and it be hid from him; when he knoweth *of it,* then he shall be guilty in one of these.

⁵And it shall be, when he shall be guilty in one of these *things,* that he shall confess that he hath sinned in that *thing:*

⁶And he shall bring his trespass offering unto the LORD for his sin which he hath sinned, a female from the flock, a lamb or a kid of the goats, for a sin offering; and the priest shall make an atonement for him concerning his sin.

⁷And if he be not able to bring a lamb, then he shall bring for his trespass, which he hath committed, two turtledoves, or two young pigeons, unto the LORD; one for a sin offering, and the other for a burnt offering.

⁸And he shall bring them unto the priest, who shall offer *that* which *is* for the sin offering first, and wring off his head from his neck, but shall not divide *it* asunder:

⁹And he shall sprinkle of the blood of the sin offering upon the side of the altar; and the rest of the blood shall be wrung out at the bottom of the altar: it *is* a sin offering.

¹⁰And he shall offer the second *for* a burnt offering, according to the manner: and the priest shall make an atonement for him for his sin which he hath sinned, and it shall be forgiven him.

¹¹But if he be not able to bring two turtledoves, or two young pigeons, then he that sinned shall bring for his offering the tenth *part* of an ephah of fine flour for a sin offering; he shall put no oil upon it, neither shall he put *any* frankincense thereon: for it *is* a sin offering.

¹²Then shall he bring it to the priest, and the priest shall take his handful of it, *even* a memorial thereof, and burn *it* on the altar, according to the offerings made by fire unto the LORD: it *is* a sin offering.

¹³And the priest shall make an atonement for him as touching his sin that he hath sinned in one of these, and it shall be forgiven him: and *the remnant* shall be the priest's, as a meat offering.

¹⁴ ¶ And the LORD spake unto Moses, saying,

¹⁵If a soul commit a trespass, and sin through ignorance, in the holy *things* of the LORD; then he shall bring for his trespass unto the LORD a ram without blemish out of the flocks, with thy estimation *by* shekels of silver, after the shekel of the sanctuary, for a trespass offering:

¹⁶And he shall make amends for the harm that

Amplified Bible

creeping things that multiply prolifically, even if he is unaware of it, and he has become unclean, he is guilty.

³Or if he touches human uncleanness, of whatever kind the uncleanness may be with which he becomes defiled, and he is unaware of it, when he does know it, then he shall be guilty.

⁴Or if anyone unthinkingly swears he will do something, whether to do evil or good, whatever it may be that a man shall pronounce rashly taking an oath, then, when he becomes aware of it, he shall be guilty in either of these.

⁵When a man is guilty in one of these, he shall confess the sin he has committed.

⁶He shall bring his guilt *or* trespass offering to the Lord for the sin which he has committed, a female from the flock, a lamb or a goat, for a sin offering; and the priest shall make atonement for his sin.

⁷But if he cannot afford a lamb, then he shall bring for his guilt offering to the Lord two turtledoves or two young pigeons, one for a sin offering and the other for a burnt offering.

⁸He shall bring them to the priest, who shall offer the one for the sin offering first, and wring its head from its neck, but shall not sever it;

⁹And he shall sprinkle some of the blood of the sin offering on the side of the altar, and the rest of the blood shall be drained out at the base of the altar; it is a sin offering.

¹⁰And he shall prepare the second bird for a burnt offering, according to the ordinance; and the priest shall make atonement for him for his sin which he has committed, and he shall be forgiven.

¹¹But if the offender cannot afford to bring two turtledoves or two young pigeons, then he shall bring for his offering the tenth part of an ephah of fine flour for a sin offering; he shall put no oil or frankincense on it, for it is a sin offering.

¹²He shall bring it to the priest, who shall take a handful of it as a memorial portion and burn it on the altar, on the offerings made by fire to the Lord; it is a sin offering.

¹³Thus the priest shall make atonement for him for the sin that he has committed in any of these things, and he shall be forgiven; and the remainder shall be for the priest, as in the cereal offering.

¹⁴And the Lord said to Moses,

¹⁵If anyone commits a breach of faith and sins unwittingly in the holy things of the Lord, he shall bring his trespass *or* guilt offering to the Lord, a ram without blemish out of the flock, valued by you in shekels of silver, that is, the shekel of the sanctuary, for a trespass *or* guilt offering.

¹⁶And he shall make restitution for what he

King James Version

he hath done in the holy *thing*, and shall add the fifth *part* thereto, and give it unto the priest: and the priest shall make an atonement for him with the ram of the trespass offering, and it shall be forgiven him.

¹⁷And if a soul sin, and commit any *of these things* which are forbidden to be done by the commandments of the LORD; though he wist *it* not, yet is he guilty, and shall bear his iniquity.

¹⁸And he shall bring a ram without blemish out of the flock, with thy estimation, for a trespass offering, unto the priest: and the priest shall make an atonement for him concerning his ignorance wherein he erred and wist *it* not, and it shall be forgiven him.

¹⁹It *is* a trespass offering: he hath certainly trespassed against the LORD.

6 And the LORD spake unto Moses, saying, ²If a soul sin, and commit a trespass against the LORD, and lie unto his neighbour in that which was delivered him to keep, or in fellowship, or in a thing taken away by violence, or hath deceived his neighbour;

³Or have found that which was lost, and lieth concerning it, and sweareth falsely; in any of all *these* that a man doeth, sinning therein:

⁴Then it shall be, because he hath sinned, and is guilty, that he shall restore that which he took violently away, or the thing which he hath deceitfully gotten, or that which was delivered him to keep, or the lost *thing* which he found,

⁵Or all *that* about which he hath sworn falsely; he shall even restore it in the principal, and shall add the fifth *part* more thereto, *and* give it unto him to whom it appertaineth, in the day of his trespass offering.

⁶And he shall bring his trespass offering unto the LORD, a ram without blemish out of the flock, with thy estimation, for a trespass offering, unto the priest:

⁷And the priest shall make an atonement for him before the LORD: and it shall be forgiven him for any *thing* of all that he hath done in trespassing therein.

⁸ ¶ And the LORD spake unto Moses, saying,

⁹Command Aaron and his sons, saying, This *is* the law of the burnt offering: It *is* the burnt offering, because of the burning upon the altar all night unto the morning, and the fire of the altar shall be burning in it.

¹⁰And the priest shall put on his linen garment, and *his* linen breeches shall he put upon his flesh, and take up the ashes which the fire hath consumed with the burnt offering on the altar, and he shall put them besides the altar.

¹¹And he shall put off his garments, and put on other garments, and carry forth the ashes without the camp unto a clean place.

¹²And the fire upon the altar shall be burning

Amplified Bible

has done amiss in the holy thing, and shall add a fifth to it, and give it to the priest; and the priest shall make atonement for him with the ram of the trespass *or* guilt offering, and he shall be forgiven.

¹⁷If anyone sins and does any of the things the Lord has forbidden, though he was not aware of it, yet he is guilty and shall bear his iniquity.

¹⁸He shall bring [to the priest] a ram without blemish out of the flock, estimated by you to the amount [of the trespass], for a guilt *or* trespass offering; and the priest shall make atonement for him for the error which he committed unknowingly, and he shall be forgiven.

¹⁹It is a trespass *or* guilt offering; he is certainly guilty before the Lord.

6 AND THE Lord said to Moses, ²If anyone sins and commits a trespass against the Lord and deals falsely with his neighbor in a matter of deposit given him to keep, or of bargain *or* pledge, or of robbery, or has oppressed his neighbor,

³Or has found what was lost and lied about it, or swears falsely, in any of all the things which men do and sin in so doing,

⁴Then if he has sinned and is guilty, he shall restore what he took by robbery, or what he secured by oppression *or* extortion, or what was delivered him to keep in trust, or the lost thing which he found,

⁵Or anything about which he has sworn falsely; he shall not only restore it in full, but shall add to it one fifth more and give it to him to whom it belongs on the day of his trespass *or* guilt offering.

⁶And he shall bring to the priest his trespass *or* guilt offering to the Lord, a ram without blemish out of the flock, valued by you to the amount of his trespass;

⁷And the priest shall make atonement for him before the Lord, and he shall be forgiven for anything of all that he may have done by which he has become guilty.

⁸And the Lord said to Moses,

⁹Command Aaron and his sons, saying, This is the law of the burnt offering: The burnt offering shall remain on the altar all night until morning; the fire shall be kept burning on the altar.

¹⁰And the priest shall put on his linen garment and put his linen breeches on his body, and take up the ashes of what the fire has consumed with the burnt offering on the altar and put them beside the altar.

¹¹And he shall put off his garments and put on other garments, and carry the ashes outside the camp to a clean place.

¹²And the fire upon the altar shall be kept

King James Version

in it; it shall not be put out: and the priest shall burn wood on it every morning, and lay the burnt offering in order upon it; and he shall burn thereon the fat of the peace offerings.

¹³The fire shall ever be burning upon the altar; it shall never go out.

¹⁴ ¶ And this *is* the law of the meat offering: the sons of Aaron shall offer it before the LORD, before the altar.

¹⁵And he shall take of it his handful, of the flour of the meat offering, and of the oil thereof, and all the frankincense which *is* upon the meat offering, and shall burn *it upon* the altar *for* a sweet savour, *even* the memorial of it, unto the LORD.

¹⁶And the remainder thereof shall Aaron and his sons eat: *with* unleavened bread shall it be eaten in the holy place; in the court of the tabernacle of the congregation they shall eat it.

¹⁷It shall not be baken *with* leaven. I have given it *unto them for* their portion of my offerings made by fire; it *is* most holy, as *is* the sin offering, and as the trespass offering.

¹⁸All the males among the children of Aaron shall eat of it. *It shall be* a statute for ever in your generations concerning the offerings of the LORD made by fire: every one that toucheth them shall be holy.

¹⁹ ¶ And the LORD spake unto Moses, saying,

²⁰This *is* the offering of Aaron and of his sons, which they shall offer unto the LORD in the day when he is anointed; the tenth *part* of an ephah of fine flour *for* a meat offering perpetual, half of it in the morning, and half thereof at night.

²¹In a pan it shall be made with oil; *and when it is* baken, thou shalt bring it in: *and* the baken pieces of the meat offering shalt thou offer *for* a sweet savour unto the LORD.

²²And the priest of his sons that is anointed in his stead shall offer it: *it is* a statute for ever unto the LORD; it shall be wholly burnt.

²³For every meat offering for the priest shall be wholly *burnt:* it shall not be eaten.

²⁴ ¶ And the LORD spake unto Moses, saying,

²⁵Speak unto Aaron and to his sons, saying, This *is* the law of the sin offering: In the place where the burnt offering is killed shall the sin offering be killed before the LORD: it *is* most holy.

²⁶The priest that offereth it for sin shall eat it: in the holy place shall it be eaten, in the court of the tabernacle of the congregation.

²⁷Whatsoever shall touch the flesh thereof shall be holy: and when there is sprinkled of the blood thereof upon *any* garment, thou shalt wash that whereon it was sprinkled in the holy place.

²⁸But the earthen vessel wherein it is sodden shall be broken: and if it be sodden in a brasen pot, it shall be both scoured, and rinsed in water.

Amplified Bible

burning on it; it shall not be allowed to go out. The priest shall burn wood on it every morning and lay the burnt offering in order upon it and he shall burn on it the fat of the peace offerings.

¹³The fire shall be burning continually upon the altar; it shall not go out.

¹⁴And this is the law of the cereal offering: The sons of Aaron shall offer it before the Lord, in front of the altar.

¹⁵One of them shall take his handful of the fine flour of the cereal offering, the oil of it, and all the frankincense which is upon the cereal offering, and burn it on the altar as the memorial of it, a sweet *and* satisfying fragrance to the Lord.

¹⁶And the remainder of it shall Aaron and his sons eat, without leaven in a holy place; in the court of the Tent of Meeting shall they eat it.

¹⁷It shall not be baked with leaven. I have given it as their portion of My offerings made by fire; it is most holy, like the sin offering and the guilt offering.

¹⁸Every male among the children of Aaron may eat of it, as his portion forever throughout your generations, from the Lord's offerings made by fire; whoever touches them shall [first] be holy (consecrated and ceremonially clean).

¹⁹And the Lord said to Moses,

²⁰This is the offering which Aaron and his sons shall offer to the Lord on the day when one is anointed (and consecrated): the tenth of an ephah of fine flour for a regular cereal offering, half of it in the morning and half of it at night.

²¹On a griddle *or* baking pan it shall be made with oil; and when it is fried you shall bring it in; in broken *and* fried pieces shall you offer the cereal offering as a sweet *and* satisfying odor to the Lord.

²²And the priest among Aaron's sons who is consecrated *and* anointed in his stead shall offer it; by a statute forever it shall be entirely burned to the Lord.

²³For every cereal offering of the priest shall be wholly burned, and not be eaten.

²⁴And the Lord said to Moses,

²⁵Say to Aaron and his sons: This is the law of the sin offering: In the place where the burnt offering is killed shall the sin offering be killed before the Lord; it is most holy.

²⁶The priest who offers it for sin shall eat it; in a sacred place shall it be eaten, in the court of the Tent of Meeting.

²⁷Whoever *or* whatever touches its flesh shall [first] be dedicated and made clean, and when any of its blood is sprinkled on a garment, you shall wash that garment in a place set apart to God's worship.

²⁸But the earthen vessel in which it is boiled shall be broken, and if it is boiled in a bronze vessel, that vessel shall be scoured and rinsed in water.

King James Version

29All the males among the priests shall eat thereof: it *is* most holy.

30And no sin offering, whereof *any* of the blood is brought into the tabernacle of the congregation to reconcile *withal* in the holy *place,* shall be eaten: it shall be burnt in the fire.

7 Likewise this *is* the law of the trespass offering: it *is* most holy.

2In the place where they kill the burnt offering shall they kill the trespass offering: and the blood thereof shall he sprinkle round about upon the altar.

3And he shall offer of it all the fat thereof; the rump, and the fat that covereth the inwards,

4And the two kidneys, and the fat that *is* on them, which *is* by the flanks, and the caul *that is* above the liver, with the kidneys, it shall he take away:

5And the priest shall burn them upon the altar *for* an offering made by fire unto the LORD: it *is* a trespass offering.

6Every male among the priests shall eat thereof: it shall be eaten in the holy place: it *is* most holy.

7As the sin offering *is,* so *is* the trespass offering: *there is* one law for them: the priest that maketh atonement therewith shall have *it.*

8And the priest that offereth *any* man's burnt offering, *even* the priest shall have to himself the skin of the burnt offering which he hath offered.

9And all the meat offering that is baken in the oven, and all *that* is dressed in the fryingpan, and in the pan, shall be the priest's that offereth it.

10And every meat offering, mingled with oil, and dry, shall all the sons of Aaron have, one *as much* as another.

11 ¶ And this *is* the law of the sacrifice of peace offerings, which he shall offer unto the LORD.

12If he offer it for a thanksgiving, then he shall offer with the sacrifice of thanksgiving unleavened cakes mingled with oil, and unleavened wafers anointed with oil, and cakes mingled with oil, of fine flour, fried.

13Besides the cakes, he shall offer *for* his offering leavened bread with the sacrifice of thanksgiving of his peace offerings.

14And of it he shall offer one out of the whole oblation *for* a heave offering unto the LORD, *and* it shall be the priest's that sprinkleth the blood of the peace offerings.

15And the flesh of the sacrifice of his peace offerings for thanksgiving shall be eaten the same day that it is offered; he shall not leave *any* of it until the morning.

16But if the sacrifice of his offering *be* a vow, or a voluntary offering, it shall be eaten the *same* day that he offereth his sacrifice: and on

Amplified Bible

29Every male among the priests may eat of this offering; it is most holy.

30But no sin offering shall be eaten of which any of the blood is brought into the Tent of Meeting to make atonement in the Holy Place; it shall be [wholly] burned with fire.

7 THIS IS the law of the guilt *or* trespass offering; it is most holy *or* sacred:

2In the place where they kill the burnt offering shall they kill the guilt *or* trespass offering; the blood of it shall the priest dash against the altar round about.

3And he shall offer all its fat, the fat tail and the fat that covers the entrails,

4And the two kidneys and the fat that is on them at the loins, and the lobe *or* appendage of the liver, which he shall take away with the kidneys.

5And the priest shall burn them on the altar for an offering made by fire to the Lord; it is a guilt *or* trespass offering.

6Every male among the priests may eat of it; it shall be eaten in a sacred place; it is most holy.

7As is the sin offering, so is the guilt *or* trespass offering; there is one law for them: the priest who makes atonement with it shall have it.

8And the priest who offers any man's burnt offering, that priest shall have for himself the hide of the burnt offering which he has offered.

9And every cereal offering that is baked in the oven and all that is prepared in a pan or on a griddle shall belong to the priest who offered it.

10And every cereal offering, mixed with oil or dry, all the sons of Aaron may have, one as well as another.

11And this is the law of the sacrifice of peace offerings which shall be offered to the Lord:

12If one offers it for a thanksgiving, then he shall offer with the thank offering unleavened cakes mixed with oil, and unleavened wafers spread with oil, and cakes of fine flour mixed with oil.

13With cakes of leavened bread he shall offer his sacrifice of thanksgiving with the sacrifice of his peace offerings.

14And of it he shall offer one cake from each offering as an offering to the Lord; it shall belong to the priest who dashes the blood of the peace offerings.

15The flesh of the sacrifice of thanksgiving presented as a peace offering shall be eaten on the day that it is offered; none of it shall be left until morning.

16But if the sacrifice of the worshiper's offering is a vow or a freewill offering, it shall be eaten the same day that he offers his sacrifice, and

King James Version

the morrow also the remainder of it shall be eaten:

¹⁷But the remainder of the flesh of the sacrifice on the third day shall be burnt with fire.

¹⁸And if *any* of the flesh of the sacrifice of his peace offerings be eaten at all on the third day, it shall not be accepted, neither shall it be imputed unto him that offereth it: it shall be an abomination, and the soul that eateth of it shall bear his iniquity.

¹⁹And the flesh that toucheth any unclean *thing* shall not be eaten; it shall be burnt with fire: and *as for* the flesh, all that be clean shall eat thereof.

²⁰But the soul that eateth *of* the flesh of the sacrifice of peace offerings, that *pertain* unto the LORD, having his uncleanness upon him, even that soul shall be cut off from his people.

²¹Moreover the soul that shall touch any unclean *thing, as* the uncleanness of man, or *any* unclean beast, or any abominable unclean *thing,* and eat of the flesh of the sacrifice of peace offerings, which *pertain* unto the LORD, even that soul shall be cut off from his people.

²² ¶ And the LORD spake unto Moses, saying,

²³Speak unto the children of Israel, saying, Ye shall eat no *manner* fat, of ox, or of sheep, or of goat.

²⁴And the fat of the beast that dieth of itself, and the fat of that which is torn *with beasts,* may be used in any *other* use: but ye shall in no wise eat of it.

²⁵For whosoever eateth the fat of the beast, of which *men* offer an offering made by fire unto the LORD, even the soul that eateth *it* shall be cut off from his people.

²⁶Moreover ye shall eat no *manner of* blood, *whether it be* of fowl or of beast, in any of your dwellings.

²⁷Whatsoever soul *it be* that eateth any *manner of* blood, even that soul shall be cut off from his people.

²⁸ ¶ And the LORD spake unto Moses, saying,

²⁹Speak unto the children of Israel, saying, He that offereth the sacrifice of his peace offerings unto the LORD shall bring his oblation unto the LORD of the sacrifice of his peace offerings.

³⁰His own hands shall bring the offerings of the LORD made by fire, the fat with the breast, it shall he bring, that the breast may be waved *for* a wave offering before the LORD.

³¹And the priest shall burn the fat upon the altar: but the breast shall be Aaron's and his sons'.

³²And the right shoulder shall ye give unto the priest *for* a heave offering of the sacrifices of your peace offerings.

³³He among the sons of Aaron, that offereth the blood of the peace offerings, and the fat, shall have the right shoulder for *his* part.

Amplified Bible

on the morrow that which remains of it shall be eaten;

¹⁷But the remainder of the flesh of the sacrifice on the third day shall be [wholly] burned with fire.

¹⁸If any of the flesh of the sacrifice of his peace offerings be eaten at all on the third day, then the one who brought it shall not be credited with it; it shall not be accepted. It shall be an abomination *and* an abhorred thing; the one who eats of it shall bear his iniquity *and* answer for it.

¹⁹The flesh that comes in contact with anything that is not clean shall not be eaten; it shall be burned with fire. As for the meat, everyone who is clean [ceremonially] may eat of it.

²⁰But the one who eats of the flesh of the sacrifice of peace offerings that belong to the Lord when he is [ceremonially] unclean, that person shall be cut off from his people [deprived of the privileges of association with them].

²¹And if anyone touches any unclean thing—the uncleanness of man or an unclean beast or any unclean abomination—and then eats of the flesh of the sacrifice of the Lord's peace offerings, that person shall be cut off from his people.

²²And the Lord said to Moses,

²³Say to the Israelites, You shall eat no kind of fat, of ox, or sheep, or goat.

²⁴The fat of the beast that dies of itself and the fat of one that is torn with beasts may be put to any other use, but under no circumstances are you to eat of it.

²⁵For whoever eats the fat of the beast from which men offer an offering made by fire to the Lord, that person shall be cut off from his people.

²⁶Moreover, you shall eat no blood of any kind, whether of bird or of beast, in any of your dwellings.

²⁷Whoever eats any kind of blood, that person shall be cut off from his people.

²⁸And the Lord said to Moses,

²⁹Tell the Israelites, He who offers the sacrifice of his peace offerings to the Lord shall bring his offering to the Lord; from the sacrifice of his peace offerings

³⁰He shall bring with his own hands the offerings made by fire to the Lord; he shall bring the fat with the breast, that the breast may be waved as a wave offering before the Lord.

³¹The priest shall burn the fat on the altar, but the breast shall be for Aaron and his sons.

³²And the right thigh you shall give to the priest for an offering from the sacrifices of your peace offerings.

³³The son of Aaron who offers the blood of the peace offerings and the fat shall have the right thigh for his portion.

King James Version

³⁴For the wave breast and the heave shoulder have I taken of the children of Israel from off the sacrifices of their peace offerings, and have given them unto Aaron the priest and unto his sons by a statute for ever from among the children of Israel.

³⁵ ¶ This *is the portion* of the anointing of Aaron, and of the anointing of his sons, out of the offerings of the LORD made by fire, in the day *when* he presented them to minister unto the LORD in the priest's office;

³⁶Which the LORD commanded to be given them of the children of Israel, in the day that he anointed them, *by* a statute for ever throughout their generations.

³⁷This *is* the law of the burnt offering, of the meat offering, and of the sin offering, and of the trespass offering, and of the consecrations, and of the sacrifice of the peace offerings;

³⁸Which the LORD commanded Moses in mount Sinai, in the day that he commanded the children of Israel to offer their oblations unto the LORD, in the wilderness of Sinai.

8 And the LORD spake unto Moses, saying, ²Take Aaron and his sons with him, and the garments, and the anointing oil, and a bullock *for* the sin offering, and two rams, and a basket of unleavened bread;

³And gather thou all the congregation together unto the door of the tabernacle of the congregation.

⁴And Moses did as the LORD commanded him; and the assembly was gathered together unto the door of the tabernacle of the congregation.

⁵And Moses said unto the congregation, This *is* the thing which the LORD commanded to be done.

⁶And Moses brought Aaron and his sons, and washed them with water.

⁷And he put upon him the coat, and girded him with the girdle, and clothed him with the robe, and put the ephod upon him, and he girded him with the curious girdle of the ephod, and bound *it* unto him therewith.

⁸And he put the breastplate upon him: also he put in the breastplate the Urim and the Thummim.

⁹And he put the mitre upon his head; also upon the mitre, *even* upon his forefront, did he put the golden plate, the holy crown; as the LORD commanded Moses.

¹⁰And Moses took the anointing oil, and anointed the tabernacle and all that *was* therein, and sanctified them.

¹¹And he sprinkled thereof upon the altar seven times, and anointed the altar and all his vessels, both the laver and his foot, to sanctify them.

Amplified Bible

³⁴For I have taken the breast that was waved and the thigh that was offered from the Israelites, out of the sacrifices of their peace offerings, and have given them to Aaron the priest and to his sons as their perpetual due from the Israelites.

³⁵This is the anointing portion of Aaron and his sons out of the offerings to the Lord made by fire on the day when they were presented to minister to the Lord in the priest's office.

³⁶The Lord commanded this to be given them of the Israelites on the day when they were anointed. It is their portion perpetually throughout their generations.

³⁷This is the law of the burnt offering, the cereal offering, the sin offering, the guilt *or* trespass offering, the consecration offering, and the sacrifice of peace offerings,

³⁸Which the Lord ordered Moses on Mount Sinai on the day He commanded the Israelites to offer their sacrifices to the Lord, in the Wilderness of Sinai.

8 AND THE Lord said to Moses, ²Take Aaron and his sons with him, and the garments [symbols of their office], and the anointing oil, and the bull of the sin offering, and the two rams, and the basket of unleavened bread;

³And assemble all the congregation at the door of the Tent of Meeting.

⁴Moses did as the Lord commanded him, and the congregation was assembled at the door of the Tent of Meeting.

⁵Moses told the congregation, This is what the Lord has commanded to be done.

⁶Moses brought Aaron and his sons and washed them with water.

⁷He put on Aaron the long undertunic, girded him with the long sash, clothed him with the robe, put the ephod (an upper vestment) upon him, and girded him with the skillfully woven cords attached to the ephod, binding it to him.

⁸And Moses put upon Aaron the breastplate; also he put in the breastplate the Urim and the Thummim [articles upon which the high priest put his hand when seeking the divine will concerning the nation].

⁹And he put the turban *or* miter on his head; on it, in front, Moses put the shining gold plate, the holy diadem, as the Lord commanded him.

¹⁰And Moses took the anointing oil and anointed the tabernacle and all that was in it, and consecrated them.

¹¹And he sprinkled some of the oil on the altar seven times and anointed the altar and all its utensils, and the laver and its base, to consecrate them.

King James Version

¹²And he poured of the anointing oil upon Aaron's head, and anointed him, to sanctify him.

¹³And Moses brought Aaron's sons, and put coats upon them, and girded them *with* girdles, and put bonnets upon them; as the LORD commanded Moses.

¹⁴And he brought the bullock *for* the sin offering: and Aaron and his sons laid their hands upon the head of the bullock *for* the sin offering.

¹⁵And he slew *it;* and Moses took the blood, and put *it* upon the horns of the altar round about with his finger, and purified the altar, and poured the blood at the bottom of the altar, and sanctified it, to make reconciliation upon it.

¹⁶And he took all the fat that *was* upon the inwards, and the caul *above* the liver, and the two kidneys, and their fat, and Moses burned *it* upon the altar.

¹⁷But the bullock, and his hide, his flesh, and his dung, he burnt with fire without the camp; as the LORD commanded Moses.

¹⁸And he brought the ram for the burnt offering: and Aaron and his sons laid their hands upon the head of the ram.

¹⁹And he killed *it;* and Moses sprinkled the blood upon the altar round about.

²⁰And he cut the ram into pieces; and Moses burnt the head, and the pieces, and the fat.

²¹And he washed the inwards and the legs in water; and Moses burnt the whole ram upon the altar: it *was* a burnt sacrifice for a sweet savour, *and* an offering made by fire unto the LORD; as the LORD commanded Moses.

²²And he brought the other ram, the ram of consecration: and Aaron and his sons laid their hands upon the head of the ram.

²³And he slew *it;* and Moses took of the blood of it, and put *it* upon the tip of Aaron's right ear, and upon the thumb of his right hand, and upon the great toe of his right foot.

²⁴And he brought Aaron's sons, and Moses put of the blood upon the tip of their right ear, and upon the thumbs of their right hands, and upon the great toes of their right feet: and Moses sprinkled the blood upon the altar round about.

²⁵And he took the fat, and the rump, and all the fat that *was* upon the inwards, and the caul *above* the liver, and the two kidneys, and their fat, and the right shoulder:

²⁶And out of the basket of unleavened bread, that *was* before the LORD, he took one unleavened cake, and a cake of oiled bread, and one wafer, and put *them* on the fat, and upon the right shoulder:

²⁷And he put all upon Aaron's hands, and upon his sons' hands, and waved them *for* a wave offering before the LORD.

²⁸And Moses took them from off their hands, and burnt *them* on the altar upon the burnt offering: they *were* consecrations for a sweet

Amplified Bible

¹²And he poured some of the anointing oil upon Aaron's head and anointed him to consecrate him.

¹³And Moses brought Aaron's sons and put undertunics on them and girded them with sashes and wound turbans on them, as the Lord commanded Moses.

¹⁴Then he brought the bull of the sin offering, and Aaron and his sons laid their hands on the head of the bull of the sin offering.

¹⁵Moses killed it and took the blood and put it on the horns of the altar round about with his finger and poured the blood at the base of the altar and purified and consecrated the altar to make atonement for it.

¹⁶He took all the fat that was on the entrails, and the lobe of the liver, and the two kidneys with their fat, and Moses burned them on the altar.

¹⁷But the bull [the sin offering] and its hide, its flesh, and its dung he burned with fire outside the camp, as the Lord commanded Moses.

¹⁸He brought the ram for the burnt offering, and Aaron and his sons laid their hands on the head of the ram.

¹⁹And Moses killed it and dashed the blood upon the altar round about.

²⁰He cut the ram into pieces and Moses burned the head, the pieces, and the fat.

²¹And he washed the entrails and the legs in water; then Moses burned the whole ram on the altar; it was a burnt sacrifice, for a sweet *and* satisfying fragrance, an offering made by fire to the Lord, as the Lord commanded Moses.

²²And he brought the other ram, the ram of consecration *and* ordination, and Aaron and his sons laid their hands upon the head of the ram.

²³And Moses killed it and took some of its blood and put it on the tip of Aaron's right ear, and on the thumb of his right hand, and on the great toe of his right foot.

²⁴And he brought Aaron's sons and Moses put some of the blood on the tips of their right ears, and the thumbs of their right hands, and the great toes of their right feet; and Moses dashed the blood upon the altar round about.

²⁵And he took the fat, the fat tail, all the fat that was on the entrails, the lobe of the liver, and the two kidneys and their fat, and the right thigh;

²⁶And out of the basket of unleavened bread, that was before the Lord, he took one unleavened cake, a cake of oiled bread, and one wafer and put them on the fat and on the right thigh;

²⁷And he put all these in Aaron's hands and his sons' hands and waved them for a wave offering before the Lord.

²⁸Then Moses took these things from their hands and burned them on the altar with the burnt offering as an ordination offering, for a

King James Version

savour: it *is* an offering made by fire unto the LORD.

²⁹And Moses took the breast, and waved it *for* a wave offering before the LORD: *for* of the ram of consecration it was Moses' part; as the LORD commanded Moses.

³⁰And Moses took of the anointing oil, and of the blood which *was* upon the altar, and sprinkled *it* upon Aaron, *and* upon his garments, and upon his sons, and upon his sons' garments with him; and sanctified Aaron, *and* his garments, and his sons, and his sons' garments with him.

³¹ ¶ And Moses said unto Aaron and to his sons, Boil the flesh *at* the door of the tabernacle of the congregation: and there eat it with the bread that *is* in the basket of consecrations, as I commanded, saying, Aaron and his sons shall eat it.

³²And that which remaineth of the flesh and of the bread shall ye burn with fire.

³³And ye shall not go out of the door of the tabernacle of the congregation *in* seven days, until the days of your consecration be at an end: for seven days shall he consecrate you.

³⁴As he hath done this day, *so* the LORD hath commanded to do, to make an atonement for you.

³⁵Therefore shall ye abide *at* the door of the tabernacle of the congregation day and night seven days, and keep the charge of the LORD, that ye die not: for so I am commanded.

³⁶So Aaron and his sons did all things which the LORD commanded by the hand of Moses.

9 And it came to pass on the eighth day, *that* Moses called Aaron and his sons, and the elders of Israel;

²And he said unto Aaron, Take thee a young calf for a sin offering, and a ram for a burnt offering, without blemish, and offer *them* before the LORD.

³And unto the children of Israel thou shalt speak, saying, Take ye a kid of the goats for a sin offering; and a calf and a lamb, both of the first year, without blemish, for a burnt offering;

⁴Also a bullock and a ram for peace offerings, to sacrifice before the LORD; and a meat offering mingled with oil: for to day the LORD will appear unto you.

⁵And they brought *that* which Moses commanded before the tabernacle of the congregation: and all the congregation drew near and stood before the LORD.

⁶And Moses said, This *is* the thing which the

Amplified Bible

sweet *and* satisfying fragrance, an offering made by fire to the Lord.

²⁹And Moses took the breast and waved it for a wave offering before the Lord; for of the ram of consecration *and* ordination it was Moses' portion, as the Lord commanded Moses.

³⁰And Moses took some of the anointing oil and some of the blood which was on the altar and sprinkled it on Aaron and his garments, and upon his sons and their garments also; so Moses consecrated Aaron and his garments, and his sons and his sons' garments.

³¹And Moses said to Aaron and his sons, Boil the flesh at the door of the Tent of Meeting and there eat it with the bread that is in the basket of consecration *and* ordination, as I commanded, saying, Aaron and his sons shall eat it.

³²And what remains of the flesh and of the bread you shall burn with fire.

³³And you shall not go out of the door of the Tent of Meeting for seven days, until the days of your consecration *and* ordination are ended; for it will take seven days to consecrate *and* ordain you.

³⁴As has been done this day, so the Lord has commanded to do for your atonement.

³⁵At the door of the Tent of Meeting you shall remain day and night for seven days, ᵃdoing what the Lord has charged you to do, that you die not; for so I am commanded.

³⁶So Aaron and his sons did all the things which the Lord commanded through Moses.

9 ON THE eighth day Moses called Aaron and his sons and the elders of Israel;

²And he said to Aaron, Take a young calf for a sin offering and a ram for a burnt offering, [each] without blemish, and offer them before the Lord.

³And say to the Israelites, Take a male goat for a sin offering, and a calf and a lamb, both a year old, without blemish, for a burnt offering,

⁴Also a bull and a ram for peace offerings to sacrifice before the Lord, and a cereal offering mixed with oil, for today the Lord will appear to you.

⁵They brought before the Tent of Meeting what Moses [had] commanded; all the congregation drew near and stood before the Lord.

⁶And Moses said, This is the thing which the

AMP notes: ᵃ We have, every one of us, a charge to keep, an eternal God to glorify, an immortal soul to provide for, needful duty to be done, our generation to serve; and it must be our daily care to keep this charge, for it is the charge of the Lord our Master (Matthew Henry, *Commentary on the Holy Bible*). The laws contained in this book, for the most part ceremonial, had an important spiritual bearing, the study of which is highly instructive (Robert Jamieson, A. R. Fausset and David Brown, *A Commentary*). The Scripture references recorded within the text are intended to be a guide to its spiritual implications.

King James Version

LORD commanded *that* ye should do: and the glory of the LORD shall appear unto you.

7And Moses said unto Aaron, Go unto the altar, and offer thy sin offering, and thy burnt offering, and make an atonement for thyself, and for the people: and offer the offering of the people, and make an atonement for them; as the LORD commanded.

8 ¶ Aaron therefore went unto the altar, and slew the calf of the sin offering, which *was* for himself.

9And the sons of Aaron brought the blood unto him: and he dipt his finger in the blood, and put *it* upon the horns of the altar, and poured out the blood at the bottom of the altar:

10But the fat, and the kidneys, and the caul above the liver of the sin offering, he burnt upon the altar; as the LORD commanded Moses.

11And the flesh and the hide he burnt with fire without the camp.

12And he slew the burnt offering; and Aaron's sons presented unto him the blood, which he sprinkled round about upon the altar.

13And they presented the burnt offering unto him, with the pieces thereof, and the head: and he burnt *them* upon the altar.

14And he did wash the inwards and the legs, and burnt *them* upon the burnt offering on the altar.

15 ¶ And he brought the people's offering, and took the goat, which *was* the sin offering for the people, and slew it, and offered it for sin, as the first.

16And he brought the burnt offering, and offered it according to the manner.

17And he brought the meat offering, and took a handful thereof, and burnt *it* upon the altar, beside the burnt sacrifice of the morning.

18He slew also the bullock and the ram *for* a sacrifice of peace offerings, which *was* for the people: and Aaron's sons presented unto him the blood, which he sprinkled upon the altar round about,

19And the fat of the bullock and of the ram, the rump, and that which covereth *the inwards,* and the kidneys, and the caul *above* the liver:

20And they put the fat upon the breasts, and he burnt the fat upon the altar:

21And the breasts and the right shoulder Aaron waved *for* a wave offering before the LORD; as Moses commanded.

22 ¶ And Aaron lift up his hand towards the people, and blessed them, and came down from offering of the sin offering, and the burnt offering, and peace offerings.

23And Moses and Aaron went into the tabernacle of the congregation, and came out, and blessed the people: and the glory of the LORD appeared unto all the people.

24And there came a fire out from before the LORD, and consumed upon the altar the burnt

Amplified Bible

Lord commanded you to do, and the glory of the Lord will appear to you.

7And Moses said to Aaron, Draw near to the altar and offer your sin offering and your burnt offering and make atonement for yourself and for the people; and offer the offering of the people and make atonement for them, as the Lord commanded.

8So Aaron drew near to the altar and killed the calf of the sin offering, which was designated for himself.

9The sons of Aaron presented the blood to him; he dipped his finger in the blood and put it on the horns of the altar and poured out the blood at the altar's base;

10But the fat, the kidneys, and the lobe of the liver from the sin offering he burned on the altar, as the Lord had commanded Moses.

11And the flesh and the hide Aaron burned with fire outside the camp.

12He killed the burnt offering, and Aaron's sons delivered to him the blood, which he dashed round about upon the altar.

13And they brought the burnt offering to him piece by piece, and the head, and Aaron burned them upon the altar.

14And he washed the entrails and the legs and burned them with the burnt offering on the altar.

15Then Aaron presented the people's offering, and took the goat of the sin offering which was for the people and killed it and offered it for sin as he did the first sin offering.

16And he presented the burnt offering and offered it according to the ordinance.

17And Aaron presented the cereal offering and took a handful of it and burned it on the altar in addition to the burnt offering of the morning.

18He also killed the bull and the ram, the sacrifice of peace offerings, for the people; and Aaron's sons presented to him the blood, which he dashed upon the altar round about,

19And the fat of the bull and of the ram, the fat tail and that which covers the entrails, and the kidneys, and the lobe of the liver.

20And they put the fat upon the breasts, and Aaron burned the fat upon the altar;

21But the breasts and the right thigh Aaron waved for a wave offering before the Lord, as Moses commanded.

22Then Aaron lifted his hands toward the people and blessed them, and came down [from the altar] after offering the sin offering, the burnt offering, and the peace offerings.

23Moses and Aaron went into the Tent of Meeting, and when they came out they blessed the people, and the glory of the Lord [the Shekinah cloud] appeared to all the people [as promised].

24Then there came a fire out from before the Lord and consumed the burnt offering and the

King James Version

offering and the fat: *which* when all the people saw, they shouted, and fell on their faces.

10 And Nadab and Abihu, the sons of Aaron, took either of them his censer, and put fire therein, and put incense thereon, and offered strange fire before the LORD, which he commanded them not.

2And there went out fire from the LORD, and devoured them, and they died before the LORD.

3Then Moses said unto Aaron, This *is it* that the LORD spake, saying, I will be sanctified in them that come nigh me, and before all the people I will be glorified. And Aaron held his peace.

4And Moses called Mishael and Elzaphan, the sons of Uzziel the uncle of Aaron, and said unto them, Come near, carry your brethren from before the sanctuary out of the camp.

5So they went near, and carried them in their coats out of the camp; as Moses had said.

6And Moses said unto Aaron, and unto Eleazar and unto Ithamar his sons, Uncover not your heads, neither rend your clothes; lest you die, and lest wrath come upon all the people: but let your brethren, the whole house of Israel, bewail the burning which the LORD hath kindled.

7And ye shall not go out from the door of the tabernacle of the congregation, lest you die: for the anointing oil of the LORD *is* upon you. And they did according to the word of Moses.

8 ¶ And the LORD spake unto Aaron, saying,

9Do not drink wine nor strong drink, thou, nor thy sons with thee, when ye go into the tabernacle of the congregation, lest ye die: *it shall be* a statute for ever throughout your generations:

10And that *ye* may put difference between holy and unholy, and between unclean and clean;

11And that *ye* may teach the children of Israel all the statutes which the LORD hath spoken unto them by the hand of Moses.

12 ¶ And Moses spake unto Aaron, and unto Eleazar and unto Ithamar his sons that were left, Take the meat offering that remaineth of

Amplified Bible

fat on the altar; and when all the people saw it, they shouted and fell on their faces.

10 AND NADAB and Abihu, the sons of Aaron, each took his censer and put fire in it, and put incense on it, and offered strange *and* unholy fire before the Lord, as He had not commanded them.

2And there came forth fire from before the Lord and killed them, and they died before the Lord.

3Then Moses said to Aaron, This is what the Lord meant when He said, I *a*[and My will, not their own] will be acknowledged as hallowed by those who come near Me, and before all the people I will be honored. And Aaron said nothing.

4Moses called Mishael and Elzaphan, sons of Uzziel uncle of Aaron, and said to them, Come near, carry your brethren from before the sanctuary out of the camp.

5So they drew near and carried them in their undertunics [stripped of their priestly vestments] out of the camp, as Moses had said.

6And Moses said to Aaron and Eleazar and Ithamar, his sons [the father and brothers of the two priests whom God had slain for offering false fire], Do not uncover your heads *or* let your hair go loose or tear your clothes, lest you die [also] and lest God's wrath should come upon all the congregation; but let your brethren, the whole house of Israel, bewail the burning which the Lord has kindled.

7And you shall not go out from the door of the Tent of Meeting, lest you die, for the Lord's anointing oil is upon you. And they did according to Moses' word.

8And the Lord said to Aaron,

9Do not drink wine or strong drink, you or your sons, when you go into the Tent of Meeting, lest you die; it shall be a statute forever in all your generations.

10You shall make a distinction *and* recognize a difference between the holy and the common *or* unholy, and between the unclean and the clean;

11And you are to teach the Israelites all the statutes which the Lord has spoken to them by Moses.

12And Moses said to Aaron and to Eleazar and Ithamar, his sons who were left, Take the cereal offering that remains of the offerings of the Lord

AMP notes: a Perhaps few believers have ever identified themselves with Nadab and Abihu, and yet few, if any, of us have not done exactly what they did in principle. Their sin, which God took so seriously and which proved fatal to them, was not a mere matter of failing to obey the letter of God's law for priests. Their inexcusable folly was in trying to please the Lord **their** way instead of **His** way. Who of us cannot recognize himself as the offerer of this prayer, with only the details lacking: "O Lord, make me rich! Then I will make large donations to Your interests!" Yet our very poverty may be the means to the end which He has in love and wisdom planned for us, the ultimate purpose of our creation, perhaps, which substitution of our will for His will would utterly defeat. No wonder God removed Nadab and Abihu from the earth! They, like ourselves, had acted like the child of a great painter who attempted to work on his father's priceless canvas instead of on the tablet assigned to him. They, like the child, were banished from the father's presence. And every believer does well to recognize the importance of being entirely surrendered to "God's will; nothing more; nothing less; nothing else; at any cost." And that does not mean first making an unholy alliance in marriage, or in business, or in thought, and then adjusting it to God's will. Remember Nadab and Abihu, who "offered strange *and* unholy fire before the Lord." It does not pay.

King James Version

the offerings of the LORD made by fire, and eat it without leaven beside the altar: for it *is* most holy:

¹³And ye shall eat it in the holy place, because it *is* thy due, and thy sons' due, of the sacrifices of the LORD made by fire: for so I am commanded.

¹⁴And the wave breast and heave shoulder shall ye eat in a clean place; thou, and thy sons, and thy daughters with thee: for *they be* thy due, and thy sons' due, *which* are given out of the sacrifices of peace offerings of the children of Israel.

¹⁵The heave shoulder and the wave breast shall they bring with the offerings made by fire of the fat, to wave *it for* a wave offering before the LORD; and it shall be thine, and thy sons' with thee, by a statute for ever; as the LORD hath commanded.

¹⁶ ¶ And Moses diligently sought the goat of the sin offering, and behold, it was burnt: and he was angry with Eleazar and Ithamar the sons of Aaron which were left *alive,* saying,

¹⁷Wherefore have ye not eaten the sin offering in the holy place, seeing it *is* most holy, and *God* hath given it you to bear the iniquity of the congregation, to make atonement for them before the LORD?

¹⁸Behold, the blood of it was not brought in within the holy *place:* ye should indeed have eaten it in the holy *place,* as I commanded.

¹⁹And Aaron said unto Moses, Behold, *this* day have they offered their sin offering and their burnt offering before the LORD; and such things have befallen me: and *if* I had eaten the sin offering to day, should it have been accepted in the sight of the LORD?

²⁰And when Moses heard *that,* he was content.

11 And the LORD spake unto Moses and to Aaron, saying unto them,

²Speak unto the children of Israel, saying, These *are* the beasts which ye shall eat among all the beasts that *are* on the earth.

³Whatsoever parteth the hoof, and *is* cloven-footed, *and* cheweth cud, among the beasts, that shall ye eat.

⁴Nevertheless these shall ye not eat of them that chew the cud, or of them that divide the

Amplified Bible

made by fire and eat it without leaven beside the altar, for it is most holy.

¹³You shall eat it in a sacred place, because it is your due and your sons' due, from the offerings made by fire to the Lord; for so I am commanded.

¹⁴But the breast that is waved and the thigh that is offered you shall eat in a clean place, you and your sons and daughters with you; for they are your due and your sons' due, given out of the sacrifices of the peace offerings of the Israelites.

¹⁵The thigh that is offered and the breast that is waved they shall bring with the offerings made by fire of the fat, to wave for a wave offering before the Lord; and it shall be yours and your sons' with you as a portion *or* due perpetually, as the Lord has commanded.

¹⁶And Moses diligently tried to find [what had become of] the goat [that had been offered] for the sin offering, and behold, it was burned up [as waste]! And he was angry with Eleazar and Ithamar, the sons of Aaron who were left alive, and said,

¹⁷Why have you not eaten the sin offering in the Holy Place? It is most holy; and God has given it to you to bear *and* take away the iniquity of the congregation, to make atonement for them before the Lord.

¹⁸Behold, the blood of it was not brought within the Holy Place; you should indeed have eaten [the flesh of it] in the Holy Place, as I commanded.

¹⁹But Aaron said to Moses, Behold, this very day in which they have [obediently] offered their sin offering and their burnt offering before the Lord, such [terrible calamities] have befallen me [and them]! If I [and they] had eaten the most holy sin offering today [humbled as we have been by the sin of our kinsmen and God's judgment upon them], would it have been acceptable in the sight of the Lord?

²⁰And when Moses heard that, he was pacified.

11 AND THE Lord said to Moses and Aaron, ²Say to the Israelites: These are the animals ᵃwhich you may eat among all the beasts that are on the earth.

³Whatever parts the hoof and is cloven-footed and chews the cud, any of these animals you may eat.

⁴Nevertheless these you shall not eat of those that chew the cud or divide the hoof: the

---

AMP notes: ᵃ At first thought the laws given here seem only to have been made obsolete by Jesus. He taught that it is not what goes into the mouth but what comes out of it that defiles a man (Matt. 15:17-20), and Paul said that when the complete and perfect came, the incomplete and imperfect would become void and superseded (I Cor. 13:9, 10), for "there is nothing unclean of itself" (Rom. 14:14 KJV). But while all these specific laws have become void, we must not lose sight of the fact that they are "superseded" by the underlying spiritual principle, which is just as binding. Christ's teaching relates to the whole area of our living, including our eating and drinking, and is dominated by the principle, "Whatever you may do, do all for the honor *and* glory of God" (I Cor. 10:31). We do well to remember that it was Jesus Christ Himself who said, "Do not think that I have come to do away with *or* undo the Law . . .; I have come not to do away with *or* undo but to complete *and* fulfill" it (Matt. 5:17).

King James Version

hoof: *as* the camel, because he cheweth the cud, but divideth not the hoof; he *is* unclean unto you.

5And the cony, because he cheweth the cud, but divideth not the hoof; he *is* unclean unto you.

6And the hare, because he cheweth the cud, but divideth not the hoof; he *is* unclean unto you.

7And the swine, though he divide the hoof, and *be* clovenfooted, yet he cheweth not the cud; he *is* unclean to you.

8Of their flesh shall ye not eat, and their carcase shall ye not touch; they *are* unclean to you.

9 ¶ These shall ye eat of all that *are* in the waters: whatsoever hath fins and scales in the waters, in the seas, and in the rivers, them shall ye eat.

10And all that have not fins nor scales in the seas, and in the rivers, of all that move in the waters, and of any living thing which *is* in the waters, they *shall be* an abomination unto you:

11They shall be even an abomination unto you: ye shall not eat of their flesh, but you shall have their carcases in abomination.

12Whatsoever hath no fins nor scales in the waters, that *shall be* an abomination unto you.

13 ¶ And these *are they which* ye shall have in abomination among the fowls; they shall not be eaten, they *are* an abomination: the eagle, and the ossifrage, and the ospray,

14And the vulture, and the kite after his kind;

15Every raven after his kind;

16And the owl, and the night hawk, and the cuckow, and the hawk after his kind,

17And the little owl, and the cormorant, and the great owl,

18And the swan, and the pelican, and the gier eagle,

19And the stork, the heron after her kind, and the lapwing, and the bat.

20 ¶ All fowls that creep, going upon *all* four, *shall be* an abomination unto you.

21Yet these may ye eat of every flying creeping thing that goeth upon *all* four, which have legs above their feet, to leap withal upon the earth;

22*Even* these of them ye may eat; the locust after his kind, and the bald locust after his kind, and the beetle after his kind, and the grasshopper after his kind.

23But all *other* flying creeping things, which have four feet, *shall be* an abomination unto you.

24And for these ye shall be unclean: whosoever toucheth the carcase of them shall be unclean until the even.

25And whosoever beareth *ought* of the carcase of them shall wash his clothes, and be unclean until the even.

26*The carcases* of every beast which divideth

Amplified Bible

camel, because it chews the cud but does not divide the hoof; it is unclean to you.

5And the coney *or* rock badger, because it chews the cud but does not divide the hoof; it is unclean to you.

6And the hare, because it chews the cud but does not divide the hoof; it is unclean to you.

7And the swine, because it divides the hoof and is cloven-footed but does not chew the cud; it is unclean to you.

8Of their flesh you shall not eat, and their carcasses you shall not touch; they are unclean to you.

9These you may eat of all that are in the waters: whatever has fins and scales in the waters, in the seas, and in the rivers, these you may eat;

10But all that have not fins and scales in the seas and in the rivers, of all the creeping things in the waters, and of all the living creatures which are in the waters, they are [to be considered] an abomination and abhorrence to you.

11They shall continue to be an abomination to you; you shall not eat of their flesh, but you shall detest their carcasses.

12Everything in the waters that has not fins or scales shall be abhorrent *and* detestable to you.

13These you shall have in abomination among the birds; they shall not be eaten, for they are detestable: the eagle, the ossifrage, the ospray,

14The kite, the whole species of falcon,

15Every kind of raven,

16The ostrich, the nighthawk, the sea gull, every species of hawk,

17The owl, the cormorant, the ibis,

18The swan, the pelican, the vulture,

19The stork, all kinds of heron, the hoopoe, and the bat.

20All winged insects that go upon all fours are to be an abomination to you;

21Yet of all winged insects that go upon all fours you may eat those which have legs above their feet with which to leap on the ground.

22Of these you may eat: the whole species of locust, of bald locust, of cricket, and of grasshopper.

23But all other winged insects which have four feet shall be detestable to you.

24And by [contact with] these you shall become unclean; whoever touches the carcass of them shall be unclean until the evening,

25And whoever carries any part of their carcass shall wash his clothes and be unclean until the evening.

26Every beast which parts the hoof but is not

King James Version

the hoof, and *is* not clovenfooted, nor cheweth the cud, *are* unclean unto you: every one that toucheth them shall be unclean.

27 And whatsoever goeth upon his paws, among all *manner of* beasts that go on *all* four, those *are* unclean unto you: whoso toucheth their carcase shall be unclean until the even.

28 And he that beareth the carcase of them shall wash his clothes, and be unclean until the even: they *are* unclean unto you.

29 ¶ These also *shall be* unclean unto you among the creeping things that creep upon the earth; the weasel, and the mouse, and the tortoise after his kind,

30 And the ferret, and the chameleon, and the lizard, and the snail, and the mole.

31 These *are* unclean to you among all that creep: whosoever doth touch them, when they be dead, shall be unclean until the even.

32 And upon whatsoever *any* of them, when they are dead, doth fall, it shall be unclean; whether *it be* any vessel of wood, or raiment, or skin, or sack, whatsoever vessel *it be,* wherein *any* work is done, it must be put into water, and it shall be unclean until the even; so it shall be cleansed.

33 And every earthen vessel, whereinto *any* of them falleth, whatsoever *is* in it shall be unclean; and ye shall break it.

34 Of all meat which may be eaten, *that* on which *such* water cometh shall be unclean: and all drink that may be drunk in every *such* vessel shall be unclean.

35 And every *thing* whereupon *any part* of their carcase falleth shall be unclean; *whether it be* oven, or ranges for pots, they shall be broken down: *for* they *are* unclean, and shall be unclean unto you.

36 Nevertheless a fountain or pit, *wherein there is* plenty of water, shall be clean: but that which toucheth their carcase shall be unclean.

37 And if *any part* of their carcase fall upon any sowing seed which is to be sown, it *shall be* clean.

38 But if *any* water be put upon the seed, and *any part* of their carcase fall thereon, it *shall be* unclean unto you.

39 And if any beast, of which ye may eat, die; he that toucheth the carcase thereof shall be unclean until the even.

40 And he that eateth of the carcase of it shall wash his clothes, and be unclean until the even: he also that beareth the carcase of it shall wash his clothes, and be unclean until the even.

41 And every creeping thing that creepeth upon the earth *shall be* an abomination; it shall not be eaten.

42 Whatsoever goeth upon the belly, and whatsoever goeth upon *all* four, or whatsoever hath more feet among all creeping things that creep

Amplified Bible

cloven-footed or does not chew the cud is unclean to you; everyone who touches them shall be unclean.

27 And all that go on their paws, among all kinds of four-footed beasts, are unclean to you; whoever touches their carcass shall be unclean until the evening,

28 And he who carries their carcass shall wash his clothes and be unclean until the evening; they are unclean to you.

29 These also are unclean to you among the creeping things [that multiply greatly] *and* creep upon the ground: the weasel, the mouse, any kind of great lizard,

30 The gecko, the land crocodile, the lizard, the sand lizard, and the chameleon.

31 These are unclean to you among all that creep; whoever touches them when they are dead shall be unclean until the evening.

32 And upon whatever they may fall when they are dead, it shall be unclean, whether it is an article of wood or clothing or skin (bottle) or sack, any vessel in which work is done; it must be put in water, and it shall be unclean until the evening; so it shall be cleansed.

33 And every earthen vessel into which any of these [creeping things] falls, whatever may be in it shall be unclean, and you shall break the vessel.

34 Of all the food [in one of these unclean vessels] which may be eaten, that on which such water comes shall be unclean, and all drink that may be drunk from every such vessel shall be unclean.

35 And everything upon which any part of their carcass falls shall be unclean; whether an oven, *or* pan with a lid, or hearth for pots, it shall be broken in pieces; they are unclean, and shall be unclean to you.

36 Yet a spring or a cistern *or* reservoir of water shall be clean; but whoever touches their carcass shall be unclean.

37 If a part of their carcass falls on seed which is to be sown, it shall be clean;

38 But if any water be put on the seed and any part of their carcass falls on it, it shall be unclean to you.

39 If any animal of which you may eat dies [unslaughtered], he who touches its carcass shall be unclean until the evening.

40 And he who eats of its carcass [ignorantly] shall wash his clothes, and be unclean until the evening; he also who carries its carcass shall wash his clothes, and be unclean until the evening.

41 And everything that creeps on the ground *and* [multiplies in] swarms shall be an abomination; it shall not be eaten.

42 Whatever goes on its belly, and whatever goes on all fours, or whatever has more [than four] feet among all things that creep on the

King James Version

upon the earth, them ye shall not eat; for they *are* an abomination.

⁴³Ye shall not make yourselves abominable with any creeping thing that creepeth, neither shall ye make yourselves unclean with them, that ye should be defiled thereby.

⁴⁴For I *am* the LORD your God: ye shall therefore sanctify yourselves, and ye shall be holy; for I *am* holy: neither shall ye defile yourselves with any *manner of* creeping thing that creepeth upon the earth.

⁴⁵For I *am* the LORD that bringeth you up out of the land of Egypt, to be your God: ye shall therefore be holy, for I *am* holy.

⁴⁶This *is* the law of the beasts, and of the fowl, and of every living creature that moveth in the waters, and of every creature that creepeth upon the earth:

⁴⁷To make a difference between the unclean and the clean, and between the beast that may be eaten and the beast that may not be eaten.

12 And the LORD spake unto Moses, saying, ²Speak unto the children of Israel, saying, If a woman have conceived seed, and born a man child: then she shall be unclean seven days; according to the days of the separation for her infirmity shall she be unclean.

³And in the eighth day the flesh of his foreskin shall be circumcised.

⁴And she shall *then* continue in the blood of her purifying three and thirty days; she shall touch no hallowed *thing*, nor come into the sanctuary, until the days of her purifying be fulfilled.

⁵But if she bear a maid child, then she shall be unclean two weeks, as *in* her separation: and she shall continue in the blood of her purifying threescore and six days.

⁶And when the days of her purifying are fulfilled, for a son, or for a daughter, she shall bring a lamb of the first year for a burnt offering, and a young pigeon, or a turtledove, for a sin offering, unto the door of the tabernacle of the congregation, unto the priest:

⁷Who shall offer it before the LORD, and make an atonement for her; and she shall be cleansed from the issue of her blood. This *is* the law for her that hath born a male or a female.

⁸And if she be not able to bring a lamb, then she shall bring two turtles, or two young pigeons; the one for the burnt offering, and the other for a sin offering: and the priest shall make an atonement for her, and she shall be clean.

13 And the LORD spake unto Moses and Aaron, saying, ²When a man shall have in the skin of his flesh a rising, a scab, or bright spot, and it be in

Amplified Bible

ground *and* swarm you shall not eat; for they are detestable.

⁴³You shall not make yourselves loathsome *and* abominable [by eating] any swarming thing that [multiplies by] swarms, neither shall you make yourselves unclean with them, that you should be defiled by them.

⁴⁴For I am the Lord your God; so consecrate yourselves and be holy, for I am holy; neither defile yourselves with any manner of thing that multiplies in large numbers *or* swarms.

⁴⁵For I am the Lord Who brought you up out of the land of Egypt to be your God; therefore you shall be holy, for I am holy.

⁴⁶This is the law of the beast, and of the bird, and of every living creature that moves in the waters, and creeps on the earth *and* multiplies in large numbers,

⁴⁷To make a difference (a distinction) between the unclean and the clean, and between the animal that may be eaten and the animal that may not be eaten.

12 AND THE Lord said to Moses, ²Say to the Israelites, If a woman conceives and bears a male child, she shall be unclean seven days, unclean as during her monthly discomfort.

³And on the eighth day the child shall be circumcised.

⁴Then she shall remain [separated] thirty-three days to be purified [from her loss] of blood; she shall touch no hallowed thing nor come into the [court of the] sanctuary until the days of her purifying are over.

⁵But if the child she bears is a girl, then she shall be unclean two weeks, as in her periodic impurity, and she shall remain separated sixty-six days to be purified [from her loss] of blood.

⁶When the days of her purifying are completed, whether for a son or for a daughter, she shall bring a lamb a year old for a burnt offering and a young pigeon or a turtledove for a sin offering to the door of the Tent of Meeting to the priest;

⁷And he shall offer it before the Lord and make atonement for her, and she shall be cleansed from the flow of her blood. This is the law for her who has borne a male or a female child.

⁸If she is unable to bring a lamb [for lack of means] then she shall bring two turtledoves or young pigeons, one for a burnt offering, the other for a sin offering; the priest shall make atonement for her, and she shall be clean.

13 AND THE Lord said to Moses and Aaron, ²When a man has a swelling on his skin, a scab, or a bright spot, and it becomes the dis-

King James Version

the skin of his flesh like the plague of leprosy; then he shall be brought unto Aaron the priest, or unto one of his sons the priests:

3And the priest shall look on the plague in the skin of the flesh: and *when* the hair in the plague is turned white, and the plague in sight *be* deeper than the skin of his flesh, it *is* a plague of leprosy: and the priest shall look on him, and pronounce him unclean.

4If the bright spot *be* white in the skin of his flesh, and in sight *be* not deeper than the skin, and the hair thereof be not turned white; then the priest shall shut up *him that hath* the plague seven days:

5And the priest shall look on him the seventh day: and behold, *if* the plague in his sight be at a stay, *and* the plague spread not in the skin; then the priest shall shut him up seven days more:

6And the priest shall look on him again the seventh day: and behold, *if* the plague *be* somewhat dark, and the plague spread not in the skin, the priest shall pronounce him clean: it *is but* a scab: and he shall wash his clothes, and be clean.

7But if the scab spread much abroad in the skin, after that he hath been seen of the priest for his cleansing, he shall be seen of the priest again:

8And *if* the priest see that behold, the scab spreadeth in the skin, then the priest shall pronounce him unclean: it *is* a leprosy.

9 ¶ When the plague of leprosy is in a man, then he shall be brought unto the priest;

10And the priest shall see *him:* and behold, *if* the rising *be* white in the skin, and it have turned the hair white, and *there be* quick raw flesh in the rising;

11It *is* an old leprosy in the skin of his flesh, and the priest shall pronounce him unclean, *and* shall not shut him up: for he *is* unclean.

12And if a leprosy break out abroad in the skin, and the leprosy cover all the skin of *him that hath* the plague from his head even to his foot, wheresoever the priest looketh;

13Then the priest shall consider: and behold, *if* the leprosy have covered all his flesh, he shall pronounce *him* clean *that hath* the plague: it is all turned white: he *is* clean.

14But when raw flesh appeareth in him, he shall be unclean.

15And the priest shall see the raw flesh, and pronounce him to be unclean: *for* the raw flesh *is* unclean: it *is* a leprosy.

Amplified Bible

ease of [a]leprosy in his skin, then he shall be brought to the priest, to Aaron or one of his sons.

3The priest shall look at the diseased spot on his skin, and if the hair in it has turned white and the disease appears depressed *and* deeper than his skin, it is a leprous disease; and the priest shall examine him, and pronounce him unclean.

4If the bright spot is white on his skin, not depressed, and the hair on it not turned white, the priest shall quarantine the person *or* bind up the spot for seven days.

5And the priest shall examine him on the seventh day, and if the disease in his estimation is at a standstill *and* has not spread in the skin, then the priest shall quarantine the person *or* bind up the spot seven more days.

6And the priest shall examine him again the seventh day, and if the diseased part has a more normal color and the disease has not spread in the skin, the priest shall pronounce him clean; it is only an eruption *or* a scab; and he shall wash his clothes and be clean.

7But if the eruption *or* scab spreads farther in the skin after he has shown himself to the priest for his cleansing, he shall be seen by the priest again.

8If the priest sees that the eruption *or* scab is spreading in the skin, then he shall pronounce him unclean; it is leprosy.

9When the disease of leprosy is in a man, he shall be brought to the priest;

10And the priest shall examine him, and if there is a white swelling in the skin and the hair on it has turned white and there is quick raw flesh in the swelling,

11It is a chronic leprosy in the skin of his body, and the priest shall pronounce him unclean; he shall not bind the spot up, for he is unclean.

12But if [supposed] leprosy breaks out in the skin, and it covers all the skin of him who has the disease from head to foot, wherever the priest looks,

13The priest shall examine him; if the [supposed] leprosy covers all his body, he shall pronounce him clean of the disease; it is all turned white, and he is clean.

14But when the raw flesh appears on him, he shall be unclean.

15And the priest shall examine the raw flesh and pronounce him unclean; for the raw flesh is unclean; it is leprosy.

AMP notes: [a] Authorities are generally agreed that there certainly was true leprosy as it is known today in the Near East in New Testament times. But from the details of the disease in Lev. 13, it is believed that other very serious skin disorders were also included under the heading of "leprosy" in earlier times. Leprosy in the Old Testament, therefore, is not to be considered as confined to the traits by which it is known today, but rather defined by the symptoms, the treatment, and the history of individual cases as recorded in Leviticus and elsewhere. That it was worse than death is implied by the words of Aaron when his sister Miriam was stricken with it: "Alas, my lord [Moses], . . . Let her not be as one dead, of whom the flesh is half consumed when he cometh out of his mother's womb" (Num. 12:11, 12 KJV).

King James Version

¹⁶Or if the raw flesh turn again, and be changed unto white, he shall come unto the priest;

¹⁷And the priest shall see him: and behold, *if* the plague be turned into white; then the priest shall pronounce *him* clean *that hath* the plague: he *is* clean.

¹⁸ ¶ The flesh also, in which, *even* in the skin thereof, was a boil, and is healed,

¹⁹And in the place of the boil there be a white rising, or a bright spot, white, *and* somewhat reddish, and it be shewed to the priest;

²⁰And if, when the priest seeth it, behold, it *be* in sight lower than the skin, and the hair thereof be turned white; the priest shall pronounce him unclean: it *is* a plague of leprosy broken out of the boil.

²¹But if the priest look on it, and behold, *there be* no white hairs therein, and *if* it *be* not lower than the skin, but *be* somewhat dark; then the priest shall shut him up seven days:

²²And if it spread much abroad in the skin, then the priest shall pronounce him unclean: it *is* a plague.

²³But if the bright spot stay in his place, *and* spread not, it *is* a burning boil; and the priest shall pronounce him clean.

²⁴ ¶ Or if there be *any* flesh, in the skin whereof *there is* a hot burning, and the quick *flesh* that burneth have a white bright spot, somewhat reddish, or white;

²⁵Then the priest shall look upon it: and behold, *if* the hair in the bright spot be turned white, and it *be* in sight deeper than the skin; it *is* a leprosy broken out of the burning: wherefore the priest shall pronounce him unclean: it *is* the plague of leprosy.

²⁶But if the priest look on it, and behold, *there be* no white hair in the bright spot, and it *be* no lower than the *other* skin, but *be* somewhat dark; then the priest shall shut him up seven days:

²⁷And the priest shall look upon him the seventh day: *and* if it be spread much abroad in the skin, then the priest shall pronounce him unclean: it *is* the plague of leprosy.

²⁸And if the bright spot stay in his place, *and* spread not in the skin, but it *be* somewhat dark; it *is* a rising of the burning, and the priest shall pronounce him clean: for it *is* an inflammation of the burning.

²⁹ ¶ If a man or woman hath a plague upon the head or the beard;

³⁰Then the priest shall see the plague: and behold, *if* it *be* in sight deeper than the skin; and *there be* in it a yellow thin hair; then the priest shall pronounce him unclean: it *is* a dry scall, *even* a leprosy upon the head or beard.

³¹And if the priest look on the plague of the scall, and, behold, it *be* not in sight deeper than the skin, and *that there is* no black hair in it; then

Amplified Bible

¹⁶But if the raw flesh turns again and becomes white, he shall come to the priest,

¹⁷And the priest shall examine him, and if the diseased part is turned to white again, then the priest shall pronounce him clean who had the disease; he is clean.

¹⁸And when there is in the skin of the body [the scar of] a boil that is healed,

¹⁹And in the place of the boil there is a white swelling or a bright spot, reddish white, and it is shown to the priest,

²⁰And if when the priest examines it it looks lower than the skin and the hair on it is turned white, the priest shall pronounce him unclean; it is the disease of leprosy; it has broken out in the boil.

²¹But if the priest examines it and finds no white hair in it and it is not lower than the skin but appears darker, then the priest shall bind it up for seven days.

²²If it spreads in the skin, [he] shall pronounce him unclean; it is diseased.

²³But if the bright spot does not spread, it is the scar of the boil, and the priest shall pronounce him clean.

²⁴Or if there is any flesh in the skin of which there is a burn by fire and the quick flesh of the burn becomes a bright spot, reddish white or white,

²⁵Then the priest shall examine it, and if the hair in the bright spot is turned white, and it appears deeper than the skin, it is leprosy broken out in the burn. Therefore the priest shall pronounce him unclean; it is the disease of leprosy.

²⁶But if the priest examines it and there is no white hair in the bright spot and it is not lower than the rest of the skin but is darker, then the priest shall bind it up for seven days.

²⁷And the priest shall examine him on the seventh day; if it is spreading in the skin, then the priest shall pronounce him unclean; it is leprosy.

²⁸But if the bright spot has not spread but is darker, it is a swelling from the burn, and the priest shall pronounce him clean; for it is the scar of the burn.

²⁹When a man or woman has a disease upon the head or in the beard,

³⁰The priest shall examine the diseased place; if it appears to be deeper than the skin, with yellow, thin hair in it, the priest shall pronounce him unclean; it is a mangelike leprosy of the head or beard.

³¹If the priest examines the spot infected by the mangelike disease, and it does not appear deeper than the skin and there is no black hair

King James Version

the priest shall shut up *him that hath* the plague of the scall seven days:

³²And in the seventh day the priest shall look on the plague: and behold, *if* the scall spread not, and there be in it no yellow hair, and the scall *be* not in sight deeper than the skin;

³³He shall be shaven, but the scall shall he not shave; and the priest shall shut up *him that hath* the scall seven days more:

³⁴And in the seventh day the priest shall look on the scall: and behold, *if* the scall be not spread in the skin, nor *be* in sight deeper than the skin; then the priest shall pronounce him clean: and he shall wash his clothes, and be clean.

³⁵But if the scall spread much in the skin after his cleansing;

³⁶Then the priest shall look on him: and behold, *if* the scall be spread in the skin, the priest shall not seek for yellow hair: he *is* unclean.

³⁷But if the scall be in his sight at a stay, and *that* there is black hair grown up therein; the scall is healed, he *is* clean: and the priest shall pronounce him clean.

³⁸ ¶ If a man also or a woman have in the skin of their flesh bright spots, *even* white bright spots;

³⁹Then the priest shall look: and behold, *if* the bright spots in the skin of their flesh *be* darkish white; it *is* a freckled spot *that* groweth in the skin: he *is* clean.

⁴⁰And the man whose hair is fallen off his head, he *is* bald: *yet is* he clean.

⁴¹And he that hath his hair fallen off from the part of *his head toward* his face, he *is* forehead bald: *yet is* he clean.

⁴²And if there be in the bald head, or bald forehead, a white reddish sore; it *is* a leprosy sprung up in his bald head, or his bald forehead.

⁴³Then the priest shall look upon it: and behold, *if* the rising of the sore *be* white reddish in his bald head, or in his bald forehead, as the leprosy appeareth in the skin of the flesh;

⁴⁴He *is* a leprous man, he *is* unclean: the priest shall pronounce him utterly unclean, his plague *is* in his head.

⁴⁵And the leper in whom the plague *is,* his clothes shall be rent, and his head bare, and he shall put a covering upon *his* upper lip, and shall cry, Unclean, unclean.

⁴⁶All the days wherein the plague *shall be* in him he shall be defiled; he *is* unclean: he shall dwell alone; without the camp *shall* his habitation *be.*

⁴⁷ ¶ The garment also that the plague of leprosy is in, *whether it be* a woollen garment, or a linen garment;

⁴⁸Whether *it be* in the warp, or woof; of linen, or of woollen; whether in a skin, or in any thing made of skin;

Amplified Bible

in it, the priest shall bind up the spot for seven days.

³²On the seventh day the priest shall examine the diseased spot; if the mange has not spread and has no yellow hair in it and does not look deeper than the skin,

³³Then the patient shall be shaved, except the mangelike spot; and the priest shall bind up the spot seven days more.

³⁴On the seventh day the priest shall look at the mangelike spot; if the mange has not spread and looks no deeper than the skin, he shall pronounce the patient clean; he shall wash his clothes and be clean.

³⁵But if the mangelike spot spreads in the skin after his cleansing,

³⁶Then the priest shall examine him, and if the mangelike spot is spread in the skin, the priest need not look for the yellow hair; the patient is unclean.

³⁷But if in his estimation the mange is at a standstill and has black hair in it, the mangelike disease is healed; he is clean; the priest shall pronounce him clean.

³⁸When a man or a woman has on the skin bright spots, even white bright spots,

³⁹Then the priest shall look, and if the bright spots in the skin are a dull white, it is a harmless eruption; he is clean.

⁴⁰If a man's hair has fallen from his head, he is bald, but he is clean.

⁴¹And if his hair has fallen out from the front of his head, he has baldness of the forehead, but he is clean.

⁴²But if there is on the bald head or forehead a reddish white diseased spot, it is leprosy breaking out on his baldness.

⁴³Then the priest shall examine him, and if the diseased swelling is reddish white on his bald head or forehead like the appearance of leprosy in the skin of the body,

⁴⁴He is a leprous man; he is unclean; the priest shall surely pronounce him unclean; his disease is on his head.

⁴⁵And the leper's clothes shall be rent, and the hair of his head shall hang loose, and he shall cover his upper lip and cry, Unclean, unclean!

⁴⁶He shall remain unclean as long as the disease is in him; he is unclean; he shall live alone [and] his dwelling shall be outside the camp.

⁴⁷The garment also that the disease of leprosy [symbolic of sin] is in, whether a wool or a linen garment,

⁴⁸Whether it be in woven or knitted stuff *or* in the warp or woof of linen or of wool, or in a skin or anything made of skin,

King James Version

⁴⁹And *if* the plague be greenish or reddish in the garment, or in the skin, either in the warp, or in the woof, or in any thing of skin; it *is* a plague of leprosy, and shall be shewed unto the priest:

⁵⁰And the priest shall look upon the plague, and shut up *it that hath* the plague seven days:

⁵¹And he shall look on the plague on the seventh day: if the plague be spread in the garment, either in the warp, or in the woof, or in a skin, *or* in any work that is made of skin; the plague *is* a fretting leprosy; it *is* unclean.

⁵²He shall therefore burn *that* garment, whether warp or woof, in woollen or in linen, or any thing of skin, wherein the plague is: for it *is* a fretting leprosy; it shall be burnt in the fire.

⁵³And if the priest shall look, and behold, the plague be not spread in the garment, either in the warp, or in the woof, or in any thing of skin;

⁵⁴Then the priest shall command that they wash *the thing* wherein the plague *is,* and he shall shut it up seven days more:

⁵⁵And the priest shall look on the plague, after *that* it is washed: and behold, *if* the plague have not changed his colour, and the plague be not spread; it *is* unclean; thou shalt burn it in the fire; it *is* fret inward, *whether* it *be* bare within or without.

⁵⁶And if the priest look, and behold, the plague *be* somewhat dark after the washing of it; then he shall rend it out of the garment, or out of the skin, or out of the warp, or out of the woof:

⁵⁷And if it appear still in the garment, either in the warp, or in the woof, or in any thing of skin; it *is* a spreading *plague:* thou shalt burn that wherein the plague *is* with fire.

⁵⁸And the garment, either warp, or woof, or whatsoever thing of skin it *be,* which thou shalt wash, if the plague be departed from them, then it shall be washed the second time, and shall be clean.

⁵⁹This *is* the law of the plague of leprosy in a garment of woollen or linen, either *in* the warp, or woof, or any thing of skins, to pronounce it clean, or to pronounce it unclean.

14 And the LORD spake unto Moses, saying, ²This shall be the law of the leper in the day of his cleansing: He shall be brought unto the priest:

³And the priest shall go forth out of the camp; and the priest shall look, and behold, *if* the plague of leprosy be healed in the leper;

⁴Then shall the priest command to take for him that is to be cleansed two birds alive *and* clean, and cedar wood, and scarlet, and hyssop:

⁵And the priest shall command that one of the birds be killed in an earthen vessel over running water:

Amplified Bible

⁴⁹If the disease is greenish or reddish in the garment, or in a skin or in the warp or woof or in anything made of skin, it is the plague of leprosy; show it to the priest.

⁵⁰The priest shall examine the diseased article and shut it up for seven days.

⁵¹He shall examine the disease on the seventh day; if [it] is spread in the garment, or in the article, whatever service it may be used for, the disease is a rotting *or* corroding leprosy; it is unclean.

⁵²He shall burn the garment, whether diseased in warp or woof, in wool or linen, or anything made of skin; for it is a rotting *or* corroding leprosy, to be burned in the fire.

⁵³But if the priest finds the disease has not spread in the garment, in the warp or the woof, or in anything made of skin,

⁵⁴Then the priest shall command that they wash the thing in which the plague is, and he shall shut it up seven days more.

⁵⁵And the priest shall examine the diseased article after it has been washed, and if the diseased portion has not changed color, though the disease has not spread, it is unclean; you shall burn it in the fire; it is a rotting *or* corroding [disease], whether the leprous spot be inside or outside.

⁵⁶If the priest looks and the diseased portion is less noticeable after it is washed, he shall tear it out of the garment, or the skin (leather), or out of the warp or woof.

⁵⁷If it appears still in the garment, either in the warp or in the woof, or in anything made of skin, it is spreading; you shall burn the diseased part with fire.

⁵⁸But the garment, or the woven or knitted stuff *or* warp or woof, or anything made of skin from which the disease departs when you have washed it, shall then be washed a second time, and be clean.

⁵⁹This is the law for a leprous disease in a garment of wool or linen, either in the warp or woof, or in anything made of skin, to pronounce it clean or unclean.

14 AND THE Lord said to Moses, ²This shall be the law of the leper on the day when he is to be pronounced clean: he shall be brought to the priest [at a meeting place outside the camp];

³The priest shall go out of the camp [to meet him]; and [he] shall examine him, and if the disease is healed in the leper,

⁴Then the priest shall command to take for him who is to be cleansed two living clean birds and cedar wood and scarlet [material] and hyssop.

⁵And the priest shall command to kill one of the birds in an earthen vessel over fresh, running water.

King James Version

⁶As for the living bird, he shall take it, and the cedar wood, and the scarlet, and the hyssop, and shall dip them and the living bird in the blood of the bird *that was* killed over the running water:

⁷And he shall sprinkle upon him that is to be cleansed from the leprosy seven times, and shall pronounce him clean, and shall let the living bird loose into the open field.

⁸And he that is to be cleansed shall wash his clothes, and shave off all his hair, and wash *himself* in water, that he may be clean: and after *that* he shall come into the camp, and shall tarry abroad out of his tent seven days.

⁹But it shall be on the seventh day, *that* he shall shave all his hair off his head and his beard and his eyebrows, even all his hair he shall shave off: and he shall wash his clothes, also he shall wash his flesh in water, and he shall be clean.

¹⁰And on the eighth day he shall take two he lambs without blemish, and one ewe lamb of the first year without blemish, and three tenth deals of fine flour *for* a meat offering, mingled with oil, and one log of oil.

¹¹And the priest that maketh *him* clean shall present the man that is to be made clean, and those *things,* before the LORD, *at* the door of the tabernacle of the congregation:

¹²And the priest shall take one he lamb, and offer him for a trespass offering, and the log of oil, and wave them *for* a wave offering before the LORD:

¹³And he shall slay the lamb in the place where he shall kill the sin offering and the burnt offering, in the holy place: for as the sin offering *is* the priest's, *so is* the trespass offering: it *is* most holy:

¹⁴And the priest shall take *some* of the blood of the trespass offering, and the priest shall put *it* upon the tip of the right ear of him that is to be cleansed, and upon the thumb of his right hand, and upon the great toe of his right foot:

¹⁵And the priest shall take *some* of the log of oil, and pour *it* into the palm of his own left hand:

¹⁶And the priest shall dip his right finger in the oil that *is* in his left hand, and shall sprinkle of the oil with his finger seven times before the LORD:

¹⁷And of the rest of the oil that *is* in his hand shall the priest put upon the tip of the right ear of him that is to be cleansed, and upon the thumb of his right hand, and upon the great toe of his right foot, upon the blood of the trespass offering:

¹⁸And the remnant of the oil that *is* in the priest's hand he shall pour upon the head of him that is to be cleansed: and the priest shall make an atonement for him before the LORD.

¹⁹And the priest shall offer the sin offering, and make an atonement for him that is to be

Amplified Bible

⁶As for the living bird, he shall take it, the cedar wood, and the scarlet [material], and the hyssop, and shall dip them and the living bird in the blood of the bird killed over the running water;

⁷And he shall sprinkle [the blood] on him who is to be cleansed from the leprosy seven times and shall pronounce him clean, and shall let go the living bird into the open field.

⁸He who is to be cleansed shall wash his clothes, shave off all his hair, and bathe himself in water; and he shall be clean. After that he shall come into the camp, but stay outside his tent seven days.

⁹But on the seventh day he shall shave all his hair off his head, his beard, his eyebrows, and his [body]; and he shall wash his clothes and bathe his body in water, and be clean.

¹⁰On the eighth day he shall take two he-lambs without blemish and one ewe lamb a year old without blemish, and three-tenths of an ephah of fine flour for a cereal offering, mixed with oil, and one log of oil.

¹¹And the priest who cleanses him shall set the man who is to be cleansed and these things before the Lord at the door of the Tent of Meeting;

¹²The priest shall take one of the male lambs and offer it for a guilt *or* trespass offering, and the log of oil, and wave them for a wave offering before the Lord.

¹³He shall kill the lamb in the place where they kill the sin offering and the burnt offering, in the sacred place [the court of the tabernacle]; for as the sin offering is the priest's, so is the guilt *or* trespass offering; it is most holy;

¹⁴And the priest shall take some of the blood of the guilt *or* trespass offering and put it on the tip of the right ear of him who is to be cleansed, and on the thumb of his right hand, and on the great toe of his right foot.

¹⁵And the priest shall take some of the log of oil and pour it into the palm of his own left hand;

¹⁶And the priest shall dip his right finger in the oil that is in his left hand and shall sprinkle some of the oil with his finger seven times before the Lord;

¹⁷And of the rest of the oil that is in his hand shall the priest put some on the tip of the right ear of him who is to be cleansed, and on the thumb of his right hand, and on the great toe of his right foot, on the blood of the guilt *or* trespass offering [which he has previously placed in each of these places].

¹⁸And the rest of the oil that is in the priest's hand he shall pour upon the head of him who is to be cleansed and make atonement for him before the Lord.

¹⁹And the priest shall offer the sin offering and make atonement for him who is to be

King James Version

cleansed from his uncleanness; and afterward he shall kill the burnt offering:

20And the priest shall offer the burnt offering and the meat offering upon the altar: and the priest shall make an atonement for him, and he shall be clean.

21 ¶ And if he *be* poor, and cannot get *so much;* then he shall take one lamb *for* a trespass offering to be waved, to make an atonement for him, and one tenth deal of fine flour mingled with oil for a meat offering, and a log of oil;

22And two turtledoves, or two young pigeons, such as he is able to get; and the one shall be a sin offering, and the other a burnt offering.

23And he shall bring them on the eighth day for his cleansing unto the priest, unto the door of the tabernacle of the congregation, before the LORD.

24And the priest shall take the lamb of the trespass offering, and the log of oil, and the priest shall wave them *for* a wave offering before the LORD:

25And he shall kill the lamb of the trespass offering, and the priest shall take *some* of the blood of the trespass offering, and put *it* upon the tip of the right ear of him that is to be cleansed, and upon the thumb of his right hand, and upon the great toe of his right foot:

26And the priest shall pour of the oil into the palm of his own left hand:

27And the priest shall sprinkle with his right finger *some* of the oil that *is* in his left hand seven times before the LORD:

28And the priest shall put of the oil that *is* in his hand upon the tip of the right ear of him that is to be cleansed, and upon the thumb of his right hand, and upon the great toe of his right foot, upon the place of the blood of the trespass offering:

29And the rest of the oil that *is* in the priest's hand he shall put upon the head of him that is to be cleansed, to make an atonement for him before the LORD.

30And he shall offer the one of the turtledoves, or of the young pigeons, such as he can get;

31*Even* such as he is able to get, the one *for* a sin offering, and the other *for* a burnt offering, with the meat offering: and the priest shall make an atonement for him that is to be cleansed before the LORD.

32This *is* the law *of him* in whom *is* the plague of leprosy, whose hand is not able to get *that which pertaineth* to his cleansing.

33 ¶ And the LORD spake unto Moses and unto Aaron, saying,

34When ye be come into the land of Canaan, which I give to you for a possession, and I put the plague of leprosy in a house of the land of your possession;

Amplified Bible

cleansed from his uncleanness, and afterward kill the burnt offering [victim].

20And the priest shall offer the burnt offering and the cereal offering on the altar; and he shall make atonement for him, and he shall be clean.

21If the cleansed leper is poor and cannot afford so much, he shall take one lamb for a guilt *or* trespass offering to be waved to make atonement for him, and one tenth of an ephah of fine flour mixed with oil for a cereal offering, and a log of oil,

22And two turtledoves or two young pigeons, such as he can afford, one for a sin offering, the other for a burnt offering.

23He shall bring them on the eighth day for his cleansing to the priest at the door of the Tent of Meeting, before the Lord.

24And the priest shall take the lamb of the guilt *or* trespass offering, and the log of oil, and shall wave them for a wave offering before the Lord.

25And he shall kill the lamb of the guilt *or* trespass offering, and the priest shall take some of the blood of the offering and put it on the tip of the right ear of him who is to be cleansed, and on the thumb of his right hand, and on the great toe of his right foot.

26And the priest shall pour some of the oil into the palm of his own left hand,

27And shall sprinkle with his right finger some of the oil that is in his left hand seven times before the Lord.

28The priest shall put some of the oil in his hand on the tip of the right ear of the one to be cleansed, and on the thumb of his right hand, and on the great toe of his right foot, on the places where he has put the blood of the guilt offering.

29The rest of the oil that is in the priest's hand he shall put on the head of the one to be cleansed, to make atonement for him before the Lord.

30And he shall offer one of the turtledoves or of the young pigeons, such as he is able to get,

31As he can afford, one for a sin offering and the other for a burnt offering, together with the cereal offering; and the priest shall make atonement for him who is to be cleansed before the Lord.

32This is the law of him in whom is the plague of leprosy, who is not able to get what is required for his cleansing.

33And the Lord said to Moses and Aaron,

34When you have come into the land of Canaan, which I give to you for a possession, and I put the disease of leprosy in a house of the land of your possession,

King James Version

³⁵And he that owneth the house shall come and tell the priest, saying, It seemeth to me *there is* as it were a plague in the house:

³⁶Then the priest shall command that they empty the house, before the priest go *into it* to see the plague, that all that *is* in the house be not *made* unclean: and afterward the priest shall go in to see the house:

³⁷And he shall look on the plague, and behold, *if* the plague *be* in the walls of the house with hollow strakes, greenish or reddish, which in sight *are* lower than the wall;

³⁸Then the priest shall go out of the house to the door of the house, and shut up the house seven days:

³⁹And the priest shall come again the seventh day, and shall look: and behold, *if* the plague be spread in the walls of the house;

⁴⁰Then the priest shall command that they take away the stones in which the plague *is,* and they shall cast them into an unclean place without the city:

⁴¹And he shall cause the house to be scraped within round about, and they shall pour out the dust that they scrape off without the city into an unclean place:

⁴²And they shall take other stones, and put *them* in the place of *those* stones; and he shall take other morter, and shall plaister the house.

⁴³And if the plague come again, and break out in the house, after *that* he hath taken away the stones, and after he hath scraped the house, and after it is plaistered;

⁴⁴Then the priest shall come and look, and behold, *if* the plague be spread in the house, it *is* a fretting leprosy in the house: it *is* unclean.

⁴⁵And he shall break down the house, the stones of it, and the timber thereof, and all the morter of the house; and he shall carry *them* forth out of the city into an unclean place.

⁴⁶Moreover he that goeth into the house all the while that it is shut up shall be unclean until the even.

⁴⁷And he that lieth in the house shall wash his clothes; and he that eateth in the house shall wash his clothes.

⁴⁸And if the priest shall come in, and look *upon it,* and behold, the plague hath not spread in the house, after the house was plaistered: then the priest shall pronounce the house clean, because the plague is healed.

⁴⁹And he shall take to cleanse the house two birds, and cedar wood, and scarlet, and hyssop:

⁵⁰And he shall kill the one of the birds in an earthen vessel over running water:

⁵¹And he shall take the cedar wood, and the hyssop, and the scarlet, and the living bird, and dip them in the blood of the slain bird, and in the running water, and sprinkle the house seven times:

⁵²And he shall cleanse the house with the

Amplified Bible

³⁵Then he who owns the house shall come and tell the priest, It seems to me there is some sort of disease in my house.

³⁶Then the priest shall command that they empty the house before [he] goes in to examine the disease, so that all that is in the house may not be declared unclean; afterward [he] shall go in to see the house.

³⁷He shall examine the disease, and if it is in the walls of the house with depressed spots of dark green or dark red appearing beneath [the surface of] the wall,

³⁸Then the priest shall go out of the door and shut up the house seven days.

³⁹The priest shall come again on the seventh day and shall look; and if the disease has spread in the walls of the house,

⁴⁰He shall command that they take out the diseased stones and cast them into an unclean place outside the city.

⁴¹He shall cause the house to be scraped within round about and the plaster *or* mortar that is scraped off to be emptied out in an unclean place outside the city.

⁴²And they shall put other stones in the place of those stones, and he shall plaster the house with fresh mortar.

⁴³If the disease returns, breaking out in the house after he has removed the stones and has scraped and plastered the house,

⁴⁴Then the priest shall come and look, and if the disease is spreading in the house, it is a rotting *or* corroding leprosy in the house; it is unclean.

⁴⁵He shall tear down the house—its stones and its timber and all the plaster *or* mortar of the house—and shall carry them forth out of the city to an unclean place.

⁴⁶Moreover, he who enters the house during the whole time that it is shut up shall be unclean until the evening.

⁴⁷And he who lies down or eats in the house shall wash his clothes.

⁴⁸But if the priest inspects it and the disease has not spread after the house was plastered, he shall pronounce the house clean, because the disease is healed.

⁴⁹He shall take to cleanse the house two birds, cedar wood, scarlet [material], and hyssop;

⁵⁰And he shall kill one of the birds in an earthen vessel over running water,

⁵¹And he shall take the cedar wood, and the hyssop, and the scarlet [material], and the living bird, and dip them in the blood of the slain bird and in the running water, and sprinkle the house seven times.

⁵²And he shall cleanse the house with the

King James Version

blood of the bird, and with the running water, and with the living bird, and with the cedar wood, and with the hyssop, and with the scarlet:

⁵³But he shall let go the living bird out of the city into the open fields, and make an atonement for the house: and it shall be clean.

⁵⁴ ¶ This *is* the law for all *manner of* plague of leprosy, and scall,

⁵⁵And for the leprosy of a garment, and of a house,

⁵⁶And for a rising, and for a scab, and for a bright spot:

⁵⁷To teach when *it is* unclean, and when *it is* clean: this *is* the law of leprosy.

15 And the LORD spake unto Moses and to Aaron, saying,

²Speak unto the children of Israel, and say unto them, When any man hath a running issue out of his flesh, *because of* his issue he *is* unclean.

³And this shall be his uncleanness in his issue: *whether* his flesh run with his issue, or his flesh be stopped from his issue, it *is* his uncleanness.

⁴Every bed, whereon he lieth that hath the issue, is unclean: and every thing, whereon he sitteth, shall be unclean.

⁵And whosoever toucheth his bed shall wash his clothes, and bathe *himself* in water, and be unclean until the even.

⁶And he that sitteth on *any* thing whereon he sat that hath the issue shall wash his clothes, and bathe *himself* in water, and be unclean until the even.

⁷And he that toucheth the flesh of him that hath the issue shall wash his clothes, and bathe *himself* in water, and be unclean until the even.

⁸And if he that hath the issue spit upon him that is clean; then he shall wash his clothes, and bathe *himself* in water, and be unclean until the even.

⁹And what saddle soever he rideth upon that hath the issue shall be unclean.

¹⁰And whosoever toucheth any *thing* that was under him shall be unclean until the even: and he that beareth *any of* those *things* shall wash his clothes, and bathe *himself* in water, and be unclean until the even.

¹¹And whomsoever he toucheth that hath the issue, and hath not rinsed his hands in water, he shall wash his clothes, and bathe *himself* in water, and be unclean until the even.

¹²And the vessel of earth, that he toucheth which hath the issue, shall be broken: and every vessel of wood shall be rinsed in water.

¹³And when he that hath an issue is cleansed of his issue; then he shall number to himself seven days for his cleansing, and wash his clothes, and bathe his flesh in running water, and shall be clean.

Amplified Bible

blood of the bird, the running water, the living bird, the cedar wood, the hyssop, and the scarlet [material].

⁵³But he shall let the living bird go out of the city into the open field; so he shall make atonement for the house, and it shall be clean.

⁵⁴This is the law for all kinds of leprous diseases, and mangelike conditions,

⁵⁵For the leprosy of a garment or of a house,

⁵⁶And for a swelling or an eruption *or* a scab or a bright spot,

⁵⁷To teach when it is unclean and when it is clean. This is the law of leprosy.

15 AND THE Lord said to Moses and Aaron, ²Say to the Israelites, When any man has a running discharge from his body, because of his discharge he is unclean.

³This shall be [the law concerning] his uncleanness in his discharge: whether his body runs with his discharge or has stopped [running], it is uncleanness in him.

⁴Every bed on which the one who has the discharge lies is unclean, and everything on which he sits shall be unclean.

⁵Whoever touches that person's bed shall wash his clothes, and bathe himself in water, and be unclean until the evening.

⁶And whoever sits on anything on which he who has the discharge has sat shall wash his clothes and bathe himself in water, and be unclean until the evening.

⁷And he who touches the flesh of him who has the discharge shall wash his clothes and bathe himself in water, and be unclean until the evening.

⁸And if he who has the discharge spits on him who is clean, then he shall wash his clothes and bathe himself in water, and be unclean until the evening.

⁹And any saddle on which he who has the discharge rides shall be unclean.

¹⁰Whoever touches anything that has been under him shall be unclean until evening; and he who carries those things shall wash his clothes and bathe himself in water, and be unclean until evening.

¹¹Whomever he who has the discharge touches without rinsing his hands in water shall wash his clothes and bathe himself in water, and be unclean until evening.

¹²The earthen vessel that he with the discharge touches shall be broken, and every vessel of wood shall be rinsed in water.

¹³When he who has a discharge is cleansed of it, he shall count seven days for his purification, then wash his clothes, bathe in running water, and be clean.

King James Version

¹⁴And on the eighth day he shall take to him two turtledoves, or two young pigeons, and come before the LORD unto the door of the tabernacle of the congregation, and give them unto the priest:

¹⁵And the priest shall offer them, the one *for* a sin offering, and the other *for* a burnt offering; and the priest shall make an atonement for him before the LORD for his issue.

¹⁶And if any man's seed of copulation go out from him, then he shall wash all his flesh in water, and be unclean until the even.

¹⁷And every garment, and every skin, whereon is the seed of copulation, shall be washed with water, and be unclean until the even.

¹⁸The woman also with whom man shall lie *with* seed of copulation, they shall *both* bathe *themselves* in water, and be unclean until the even.

¹⁹ ¶ And if a woman have an issue, *and* her issue in her flesh be blood, she shall be put apart seven days: and whosoever toucheth her shall be unclean until the even.

²⁰And every *thing* that she lieth upon in her separation shall be unclean: every *thing* also that she sitteth upon shall be unclean.

²¹And whosoever toucheth her bed shall wash his clothes, and bathe *himself* in water, and be unclean until the even.

²²And whosoever toucheth any thing that she sat upon shall wash his clothes, and bathe *himself* in water, and be unclean until the even.

²³And if it *be* on *her* bed, or on *any* thing whereon she sitteth, when he toucheth it, he shall be unclean until the even.

²⁴And if any man lie with her at all, and her flowers be upon him, he shall be unclean seven days; and all the bed whereon he lieth shall be unclean.

²⁵And if a woman have an issue of her blood many days out of the time of her separation, or if it run beyond the time of her separation; all the days of the issue of her uncleanness shall be as the days of her separation: she *shall be* unclean.

²⁶Every bed whereon she lieth all the days of her issue shall be unto her as the bed of her separation: and whatsoever she sitteth upon shall be unclean, as the uncleanness of her separation.

²⁷And whosoever toucheth those *things* shall be unclean, and shall wash his clothes, and bathe *himself* in water, and be unclean until the even.

²⁸But if she be cleansed of her issue, then she shall number to herself seven days, and after *that* she shall be clean.

²⁹And on the eighth day she shall take unto her two turtles, or two young pigeons, and bring them unto the priest, to the door of the tabernacle of the congregation.

Amplified Bible

¹⁴On the eighth day he shall take two turtledoves or two young pigeons and come before the Lord to the door of the Tent of Meeting and give them to the priest;

¹⁵And the priest shall offer them, one for a sin offering and the other for a burnt offering; and [he] shall make atonement for the man before the Lord for his discharge.

¹⁶And if any man has a discharge of semen, he shall wash all his body in water, and be unclean until evening.

¹⁷And every garment and every skin on which the sperm comes shall be washed with water, and be unclean until evening.

¹⁸The woman also with whom a man with emission of semen shall lie, they shall both bathe themselves in water, and be unclean until evening.

¹⁹And if a woman has a discharge, her [regular] discharge of blood of her body, she shall be in her impurity *or* separation for seven days, and whoever touches her shall be unclean until evening.

²⁰And everything that she lies on in her separation shall be unclean; everything also that she sits on shall be unclean.

²¹And whoever touches her bed shall wash his clothes and bathe himself in water, and be unclean until evening.

²²Whoever touches anything she sat on shall wash his clothes and bathe himself in water, and be unclean until evening.

²³And if her flow has stained her bed or anything on which she sat, when he touches it, he shall be unclean until evening.

²⁴And if any man lie with her and her impurity be upon him, he shall be unclean seven days; and every bed on which he lies shall be unclean.

²⁵And if a woman has an issue of blood for many days, not during the time of her separation, or if she has a discharge beyond the time of her [regular] impurity, all the days of the issue of her uncleanness she shall be as in the days of her impurity; she shall be unclean.

²⁶Every bed on which she lies all the days of her discharge shall be as the bed of her impurity, and whatever she sits on shall be unclean, as in her impurity.

²⁷And whoever touches those things shall be unclean, and shall wash his clothes and bathe himself in water, and be unclean until evening.

²⁸But if she is cleansed of her discharge, then she shall wait seven days, and after that she shall be clean.

²⁹And on the eighth day she shall take two turtledoves or two young pigeons and bring them to the priest at the door of the Tent of Meeting;

King James Version

³⁰And the priest shall offer the one *for* a sin offering, and the other *for* a burnt offering; and the priest shall make an atonement for her before the LORD for the issue of her uncleanness.

³¹ ¶ Thus shall ye separate the children of Israel from their uncleanness; that they die not in their uncleanness, when they defile my tabernacle that *is* among them.

³²This *is* the law of him that hath an issue, and *of him* whose seed goeth from him, and is defiled therewith;

³³And of her that is sick of her flowers, and of him that hath an issue, of the man, and of the woman, and of him that lieth with her which is unclean.

16 And the LORD spake unto Moses after the death of the two sons of Aaron, when they offered before the LORD, and died;

²And the LORD said unto Moses, Speak unto Aaron thy brother, that he come not at all times into the holy *place* within the vail before the mercy seat, which *is* upon the ark; that he die not: for I will appear in the cloud upon the mercy seat.

³Thus shall Aaron come into the holy *place:* with a young bullock for a sin offering, and a ram for a burnt offering.

⁴He shall put on the holy linen coat, and he shall have the linen breeches upon his flesh, and shall be girded with a linen girdle, and with the linen mitre shall he be attired: these *are* holy garments; therefore shall he wash his flesh in water, and *so* put them on.

⁵And he shall take of the congregation of the children of Israel two kids of the goats for a sin offering, and one ram for a burnt offering.

⁶And Aaron shall offer *his* bullock of the sin offering, which *is* for himself, and make an atonement for himself, and for his house.

⁷And he shall take the two goats, and present them before the LORD *at* the door of the tabernacle of the congregation.

⁸And Aaron shall cast lots upon the two goats; one lot for the LORD, and the other lot for the scapegoat.

⁹And Aaron shall bring the goat upon which the LORD'S lot fell, and offer him *for* a sin offering.

¹⁰But the goat, on which the lot fell to be the scapegoat, shall be presented alive before the LORD, to make an atonement with him, *and* to let him go for a scapegoat into the wilderness.

Amplified Bible

³⁰He shall offer one for a sin offering and the other for a burnt offering; and he shall make atonement for her before the Lord for her unclean discharge.

³¹Thus you shall separate the Israelites from their uncleanness, lest they die in their uncleanness by defiling My tabernacle that is in the midst of them.

³²This is the law for him who has a discharge and for him who has emissions of sperm, being made unclean by it;

³³And for her who is sick with her impurity, and for any person who has a discharge, whether man or woman, and for him who lies with her who is unclean.

16 AFTER THE death of Aaron's two sons, when they drew near before the Lord [offered false fire] and died,

²The Lord said to Moses, Tell Aaron your brother he ᵃmust not come at all times into the Holy of Holies within the veil before the mercy seat upon the ark, lest he die; for I will appear in the cloud on the mercy seat.

³But Aaron shall come into the holy enclosure in this way: with a young bull for a sin offering and a ram for a burnt offering.

⁴He shall put on the holy linen undergarment, and he shall have the linen breeches upon his body, and be girded with the linen girdle *or* sash, and with the linen turban *or* miter shall he be attired; these are the holy garments; he shall bathe his body in water and then put them on.

⁵He shall take [at the expense] of the congregation of the Israelites two male goats for a sin offering and one ram for a burnt offering.

⁶And Aaron shall present the bull as the sin offering for himself and make atonement for himself and for his house [the other priests].

⁷He shall take the two goats and present them before the Lord at the door of the Tent of Meeting.

⁸Aaron shall cast lots on the two goats—one lot for the Lord, the other lot for Azazel *or* removal.

⁹And Aaron shall bring the goat on which the Lord's lot fell and offer him as a sin offering.

¹⁰But the goat on which the lot fell for Azazel *or* removal shall be presented alive before the Lord to make atonement over him, that he may be let go into the wilderness for Azazel (for dismissal).

AMP notes: ᵃ Since the priests have been warned by the death of Nadab and Abihu to approach God with reverence and godly fear, directions are here given how the nearest approach might be made . . . Within the veil none must ever come but the high priest only, and he but one day in the year. But see what a blessed change is made by the Gospel of Christ; all good Christians now have boldness to enter into the Holy of Holies, through the veil, every day (Heb. 10:19, 20); and we come **boldly** (not as Aaron must, with fear and trembling) to the throne of grace, or mercy seat (Heb. 4:16) . . . Now therefore we are welcome to come at all times into the Holy Place "not made with hands." In the past Aaron could not come near "at all times," lest he die; we now must come near "at all times," that we may live. It is [keeping our] distance only that is our death (Matthew Henry, *A Commentary*).

King James Version

¹¹And Aaron shall bring the bullock of the sin offering, which *is* for himself, and shall make an atonement for himself, and for his house, and shall kill the bullock of the sin offering which *is* for himself:

¹²And he shall take a censer full of burning coals of fire from off the altar before the LORD, and his hands full of sweet incense beaten small, and bring *it* within the vail:

¹³And he shall put the incense upon the fire before the LORD, that the cloud of the incense may cover the mercy seat that *is* upon the Testimony, that he die not:

¹⁴And he shall take of the blood of the bullock, and sprinkle *it* with his finger upon the mercy seat eastward; and before the mercy seat shall he sprinkle of the blood with his finger seven times.

¹⁵Then shall he kill the goat of the sin offering, that *is* for the people, and bring his blood within the vail, and do with that blood as he did with the blood of the bullock, and sprinkle it upon the mercy seat, and before the mercy seat:

¹⁶And he shall make an atonement for the holy *place,* because of the uncleanness of the children of Israel, and because of their transgressions in all their sins: and so shall he do for the tabernacle of the congregation, that remaineth among them in the midst of their uncleanness.

¹⁷And there shall be no man in the tabernacle of the congregation when he goeth in to make an atonement in the holy *place,* until he come out, and have made an atonement for himself, and for his household, and for all the congregation of Israel.

¹⁸And he shall go out unto the altar that *is* before the LORD, and make an atonement for it; and shall take of the blood of the bullock, and of the blood of the goat, and put *it* upon the horns of the altar round about.

¹⁹And he shall sprinkle of the blood upon it with his finger seven times, and cleanse it, and hallow it from the uncleanness of the children of Israel.

²⁰And when he hath made an end of reconciling the holy *place,* and the tabernacle of the congregation, and the altar, he shall bring the live goat:

²¹And Aaron shall lay both his hands upon the head of the live goat, and confess over him all the iniquities of the children of Israel, and all their transgressions in all their sins, putting them upon the head of the goat, and shall send *him* away by the hand of a fit man into the wilderness:

Amplified Bible

¹¹Aaron shall present the bull as the sin offering for his own sins and shall make atonement for himself and for his house [the other priests], and shall kill the bull as the sin offering for himself.

¹²He shall take a censer full of burning coals of fire from off the [bronze] altar before the Lord, and his two hands full of sweet incense beaten small, and bring it within the veil [into the Holy of Holies],

¹³And put the incense on the fire [in the censer] before the Lord, that the cloud of the incense may cover the mercy seat that is upon [the ark of] the Testimony, lest he die.

¹⁴He shall take of the bull's blood and sprinkle it with his finger on the front [the east side] of the mercy seat, and before the mercy seat he shall sprinkle of the blood with his finger seven times.

¹⁵Then shall he kill the goat of the sin offering that is for [the sins of] the people and bring its blood within the veil [into the Holy of Holies] and do with that blood as he did with the blood of the bull, and sprinkle it on the mercy seat and before the mercy seat.

¹⁶Thus he shall make atonement for the Holy Place because of the uncleanness of the Israelites and because of their transgressions, even all their sins; and so shall he do for the Tent of Meeting, that remains among them in the midst of their uncleanness.

¹⁷There shall be no man in the Tent of Meeting when the high priest goes in to make atonement in the Holy of Holies [within the veil] until he comes out and has made atonement for his own sins and those of his house [the other priests] and of all the congregation of Israel.

¹⁸And he shall go out to the altar [of burnt offering in the court] which is before the Lord and make atonement for it, and shall take some of the blood of the bull and of the goat and put it on the horns of the altar round about.

¹⁹And he shall sprinkle some of the blood on it with his fingers seven times and cleanse it and hallow it from the uncleanness of the Israelites.

²⁰And when he has finished atoning for the Holy of Holies and the Tent of Meeting and the altar [of burnt offering], he shall present the live goat;

²¹And Aaron shall lay both his hands upon the head of the live goat and confess over him all the iniquities of the Israelites and all their transgressions, all their sins; and he shall put them upon the head of the goat [the sin-bearer], and send him away into the wilderness by the hand of a man ^awho is timely (ready, fit).

AMP notes: ^a This is suggestive of the part the personal worker has to play in showing the sinner that Christ the great Sin-bearer has made full substitution for him, if he will accept it. Notice the qualifications of this man, sent along to complete the picture of the transaction between the sinner and his only sin-bearer. He is to be a man, says the Hebrew, "timely (ready, fit)" to do such a task.

King James Version

22And the goat shall bear upon him all their iniquities unto a land not inhabited: and he shall let go the goat in the wilderness.

23And Aaron shall come into the tabernacle of the congregation, and shall put off the linen garments, which he put on when he went into the holy *place,* and shall leave them there:

24And he shall wash his flesh with water in the holy place, and put on his garments, and come forth, and offer his burnt offering, and the burnt offering of the people, and make an atonement for himself, and for the people.

25And the fat of the sin offering shall he burn upon the altar.

26And he that let go the goat for the scapegoat shall wash his clothes, and bathe his flesh in water, and afterward come into the camp.

27And the bullock for the sin offering, and the goat for the sin offering, whose blood was brought in to make atonement in the holy *place,* shall *one* carry forth without the camp; and they shall burn in the fire their skins, and their flesh, and their dung.

28And he that burneth them shall wash his clothes, and bathe his flesh in water, and afterward he shall come into the camp.

29 ¶ And *this* shall be a statute for ever unto you: *that* in the seventh month, on the tenth *day* of the month, ye shall afflict your souls, and do no work *at all, whether it be* one of your own country, or a stranger that sojourneth among you:

30For on that day shall *the priest* make an atonement for you, to cleanse you, *that* ye may be clean from all your sins before the LORD.

31It *shall be* a sabbath of rest unto you, and ye shall afflict your souls, *by* a statute for ever.

32And the priest, whom he shall anoint, and whom he shall consecrate to minister in the priest's office in his father's stead, shall make the atonement, and shall put on the linen clothes, *even* the holy garments:

33And he shall make an atonement for the holy sanctuary, and he shall make an atonement for the tabernacle of the congregation, and for the altar, and he shall make an atonement for the priests, and for all the people of the congregation.

34And this shall be an everlasting statute unto you, to make an atonement for the children of Israel for all their sins once a year. And he did as the LORD commanded Moses.

17 And the LORD spake unto Moses, saying, 2Speak unto Aaron, and unto his sons, and unto all the children of Israel, and say unto them; This *is* the thing which the LORD hath commanded, saying,

Amplified Bible

22The goat shall bear upon himself all their iniquities, carrying them to a land cut off (a land of forgetfulness *and* separation, not inhabited)! And the man leading it shall let the goat go in the wilderness.

23Aaron shall come into the Tent of Meeting and put off the linen garments which he put on when he went into the Holy of Holies, and leave them there;

24And he shall bathe his body with water in a sacred place and put on his garments, and come forth and offer his burnt offering and that of the people, and make atonement for himself and for them.

25And the fat of the sin offering he shall burn upon the altar.

26The man who led the sin-bearing goat out and let him go for Azazel *or* removal shall wash his clothes and bathe his body, and afterward he may come into the camp.

27The bull and the goat for the sin offering, whose blood was brought in to make atonement in the Holy of Holies, shall be carried forth without the camp; their skins, their flesh, and their dung shall be burned with fire.

28And he who burns them shall wash his clothes and bathe his body in water, and afterward he may come into the camp.

29It shall be a statute to you forever that in the seventh month [nearly October] on the tenth day of the month you shall afflict yourselves [by fasting with penitence and humiliation] and do no work at all, either the native-born or the stranger who dwells temporarily among you.

30For on this day atonement shall be made for you, to cleanse you; from all your sins you shall be clean before the Lord.

31It is a sabbath of [solemn] rest to you, and you shall afflict yourselves [by fasting with penitence and humiliation]; it is a statute forever.

32And the priest who shall be anointed and consecrated to minister in the priest's office in his father's stead shall make atonement, wearing the holy linen garments;

33He shall make atonement for the Holy Sanctuary, for the Tent of Meeting, and for the altar [of burnt offering in the court], and shall make atonement for the priests and for all the people of the assembly.

34This shall be an everlasting statute for you, that atonement may be made for the Israelites for all their sins once a year. And Moses did as the Lord commanded him.

17 AND THE Lord said to Moses, 2Tell Aaron, his sons, and all the Israelites, This is what the Lord has commanded:

King James Version

3What man soever *there be* of the house of Israel, that killeth an ox, or lamb, or goat, in the camp, or that killeth *it* out of the camp,

4And bringeth it not unto the door of the tabernacle of the congregation, to offer an offering unto the LORD before the tabernacle of the LORD; blood shall be imputed unto that man; he hath shed blood; and that man shall be cut off from among his people:

5To the end that the children of Israel may bring their sacrifices, which they offer in the open field, even that they may bring them unto the LORD, unto the door of the tabernacle of the congregation, unto the priest, and offer them *for* peace offerings unto the LORD.

6And the priest shall sprinkle the blood upon the altar of the LORD *at* the door of the tabernacle of the congregation, and burn the fat for a sweet savour unto the LORD.

7And they shall no more offer their sacrifices unto devils, after whom they have gone a whoring. This shall be a statute for ever unto them throughout their generations.

8And thou shalt say unto them, Whatsoever man *there be* of the house of Israel, or of the strangers which sojourn among you, that offereth a burnt offering or sacrifice,

9And bringeth it not unto the door of the tabernacle of the congregation, to offer it unto the LORD; even that man shall be cut off from among his people.

10 ¶ And whatsoever man *there be* of the house of Israel, or of the strangers that sojourn among you, that eateth any *manner of* blood; I will even set my face against *that* soul that eateth blood, and will cut him off from among his people.

11For the life of the flesh *is* in the blood: and I have given it to you upon the altar to make an atonement for your souls: for it *is* the blood *that* maketh an atonement for the soul.

12Therefore I said unto the children of Israel, No soul of you shall eat blood, neither shall any stranger that sojourneth among you eat blood.

13And whatsoever man *there be* of the children of Israel, or of the strangers that sojourn among you, which hunteth and catcheth *any* beast or fowl that may be eaten; he shall even pour out the blood thereof, and cover it with dust.

14For *it is* the life of all flesh; the blood of it *is* for the life thereof: therefore I said unto the children of Israel, Ye shall eat the blood of no *manner of* flesh: for the life of all flesh *is* the blood thereof: whosoever eateth it shall be cut off.

15And every soul that eateth that which died of itself, or that which was torn *with beasts,* *whether it be* one of your own country, or a stranger, he shall both wash his clothes, and

Amplified Bible

3If any man of the house of Israel kills an ox or lamb or goat in the camp or kills it outside the camp

4And does not bring it to the door of the Tent of Meeting to offer it as an offering to the Lord before the Lord's tabernacle, [guilt for shedding] *a*blood shall be imputed to that man; he has shed blood and shall be cut off from among his people.

5This is so that the Israelites, rather than offer their sacrifices [to idols] in the open field [where they slew them], may bring them to the Lord at the door of the Tent of Meeting, to the priest, to offer them as peace offerings to the Lord.

6And the priest shall dash the blood on the altar of the Lord at the door of the Tent of Meeting and burn the fat for a sweet *and* satisfying fragrance to the Lord.

7So they shall no more offer their sacrifices to goatlike gods *or* demons *or* field spirits after which they have played the harlot. This shall be a statute forever to them throughout their generations.

8And you shall say to them, Whoever of the house of Israel or of the strangers who dwell temporarily among you offers a burnt offering or sacrifice

9And does not bring it to the door of the Tent of Meeting to offer it to the Lord shall be cut off from among his people.

10Any one of the house of Israel or of the strangers who dwell temporarily among them who eats any kind of blood, against that person I will set My face and I will cut him off from among his people [that he may not be included in the atonement made for them].

11For the life (the animal soul) is in the blood, and I have given it for you upon the altar to make atonement for your souls; for it is the blood that makes atonement, by reason of the life [which it represents].

12Therefore I have said to the Israelites, No person among you shall eat blood, neither shall any stranger who dwells temporarily among you eat blood.

13And any of the Israelites or of the strangers who sojourn among them who takes in hunting any clean beast or bird shall pour out its blood and cover it with dust.

14As for the life of all flesh, the blood of it represents the life of it; therefore I said to the Israelites, You shall partake of the blood of no kind of flesh, for the life of all flesh is its blood. Whoever eats of it shall be cut off.

15And every person who eats what dies of itself or was torn by beasts, whether he is native-born or a temporary resident, shall wash his

AMP notes: a This requirement, that an animal to be killed was to be brought as an offering to the Lord, was no privation for the owner, for after offering it on the altar of burnt offering he received most of it back as a gift from God.

King James Version

bathe *himself* in water, and be unclean until the even: then shall he be clean.

¹⁶But if he wash *them* not, nor bathe his flesh; then he shall bear his iniquity.

18 And the LORD spake unto Moses, saying, ²Speak unto the children of Israel, and say unto them, I *am* the LORD your God.

³After the doings of the land of Egypt, wherein ye dwelt, shall ye not do: and after the doings of the land of Canaan, whither I bring you, shall ye not do: neither shall ye walk in their ordinances. *=laws*

⁴Ye shall do my judgments, and keep mine ordinances, to walk therein: I *am* the LORD your God.

⁵Ye shall therefore keep my statutes, and my judgments: which if a man do, he shall live in them: I *am* the LORD.

⁶ ¶ None of you shall approach to any that is near of kin to him, to uncover *their* nakedness: I *am* the LORD.

⁷The nakedness of thy father, or the nakedness of thy mother, shalt thou not uncover: she *is* thy mother; thou shalt not uncover her nakedness.

⁸The nakedness of thy father's wife shalt thou not uncover: it *is* thy father's nakedness.

⁹The nakedness of thy sister, the daughter of thy father, or daughter of thy mother, *whether she be* born at home, or born abroad, *even* their nakedness thou shalt not uncover.

¹⁰The nakedness of thy son's daughter, or of thy daughter's daughter, *even* their nakedness thou shalt not uncover: for theirs *is* thine own nakedness.

¹¹The nakedness of thy father's wife's daughter, begotten of thy father, she *is* thy sister, thou shalt not uncover her nakedness.

¹²Thou shalt not uncover the nakedness of thy father's sister: she *is* thy father's near kinswoman.

¹³Thou shalt not uncover the nakedness of thy mother's sister: for she *is* thy mother's near kinswoman.

¹⁴Thou shalt not uncover the nakedness of thy father's brother, thou shalt not approach to his wife: she *is* thine aunt.

¹⁵Thou shalt not uncover the nakedness of thy daughter in law: she *is* thy son's wife; thou shalt not uncover her nakedness.

¹⁶Thou shalt not uncover the nakedness of thy brother's wife: it *is* thy brother's nakedness.

¹⁷Thou shalt not uncover the nakedness of a woman and her daughter, neither shalt thou take her son's daughter, or her daughter's daughter, to uncover her nakedness; *for* they *are* her near kinswomen: it *is* wickedness.

¹⁸Neither shalt thou take a wife to her sister,

Amplified Bible

clothes and bathe himself in water, and be unclean until evening; then shall he be clean.

¹⁶But if he does not wash his clothes or bathe his body, he shall bear his own iniquity [for it shall not be borne by the sacrifice of atonement].

18 AND THE Lord said to Moses, ²Say to the Israelites, I am the Lord your God.

³You shall not do as was done in the land of Egypt in which you dwelt, nor shall you do as is done in the land of Canaan to which I am bringing you; neither shall you walk in their statutes.

⁴You shall do My ordinances and keep My statutes and walk in them. I am the Lord your God.

⁵You shall therefore keep My statutes and My ordinances which, if a man does, he shall live by them. I am the Lord.

⁶None of you shall approach anyone close of kin to him to have sexual relations. I am the Lord.

⁷The nakedness of your father, which is the nakedness of your mother, you shall not uncover; she is your mother; you shall not have intercourse with her.

⁸The nakedness of your father's wife you shall not uncover; it is your father's nakedness.

⁹You shall not have intercourse with *or* uncover the nakedness of your sister, the daughter of your father or of your mother, whether born at home or born abroad.

¹⁰You must not have sexual relations with your son's daughter or your daughter's daughter; their nakedness you shall not uncover, for they are your own flesh.

¹¹You must not have intercourse with your father's wife's daughter; begotten by your father, she is your sister; you shall not uncover her nakedness.

¹²You shall not have intercourse with your father's sister; she is your father's near kinswoman.

¹³You shall not have sexual relations with your mother's sister, for she is your mother's near kinswoman.

¹⁴You shall not have intercourse with your father's brother's wife; you shall not approach his wife; she is your aunt.

¹⁵You shall not uncover the nakedness of your daughter-in-law; she is your son's wife; you shall not have intercourse with her.

¹⁶You shall not have intercourse with your brother's wife; she belongs to your brother.

¹⁷You shall not marry a woman and her daughter, nor shall you take her son's daughter or her daughter's daughter to have intercourse; they are [her] near kinswomen; it is wickedness *and* an outrageous offense.

¹⁸You must not marry a woman in addition to her sister, to be a rival to her, having sexual re-

King James Version

to vex *her,* to uncover her nakedness, besides the other in her life *time.*

19Also thou shalt not approach unto a woman to uncover her nakedness, as long as she is put apart for her uncleanness.

20Moreover thou shalt not lie carnally with thy neighbour's wife, to defile *thyself* with her.

21And thou shalt not let *any* of thy seed pass through *the* fire to Molech, neither shalt thou profane the name of thy God: I *am* the LORD.

22Thou shalt not lie with mankind, as with womankind: it *is* abomination.

23Neither shalt thou lie with any beast to defile *thyself* therewith: neither shall any woman stand before a beast to lie down thereto: it *is* confusion.

24Defile not you yourselves in any of these *things:* for in all these the nations are defiled which I cast out before you:

25And the land is defiled: therefore I do visit the iniquity thereof upon it, and the land *itself* vomiteth out her inhabitants.

26Ye shall therefore keep my statutes and my judgments, and shall not commit any of these abominations; *neither* any of your own nation, nor any stranger that sojourneth among you:

27(For all these abominations have the men of the land done, which *were* before you, and the land is defiled;)

28That the land spue not you out also, when ye defile it, as it spued out the nations that *were* before you.

29For whosoever shall commit any of these abominations, even the souls that commit *them* shall be cut off from among their people.

30Therefore ye shall keep mine ordinance, that *ye* commit not *any one* of *these* abominable customs, which were committed before you, and that ye defile not yourselves therein: I *am* the LORD your God.

19 And the LORD spake unto Moses, saying, 2Speak unto all the congregation of the children of Israel, and say unto them, Ye shall be holy: for I the LORD your God *am* holy.

3Ye shall fear every man his mother, and his father, and keep my sabbaths: I *am* the LORD your God.

4Turn ye not unto idols, nor make to yourselves molten gods: I *am* the LORD your God.

5 ¶ And if ye offer a sacrifice of peace offerings unto the LORD, ye shall offer it at your own will.

6It shall be eaten the *same* day ye offer it, and on the morrow: and if ought remain until the third day, it shall be burnt in the fire.

7And if it be eaten at all on the third day, it *is* abominable; it shall not be accepted.

Amplified Bible

lations with the second sister when the first one is alive.

19Also you shall not have intercourse with a woman during her [menstrual period or similar] uncleanness.

20Moreover, you shall not lie carnally with your neighbor's wife, to defile yourself with her.

21You shall not give any of your children to pass through the fire *and* sacrifice them to Molech [the fire god], nor shall you profane the name of your God [by giving it to false gods]. I am the Lord.

22You shall not lie with a man as with a woman; it is an abomination.

23Neither shall you lie with any beast and defile yourself with it; neither shall any woman yield herself to a beast to lie with it; it is confusion, perversion, *and* degradedly carnal.

24Do not defile yourselves in any of these ways, for in all these things the nations are defiled which I am casting out before you.

25And the land is defiled; therefore I visit the iniquity of it upon it, and the land itself vomits out her inhabitants.

26So you shall keep My statutes and My ordinances and shall not commit any of these abominations, neither the native-born nor any stranger who sojourns among you,

27For all these abominations have the men of the land done who were before you, and the land is defiled—

28[Do none of these things] lest the land spew you out when you defile it as it spewed out the nation that was before you.

29Whoever commits any of these abominations shall be cut off from among [his] people.

30So keep My charge: do not practice any of these abominable customs which were practiced before you and defile yourselves by them. I am the Lord your God.

19 AND THE Lord said to Moses, 2Say to all the assembly of the Israelites, You shall be holy, for I the Lord your God am holy.

3Each of you shall give due respect to his mother and his father, and keep My Sabbaths holy. I the Lord am your God.

4Do not turn to idols *and* things of nought or make for yourselves molten gods. I the Lord am your God.

5And when you offer a sacrifice of peace offering to the Lord, you shall offer it so that you may be accepted.

6It shall be eaten the same day you offer it and on the day following; and if anything remains until the third day, it shall be burned in the fire.

7If it is eaten at all the third day, it is loathsome; it will not be accepted.

King James Version

⁸Therefore *every one* that eateth it shall bear his iniquity, because he hath profaned the hallowed *thing* of the LORD: and that soul shall be cut off from among his people.

⁹ ¶ And when ye reap the harvest of your land, thou shalt not wholly reap the corners of thy field, neither shalt thou gather the gleanings of thy harvest.

¹⁰And thou shalt not glean thy vineyard, neither shalt thou gather *every* grape of thy vineyard; thou shalt leave them for the poor and stranger: I *am* the LORD your God.

¹¹Ye shall not steal, neither deal falsely, neither lie one to another.

¹²And ye shall not swear by my name falsely, neither shalt thou profane the name of thy God: I *am* the LORD.

¹³Thou shalt not defraud thy neighbour, neither rob *him:* the wages of him that is hired shall not abide with thee all night until the morning.

¹⁴Thou shalt not curse the deaf, nor put a stumblingblock before the blind, but shalt fear thy God: I *am* the LORD.

¹⁵Ye shall do no unrighteousness in judgment: thou shalt not respect the person of the poor, nor honour the person of the mighty: *but* in righteousness shalt thou judge thy neighbour.

¹⁶Thou shalt not go up and down *as* a talebearer among thy people: neither shalt thou stand against the blood of thy neighbour: I *am* the LORD.

¹⁷Thou shalt not hate thy brother in thine heart: thou shalt in any wise rebuke thy neighbour, and not suffer sin upon him.

¹⁸Thou shalt not avenge, nor bear any grudge against the children of thy people, but thou shalt love thy neighbour as thyself: I *am* the LORD.

¹⁹ ¶ Ye shall keep my statutes. Thou shalt not let thy cattle gender with a diverse kind: thou shalt not sow thy field with mingled seed: neither shall a garment mingled of linen and woollen come upon thee.

²⁰And whosoever lieth carnally with a woman that *is* a bondmaid, betrothed to a husband, and not at all redeemed, nor freedom given her; she shall be scourged, they shall not be put to death, because she was not free.

²¹And he shall bring his trespass offering unto the LORD, unto the door of the tabernacle of the congregation, *even* a ram for a trespass offering.

²²And the priest shall make an atonement for him with the ram of the trespass offering before the LORD for his sin which he hath done: and the sin which he hath done shall be forgiven him.

²³And when ye shall come into the land, and shall have planted all *manner of* trees for food, then ye shall count the fruit thereof as uncircumcised: three years shall it be as uncircumcised unto you: it shall not be eaten of.

Amplified Bible

⁸But everyone who eats it shall bear his iniquity, for he has profaned a holy thing of the Lord; and that soul shall be cut off from his people [and not be included in the atonement made for them].

⁹And when you reap the harvest of your land, you shall not reap your field to its very corners, neither shall you gather the fallen ears *or* gleanings of your harvest.

¹⁰And you shall not glean your vineyard bare, neither shall you gather its fallen grapes; you shall leave them for the poor and the stranger. I am the Lord your God.

¹¹You shall not steal, or deal falsely, or lie one to another.

¹²And you shall not swear by My name falsely, neither shall you profane the name of your God. I am the Lord.

¹³You shall not defraud *or* oppress your neighbor or rob him; the wages of a hired servant shall not remain with you all night until morning.

¹⁴You shall not curse the deaf or put a stumbling block before the blind, but you shall [reverently] fear your God. I am the Lord.

¹⁵You shall do no injustice in judging a case; you shall not be partial to the poor or show a preference for the mighty, but in righteousness *and* according to the merits of the case judge your neighbor.

¹⁶You shall not go up and down as a dispenser of gossip *and* scandal among your people, nor shall you [secure yourself by false testimony or by silence and] endanger the life of your neighbor. I am the Lord.

¹⁷You shall not hate your brother in your heart; but you shall surely rebuke your neighbor, lest you incur sin because of him.

¹⁸You shall not take revenge or bear any grudge against the sons of your people, but you shall love your neighbor as yourself. I am the Lord.

¹⁹You shall keep My statutes. You shall not let your domestic animals breed with a different kind [of animal]; you shall not sow your field with mixed seed, neither wear a garment of linen mixed with wool.

²⁰And if a man lies carnally with a woman who is a slave betrothed to a husband and not yet ransomed or given her freedom, they shall be punished [after investigation]; they shall not be put to death, because she was not free;

²¹But he shall bring his guilt *or* trespass offering to the Lord to the door of the Tent of Meeting, a ram for a guilt *or* trespass offering.

²²The priest shall make atonement for him with the ram of the guilt *or* trespass offering before the Lord for his sin, and he shall be forgiven for committing the sin.

²³And when you come into the land and have planted all kinds of trees for food, then you shall count the fruit of them as inedible *and* forbidden to you for three years; it shall not be eaten.

King James Version

24 But in the fourth year all the fruit thereof shall be holy to praise the LORD *withal*.

25 And in the fifth year shall ye eat of the fruit thereof, that *it* may yield unto you the increase thereof: I *am* the LORD your God.

26 ¶ Ye shall not eat *any thing* with the blood: neither shall ye use enchantment, nor observe times.

27 Ye shall not round the corners of your heads, neither shalt thou mar the corners of thy beard.

28 Ye shall not make any cuttings in your flesh for the dead, nor print any marks upon you: I *am* the LORD. *Brings attention to the flesh.*

29 Do not prostitute thy daughter, to cause her to be a whore; lest the land fall to whoredom, and the land become full of wickedness.

30 Ye shall keep my sabbaths, and reverence my sanctuary: I *am* the LORD.

31 Regard not them that have familiar spirits, neither seek after wizards, to be defiled by them: I *am* the LORD your God.

32 Thou shalt rise up before the hoary head, and honour the face of the old man, and fear thy God: I *am* the LORD.

33 And if a stranger sojourn with thee in your land, ye shall not vex him.

34 *But* the stranger that dwelleth with you shall be unto you as one born amongst you, and thou shalt love him as thyself; for ye were strangers in the land of Egypt: I *am* the LORD your God.

35 Ye shall do no unrighteousness in judgment, in meteyard, in weight, or in measure.

36 Just balances, just weights, a just ephah, and a just hin, shall ye have: I *am* the LORD your God, which brought you out of the land of Egypt.

37 Therefore shall ye observe all my statutes, and all my judgments, and do them: I *am* the LORD.

Vs 28 ✗ *The Cannanites did this in the promised land.*

20 And the LORD spake unto Moses, saying, 2 Again, thou shalt say to the children of Israel, Whosoever *he be* of the children of Israel, or of the strangers that sojourn in Israel, that giveth *any* of his seed unto Molech; he shall surely be put to death: the people of the land shall stone him with stones.

3 And I will set my face against that man, and will cut him off from among his people; because he hath given of his seed unto Molech, to defile my sanctuary, and to profane my holy name.

4 And if the people of the land do any ways hide their eyes from the man, when he giveth of his seed unto Molech, and kill him not:

Amplified Bible

24 In the fourth year all their fruit shall be holy for giving praise to the Lord.

25 But in the fifth year you may eat of the fruit [of the trees], that their produce may enrich you; I am the Lord your God.

26 You shall not eat anything with the blood; neither shall you use magic, omens, *or* witchcraft [or predict events by horoscope or signs and lucky days].

27 You shall not round the corners of the hair of your heads nor trim the corners of your beard [as some idolaters do].

28 You shall not make any cuttings in your flesh for the dead nor print *or* tattoo any marks upon you; I am the Lord.

29 Do not profane your daughter by causing her to be a harlot, lest the land fall into harlotry and become full of wickedness.

30 You shall keep My Sabbaths and reverence My sanctuary. I am the Lord.

31 Turn not to those [mediums] who have familiar spirits or to wizards; do not seek them out to be defiled by them. I am the Lord your God.

32 You shall rise up before the hoary head and honor the face of the old man and [reverently] fear your God. I am the Lord.

33 And if a stranger dwells temporarily with you in your land, you shall not suppress *and* mistreat him.

34 But the stranger who dwells with you shall be to you as one born among you; and you shall love him as yourself, for you were strangers in the land of Egypt. I am the Lord your God.

35 You shall do no unrighteousness in judgment, in measures of length or weight or quantity.

36 You shall have accurate *and* just balances, just weights, just ephah and hin measures. I am the Lord your God, Who brought you out of the land of Egypt.

37 You shall observe all My statutes and ordinances and do them. I am the Lord.

20 AND THE Lord said to Moses, 2 Moreover, you shall say to the Israelites, Any one of the Israelites or of the strangers that sojourn in Israel who gives any of his children to Molech [the fire god worshiped with human sacrifices] shall surely be put to death; the people of the land shall stone him with stones.

3 I also will set My face against that man [opposing him, withdrawing My protection from him, and excluding him from My covenant] and will cut him off from among his people, because he has given of his children to Molech, defiling My sanctuary and profaning My holy name.

4 And if the people of the land do at all hide their eyes from the man when he gives one of his children [as a burnt offering] to Molech [the fire god] *and* they overlook it *or* neglect to take legal action to punish him, winking at his sin, and do not kill him [as My law requires],

King James Version

⁵Then I will set my face against that man, and against his family, and will cut him off, and all that go a whoring after him, to commit whoredom with Molech, from among their people.

⁶And the soul that turneth after such as have familiar spirits, and after wizards, to go a whoring after them, I will even set my face against that soul, and will cut him off from among his people.

⁷Sanctify yourselves therefore, and be ye holy: for I *am* the LORD your God.

⁸And ye shall keep my statutes, and do them: I *am* the LORD which sanctify you.

⁹For every one that curseth his father or his mother shall be surely put to death: he hath cursed his father or his mother; his blood *shall be* upon him.

¹⁰ ¶ And the man that committeth adultery with *another* man's wife, *even he* that committeth adultery with his neighbour's wife, the adulterer and the adulteress shall surely be put to death.

¹¹And the man that lieth with his father's wife hath uncovered his father's nakedness: both of them shall surely be put to death; their blood *shall be* upon them.

¹²And if a man lie with his daughter in law, both of them shall surely be put to death: they have wrought confusion; their blood *shall be* upon them.

¹³If a man also lie with mankind, as he lieth with a woman, both of them have committed an abomination: they shall surely be put to death; their blood *shall be* upon them.

¹⁴And if a man take a wife and her mother, it *is* wickedness: they shall be burnt with fire, both he and they; that there be no wickedness among you.

¹⁵And if a man lie with a beast, he shall surely be put to death: and ye shall slay the beast.

¹⁶And if a woman approach unto any beast, and lie down thereto, thou shalt kill the woman and the beast: they shall surely be put to death; their blood *shall be* upon them.

¹⁷And if a man shall take his sister, his father's daughter, or his mother's daughter, and see her nakedness, and she see his nakedness; it *is* a wicked thing; and they shall be cut off in the sight of their people: he hath uncovered his sister's nakedness; he shall bear his iniquity.

¹⁸And if a man shall lie with a woman having her sickness, and shall uncover her nakedness; he hath discovered her fountain, and she hath uncovered the fountain of her blood: and both of them shall be cut off from among their people.

Amplified Bible

⁵Then I will set My face against that man and against his family and will cut him off from among their people, him and all who follow him to [unfaithfulness to Me, and thus] play the harlot after Molech.

⁶The person who turns to those who have familiar spirits and to wizards, [being unfaithful to Israel's Maker Who is her Husband, and thus] playing the harlot after them, I will set My face against that person and will cut him off from among his people [that he may not be included in the atonement made for them].

⁷Consecrate yourselves therefore, and be holy; for I am the Lord your God.

⁸And you shall keep My statutes and do them. I am the Lord Who sanctifies you.

⁹Everyone who curses his father or mother shall surely be put to death; he has cursed his father or mother; his bloodguilt is upon him.

¹⁰The man who commits adultery with another's wife, even his neighbor's wife, the adulterer and the adulteress shall surely be put to death.

¹¹And the man who lies carnally with his father's wife has uncovered his father's nakedness; both of the guilty ones shall surely be put to death; their blood shall be upon their own heads.

¹²And if a man lies carnally with his daughter-in-law, both of them shall surely be put to death; they have wrought confusion, perversion, *and* defilement; their blood shall be upon their own heads.

¹³If a man lies with a male as if he were a woman, both men have committed an offense (something perverse, unnatural, abhorrent, and detestable); they shall surely be put to death; their blood shall be upon them.

¹⁴And if a man takes a wife and her mother, it is wickedness *and* an outrageous offense; all three shall be burned with fire, both he and they [after being stoned to death], that there be no wickedness among you.

¹⁵And if a man lies carnally with a beast, he shall surely be [stoned] to death, and you shall slay the beast.

¹⁶If a woman approaches any beast and lies carnally with it, you shall [stone] the woman and the beast; they shall surely be put to death; their blood is upon them.

¹⁷If a man takes his sister, his father's or his mother's daughter, and sees her nakedness and she sees his nakedness, it is a wicked *and* shameful thing; and they shall be cut off in the sight of their people; he has had sexual relations with his sister; he shall bear his iniquity.

¹⁸And if a man shall lie with a woman having her menstrual pains and shall uncover her nakedness, he has made naked her fountain, and she has uncovered the fountain of her blood; and both of them shall be cut off from among their people.

King James Version

19And thou shalt not uncover the nakedness of thy mother's sister, nor of thy father's sister: for he uncovereth his near kin: they shall bear their iniquity.

20And if a man shall lie with his uncle's wife, he hath uncovered his uncle's nakedness: they shall bear their sin; they shall die childless.

21And if a man shall take his brother's wife, it *is* an unclean thing: he hath uncovered his brother's nakedness; they shall be childless.

22 ¶ Ye shall therefore keep all my statutes, and all my judgments, and do them: that the land, whither I bring you to dwell therein, spue you not out.

23And ye shall not walk in the manners of the nation, which I cast out before you: for they committed all these *things,* and therefore I abhorred them.

24But I have said unto you, Ye shall inherit their land, and I will give it unto you to possess it, a land that floweth with milk and honey: I *am* the LORD your God, which have separated you from *other* people.

25Ye shall therefore put difference between clean beasts and unclean, and between unclean fowls and clean: and ye shall not make your souls abominable by beast, or by fowl, or by any *manner of living thing* that creepeth *on* the ground, which I have separated from you as unclean.

26And ye shall be holy unto me: for I the LORD *am* holy, and have severed you from *other* people, that *ye* should be mine.

27A man also or woman that hath a familiar spirit, or that is a wizard, shall surely be put to death: they shall stone them with stones: their blood *shall be* upon them.

21 And the LORD said unto Moses, Speak unto the priests the sons of Aaron, and say unto them, There shall none be defiled for the dead among his people:

2But for his kin, that is near unto him, *that is,* for his mother, and for his father, and for his son, and for his daughter, and for his brother,

3And for his sister a virgin, that is nigh unto him, which hath had no husband; for her may he be defiled.

4*But* he shall not defile himself, *being* a chief man among his people, to profane himself.

5They shall not make baldness upon their head, neither shall they shave off the corner of their beard, nor make any cuttings in their flesh.

6They shall be holy unto their God, and not profane the name of their God: for the offerings

Amplified Bible

19You shall not uncover the nakedness of your mother's sister or of your father's sister, for that is to make naked his close kin; they shall bear their iniquity.

20And if a man shall lie carnally with his uncle's wife, he has uncovered his uncle's nakedness; they shall bear their sin; they shall die childless [not literally, but in a legal sense].

21And if a man shall take his brother's wife, it is impurity; he has uncovered his brother's nakedness; they shall be childless [not literally, but in a legal sense].

22You shall therefore keep all My statutes and all My ordinances and do them, that the land where I am bringing you to dwell may not vomit you out [as it did those before you].

23You shall not walk in the customs of the nation which I am casting out before you; for they did all these things, and therefore I was wearied *and* grieved by them.

24But I have said to you, You shall inherit their land, and I will give it to you to possess, a land flowing with milk and honey. I am the Lord your God, Who has separated you from the peoples.

25You shall therefore make a distinction between the clean beast and the unclean, and between the unclean fowl and the clean; and you shall not make yourselves detestable with beast or with bird or with anything with which the ground teems *or* that creeps, which I have set apart from you as unclean.

26And you shall be holy to Me; for I the Lord am holy, and have separated you from the peoples, that you should be Mine.

27A man or woman who is a medium *and* has a familiar spirit or is a wizard shall surely be put to death, be stoned with stones; their blood shall be upon them.

21 THE LORD said to Moses, Speak to the priests [exclusive of the high priest], the sons of Aaron, and say to them that none of them shall defile himself for the dead among his people [by touching a corpse or assisting in preparing it for burial],

2Except for his near [blood] kin, for his mother, father, son, daughter, brother,

3And for his sister, a virgin, who is near to him because she has had no husband; for her he may be defiled.

4He shall not even defile himself, being a [bereaved] husband [his wife not being his blood kin] *or* being a chief man among his people, and so profane himself.

5The priests [like the other Israelite men] shall not shave the crown of their heads or clip off the corners of their beard or make any cuttings in their flesh.

6They shall be holy to their God and not profane the name of their God; for they offer the of-

King James Version

of the LORD made by fire, *and* the bread of their God, they do offer: therefore they shall be holy.

⁷They shall not take a wife *that is* a whore, or profane; neither shall they take a woman put away from her husband: for he *is* holy unto his God.

⁸Thou shalt sanctify him therefore; for he offereth the bread of thy God: he shall be holy unto thee: for I the LORD, which sanctify you, *am* holy.

⁹And the daughter of any priest, if she profane herself by playing the whore, she profaneth her father: she shall be burnt with fire.

¹⁰ ¶ And *he that is* the high priest among his brethren, upon whose head the anointing oil was poured, and that is consecrated to put on the garments, shall not uncover his head, nor rend his clothes;

¹¹Neither shall he go in to any dead body, nor defile himself for his father, or for his mother;

¹²Neither shall he go out of the sanctuary, nor profane the sanctuary of his God; for the crown of the anointing oil of his God *is* upon him: I *am* the LORD.

¹³And he shall take a wife in her virginity.

¹⁴A widow, or a divorced *woman*, or profane, *or* a harlot, these shall he not take: but he shall take a virgin of his own people to wife.

¹⁵Neither shall he profane his seed among his people: for I the LORD do sanctify him.

¹⁶ ¶ And the LORD spake unto Moses, saying,

¹⁷Speak unto Aaron, saying, Whosoever *he be* of thy seed in their generations that hath *any* blemish, let him not approach to offer the bread of his God.

¹⁸For whatsoever man *he be* that hath a blemish, he shall not approach: a blind man, or a lame, or he that hath a flat nose, or any thing superfluous,

¹⁹Or a man that is brokenfooted, or brokenhanded,

²⁰Or crookbackt, or a dwarf, or that hath a blemish in his eye, or be scurvy, or scabbed, or hath his stones broken;

²¹No man that hath a blemish, of the seed of Aaron the priest, shall come nigh to offer the offerings of the LORD made by fire: he hath a blemish; he shall not come nigh to offer the bread of his God.

²²He shall eat the bread of his God, *both* of the most holy, and of the holy.

²³Only he shall not go in unto the vail, nor come nigh unto the altar, because he hath a blemish; that he profane not my sanctuaries: for I the LORD do sanctify them.

²⁴And Moses told *it* unto Aaron, and to his sons, and unto all the children of Israel.

Amplified Bible

ferings made by fire to the Lord, the bread of their God; therefore they shall be holy.

⁷They shall not take a wife who is a harlot or polluted *or* profane or divorced, for [the priest] is holy to his God.

⁸You shall consecrate him therefore, for he offers the bread of your God; he shall be holy to you, for I the Lord Who sanctifies you am holy.

⁹The daughter of any priest who profanes herself by playing the harlot profanes her father; she shall be burned with fire [after being stoned].

¹⁰But he who is the high priest among his brethren, upon whose head the anointing oil was poured and who is consecrated to put on the [sacred] garments, shall not let the hair of his head hang loose or rend his clothes [in mourning],

¹¹Neither shall he go in where any dead body lies nor defile himself [by doing so, even] for his father or for his mother;

¹²Neither shall he go out of the sanctuary nor desecrate *or* make ceremonially unclean the sanctuary of his God, for the crown *or* consecration of the anointing oil of his God is upon him. I am the Lord.

¹³He shall take a wife in her virginity.

¹⁴A widow or a divorced woman or a woman who is polluted *or* profane or a harlot, these shall not marry, but he shall take as his wife a virgin of his own people,

¹⁵That he may not profane *or* dishonor his children among his people; for I the Lord do sanctify the high priest.

¹⁶And the Lord said to Moses,

¹⁷Say to Aaron, Any one of your sons in their successive generations who has any blemish, let him not come near to offer the bread of his God.

¹⁸For no man who has a blemish shall approach [God's altar to serve as priest], a man blind or lame, or he who has a disfigured face or a limb too long,

¹⁹Or who has a fractured foot or hand,

²⁰Or is a hunchback, or a dwarf, or has a defect in his eye, or has scurvy *or* itch, or scabs *or* skin trouble, or has damaged testicles.

²¹No man of the offspring of Aaron the priest who has a blemish *and* is disfigured *or* deformed shall come near [the altar] to offer the offerings of the Lord made by fire. He has a blemish; he shall not come near to offer the bread of his God.

²²He may eat the bread of his God, both of the most holy and of the holy things,

²³But he shall not come within the veil or come near the altar [of incense], because he has a blemish, that he may not desecrate *and* make unclean My sanctuaries *and* hallowed things; for I the Lord do sanctify them.

²⁴And Moses told it to Aaron and to his sons and to all the Israelites.

King James Version

22 And the LORD spake unto Moses, saying, ²Speak unto Aaron and to his sons, that they separate themselves from the holy *things* of the children of Israel, and that they profane not my holy name *in those things* which they hallow unto me: I *am* the LORD.

³Say unto them, Whosoever *he be* of all your seed among your generations, that goeth unto the holy *things* which the children of Israel hallow unto the LORD, having his uncleanness upon him, that soul shall be cut off from my presence: I *am* the LORD.

⁴What man soever of the seed of Aaron *is* a leper, or hath a running issue; he shall not eat of the holy *things*, until he be clean. And whoso toucheth any *thing that is* unclean *by* the dead, or a man whose seed goeth from him;

⁵Or whosoever toucheth any creeping thing, whereby he may be made unclean, or a man of whom he may take uncleanness, whatsoever uncleanness he hath;

⁶The soul which hath touched *any* such shall be unclean until even, and shall not eat of the holy *things*, unless he wash his flesh with water.

⁷And when the sun is down, he shall be clean, and shall afterward eat of the holy *things;* because it *is* his food.

⁸That which dieth of itself, or is torn *with beasts*, he shall not eat to defile *himself* therewith: I *am* the LORD.

⁹They shall therefore keep mine ordinance, lest they bear sin for it, and die therefore, if they profane it: I the LORD do sanctify them.

¹⁰ ¶ There shall no stranger eat *of* the holy *thing:* a sojourner of the priest's, or a hired servant, shall not eat *of* the holy *thing*.

¹¹But if the priest buy *any* soul with his money, he shall eat of it, and he that is born in his house: they shall eat of his meat.

¹²If the priest's daughter also be *married* unto a stranger, she may not eat of an offering of the holy *things*.

¹³But if the priest's daughter be a widow, or divorced, and have no child, and is returned unto her father's house, as *in* her youth, she shall eat of her father's meat: but there shall no stranger eat thereof.

¹⁴And if a man eat *of* the holy *thing* unwittingly, then he shall put the fifth *part* thereof unto it, and shall give *it* unto the priest with the holy *thing*.

¹⁵And they shall not profane the holy *things* of the children of Israel, which they offer unto the LORD;

¹⁶Or suffer them to bear the iniquity of trespass, when they eat their holy *things:* for I the LORD do sanctify them.

¹⁷ ¶ And the LORD spake unto Moses, saying,

Amplified Bible

22 AND THE Lord said to Moses, ²Say to Aaron and his sons that they shall stay away from the holy things which the Israelites dedicate to Me, that they may not profane My holy name; I am the Lord.

³Tell them, Any one of your offspring throughout your generations who goes to the holy things which the Israelites dedicate to the Lord when he is unclean, that [priest] shall be cut off from My presence *and* excluded from the sanctuary; I am the Lord.

⁴No man of the offspring of Aaron who is a leper or has a discharge shall eat of the holy things [the offerings and the showbread] until he is clean. And whoever touches any person *or* thing made unclean by contact with a corpse or a man who has had a discharge of semen,

⁵Or whoever touches any dead creeping thing by which he may be made unclean, or a man from whom he may acquire uncleanness, whatever it may be,

⁶The priest who has touched any such thing shall be unclean until evening and shall not eat of the holy things unless he has bathed with water.

⁷When the sun is down, he shall be clean, and afterward may eat of the holy things, for they are his food.

⁸That which dies of itself or is torn by beasts he shall not eat, defiling himself with it. I am the Lord.

⁹The priests therefore shall observe My ordinance, lest they bear sin for it and die thereby if they profane it. I am the Lord, Who sanctifies them.

¹⁰No outsider [not of the family of Aaron] shall eat of the holy thing [which has been offered to God]; a sojourner with the priest or a hired servant shall not eat of the holy thing.

¹¹But if a priest buys a slave with his money, the slave may eat of the holy thing, and he also who is born in the priest's house; they may eat of his food.

¹²If a priest's daughter is married to an outsider [not of the priestly tribe], she shall not eat of the offering of the holy things.

¹³But if a priest's daughter is a widow or divorced, and has no child, and returns to her father's house as in her youth, she shall eat of her father's food; but no stranger shall eat of it.

¹⁴And if a man eats unknowingly of the holy thing [which has been offered to God], then he shall add one-fifth of its value to it and repay that amount to the priest for the holy thing.

¹⁵The priests shall not profane the holy things the Israelites offer to the Lord,

¹⁶And so cause them [by neglect of any essential observance] to bear the iniquity when they eat their holy things; for I the Lord sanctify them.

¹⁷And the Lord said to Moses,

King James Version

18Speak unto Aaron, and to his sons, and unto all the children of Israel, and say unto them, Whatsoever *he be* of the house of Israel, or of the strangers in Israel, that will offer his oblation for all his vows, and for all his freewill offerings, which they will offer unto the LORD for a burnt offering;

19*Ye shall offer* at your own will a male without blemish, of the beeves, of the sheep, or of the goats.

20*But* whatsoever hath a blemish, *that* shall ye not offer: for it shall not be acceptable for you.

21And whosoever offereth a sacrifice of peace offerings unto the LORD to accomplish *his* vow, or a freewill offering in beeves or sheep, it shall be perfect to be accepted; there shall be no blemish therein.

22Blind, or broken, or maimed, or having a wen, or scurvy, or scabbed, ye shall not offer these unto the LORD, nor make an offering by fire of them upon the altar unto the LORD.

23Either a bullock or a lamb that hath any thing superfluous or lacking in his parts, that mayest thou offer *for* a freewill offering; but for a vow it shall not be accepted.

24Ye shall not offer unto the LORD that which is bruised, or crushed, or broken, or cut; neither shall you make *any* offering *thereof* in your land.

25Neither from a stranger's hand shall ye offer the bread of your God of any of these; because their corruption *is* in them, *and* blemishes *be* in them: they shall not be accepted for you.

26 ¶ And the LORD spake unto Moses, saying,

27When a bullock, or a sheep, or a goat, is brought forth, then it shall be seven days under the dam; and from the eighth day and thenceforth it shall be accepted for an offering made by fire unto the LORD.

28And *whether it be* cow or ewe, ye shall not kill it and her young both in one day.

29And when ye will offer a sacrifice of thanksgiving unto the LORD, offer *it* at your own will.

30On the same day it shall be eaten up; ye shall leave none of it until the morrow: I *am* the LORD.

31 ¶ Therefore shall ye keep my commandments, and do them: I *am* the LORD.

32Neither shall ye profane my holy name; but I will be hallowed among the children of Israel: I *am* the LORD which hallow you,

33That brought you out of the land of Egypt, to be your God: I *am* the LORD.

23 And the LORD spake unto Moses, saying, 2Speak unto the children of Israel, and say unto them, *Concerning* the feasts of the LORD, which ye shall proclaim *to be* holy convocations, *even* these *are* my feasts.

Amplified Bible

18Say to Aaron and his sons and to all the Israelites, Whoever of the house of Israel and of the foreigners in Israel brings his offering, whether to pay a vow or as a freewill offering which is offered to the Lord for a burnt offering

19That you may be accepted, you shall offer a male without blemish of the young bulls, the sheep, or the goats.

20But you shall not offer anything which has a blemish, for it will not be acceptable for you.

21And whoever offers a sacrifice of peace offering to the Lord to make a special vow to the Lord or for a freewill offering from the herd or from the flock must bring what is perfect to be accepted; there shall be no blemish in it.

22Animals blind or made infirm *and* weak or maimed, or having sores *or* a wen or an itch or scabs, you shall not offer to the Lord or make an offering of them by fire upon the altar to the Lord.

23For a freewill offering you may offer either a bull or a lamb which has some part too long or too short, but for [the payment of] a vow it shall not be accepted.

24You shall not offer to the Lord any animal which has its testicles bruised or crushed or broken or cut, neither sacrifice it in your land.

25Neither shall you offer as the bread of your God any such animals obtained from a foreigner [who may wish to pay respect to the true God], because their defects render them unfit; there is a blemish in them; they will not be accepted for you.

26And the Lord said to Moses,

27When a bull or a sheep or a goat is born, it shall remain for seven days with its mother; and from the eighth day on it shall be accepted for an offering made by fire to the Lord.

28And whether [the mother] is a cow or a ewe, you shall not kill her and her young both in one day.

29And when you sacrifice an offering of thanksgiving to the Lord, sacrifice it so that you may be accepted.

30It shall be eaten on the same day; you shall leave none of it until the next day. I am the Lord.

31So shall you heartily accept My commandments *and* conform your life and conduct to them. I am the Lord.

32Neither shall you profane My holy name [applying it to an idol, or treating it with irreverence or contempt or as a byword]; but I will be hallowed among the Israelites. I am the Lord, Who consecrates *and* makes you holy,

33Who brought you out of the land of Egypt to be your God. I am the Lord.

23 THE LORD said to Moses, 2Say to the Israelites, The set feasts *or* appointed seasons of the Lord which you shall proclaim as holy convocations, even My set feasts, are these:

King James Version

3 ¶ Six days shall work be done: but the seventh day *is* the sabbath of rest, a holy convocation; ye shall do no work *therein:* it *is* the sabbath of the LORD in all your dwellings.

4 ¶ These *are* the feasts of the LORD, *even* holy convocations, which ye shall proclaim in their seasons.

5In the fourteenth *day* of the first month at even *is* the LORD'S passover.

6And on the fifteenth day of the same month *is* the feast of unleavened bread unto the LORD: seven days ye must eat unleavened bread.

7In the first day ye shall have a holy convocation: ye shall do no servile work *therein.*

8But ye shall offer an offering made by fire unto the LORD seven days: in the seventh day *is* a holy convocation: ye shall do no servile work *therein.*

9 ¶ And the LORD spake unto Moses, saying,

10Speak unto the children of Israel, and say unto them, When ye be come into the land which I give unto you, and shall reap the harvest thereof, then ye shall bring a sheaf of the firstfruits of your harvest unto the priest:

11And he shall wave the sheaf before the LORD, to be accepted for you: on the morrow after the sabbath the priest shall wave it.

12And ye shall offer that day when ye wave the sheaf a he lamb without blemish of the first year for a burnt offering unto the LORD.

13And the meat offering thereof *shall be* two tenth deals *of* fine flour mingled with oil, an offering made by fire unto the LORD *for* a sweet savour: and the drink offering thereof *shall be of* wine, the fourth *part* of a hin.

14And ye shall eat neither bread, nor parched *corn,* nor green ears, until the selfsame day that ye have brought an offering unto your God: *it shall be* a statute for ever throughout your generations in all your dwellings.

15 ¶ And ye shall count unto you from the morrow after the sabbath, from the day that ye brought the sheaf of the wave offering; seven sabbaths shall be complete:

16Even unto the morrow after the seventh sabbath shall ye number fifty days; and ye shall offer a new meat offering unto the LORD.

17Ye shall bring out of your habitations two wave loaves of two tenth deals: they shall be *of* fine flour; they shall be baken *with* leaven; *they are* the firstfruits unto the LORD.

18And ye shall offer with the bread seven lambs without blemish of the first year, and one young bullock, and two rams: they shall be *for* a burnt offering unto the LORD, with their meat offering, and their drink offerings, *even* an offering made by fire, of sweet savour unto the LORD.

Amplified Bible

3Six days shall work be done, but the seventh day is the Sabbath of rest, a holy convocation *or* assembly by summons. You shall do no work on that day; it is the Sabbath of the Lord in all your dwellings.

4These are the set feasts *or* appointed seasons of the Lord, holy convocations you shall proclaim at their stated times:

5On the fourteenth day of the first month at twilight is the Lord's Passover.

6On the fifteenth day of the same month is the Feast of Unleavened Bread to the Lord; for seven days you shall eat unleavened bread.

7On the first day you shall have a holy "calling together;" you shall do no servile *or* laborious work on that day.

8But you shall offer an offering made by fire to the Lord for seven days; on the seventh day is a holy convocation; you shall do no servile *or* laborious work on that day.

9And the Lord said to Moses,

10Tell the Israelites, When you have come into the land I give you and reap its harvest, you shall bring the sheaf of the firstfruits of your harvest to the priest.

11And he shall wave the sheaf before the Lord, that you may be accepted; on the next day after the Sabbath the priest shall wave it [before the Lord].

12You shall offer on the day when you wave the sheaf a male lamb a year old without blemish for a burnt offering to the Lord.

13Its cereal offering shall be two-tenths of an ephah of fine flour mixed with oil, an offering made by fire to the Lord for a sweet, pleasing, *and* satisfying fragrance; and the drink offering of it [to be poured out] shall be of wine, a fourth of a hin.

14And you shall eat neither bread nor parched grain nor green ears, until this same day when you have brought the offering of your God; it is a statute forever throughout your generations in all your houses.

15And you shall count from the day after the Sabbath, from the day that you brought the sheaf of the wave offering, seven Sabbaths; [seven full weeks] shall they be.

16Count fifty days to the day after the seventh Sabbath; then you shall present a cereal offering of new grain to the Lord.

17You shall bring from your dwellings two loaves of bread to be waved, made from two-tenths of an ephah of fine flour; they shall be baked with leaven, for firstfruits to the Lord.

18And you shall offer with the bread seven lambs, a year old and without blemish, and one young bull and two rams. They shall be a burnt offering to the Lord, with their cereal offering and their drink offerings, an offering made by fire, of a sweet *and* satisfying fragrance to the Lord.

King James Version

¹⁹Then ye shall sacrifice one kid of the goats for a sin offering, and two lambs of the first year for a sacrifice of peace offerings.

²⁰And the priest shall wave them with the bread of the firstfruits *for* a wave offering before the LORD, with the two lambs: they shall be holy to the LORD for the priest.

²¹And ye shall proclaim on the selfsame day, *that* it may be a holy convocation unto you: ye shall do no servile work *therein: it shall be* a statute for ever in all your dwellings throughout your generations.

²²And when ye reap the harvest of your land, thou shalt not make clean riddance of the corners of thy field when thou reapest, neither shalt thou gather *any* gleaning of thy harvest: thou shalt leave them unto the poor, and to the stranger: I *am* the LORD your God.

²³ ¶ And the LORD spake unto Moses, saying,

²⁴Speak unto the children of Israel, saying, In the seventh month, in the first *day* of the month, shall ye have a sabbath, a memorial of blowing of trumpets, a holy convocation.

²⁵Ye shall do no servile work *therein:* but ye shall offer an offering made by fire unto the LORD.

²⁶ ¶ And the LORD spake unto Moses, saying,

²⁷Also on the tenth *day* of this seventh month *there shall be* a day of atonement: it shall be a holy convocation unto you; and ye shall afflict your souls, and offer an offering made by fire unto the LORD.

²⁸And ye shall do no work in that same day: for it *is* a day of atonement, to make an atonement for you before the LORD your God.

²⁹For whatsoever soul *it be* that shall not be afflicted in that same day, he shall be cut off from among his people.

³⁰And whatsoever soul *it be* that doeth any work in that same day, the same soul will I destroy from among his people.

³¹Ye shall do no *manner of* work: *it shall be* a statute for ever throughout your generations in all your dwellings.

³²It *shall be* unto you a sabbath of rest, and ye shall afflict your souls: in the ninth *day* of the month at even, from even unto even, shall ye celebrate your sabbath.

³³ ¶ And the LORD spake unto Moses, saying,

³⁴Speak unto the children of Israel, saying, The fifteenth day of this seventh month *shall be* the feast of tabernacles *for* seven days unto the LORD.

³⁵On the first day *shall be* a holy convocation: ye shall do no servile work *therein.*

³⁶Seven days ye shall offer an offering made by fire unto the LORD: on the eighth day shall be a holy convocation unto you; and ye shall offer an offering made by fire unto the LORD: it *is* a solemn assembly; *and* ye shall do no servile work *therein.*

³⁷These *are* the feasts of the LORD, which ye

Amplified Bible

¹⁹Then you shall sacrifice one he-goat for a sin offering and two he-lambs, a year old, for a sacrifice of peace offering.

²⁰The priest shall wave the two lambs, together with the bread of the firstfruits, for a wave offering before the Lord. They shall be holy to the Lord for the priest.

²¹You shall make proclamation the same day, summoning a holy assembly; you shall do no servile work that day. It shall be a statute forever in all your dwellings throughout your generations.

²²And when you reap the harvest of your land, you shall not wholly reap the corners of your field, neither shall you gather the gleanings of your harvest; you shall leave them for the poor and the stranger. I am the Lord your God.

²³And the Lord said to Moses,

²⁴Say to the Israelites, On the first day of the seventh month [almost October], you shall observe a day of solemn [sabbatical] rest, a memorial day announced by blowing of trumpets, a holy [called] assembly.

²⁵You shall do no servile work on it, but you shall present an offering made by fire to the Lord.

²⁶And the Lord said to Moses,

²⁷Also the tenth day of this seventh month is the Day of Atonement; it shall be a holy [called] assembly, and you shall afflict yourselves [by fasting in penitence and humility] and present an offering made by fire to the Lord.

²⁸And you shall do no work on this day, for it is the Day of Atonement, to make atonement for you before the Lord your God.

²⁹For whoever is not afflicted [by fasting in penitence and humility] on this day shall be cut off from among his people [that he may not be included in the atonement made for them].

³⁰And whoever does any work on that same day I will destroy from among his people.

³¹You shall do no kind of work [on that day]. It is a statute forever throughout your generations in all your dwellings.

³²It shall be to you a sabbath of rest, and you shall afflict yourselves [by fasting in penitence and humility]. On the ninth day of the month from evening to evening you shall keep your sabbath.

³³And the Lord said to Moses,

³⁴Say to the Israelites, The fifteenth day of this seventh month, and for seven days, is the Feast of Tabernacles *or* Booths to the Lord.

³⁵On the first day shall be a holy convocation; you shall do no servile work on that day.

³⁶For seven days you shall offer an offering made by fire to the Lord; on the eighth day shall be a holy convocation and you shall present an offering made by fire to the Lord. It is a solemn assembly; you shall do no laborious work on that day.

³⁷These are the set feasts *or* appointed seasons of the Lord, which you shall proclaim to be

King James Version

shall proclaim *to be* holy convocations, to offer an offering made by fire unto the LORD, a burnt offering, and a meat offering, a sacrifice, and drink offerings, every thing upon his day:

38Beside the sabbaths of the LORD, and beside your gifts, and beside all your vows, and beside all your freewill offerings, which ye give unto the LORD.

39Also in the fifteenth day of the seventh month, when ye have gathered in the fruit of the land, ye shall keep a feast unto the LORD seven days: on the first day *shall be* a sabbath, and on the eighth day *shall be* a sabbath.

40And ye shall take you on the first day the boughs of goodly trees, branches of palm trees, and the boughs of thick trees, and willows of the brook; and ye shall rejoice before the LORD your God seven days.

41And ye shall keep it a feast unto the LORD seven days in the year. *It shall be* a statute for ever in your generations: ye shall celebrate it in the seventh month.

42Ye shall dwell in booths seven days; all that are Israelites born shall dwell in booths:

43That your generations may know that I made the children of Israel to dwell in booths, when I brought them out of the land of Egypt: I *am* the LORD your God.

44And Moses declared unto the children of Israel the feasts of the LORD.

24 And the LORD spake unto Moses, saying, 2Command the children of Israel, that they bring unto thee pure oil olive beaten for the light, to cause the lamps to burn continually.

3Without the vail of the Testimony, in the tabernacle of the congregation, shall Aaron order it from the evening unto the morning before the LORD continually: *it shall be* a statute for ever in your generations.

4He shall order the lamps upon the pure candlestick before the LORD continually.

5 ¶ And thou shalt take fine flour, and bake twelve cakes thereof: two tenth deals shall be *in* one cake.

6And thou shalt set them *in* two rows, six on a row, upon the pure table before the LORD.

7And thou shalt put pure frankincense upon *each* row, that it may be on the bread for a memorial, *even* an offering made by fire unto the LORD.

8Every sabbath he shall set it in order before the LORD continually, *being taken* from the children of Israel *by* an everlasting covenant.

Amplified Bible

holy convocations, to present an offering made by fire to the Lord, a burnt offering and a cereal offering, sacrifices and drink offerings, each on its own day.

38This is in addition to the Sabbaths of the Lord and besides your gifts and all your vowed offerings and all your freewill offerings which you give to the Lord.

39Also on the fifteenth day of the seventh month [nearly October], when you have gathered in the fruit of the land, you shall keep the feast of the Lord for seven days, the first day and the eighth day each a Sabbath.

40And on the first day you shall take the fruit of pleasing trees [and make booths of them], branches of palm trees, and boughs of thick (leafy) trees, and willows of the brook; and you shall rejoice before the Lord your God for seven days.

41You shall keep it as a feast to the Lord for seven days in the year, a statute forever throughout your generations; you shall keep it in the seventh month.

42You shall dwell in booths (shelters) for seven days: All native Israelites shall dwell in booths,

43That your generations may know that I made the Israelites dwell in booths when I brought them out of the land of Egypt. I am the Lord your God.

44Thus Moses declared to the Israelites the set *or* appointed feasts of the Lord.

24 AND THE Lord said to Moses, 2Command the Israelites that they bring to you pure oil from beaten olives for the light [of the golden lampstand] to cause a lamp to burn continually.

3Outside the veil of the Testimony [between the Holy and the Most Holy Places] in the Tent of Meeting, Aaron shall keep it in order from evening to morning before the Lord continually; it shall be a statute forever throughout your generations.

4He shall keep the lamps in order upon the lampstand of pure gold before the Lord continually.

5And you shall take fine flour and bake twelve cakes with it; two-tenths of an ephah shall be in each cake [of the showbread *or* bread of the Presence].

6And you shall set them in two rows, six in a row, upon the table of pure gold before the Lord.

7You shall put pure frankincense [in a bowl or spoon] beside each row, that it may be with the bread as a memorial portion, an offering to be made by fire to the Lord.

8Every Sabbath day Aaron shall set the showbread in order before the Lord continually; it is on behalf of the Israelites, an everlasting covenant.

King James Version

9And it shall be Aaron's and his sons'; and they shall eat it in the holy place: for it *is* most holy unto him of the offerings of the LORD made by fire, *by* a perpetual statute.

10 ¶ And the son of an Israelitish woman, whose father *was* an Egyptian, went out among the children of Israel: and *this* son of the Israelitish *woman* and a man of Israel strove together in the camp;

11And the Israelitish woman's son blasphemed the name *of the LORD,* and cursed. And they brought him unto Moses: (and his mother's name *was* Shelomith, the daughter of Dibri, of the tribe of Dan:)

12And they put him in ward, that the mind of the LORD might be shewed them.

13And the LORD spake unto Moses, saying,

14Bring forth him that hath cursed without the camp; and let all that heard *him* lay their hands upon his head, and let all the congregation stone him.

15And thou shalt speak unto the children of Israel, saying, Whosoever curseth his God shall bear his sin.

16And he that blasphemeth the name of the LORD, he shall surely be put to death, *and* all the congregation shall certainly stone him: as well the stranger, as he that is born in the land, when he blasphemeth the name *of the LORD,* shall be put to death.

17And he that killeth any man shall surely be put to death.

18And he that killeth a beast shall make it good; beast for beast.

19And if a man cause a blemish in his neighbour; as he hath done, so shall it be done to him;

20Breach for breach, eye for eye, tooth for tooth: as he hath caused a blemish in a man, so shall it be done to him *again.*

21And he that killeth a beast, he shall restore it: and he that killeth a man, he shall be put to death.

22Ye shall have one manner of law, as well for the stranger, as for one of your own country: for I *am* the LORD your God.

23And Moses spake to the children of Israel, that they should bring forth him that had cursed out of the camp, and stone him with stones. And the children of Israel did as the LORD commanded Moses.

25 And the LORD spake unto Moses in mount Sinai, saying,

2Speak unto the children of Israel, and say unto them, When ye come into the land which I give you, then shall the land keep a sabbath unto the LORD.

3Six years thou shalt sow thy field, and six years thou shalt prune thy vineyard, and gather in the fruit thereof;

4But in the seventh year shall be a sabbath of

Amplified Bible

9And the bread shall be for Aaron and his sons, and they shall eat it in a sacred place, for it is for [Aaron] a most holy portion of the offerings to the Lord made by fire, a perpetual due [to the high priest].

10Now the son of an Israelite woman, whose father was an Egyptian, went out among the Israelites, and he and a man of Israel quarreled *and* strove together in the camp.

11The Israelite woman's son blasphemed the Name [of the Lord] and cursed. They brought him to Moses—his mother was Shelomith, the daughter of Dibri, of the tribe of Dan.

12And they put him in custody until the will of the Lord might be declared to them.

13And the Lord said to Moses,

14Bring him who has cursed out of the camp, and let all who heard him lay their hands upon his head; then let all the congregation stone him.

15And you shall say to the Israelites, Whoever curses his God shall bear his sin.

16And he who blasphemes the Name of the Lord, he shall surely be put to death, and all the congregation shall certainly stone him; the stranger as well as he who was born in the land shall be put to death when he blasphemes the Name [of the Lord].

17And he who kills any man shall surely be put to death.

18And he who kills a beast shall make it good, beast for beast.

19And if a man causes a blemish *or* disfigurement on his neighbor, it shall be done to him as he has done:

20Fracture for fracture, eye for eye, tooth for tooth; as he has caused a blemish *or* disfigurement on a man, so shall it be done to him.

21He who kills a beast shall replace it; he who kills a man shall be put to death.

22You shall have the same law for the sojourner among you as for one of your own nationality, for I am the Lord your God.

23Moses spoke to the Israelites, and they brought him who had cursed out of the camp and stoned him with stones. Thus the Israelites did as the Lord commanded Moses.

25 THE LORD said to Moses on Mount Sinai,

2Say to the Israelites, When you come into the land which I give you, then shall the land keep a sabbath to the Lord.

3For six years you shall sow your field, and for six years you shall prune your vineyard and gather in its fruits.

4But in the seventh year there shall be a sab-

King James Version

rest unto the land, a sabbath for the LORD: thou shalt neither sow thy field, nor prune thy vineyard.

5That which groweth of it own accord of thy harvest thou shalt not reap, neither gather the grapes of thy vine undressed: *for* it is a year of rest unto the land.

6And the sabbath of the land shall be meat for you; for thee, and for thy servant, and for thy maid, and for thy hired servant, and for thy stranger that sojourneth with thee,

7And for thy cattle, and for the beast that *are* in thy land, shall all the increase thereof be meat.

8 ¶ And thou shalt number seven sabbaths of years unto thee, seven times seven years; and the space of the seven sabbaths of years shall be unto thee forty and nine years.

9Then shalt thou cause the trumpet of the jubile to sound on the tenth *day* of the seventh month, in the day of atonement shall ye make the trumpet sound throughout all your land.

10And ye shall hallow the fiftieth year, and proclaim liberty throughout *all* the land unto all the inhabitants thereof: it shall be a jubile unto you; and ye shall return every man unto his possession, and ye shall return every man unto his family.

11A jubile shall that fiftieth year be unto you: ye shall not sow, neither reap that which groweth of itself in it, nor gather *the grapes* in it of thy vine undressed.

12For it *is* the jubile; it shall be holy unto you: ye shall eat the increase thereof out of the field.

13In the year of this jubile ye shall return every man unto his possession.

14And if thou sell ought unto thy neighbour, or buyest *ought* of thy neighbour's hand, ye shall not oppress one another:

15According to the number of years after the jubile thou shalt buy of thy neighbour, *and* according unto the number of years of the fruits he shall sell unto thee:

16According to the multitude of years thou shalt increase the price thereof, and according to the fewness of years thou shalt diminish the price of it: for *according to* the number *of the years* of the fruits doth he sell unto thee.

17Ye shall not therefore oppress one another; but thou shalt fear thy God: for I *am* the LORD your God.

18 ¶ Wherefore ye shall do my statutes, and keep my judgments, and do them; and ye shall dwell in the land in safety.

19And the land shall yield her fruit, and ye shall eat *your* fill, and dwell therein in safety.

20And if ye say, What shall we eat the

Amplified Bible

bath of solemn rest for the land, a sabbath to the Lord; you shall neither sow your field nor prune your vineyard.

5What grows of itself in your harvest you shall not reap and the grapes on your uncultivated vine you shall not gather, for it is a year of rest to the land.

6And the sabbath rest of the [untilled] land shall [in its increase] furnish food for you, for your male and female slaves, your hired servant, and the temporary resident who lives with you,

7For your domestic animals also and for the [wild] beasts in your land; all its yield shall be for food.

8And you shall number seven sabbaths *or* weeks of years for you, seven times seven years, so the total time of the seven weeks of years shall be forty-nine years.

9Then you shall sound abroad the loud trumpet on the tenth day of the seventh month [almost October]; on the Day of Atonement blow the trumpet in all your land.

10And you shall hallow the fiftieth year and proclaim liberty throughout all the land to all its inhabitants. It shall be a jubilee for you; and each of you shall return to his ancestral possession [which through poverty he was compelled to sell], and each of you shall return to his family [from whom he was separated in bond service].

11That fiftieth year shall be a jubilee for you; in it you shall not sow, or reap and store what grows of itself, or gather the grapes of the uncultivated vines.

12For it is a jubilee; it shall be holy to you; you shall eat the [sufficient] increase of it out of the field.

13In this Year of Jubilee each of you shall return to his ancestral property.

14And if you sell anything to your neighbor or buy from your neighbor, you shall not wrong one another.

15According to the number of years after the Jubilee, you shall buy from your neighbor. And he shall sell to you according to the number of years [remaining in which you may gather] the crops [before you must restore the property to him].

16If the years [to the next Jubilee] are many, you may increase the price, and if the years remaining are few, you shall diminish the price, for the number of the crops is what he is selling to you.

17You shall not oppress *and* wrong one another, but you shall [reverently] fear your God. For I am the Lord your God.

18Therefore you shall do *and* give effect to My statutes and keep My ordinances and perform them, and you will dwell in the land in safety.

19The land shall yield its fruit; you shall eat your fill and dwell there in safety.

20And if you say, What shall we eat in the sev-

King James Version

seventh year? behold, we shall not sow, nor gather in our increase:

²¹Then I will command my blessing upon you in the sixth year, and it shall bring forth fruit for three years.

²²And ye shall sow the eighth year, and eat *yet* of old fruit until the ninth year; until her fruits come in ye shall eat *of* the old *store.*

²³ ¶ The land shall not be sold for ever: for the land *is* mine; for ye *were* strangers and sojourners with me.

²⁴And in all the land of your possession ye shall grant a redemption for the land.

²⁵If thy brother be waxen poor, and hath sold away *some* of his possession, and *if any of* his kin come to redeem it, then shall he redeem that which his brother sold.

²⁶And if the man have none to redeem *it,* and himself be able to redeem it;

²⁷Then let him count the years of the sale thereof, and restore the overplus unto the man to whom he sold it; that he may return unto his possession.

²⁸But if he be not able to restore *it* to him, then that which is sold shall remain in the hand of him that hath bought it until the year of jubile: and in the jubile it shall go out, and he shall return unto his possession.

²⁹And if a man sell a dwelling house in a walled city, then he may redeem it within a whole year after it is sold; *within* a full year may he redeem it.

³⁰And if it be not redeemed within the space of a full year, then the house that *is* in the walled city shall be stablished for ever to him that bought it throughout his generations: it shall not go out in the jubile.

³¹But the houses of the villages which have no wall round about them shall be counted as the fields of the country: they may be redeemed, and they shall go out in the jubile.

³²Notwithstanding the cities of the Levites, *and* the houses of the cities of their possession, may the Levites redeem at any time.

³³And if a man purchase of the Levites, then the house that was sold, and the city of his possession, shall go out in the *year of* jubile: for the houses of the cities of the Levites *are* their possession among the children of Israel.

³⁴But the field of the suburbs of their cities may not be sold; for it *is* their perpetual possession.

³⁵ ¶ And if thy brother be waxen poor, and fallen in decay with thee; then thou shalt relieve

Amplified Bible

enth year if we are not to sow or gather in our increase?

²¹Then [this is My answer:] I will command My [special] blessings on you in the sixth year, so that it shall bring forth [sufficient] fruit for three years.

²²And you shall sow in the eighth year, but eat of the old store of produce; until the crops of the ninth year come in you shall eat of the old supply.

²³The land shall not be sold into perpetual ownership, for the land is Mine; you are [only] strangers and temporary residents with Me.

²⁴And in all the country you possess you shall grant a redemption for the land [in the Year of Jubilee].

²⁵If your brother has become poor and has sold some of his property, if any of his kin comes to redeem it, he shall [be allowed to] redeem what his brother has sold.

²⁶And if the man has no one to redeem his property, and he himself has become more prosperous *and* has enough to redeem it,

²⁷Then let him count the years since he sold it and restore the overpayment to the man to whom he sold it, and return to his ancestral possession.

²⁸But if he is unable to redeem it, it shall remain in the buyer's possession until the Year of Jubilee, when it shall be set free and he may return to it.

²⁹If a man sells a dwelling house in a fortified city, he may redeem it within a whole year after it is sold; for a full year he may have the right of redemption.

³⁰And if it is not redeemed within a full year, then the house that is in the fortified city shall be made sure, permanently *and* without limitations, for him who bought it, throughout his generations. It shall not go free in the Year of Jubilee.

³¹But the houses of the unwalled villages shall be counted with the fields of the country. They may be redeemed, and they shall go free in the Year of Jubilee.

³²Nevertheless, the cities of the Levites, the houses in the cities of their possession, the Levites may redeem at any time.

³³But if a house is not redeemed by a Levite, the sold house in the city they possess shall go free in the Year of Jubilee, for the houses in the Levite cities are their ancestral possession among the Israelites.

³⁴But the field of unenclosed *or* pasture lands of their cities may not be sold; it is their perpetual possession.

³⁵And if your [Israelite] brother has become poor and his hand wavers [from poverty, sickness, or age and he is unable to support himself], then you shall uphold (strengthen, relieve) him, [treating him with the courtesy and consideration that you would] a stranger or a

King James Version

him: *yea, though he be* a stranger, or a sojourner; that he may live with thee.

36Take thou no usury of him, or increase: but fear thy God; that thy brother may live with thee.

37Thou shalt not give him thy money upon usury, nor lend him thy victuals for increase.

38I *am* the LORD your God, which brought you forth out of the land of Egypt, to give you the land of Canaan, *and* to be your God.

39 ¶ And if thy brother *that dwelleth* by thee be waxen poor, and be sold unto thee; thou shalt not compel him to serve as a bondservant:

40But as a hired servant, *and* as a sojourner, he shall be with thee, *and* shall serve thee unto the year of jubile:

41And *then* shall he depart from thee, *both* he and his children with him, and shall return unto his own family, and unto the possession of his fathers shall he return.

42For they *are* my servants, which I brought forth out of the land of Egypt: they shall not be sold as bondmen.

43Thou shalt not rule over him with rigour; but shalt fear thy God.

44Both thy bondmen, and thy bondmaids, which thou shalt have, *shall be* of the heathen that *are* round about you; of them shall ye buy bondmen and bondmaids.

45Moreover of the children of the strangers that do sojourn among you, of them shall ye buy, and of their families that *are* with you, which they begat in your land: and they shall be your possession.

46And ye shall take them as an inheritance for your children after you, to inherit *them for* a possession; they shall be your bondmen for ever: but over your brethren the children of Israel, ye shall not rule one over another with rigour.

47 ¶ And if a sojourner or stranger wax rich by thee, and thy brother *that dwelleth* by him wax poor, and sell himself unto the stranger *or* sojourner by thee, or to the stock of the stranger's family:

48After *that* he is sold he may be redeemed again; one of his brethren may redeem him:

49Either his uncle, or his uncle's son, may redeem him, or *any* that is nigh of kin unto him of his family may redeem him; or if he be able, he may redeem himself.

50And he shall reckon with him that bought him from the year that he was sold to him unto the year of jubile: and the price of his sale shall be according unto the number of years, according to the time of a hired servant shall it be with him.

51If *there be* yet many years *behind,* according

Amplified Bible

temporary resident with you [without property], so that he may live [along] with you.

36Charge him no interest or [portion of] increase, but fear your God, so your brother may [continue to] live along with you.

37You shall not give him your money at interest nor lend him food at a profit.

38I am the Lord your God, Who brought you forth out of the land of Egypt to give you the land of Canaan and to be your God.

39And if your brother becomes poor beside you and sells himself to you, you shall not compel him to serve as a bondman (a slave not eligible for redemption),

40But as a hired servant and as a temporary resident he shall be with you; he shall serve you till the Year of Jubilee,

41And then he shall depart from you, he and his children with him, and shall go back to his own family and return to the possession of his fathers.

42For the Israelites are My servants; I brought them out of the land of Egypt; they shall not be sold as bondmen.

43You shall not rule over him with harshness (severity, oppression), but you shall [reverently] fear your God.

44As for your bondmen and your bondmaids whom you may have, they shall be from the nations round about you, of whom you may buy bondmen and bondmaids.

45Moreover, of the children of the strangers who sojourn among you, of them you may buy and of their families that are with you which they have begotten in your land, and they shall be your possession.

46And you shall make them an inheritance for your children after you, to hold for a possession; of them shall you take your bondmen always, but over your brethren the Israelites you shall not rule one over another with harshness (severity, oppression).

47And if a sojourner or stranger with you becomes rich and your [Israelite] brother becomes poor beside him and sells himself to the stranger or sojourner with you or to a member of the stranger's family,

48After he is sold he may be redeemed. One of his brethren may redeem him:

49Either his uncle or his uncle's son may redeem him, or a near kinsman may redeem him; or if he has enough *and* is able, he may redeem himself.

50And [the redeemer] shall reckon with the purchaser of the servant from the year when he sold himself to the purchaser to the Year of Jubilee, and the price of his release shall be adjusted according to the number of years. The time he was with his owner shall be counted as that of a hired servant.

51If there remain many years [before the Year

King James Version

unto them he shall give again the price of his redemption out of the money that he was bought for.

⁵²And if there remain but few years unto the year of jubile, then he shall count with him, *and* according unto his years shall he give *him* again the price of his redemption.

⁵³*And* as a yearly hired servant shall he be with him: *and the other* shall not rule with rigour over him in thy sight.

⁵⁴And if he be not redeemed in these *years,* then he shall go out in the year of jubile, *both* he, and his children with him.

⁵⁵For unto me the children of Israel *are* servants; they *are* my servants whom I brought forth out of the land of Egypt: I *am* the LORD your God.

26 Ye shall make you no idols nor graven image, neither rear you up a standing image, neither shall ye set up *any* image of stone in your land, to bow down unto it: for I *am* the LORD your God.

²Ye shall keep my sabbaths, and reverence my sanctuary: I *am* the LORD.

³ ¶ If ye walk in my statutes, and keep my commandments, and do them;

⁴Then I will give you rain in due season, and the land shall yield her increase, and the trees of the field shall yield their fruit.

⁵And your threshing shall reach unto the vintage, and the vintage shall reach unto the sowing time: and ye shall eat your bread to the full, and dwell in your land safely.

⁶And I will give peace in the land, and ye shall lie down, and none shall make *you* afraid: and I will rid evil beasts out of the land, neither shall the sword go through your land.

⁷And ye shall chase your enemies, and they shall fall before you by the sword.

⁸And five of you shall chase an hundred, and an hundred of you shall put ten thousand to flight: and your enemies shall fall before you by the sword.

⁹For I will have respect unto you, and make you fruitful, and multiply you, and establish my covenant with you.

¹⁰And ye shall eat old store, and bring forth the old because of the new.

¹¹And I will set my tabernacle amongst you: and my soul shall not abhor you.

¹²And I will walk among you, and will be your God, and ye shall be my people.

¹³I *am* the LORD your God, which brought you forth out of the land of Egypt, that ye should not be their bondmen; and I have broken the bands of your yoke, and made you go upright.

Amplified Bible

of Jubilee], in proportion to them he must refund [to the purchaser] for his release [the overpayment] for his acquisition.

⁵²And if little time remains until the Year of Jubilee, he shall count it over with him and he shall refund the proportionate amount for his release.

⁵³And as a servant hired year by year shall he deal with him; he shall not rule over him with harshness (severity, oppression) in your sight [make sure of that].

⁵⁴And if he is not redeemed during these years *and* by these means, then he shall go free in the Year of Jubilee, he and his children with him.

⁵⁵For to Me the Israelites are servants, My servants, whom I brought forth out of the land of Egypt. I am the Lord your God.

26 YOU SHALL make for yourselves no idols nor shall you erect a graven image, pillar, *or* obelisk, nor shall you place any figured stone in your land to which *or* on which to bow down; for I am the Lord your God.

²You shall keep My Sabbaths and reverence My sanctuary. I am the Lord.

³If you walk in My statutes and keep My commandments and do them,

⁴I will give you rain in due season, and the land shall yield her increase and the trees of the field yield their fruit.

⁵And your threshing [time] shall reach to the vintage and the vintage [time] shall reach to the sowing time, and you shall eat your bread to the full and dwell in your land securely.

⁶I will give peace in the land; you shall lie down and none shall fill you with dread *or* make you afraid; and I will clear ferocious (wild) beasts out of the land, and no sword shall go through your land.

⁷And you shall chase your enemies, and they shall fall before you by the sword.

⁸Five of you shall chase a hundred, and a hundred of you shall put ten thousand to flight; your enemies shall fall before you by the sword.

⁹For I will be leaning toward you with favor *and* regard for you, rendering you fruitful, multiplying you, and establishing *and* ratifying My covenant with you.

¹⁰And you shall eat the [abundant] old store of produce long kept, and clear out the old [to make room] for the new.

¹¹I will set My dwelling in *and* among you, and My soul shall not despise *or* reject *or* separate itself from you.

¹²And I will walk in *and* with *and* among you and will be your God, and you shall be My people.

¹³I am the Lord your God, Who brought you forth out of the land of Egypt, that you should no more be slaves; and I have broken the bars of your yoke and made you walk erect [as free men].

King James Version

14 ¶ But if ye will not hearken unto me, and will not do all these commandments;

15And if ye shall despise my statutes, or if your soul abhor my judgments, so that *ye* will not do all my commandments, *but* that ye break my covenant:

16I also will do this unto you; I will even appoint over you terror, consumption, and the burning ague, that shall consume the eyes, and cause sorrow of heart: and ye shall sow your seed in vain, for your enemies shall eat it.

17And I will set my face against you, and ye shall be slain before your enemies; they that hate you shall reign over you; and ye shall flee when none pursueth you.

18And if ye will not yet for *all* this hearken unto me, then I will punish you seven *times* more for your sins.

19And I will break the pride of your power; and I will make your heaven as iron, and your earth as brass:

20And your strength shall be spent in vain: for your land shall not yield her increase, neither shall the trees of the land yield their fruits.

21And if ye walk contrary unto me, and will not hearken unto me; I will bring seven *times* more plagues upon you according to your sins.

22I will also send wild beasts among you, which shall rob you of your children, and destroy your cattle, and make you few in number; and your *high* ways shall be desolate.

23And if ye will not be reformed by me by these *things*, but will walk contrary unto me;

24Then will I also walk contrary unto you, and will punish you yet seven *times* for your sins.

25And I will bring a sword upon you, that shall avenge the quarrel of *my* covenant: and when ye are gathered together within your cities, I will send the pestilence among you; and ye shall be delivered into the hand of the enemy.

26*And* when I have broken the staff of your bread, ten women shall bake your bread in one oven, and they shall deliver *you* your bread again by weight: and ye shall eat, and not be satisfied.

27And if ye will not for *all* this hearken unto me, but walk contrary unto me;

28Then I will walk contrary unto you also in fury; and I, even I, will chastise you seven *times* for your sins.

29And ye shall eat the flesh of your sons, and the flesh of your daughters shall ye eat.

Amplified Bible

14But if you will not hearken to Me and will not do all these commandments,

15And if you spurn *and* despise My statutes, and if your soul despises *and* rejects My ordinances, so that you will not do all My commandments, but break My covenant,

16I will do this: I will appoint over you [sudden] terror (trembling, trouble), even consumption and fever that consume *and* waste the eyes and make the [physical] life pine away. You shall sow your seed in vain, for your enemies shall eat it.

17I [the Lord] will set My face against you and [a]you shall be defeated *and* slain before your enemies; they who hate you shall rule over you; you shall flee when no one pursues you.

18And if in spite of all this you still will not listen *and* be obedient to Me, then I will chastise *and* discipline you seven times more for your sins.

19And I will break *and* humble your pride in your power, and I will make your heavens as iron [yielding no answer, no blessing, no rain] and your earth [as sterile] as brass.

20And your strength shall be spent in vain, for your land shall not yield its increase, neither shall the trees of the land yield their fruit.

21If you walk contrary to Me and will not heed Me, I will bring seven times more plagues upon you, according to your sins.

22I will loose the wild beasts of the field among you, which shall rob you of your children, destroy your livestock, and make you few so that your roads shall be deserted *and* desolate.

23If by these means you are not turned to Me but determine to walk contrary to Me,

24I also will walk contrary to you, and I will smite you seven times for your sins.

25And I will bring a sword upon you that shall execute the vengeance [for the breaking] of My covenant; and you shall be gathered together within your cities, and I will send the pestilence among you, and you shall be delivered into the hands of the enemy.

26When I break your staff of bread *and* cut off your supply of food, ten women shall bake your bread in one oven, and they shall ration your bread *and* deliver it again by weight; and you shall eat, and not be satisfied.

27And if in spite of all this you will not listen *and* give heed to Me but walk contrary to Me,

28Then I will walk contrary to you in wrath, and I also will chastise you seven times for your sins.

29You shall eat the flesh of your sons *and* of your daughters.

AMP notes: *a* This chapter abounds in prophecies of what God would do for, or against, His people if they did, or did not, meet His conditions. Each of these prophecies was literally fulfilled in the following centuries. The Scripture references indicate where these fulfillments are recorded; there are at least a dozen of them. Yet some people do not seem to have awakened to the fact that God **keeps His word,** whether for us or against us. It all depends on us.

King James Version

30And I will destroy your high places, and cut down your images, and cast your carcases upon the carcases of your idols, and my soul shall abhor you.

31And I will make your cities waste, and bring your sanctuaries unto desolation, and I will not smell the savour of your sweet odours.

32And I will bring the land into desolation: and your enemies which dwell therein shall be astonished at it.

33And I will scatter you among the heathen, and will draw out a sword after you: and your land shall be desolate, and your cities waste.

34Then shall the land enjoy her sabbaths, as long as it lieth desolate, and ye be in your enemies' land; even then shall the land rest, and enjoy her sabbaths.

35As long as it lieth desolate it shall rest; because it did not rest in your sabbaths, when ye dwelt upon it.

36And upon them that are left alive of you I will send a faintness into their hearts in the lands of their enemies; and the sound of a shaken leaf shall chase them; and they shall flee, as fleeing from a sword; and they shall fall when none pursueth.

37And they shall fall one upon another, as it were before a sword, when none pursueth: and ye shall have no power to stand before your enemies.

38And ye shall perish among the heathen, and the land of your enemies shall eat you up.

39And they that are left of you shall pine away in their iniquity in your enemies' lands; and also in the iniquities of their fathers shall they pine away with them.

40If they shall confess their iniquity, and the iniquity of their fathers, with their trespass which they trespassed against me, and that also they have walked contrary unto me;

41And that I also have walked contrary unto them, and have brought them into the land of their enemies; if then their uncircumcised hearts be humbled, and they then accept of the punishment of their iniquity:

42Then will I remember my covenant with Jacob, and also my covenant with Isaac, and also my covenant with Abraham will I remember; and I will remember the land.

43The land also shall be left of them, and shall enjoy her sabbaths, while she lieth desolate without them: and they shall accept of the punishment of their iniquity: because, even because they despised my judgments, and because their soul abhorred my statutes.

Amplified Bible

30And I will destroy your high places [devoted to idolatrous worship], and cut down your sun-images, and throw your dead bodies upon the [wrecked] bodies of your idols, and My soul shall abhor you [with deep and unutterable loathing].

31I will lay your cities waste, bring your sanctuaries to desolation, and I will not smell the fragrance of your sweet and soothing odors [of offerings made by fire].

32And I will bring the land into desolation, and your enemies who dwell in it shall be astonished at it.

33I will scatter you among the nations and draw out [your enemies'] sword after you; and your land shall be desolate and your cities a waste.

34Then shall the land [of Israel have the opportunity to] enjoy its sabbaths as long as it lies desolate and you are in your enemies' land; then shall the land rest, to enjoy and receive payments for its sabbaths [divinely ordained for it].

35As long as it lies desolate and waste, it shall have rest, the rest it did not have in your sabbaths when you dwelt upon it.

36As for those who are left of you, I will send dejection (lack of courage, a faintness) into their hearts in the lands of their enemies; the sound of a driven leaf shall put them to hasty and tumultuous flight, and they shall flee as if from the sword, and fall when no one pursues them.

37They shall stumble over one another as if to escape a sword when no one pursues them; and you shall have no power to stand before your enemies.

38You shall perish among the nations; the land of your enemies shall eat you up.

39And those of you who are left shall pine away in their iniquity in your enemies' lands; also in the iniquities of their fathers shall they pine away like them.

40But if they confess their own and their fathers' iniquity in their treachery which they committed against Me—and also that because they walked contrary to Me

41I also walked contrary to them and brought them into the land of their enemies—if then their uncircumcised hearts are humbled and they then accept the punishment for their iniquity,

42Then will I [earnestly] remember My covenant with Jacob, My covenant with Isaac, and My covenant with Abraham, and [earnestly] remember the land.

43But the land shall be left behind them and shall enjoy its sabbaths while it lies desolate without them; and they shall accept the punishment for their sins and make amends because they despised and rejected My ordinances and their soul scorned and rejected My statutes.

King James Version

⁴⁴And yet for all that, when they be in the land of their enemies, I will not cast them away, neither will I abhor them, to destroy them utterly, and to break my covenant with them: for I *am* the LORD their God.

⁴⁵But I will for their sakes remember the covenant of their ancestors, whom I brought forth out of the land of Egypt in the sight of the heathen, that *I* might be their God: I *am* the LORD.

⁴⁶These *are* the statutes and judgments and laws, which the LORD made between him and the children of Israel in mount Sinai by the hand of Moses.

27 And the LORD spake unto Moses, saying, ²Speak unto the children of Israel, and say unto them, When a man shall make a singular vow, the persons *shall be* for the LORD by thy estimation.

³And thy estimation shall be, of the male from twenty years old even unto sixty years old, even thy estimation shall be fifty shekels of silver, after the shekel of the sanctuary.

⁴And if it *be* a female, then thy estimation shall be thirty shekels.

⁵And if *it be* from five years old even unto twenty years old, then thy estimation shall be of the male twenty shekels, and for the female ten shekels.

⁶And if *it be* from a month old even unto five years old, then thy estimation shall be of the male five shekels of silver, and for the female thy estimation *shall be* three shekels of silver.

⁷And if *it be* from sixty years old and above; if *it be* a male, then thy estimation shall be fifteen shekels, and for the female ten shekels.

⁸But if he be poorer than thy estimation, then he shall present himself before the priest, and the priest shall value him; according to his ability that vowed shall the priest value him.

⁹ ¶ And if *it be* a beast, whereof *men* bring an offering unto the LORD, all that *any man* giveth of such unto the LORD shall be holy.

¹⁰He shall not alter it, nor change it, a good for a bad, or a bad for a good: and if he shall at all change beast for beast, then it and the exchange thereof shall be holy.

¹¹And if *it be* any unclean beast, of which they do not offer a sacrifice unto the LORD, then he shall present the beast before the priest:

¹²And the priest shall value it, whether it be good or bad: as thou valuest it, *who art* the priest, so shall it be.

Amplified Bible

⁴⁴And ^ayet for all that, when they are in the land of their enemies, I will not spurn *and* cast them away, neither will I despise *and* abhor them to destroy them utterly and to break My covenant with them, for I am the Lord their God.

⁴⁵But I will for their sake [earnestly] remember the covenant with their forefathers whom I brought forth out of the land of Egypt in the sight of the nations, that I might be their God. I am the Lord.

⁴⁶These are the statutes, ordinances, and laws which the Lord made between Him and the Israelites on Mount Sinai through Moses.

27 AND THE Lord said to Moses, ²Say to the Israelites, When a man shall make a special vow of persons to the Lord at your valuation,

³Then your valuation of a male from twenty years old to sixty years old shall be fifty shekels of silver, according to the shekel of the sanctuary.

⁴And if the person is a female, your valuation shall be thirty shekels.

⁵And if the person is from five years old up to twenty years old, then your valuation shall be for the male twenty shekels and for the female ten shekels.

⁶And if a child is from a month up to five years old, then your valuation shall be for the male five shekels of silver and for the female three shekels.

⁷And if the person is from sixty years old and above, if it be a male, then your valuation shall be fifteen shekels and for the female ten shekels.

⁸But if the man is too poor to pay your valuation, then he shall be set before the priest, and the priest shall value him; according to the ability of him who vowed shall the priest value him.

⁹If it is a beast of which men offer an offering to the Lord, all that any man gives of such to the Lord shall be holy.

¹⁰He shall not replace it or exchange it, a good for a bad, or a bad for a good; and if he makes any exchange of a beast for a beast, then both the original offering and that exchanged for it shall be holy.

¹¹If it is an unclean animal, such as is not offered as an offering to the Lord, he shall bring the animal before the priest,

¹²And the priest shall value it, whether it be good or bad; as you, the priest, value it, so shall it be.

AMP notes: ^a No greater evidence that God keeps His word is available than the fact of the existence today of the Jews as a nation. Scattered for twenty-five centuries throughout the world with powerful forces determined to wipe them out, yet they are restored to their homeland because, in spite of all their sins against Him, God refuses to break His covenant with their forefathers and with them. The presence of even a small number of Jews in the world, after all the centuries of diabolical effort to exterminate them, would alone be sufficient assurance that God will keep His promises, whether good or bad, to individuals or to nations.

King James Version

¹³But if he will at all redeem it, then he shall add a fifth *part* thereof unto thy estimation.

¹⁴ ¶ And when a man shall sanctify his house *to be* holy unto the LORD, then the priest shall estimate it, whether it be good or bad: as the priest shall estimate it, so shall it stand.

¹⁵And if he that sanctified *it* will redeem his house, then he shall add the fifth *part* of the money of thy estimation unto it, and it shall be his.

¹⁶And if a man shall sanctify unto the LORD *some part* of a field of his possession, then thy estimation shall be according to the seed thereof: a homer of barley seed *shall be valued* at fifty shekels of silver.

¹⁷If he sanctify his field from the year of jubile, according to thy estimation it shall stand.

¹⁸But if he sanctify his field after the jubile, then the priest shall reckon unto him the money according to the years that remain, *even* unto the year of the jubile, and it shall be abated from thy estimation.

¹⁹And if he that sanctified the field will in any wise redeem it, then he shall add the fifth *part* of the money of thy estimation unto it, and it shall be assured to him.

²⁰And if he will not redeem the field, or if he have sold the field to another man, it shall not be redeemed any more.

²¹But the field, when it goeth out in the jubile, shall be holy unto the LORD, as a field devoted; the possession thereof shall be the priest's.

²²And if *a man* sanctify unto the LORD a field which he hath bought, which *is* not of the fields of his possession;

²³Then the priest shall reckon unto him the worth of thy estimation, *even* unto the year of the jubile: and he shall give thine estimation in that day, *as* a holy *thing* unto the LORD.

²⁴In the year of the jubile the field shall return unto him of whom it was bought, *even* to him to whom the possession of the land *did belong.*

²⁵And all thy estimations shall be according to the shekel of the sanctuary: twenty gerahs shall be the shekel.

²⁶ ¶ Only the firstling of the beasts, which should be the LORD's firstling, no man shall sanctify it; whether *it be* ox, or sheep: it *is* the LORD's.

²⁷And if *it be* of an unclean beast, then he shall redeem *it* according to thine estimation, and shall add a fifth *part* of it thereto: or if it be not redeemed, then it shall be sold according to thy estimation.

²⁸Notwithstanding no devoted thing, that a man shall devote unto the LORD of all that he hath, *both* of man and beast, and of the field of his possession, shall be sold or redeemed: every devoted thing *is* most holy unto the LORD.

Amplified Bible

¹³But if he wishes to redeem it, he shall add a fifth to your valuation.

¹⁴If a man dedicates his house to be sacred to the Lord, the priest shall appraise it, whether it be good or bad; as the priest appraises it, so shall it stand.

¹⁵If he who dedicates his house wants to redeem it, he shall add a fifth of your valuation to it, and it shall be his.

¹⁶And if a man shall dedicate to the Lord some part of a field of his possession, then your valuation shall be according to the seed [required] for it; [a sowing of] a homer of barley shall be valued at fifty shekels of silver.

¹⁷If he dedicates his field during the Year of Jubilee, it shall stand according to your full valuation.

¹⁸But if he dedicates his field after the Jubilee, then the priest shall count the money value in proportion to the years that remain until the Year of Jubilee, and it shall be deducted from your valuation.

¹⁹If he who dedicates the field wishes to redeem it, then he shall add a fifth of the money of your appraisal to it, and it shall remain his.

²⁰But if he does not want to redeem the field, or if he has sold it to another man, it shall not be redeemed any more.

²¹But the field, when it is released in the Jubilee, shall be holy to the Lord, as a field devoted [to God or destruction]; the priest shall have possession of it.

²²And if a man dedicates to the Lord a field he has bought, which is not of the fields of his [ancestral] possession,

²³The priest shall compute the amount of your valuation for it up to the Year of Jubilee; the man shall give that amount on that day as a holy thing to the Lord.

²⁴In the Year of Jubilee the field shall return to him of whom it was bought, to him to whom the land belonged [as his ancestral inheritance].

²⁵And all your valuations shall be according to the sanctuary shekel; twenty gerahs shall make a shekel.

²⁶But the firstling of the animals, since a firstling belongs to the Lord, no man may dedicate, whether it be ox or sheep. It is the Lord's [already].

²⁷If it be of an unclean animal, the owner may redeem it according to your valuation, and shall add a fifth to it; or if it is not redeemed, then it shall be sold according to your valuation.

²⁸But nothing that a man shall devote to the Lord of all that he has, whether of man or beast or of the field of his possession, shall be sold or redeemed; every devoted thing is most holy to the Lord.

King James Version

²⁹None devoted, which shall be devoted of men, shall be redeemed; *but* shall surely be put to death.

³⁰ ¶ And all the tithe of the land, *whether* of the seed of the land, *or* of the fruit of the tree, *is* the LORD'S: *it is* holy unto the LORD.⋆

³¹And if a man will at all redeem *ought* of his tithes, he shall add thereto the fifth *part* thereof.

³²And *concerning* the tithe of the herd, or of the flock, *even of* whatsoever passeth under the rod, the tenth shall be holy unto the LORD.

³³He shall not search whether it be good or bad, neither shall he change it: and if he change it at all, then both it and the change thereof shall be holy; it shall not be redeemed.

³⁴These *are* the commandments, which the LORD commanded Moses for the children of Israel in mount Sinai.

⋆30: Set apart and sanctified to God.

Amplified Bible

²⁹No one doomed to death [under the claim of divine justice], who is to be completely destroyed from among men, shall be ransomed [from suffering the death penalty]; he shall surely be put to death.

³⁰And all the tithe of the land, whether of the seed of the land or of the fruit of the tree, is the Lord's; it is holy to the Lord.

³¹And if a man wants to redeem any of his tithe, he shall add a fifth to it.

³²And all the tithe of the herd or of the flock, whatever passes under the herdsman's staff [by means of which each tenth animal as it passes through a small door is selected and marked], the tenth shall be holy to the Lord.

³³The man shall not examine whether the animal is good or bad nor shall he exchange it. If he does exchange it, then both it and the animal substituted for it shall be holy; it shall not be redeemed.

³⁴These are the commandments which the Lord commanded Moses on Mount Sinai for the Israelites.

King James Version	Amplified Bible

THE FOURTH BOOK OF MOSES, CALLED
Numbers

1 And the LORD spake unto Moses in the wilderness of Sinai, in the tabernacle of the congregation, on the first *day* of the second month, in the second year after they were come out of the land of Egypt, saying,

2 Take ye the sum of all the congregation of the children of Israel, after their families, by the house of their fathers, with the number of *their* names, every male by their polls;

3 From twenty years old and upward, all that *are able to* go forth *to* war in Israel: thou and Aaron shall number them by their armies.

4 And with you there shall be a man of every tribe; every one head of the house of his fathers.

5 ¶ And these *are* the names of the men that shall stand with you: of *the tribe of* Reuben; Elizur the son of Shedeur.

6 Of Simeon; Shelumiel the son of Zurishaddai.

7 Of Judah; Nahshon the son of Amminadab.

8 Of Issachar; Nethaneel the son of Zuar.

9 Of Zebulun; Eliab the son of Helon.

10 Of the children of Joseph: of Ephraim; Elishama the son of Ammihud: of Manasseh; Gamaliel the son of Pedahzur.

11 Of Benjamin; Abidan the son of Gideoni.

12 Of Dan; Ahiezer the son of Ammishaddai.

13 Of Asher; Pagiel the son of Ocran.

14 Of Gad; Eliasaph the son of Deuel.

15 Of Naphtali; Ahira the son of Enan.

16 These *were* the renowned of the congregation, princes of the tribes of their fathers, heads of thousands in Israel.

17 And Moses and Aaron took these men which are expressed by *their* names:

18 And they assembled all the congregation together on the first *day* of the second month, and they declared their pedigrees after their families, by the house of their fathers, according to the number of the names, from twenty years old and upward, by their polls.

19 As the LORD commanded Moses, so he numbered them in the wilderness of Sinai.

20 ¶ And the children of Reuben, Israel's eldest son, *by* their generations, after their families, by the house of their fathers, according to the number of the names, by their polls, every male from twenty years old and upward, all that *were able to* go forth *to* war;

21 Those that were numbered of them, *even* of the tribe of Reuben, *were* forty and six thousand and five hundred.

THE FOURTH BOOK OF MOSES, CALLED
Numbers

1 THE LORD spoke to Moses in the Wilderness of Sinai in the Tent of Meeting on the first day of the second month in the second year after they came out of the land of Egypt, saying,

2 Take a census of all the males of the congregation of the Israelites by families, by their fathers' houses, according to the number of names, head by head.

3 From twenty years old and upward, all in Israel who are able to go forth to war you and Aaron shall number, company by company.

4 And with you there shall be a man [to assist you] from each tribe, each being the head of his father's house.

5 And these are the names of the men who shall attend you: Of Reuben, Elizur son of Shedeur;

6 Of Simeon, Shelumiel son of Zurishaddai;

7 Of Judah, Nahshon son of Amminadab;

8 Of Issachar, Nethanel son of Zuar;

9 Of Zebulun, Eliab son of Helon;

10 Of the sons of Joseph: of Ephraim, Elishama son of Ammihud; of Manasseh, Gamaliel son of Pedahzur;

11 Of Benjamin, Abidan son of Gideoni;

12 Of Dan, Ahiezer son of Ammishaddai;

13 Of Asher, Pagiel son of Ochran;

14 Of Gad, Eliasaph son of Deuel;

15 Of Naphtali, Ahira son of Enan.

16 These were those chosen from the congregation, the leaders of their ancestral tribes, heads of thousands [the highest class of officers] in Israel.

17 And Moses and Aaron took these men who have been named,

18 And assembled all the congregation on the first day of the second month, and they declared their ancestry after their families, by their fathers' houses, according to the number of names from twenty years old and upward, head by head,

19 As the Lord commanded Moses. So he numbered them in the Wilderness of Sinai.

20 The sons of Reuben, Israel's firstborn, their generations, by their families, by their fathers' houses, according to the number of names, head by head, every male from twenty years old and upward, all who were able to go to war:

21 Those of the tribe of Reuben numbered 46,500.

King James Version

22Of the children of Simeon, *by* their generations, after their families, by the house of their fathers, those that were numbered of them, according to the number of the names, by their polls, every male from twenty years old and upward, all that *were able to* go forth *to* war;

23Those that were numbered of them, *even* of the tribe of Simeon, *were* fifty and nine thousand and three hundred.

24Of the children of Gad, *by* their generations, after their families, by the house of their fathers, according to the number of the names, from twenty years old and upward, all that *were able to* go forth *to* war;

25Those that were numbered of them, *even* of the tribe of Gad, *were* forty and five thousand six hundred and fifty.

26Of the children of Judah, *by* their generations, after their families, by the house of their fathers, according to the number of the names, from twenty years old and upward, all that *were able to* go forth *to* war;

27Those that were numbered of them, *even* of the tribe of Judah, *were* threescore and fourteen thousand and six hundred.

28Of the children of Issachar, *by* their generations, after their families, by the house of their fathers, according to the number of the names, from twenty years old and upward, all that *were able to* go forth *to* war;

29Those that were numbered of them, *even* of the tribe of Issachar, *were* fifty and four thousand and four hundred.

30Of the children of Zebulun, *by* their generations, after their families, by the house of their fathers, according to the number of the names, from twenty years old and upward, all that *were able to* go forth *to* war;

31Those that were numbered of them, *even* of the tribe of Zebulun, *were* fifty and seven thousand and four hundred.

32Of the children of Joseph, *namely,* of the children of Ephraim, *by* their generations, after their families, by the house of their fathers, according to the number of the names, from twenty years old and upward, all that *were able to* go forth *to* war;

33Those that were numbered of them, *even* of the tribe of Ephraim, *were* forty thousand and five hundred.

34Of the children of Manasseh, *by* their generations, after their families, by the house of their fathers, according to the number of the names, from twenty years old and upward, all that *were able to* go forth *to* war;

35Those that were numbered of them, *even* of the tribe of Manasseh, *were* thirty and two thousand and two hundred.

36Of the children of Benjamin, *by* their generations, after their families, by the house of their

Amplified Bible

22Of the sons of Simeon, their generations, by their families, by their fathers' houses, those numbered of them according to the number of names, head by head, every male from twenty years old and upward, all who were able to go to war:

23Those of the tribe of Simeon numbered 59,300.

24Of the sons of Gad, their generations, by their families, by their fathers' houses, according to the number of names, from twenty years old and upward, all who were able to go to war:

25Those of the tribe of Gad numbered 45,650.

26Of the sons of Judah, their generations, by their families, by their fathers' houses, according to the number of names, from twenty years old and upward, all able to go to war:

27Those of the tribe of Judah numbered 74,600.

28Of the sons of Issachar, their generations, by their families, by their fathers' houses, according to the number of names, from twenty years old and upward, all able to go to war:

29Those of the tribe of Issachar numbered 54,400.

30Of the sons of Zebulun, their generations, by their families, by their fathers' houses, according to the number of names, from twenty years old and upward, all able to go to war:

31Those of the tribe of Zebulun numbered 57,400.

32Of the sons of Joseph: the sons of Ephraim, their generations, by their families, by their fathers' houses, according to the number of names, from twenty years old and upward, all able to go to war:

33Those of the tribe of Ephraim numbered 40,500.

34Of the sons of Manasseh, their generations, by their families, by their fathers' houses, according to the number of names, from twenty years old and upward, all able to go to war:

35Those of the tribe of Manasseh numbered 32,200.

36Of the sons of Benjamin, their generations, by their families, by their fathers' houses, ac-

King James Version

fathers, according to the number of the names, from twenty years old and upward, all that *were able to* go forth *to* war;

³⁷Those that were numbered of them, *even* of the tribe of Benjamin, *were* thirty and five thousand and four hundred.

³⁸Of the children of Dan, *by* their generations, after their families, by the house of their fathers, according to the number of the names, from twenty years old and upward, all that *were able to* go forth *to* war;

³⁹Those that were numbered of them, *even* of the tribe of Dan, *were* threescore and two thousand and seven hundred.

⁴⁰Of the children of Asher, *by* their generations, after their families, by the house of their fathers, according to the number of the names, from twenty years old and upward, all that *were able to* go forth *to* war;

⁴¹Those that were numbered of them, *even* of the tribe of Asher, *were* forty and one thousand and five hundred.

⁴²*Of* the children of Naphtali, *throughout* their generations, after their families, by the house of their fathers, according to the number of the names, from twenty years old and upward, all that *were able to* go forth *to* war;

⁴³Those that were numbered of them, *even* of the tribe of Naphtali, *were* fifty and three thousand and four hundred.

⁴⁴These *are* those that were numbered, which Moses and Aaron numbered, and the princes of Israel, *being* twelve men: each one was for the house of his fathers.

⁴⁵So were all those that were numbered of the children of Israel, by the house of their fathers, from twenty years old and upward, all that *were able to* go forth *to* war in Israel;

⁴⁶Even all they that were numbered were six hundred thousand and three thousand and five hundred and fifty.

⁴⁷ ¶ But the Levites after the tribe of their fathers were not numbered among them.

⁴⁸For the LORD had spoken unto Moses, saying,

⁴⁹Only thou shalt not number the tribe of Levi, neither take the sum of them among the children of Israel:

⁵⁰But thou shalt appoint the Levites over the tabernacle of Testimony, and over all the vessels thereof, and over all *things* that *belong* to it: they shall bear the tabernacle, and all the vessels thereof; and they shall minister unto it, and shall encamp round about the tabernacle.

⁵¹And when the tabernacle setteth forward, the Levites shall take it down: and when the tabernacle is to be pitched, the Levites shall set it up: and the stranger that cometh nigh shall be put to death.

⁵²And the children of Israel shall pitch their

Amplified Bible

cording to the number of names, from twenty years old and upward, all able to go to war:

³⁷Those of the tribe of Benjamin numbered 35,400.

³⁸Of the sons of Dan, their generations, by their families, by their fathers' houses, according to the number of names, from twenty years old and upward, all able to go to war:

³⁹Those of the tribe of Dan numbered 62,700.

⁴⁰Of the sons of Asher, their generations, by their families, by their fathers' houses, according to the number of names, from twenty years old and upward, all able to go to war:

⁴¹Those of the tribe of Asher numbered 41,500.

⁴²Of the sons of Naphtali, their generations, by their families, by their fathers' houses, according to the number of names, from twenty years old and upward, all able to go to war:

⁴³Those of the tribe of Naphtali numbered 53,400.

⁴⁴These were numbered by Moses and Aaron, and the leaders of Israel, twelve men, each representing his father's house.

⁴⁵So all those numbered of the Israelites, by their fathers' houses, from twenty years old and upward, able to go to war in Israel,

⁴⁶All who were numbered were 603,550.

⁴⁷But the Levites by their fathers' tribe were not numbered with them.

⁴⁸For the Lord had said to Moses,

⁴⁹Only the tribe of Levi you shall not number in the census of the Israelites.

⁵⁰But appoint the Levites over the tabernacle of the Testimony, and over all its vessels and furnishings and all things that belong to it. They shall carry the tabernacle [when journeying] and all its furnishings, and they shall minister to it and encamp around it.

⁵¹When the tabernacle is to go forward, the Levites shall take it down, and when the tabernacle is to be pitched, the Levites shall set it up. And the excluded [any not of the tribe of Levi] who approach the tabernacle shall be put to death.

⁵²The Israelites shall pitch their tents by

King James Version

tents, every man by his own camp, and every man by his own standard, throughout their hosts.

53But the Levites shall pitch round about the tabernacle of Testimony, that there be no wrath upon the congregation of the children of Israel: and the Levites shall keep the charge of the tabernacle of Testimony.

54And the children of Israel did according to all that the LORD commanded Moses, so did they.

2 And the LORD spake unto Moses and unto Aaron, saying,

2Every man of the children of Israel shall pitch by his own standard, with the ensign of their father's house: far off about the tabernacle of the congregation shall they pitch.

3 ¶ And on the east side toward the rising of the sun *shall* they of the standard of the camp of Judah pitch throughout their armies: and Nahshon the son of Amminadab *shall be* captain of the children of Judah.

4And his host, and those that were numbered of them, *were* threescore and fourteen thousand and six hundred.

5And those that do pitch next unto him *shall be* the tribe of Issachar: and Nethaneel the son of Zuar *shall be* captain of the children of Issachar.

6And his host, and those that were numbered thereof, *were* fifty and four thousand and four hundred.

7*Then* the tribe of Zebulun: and Eliab the son of Helon *shall be* captain of the children of Zebulun.

8And his host, and those that were numbered thereof, *were* fifty and seven thousand and four hundred.

9All that were numbered in the camp of Judah *were* an hundred thousand and fourscore thousand and six thousand and four hundred, throughout their armies. *These* shall first set forth.

10 ¶ On the south side *shall be* the standard of the camp of Reuben according to their armies: and the captain of the children of Reuben *shall be* Elizur the son of Shedeur.

11And his host, and those that were numbered thereof, *were* forty and six thousand and five hundred.

12And those which pitch by him *shall be* the tribe of Simeon: and the captain of the children of Simeon *shall be* Shelumiel the son of Zurishaddai.

13And his host, and those that were numbered of them, *were* fifty and nine thousand and three hundred.

14Then the tribe of Gad: and the captain of the sons of Gad *shall be* Eliasaph the son of Reuel.

Amplified Bible

their companies, every man by his own camp and every man by his own [tribal] standard.

53But the Levites shall encamp around the tabernacle of the Testimony, that there may be no wrath upon the congregation of the Israelites; and the Levites shall keep charge of the tabernacle of the Testimony.

54Thus did the Israelites; according to all that the Lord commanded Moses, so they did.

2 THE LORD said to Moses and Aaron, 2The Israelites shall encamp, each by his own [tribal] standard *or* banner with the ensign of his father's house, opposite the Tent of Meeting *and* facing it on every side.

3On the east side toward the sunrise shall they of the standard of the camp of Judah encamp by their companies; Nahshon son of Amminadab being the leader of the sons of Judah.

4Judah's host as numbered totaled 74,600.

5Next to Judah the tribe of Issachar shall encamp, Nethanel son of Zuar being the leader of the sons of Issachar.

6Issachar's host as numbered totaled 54,400.

7Then the tribe of Zebulun, Eliab son of Helon being the leader of the sons of Zebulun.

8Zebulun's host as numbered totaled 57,400.

9All these [three tribes] numbered in the camp of Judah totaled 186,400. They shall set forth first [on the march].

10On the south side shall be the standard of the camp of Reuben by their companies, the leader of the sons of Reuben being Elizur son of Shedeur.

11Reuben's host as numbered totaled 46,500.

12Those who encamp next to Reuben shall be the tribe of Simeon, the leader of the sons of Simeon being Shelumiel son of Zurishaddai.

13Simeon's host as numbered totaled 59,300.

14Then the tribe of Gad, the leader of the sons of Gad being Eliasaph son of Reuel (Deuel).

King James Version

15And his host, and those that were numbered of them, *were* forty and five thousand and six hundred and fifty.

16All that were numbered in the camp of Reuben *were* an hundred thousand and fifty and one thousand and four hundred and fifty, throughout their armies. And they shall set forth in the second rank.

17 ¶ Then the tabernacle of the congregation shall set forward *with* the camp of the Levites in the midst of the camp: as they encamp, so shall they set forward, every man in his place by their standards.

18 ¶ On the west side *shall be* the standard of the camp of Ephraim according to their armies: and the captain of the sons of Ephraim *shall be* Elishama the son of Ammihud.

19And his host, and those that were numbered of them, *were* forty thousand and five hundred.

20And by him *shall be* the tribe of Manasseh: and the captain of the children of Manasseh *shall be* Gamaliel the son of Pedahzur.

21And his host, and those that were numbered of them, *were* thirty and two thousand and two hundred.

22Then the tribe of Benjamin: and the captain of the sons of Benjamin *shall be* Abidan the son of Gideoni.

23And his host, and those that were numbered of them, *were* thirty and five thousand and four hundred.

24All that were numbered of the camp of Ephraim *were* an hundred thousand and eight thousand and an hundred, throughout their armies. And they shall go forward in the third rank.

25 ¶ The standard of the camp of Dan *shall be* on the north side by their armies: and the captain of the children of Dan *shall be* Ahiezer the son of Ammishaddai.

26And his host, and those that were numbered of them, *were* threescore and two thousand and seven hundred.

27And those that encamp by him *shall be* the tribe of Asher: and the captain of the children of Asher *shall be* Pagiel the son of Ocran.

28And his host, and those that were numbered of them, *were* forty and one thousand and five hundred.

29Then the tribe of Naphtali: and the captain of the children of Naphtali *shall be* Ahira the son of Enan.

30And his host, and those that were numbered of them, *were* fifty and three thousand and four hundred.

31All they that were numbered in the camp of Dan *were* an hundred thousand and fifty and seven thousand and six hundred. They shall go hindmost with their standards.

32 ¶ These *are* those which were numbered of the children of Israel by the house of their fa-

Amplified Bible

15Gad's host as numbered totaled 45,650.

16The whole number in [the three tribes of] the camp of Reuben was 151,450. They shall take second place [on the march].

17Then the Tent of Meeting shall set out, with the camp of the Levites in the midst of the camps; as they encamp so shall they set forward, every man in his place, standard after standard.

18On the west side shall be the standard of the camp of Ephraim by their companies, the leader of the sons of Ephraim being Elishama son of Ammihud.

19Ephraim's host as numbered totaled 40,500.

20Beside Ephraim shall be the tribe of Manasseh, the leader of the sons of Manasseh being Gamaliel son of Pedahzur.

21Manasseh's host as numbered totaled 32,200.

22Then the tribe of Benjamin, the leader of the sons of Benjamin being Abidan son of Gideoni.

23Benjamin's host as numbered totaled 35,400.

24The whole number [of the three tribes] in the camp of Ephraim totaled 108,100. They shall go forward in third place.

25The standard of the camp of Dan shall be on the north side [of the tabernacle] by their companies, the leader of the sons of Dan being Ahiezer son of Ammishaddai.

26Dan's host as numbered totaled 62,700.

27Encamped next to Dan shall be the tribe of Asher, the leader of the sons of Asher being Pagiel son of Ochran.

28Asher's host as numbered totaled 41,500.

29Then the tribe of Naphtali, the leader of the sons of Naphtali being Ahira son of Enan.

30Naphtali's host as numbered totaled 53,400.

31The whole number [of the three tribes] in the camp of Dan totaled 157,600. They shall set out last, standard after standard.

32These are the Israelites as numbered by

King James Version

thers: all those that were numbered of the camps throughout their hosts *were* six hundred thousand and three thousand and five hundred and fifty.

³³But the Levites were not numbered among the children of Israel; as the LORD commanded Moses.

³⁴And the children of Israel did according to all that the LORD commanded Moses: so they pitched by their standards, and so they set forward, every one after their families, according to the house of their fathers.

3 These also *are* the generations of Aaron and Moses in the day that the LORD spake with Moses in mount Sinai.

²And these *are* the names of the sons of Aaron; Nadab the firstborn, and Abihu, Eleazar, and Ithamar.

³These *are* the names of the sons of Aaron, the priests which were anointed, whom he consecrated to minister in the priest's office.

⁴And Nadab and Abihu died before the LORD, when they offered strange fire before the LORD, in the wilderness of Sinai, and they had no children: and Eleazar and Ithamar ministered in the priest's office in the sight of Aaron their father.

⁵ ¶ And the LORD spake unto Moses, saying,

⁶Bring the tribe of Levi near, and present them before Aaron the priest, that they may minister unto him.

⁷And they shall keep his charge, and the charge of the whole congregation before the tabernacle of the congregation, to do the service of the tabernacle.

⁸And they shall keep all the instruments of the tabernacle of the congregation, and the charge of the children of Israel, to do the service of the tabernacle.

⁹And thou shalt give the Levites unto Aaron and to his sons: they *are* wholly given unto him out of the children of Israel.

¹⁰And thou shalt appoint Aaron and his sons, and they shall wait on their priest's office: and the stranger that cometh nigh shall be put to death.

¹¹And the LORD spake unto Moses, saying,

¹²And I, behold, I have taken the Levites from among the children of Israel instead of all the firstborn that openeth the matrix among the children of Israel: therefore the Levites shall be mine;

¹³Because all the firstborn *are* mine; *for* on the day that I smote all the firstborn in the land of Egypt I hallowed unto me all the firstborn in Israel, both man and beast: mine they shall be: I *am* the LORD.

Amplified Bible

their fathers' houses. All in the camps who were numbered by their companies were 603,550.

³³But the Levites were not numbered with the Israelites, for so the Lord commanded Moses.

³⁴Thus the Israelites did according to all the Lord commanded Moses; so they encamped by their standards, and so they set forward, everyone with his [tribal] families, according to his father's house.

3 NOW THESE are the generations of Aaron and Moses when the Lord spoke with Moses on Mount Sinai.

²These are the names of the sons of Aaron: Nadab the firstborn, Abihu, Eleazar, and Ithamar.

³These are the names of the sons of Aaron, the priests who were anointed, whom Aaron consecrated *and* ordained to minister in the priest's office.

⁴But Nadab and Abihu died before the Lord when they offered strange fire before the Lord in the Wilderness of Sinai; and they had no children. So Eleazar and Ithamar ministered in the priest's office in the presence *and* under the supervision of Aaron their father.

⁵And the Lord said to Moses,

⁶Bring the tribe of Levi near and set them before Aaron the priest, that they may minister to him.

⁷And they shall carry out his instructions and the duties connected with the whole assembly before the Tent of Meeting, doing the service of the tabernacle.

⁸And they shall keep all the instruments *and* furnishings of the Tent of Meeting and take charge of [attending] the Israelites, to serve in the tabernacle.

⁹And you shall give the Levites [as servants and helpers] to Aaron and his sons; they are wholly given to him from among the Israelites.

¹⁰And you shall appoint Aaron and his sons, and they shall observe *and* attend to their priest's office; but the excluded [anyone daring to assume priestly duties or privileges who is not of the house of Aaron and called of God] who comes near [the holy things] shall be put to death.

¹¹And the Lord said to Moses,

¹²Behold, I have taken the Levites from among the Israelites instead of every firstborn who opens the womb among the Israelites; and the Levites shall be Mine,

¹³For all the firstborn are Mine. On the day that I slew all the firstborn in the land of Egypt, I consecrated for Myself all the firstborn in Israel, both man and beast; Mine they shall be. I am the Lord.

King James Version

14 ¶ And the LORD spake unto Moses in the wilderness of Sinai, saying,

15 Number the children of Levi after the house of their fathers, by their families: every male from a month old and upward shalt thou number them.

16 And Moses numbered them according to the word of the LORD, as he was commanded.

17 And these were the sons of Levi by their names; Gershon, and Kohath, and Merari.

18 And these *are* the names of the sons of Gershon by their families; Libni, and Shimei.

19 And the sons of Kohath by their families; Amram, and Izehar, Hebron, and Uzziel.

20 And the sons of Merari by their families; Mahli, and Mushi. These *are* the families of the Levites according to the house of their fathers.

21 ¶ Of Gershon *was* the family of the Libnites, and the family of the Shimites: these *are* the families of the Gershonites.

22 Those that were numbered of them, according to the number of all the males, from a month old and upward, *even* those that were numbered of them *were* seven thousand and five hundred.

23 The families of the Gershonites shall pitch behind the tabernacle westward.

24 And the chief of the house of the father of the Gershonites *shall be* Eliasaph the son of Lael.

25 And the charge of the sons of Gershon in the tabernacle of the congregation *shall be* the tabernacle, and the tent, the covering thereof, and the hanging for the door of the tabernacle of the congregation,

26 And the hangings of the court, and the curtain for the door of the court, which *is* by the tabernacle, and by the altar round about, and the cords of it for all the service thereof.

27 ¶ And of Kohath *was* the family of the Amramites, and the family of the Izeharites, and the family of the Hebronites, and the family of the Uzzielites: these *are* the families of the Kohathites.

28 In the number of all the males, from a month old and upward, *were* eight thousand and six hundred, keeping the charge of the sanctuary.

29 The families of the sons of Kohath shall pitch on the side of the tabernacle southward.

30 And the chief of the house of the father of the families of the Kohathites *shall be* Elizaphan the son of Uzziel.

31 And their charge *shall be* the ark, and the table, and the candlestick, and the altars, and the vessels of the sanctuary wherewith they minister, and the hanging, and all the service thereof.

32 And Eleazar the son of Aaron the priest *shall be* chief over the chief of the Levites, *and* have the oversight of them that keep the charge of the sanctuary.

Amplified Bible

14 And the Lord said to Moses in the Wilderness of Sinai,

15 Number the sons of Levi by their fathers' houses and by families. Every male from a month old and upward you shall number.

16 So Moses numbered them as he was commanded by the word of the Lord.

17 These were the sons of Levi by their names: Gershon, Kohath, and Merari.

18 And these are the names of the sons of Gershon by their families: Libni and Shimei.

19 The sons of Kohath by their families: Amram, Izhar, Hebron, and Uzziel.

20 The sons of Merari by their families: Mahli and Mushi. These are the families of the Levites by their fathers' houses.

21 Of Gershon were the families of the Libnites and of the Shimeites. These are the families of the Gershonites.

22 The males who were numbered of them from a month old and upward totaled 7,500.

23 The families of the Gershonites were to encamp behind the tabernacle on the west,

24 The leader of the fathers' houses of the Gershonites being Eliasaph son of Lael.

25 And the responsibility of the sons of Gershon in the Tent of Meeting was to be the tabernacle, the tent, its covering, and the hangings for the door of the Tent of Meeting,

26 And the hangings of the court, the curtain for the door of the court which is around the tabernacle and the altar, its cords, and all the service pertaining to them.

27 Of Kohath were the families of the Amramites, the Izharites, the Hebronites, and the Uzzielites; these are the families of the Kohathites.

28 The number of all the males from a month old and upward totaled 8,600, attending to the duties of the sanctuary.

29 The families of the sons of Kohath were to encamp on the south side of the tabernacle,

30 The chief of the fathers' houses of the families of the Kohathites being Elizaphan son of Uzziel.

31 Their charge was to be the ark, the table, the lampstand, the altars, and the utensils of the sanctuary with which the priests minister, and the screen, and all the service having to do with these.

32 Eleazar son of Aaron the priest was to be chief over the leaders of the Levites, and have the oversight of those who had charge of the sanctuary.

King James Version

33 ¶ Of Merari *was* the family of the Mahlites, and the family of the Mushites: these *are* the families of Merari.

34 And those that were numbered of them, according to the number of all the males, from a month old and upward, *were* six thousand and two hundred.

35 And the chief of the house of the father of the families of Merari *was* Zuriel the son of Abihail: *these* shall pitch on the side of the tabernacle northwards.

36 And under the custody and charge of the sons of Merari *shall be* the boards of the tabernacle, and the bars thereof, and the pillars thereof, and the sockets thereof, and all the vessels thereof, and all that serveth thereto,

37 And the pillars of the court round about, and their sockets, and their pins, and their cords.

38 ¶ But those that encamp before the tabernacle toward the east, *even* before the tabernacle of the congregation eastward, *shall be* Moses, and Aaron and his sons, keeping the charge of the sanctuary for the charge of the children of Israel; and the stranger that cometh nigh shall be put to death.

39 All that were numbered of the Levites, which Moses and Aaron numbered at the commandment of the LORD, throughout their families, all the males from a month old and upward, *were* twenty and two thousand.

40 ¶ And the LORD said unto Moses, Number all the firstborn of the males of the children of Israel from a month old and upward, and take the number of their names.

41 And thou shalt take the Levites for me (I *am* the LORD) instead of all the firstborn among the children of Israel; and the cattle of the Levites instead of all the firstlings among the cattle of the children of Israel.

42 And Moses numbered, as the LORD commanded him, all the firstborn among the children of Israel.

43 And all the firstborn males by the number of names, from a month old and upward, of those that were numbered of them, were twenty and two thousand two hundred and threescore and thirteen.

44 And the LORD spake unto Moses, saying,

45 Take the Levites instead of all the firstborn among the children of Israel, and the cattle of

Amplified Bible

33 Of Merari were the families of the Mahlites and the Mushites; these are the families of Merari.

34 Their number of all the males from a month old and upward totaled 6,200.

35 And the head of the fathers' houses of the families of Merari was Zuriel son of Abihail; the Merarites were to encamp on the north side of the tabernacle.

36 And the appointed charge of the sons of Merari was the boards *or* frames of the tabernacle, and its bars, pillars, sockets *or* bases, and all the accessories *or* instruments of it, and all the work connected with them,

37 And the pillars of the surrounding court and their sockets *or* bases, with their pegs and their cords.

38 But those to encamp before the tabernacle toward the east, before the Tent of Meeting, toward the sunrise, were to be Moses and Aaron and his sons, keeping the full charge of the rites of the sanctuary in whatever was required for the Israelites; and the [a]excluded [one not a descendant of Aaron and called of God] who came near [the sanctuary] was to be put to death.

39 All the Levites whom Moses and Aaron numbered at the command of the Lord, by their families, all the males from a month old and upward, were 22,000.

40 And the Lord said to Moses, Number all the firstborn of the males of the Israelites from a month old and upward, and take the number of their names.

41 You shall take the Levites for Me instead of all the firstborn among the Israelites. I am the Lord; and you shall take the cattle of the Levites for Me instead of all the firstlings among the cattle of the Israelites.

42 So Moses numbered, as the Lord commanded him, all the firstborn Israelites.

43 But all the firstborn males from a month old and upward as numbered were 22,273 [273 more than the Levites].

44 And the Lord said to Moses,

45 Take the Levites [for Me] instead of all the firstborn Israelites, and the Levites' cattle in-

AMP notes: *a* This ban against "the excluded" from coming near the sanctuary (the sacred tent, the tabernacle proper) is not to be construed as discrimination against people who were not Israelites. It included everyone except the ordained descendants of Levi of the house of Aaron. The tabernacle proper was made up of two small rooms which no one except the priest or priests who had the assignment was ever to enter. The congregation entered the outside enclosure only. This was true also of the later temples. Neither Jesus nor any of his disciples or Paul ever entered the sanctuary. When Jesus "taught in the temple" or "entered into the temple," the Greek word invariably indicates that He was in the temple enclosure (*hieron*) and not in the sanctuary (*naos*). (For more information, see Richard Trench, *Synonyms of The New Testament*). For a violation of this ban see II Chron. 26:16-21, which tells of King Uzziah, who attempted to enter the sanctuary to burn incense and while being forcibly put out by eighty priests became a leper—for the rest of his life.

King James Version

the Levites instead of their cattle; and the Levites shall be mine: I *am* the LORD.

⁴⁶And for those that are *to be* redeemed of the two hundred and threescore and thirteen of the firstborn of the children of Israel, which are more than the Levites;

⁴⁷Thou shalt even take five shekels apiece by the poll, after the shekel of the sanctuary shalt thou take *them:* (the shekel *is* twenty gerahs:)

⁴⁸And thou shalt give the money, wherewith the odd number of them is *to be* redeemed, unto Aaron and to his sons.

⁴⁹And Moses took the redemption money of them that were over and above them that were redeemed by the Levites:

⁵⁰Of the firstborn of the children of Israel took he the money; a thousand three hundred and threescore and five *shekels,* after the shekel of the sanctuary:

⁵¹And Moses gave the money of them that were redeemed unto Aaron and to his sons, according to the word of the LORD, as the LORD commanded Moses.

4 And the LORD spake unto Moses and unto Aaron, saying,

²Take the sum of the sons of Kohath from among the sons of Levi, after their families, by the house of their fathers,

³From thirty years old and upward even until fifty years old, all that enter into the host, to do the work in the tabernacle of the congregation.

⁴This *shall be* the service of the sons of Kohath in the tabernacle of the congregation, *about* the most holy *things:*

⁵And when the camp setteth forward, Aaron shall come, and his sons, and they shall take down the covering vail, and cover the ark of Testimony with it:

⁶And shall put thereon the covering of badgers' skins, and shall spread over *it* a cloth wholly of blue, and shall put in the staves thereof.

⁷And upon the table of shewbread they shall spread a cloth of blue, and put thereon the dishes, and the spoons, and the bowls, and covers to cover withal: and the continual bread shall be thereon:

⁸And they shall spread upon them a cloth of scarlet, and cover the same with a covering of badgers' skins, and shall put in the staves thereof.

⁹And they shall take a cloth of blue, and cover the candlestick of the light, and his lamps, and his tongs, and his snuffdishes, and all the oil vessels thereof, wherewith they minister unto it:

¹⁰And they shall put it and all the vessels thereof within a covering of badgers' skins, and shall put *it* upon a bar.

¹¹And upon the golden altar they shall spread

Amplified Bible

stead of their cattle; and the Levites shall be Mine. I am the Lord.

⁴⁶And for those 273 who are to be redeemed of the firstborn of the Israelites who outnumber the Levites,

⁴⁷You shall take five shekels apiece, reckoning by the sanctuary shekel of twenty gerahs; you shall collect them,

⁴⁸And you shall give the ransom silver from the excess number [over the Levites] to be redeemed to Aaron and his sons.

⁴⁹So Moses took the redemption money from those who were left over from the number who were redeemed by the Levites.

⁵⁰From the firstborn of the Israelites he took the money, 1,365 shekels, after the shekel of the sanctuary.

⁵¹And Moses gave the money from those who were ransomed to Aaron and his sons, as the Lord commanded Moses.

4 AND THE Lord said to Moses and Aaron,

²Take a census of the Kohathite division among the sons of Levi, by their families, by their fathers' houses,

³From thirty years old and up to fifty years old, all who can enter the service to do the work in the Tent of Meeting.

⁴This shall be the responsibility of the sons of Kohath in the Tent of Meeting: the most holy things.

⁵When the camp prepares to set forward, Aaron and his sons shall take down the veil [screening the Holy of Holies] and cover the ark of the Testimony with it,

⁶And shall put on it the covering of dolphin *or* porpoise skin, and shall spread over that a cloth wholly of blue, and shall put in place the poles of the ark.

⁷And upon the table of showbread they shall spread a cloth of blue and put on it the plates, the dishes for incense, the bowls, the flagons for the drink offering, and also the continual showbread.

⁸And they shall spread over them a cloth of scarlet, and put over that a covering of dolphin *or* porpoise skin, and put in place the poles [for carrying].

⁹And they shall take a cloth of blue and cover the lampstand for the light and its lamps, its snuffers, its ashtrays, and all the oil vessels from which it is supplied.

¹⁰And they shall put the lampstand and all its utensils within a covering of dolphin *or* porpoise skin and shall put it upon the frame [for carrying].

¹¹And upon the golden [incense] altar they

King James Version

a cloth of blue, and cover it with a covering of badgers' skins, and shall put to the staves thereof:

¹²And they shall take all the instruments of ministry, wherewith they minister in the sanctuary, and put *them* in a cloth of blue, and cover them with a covering of badgers' skins, and shall put *them* on a bar:

¹³And they shall take away the ashes from the altar, and spread a purple cloth thereon:

¹⁴And they shall put upon it all the vessels thereof, wherewith they minister about it, *even* the censers, the fleshhooks, and the shovels, and the basons, all the vessels of the altar; and they shall spread upon it a covering of badgers' skins, and put to the staves of it.

¹⁵And when Aaron and his sons have made an end of covering the sanctuary, and all the vessels of the sanctuary, as the camp is to set forward; after that, the sons of Kohath shall come to bear *it:* but they shall not touch *any* holy *thing,* lest they die. These *things are* the burden of the sons of Kohath in the tabernacle of the congregation.

¹⁶And *to* the office of Eleazar the son of Aaron the priest *pertaineth* the oil for the light, and the sweet incense, and the daily meat offering, and the anointing oil, *and* the oversight of all the tabernacle, and of all that therein *is,* in the sanctuary, and in the vessels thereof.

¹⁷And the LORD spake unto Moses and unto Aaron, saying,

¹⁸Cut ye not off the tribe of the families of the Kohathites from among the Levites:

¹⁹But thus do unto them, that they may live, and not die, when they approach unto the most holy *things:* Aaron and his sons shall go in, and appoint them every one to his service and to his burden:

²⁰But they shall not go in to see when the holy *things* are covered, lest they die.

²¹ ¶ And the LORD spake unto Moses, saying,

²²Take also the sum of the sons of Gershon, throughout the houses of their fathers, by their families;

²³From thirty years old and upward until fifty years old shalt thou number them; all that enter in to perform the service, to do the work in the tabernacle of the congregation.

²⁴This *is* the service of the families of the Gershonites, to serve, and for burdens:

²⁵And they shall bear the curtains of the tabernacle, and the tabernacle of the congregation, his covering, and the covering of the badgers' skins that *is* above upon it, and the hanging for the door of the tabernacle of the congregation,

Amplified Bible

shall spread a cloth of blue, and cover it with a covering of dolphin *or* porpoise skin, and shall put in place its poles [for carrying].

¹²And they shall take all the utensils of the service with which they minister in the sanctuary, and put them in a cloth of blue, and cover them with a covering of dolphin *or* porpoise skin, and shall put them on the frame [for carrying].

¹³And they shall take away the ashes from the altar [of burnt offering] and spread a purple cloth over it.

¹⁴And they shall put upon it all its vessels *and* utensils with which they minister there, the firepans, the fleshhooks *or* forks, the shovels, the basins, and all the vessels *and* utensils of the altar, and they shall spread over it all a covering of dolphin *or* porpoise skin, and shall put in its poles [for carrying].

¹⁵When Aaron and his sons have finished covering the sanctuary and all its furniture, as the camp sets out, after all that [is done but not before], the sons of Kohath shall come to carry them. But they shall not touch the holy things, lest they die. These are the things of the Tent of Meeting which the sons of Kohath are to carry.

¹⁶And Eleazar son of Aaron the priest shall have charge of the oil for the light, the fragrant incense, the continual cereal offering, and the anointing oil, with the oversight of all the tabernacle and of all that is in it, of the sanctuary and its utensils.

¹⁷And the Lord said to Moses and Aaron,

¹⁸[Since] the tribe of the families of the Kohathites [are only Levites and not priests], do not [by exposing them to the sin of touching the most holy things] cut them off from among the Levites.

¹⁹But deal thus with them, that they may live and not die when they approach the most holy things: Aaron and his sons shall go in and appoint them each to his work and to his burden [to be carried on the march].

²⁰But [the Kohathites] shall not go in to see the sanctuary [the Holy Place and the Holy of Holies] *or* its holy things, even for an instant, lest they die.

²¹And the Lord said to Moses,

²²Take a census of the sons of Gershon, by their fathers' houses, by their families.

²³From thirty years old and up to fifty years old you shall number them, all who enter for service to do the work in the Tent of Meeting.

²⁴This is the service of the families of the Gershonites, in serving and in bearing burdens [when on the march]:

²⁵And they shall carry the curtains of the tabernacle, and the Tent of Meeting, its covering, and the covering of dolphin *or* porpoise skin that is on top of it, and the hanging *or* screen for the door of the Tent of Meeting,

King James Version

26And the hangings of the court, and the hanging for the door of the gate of the court, which *is* by the tabernacle and by the altar round about, and their cords, and all the instruments of their service, and all that is made for them: so shall they serve.

27At the appointment of Aaron and his sons shall be all the service of the sons of the Gershonites, in all their burdens, and in all their service: and ye shall appoint unto them in charge all their burdens.

28This *is* the service of the families of the sons of Gershon in the tabernacle of the congregation: and their charge *shall be* under the hand of Ithamar the son of Aaron the priest.

29 ¶ *As for* the sons of Merari, thou shalt number them after their families, by the house of their fathers;

30From thirty years old and upward even unto fifty years old shalt thou number them, every one that entereth into the service, to do the work of the tabernacle of the congregation.

31And this *is* the charge of their burden, according to all their service in the tabernacle of the congregation; the boards of the tabernacle, and the bars thereof, and the pillars thereof, and sockets thereof,

32And the pillars of the court round about, and their sockets, and their pins, and their cords, with all their instruments, and with all their service: and by name ye shall reckon the instruments of the charge of their burden.

33This *is* the service of the families of the sons of Merari, according to all their service, in the tabernacle of the congregation, under the hand of Ithamar the son of Aaron the priest.

34 ¶ And Moses and Aaron and the chief of the congregation numbered the sons of the Kohathites after their families, and after the house of their fathers,

35From thirty years old and upward even unto fifty years old, every one that entereth into the service, for the work in the tabernacle of the congregation:

36And those that were numbered of them by their families were two thousand seven hundred and fifty.

37These *were* they that were numbered of the families of the Kohathites, all that *might* do service in the tabernacle of the congregation, which Moses and Aaron did number according to the commandment of the LORD by the hand of Moses.

38And those that were numbered of the sons of Gershon, throughout their families, and by the house of their fathers,

39From thirty years old and upward even unto fifty years old, every one that entereth into the service, for the work in the tabernacle of the congregation,

Amplified Bible

26And the hangings of the court, and the hanging *or* screen for the entrance of the gate of the court which is around the tabernacle and the altar [of burnt offering], and their cords, and all the equipment for their service; whatever needs to be done with them, that they shall do.

27Under the direction of Aaron and his sons shall be all the service of the sons of the Gershonites, in all they have to carry and in all they have to do; and you shall assign to their charge all that they are to carry [on the march].

28This is the service of the families of the sons of Gershon in the Tent of Meeting; and their work shall be under the direction of Ithamar son of Aaron, the [high] priest.

29As for the sons of Merari, you shall number them by their families and their fathers' houses;

30From thirty years old up to fifty years old you shall number them, everyone who enters the service to do the work of the Tent of Meeting.

31And this is what they are assigned to carry *and* to guard [on the march], according to all their service in the Tent of Meeting: the boards *or* frames of the tabernacle, and its bars, and its pillars, and its sockets *or* bases,

32And the pillars of the court round about with their sockets *or* bases, and pegs, and cords, with all their equipment and all their accessories for service; and you shall assign to them by name the articles which they are to carry [on the march].

33This is the work of the families of the sons of Merari, according to all their tasks in the Tent of Meeting, under the direction of Ithamar son of Aaron, the [high] priest.

34And Moses and Aaron and the leaders of the congregation numbered the sons of the Kohathites by their families and their fathers' houses,

35From thirty years old up to fifty years old, everyone who enters the service to do the work of the Tent of Meeting;

36And those who were numbered of them by their families were 2,750.

37These were numbered of the families of the Kohathites, all who did service in the Tent of Meeting, whom Moses and Aaron numbered according to the command of the Lord through Moses.

38And those that were numbered of the sons of Gershon, by their families, and by their fathers' houses,

39From thirty years old up to fifty years old, everyone who entered the service to do the work of the Tent of Meeting,

King James Version

40 Even those that were numbered of them, throughout their families, by the house of their fathers, were two thousand and six hundred and thirty.

41 These *are* they that were numbered of the families of the sons of Gershon, of all that *might* do service in the tabernacle of the congregation, whom Moses and Aaron did number according to the commandment of the LORD.

42 And those that were numbered of the families of the sons of Merari, throughout their families, by the house of their fathers,

43 From thirty years old and upward even unto fifty years old, every one that entereth into the service, for the work in the tabernacle of the congregation,

44 Even those that were numbered of them after their families, were three thousand and two hundred.

45 These *be* those that were numbered of the families of the sons of Merari, whom Moses and Aaron numbered according to the word of the LORD by the hand of Moses.

46 All those that were numbered of the Levites, whom Moses and Aaron and the chief of Israel numbered, after their families, and after the house of their fathers,

47 From thirty years old and upward even unto fifty years old, every one that came to do the service of the ministry, and the service of the burden in the tabernacle of the congregation,

48 Even those that were numbered of them, were eight thousand and five hundred and fourscore.

49 According to the commandment of the LORD they were numbered by the hand of Moses, every one according to his service, and according to his burden: thus *were they* numbered of him, as the LORD commanded Moses.

5 And the LORD spake unto Moses, saying,
2 Command the children of Israel, that they put out of the camp every leper, and every one that hath an issue, and whosoever is defiled by the dead:

3 Both male and female shall ye put out, without the camp shall ye put them; that they defile not their camps, in the midst whereof I dwell.

4 And the children of Israel did so, and put them out without the camp: as the LORD spake unto Moses, so did the children of Israel.

5 ¶ And the LORD spake unto Moses, saying,
6 Speak unto the children of Israel, When a man or woman shall commit any sin that men commit, to do a trespass against the LORD, and that person be guilty;

7 Then they shall confess their sin which they have done: and he shall recompense his trespass with the principal thereof, and add unto it the fifth *part* thereof, and give *it* unto *him* against whom he hath trespassed.

Amplified Bible

40 Those who were enrolled of them, by their families, by their fathers' houses, were 2,630.

41 These were numbered of the families of the sons of Gershon, all who served in the Tent of Meeting, whom Moses and Aaron numbered as the Lord commanded.

42 And those numbered of the families of the sons of Merari, by their families, by their fathers' houses,

43 From thirty years old up to fifty years old, everyone who entered into the service for work in the Tent of Meeting,

44 Even those who were numbered of them by their families, were 3,200.

45 These are those who were numbered of the families of the sons of Merari, whom Moses and Aaron numbered according to the command of the Lord by Moses.

46 All those who were numbered of the Levites, whom Moses and Aaron and the leaders of Israel counted by their families and by their fathers' houses,

47 From thirty years old up to fifty years old, everyone who could enter to do the work of service and of burden bearing in the Tent of Meeting,

48 Those that were numbered of them were 8,580.

49 According to the command of the Lord through Moses, they were assigned each to his work of serving and carrying. Thus they were numbered by him, as the Lord had commanded Moses.

5 THE LORD said to Moses,
2 Command the Israelites that they put outside the camp every leper and everyone who has a discharge, and whoever is defiled by [coming in contact with] the dead;

3 Both male and female you shall put out; without the camp you shall put them, that they may not defile their camp, in the midst of which I dwell.

4 The Israelites did so, and put them outside the camp; as the Lord said to Moses, so the Israelites did.

5 And the Lord said to Moses,
6 Say to the Israelites, When a man or woman commits any sin that men commit by breaking faith with the Lord, and that person is guilty,

7 Then he shall confess the sin which he has committed, and he shall make restitution for his wrong in full, and add a fifth to it, and give it to him whom he has wronged.

King James Version

8But if the man have no kinsman to recompense the trespass unto, *let* the trespass *be* recompensed unto the LORD, *even* to the priest; beside the ram of the atonement, whereby an atonement shall be made for him.

9And every offering of all the holy *things* of the children of Israel, which they bring unto the priest, shall be his.

10And every man's hallowed *things* shall be his: whatsoever any man giveth the priest, it shall be his.

11 ¶ And the LORD spake unto Moses, saying,

12Speak unto the children of Israel, and say unto them, If any man's wife go aside, and commit a trespass against him,

13And a man lie with her carnally, and it be hid from the eyes of her husband, and be kept close, and she be defiled, and *there be* no witness against her, neither she be taken *with the manner;*

14And the spirit of jealousy come upon him, and he be jealous of his wife, and she be defiled: or if the spirit of jealousy come upon him, and he be jealous of his wife, and she be not defiled:

15Then shall the man bring his wife unto the priest, and he shall bring her offering for her, the tenth *part* of an ephah of barley meal; he shall pour no oil upon it, nor put frankincense thereon; for it *is* an offering of jealousy, an offering of memorial, bringing iniquity to remembrance.

16And the priest shall bring her near, and set her before the LORD:

17And the priest shall take holy water in an earthen vessel; and of the dust that is in the floor of the tabernacle the priest shall take, and put *it* into the water:

18And the priest shall set the woman before the LORD, and uncover the woman's head, and put the offering of memorial in her hands, which *is* the jealousy offering: and the priest shall have in his hand the bitter water that causeth the curse:

19And the priest shall charge her by an oath, and say unto the woman, If no man have lain with thee, and if thou hast not gone aside *to* uncleanness *with another* instead of thy husband, be thou free from this bitter water that causeth the curse:

20But if thou hast gone aside *to another* instead of thy husband, and if thou be defiled, and *some* man hath lain with thee beside thine husband:

21Then the priest shall charge the woman with an oath of cursing, and the priest shall say unto the woman, The LORD make thee a curse and an oath among thy people, when the LORD doth make thy thigh to rot, and thy belly to swell;

Amplified Bible

8But if the man [wronged] has no kinsman to whom the restitution may be made, let it be given to the Lord for the priest, besides the ram of atonement with which atonement shall be made for the offender.

9And every offering of all the holy things of the Israelites which they bring to the priest shall be his.

10And every man's hallowed things shall be the priest's; whatever any man gives the priest shall be his.

11And the Lord said to Moses,

12Say to the Israelites, If any man's wife goes astray and commits an offense of guilt against him,

13And a man lies with her carnally, and it is hidden from the eyes of her husband and it is kept secret though she is defiled, and there is no witness against her nor was she taken in the act,

14And if the spirit of jealousy comes upon him and he is jealous *and* suspicious of his wife who has defiled herself—or if the spirit of jealousy comes upon him and he is jealous *and* suspicious of his wife though she has not defiled herself—

15Then shall the man bring his wife to the priest, and he shall bring the offering required of her, a tenth of an ephah of barley meal; but he shall pour no oil upon it nor put frankincense on it [symbols of favor and joy], for it is a cereal offering of jealousy *and* suspicion, a memorial offering bringing iniquity to remembrance.

16And the priest shall bring her near and set her before the Lord.

17And the priest shall take holy water [probably from the sacred laver] in an earthen vessel and take some of the dust that is on the floor of the tabernacle and put it in the water.

18And the priest shall set the woman before the Lord, and let the hair of the woman's head hang loose, and put the meal offering of remembrance in her hands, which is the jealousy *and* suspicion offering. And the priest shall have in his hand the water of bitterness that brings the curse.

19Then the priest shall make her take an oath, and say to the woman, If no man has lain with you and if you have not gone astray to uncleanness with another instead of your husband, then be free from any effect of this water of bitterness which brings the curse.

20But if you have gone astray and you are defiled, some man having lain with you beside your husband,

21Then the priest shall make the woman take the oath of the curse, and say to the woman, The Lord make you a curse and an oath among your people when the Lord makes your thigh fall away and your body swell.

King James Version

²²And this water that causeth the curse shall go into thy bowels, to make *thy* belly to swell, and *thy* thigh to rot: And the woman shall say, Amen, amen.

²³And the priest shall write these curses in a book, and he shall blot *them* out with the bitter water:

²⁴And he shall cause the woman to drink the bitter water that causeth the curse: and the water that causeth the curse shall enter into her, and become bitter.

²⁵Then the priest shall take the jealousy offering out of the woman's hand, and shall wave the offering before the LORD, and offer it upon the altar:

²⁶And the priest shall take a handful of the offering, *even* the memorial thereof, and burn *it* upon the altar, and afterward shall cause the woman to drink the water.

²⁷And when he hath made her to drink the water, then it shall come to pass, *that,* if she be defiled, and have done trespass against her husband, that the water that causeth the curse shall enter into her, and become bitter, and her belly shall swell, and her thigh shall rot: and the woman shall be a curse among her people.

²⁸And if the woman be not defiled, but *be* clean; then she shall be free, and shall conceive seed.

²⁹This *is* the law of jealousies, when a wife goeth aside *to another* instead of her husband, and is defiled;

³⁰Or when the spirit of jealousy cometh upon him, and he be jealous over his wife, and shall set the woman before the LORD, and the priest shall execute upon her all this law.

³¹Then shall the man be guiltless from iniquity, and this woman shall bear her iniquity.

6 And the LORD spake unto Moses, saying,
²Speak unto the children of Israel, and say unto them, When either man or woman shall separate *themselves* to vow a vow of a Nazarite, to separate *themselves* unto the LORD:

³He shall separate *himself* from wine and strong drink, *and* shall drink no vinegar of wine, or vinegar of strong drink, neither shall he drink any liquor of grapes, nor eat moist grapes, or dried.

⁴All the days of his separation shall he eat nothing that is made of the vine tree, from the kernels even to the husk.

⁵All the days of the vow of his separation there shall no rasor come upon his head: until the days be fulfilled, *in* the which he separateth *himself* unto the LORD, he shall be holy, *and* shall let the locks of the hair of his head grow.

⁶All the days that he separateth *himself* unto the LORD he shall come at no dead body.

Amplified Bible

²²May this water that brings the curse go into your bowels and make your body swell and your thigh fall away. And the woman shall say, So let it be, so let it be.

²³The priest shall then write these curses in a book and shall wash them off into the water of bitterness;

²⁴And he shall cause the woman to drink the water of bitterness that brings the curse, and the water that brings the curse shall enter into her [to try her] bitterly.

²⁵Then the priest shall take the cereal offering of jealousy *and* suspicion out of the woman's hand and shall wave the offering before the Lord and offer it upon the altar.

²⁶And the priest shall take a handful of the cereal offering as the memorial portion of it and burn it on the altar, and afterward shall cause the woman to drink the water.

²⁷And when he has made her drink the water, then if she is defiled and has committed a trespass against her husband, the curse water which she drank shall be bitterness and cause her body to swell and her thigh to fall away, and the woman shall be a curse among her people.

²⁸But if the woman is not defiled and is clean, then she shall be free [from the curse] and be able to have children.

²⁹This is the law of jealousy *and* suspicion when a wife goes aside to another instead of her husband and is defiled,

³⁰Or when the spirit of jealousy *and* suspicion comes upon a man and he is jealous *and* suspicious of his wife; then shall he set the woman before the Lord, and the priest shall execute on her all this law.

³¹The [husband] shall be free from iniquity *and* guilt, and that woman [if guilty] shall bear her iniquity.

6 AND THE Lord said to Moses,
²Say to the Israelites, When either a man or a woman shall make a special vow, the vow of a Nazirite, that is, one separated *and* consecrated to the Lord,

³He shall separate himself from wine and strong drink; he shall drink no vinegar of wine or of strong drink, and shall drink no grape juice, or eat grapes, fresh or dried.

⁴All the days of his separation he shall eat nothing produced from the grapevine, not even the seeds or the skins.

⁵All the days of the vow of his separation *and* abstinence there shall no razor come upon his head. Until the time is completed for which he separates himself to the Lord, he shall be holy, and shall let the locks of the hair of his head grow long.

⁶All the days that he separates himself to the Lord he shall not go near a dead body.

King James Version

⁷He shall not make himself unclean for his father, or for his mother, for his brother, or for his sister, when they die: because the consecration of his God *is* upon his head.

⁸All the days of his separation he *is* holy unto the LORD.

⁹And if any man die very suddenly by him, and he hath defiled the head of his consecration; then he shall shave his head in the day of his cleansing, on the seventh day shall he shave it.

¹⁰And on the eighth day he shall bring two turtles, or two young pigeons, to the priest, to the door of the tabernacle of the congregation:

¹¹And the priest shall offer the one for a sin offering, and the other for a burnt offering, and make an atonement for him, for that he sinned by the dead, and shall hallow his head that *same* day.

¹²And he shall consecrate unto the LORD the days of his separation, and shall bring a lamb of the first year for a trespass offering: but the days that were before shall be lost, because his separation was defiled.

¹³And this *is* the law of the Nazarite, when the days of his separation are fulfilled: he shall be brought unto the door of the tabernacle of the congregation:

¹⁴And he shall offer his offering unto the LORD, one he lamb of the first year without blemish for a burnt offering, and one ewe lamb of the first year without blemish for a sin offering, and one ram without blemish for peace offerings,

¹⁵And a basket of unleavened bread, cakes *of* fine flour mingled with oil, and wafers of unleavened bread anointed with oil, and their meat offering, and their drink offerings.

¹⁶And the priest shall bring *them* before the LORD, and shall offer his sin offering, and his burnt offering:

¹⁷And he shall offer the ram *for* a sacrifice of peace offerings unto the LORD, with the basket of unleavened bread: the priest shall offer also his meat offering, and his drink offering.

¹⁸And the Nazarite shall shave the head of his separation *at* the door of the tabernacle of the congregation, and shall take the hair of the head of his separation, and put *it* in the fire which *is* under the sacrifice of the peace offerings.

¹⁹And the priest shall take the sodden shoulder of the ram, and one unleavened cake out of the basket, and one unleavened wafer, and shall put *them* upon the hands of the Nazarite, after *the hair of* his separation is shaven:

²⁰And the priest shall wave them *for* a wave offering before the LORD: this *is* holy for the priest, with the wave breast and heave shoulder: and after *that* the Nazarite may drink wine.

²¹This *is* the law of the Nazarite who hath vowed, *and of* his offering unto the LORD for his

Amplified Bible

⁷He shall not make himself unclean for his father, mother, brother, or sister, when they die, because his separation *and* abstinence to his God is upon his head.

⁸All the days of his separation *and* abstinence he is holy to the Lord.

⁹And if any man dies very suddenly beside him, and he has defiled his consecrated head, then he shall shave his head on the day of his cleansing; on the seventh day shall he shave it.

¹⁰On the eighth day he shall bring two turtledoves or two young pigeons to the priest to the door of the Tent of Meeting,

¹¹And the priest shall offer the one for a sin offering and the other for a burnt offering and make atonement for him because he sinned by reason of the dead body. He shall consecrate his head the same day,

¹²And he shall consecrate *and* separate himself to the Lord for the days of his separation and shall bring a male lamb a year old for a trespass *or* guilt offering; but the previous days shall be void *and* lost, because his separation was defiled.

¹³And this is the law of the Nazirite when the days of his separation *and* abstinence are fulfilled. He shall be brought to the door of the Tent of Meeting,

¹⁴And he shall offer his gift to the Lord, one he-lamb a year old without blemish for a burnt offering, and one ewe lamb a year old without blemish for a sin offering, and one ram without blemish for a peace offering,

¹⁵And a basket of unleavened bread, cakes of fine flour mingled with oil, and wafers of unleavened bread spread with oil, and their cereal offering, and their drink offering.

¹⁶And the priest shall present them before the Lord and shall offer the person's sin offering and his burnt offering.

¹⁷And he shall offer the ram for a sacrifice of peace offering to the Lord, with the basket of unleavened bread; the priest shall offer also its cereal offering and its drink offering.

¹⁸And the Nazirite shall shave his consecrated head at the door of the Tent of Meeting, and shall take the hair and put it on the fire which is under the sacrifice of the peace offerings.

¹⁹And the priest shall take the boiled shoulder of the ram, and one unleavened cake out of the basket, and one unleavened wafer and shall put them upon the hands of the Nazirite, after he has shaven the hair of his separation *and* abstinence.

²⁰And the priest shall wave them for a wave offering before the Lord; they are a holy portion for the priest, with the breast that is waved and the thigh *or* shoulder that is offered; and after that the Nazirite may drink wine.

²¹This is the law for the Nazirite who has made a vow. His offering to the Lord, besides

King James Version

separation, besides *that* that his hand shall get: according to the vow which he vowed, so he must do after the law of his separation.

22 ¶ And the LORD spake unto Moses, saying,

23Speak unto Aaron and unto his sons, saying, On this wise ye shall bless the children of Israel, saying unto them,

24 ¶ The LORD bless thee, and keep thee:

25 ¶ The LORD make his face shine upon thee, and be gracious unto thee:

26 ¶ The LORD lift up his countenance upon thee, and give thee peace.

27 ¶ And they shall put my name upon the children of Israel; and I will bless them.

7 And it came to pass on the day that Moses had fully set up the tabernacle, and had anointed it, and sanctified it, and all the instruments thereof, both the altar and all the vessels thereof, and had anointed them, and sanctified them;

2That the princes of Israel, heads of the house of their fathers, who *were* the princes of the tribes, and were over them that were numbered, offered:

3And they brought their offering before the LORD, six covered wagons, and twelve oxen; a wagon for two of the princes, and for *each* one an ox: and they brought them before the tabernacle.

4And the LORD spake unto Moses, saying,

5Take *it* of them, that they may be to do the service of the tabernacle of the congregation; and thou shalt give them unto the Levites, to every man according to his service.

6And Moses took the wagons and the oxen, and gave them unto the Levites.

7Two wagons and four oxen he gave unto the sons of Gershon, according to their service:

8And four wagons and eight oxen he gave unto the sons of Merari, according unto their service, under the hand of Ithamar the son of Aaron the priest.

9But unto the sons of Kohath he gave none: because the service of the sanctuary belonging unto them *was that* they should bear upon *their* shoulders.

10And the princes offered *for* dedicating of the altar in the day that it was anointed, even the princes offered their offering before the altar.

11And the LORD said unto Moses, They shall offer their offering, each prince on *his* day, for the dedicating of the altar.

12 ¶ And he that offered his offering the first day was Nahshon the son of Amminadab, of the tribe of Judah:

13And his offering *was* one silver charger, the weight thereof *was* an hundred and thirty

Amplified Bible

what else he is able to afford, shall be according to the vow which he has vowed; so shall he do according to the law for his separation *and* abstinence [as a Nazirite].

22And the Lord said to Moses,

23Say to Aaron and his sons, This is the way you shall bless the Israelites. Say to them,

24The Lord bless you and watch, guard, *and* keep you;

25The Lord make His face to shine upon *and* enlighten you and be gracious (kind, merciful, and giving favor) to you;

26The Lord lift up His [approving] countenance upon you and give you peace (tranquility of heart and life continually).

27And they shall put My name upon the Israelites, and I will bless them.

7 ON THE day that Moses had fully completed setting up the tabernacle and had anointed and consecrated it and all its furniture, and the altar and all its utensils, and had anointed and set them apart for holy use,

2The princes *or* leaders of Israel, heads of their fathers' houses, made offerings. These were the leaders of the tribes and were over those who were numbered.

3And they brought their offering before the Lord, six covered wagons and twelve oxen; a wagon for each two of the princes *or* leaders and an ox for each one; and they brought them before the tabernacle.

4Then the Lord said to Moses,

5Accept the things from them, that they may be used in doing the service of the Tent of Meeting, and give them to the Levites, to each man according to his service.

6So Moses took the wagons and the oxen and gave them to the Levites.

7Two wagons and four oxen he gave to the sons of Gershon, according to their service;

8And four wagons and eight oxen he gave to the sons of Merari, according to their service, under the supervision of Ithamar son of Aaron, the [high] priest.

9But to the sons of Kohath he gave none, because they were assigned the care of the sanctuary *and* the holy things which had to be carried on their shoulders.

10And the princes *or* leaders offered sacrifices for the dedication of the altar [of burnt offering] on the day that it was anointed; and they offered their sacrifice before the altar.

11And the Lord said to Moses, They shall offer their offerings, each prince *or* leader on his day, for the dedication of the altar.

12He who offered his offering on the first day was Nahshon son of Amminadab, of the tribe of Judah.

13And his offering was one silver platter, the weight of which was 130 shekels, one silver

King James Version

shekels, one silver bowl of seventy shekels, after the shekel of the sanctuary; both of them *were* full *of* fine flour mingled with oil for a meat offering:

14One spoon of ten *shekels* of gold, full *of* incense:

15One young bullock, one ram, one lamb of the first year, for a burnt offering:

16One kid of the goats for a sin offering:

17And for a sacrifice of peace offerings, two oxen, five rams, five he goats, five lambs of the first year: this *was* the offering of Nahshon the son of Amminadab.

18 ¶ On the second day Nethaneel the son of Zuar, prince of Issachar, did offer:

19He offered *for* his offering one silver charger, the weight whereof *was* an hundred and thirty *shekels,* one silver bowl of seventy shekels, after the shekel of the sanctuary; both of them full *of* fine flour mingled with oil for a meat offering:

20One spoon of gold of ten *shekels,* full *of* incense:

21One young bullock, one ram, one lamb of the first year, for a burnt offering:

22One kid of the goats for a sin offering:

23And for a sacrifice of peace offerings, two oxen, five rams, five he goats, five lambs of the first year: this *was* the offering of Nethaneel the son of Zuar.

24 ¶ On the third day Eliab the son of Helon, prince of the children of Zebulun, *did offer:*

25His offering *was* one silver charger, the weight whereof *was* an hundred and thirty *shekels,* one silver bowl of seventy shekels, after the shekel of the sanctuary; both of them full *of* fine flour mingled with oil for a meat offering:

26One golden spoon of ten *shekels,* full *of* incense:

27One young bullock, one ram, one lamb of the first year, for a burnt offering:

28One kid of the goats for a sin offering:

29And for a sacrifice of peace offerings, two oxen, five rams, five he goats, five lambs of the first year: this *was* the offering of Eliab the son of Helon.

30 ¶ On the fourth day Elizur the son of Shedeur, prince of the children of Reuben, *did offer:*

31His offering *was* one silver charger of the

Amplified Bible

basin of seventy shekels, according to the shekel of the sanctuary, both of them full of fine flour mixed with oil for a cereal offering;

14One golden bowl of ten shekels, full of incense;

15One young bull, one ram, one male lamb a year old, for a burnt offering;

16One male goat for a sin offering;

17And [a]for the sacrifice of peace offerings, two oxen, five rams, five male goats, five male lambs a year old. This was the offering of Nahshon son of Amminadab.

18The second day Nethanel son of Zuar, leader [of the tribe] of Issachar, offered.

19He gave for his offering one silver platter, the weight of which was 130 shekels, one silver basin of seventy shekels, after the shekel of the sanctuary, both of them full of fine flour mixed with oil for a cereal offering;

20One golden bowl of ten shekels, full of incense;

21One young bull, one ram, one male lamb a year old, for a burnt offering;

22One male goat for a sin offering;

23And for the sacrifice of peace offerings, two oxen, five rams, five male goats, five male lambs a year old. This was the offering of Nethanel son of Zuar.

24The third day Eliab son of Helon, leader of the sons of Zebulun, offered.

25His offering was one silver platter, the weight of which was 130 shekels, one silver basin of seventy shekels, after the shekel of the sanctuary, both of them full of fine flour mixed with oil for a cereal offering;

26One golden bowl of ten shekels, full of incense;

27One young bull, one ram, one male lamb a year old, for a burnt offering;

28One male goat for a sin offering;

29And for the sacrifice of peace offerings, two oxen, five rams, five male goats, five male lambs a year old. This was the offering of Eliab son of Helon.

30The fourth day Elizur son of Shedeur, leader of the sons of Reuben, offered.

31His offering was one silver platter of the

AMP notes: [a] Verses 12 to 17 give the detailed description of one tribe leader's offering. Then, instead of saying that the gifts of the other tribe leaders were exactly like this one and naming the leaders, the record goes on for **seventy** verses repeating what has already been said **eleven** more times! Why? These things "were written for our learning" (Rom. 15:4 KJV). Let us seek the answer. Other commentators give Matthew Henry credit for giving the correct view. He says that both in dictating that each tribal leader have a separate day for his gift and in giving the reports equal space, regardless of the contrast in the tribe's strength and rank in the camp, God had a definite purpose: "that an equal honor might thereby be put on each several tribe . . . Thus it was intimated that all the tribes of Israel had an equal share in the altar and an equal share in the sacrifices that were offered upon it. Though one tribe was posted more honorably in the camp than another, yet they and their services were all alike acceptable to God . . . Rich and poor meet together before God . . . He was letting us know that what is given is lent to the Lord, and He carefully records it, with everyone's name prefixed to his gift, because what is so given as a labor of love (Heb. 6:10 KJV) He will repay. Christ took particular notice of what was cast into the treasury (Mark 12:41)" (Matthew Henry, *A Commentary*).

King James Version

weight of an hundred and thirty *shekels,* one silver bowl of seventy shekels, after the shekel of the sanctuary; both of them full *of* fine flour mingled with oil for a meat offering:

³²One golden spoon *of* ten *shekels,* full *of* incense:

³³One young bullock, one ram, one lamb of the first year, for a burnt offering:

³⁴One kid of the goats for a sin offering:

³⁵And for a sacrifice of peace offerings, two oxen, five rams, five he goats, five lambs of the first year: this *was* the offering of Elizur the son of Shedeur.

³⁶ ¶ On the fifth day Shelumiel the son of Zurishaddai, prince of the children of Simeon, *did offer:*

³⁷His offering *was* one silver charger, the weight whereof *was* an hundred and thirty *shekels,* one silver bowl of seventy shekels, after the shekel of the sanctuary; both of them full *of* fine flour mingled with oil for a meat offering:

³⁸One golden spoon of ten *shekels,* full *of* incense:

³⁹One young bullock, one ram, one lamb of the first year, for a burnt offering:

⁴⁰One kid of the goats for a sin offering:

⁴¹And for a sacrifice of peace offerings, two oxen, five rams, five he goats, five lambs of the first year: this *was* the offering of Shelumiel the son of Zurishaddai.

⁴² ¶ On the sixth day Eliasaph the son of Deuel, prince of the children of Gad, *offered:*

⁴³His offering *was* one silver charger of the weight of an hundred and thirty *shekels,* a silver bowl of seventy shekels, after the shekel of the sanctuary; both of them full *of* fine flour mingled with oil for a meat offering:

⁴⁴One golden spoon of ten *shekels,* full *of* incense:

⁴⁵One young bullock, one ram, one lamb of the first year, for a burnt offering:

⁴⁶One kid of the goats for a sin offering:

⁴⁷And for a sacrifice of peace offerings, two oxen, five rams, five he goats, five lambs of the first year: this *was* the offering of Eliasaph the son of Deuel.

⁴⁸ ¶ On the seventh day Elishama the son of Ammihud, prince of the children of Ephraim, *offered:*

⁴⁹His offering *was* one silver charger, the weight whereof *was* an hundred and thirty *shekels,* one silver bowl of seventy shekels, after the shekel of the sanctuary; both of them full *of* fine flour mingled with oil for a meat offering:

⁵⁰One golden spoon of ten *shekels,* full *of* incense:

⁵¹One young bullock, one ram, one lamb of the first year, for a burnt offering:

⁵²One kid of the goats for a sin offering:

⁵³And for a sacrifice of peace offerings, two oxen, five rams, five he goats, five lambs of the

Amplified Bible

weight of 130 shekels, one silver basin of seventy shekels, after the shekel of the sanctuary, both of them full of fine flour mixed with oil for a cereal offering;

³²One golden bowl of ten shekels, full of incense;

³³One young bull, one ram, one male lamb a year old, for a burnt offering;

³⁴One male goat for a sin offering;

³⁵And for the sacrifice of peace offerings, two oxen, five rams, five male goats, five male lambs a year old. This was the offering of Elizur son of Shedeur.

³⁶The fifth day Shelumiel son of Zurishaddai, leader of the sons of Simeon, offered.

³⁷His offering was one silver platter, the weight of which was 130 shekels, one silver basin of seventy shekels, after the shekel of the sanctuary, both of them full of fine flour mixed with oil for a cereal offering;

³⁸One golden bowl of ten shekels, full of incense;

³⁹One young bull, one ram, one male lamb a year old, for a burnt offering;

⁴⁰One male goat for a sin offering;

⁴¹And for the sacrifice of peace offerings, two oxen, five rams, five male goats, five male lambs a year old. This was the offering of Shelumiel son of Zurishaddai.

⁴²The sixth day Eliasaph son of Deuel, leader of the sons of Gad, offered.

⁴³His offering was one silver platter of the weight of 130 shekels, a silver basin of seventy shekels, after the shekel of the sanctuary, both of them full of fine flour mixed with oil for a cereal offering;

⁴⁴One golden bowl of ten shekels, full of incense;

⁴⁵One young bull, one ram, one male lamb a year old, for a burnt offering;

⁴⁶One male goat for a sin offering;

⁴⁷And for the sacrifice of peace offerings, two oxen, five rams, five male goats, [and] five male lambs a year old. This was the offering of Eliasaph son of Deuel.

⁴⁸The seventh day Elishama son of Ammihud, leader of the sons of Ephraim, offered.

⁴⁹His offering was one silver platter, the weight of which was 130 shekels, one silver basin of seventy shekels, after the shekel of the sanctuary, both of them full of fine flour mixed with oil for a cereal offering;

⁵⁰One golden bowl of ten shekels, full of incense;

⁵¹One young bull, one ram, one male lamb a year old, for a burnt offering;

⁵²One male goat for a sin offering;

⁵³And for the sacrifice of peace offerings, two oxen, five rams, five male goats, [and] five male

King James Version

first year: this *was* the offering of Elishama the son of Ammihud.

54 ¶ On the eighth day *offered* Gamaliel the son of Pedahzur, prince of the children of Manasseh:

55His offering *was* one silver charger, the weight of an hundred and thirty *shekels,* one silver bowl of seventy shekels, after the shekel of the sanctuary; both of them full *of* fine flour mingled with oil for a meat offering:

56One golden spoon of ten *shekels,* full *of* incense:

57One young bullock, one ram, one lamb of the first year, for a burnt offering:

58One kid of the goats for a sin offering:

59And for a sacrifice of peace offerings, two oxen, five rams, five he goats, five lambs of the first year: this *was* the offering of Gamaliel the son of Pedahzur.

60 ¶ On the ninth day Abidan the son of Gideoni, prince of the children of Benjamin, *offered:*

61His offering *was* one silver charger, the weight whereof *was* an hundred and thirty *shekels,* one silver bowl of seventy shekels, after the shekel of the sanctuary; both of them full *of* fine flour mingled with oil for a meat offering:

62One golden spoon of ten *shekels,* full *of* incense:

63One young bullock, one ram, one lamb of the first year, for a burnt offering:

64One kid of the goats for a sin offering:

65And for a sacrifice of peace offerings, two oxen, five rams, five he goats, five lambs of the first year: this *was* the offering of Abidan the son of Gideoni.

66 ¶ On the tenth day Ahiezer the son of Ammishaddai, prince of the children of Dan, *offered:*

67His offering *was* one silver charger, the weight whereof *was* an hundred and thirty *shekels,* one silver bowl of seventy shekels, after the shekel of the sanctuary; both of them full *of* fine flour mingled with oil for a meat offering:

68One golden spoon of ten *shekels,* full *of* incense:

69One young bullock, one ram, one lamb of the first year, for a burnt offering:

70One kid of the goats for a sin offering:

71And for a sacrifice of peace offerings, two oxen, five rams, five he goats, five lambs of the first year: this *was* the offering of Ahiezer the son of Ammishaddai.

72 ¶ On the eleventh day Pagiel the son of Ocran, prince of the children of Asher, *offered:*

73His offering *was* one silver charger, the weight whereof *was* an hundred and thirty *shekels,* one silver bowl of seventy shekels, after the shekel of the sanctuary; both of them full *of* fine flour mingled with oil for a meat offering:

74One golden spoon of ten *shekels,* full *of* incense:

Amplified Bible

lambs a year old. This was the offering of Elishama son of Ammihud.

54The eighth day Gamaliel son of Pedahzur, leader of the sons of Manasseh, offered.

55His offering was one silver platter of the weight of 130 shekels, one silver basin of seventy shekels, after the shekel of the sanctuary, both of them full of fine flour mixed with oil for a cereal offering;

56One golden bowl of ten shekels, full of incense;

57One young bull, one ram, one male lamb a year old, for a burnt offering;

58One male goat for a sin offering;

59And for the sacrifice of peace offerings, two oxen, five rams, five male goats, five male lambs a year old. This was the offering of Gamaliel son of Pedahzur.

60The ninth day Abidan son of Gideoni, prince *or* leader of the sons of Benjamin, offered.

61His offering was one silver platter, the weight of which was 130 shekels, one silver basin of seventy shekels, after the shekel of the sanctuary, both of them full of fine flour mixed with oil for a cereal offering;

62One golden bowl of ten shekels, full of incense;

63One young bull, one ram, one male lamb a year old, for a burnt offering;

64One male goat for a sin offering;

65And for the sacrifice of peace offerings, two oxen, five rams, five male goats, five male lambs a year old. This was the offering of Abidan son of Gideoni.

66The tenth day Ahiezer son of Ammishaddai, leader of the sons of Dan, offered.

67His offering was one silver platter, the weight of which was 130 shekels, one silver basin of seventy shekels, after the shekel of the sanctuary, both of them full of fine flour mixed with oil for a cereal offering;

68One golden bowl of ten shekels, full of incense;

69One young bull, one ram, one male lamb a year old, for a burnt offering;

70One male goat for a sin offering;

71And for the sacrifice of peace offerings, two oxen, five rams, five male goats, five male lambs a year old. This was the offering of Ahiezer son of Ammishaddai.

72The eleventh day Pagiel son of Ochran, leader of the sons of Asher, offered.

73His offering was one silver platter, the weight of which was 130 shekels, one silver basin of seventy shekels, after the shekel of the sanctuary, both of them full of fine flour mixed with oil for a cereal offering;

74One golden bowl of ten shekels, full of incense;

King James Version

75One young bullock, one ram, one lamb of the first year, for a burnt offering:

76One kid of the goats for a sin offering:

77And for a sacrifice of peace offerings, two oxen, five rams, five he goats, five lambs of the first year: this was the offering of Pagiel the son of Ocran.

78 ¶ On the twelfth day Ahira the son of Enan, prince of the children of Naphtali, offered:

79His offering was one silver charger, the weight whereof was an hundred and thirty shekels, one silver bowl of seventy shekels, after the shekel of the sanctuary; both of them full of fine flour mingled with oil for a meat offering:

80One golden spoon of ten shekels, full of incense:

81One young bullock, one ram, one lamb of the first year, for a burnt offering:

82One kid of the goats for a sin offering:

83And for a sacrifice of peace offerings, two oxen, five rams, five he goats, five lambs of the first year: this was the offering of Ahira the son of Enan.

84 ¶ This was the dedication of the altar, in the day when it was anointed, by the princes of Israel: twelve chargers of silver, twelve silver bowls, twelve spoons of gold:

85Each charger of silver weighing an hundred and thirty shekels, each bowl seventy: all the silver vessels weighed two thousand and four hundred shekels, after the shekel of the sanctuary:

86The golden spoons were twelve, full of incense, weighing ten shekels apiece, after the shekel of the sanctuary: all the gold of the spoons was an hundred and twenty shekels.

87All the oxen for the burnt offering were twelve bullocks, the rams twelve, the lambs of the first year twelve, with their meat offering: and the kids of the goats for sin offering twelve.

88And all the oxen for the sacrifice of the peace offerings were twenty and four bullocks, the rams sixty, the he goats sixty, the lambs of the first year sixty. This was the dedication of the altar, after that it was anointed.

89 ¶ And when Moses was gone into the tabernacle of the congregation to speak with him, then he heard the voice of one speaking unto him from off the mercy seat that was upon the ark of Testimony, from between the two cherubims: and he spake unto him.

8 And the LORD spake unto Moses, saying,
2Speak unto Aaron, and say unto him, When thou lightest the lamps, the seven lamps shall give light over against the candlestick.

3And Aaron did so; he lighted the lamps thereof over against the candlestick, as the LORD commanded Moses.

4And this work of the candlestick was of beaten gold, unto the shaft thereof, unto the flowers

Amplified Bible

75One young bull, one ram, one male lamb a year old, for a burnt offering;

76One male goat for a sin offering;

77And for the sacrifice of peace offerings, two oxen, five rams, five male goats, five male lambs a year old. This was the offering of Pagiel son of Ochran.

78The twelfth day Ahira son of Enan, leader of the sons of Naphtali, offered.

79His offering was one silver platter, the weight of which was 130 shekels, one silver basin of seventy shekels, after the shekel of the sanctuary, both of them full of fine flour mixed with oil for a cereal offering;

80One golden bowl of ten shekels, full of incense;

81One young bull, one ram, one male lamb a year old, for a burnt offering;

82One male goat for a sin offering;

83And for the sacrifice of peace offerings, two oxen, five rams, five male goats, five male lambs a year old. This was the offering of Ahira son of Enan.

84This was the dedication offering for the altar [of burnt offering] from the leaders of Israel on the day when it was anointed: twelve platters of silver, twelve silver basins, twelve golden bowls;

85Each platter of silver weighing 130 shekels, each basin seventy; all the silver vessels weighed 2,400 shekels, after the shekel of the sanctuary.

86The twelve golden bowls full of incense, weighing ten shekels apiece, after the shekel of the sanctuary, all the gold of the bowls being 120 shekels.

87All the oxen for the burnt offering were twelve bulls, the rams twelve, the male lambs a year old twelve, together with their cereal offering; and the male goats for a sin offering twelve.

88And all the oxen for the sacrifice of the peace offerings were twenty-four bulls, the rams sixty, the male goats sixty, the male lambs a year old sixty. This was the dedication of the altar [of burnt offering] after it was anointed.

89And when Moses went into the Tent of Meeting to speak with the Lord, he heard the voice speaking to him from above the mercy seat that was upon the ark of the Testimony from between the two cherubim; and He spoke to [Moses].

8 AND THE Lord said to Moses,
2Say to Aaron, When you set up and light the lamps, the seven lamps shall be made to give light in front of the lampstand.

3And Aaron did so; he lighted the lamps of the lampstand to give light in front of it, as the Lord commanded Moses.

4And this was the workmanship of the candlestick: beaten or turned gold, beaten work [of

King James Version

thereof, *was* beaten work: according unto the pattern which the LORD had shewed Moses, so he made the candlestick.

5 ¶ And the LORD spake unto Moses, saying,

6 Take the Levites from among the children of Israel, and cleanse them.

7 And thus shalt thou do unto them, to cleanse them: Sprinkle water of purifying upon them, and let them shave all their flesh, and let them wash their clothes, and *so* make themselves clean.

8 Then let them take a young bullock with his meat offering, *even* fine flour mingled with oil, and another young bullock shalt thou take for a sin offering.

9 And thou shalt bring the Levites before the tabernacle of the congregation: and thou shalt gather the whole assembly of the children of Israel together:

10 And thou shalt bring the Levites before the LORD: and the children of Israel shall put their hands upon the Levites:

11 And Aaron shall offer the Levites before the LORD *for* an offering of the children of Israel, that they may execute the service of the LORD.

12 And the Levites shall lay their hands upon the heads of the bullocks: and thou shalt offer the one *for* a sin offering, and the other *for* a burnt offering, unto the LORD, to make an atonement for the Levites.

13 And thou shalt set the Levites before Aaron, and before his sons, and offer them *for* an offering unto the LORD.

14 Thus shalt thou separate the Levites from among the children of Israel: and the Levites shall be mine.

15 And after that shall the Levites go in to do the service of the tabernacle of the congregation: and thou shalt cleanse them, and offer them *for* an offering.

16 For they *are* wholly given unto me from among the children of Israel; instead of such as open every womb, *even instead of* the firstborn of all the children of Israel, have I taken them unto me.

17 For all the firstborn of the children of Israel *are* mine, *both* man and beast: on the day that I smote every firstborn in the land of Egypt, I sanctified them for myself.

18 And I have taken the Levites for all the firstborn of the children of Israel.

19 And I have given the Levites *as* a gift to Aaron and to his sons from among the children of Israel, to do the service of the children of Is-

Amplified Bible

gold] from its base to its flowers; according to the pattern which the Lord had shown Moses, so he made the lampstand.

5 And the Lord said to Moses,

6 Take the *a*Levites from among the Israelites and cleanse them.

7 And thus you shall do to them to cleanse them: sprinkle the water of purification [water to be used in case of sin] upon them, and let them pass a razor over all their flesh and wash their clothes and cleanse themselves.

8 Then let them take a young bull and its cereal offering of fine flour mixed with oil, and another young bull you shall take for a sin offering.

9 You shall present the Levites before the Tent of Meeting, and you shall assemble the whole Israelite congregation.

10 And you shall present the Levites before the Lord, and the Israelites shall put their hands upon the Levites,

11 And Aaron shall offer the Levites before the Lord as a wave offering from the Israelites *and* on their behalf, that they may do the service of the Lord.

12 Then the Levites shall lay their hands upon the heads of the bulls, and you shall offer the one for a sin offering and the other for a burnt offering to the Lord, to make atonement for the Levites.

13 And you shall present the Levites before Aaron and his sons and offer them as a wave offering to the Lord.

14 Thus you shall separate the Levites from among the Israelites, and the Levites shall be Mine [in a very special sense].

15 And after that the Levites shall go in to do service at the Tent of Meeting, when you have cleansed them and offered them as a wave offering.

16 For they are wholly given to Me from among the Israelites; instead of all who open the womb, the firstborn of all the Israelites, I have taken the Levites for Myself.

17 For all the firstborn of the Israelites are Mine, both of man and beast; on the day that I smote every firstborn in the land of Egypt [not of Israel], I consecrated them *and* set them apart for Myself.

18 And I have taken the Levites instead of all the firstborn of the Israelites.

19 And I have given the Levites as a gift to Aaron and to his sons from among the Israelites to do the service of the Israelites at the Tent of

AMP notes: *a* There are many lessons for the Christian in this section (Num. 8:5-22). He sees here the importance of each member of God's family having his own particular task (I Cor. 12). It is necessary that special men be designated for particular duties in order that the work of God's kingdom shall be done in orderly fashion. Those who do the work of God must be cleansed from all defilement of flesh and spirit. No one is fit in himself to serve God. It is only as we see ourselves as guilty sinners saved through the sacrifice of the Lord Jesus Christ at Calvary that we can do anything that is worthwhile in God's sight. Apart from Him, "all our righteousnesses *are* as filthy rags" (Isa. 64:6 KJV). (F. Davidson, ed., *The New Bible Commentary*).

King James Version

rael in the tabernacle of the congregation, and to make an atonement for the children of Israel: that there be no plague among the children of Israel, when the children of Israel come nigh unto the sanctuary.

20And Moses, and Aaron, and all the congregation of the children of Israel, did to the Levites according unto all that the LORD commanded Moses concerning the Levites, so did the children of Israel unto them.

21And the Levites were purified, and they washed their clothes; and Aaron offered them *as* an offering before the LORD; and Aaron made an atonement for them to cleanse them.

22And after that went the Levites in to do their service in the tabernacle of the congregation before Aaron, and before his sons: as the LORD had commanded Moses concerning the Levites, so did they unto them.

23 ¶ And the LORD spake unto Moses, saying,

24This *is it* that *belongeth* unto the Levites: from twenty and five years old and upward they shall go in to wait upon the service of the tabernacle of the congregation:

25And from the age of fifty years they shall cease waiting upon the service *thereof,* and shall serve no more:

26But shall minister with their brethren in the tabernacle of the congregation, to keep the charge, and shall do no service. Thus shalt thou do unto the Levites touching their charge.

9 And the LORD spake unto Moses in the wilderness of Sinai, in the first month of the second year after they were come out of the land of Egypt, saying,

2Let the children of Israel also keep the passover at his appointed season.

3In the fourteenth day of this month, at even, ye shall keep it in his appointed season: according to all the rites of it, and according to all the ceremonies thereof, shall ye keep it.

4And Moses spake unto the children of Israel, that they should keep the passover.

5And they kept the passover on the fourteenth day of the first month at even in the wilderness of Sinai: according to all that the LORD commanded Moses, so did the children of Israel.

6 ¶ And there were *certain* men, who were defiled by the dead body of a man, that they could not keep the passover on that day: and they came before Moses and before Aaron on that day:

7And those men said unto him, We *are* defiled by the dead body of a man: wherefore are we kept back, that *we* may not offer an offering of the LORD in his appointed season among the children of Israel?

8And Moses said unto them, Stand still, and I

Amplified Bible

Meeting and to make atonement for them, that there may be no plague among the Israelites if they should come near the sanctuary.

20So Moses and Aaron and all the congregation of the Israelites did thus to the Levites; according to all that the Lord commanded Moses concerning [them], so did the Israelites to them.

21The Levites cleansed *and* purified themselves and they washed their clothes; and Aaron offered them as a wave offering before the Lord and Aaron made atonement for them to cleanse them.

22And after that the Levites went in to do their service in the Tent of Meeting with the attendance of Aaron and his sons; as the Lord had commanded Moses concerning the Levites, so did they to them.

23And the Lord said to Moses,

24This is what applies to the Levites: from twenty-five years old and upward they shall go in to perform the work of the service of the Tent of Meeting,

25And at the age of fifty years, they shall retire from the warfare of the service and serve no more,

26But shall help their brethren in the Tent of Meeting [attend to protecting the sacred things from being profaned], but shall do no regular *or* heavy service. Thus shall you direct the Levites in regard to their duties.

9 THE LORD said to Moses in the Wilderness of Sinai in the first month of the second year after they had come out of the land of Egypt,

2Let the Israelites keep the Passover at its appointed time.

3On the fourteenth day of this month in the evening, you shall keep it at its appointed time; according to all its statutes and ordinances you shall keep it.

4So Moses told the Israelites they should keep the Passover.

5And they kept the Passover on the fourteenth day of the first month in the evening in the Wilderness of Sinai; according to all that the Lord commanded Moses, so the Israelites did.

6And there were certain men who were defiled by touching the dead body of a man, so they could not keep the Passover on that day; and they came before Moses and Aaron on that day.

7Those men said to [Moses], We are defiled by touching the dead body. Why are we prevented from offering the Lord's offering at its appointed time among the Israelites?

8And Moses said to them, Stand still, and I

King James Version

will hear what the LORD will command concerning you.

9 ¶ And the LORD spake unto Moses, saying,

10Speak unto the children of Israel, saying, If any man of you or of your posterity shall be unclean by reason of a dead body, or *be* in a journey afar off, yet he shall keep the passover unto the LORD.

11The fourteenth day of the second month at even they shall keep it, *and* eat it with unleavened bread and bitter *herbs.*

12They shall leave none of it unto the morning, nor break any bone of it: according to all the ordinances of the passover they shall keep it.

13But the man that *is* clean, and is not in a journey, and forbeareth to keep the passover, even the same soul shall be cut off from among his people: because he brought not the offering of the LORD in his appointed season, that man shall bear his sin.

14And if a stranger shall sojourn among you, and will keep the passover unto the LORD; according to the ordinance of the passover, and according to the manner thereof, so shall he do: ye shall have one ordinance, both for the stranger, and for him that was born in the land.

15 ¶ And on the day that the tabernacle was reared up, the cloud covered the tabernacle, *namely,* the tent of the Testimony: and at even there was upon the tabernacle as it were the appearance of fire, until the morning.

16So it was alway: the cloud covered it *by day,* and the appearance of fire by night.

17And when the cloud was taken up from the tabernacle, then after that the children of Israel journeyed: and in the place where the cloud abode, there the children of Israel pitched their tents.

18At the commandment of the LORD the children of Israel journeyed, and at the commandment of the LORD they pitched: as long as the cloud abode upon the tabernacle they rested in the tents.

19And when the cloud tarried long upon the tabernacle many days, then the children of Israel kept the charge of the LORD, and journeyed not.

20And *so* it was, when the cloud was a few days upon the tabernacle; according to the commandment of the LORD they abode in their tents, and according to the commandment of the LORD they journeyed.

21And *so* it was, when the cloud abode from even unto the morning, and *that* the cloud was taken up in the morning, then they journeyed: whether *it was* by day or by night that the cloud was taken up, they journeyed.

22Or *whether it were* two days, or a month, or a year, that the cloud tarried upon the tabernacle, remaining thereon, the children of Israel abode

Amplified Bible

will hear what the Lord will command concerning you.

9And the Lord said to Moses,

10Say to the Israelites, If any man of you or of your posterity shall be unclean by reason of touching a dead body or is far off on a journey, still he shall keep the Passover to the Lord.

11On the fourteenth day of the second month in the evening they shall keep it, and eat it with unleavened bread and bitter herbs.

12They shall leave none of it until the morning nor break any bone of it; according to all the statutes for the Passover they shall keep it.

13But the man who is clean and is not on a journey, yet does not keep the Passover, that person shall be cut off from among his people because he did not bring the Lord's offering at its appointed time; that man shall bear [the penalty of] his sin.

14And if a stranger sojourns among you and will keep the Passover to the Lord, according to [its] statutes and its ordinances, so shall he do; you shall have one statute both for the temporary resident and for him who was born in the land.

15And on the day that the tabernacle was erected, the cloud [of God's presence] covered the tabernacle, that is, the Tent of the Testimony; and at evening it was over the tabernacle, having the appearance of [a pillar of] fire until the morning.

16So it was constantly; the cloud covered it by day, and the appearance of fire by night.

17Whenever the cloud was taken up from over the Tent, after that the Israelites journeyed; and in the place where the cloud rested, there the Israelites encamped.

18At the Lord's command the Israelites journeyed, and at [His] command they encamped. As long as the cloud rested upon the tabernacle they remained encamped.

19Even when the cloud tarried upon the tabernacle many days, the Israelites kept the Lord's charge and did not set out.

20And sometimes the cloud was only a few days upon the tabernacle, but according to the command of the Lord they remained encamped, and at His command they journeyed.

21And sometimes the cloud remained [over the tabernacle] from evening only until morning, but when the cloud was taken up, they journeyed; whether it was taken up by day or by night, they journeyed.

22Whether it was two days or a month or a longer time that the cloud tarried upon the tabernacle, dwelling on it, the Israelites remained

King James Version

in their tents, and journeyed not: but when it was taken up, they journeyed.

23At the commandment of the LORD they rested in the tents, and at the commandment of the LORD they journeyed: they kept the charge of the LORD, at the commandment of the LORD by the hand of Moses.

10 And the LORD spake unto Moses, saying, 2Make thee two trumpets of silver; of a whole piece thou shalt make them: that thou mayest use them for the calling of the assembly, and for the journeying of the camps.

3And when they shall blow with them, all the assembly shall assemble themselves to thee at the door of the tabernacle of the congregation.

4And if they blow *but* with one *trumpet,* then the princes, *which are* heads of the thousands of Israel, shall gather themselves unto thee.

5When ye blow an alarm, then the camps that lie on the east parts shall go forward.

6When you blow an alarm the second time, then the camps that lie on the south side shall take their journey: they shall blow an alarm for their journeys.

7But when the congregation is to be gathered together, you shall blow, but you shall not sound an alarm.

8And the sons of Aaron, the priests, shall blow with the trumpets; and they shall be to you for an ordinance for ever throughout your generations.

9And if ye go *to* war in your land against the enemy that oppresseth you, then ye shall blow an alarm with the trumpets; and ye shall be remembered before the LORD your God, and ye shall be saved from your enemies.

10Also in the day of your gladness, and in your solemn days, and in the beginnings of your months, ye shall blow with the trumpets over your burnt offerings, and over the sacrifices of your peace offerings; that they may be to you for a memorial before your God: I *am* the LORD your God.

11 ¶ And it came to pass on the twentieth *day* of the second month, in the second year, *that* the cloud was taken up from off the tabernacle of the Testimony.

12And the children of Israel took their journeys out of the wilderness of Sinai; and the cloud rested in the wilderness of Paran.

13And they first took their journey according to the commandment of the LORD by the hand of Moses.

14In the first *place* went the standard of the camp of the children of Judah according to their armies: and over his host *was* Nahshon the son of Amminadab.

15And over the host of the tribe of the children of Issachar *was* Nethaneel the son of Zuar.

Amplified Bible

encamped; but when it was taken up, they journeyed.

23At the command of the Lord they remained encamped, and at [His] command they journeyed; they kept the charge of the Lord, at the command of the Lord through Moses.

10 AND THE Lord said to Moses, 2Make two trumpets of silver; of hammered *or* turned work you shall make them, that you may use them to call the congregation and for breaking camp.

3When they both are blown, all the congregation shall assemble before you at the door of the Tent of Meeting.

4And if one blast on a single trumpet is blown, then the princes *or* leaders, heads of the tribes of Israel, shall gather themselves to you.

5When you blow an alarm, the camps on the east side [of the tabernacle] shall set out.

6When you blow an alarm the second time, then the camps on the south side shall set out. An alarm shall be blown whenever they are to set out on their journeys.

7When the congregation is to be assembled, you shall blow [the trumpets in short, sharp tones], but not the blast of an alarm.

8And the sons of Aaron, the priests, shall blow the trumpets, and the trumpets shall be to you for a perpetual statute throughout your generations.

9When you go to war in your land against the enemy that oppresses you, then blow an alarm with the trumpets, that you may be remembered before the Lord your God, and you shall be saved from your enemies.

10Also in the day of rejoicing, and in your set feasts, and at the beginnings of your months, you shall blow the trumpets over your burnt offerings and your peace offerings; thus they may be a remembrance before your God. I am the Lord your God.

11On the twentieth day of the second month in the second year [since leaving Egypt], the cloud [of the Lord's presence] was taken up from over the tabernacle of the Testimony,

12And the Israelites took their journey by stages out of the Wilderness of Sinai, and the [guiding] cloud rested in the Wilderness of Paran.

13When the journey was to begin, at the command of the Lord through Moses,

14In the first place went the standard of the camp of the sons of Judah by their companies; and over their host was Nahshon son of Amminadab.

15And over the host of the tribe of the sons of Issachar was Nethanel son of Zuar.

King James Version

¹⁶And over the host of the tribe of the children of Zebulun *was* Eliab the son of Helon.

¹⁷And the tabernacle was taken down; and the sons of Gershon and the sons of Merari set forward, bearing the tabernacle.

¹⁸ ¶ And the standard of the camp of Reuben set forward according to their armies: and over his host *was* Elizur the son of Shedeur.

¹⁹And over the host of the tribe of the children of Simeon *was* Shelumiel the son of Zurishaddai.

²⁰And over the host of the tribe of the children of Gad *was* Eliasaph the son of Deuel.

²¹And the Kohathites set forward, bearing the sanctuary: and *the other* did set up the tabernacle against they came.

²² ¶ And the standard of the camp of the children of Ephraim set forward according to their armies: and over his host *was* Elishama the son of Ammihud.

²³And over the host of the tribe of the children of Manasseh *was* Gamaliel the son of Pedahzur.

²⁴And over the host of the tribe of the children of Benjamin *was* Abidan the son of Gideoni.

²⁵ ¶ And the standard of the camp of the children of Dan set forward, *which was* the rereward of all the camps throughout their hosts: and over his host *was* Ahiezer the son of Ammishaddai.

²⁶And over the host of the tribe of the children of Asher *was* Pagiel the son of Ocran.

²⁷And over the host of the tribe of the children of Naphtali *was* Ahira the son of Enan.

²⁸Thus *were* the journeyings of the children of Israel according to their armies, when they set forward.

²⁹ ¶ And Moses said unto Hobab, the son of Raguel the Midianite, Moses' father in law, We *are* journeying unto the place of which the LORD said, I will give it you: come thou with us, and we will do thee good: for the LORD hath spoken good concerning Israel.

³⁰And he said unto him, I will not go; but I will depart to mine own land, and to my kindred.

³¹And he said, Leave us not, I pray thee; forasmuch as thou knowest how we are to encamp in the wilderness, and thou mayest be to us instead of eyes.

³²And it shall be, if thou go with us, yea, it shall be, *that* what goodness the LORD shall do unto us, the same will we do unto thee.

³³ ¶ And they departed from the mount of the LORD three days' journey: and the ark of the covenant of the LORD went before them *in* the three days' journey, to search out a resting place for them.

Amplified Bible

¹⁶And over the host of the tribe of the sons of Zebulun was Eliab son of Helon.

¹⁷When the tabernacle was taken down, the sons of Gershon and Merari, bearing [it] on their shoulders, set out.

¹⁸The standard of the camp of Reuben set forward by their companies; and over Reuben's host was Elizur son of Shedeur.

¹⁹And over the host of the tribe of the sons of Simeon was Shelumiel son of Zurishaddai.

²⁰And over the host of the tribe of the sons of Gad was Eliasaph son of Deuel.

²¹Then the Kohathites set forward, bearing the holy things, and the tabernacle was set up before they arrived.

²²And the standard of the camp of the sons of Ephraim set forward according to their companies; and over Ephraim's host was Elishama son of Ammihud.

²³Over the host of the tribe of the sons of Manasseh was Gamaliel son of Pedahzur.

²⁴And over the host of the tribe of the sons of Benjamin was Abidan son of Gideoni.

²⁵Then the standard of the camp of the sons of Dan, which was the rear guard of all the camps, set forward according to their companies; and over Dan's host was Ahiezer son of Ammishaddai.

²⁶And over the host of the tribe of the sons of Asher was Pagiel son of Ochran.

²⁷And over the host of the tribe of the sons of Naphtali was Ahira son of Enan.

²⁸This was the Israelites' order of march by their hosts when they set out.

²⁹And Moses said to Hobab son of Reuel the Midianite, Moses' father-in-law, We are journeying to the place of which the Lord said, I will give it to you. Come with us, and we will do you good, for the Lord has promised good concerning Israel.

³⁰And Hobab said to him, I will not go; I will depart to my own land and to my family.

³¹And Moses said, ᵃDo not leave us, I pray you; for you know how we are to encamp in the wilderness, and you will serve as eyes for us.

³²And if you will go with us, it shall be that whatever good the Lord does to us, the same we will do to you.

³³They departed from the mountain of the Lord [Mount Sinai] three days' journey; and the ark of the covenant of the Lord went before them during the three days' journey to seek out a resting-place for them.

AMP notes: ᵃ The record does not say so, but Hobab seems to have remained with the Israelites, for later history shows that his descendants lived in Canaan (Judg. 1:16; I Sam. 15:6).

King James Version

34And the cloud of the LORD *was* upon them by day, when they went out of the camp. 35And it came to pass, when the ark set forward, that Moses said, Rise up, LORD, and let thine enemies be scattered; and let them that hate thee flee before thee. 36 ¶ And when it rested, he said, Return, O LORD, *unto* the many thousands of Israel.

11 And *when* the people complained, it displeased the LORD: and the LORD heard *it;* and his anger was kindled; and the fire of the LORD burnt among them, and consumed *them that were* in the uttermost parts of the camp. 2And the people cried unto Moses; and when Moses prayed unto the LORD, the fire was quenched. 3And he called the name of the place Taberah: because the fire of the LORD burnt among them. 4 ¶ And the mixt multitude that *was* among them fell a lusting: and the children of Israel also wept again, and said, Who shall give us flesh to eat? 5We remember the fish, which we did eat in Egypt freely; the cucumbers, and the melons, and the leeks, and the onions, and the garlick: 6But now our soul *is* dried away: *there is* nothing at all, beside *this* manna, *before* our eyes. 7And the manna *was* as coriander seed, and the colour thereof as the colour of bdellium. 8*And* the people went about, and gathered *it,* and ground *it* in mills, or beat *it* in a mortar, and baked *it* in pans, and made cakes *of* it: and the taste of it was as the taste of fresh oil. 9And when the dew fell upon the camp in the night, the manna fell upon it. 10Then Moses heard the people weep throughout their families, every man in the door of his tent: and the anger of the LORD was kindled greatly; Moses also was displeased. 11And Moses said unto the LORD, Wherefore hast thou afflicted thy servant? and wherefore have I not found favour in thy sight, that *thou* layest the burden of all this people upon me? 12Have I conceived all this people? have I begotten them, that thou shouldest say unto me, Carry them in thy bosom, as a nursing father beareth the sucking child, unto the land which thou swarest unto their fathers? 13Whence should I have flesh to give unto all this people? for they weep unto me, saying, Give us flesh, that we may eat. 14I am not able to bear all this people alone, because *it is* too heavy for me. 15And if thou deal thus with me, kill me, I

Amplified Bible

34The cloud of the Lord was over them by day when they went forward from the camp. 35Whenever the ark set out, Moses said, Rise up, Lord; let Your enemies be scattered; and let those who hate You flee before You. 36And when it rested, he said, Return, O Lord, to the ten thousand thousands in Israel.

11 AND THE people grumbled *and* deplored their hardships, which was evil in the ears of the Lord, and when the Lord heard it, His anger was kindled; and the fire of the Lord burned among them and devoured those in the outlying parts of the camp. 2The people cried to Moses, and when Moses prayed to the Lord, the fire subsided. 3He called the name of the place Taberah [burning], because the fire of the Lord burned among them. 4And the mixed multitude among them [the rabble who followed Israel from Egypt] began to lust greatly [for familiar and dainty food], and the Israelites wept again and said, Who will give us meat to eat? 5We remember the fish we ate freely in Egypt *and* without cost, the cucumbers, melons, leeks, onions, and garlic. 6But now our soul (our strength) is dried up; there is nothing at all [in the way of food] to be seen but this manna. 7The manna was like coriander seed and its appearance was like that of bdellium [perhaps a precious stone]. 8The people went about and gathered it, and ground it in mills or beat it in mortars, and boiled it in pots, and made cakes of it; and it tasted like cakes baked with fresh oil. 9And when the dew fell on the camp in the night, the manna fell with it. 10And Moses heard the people weeping throughout their families, every man at the door of his tent; and the anger of the Lord blazed hotly, and in the eyes of Moses it was evil. 11And Moses said to the Lord, Why have You dealt ill with Your servants? And why have I not found favor in Your sight, that You lay the burden of all this people on me? 12Have I conceived all this people? Have I brought them forth, that You should say to me, Carry them in your bosom, as a nursing father carries the sucking child, to the land which You swore to their fathers [to give them]? 13Where should I get meat to give to all these people? For they weep before me and say, Give us meat, that we may eat. 14I am not able to carry all these people alone, because the burden is too heavy for me. 15And if this is the way You deal with me, kill

King James Version

pray thee, out of hand, if I have found favour in thy sight; and let me not see my wretchedness.

16 ¶ And the LORD said unto Moses, Gather unto me seventy men of the elders of Israel, whom thou knowest to be the elders of the people, and officers over them; and bring them unto the tabernacle of the congregation, that they may stand there with thee.

17And I will come down and talk with thee there: and I will take of the spirit which *is* upon thee, and will put *it* upon them; and they shall bear the burden of the people with thee, that thou bear *it* not thyself alone.

18And say thou unto the people, Sanctify yourselves against to morrow, and ye shall eat flesh: for you have wept in the ears of the LORD, saying, Who shall give us flesh to eat? for *it was* well with us in Egypt: therefore the LORD will give you flesh, and ye shall eat.

19Ye shall not eat one day, nor two days, nor five days, neither ten days, nor twenty days;

20*But* even a whole month, until it come out at your nostrils, and it be loathsome unto you: because that ye have despised the LORD which *is* among you, and have wept before him, saying, Why came we forth out of Egypt?

21And Moses said, The people, amongst whom I *am, are* six hundred thousand footmen; and thou hast said, I will give them flesh, that they may eat a whole month.

22Shall the flocks and the herds be slain for them, to suffice them? or shall all the fish of the sea be gathered together for them, to suffice them?

23And the LORD said unto Moses, Is the LORD's hand waxed short? thou shalt see now whether my word shall come to pass unto thee or not.

24And Moses went out, and told the people the words of the LORD, and gathered the seventy men of the elders of the people, and set them round about the tabernacle.

25And the LORD came down in a cloud, and spake unto him, and took of the spirit that *was* upon him, and gave *it* unto the seventy elders: and it came to pass, that when the spirit rested upon them, they prophesied, and did not cease.

26But there remained two *of the* men in the camp, the name of the one *was* Eldad, and the name of the other Medad: and the spirit rested upon them; and they *were* of them that were written, but went not out unto the tabernacle: and they prophesied in the camp.

27And there ran a young man, and told Moses, and said, Eldad and Medad do prophesy in the camp.

Amplified Bible

me, I pray You, at once, and be granting me a favor and let me not see my wretchedness [in the failure of all my efforts].

16And the Lord said to Moses, Gather for Me *a* seventy men of the elders of Israel whom you know to be the elders of the people and officers over them; and bring them to the Tent of Meeting and let them stand there with you.

17And I will come down and talk with you there; and I will take of the Spirit which is upon you and will put It upon them; and they shall bear the burden of the people with you, so that you may not have to bear it yourself alone.

18And say to the people, Consecrate yourselves for tomorrow, and you shall eat meat; for you have wept in the hearing of the Lord, saying, Who will give us meat to eat? For it was well with us in Egypt. Therefore the Lord will give you meat, and you shall eat.

19You shall not eat one day, or two, or five, or ten, or twenty days,

20But a whole month—until [you are satiated and vomit it up violently and] it comes out at your nostrils and is disgusting to you—because you have rejected *and* despised the Lord Who is among you, and have wept before Him, saying, Why did we come out of Egypt?

21But Moses said, The people among whom I am are 600,000 footmen [besides all the women and children], and You have said, I will give them meat, that they may eat a whole month!

22Shall flocks and herds be killed to suffice them? Or shall all the fish of the sea be collected to satisfy them?

23The Lord said to Moses, Has the Lord's hand (His ability and power) become short (thwarted and inadequate)? You shall see now whether My word shall come to pass for you or not.

24So Moses went out and told the people the words of the Lord, and he gathered seventy men of the elders of the people and set them round about the Tent.

25And the Lord came down in the cloud and spoke to him, and took of the Spirit that was upon him and put It upon the seventy elders; and when the Spirit rested upon them, they prophesied [sounding forth the praises of God and declaring His will]. Then they did so no more.

26But there remained two men in the camp named Eldad and Medad. The Spirit rested upon them, and they were of those who were selected *and* listed, yet they did not go out to the Tent [as told to do], but they prophesied in the camp.

27And a young man ran to Moses and said, Eldad and Medad are prophesying [sounding forth the praises of God and declaring His will] in the camp.

AMP notes: *a* A council of seventy elders had existed the year before this (Exod. 24:9). It appears to be the source of the Sanhedrin, the highest Jewish assembly for government in the time of our Lord—usually translated "council."

King James Version

²⁸And Joshua the son of Nun, the servant of Moses, *one* of his young men, answered and said, My lord Moses, forbid them.

²⁹And Moses said unto him, Enviest thou for my sake? would God that all the LORD's people were prophets, *and* that the LORD would put his spirit upon them!

³⁰And Moses gat him into the camp, he and the elders of Israel.

³¹ ¶ And there went forth a wind from the LORD, and brought quails from the sea, and let *them* fall by the camp, as it were a day's journey on this side, and as it were a day's journey on the other side, round about the camp, and as it were two cubits *high* upon the face of the earth.

³²And the people stood up all that day, and all *that* night, and all the next day, and they gathered the quails: he that gathered least gathered ten homers: and they spread *them* all abroad for themselves round about the camp.

³³And while the flesh *was* yet between their teeth, ere it was chewed, the wrath of the LORD was kindled against the people, and the LORD smote the people *with* a very great plague.

³⁴And he called the name of that place Kibroth-hattaavah: because there they buried the people that lusted.

³⁵*And* the people journeyed from Kibroth-hattaavah *unto* Hazeroth; and abode at Hazeroth.

12 And Miriam and Aaron spake against Moses because of the Ethiopian woman whom he had married: for he had married an Ethiopian woman.

²And they said, Hath the LORD indeed spoken only by Moses? hath he not spoken also by us? And the LORD heard *it*.

³(Now the man Moses *was* very meek, above all the men which *were* upon the face of the earth.)

⁴And the LORD spake suddenly unto Moses, and unto Aaron, and unto Miriam, Come out ye three unto the tabernacle of the congregation. And they three came out.

⁵And the LORD came down in the pillar of the cloud, and stood *in* the door of the tabernacle, and called Aaron and Miriam: and they both came forth.

⁶And he said, Hear now my words: If there be a prophet among you, *I* the LORD will make myself known unto him in a vision, *and* will speak unto him in a dream.

⁷My servant Moses *is* not so, who *is* faithful in all mine house.

⁸With him will I speak mouth to mouth, even

Amplified Bible

²⁸Joshua son of Nun, the minister of Moses, one of his chosen men, said, My lord Moses, forbid them!

²⁹But Moses said to him, Are you ᵃenvious *or* jealous for my sake? Would that all the Lord's people were prophets and that the Lord would put His Spirit upon them!

³⁰And Moses went back into the camp, he and the elders of Israel.

³¹And there went forth a wind from the Lord and brought quails from the sea, and let them fall [so they flew low] beside the camp, about a day's journey on this side and on the other side, all around the camp, about two cubits above the ground.

³²And the people rose all that day and all night and all the next day and caught *and* gathered the quails. He who gathered least gathered ten homers; and they spread them out for themselves round about the camp [to cure them by drying].

³³While the meat was yet between their teeth, before it was consumed, the anger of the Lord was kindled against the people, and the Lord smote them with a very great plague.

³⁴That place was called Kibroth-hattaavah [the graves of sensuous desire], because there they buried the people who lusted, whose physical appetite caused them to sin.

³⁵The Israelites journeyed from Kibroth-hattaavah to Hazeroth, where they remained.

12 NOW MIRIAM and Aaron talked against Moses [their brother] because of his ᵇCushite wife, for he had married a Cushite woman.

²And they said, Has the Lord indeed spoken only by Moses? Has He not spoken also by us? And the Lord heard it.

³Now the man Moses was very meek (gentle, kind, and humble) *or* above all the men on the face of the earth.

⁴Suddenly the Lord said to Moses, Aaron, and Miriam, Come out, you three, to the Tent of Meeting. And the three of them came out.

⁵The Lord came down in a pillar of cloud, and stood at the Tent door and called Aaron and Miriam, and they came forward.

⁶And He said, Hear now My words: If there is a prophet among you, I the Lord make Myself known to him in a vision and speak to him in a dream.

⁷But not so with My servant Moses; he is entrusted *and* faithful in all My house.

⁸With him I speak mouth to mouth [directly],

AMP notes: ᵃ "Moses, the minister of God, rebukes our partial love, / Who envy at the gifts bestow'd on those we disapprove. / We do not our own spirit know, who wish to see suppressed, / The men that Jesus' spirit show, the men whom God hath blest" (Charles Wesley). ᵇ Zipporah, Moses' wife, seems to have died some time before. Marriage with a Canaanite was forbidden, but not with an Egyptian or Cushite. Joseph's wife was an Egyptian (Gen. 41:45).

King James Version

apparently, and not in dark speeches; and the similitude of the LORD shall he behold: wherefore then were ye not afraid to speak against my servant Moses?

⁹And the anger of the LORD was kindled against them; and he departed.

¹⁰And the cloud departed from off the tabernacle; and behold, Miriam *became* leprous, *white* as snow: and Aaron looked upon Miriam, and behold, *she was* leprous.

¹¹And Aaron said unto Moses, Alas, my lord, I beseech thee, lay not the sin upon us, wherein we have done foolishly, and wherein we have sinned.

¹²Let her not be as one dead, of whom the flesh is half consumed when he cometh out of his mother's womb.

¹³And Moses cried unto the LORD, saying, Heal her now, O God, I beseech thee.

¹⁴And the LORD said unto Moses, If her father had but spit in her face, should she not be ashamed seven days? let her be shut out from the camp seven days, and after *that* let her be received in *again*.

¹⁵And Miriam was shut out from the camp seven days: and the people journeyed not till Miriam was brought in *again*.

¹⁶And afterward the people removed from Hazeroth, and pitched in the wilderness of Paran.

13 And the LORD spake unto Moses, saying, ²Send thou men, that they may search the land of Canaan, which I give unto the children of Israel: of every tribe of their fathers shall ye send a man, every one a ruler among them.

³And Moses by the commandment of the LORD sent them from the wilderness of Paran: all those men *were* heads of the children of Israel.

⁴And these *were* their names: of the tribe of Reuben, Shammua the son of Zaccur.

⁵Of the tribe of Simeon, Shaphat the son of Hori.

⁶Of the tribe of Judah, Caleb the son of Jephunneh.

⁷Of the tribe of Issachar, Igal the son of Joseph.

⁸Of the tribe of Ephraim, Oshea the son of Nun.

⁹Of the tribe of Benjamin, Palti the son of Raphu.

¹⁰Of the tribe of Zebulun, Gaddiel the son of Sodi.

¹¹Of the tribe of Joseph, *namely,* of the tribe of Manasseh, Gaddi the son of Susi.

¹²Of the tribe of Dan, Ammiel the son of Gemalli.

Amplified Bible

clearly and not in dark speeches; and he beholds the form of the Lord. Why then were you not afraid to speak against My servant Moses?

⁹And the anger of the Lord was kindled against them, and He departed.

¹⁰And when the cloud departed from over the Tent, behold, Miriam was leprous, as white as snow. And Aaron looked at Miriam, and, behold, she was leprous!

¹¹And Aaron said to Moses, Oh, my lord, I plead with you, lay not the sin upon us in which we have done foolishly and in which we have sinned.

¹²Let her not be as one dead, already half decomposed when he comes out of his mother's womb.

¹³And Moses cried to the Lord, saying, Heal her now, O God, I beseech You!

¹⁴And the Lord said to Moses, If her father had but spit in her face, should she not be ashamed for seven days? Let her be shut up outside the camp for seven days, and after that let her be brought in again.

¹⁵So Miriam was shut up without the camp for seven days, and the people did not journey on until Miriam was brought in again.

¹⁶Afterward [they] removed from Hazeroth and encamped in the Wilderness of Paran.

13 AND THE Lord said to Moses, ²Send men to explore *and* scout out [for yourselves] the land of Canaan, which I give to the Israelites. From each tribe of their fathers you shall send a man, every one a leader *or* head among them.

³So Moses by the command of the Lord sent scouts from the Wilderness of Paran, all of them men who were heads of the Israelites.

⁴These were their names: of the tribe of Reuben, Shammua son of Zaccur;

⁵Of the tribe of Simeon, Shaphat son of Hori;

⁶Of the tribe of Judah, Caleb son of Jephunneh;

⁷Of the tribe of Issachar, Igal son of Joseph;

⁸Of the tribe of Ephraim, Hoshea [that is, Joshua] son of Nun;

⁹Of the tribe of Benjamin, Palti son of Raphu;

¹⁰Of the tribe of Zebulun, Gaddiel son of Sodi;

¹¹Of the tribe of Joseph, that is, of the tribe of Manasseh, Gaddi son of Susi;

¹²Of the tribe of Dan, Ammiel son of Gemalli;

King James Version

13Of the tribe of Asher, Sethur the son of Michael.

14Of the tribe of Naphtali, Nahbi the son of Vophsi.

15Of the tribe of Gad, Geuel the son of Machi.

16These *are* the names of the men which Moses sent to spy out the land. And Moses called Oshea the son of Nun, Jehoshua.

17And Moses sent them to spy out the land of Canaan, and said unto them, Get you up this *way* southward, and go up into the mountain:

18And see the land, what it *is;* and the people that dwelleth therein, whether they *be* strong or weak, few or many;

19And what the land *is* that they dwell in, whether it *be* good or bad; and what cities *they be* that they dwell in, whether in tents, or in strong holds;

20And what the land *is,* whether it *be* fat or lean, whether there be wood therein, or not. And be ye of good courage, and bring of the fruit of the land. Now the time *was* the time of the first ripe grapes.

21So they went up, and searched the land from the wilderness of Zin unto Rehob, as *men* come to Hamath.

22And they ascended by the south, and came unto Hebron; where Ahiman, Sheshai, and Talmai, the children of Anak, *were.* (Now Hebron was built seven years before Zoan in Egypt.)

23And they came unto the brook of Eshcol, and cut down from thence a branch with one cluster of grapes, and they bare it between two upon a staff; and *they brought* of the pomegranates, and of the figs.

24The place was called the brook Eshcol, because of the cluster of grapes which the children of Israel cut down from thence.

25And they returned from searching of the land after forty days.

26 ¶ And they went and came to Moses, and to Aaron, and to all the congregation of the children of Israel, unto the wilderness of Paran, to Kadesh; and brought back word unto them, and unto all the congregation, and shewed them the fruit of the land.

27And they told him, and said, We came unto the land whither thou sentest us, and surely it floweth with milk and honey; and this *is* the fruit of it.

28Nevertheless the people *be* strong that dwell in the land, and the cities *are* walled, *and* very great: and moreover we saw the children of Anak there.

29The Amalekites dwell in the land of the south: and the Hittites, and the Jebusites, and the Amorites, dwell in the mountains: and the

Amplified Bible

13Of the tribe of Asher, Sethur son of Michael;

14Of the tribe of Naphtali, Nahbi son of Vophsi;

15Of the tribe of Gad, Geuel son of Machi.

16These are the names of the men whom Moses sent to explore *and* scout out the land. And Moses called Hoshea son of Nun, Joshua.

17Moses sent them to scout out the land of Canaan, and said to them, Get up this way by the South (the Negeb) and go up into the hill country,

18And see what the land is and whether the people who dwell there are strong or weak, few or many,

19And whether the land they live in is good or bad, and whether the cities they dwell in are camps or strongholds,

20And what the land is, whether it is fat or lean, whether there is timber on it or not. And be of good courage and bring some of the fruit of the land. Now the time was the time of the first ripe grapes.

21So they went up and scouted through the land from the Wilderness of Zin to Rehob, to the entrance of Hamath.

22And then went up into the South (the Negeb) and came to Hebron; and Ahiman, Sheshai, and Talmai [probably three tribes of] the sons of Anak were there. (Hebron was built seven years before Zoan in Egypt.)

23And they came to the Valley of Eshcol, and cut down from there a branch with one cluster of grapes, and they carried it on a pole between two [of them]; they brought also some pomegranates and figs.

24That place was called the Valley of Eshcol [cluster] because of the cluster which the Israelites cut down there.

25And they returned from scouting out the land after forty days.

26They came to Moses and Aaron and to all the Israelite congregation in the Wilderness of Paran at Kadesh, and brought them word, and showed them the land's fruit.

27They told Moses, We came to the land to which you sent us; surely it flows with milk and honey. This is its fruit.

28But the people who dwell there are strong, and the cities are afortified *and* very large; moreover, there we saw the sons of Anak [of great stature and courage].

29Amalek dwells in the land of the South (the Negeb); the Hittite, the Jebusite, and the Amorite dwell in the hill country; and the Canaanite

---

AMP notes: *a* The scouts probably had not seen walled cities before, having lived their childhood in Goshen in Egypt. Those who forgot God's power to help them naturally found the situation formidable, as happens in the lives of most people. " 'But God' makes all the difference between cowards and Calebs."

King James Version

Canaanites dwell by the sea, and by the coast of Jordan.

30 And Caleb stilled the people before Moses, and said, Let us go up at once, and possess it; for we are well able to overcome it.

31 But the men that went up with him said, We be not able to go up against the people; for they *are* stronger than we.

32 And they brought up an evil report of the land which they had searched unto the children of Israel, saying, The land, through which we have gone to search it, *is* a land that eateth up the inhabitants thereof; and all the people that we saw in it *are* men of a great stature.

33 And there we saw the giants, the sons of Anak, *which come* of the giants: and we were in our own sight as grasshoppers, and so we were in their sight.

14 And all the congregation lifted up their voice, and cried; and the people wept that night.

2 And all the children of Israel murmured against Moses and against Aaron: and the whole congregation said unto them, Would God that we had died in the land of Egypt! or would God we had died in this wilderness!

3 And wherefore *hath* the LORD brought us unto this land, to fall by the sword, *that* our wives and our children should be a prey? were it not better for us to return into Egypt?

4 And they said one to another, Let us make a captain, and let us return into Egypt.

5 Then Moses and Aaron fell on their faces before all the assembly of the congregation of the children of Israel.

6 And Joshua the son of Nun, and Caleb the son of Jephunneh, *which were* of them that searched the land, rent their clothes:

7 And they spake unto all the company of the children of Israel, saying, The land, which we passed through to search it, *is* an exceeding good land.

8 If the LORD delight in us, then he will bring us into this land, and give it us; a land which floweth with milk and honey.

9 Only rebel not ye against the LORD, neither fear ye the people of the land; for they *are* bread for us: their defence is departed from them, and the LORD *is* with us: fear them not.

10 But all the congregation bade stone them with stones. And the glory of the LORD appeared in the tabernacle of the congregation before all the children of Israel.

11 And the LORD said unto Moses, How long will this people provoke me? and how long will it be ere they believe me, for all the signs which I have shewed among them?

12 I will smite them with the pestilence, and disinherit them, and will make of thee a greater nation and mightier than they.

Amplified Bible

dwells by the sea and along by the side of the Jordan [River].

30 Caleb quieted the people before Moses, and said, Let us go up at once and possess it; we are well able to conquer it.

31 But his fellow scouts said, We are not able to go up against the people [of Canaan], for they are stronger than we are.

32 So they brought the Israelites an evil report of the land which they had scouted out, saying, The land through which we went to spy it out is a land that devours its inhabitants. And all the people that we saw in it are men of great stature.

33 There we saw the Nephilim [or giants], the sons of Anak, who come from the giants; and we were in our own sight as grasshoppers, and so we were in their sight.

14 AND ALL the congregation cried out with a loud voice, and [they] wept that night.

2 All the Israelites grumbled *and* deplored their situation, accusing Moses and Aaron, to whom the whole congregation said, Would that we had died in Egypt! Or that we had died in this wilderness!

3 Why does the Lord bring us to this land to fall by the sword? Our wives and little ones will be a prey. Is it not better for us to return to Egypt?

4 And they said one to another, Let us choose a captain and return to Egypt.

5 Then Moses and Aaron fell on their faces before all the assembly of Israelites.

6 And Joshua son of Nun and Caleb son of Jephunneh, who were among the scouts who had searched the land, rent their clothes,

7 And they said to all the company of Israelites, The land through which we passed as scouts is an exceedingly good land.

8 If the Lord delights in us, then He will bring us into this land and give it to us, a land flowing with milk and honey.

9 Only do not rebel against the Lord, neither fear the people of the land, for they are bread for us. Their defense *and* the shadow [of protection] is removed from over them, but the Lord is with us. Fear them not.

10 But all the congregation said to stone [Joshua and Caleb] with stones. But the glory of the Lord appeared at the Tent of Meeting before all the Israelites.

11 And the Lord said to Moses, How long will this people provoke (spurn, despise) Me? And how long will it be before they believe Me [trusting in, relying on, clinging to Me], for all the signs which I have performed among them?

12 I will smite them with the pestilence and disinherit them, and will make of you [Moses] a nation greater and mightier than they.

King James Version

13And Moses said unto the LORD, Then the Egyptians shall hear *it*, (for thou broughtest up this people in thy might from among them;)

14And they will tell *it* to the inhabitants of this land: *for* they have heard that thou LORD *art* among this people, that thou LORD *art* seen face to face, and *that* thy cloud standeth over them, and *that* thou goest before them, by day time in a pillar of a cloud, and in a pillar of fire by night.

15Now *if* thou shalt kill *all* this people as one man, then the nations which have heard the fame of thee will speak, saying,

16Because the LORD was not able to bring this people into the land which he sware unto them, therefore he hath slain them in the wilderness.

17And now, I beseech thee, let the power of my Lord be great, according as thou hast spoken, saying,

18The LORD *is* longsuffering, and of great mercy, forgiving iniquity and transgression, and by no means clearing *the guilty*, visiting the iniquity of the fathers upon the children unto the third and fourth *generation*.

19Pardon, I beseech thee, the iniquity of this people according unto the greatness of thy mercy, and as thou hast forgiven this people, from Egypt even until now.

20And the LORD said, I have pardoned according to thy word:

21But *as* truly *as* I live, all the earth shall be filled *with* the glory of the LORD.

22Because all *those* men which have seen my glory, and my miracles, which I did in Egypt and in the wilderness, and have tempted me *now* these ten times, and have not hearkened to my voice;

23Surely they shall not see the land which I sware unto their fathers, neither shall any of them that provoked me see it:

24But my servant Caleb, because he had another spirit with him, and hath followed me fully, him will I bring into the land whereinto he went; and his seed shall possess it.

25(Now the Amalekites and the Canaanites dwelt in the valley.) To morrow turn you, and get you *into* the wilderness *by* the way of the Red sea.

26 ¶ And the LORD spake unto Moses and unto Aaron, saying,

27How long *shall I bear* with this evil congregation, which murmur against me? I have heard the murmurings of the children of Israel, which they murmur against me.

28Say unto them, *As truly as* I live, saith the LORD, as ye have spoken in mine ears, so will I do to you:

29Your carcases shall fall in this wilderness; and all that were numbered of you, according to your whole number, from twenty years old and upward, which have murmured against me,

30Doubtless ye shall not come into the land,

Amplified Bible

13But Moses said to the Lord, Then the Egyptians will hear of it, for You brought up this people in Your might from among them.

14And they will tell it to the inhabitants of this land. They have heard that You, Lord, are in the midst of this people [of Israel], that You, Lord, are seen face to face, and that Your cloud stands over them, and that You go before them in a pillar of cloud by day and in a pillar of fire by night.

15Now if You kill all this people as one man, then the nations that have heard Your fame will say,

16Because the Lord was not able to bring this people into the land which He swore to give to them, therefore He has slain them in the wilderness.

17And now, I pray You, let the power of my Lord be great, as You have promised, saying,

18The Lord is long-suffering *and* slow to anger, and abundant in mercy *and* loving-kindness, forgiving iniquity and transgression; but He will by no means clear the guilty, visiting the iniquity of the fathers upon the children, upon the third and fourth generation.

19Pardon, I pray You, the iniquity of this people according to the greatness of Your mercy *and* loving-kindness, just as You have forgiven [them] from Egypt until now.

20And the Lord said, I have pardoned according to your word,

21But truly as I live and as all the earth shall be filled with the glory of the Lord,

22Because all those men who have seen My glory and My [miraculous] signs which I performed in Egypt and in the wilderness, yet have tested *and* proved Me these ten times and have not heeded My voice,

23Surely they shall not see the land which I swore to give to their fathers; nor shall any who provoked (spurned, despised) Me see it.

24But My servant Caleb, because he has a different spirit and has followed Me fully, I will bring into the land into which he went, and his descendants shall possess it.

25Now because the Amalekites and the Canaanites dwell in the valley, tomorrow turn and go into the wilderness by way of the Red Sea.

26And the Lord said to Moses and Aaron,

27How long will this evil congregation murmur against Me? I have heard the complaints the Israelites murmur against Me.

28Tell them, As I live, says the Lord, what you have said in My hearing I will do to you:

29Your dead bodies shall fall in this wilderness—of all who were numbered of you, from twenty years old and upward, who have murmured against Me,

30Surely none shall come into the land in

King James Version

concerning which I sware to make you dwell therein, save Caleb the son of Jephunneh, and Joshua the son of Nun.

³¹But your little ones, which ye said should be a prey, them will I bring in, and they shall know the land which ye have despised.

³²But *as for* you, your carcases, they shall fall in this wilderness.

³³And your children shall wander in the wilderness forty years, and bear your whoredoms, until your carcases be wasted in the wilderness.

³⁴After the number of the days *in* which ye searched the land, *even* forty days, each day for a year, shall ye bear your iniquities, *even* forty years, and ye shall know my breach of promise.

³⁵I the LORD have said, I will surely do it unto all this evil congregation, that are gathered together against me: in this wilderness they shall be consumed, and there they shall die.

³⁶And the men, which Moses sent to search the land, who returned, and made all the congregation to murmur against him, by bringing up a slander upon the land,

³⁷Even *those* men that did bring up the evil report upon the land, died by the plague before the LORD.

³⁸But Joshua the son of Nun, and Caleb the son of Jephunneh, *which were* of the men that went to search the land, lived *still.*

³⁹And Moses told these sayings unto all the children of Israel: and the people mourned greatly.

⁴⁰ ¶ And they rose up early in the morning, and gat them up into the top of the mountain, saying, Lo, we *be here,* and will go up unto the place which the LORD hath promised: for we have sinned.

⁴¹And Moses said, Wherefore now do ye transgress the commandment of the LORD? but it shall not prosper.

⁴²Go not up, for the LORD *is* not among you; that ye be not smitten before your enemies.

⁴³For the Amalekites and the Canaanites *are* there before you, and ye shall fall by the sword: because ye are turned away from the LORD, therefore the LORD will not be with you.

⁴⁴But they presumed to go up unto the hill top: nevertheless the ark of the covenant of the LORD, and Moses, departed not out of the camp.

⁴⁵Then the Amalekites came down, and the Canaanites which dwelt in that hill, and smote them, and discomfited them, *even* unto Hormah.

15 And the LORD spake unto Moses, saying, ²Speak unto the children of Israel, and

Amplified Bible

which I swore to make you dwell, except Caleb son of Jephunneh and Joshua son of Nun.

³¹But your little ones whom you said would be a prey, them will I bring in and they shall know the land which you have despised *and* rejected.

³²But as for you, your dead bodies shall fall in this wilderness.

³³And your children shall be wanderers *and* shepherds in the wilderness for forty years and shall suffer for your whoredoms (your infidelity to your espoused God), until your corpses are consumed in the wilderness.

³⁴After the number of the days in which you spied out the land [of Canaan], even forty days, for each day a year shall you bear *and* suffer for your iniquities, even for forty years, and you shall know My displeasure [the revoking of My promise and My estrangement].

³⁵I the Lord have spoken; surely this will I do to all this evil congregation who is gathered together against Me. In this wilderness they shall be consumed [by war, disease, plagues], and here they shall die.

³⁶And the men whom Moses sent to search the land, who returned and made all the congregation grumble *and* complain against him by bringing back a slanderous report of the land,

³⁷Even those men who brought the evil report of the land died by a plague before the Lord.

³⁸But Joshua son of Nun and Caleb son of Jephunneh, who were among the men who went to search the land, lived still.

³⁹Moses told [the Lord's] words to all the Israelites, and [they] mourned greatly.

⁴⁰And they rose early in the morning and went up to the top of the mountain, saying, Behold, we are here, and we intend to go up to the place which the Lord has promised, for we have sinned.

⁴¹But Moses said, Why now do you transgress the command of the Lord [to turn back by way of the Red Sea], since it will not succeed?

⁴²Go not up, for the Lord is not among you, that you be not struck down before your enemies.

⁴³For the Amalekites and the Canaanites are there before you, and you shall fall by the sword. Because you have turned away from following after the Lord, therefore the Lord will not be with you.

⁴⁴But they presumed to go up to the heights of the hill country; however, neither the ark of the covenant of the Lord nor Moses departed out of the camp.

⁴⁵Then the Amalekites came down and the Canaanites who dwelt in that hill country and smote the Israelites and beat them back, even as far as Hormah.

15 AND THE Lord said to Moses, ²Say to the Israelites, When you come

King James Version

say unto them, When ye be come into the land of your habitations, which I give unto you,

³And will make an offering by fire unto the LORD, a burnt offering, or a sacrifice in performing a vow, or in a freewill offering, or in your solemn feasts, to make a sweet savour unto the LORD, of the herd, or of the flock:

⁴Then shall he that offereth his offering unto the LORD bring a meat offering of a tenth deal *of* flour mingled with the fourth *part* of a hin of oil.

⁵And the fourth *part* of a hin *of* wine for a drink offering shalt thou prepare with the burnt offering or sacrifice, for one lamb.

⁶Or for a ram, thou shalt prepare *for* a meat offering two tenth deals *of* flour mingled with the third *part* of a hin of oil.

⁷And for a drink offering thou shalt offer the third *part* of a hin *of* wine, *for* a sweet savour unto the LORD.

⁸And when thou preparest a bullock *for* a burnt offering, or *for* a sacrifice in performing a vow, or peace offerings unto the LORD:

⁹Then shall he bring with a bullock a meat offering of three tenth deals *of* flour mingled with half a hin of oil.

¹⁰And thou shalt bring for a drink offering half a hin *of* wine, *for* an offering made by fire, of a sweet savour unto the LORD.

¹¹Thus shall it be done for one bullock, or for one ram, or for a lamb, or a kid.

¹²According to the number that ye shall prepare, so shall ye do to *every* one according to their number.

¹³All that are born of the country shall do these *things* after this manner, in offering an offering made by fire, of a sweet savour unto the LORD.

¹⁴And if a stranger sojourn with you, or whosoever *be* among you in your generations, and will offer an offering made by fire, of a sweet savour unto the LORD; as ye do, so he shall do.

¹⁵One ordinance *shall be both* for you *of* the congregation, and also for the stranger that sojourneth *with you,* an ordinance for ever in your generations: as ye *are,* so shall the stranger be before the LORD.

¹⁶One law and one manner shall be for you, and for the stranger that sojourneth with you.

¹⁷ ¶ And the LORD spake unto Moses, saying,

¹⁸Speak unto the children of Israel, and say unto them, When ye come into the land whither I bring you,

¹⁹Then it shall be, *that* when ye eat of the bread of the land, ye shall offer up a heave offering unto the LORD.

²⁰Ye shall offer up a cake *of* the first of your dough *for* a heave offering: as *ye do* the heave offering of the threshingfloor, so shall ye heave it.

Amplified Bible

into the land where you are to live, which I am giving you,

³And will make an offering by fire to the Lord from the herd or from the flock, a burnt offering or a sacrifice to fulfill a special vow or as a freewill offering or in your set feasts, to make a pleasant *and* soothing fragrance to the Lord,

⁴Then shall he who brings his offering to the Lord bring a cereal offering of a tenth of an ephah of fine flour mixed with a fourth of a hin of oil.

⁵And a fourth of a hin of wine for the drink offering you shall prepare with the burnt offering or for the sacrifice, for each lamb.

⁶Or for a ram you shall prepare for a cereal offering two tenths of an ephah of fine flour mixed with a third of a hin of oil.

⁷And for the drink offering you shall offer a third of a hin of wine, for a sweet *and* pleasing odor to the Lord.

⁸And when you prepare a bull for a burnt offering or for a sacrifice, in fulfilling a special vow or peace offering to the Lord,

⁹Then shall one offer with the bull a cereal offering of three tenths of an ephah of fine flour mixed with half a hin of oil.

¹⁰And you shall bring for the drink offering half a hin of wine for an offering made by fire, of a pleasant *and* soothing fragrance to the Lord.

¹¹Thus shall it be done for each bull or for each ram, or for each of the male lambs or of the kids.

¹²According to the number that you shall prepare, so shall you do to everyone according to their number.

¹³All who are native-born shall do these things in this way in bringing an offering made by fire of a sweet *and* pleasant odor to the Lord.

¹⁴And if a stranger sojourns with you or whoever may be among you throughout your generations, and he wishes to offer an offering made by fire, of a pleasing *and* soothing fragrance to the Lord, as you do, so shall he do.

¹⁵There shall be one [and the same] statute [both] for you [of the congregation] and for the stranger who is a temporary resident with you, a statute forever throughout your generations: as you are, so shall the stranger be before the Lord.

¹⁶One law and one ordinance shall be for you and for the stranger who sojourns with you.

¹⁷And the Lord said to Moses,

¹⁸Say to the Israelites, When you come into the land to which I am bringing you,

¹⁹Then, when you eat of the food of the land, you shall set apart a portion for a gift to the Lord [called a heave or taken-out offering].

²⁰You shall set apart a cake made of the first of your coarse meal as a gift [to the Lord]; as an offering set apart from the threshing floor, so shall you lift it out *or* heave it.

King James Version

21Of the first of your dough ye shall give unto the LORD a heave offering in your generations.

22And if ye have erred, and not observed all these commandments, which the LORD hath spoken unto Moses,

23*Even* all that the LORD hath commanded you by the hand of Moses, from the day that the LORD commanded *Moses,* and henceforward among your generations;

24Then it shall be, if *ought* be committed by ignorance without the knowledge of the congregation, that all the congregation shall offer one young bullock for a burnt offering, for a sweet savour unto the LORD, with his meat offering, and his drink offering, according to the manner, and one kid of the goats for a sin offering.

25And the priest shall make an atonement for all the congregation of the children of Israel, and it shall be forgiven them; for it *is* ignorance: and they shall bring their offering, a sacrifice made by fire unto the LORD, and their sin offering before the LORD, for their ignorance:

26And it shall be forgiven all the congregation of the children of Israel, and the stranger that sojourneth among them; seeing all the people were in ignorance.

27And if any soul sin through ignorance, then he shall bring a she goat of the first year for a sin offering.

28And the priest shall make an atonement for the soul that sinneth ignorantly, when he sinneth by ignorance before the LORD, to make an atonement for him; and it shall be forgiven him.

29You shall have one law for him that sinneth through ignorance, *both for* him that is born amongst the children of Israel, and for the stranger that sojourneth among them.

30But the soul that doeth *ought* presumptuously, *whether he be* born in the land, or a stranger, the same reproacheth the LORD; and that soul shall be cut off from among his people.

31Because he hath despised the word of the LORD, and hath broken his commandment, that soul shall utterly be cut off; his iniquity *shall be* upon him.

32 ¶ And while the children of Israel were in the wilderness, they found a man that gathered sticks upon the sabbath day.

33And they that found him gathering sticks brought him unto Moses and Aaron, and unto all the congregation.

34And they put him in ward, because it was not declared what should be done to him.

35And the LORD said unto Moses, The man shall be surely put to death: all the congregation shall stone him with stones without the camp.

36And all the congregation brought him with-

Amplified Bible

21Of the first of your coarse meal you shall give to the Lord a portion for a gift throughout your generations [your heave or lifted-out offering].

22When you have erred and have not observed all these commandments which the Lord has spoken to Moses,

23Even all that the Lord has commanded you through Moses, from the day that the Lord gave commandment and onward throughout your generations,

24Then it shall be, if it was done unwittingly *or* in error without the knowledge of the congregation, that all the congregation shall offer one young bull for a burnt offering, for a pleasant *and* soothing fragrance to the Lord, with its cereal offering and its drink offering, according to the ordinance, and one male goat for a sin offering.

25And the priest shall make atonement for all the congregation of the Israelites, and they shall be forgiven, for it was an error and they have brought their offering, an offering made by fire to the Lord, and their sin offering before the Lord for their error.

26And all the congregation of the Israelites shall be forgiven and the stranger who lives temporarily among them, because all the people were involved in the error.

27And if any person sins unknowingly *or* unintentionally, he shall offer a female goat a year old for a sin offering.

28And the priest shall make atonement before the Lord for the person who commits an error when he sins unknowingly *or* unintentionally, to make atonement for him; and he shall be forgiven.

29You shall have one law for him who sins unknowingly *or* unintentionally, whether he is native born among the Israelites or a stranger who is sojourning among them.

30But the person who does anything [wrong] willfully *and* openly, whether he is native-born or a stranger, that one reproaches, reviles, *and* blasphemes the Lord, and that person shall be cut off from among his people [that the atonement made for them may not include him].

31Because he has despised and rejected the word of the Lord, and has broken His commandment, that person shall be utterly cut off; his iniquity shall be upon him.

32While the Israelites were in the wilderness, they found a man who was gathering sticks on the Sabbath day.

33Those who found him gathering sticks brought him to Moses and Aaron and to all the congregation.

34They put him in custody, because it was not certain *or* clear what should be done to him.

35And the Lord said to Moses, The man shall surely be put to death. All the congregation shall stone him with stones without the camp.

36And all the congregation brought him with-

King James Version

out the camp, and stoned him with stones, and he died; as the LORD commanded Moses.

37 ¶ And the LORD spake unto Moses, saying,

38Speak unto the children of Israel, and bid them that they make them fringes in the borders of their garments throughout their generations, and that they put upon the fringe of the borders a ribband of blue:

39And it shall be unto you for a fringe, that ye may look upon it, and remember all the commandments of the LORD, and do them; and that ye seek not after your own heart and your own eyes, after which ye use to go a whoring:

40That ye may remember, and do all my commandments, and be holy unto your God.

41I am the LORD your God, which brought you out of the land of Egypt, to be your God: I am the LORD your God.

16 Now Korah, the son of Izhar, the son of Kohath, the son of Levi, and Dathan and Abiram, the sons of Eliab, and On, the son of Peleth, sons of Reuben, took men:

2And they rose up before Moses, with certain of the children of Israel, two hundred and fifty princes of the assembly, famous in the congregation, men of renown:

3And they gathered themselves together against Moses and against Aaron, and said unto them, Ye take too much upon you, seeing all the congregation are holy, every one of them, and the LORD is among them: wherefore then lift you up yourselves above the congregation of the LORD?

4And when Moses heard it, he fell upon his face:

5And he spake unto Korah and unto all his company, saying, Even to morrow the LORD will shew who are his, and who is holy; and will cause him to come near unto him: even him whom he hath chosen will he cause to come near unto him.

6This do; Take you censers, Korah, and all his company;

7And put fire therein, and put incense in them before the LORD to morrow: and it shall be that the man whom the LORD doth choose, he shall be holy: ye take too much upon you, ye sons of Levi.

8And Moses said unto Korah, Hear, I pray you, ye sons of Levi:

9Seemeth it but a small thing unto you, that the God of Israel hath separated you from the congregation of Israel, to bring you near to himself to do the service of the tabernacle of the LORD, and to stand before the congregation to minister unto them?

10And he hath brought thee near to him, and

Amplified Bible

out the camp and stoned him to death with stones, as the Lord commanded Moses.

37And the Lord said to Moses,

38Speak to the Israelites and bid them make fringes or tassels on the corners in the borders of their garments throughout their generations, and put upon the fringe of the borders or upon the tassel of each corner a cord of blue.

39And it shall be to you a fringe or tassel that you may look upon and remember all the commandments of the Lord and do them, that you may not spy out and follow after [the desires of] your own heart and your own eyes, after which you used to follow and play the harlot [spiritually, if not physically],

40That you may remember and do all My commandments and be holy to your God.

41I am the Lord your God, Who brought you out of the land of Egypt to be your God. I am the Lord your God.

16 NOW KORAH son of Izhar, the son of Kohath, the son of Levi, with Dathan and Abiram sons of Eliab, and On son of Peleth, sons of Reuben, took men,

2And they rose up before Moses, with certain of the Israelites, 250 princes or leaders of the congregation called to the assembly, men well known and of distinction.

3And they gathered together against Moses and Aaron, and said to them, [Enough of you!] You take too much upon yourselves, seeing that all the congregation is holy, every one of them, and the Lord is among them. Why then do you lift yourselves up above the assembly of the Lord?

4And when Moses heard it, he fell upon his face.

5And he said to Korah and all his company, In the morning the Lord will show who are His and who is holy, and will cause him to come near to Him; him whom He has chosen will He cause to come near to Him.

6Do this: Take censers, Korah and all your company,

7And put fire in them and put incense upon them before the Lord tomorrow; and the man whom the Lord chooses shall be holy. You take too much upon yourselves, you sons of Levi.

8And Moses said to Korah, Hear, I pray you, you sons of Levi:

9Does it seem but a small thing to you that the God of Israel has separated you from the congregation of Israel, to bring you near to Himself to do the service of the tabernacle of the Lord and to stand before the congregation to minister to them,

10And that He has brought you near to Him,

King James Version

all thy brethren the sons of Levi with thee: and seek ye the priesthood also?

¹¹For which cause *both* thou and all thy company *are* gathered together against the LORD: and what *is* Aaron, that ye murmur against him?

¹²And Moses sent to call Dathan and Abiram, the sons of Eliab: which said, We will not come up:

¹³*Is it* a small thing that thou hast brought us up out of a land that floweth with milk and honey, to kill us in the wilderness, except thou make thyself altogether a prince over us?

¹⁴Moreover thou hast not brought us into a land that floweth with milk and honey, or given us inheritance of fields and vineyards: wilt thou put out the eyes of these men? we will not come up.

¹⁵And Moses was very wroth, and said unto the LORD, Respect not thou their offering: I have not taken one ass from them, neither have I hurt one of them.

¹⁶And Moses said unto Korah, Be thou and all thy company before the LORD, thou, and they, and Aaron, to morrow:

¹⁷And take every man his censer, and put incense in them, and bring ye before the LORD every man his censer, two hundred and fifty censers; thou also, and Aaron, each *of you* his censer.

¹⁸And they took every man his censer, and put fire in them, and laid incense thereon, and stood *in* the door of the tabernacle of the congregation with Moses and Aaron.

¹⁹And Korah gathered all the congregation against them unto the door of the tabernacle of the congregation: and the glory of the LORD appeared unto all the congregation.

²⁰And the LORD spake unto Moses and unto Aaron, saying,

²¹Separate yourselves from among this congregation, that I may consume them in a moment.

²²And they fell upon their faces, and said, O God, the God of the spirits of all flesh, shall one man sin, and wilt thou be wroth with all the congregation?

²³And the LORD spake unto Moses, saying,

²⁴Speak unto the congregation, saying, Get you up from about the tabernacle of Korah, Dathan, and Abiram.

²⁵And Moses rose up and went unto Dathan and Abiram; and the elders of Israel followed him.

²⁶And he spake unto the congregation, saying, Depart, I pray you, from the tents of these wicked men, and touch nothing of theirs, lest ye be consumed in all their sins.

²⁷So they gat up from the tabernacle of Korah, Dathan, and Abiram, on every side: and Dathan and Abiram came out, and stood *in* the door of their tents, and their wives, and their sons, and their little children.

Amplified Bible

and all your brethren the sons of Levi with you? Would you seek the priesthood also?

¹¹Therefore you and all your company are gathered together against the Lord. And Aaron, what is he that you murmur against him?

¹²And Moses sent to call Dathan and Abiram, the sons of Eliab, and they said, We will not come up.

¹³Is it a small thing that you have brought us up out of a land flowing with milk and honey to kill us in the wilderness, but you must also make yourself a prince over us?

¹⁴Moreover, you have not brought us into a land that flows with milk and honey or given us an inheritance of fields and vineyards. Will you bore out the eyes of these men? We will not come up!

¹⁵And Moses was very angry and said to the Lord, Do not respect their offering! I have not taken one donkey from them, nor have I hurt one of them.

¹⁶And Moses said to Korah, You and all your company be before the Lord tomorrow, you and they and Aaron.

¹⁷And let every man take his censer and put incense upon it and bring before the Lord every man his censer, 250 censers; you also and Aaron, each his censer.

¹⁸So they took every man his censer, and they put fire in them and laid incense upon it, and they stood at the entrance of the Tent of Meeting with Moses and Aaron.

¹⁹Then Korah assembled all the congregation against Moses and Aaron before the entrance of the Tent of Meeting, and the glory of the Lord appeared to all the congregation.

²⁰And the Lord said to Moses and Aaron,

²¹Separate yourselves from among this congregation, that I may consume them in a moment.

²²And they fell upon their faces, and said, O God, the God of the spirits of all flesh, shall one man sin and will You be angry with all the congregation?

²³And the Lord said to Moses,

²⁴Say to the congregation, Get away from around the tents of Korah, Dathan, and Abiram.

²⁵Then Moses rose up and went to Dathan and Abiram, and the elders of Israel followed him.

²⁶And he said to the congregation, Depart, I pray you, from the tents of these wicked men, and touch nothing of theirs, lest you be consumed in all their sins.

²⁷So they got away from around the tents of Korah, Dathan, and Abiram. And Dathan and Abiram came out and stood in the door of their tents with their wives, and their sons, and their little ones.

King James Version

28And Moses said, Hereby ye shall know that the LORD hath sent me to do all these works; for *I have* not *done them* of mine own mind.

29If these *men* die the common death of all men, or if they be visited after the visitation of all men; *then* the LORD hath not sent me.

30But if the LORD make a new thing, and the earth open her mouth, and swallow them up, with all that *appertain* unto them, and they go down quick into the pit; then ye shall understand that these men have provoked the LORD.

31And it came to pass, as he had made an end of speaking all these words, that the ground clave asunder that *was* under them:

32And the earth opened her mouth, and swallowed them up, and their houses, and all the men that *appertained* unto Korah, and all *their* goods.

33They, and all that *appertained* to them, went down alive into the pit, and the earth closed upon them: and they perished from among the congregation.

34And all Israel that *were* round about them fled at the cry of them: for they said, Lest the earth swallow us up *also.*

35And there came out a fire from the LORD, and consumed the two hundred and fifty men that offered incense.

36 ¶ And the LORD spake unto Moses, saying,

37Speak unto Eleazar the son of Aaron the priest, that he take up the censers out of the burning, and scatter thou the fire yonder; for they are hallowed.

38The censers of these sinners against their own souls, let them make them broad plates *for* a covering of the altar: for they offered them before the LORD, therefore they are hallowed: and they shall be a sign unto the children of Israel.

39And Eleazar the priest took the brasen censers, wherewith they that were burnt had offered; and they were made broad *plates for* a covering of the altar:

40*To be* a memorial unto the children of Israel, that no stranger, which *is* not of the seed of Aaron, come near to offer incense before the LORD; that he be not as Korah, and as his company: as the LORD said to him by the hand of Moses.

41 ¶ But on the morrow all the congregation of the children of Israel murmured against Moses and against Aaron, saying, Ye have killed the people of the LORD.

42And it came to pass, when the congregation was gathered against Moses and against Aaron, that they looked toward the tabernacle of the congregation: and behold, the cloud covered it, and the glory of the LORD appeared.

43And Moses and Aaron came before the tabernacle of the congregation.

44And the LORD spake unto Moses, saying,

45Get you up from among this congregation,

Amplified Bible

28And Moses said, By this you shall know that the Lord has sent me to do all these works, for I do not act of my own accord:

29If these men die the common death of all men or if [only] what happens to everyone happens to them, then the Lord has not sent me.

30But if the Lord causes a new thing [to happen], and the earth opens its mouth and swallows them up, with all that belongs to them, and they go down alive into Sheol (the place of the dead), then you shall understand that these men have provoked (spurned, despised) the Lord!

31As soon as he stopped speaking, the ground under the offenders split apart

32And the earth opened its mouth and swallowed them and their households and [Korah and] all [his] men and all their possessions.

33They and all that belonged to them went down alive into Sheol (the place of the dead); and the earth closed upon them, and they perished from among the assembly.

34And all Israel who were round about them fled at their cry, for they said, Lest the earth swallow us up also.

35And fire came forth from the Lord and devoured the 250 men who offered the incense.

36And the Lord said to Moses,

37Speak to Eleazar son of Aaron, the priest, that he take up the censers out of the burning and scatter the fire at a distance. For the censers are hallowed—

38The censers of these men who have sinned against themselves *and* at the cost of their own lives. Let the censers be made into hammered plates for a covering of the altar [of burnt offering], for they were used in offering before the Lord and therefore they are sacred. They shall be a sign [of warning] to the Israelites.

39Eleazar the priest took the bronze censers with which the Levites who were burned had offered incense, and they were hammered into broad sheets for a covering of the [brazen] altar [of burnt offering],

40To be a memorial [a warning forever] to the Israelites, so that no outsider, that is, no one not of the descendants of Aaron, should come near to offer incense before the Lord, lest he become as Korah and as his company, as the Lord said to Eleazar through Moses.

41But on the morrow all the congregation of the Israelites murmured against Moses and Aaron, saying, You have killed the people of the Lord.

42When the congregation was gathered against Moses and Aaron, they looked at the Tent of Meeting, and behold, the cloud covered it and they saw the Lord's glory.

43And Moses and Aaron came to the front of the Tent of Meeting.

44And the Lord said to Moses,

45Get away from among this congregation,

King James Version

that I may consume them as in a moment. And they fell upon their faces.

⁴⁶And Moses said unto Aaron, Take a censer, and put fire therein from off the altar, and put on incense, and go quickly unto the congregation, and make an atonement for them: for there is wrath gone out from the LORD; the plague is begun.

⁴⁷And Aaron took as Moses commanded, and ran into the midst of the congregation; and behold, the plague was begun among the people: and he put on incense, and made an atonement for the people.

⁴⁸And he stood between the dead and the living; and the plague was stayed.

⁴⁹Now they that died in the plague were fourteen thousand and seven hundred, beside them that died about the matter of Korah.

⁵⁰And Aaron returned unto Moses unto the door of the tabernacle of the congregation: and the plague was stayed.

17 And the LORD spake unto Moses, saying, ²Speak unto the children of Israel, and take of every one of them a rod according to the house of *their* fathers, of all their princes according to the house of their fathers twelve rods: write thou every man's name upon his rod.

³And thou shalt write Aaron's name upon the rod of Levi: for one rod *shall be* for the head of the house of their fathers.

⁴And thou shalt lay them up in the tabernacle of the congregation before the Testimony, where I will meet with you.

⁵And it shall come to pass, *that* the man's rod, whom I shall choose, shall blossom: and I will make to cease from me the murmurings of the children of Israel, whereby they murmur against you.

⁶And Moses spake unto the children of Israel, and every one of their princes gave him a rod apiece, for each prince one, according to their fathers' houses, *even* twelve rods: and the rod of Aaron *was* among their rods.

⁷And Moses laid up the rods before the LORD in the tabernacle of Witness.

⁸And it came to pass, that on the morrow Moses went into the tabernacle of Witness; and behold, the rod of Aaron for the house of Levi was budded, and brought forth buds, and bloomed blossoms, and yielded almonds.

⁹And Moses brought out all the rods from before the LORD unto all the children of Israel: and they looked, and took every man his rod.

¹⁰And the LORD said unto Moses, Bring Aaron's rod again before the Testimony, to be kept for a token against the rebels; and thou shalt quite take away their murmurings from me, that they die not.

¹¹And Moses did *so:* as the LORD commanded him, so did he.

Amplified Bible

that I may consume them in a moment. And Moses and Aaron fell on their faces.

⁴⁶And Moses said to Aaron, Take a censer and put fire in it from off the altar and lay incense on it, and carry it quickly to the congregation and make atonement for them. For there is wrath gone out from the Lord; the plague has begun!

⁴⁷So Aaron took the burning censer as Moses commanded, and ran into the midst of the congregation; and behold, the plague was begun among the people; and he put on the incense and made atonement for the people.

⁴⁸And he stood between the dead and the living, and the plague was stayed.

⁴⁹Now those who died in the plague were 14,700, besides those who died in the matter of Korah.

⁵⁰And Aaron returned to Moses to the door of the Tent of Meeting, since the plague was stayed.

17 AND THE Lord said to Moses, ²Speak to the Israelites and get from them rods *or* staves, one for each father's house, from all their leaders according to their father's houses, twelve rods. Write every man's name on his rod.

³And you shall write Aaron's name on the rod of Levi [his great-grandfather]. For there shall be one rod for the head of each father's house.

⁴You shall lay them up in the Tent of Meeting before [the ark of] the Testimony, where I meet with you.

⁵And the rod of the man whom I choose shall bud, and I will make to cease from Me the murmurings of the Israelites, which they murmur against you.

⁶And Moses spoke to the Israelites, and every one of their leaders gave him a rod *or* staff, one for each leader according to their fathers' houses, twelve rods, and the rod of Aaron was among their rods.

⁷And Moses deposited the rods before the Lord in the Tent of the Testimony.

⁸And the next day Moses went into the Tent of the Testimony, and behold, the rod of Aaron for the house of Levi had sprouted and brought forth buds and produced blossoms and yielded [ripe] almonds.

⁹Moses brought out all the rods from before the Lord to all the Israelites; and they looked, and each man took his rod.

¹⁰And the Lord told Moses, Put Aaron's rod back before the Testimony [in the ark], to be kept as a [warning] sign for the rebels; and you shall make an end of their murmurings against Me, lest they die.

¹¹And Moses did so; as the Lord commanded him, so he did.

King James Version

¹²And the children of Israel spake unto Moses, saying, Behold, we die, we perish, we all perish.

¹³Whosoever cometh any thing near unto the tabernacle of the LORD shall die: shall we be consumed with dying?

18 And the LORD said unto Aaron, Thou and thy sons and thy father's house with thee shall bear the iniquity of the sanctuary: and thou and thy sons with thee shall bear the iniquity of your priesthood.

²And thy brethren also *of* the tribe of Levi, the tribe of thy father, bring thou with thee, that they may be joined unto thee, and minister unto thee: but thou and thy sons with thee shall *minister* before the tabernacle of Witness.

³And they shall keep thy charge, and the charge of all the tabernacle: only they shall not come nigh the vessels of the sanctuary and the altar, that neither they, nor you also, die.

⁴And they shall be joined unto thee, and keep the charge of the tabernacle of the congregation, for all the service of the tabernacle: and a stranger shall not come nigh unto you.

⁵And ye shall keep the charge of the sanctuary, and the charge of the altar: that there be no wrath any more upon the children of Israel.

⁶And I, behold, I have taken your brethren the Levites from among the children of Israel: to you *they are* given *as* a gift for the LORD, to do the service of the tabernacle of the congregation.

⁷Therefore thou and thy sons with thee shall keep your priest's office for every thing of the altar, and within the vail; and ye shall serve: I have given your priest's office *unto you as* a service of gift: and the stranger that cometh nigh shall be put to death.

⁸And the LORD spake unto Aaron, Behold, I also have given thee the charge of mine heave offerings of all the hallowed *things* of the children of Israel; unto thee have I given them by reason of the anointing, and to thy sons, by an ordinance for ever.

⁹This shall be thine of the most holy *things,* *reserved* from the fire: every oblation of theirs, every meat offering of theirs, and every sin of-

Amplified Bible

¹²The Israelites said to Moses, Behold, we perish, we are undone, all undone!

¹³Everyone who comes near, who comes near the tabernacle of the Lord, dies *or* shall die! Are we all to perish?

18 AND THE Lord said to Aaron, You and your sons and your father's house with you shall bear *and* remove the iniquity of the sanctuary [that is, the guilt for the offenses which the people unknowingly commit when brought into contact with the manifestations of God's presence]. And you and your sons with you shall bear *and* remove the iniquity of your priesthood [your own unintentional offenses].

²And your brethren also of the tribe of Levi, the tribe of your [fore]father, bring with you, that they may be joined to you and minister to you; but only you and your sons with you shall come before the Tent of the Testimony [into the Holy Place where only priests may go and into the Most Holy Place which only the high priest dares enter].

³And the Levites shall attend you [as servants] and attend to all the duties of the Tent; only they shall not come near the sacred vessels of the sanctuary or to the brazen altar, that they and also you [Aaron] die not.

⁴And they shall be joined to you and attend to the duties of the Tent of Meeting—all the [menial] service of the Tent—and no stranger [no layman, anyone who is not a Levite] shall come near you [Aaron and your sons].

⁵And you shall attend to the duties of the sanctuary and attend to the altar [of burnt offering and the altar of incense], that there be no wrath any more upon the Israelites [as in the incident of Korah, Dathan, and Abiram].

⁶And I, behold, I have taken your brethren the Levites from among the Israelites; to you they are a gift, given to the Lord, to do the [menial] service of the Tent of Meeting.

⁷Therefore you and your sons with you shall attend to your priesthood for everything of the altar [of burnt offering and the altar of incense] and [of the Holy of Holies] within the veil, and you shall serve. I give you your priesthood as a service of gift. And the stranger [anyone other than Moses or your sons, Aaron] who comes near shall be put to death.

⁸And the Lord said to Aaron, And I, behold, I have given you the charge of My heave offerings [whatever is taken out and kept of the offerings made to Me], all the dedicated *and* consecrated things of the Israelites; to you have I given them [as your portion] and to your sons as a continual allowance forever by reason of your anointing as priests.

⁹This shall be yours of the most holy things, reserved from the fire: every offering of the people, every cereal offering and sin offering

King James Version

fering of theirs, and every trespass offering of theirs, which they shall render unto me, *shall be* most holy for thee and for thy sons.

¹⁰In the most holy *place* shalt thou eat it; every male shall eat it: it shall be holy unto thee.

¹¹And this *is* thine; the heave offering of their gift, with all the wave offerings of the children of Israel: I have given them unto thee, and to thy sons and to thy daughters with thee, by a statute for ever: every one *that is* clean in thy house shall eat of it.

¹²All the best of the oil, and all the best of the wine, and of the wheat, the firstfruits of them which they shall offer unto the LORD, them have I given thee.

¹³*And* whatsoever is first ripe in the land, which they shall bring unto the LORD, shall be thine; every one *that is* clean in thine house shall eat *of* it.

¹⁴Every thing devoted in Israel shall be thine.

¹⁵Every thing that openeth the matrix in all flesh, which they bring unto the LORD, *whether it be* of men or beasts, shall be thine: nevertheless the firstborn of man shalt thou surely redeem, and the firstling of unclean beasts shalt thou redeem.

¹⁶And those that are *to be* redeemed from a month old shalt thou redeem, according to thine estimation, *for* the money of five shekels, after the shekel of the sanctuary, which *is* twenty gerahs.

¹⁷But the firstling of a cow, or the firstling of a sheep, or the firstling of a goat, thou shalt not redeem; they *are* holy: thou shalt sprinkle their blood upon the altar, and shalt burn their fat *for* an offering made by fire, for a sweet savour unto the LORD.

¹⁸And the flesh of them shall be thine, as the wave breast and as the right shoulder are thine.

¹⁹All the heave offerings of the holy *things,* which the children of Israel offer unto the LORD, have I given thee, and thy sons and thy daughters with thee, by a statute for ever: it *is* a covenant of salt for ever before the LORD unto thee and to thy seed with thee.

²⁰ ¶ And the LORD spake unto Aaron, Thou shalt have no inheritance in their land, neither shalt thou have any part among them: I *am* thy part and thine inheritance among the children of Israel.

²¹And behold, I have given the children of Levi all the tenth in Israel for an inheritance, for their service which they serve, *even* the service of the tabernacle of the congregation.

²²Neither must the children of Israel henceforth come nigh the tabernacle of the congregation, lest they bear sin, and die.

Amplified Bible

and trespass offering of theirs, which they shall render to Me, shall be most holy for you [Aaron] and for your sons.

¹⁰As the most holy thing *and* in a sacred place shall you eat of it; every male [of your house] shall eat of it. It shall be holy to you.

¹¹And this also is yours: the heave offering of their gift, with all the wave offerings of the Israelites. I have given them to you and to your sons and to your daughters with you as a continual allowance forever; everyone in your house who is [ceremonially] clean may eat of it.

¹²All the best of the oil, and all the best of the [fresh] wine and of the grain, the firstfruits of what they give to the Lord, to you have I given them.

¹³Whatever is first ripe in the land, which they bring to the Lord, shall be yours. Everyone who is [ceremonially] clean in your house may eat of it.

¹⁴Every devoted thing in Israel [everything that has been vowed to the Lord] shall be yours.

¹⁵Everything that first opens the womb in all flesh, which they bring to the Lord, whether it be of men or beasts, shall be yours. Nevertheless the firstborn of man you shall surely redeem, and the firstling of unclean beasts shall redeem.

¹⁶And those that are to be redeemed of them, from a month old shall you redeem, according to your estimate [of their age], for the fixed price of five shekels in silver, according to the shekel of the sanctuary, which is twenty gerahs.

¹⁷But the firstling of a cow or of a sheep or of a goat you shall not redeem. They [as the firstborn of clean beasts belong to God and] are holy. You shall sprinkle their blood upon the altar and shall burn their fat for an offering made by fire, for a sweet *and* soothing odor to the Lord.

¹⁸And the flesh of them shall be yours, as the wave breast and as the right shoulder are yours.

¹⁹All the heave offerings [the lifted-out and kept portions] of the holy things which the Israelites give to the Lord I give to you and to your sons and your daughters with you, as a continual debt forever. It is a covenant of salt [that cannot be dissolved or violated] forever before the Lord for you [Aaron] and for your posterity with you.

²⁰And the Lord said to Aaron, You shall have no inheritance in the land [of the Israelites], neither shall you have any part among them. I am your portion and your inheritance among the Israelites.

²¹And, behold, I have given the Levites all the tithes in Israel for an inheritance in return for their service which they serve, the [menial] service of the Tent of Meeting.

²²Henceforth the Israelites shall not come near the Tent of Meeting [the covered sanctuary, the Holy Place, and the Holy of Holies], lest they incur guilt and die.

King James Version

23But the Levites shall do the service of the tabernacle of the congregation, and they shall bear their iniquity: *it shall be* a statute for ever throughout your generations, that among the children of Israel they have no inheritance.

24But the tithes of the children of Israel, which they offer *as* a heave offering unto the LORD, I have given to the Levites to inherit: therefore I have said unto them, Among the children of Israel they shall have no inheritance.

25 ¶ And the LORD spake unto Moses, saying,

26Thus speak unto the Levites, and say unto them, When ye take of the children of Israel the tithes which I have given you from them for your inheritance, then ye shall offer up a heave offering of it for the LORD, *even* a <u>tenth</u> *part* of the tithe.

27And *this* your heave offering shall be reckoned unto you, as though it were the corn of the threshingfloor, and as the fulness of the winepress.

28Thus you also shall offer a heave offering unto the LORD of all your tithes, which ye receive of the children of Israel; and ye shall give thereof the LORD'S heave offering to Aaron the priest.

29Out of all your gifts ye shall offer every heave offering of the LORD, of all the best thereof, *even* the hallowed *part* thereof out of it.

30Therefore thou shalt say unto them, When ye have heaved the best thereof from it, then it shall be counted unto the Levites as the increase of the threshingfloor, and as the increase of the winepress.

31And ye shall eat it in every place, ye and your households: for it *is* your reward for your service in the tabernacle of the congregation.

32And ye shall bear no sin by reason of it, when ye have heaved from it the best of it: neither shall ye pollute the holy *things* of the children of Israel, lest ye die.

26: The Ministry is to get 1/10th of the tithes

19 And the LORD spake unto Moses and unto Aaron, saying,

2This *is* the ordinance of the law which the LORD hath commanded, saying, Speak unto the children of Israel, that they bring thee a red heifer without spot, wherein *is* no blemish, *and* upon which never came yoke:

3And ye shall give her unto Eleazar the priest, that he may bring her forth without the camp, and *one* shall slay her before his face:

Amplified Bible

23But the Levites shall do the [menial] service of the Tent of Meeting, and they shall bear and remove the iniquity of the people [that is, be answerable for the legal pollutions of the holy things and offer the necessary atonements for unintentional offenses in these matters]. It shall be a statute forever in all your generations, that among the Israelites the Levites have no inheritance [of land].

24But the tithes of the Israelites, which they present as an offering to the Lord, I have given to the Levites to inherit; therefore I have said to them, Among the Israelites they shall have no inheritance. [They have homes and cities and pasturage to use but not to possess as their personal inheritance.]

25And the Lord said to Moses,

26Moreover, you shall say to the Levites, When you take from the Israelites the tithe which I have given you from them for your inheritance, then you shall present an offering from it to the Lord, even a tenth of the tithe [paid by the people].

27And what you lift out and keep [your heave offering] shall be credited to you as though it were the grain of the threshing floor or as the fully ripe produce of the vine.

28Likewise you shall also present an offering to the Lord of all your tithes which you receive from the Israelites; and therefore you shall give this heave offering [lifted out and kept] for the Lord to Aaron the priest.

29Out of all the gifts to you, you shall present every offering due to the Lord, of all the best of it, even the hallowed part lifted out *and* held back out of it [for the Levites].

30Therefore you shall say to them, When you have lifted out *and* held back the best from it [and presented it to the Lord by giving it to yourselves, the Levites], then it shall be counted to [you] the Levites just as if it were the increase of the threshing floor or of the winepress.

31And you may eat it in every place, you and your households, for it is your reward for your service in the Tent of Meeting.

32And you shall be guilty of no sin by reason of it when you have lifted out *and* held back the best of it; neither shall you have polluted the holy things of the Israelites, neither shall you die [because of it].

19 AND THE Lord said to Moses and Aaron, 2This is the ritual of the law which the Lord has commanded: Tell the Israelites to bring you a red heifer without spot, in which is no blemish, upon which a yoke has never come.

3And you shall give her to Eleazar the priest, and he shall bring her outside the camp, and she shall be slaughtered before him.

King James Version

4And Eleazar the priest shall take of her blood with his finger, and sprinkle of her blood directly before the tabernacle of the congregation seven times:

5And one shall burn the heifer in his sight; her skin, and her flesh, and her blood, with her dung, shall he burn:

6And the priest shall take cedar wood, and hyssop, and scarlet, and cast it into the midst of the burning of the heifer.

7Then the priest shall wash his clothes, and he shall bathe his flesh in water, and afterward he shall come into the camp, and the priest shall be unclean until the even.

8And he that burneth her shall wash his clothes in water, and bathe his flesh in water, and shall be unclean until the even.

9And a man that is clean shall gather up the ashes of the heifer, and lay them up without the camp in a clean place, and it shall be kept for the congregation of the children of Israel for a water of separation: it is a purification for sin.

10And he that gathereth the ashes of the heifer shall wash his clothes, and be unclean until the even: and it shall be unto the children of Israel, and unto the stranger that sojourneth among them, for a statute for ever.

11 ¶ He that toucheth the dead body of any man shall be unclean seven days.

12He shall purify himself with it on the third day, and on the seventh day he shall be clean: but if he purify not himself the third day, then the seventh day he shall not be clean.

13Whosoever toucheth the dead body of any man that is dead, and purifieth not himself, defileth the tabernacle of the LORD; and that soul shall be cut off from Israel: because the water of separation was not sprinkled upon him, he shall be unclean; his uncleanness is yet upon him.

14This is the law, when a man dieth in a tent: all that come into the tent, and all that is in the tent, shall be unclean seven days.

15And every open vessel, which hath no covering bound upon it, is unclean.

16And whosoever toucheth one that is slain with a sword in the open fields, or a dead body, or a bone of a man, or a grave, shall be unclean seven days.

17And for an unclean person they shall take of the ashes of the burnt heifer of purification for sin, and running water shall be put thereto in a vessel:

18And a clean person shall take hyssop, and dip it in the water, and sprinkle it upon the tent, and upon all the vessels, and upon the persons that were there, and upon him that touched a bone, or one slain, or one dead, or a grave:

19And the clean person shall sprinkle upon the unclean on the third day, and on the seventh day: and on the seventh day he shall purify him-

Amplified Bible

4Eleazar the priest shall take some of her blood with his finger and sprinkle it toward the front of the Tent of Meeting seven times.

5The heifer shall be burned in his sight, her skin, flesh, blood, and dung.

6And the priest shall take cedar wood, and hyssop, and scarlet [stuff] and cast them into the midst of the burning heifer.

7Then the priest shall wash his clothes and bathe his body in water; afterward he shall come into the camp, but he shall be unclean until evening.

8He who burns the heifer shall wash his clothes and bathe his body in water, and shall be unclean until evening.

9And a man who is clean shall collect the ashes of the heifer and put them outside the camp in a clean place, and they shall be kept for the congregation of the Israelites for the water for impurity; it is a sin offering.

10And he who gathers the ashes of the heifer shall wash his clothes, and be unclean until evening. This shall be to the Israelites and to the stranger who sojourns among them a perpetual statute.

11He who touches the dead body of any person shall be unclean for seven days.

12He shall purify himself with the water for impurity [made with the ashes of the burned heifer] on the third day, and on the seventh day he shall be clean. But if he does not purify himself the third day, then the seventh day he shall not be clean.

13Whoever touches the corpse of any who has died and does not purify himself defiles the tabernacle of the Lord, and that person shall be cut off from Israel. Because the water for impurity was not sprinkled upon him, he shall be unclean; his uncleanness is still upon him.

14This is the law when a man dies in a tent: all who come into the tent and all who are in the tent shall be unclean for seven days.

15And every open vessel, which has no covering fastened upon it, is unclean.

16And whoever in the open field touches one who is slain with a sword, or a dead body, or a bone of a dead man, or a grave, shall be unclean for seven days.

17And for the unclean, they shall take of the ashes of the burning of the sin offering, and the running water shall be put with it in a vessel.

18And a clean person shall take hyssop and dip it in the water and sprinkle it upon the tent, and upon all the vessels, and upon the persons who were there, and upon him who touched the bone, or the slain, or the naturally dead, or the grave.

19And the clean person shall sprinkle [the water for purification] upon the unclean person on the third day and on the seventh day, and on the seventh day the unclean man shall purify him-

King James Version

self, and wash his clothes, and bathe *himself* in water, and shall be clean at even.

²⁰But the man that shall be unclean, and shall not purify himself, that soul shall be cut off from among the congregation, because he hath defiled the sanctuary of the LORD: the water of separation hath not been sprinkled upon him; he *is* unclean.

²¹And it shall be a perpetual statute unto them, that he that sprinkleth the water of separation shall wash his clothes; and he that toucheth the water of separation shall be unclean until even.

²²And whatsoever the unclean *person* toucheth shall be unclean; and the soul that toucheth *it* shall be unclean until even.

20 Then came the children of Israel, *even* the whole congregation, *into* the desert of Zin in the first month: and the people abode in Kadesh; and Miriam died there, and was buried there.

²And there was no water for the congregation: and they gathered themselves together against Moses and against Aaron.

³And the people chode with Moses, and spake, saying, Would God that we had died when our brethren died before the LORD!

⁴And why have ye brought up the congregation of the LORD into this wilderness, that we and our cattle should die there?

⁵And wherefore have ye made us to come up out of Egypt, to bring us in unto this evil place? it *is* no place of seed, or of figs, or vines, or of pomegranates; neither *is there any* water to drink.

⁶And Moses and Aaron went from the presence of the assembly unto the door of the tabernacle of the congregation, and they fell upon their faces: and the glory of the LORD appeared unto them.

⁷And the LORD spake unto Moses, saying,

⁸Take the rod, and gather thou the assembly together, thou, and Aaron thy brother, and speak ye unto the rock before their eyes; and it shall give forth his water, and thou shalt bring forth to them water out of the rock: so thou shalt give the congregation and their beasts drink.

⁹And Moses took the rod from before the LORD, as he commanded him.

¹⁰And Moses and Aaron gathered the congregation together before the rock, and he said unto them, Hear now, ye rebels; must we fetch you water out of this rock?

¹¹And Moses lift up his hand, and with his rod he smote the rock twice: and the water came

Amplified Bible

self, and wash his clothes and bathe himself in water, and shall be clean at evening.

²⁰But the man who is unclean and does not purify himself, that person shall be cut off from among the congregation, because he has defiled the sanctuary of the Lord. The water for purification has not been sprinkled upon him; he is unclean.

²¹And it shall be a perpetual statute to them. He who sprinkles the water for impurity [upon another] shall wash his clothes, and he who touches the water for impurity shall be unclean until evening.

²²And whatever the unclean person touches shall be unclean, and anyone who touches it shall be unclean until evening.

20 AND THE Israelites, the whole congregation, came into the Wilderness of Zin in the first month. And the people dwelt in Kadesh. Miriam died and was buried there.

²Now there was no water for the congregation, and they assembled together against Moses and Aaron.

³And the people contended with Moses, and said, Would that we had died when our brethren died [in the plague] before the Lord!

⁴And why have you brought up the congregation of the Lord into this wilderness, that we should die here, we and our livestock?

⁵And why have you made us come up out of Egypt to bring us into this evil place? It is no place of grain or of figs or of vines or of pomegranates. And there is no water to drink.

⁶Then Moses and Aaron went from the presence of the assembly to the door of the Tent of Meeting and fell on their faces. Then the glory of the Lord appeared to them.

⁷And the Lord said to Moses,

⁸Take the rod, and assemble the congregation, you and Aaron your brother, and tell the rock before their eyes to give forth its water, and you shall bring forth to them water out of the rock; so you shall give the congregation and their livestock drink.

⁹So Moses took the rod from before the Lord, as He commanded him.

¹⁰And Moses and Aaron assembled the congregation before the rock and Moses said to them, Hear now, you rebels; must we bring you water out of this rock?

¹¹And Moses lifted up his hand and with his rod he smote the rock ªtwice. And the water

---

AMP notes: ª "And the Rock was Christ," as I Cor. 10:4 explains. Once smitten at Rephidim (Exod. 17:6ff.), He did not need to be smitten, crucified, again. To smite the rock twice was to imply that Christ's death on the cross was not effectual or sufficient for time and eternity.

King James Version

out abundantly, and the congregation drank, and their beasts *also.*

¹²And the LORD spake unto Moses and Aaron, Because ye believed me not, to sanctify me in the eyes of the children of Israel, therefore ye shall not bring this congregation into the land which I have given them.

¹³This *is* the water of Meribah; because the children of Israel strove with the LORD, and he was sanctified in them.

¹⁴ ¶ And Moses sent messengers from Kadesh unto the king of Edom, Thus saith thy brother Israel, Thou knowest all the travail that hath befallen us:

¹⁵How our fathers went down into Egypt, and we have dwelt in Egypt a long time; and the Egyptians vexed us, and our fathers:

¹⁶And when we cried unto the LORD, he heard our voice, and sent an angel, and hath brought us forth out of Egypt: and behold, we *are* in Kadesh, a city in the uttermost of thy border:

¹⁷Let us pass, I pray thee, through thy country: we will not pass through the fields, or through the vineyards, neither will we drink *of* the water of the wells: we will go *by* the king's *high* way, we will not turn *to* the right hand nor *to* the left, until we have passed thy borders.

¹⁸And Edom said unto him, Thou shalt not pass by me, lest I come out against thee with the sword.

¹⁹And the children of Israel said unto him, We will go by the high way: and if I and my cattle drink *of* thy water, then I will pay for it: I will only, without *doing any* thing *else,* go through on my feet.

²⁰And he said, Thou shalt not go through. And Edom came out against him with much people, and with a strong hand.

²¹Thus Edom refused to give Israel passage through his border: wherefore Israel turned away from him.

²² ¶ And the children of Israel, *even* the whole congregation, journeyed from Kadesh, and came *unto* mount Hor.

²³And the LORD spake unto Moses and Aaron in mount Hor, by the coast of the land of Edom, saying,

²⁴Aaron shall be gathered unto his people: for he shall not enter into the land which I have given unto the children of Israel, because ye rebelled against my word at the water of Meribah.

Amplified Bible

came out abundantly, and the congregation drank, and their livestock.

¹²And the Lord said to Moses and Aaron, Because you did not believe in (rely on, cling to) Me to sanctify Me in the eyes of the Israelites, you therefore *ᵃ*shall not bring this congregation into the land which I have given them.

¹³These are the waters of Meribah [strife], where the Israelites contended with the Lord and He showed Himself holy among them.

¹⁴And Moses sent messengers from Kadesh to the king of Edom, saying, Thus says your kinsman Israel: You know all the adversity *and* birth pangs that have come upon us [as a nation]:

¹⁵How our fathers went down to Egypt; we dwelt there a long time, and the Egyptians dealt evilly with us and our fathers.

¹⁶But when we cried to the Lord, He heard us and sent an angel and brought us forth out of Egypt. Now behold, we are in Kadesh, a city on your country's edge.

¹⁷Let us pass, I pray you, through your country. We will not pass through field or vineyard, or drink of the water of the wells. We will go along the king's highway; we will not turn aside to the right hand or to the left until we have passed your borders.

¹⁸But Edom said to him, You shall not go through, lest I come out against you with the sword.

¹⁹And the Israelites said to him, We will go by the highway, and if I and my livestock drink of your water, I will pay for it. Only let me pass through on foot, nothing else.

²⁰But Edom said, You shall not go through. And Edom came out against Israel with many people and a strong hand.

²¹Thus Edom refused to give Israel passage through his territory, *ᵇ*so Israel turned away from him.

²²They journeyed from Kadesh, and the Israelites, even the whole congregation, came to Mount Hor.

²³And the Lord said to Moses and Aaron at Mount Hor, on the border of the land of Edom,

²⁴Aaron shall be gathered to his people. For he shall not enter the land which I have given to the Israelites, because you both rebelled against My instructions at the waters of Meribah.

AMP notes: ᵃ Possibly Moses was not aware of the significance of what he had been ordered to do, but nevertheless God held him responsible for not obeying Him exactly. Obedience to His will is vitally important, whether we understand His purpose or not. The motto "God's will: nothing more; nothing less; nothing else; at any cost" would have been priceless to Moses and Aaron that day, if they had only followed it.   ᵇ Israel (Jacob's offspring) did not fight Edom, the offspring of Jacob's brother Esau, because of the Lord's warning, later conveyed in definite instructions (Deut. 23:7). But what had begun as only a quarrel between twin brothers (Gen. 27:41) had now been passed on for generations and was to cost countless lives, extending throughout the Old Testament and into the New, where Herod, remotely related to Esau, tried to take the life of the Babe of Bethlehem, a descendant of Jacob. "See how much wood *or* how great a forest a tiny spark can set ablaze!" (James 3:5).

King James Version

25 Take Aaron and Eleazar his son, and bring them up *unto* mount Hor:

26 And strip Aaron of his garments, and put them upon Eleazar his son: and Aaron shall be gathered *unto his people,* and shall die there.

27 And Moses did as the LORD commanded: and they went up into mount Hor in the sight of all the congregation.

28 And Moses stripped Aaron of his garments, and put them upon Eleazar his son; and Aaron died there in the top of the mount: and Moses and Eleazar came down from the mount.

29 And when all the congregation saw that Aaron was dead, they mourned for Aaron thirty days, *even* all the house of Israel.

21 And *when* king Arad the Canaanite, which dwelt *in* the south, heard *tell* that Israel came *by* the way of the spies; then he fought against Israel, and took *some* of them prisoners.

2 And Israel vowed a vow unto the LORD, and said, If thou wilt indeed deliver this people into my hand, then I will utterly destroy their cities.

3 And the LORD hearkened to the voice of Israel, and delivered up the Canaanites; and they utterly destroyed them and their cities: and he called the name of the place Hormah.

4 ¶ And they journeyed from mount Hor *by* the way of the Red sea, to compass the land of Edom: and the soul of the people was much discouraged because of the way.

5 And the people spake against God, and against Moses, Wherefore have ye brought us up out of Egypt to die in the wilderness? for *there is* no bread, neither *is there any* water; and our soul loatheth *this* light bread.

6 And the LORD sent fiery serpents among the people, and they bit the people; and much people of Israel died.

7 Therefore the people came to Moses, and said, We have sinned, for we have spoken against the LORD, and against thee; pray unto the LORD, that he take away the serpents from us. And Moses prayed for the people.

8 And the LORD said unto Moses, Make thee a fiery *serpent,* and set it upon a pole: and it shall come to pass, that every one that is bitten, when he looketh upon it, shall live.

9 And Moses made a serpent of brass, and put it upon a pole, and it came to pass, that if a serpent had bitten *any* man, when he beheld the serpent of brass, he lived.

Amplified Bible

25 Take Aaron and Eleazar his son and bring them up to Mount Hor.

26 Strip Aaron of his vestments and put them on Eleazar his son, and Aaron shall be gathered to his people, and shall die there.

27 And Moses did as the Lord commanded; and they went up Mount Hor in the sight of all the congregation.

28 And Moses stripped Aaron of his [priestly] garments and put them on Eleazar his son. And Aaron died there on the mountain top; and Moses and Eleazar came down from the mountain.

29 When all the congregation saw that Aaron was dead, they wept *and* mourned for him thirty days, all the house of Israel.

21 WHEN THE Canaanite king of Arad, who dwelt in the South (the Negeb), heard that Israel was coming by the way of Atharim [the route traveled by the spies sent out by Moses], he fought against Israel and took some of them captive.

2 And Israel vowed a vow to the Lord, and said, If You will indeed deliver this people into my hand, then I will utterly destroy their cities.

3 And the Lord hearkened to Israel and gave over the Canaanites. And they utterly destroyed them and their cities; and the name of the place was called Hormah [a banned or devoted thing].

4 And they journeyed from Mount Hor by the way to the Red Sea, to go around the land of Edom, and the people became impatient (depressed, much discouraged), because [of the trials] of the way.

5 And the people spoke against God and against Moses, Why have you brought us out of Egypt to die in the wilderness? For there is no bread, neither is there any water, and we loathe this light (contemptible, unsubstantial) manna.

6 Then the Lord sent fiery (burning) serpents among the people; and they bit the people, and many Israelites died.

7 And the people came to Moses, and said, We have sinned, for we have spoken against the Lord and against you; pray to the Lord, that He may take away the serpents from us. So Moses prayed for the people.

8 And the Lord said to Moses, Make a fiery serpent [of bronze] and set it on a pole; and everyone who is bitten, when he looks at it, shall live.

9 And Moses made a serpent of bronze and put it on a pole, and if a serpent had bitten any man, when he looked to the serpent of bronze [*a* at-

AMP notes: *a* Jesus said that as Moses lifted up the serpent in the wilderness, so must the Son of Man be lifted up, "that everyone who believes in Him [who cleaves to Him, trusts Him and relies on Him] may *not perish, but* have eternal life *and* [actually] live forever!" (John 3:14, 15). Obviously this implies that the look that caused the victim of a fiery serpent to be healed was something far more than a casual glance. A "look" would save, but what kind of a look? The Hebrew text here means "look attentively, expectantly, with a steady and absorbing gaze." Or, as Jesus said in the last verse of the chapter quoted above (John 3:36), "He who believes in (has faith in, clings to, relies on) the Son has (now possesses) eternal life." But whoever does not so believe in, cling to, and rely on the Son "will never see . . . life." The look that saves is not just a fleeting glance; it is a God-honoring, God-answered, fixed, and absorbing gaze!

King James Version

¹⁰And the children of Israel set forward, and pitched in Oboth.

¹¹And they journeyed from Oboth, and pitched at Ije-abarim, in the wilderness which *is* before Moab, toward the sunrising.

¹²From thence they removed, and pitched in the valley of Zared.

¹³From thence they removed, and pitched on the *other* side of Arnon, which *is* in the wilderness that cometh out of the coasts of the Amorites: for Arnon *is* the border of Moab, between Moab and the Amorites.

¹⁴Wherefore it is said in the book of the wars of the LORD, What he did in the Red sea, and *in* the brooks of Arnon,

¹⁵And *at* the stream of the brooks that goeth down to the dwelling of Ar, and lieth upon the border of Moab.

¹⁶And from thence *they went* to Beer: that *is* the well whereof the LORD spake unto Moses, Gather the people together, and I will give them water.

¹⁷Then Israel sang this song, Spring up, O well; sing ye unto it:

¹⁸The princes digged the well, the nobles of the people digged it, by the direction of the lawgiver, with their staves. And from the wilderness *they went to* Mattanah:

¹⁹And from Mattanah *to* Nahaliel: and from Nahaliel *to* Bamoth:

²⁰And from Bamoth *in* the valley, that *is* in the country of Moab, *to* the top of Pisgah, which looketh toward Jeshimon.

²¹ ¶ And Israel sent messengers unto Sihon king of the Amorites, saying,

²²Let me pass through thy land: we will not turn into the fields, or into the vineyards; we will not drink *of* the waters of the well: *but* we will go along by the king's *high* way, until we be past thy borders.

²³And Sihon would not suffer Israel to pass through his border: but Sihon gathered all his people together, and went out against Israel into the wilderness: and he came *to* Jahaz, and fought against Israel.

²⁴And Israel smote him with the edge of the sword, and possessed his land from Arnon unto Jabbok, *even* unto the children of Ammon: for the border of the children of Ammon *was* strong.

²⁵And Israel took all these cities: and Israel dwelt in all the cities of the Amorites, in Heshbon, and in all the villages thereof.

²⁶For Heshbon *was* the city of Sihon the king of the Amorites, who had fought against the former king of Moab, and taken all his land out of his hand, *even* unto Arnon.

²⁷Wherefore they that speak in proverbs say,

Amplified Bible

tentively, expectantly, with a steady and absorbing gaze], he lived.

¹⁰And the Israelites journeyed on and encamped at Oboth.

¹¹They journeyed from Oboth and encamped at Iye-abarim, in the wilderness opposite Moab, toward the sunrise.

¹²From there they journeyed and encamped in the Valley of Zared.

¹³From there they journeyed and encamped on the other side of [the river] Arnon, which is in the desert *or* wilderness that extends from the frontier of the Amorites; for [the river] Arnon is the boundary of Moab, between Moab and the Amorites.

¹⁴That is why it is said in the Book of the Wars of the Lord: Waheb in Suphah, and the valleys of [the branches of] the Arnon [River],

¹⁵And the slope of the valleys that stretch toward the site of Ar and find support on the border of Moab.

¹⁶From there the Israelites went on to Beer [a well], the well of which the Lord had said to Moses, Assemble the people together and I will give them water.

¹⁷Then Israel sang this song, Spring up, O well! Let all sing to it,

¹⁸The fountain that the princes opened, that the nobles of the people hollowed out from their staves. And from the wilderness *or* desert [Israel journeyed] to Mattanah,

¹⁹And from Mattanah to Nahaliel, and from Nahaliel to Bamoth,

²⁰And from Bamoth to the valley that is in the field of Moab, to the top of Pisgah which looks down upon Jeshimon *and* the desert.

²¹And Israel sent messengers to Sihon king of the Amorites, saying,

²²Let me pass through your land. We will not turn aside into field or vineyard; we will not drink the water of the wells. We will go by the king's highway until we have passed your border.

²³But Sihon would not allow Israel to pass through his border. Instead Sihon gathered all his people together and went out against Israel into the wilderness, and came to Jahaz, and he fought against Israel.

²⁴And Israel smote the king of the Amorites with the edge of the sword and possessed his land from the river Arnon to the river Jabbok, as far as the Ammonites, for the boundary of the Ammonites was strong.

²⁵And Israel took all these cities and dwelt in all the cities of the Amorites, in Heshbon and in all its towns.

²⁶For Heshbon was the city of Sihon king of the Amorites, who had fought against the former king of Moab and taken all his land out of his hand, as far as [the river] Arnon.

²⁷That is why those who sing ballads say,

King James Version

Come *into* Heshbon, let the city of Sihon be built and prepared:

²⁸For there is a fire gone out of Heshbon, a flame from the city of Sihon: it hath consumed Ar of Moab, *and* the lords of the high places of Arnon.

²⁹Woe to thee, Moab! thou art undone, O people of Chemosh: he hath given his sons that escaped, and his daughters into captivity unto Sihon king of the Amorites.

³⁰We have shot at them; Heshbon is perished even unto Dibon, and we have laid *them* waste even unto Nophah, which *reacheth* unto Medeba.

³¹Thus Israel dwelt in the land of the Amorites.

³²And Moses sent to spy out Jaazer, and they took the villages thereof, and drove out the Amorites that *were* there.

³³And they turned and went up *by* the way of Bashan: and Og the king of Bashan went out against them, he, and all his people, to the battle *at* Edrei.

³⁴And the LORD said unto Moses, Fear him not: for I have delivered him into thy hand, and all his people, and his land; and thou shalt do to him as thou didst unto Sihon king of the Amorites, which dwelt at Heshbon.

³⁵So they smote him, and his sons, and all his people, until there was none left him alive: and they possessed his land.

22 And the children of Israel set forward, and pitched in the plains of Moab on *this* side Jordan *by* Jericho.

²And Balak the son of Zippor saw all that Israel had done to the Amorites.

³And Moab was sore afraid of the people, because they *were* many: and Moab was distressed because of the children of Israel.

⁴And Moab said unto the elders of Midian, Now shall *this* company lick up all *that are* round about us, as the ox licketh up the grass of the field. And Balak the son of Zippor *was* king of the Moabites at that time.

⁵He sent messengers therefore unto Balaam the son of Beor to Pethor, which *is* by the river *of* the land of the children of his people, to call him, saying, Behold, there is a people come out from Egypt: behold, they cover the face of the earth, and they abide over against me:

⁶Come now therefore, I pray thee, curse me this people; for they *are* too mighty for me: peradventure I shall prevail, *that* we may smite them, and *that* I may drive them out of the land: for I wot that *he* whom thou blessest *is* blessed, and *he* whom thou cursest is cursed.

⁷And the elders of Moab and the elders of Midian departed with the rewards of divination

Amplified Bible

Come to Heshbon, let the city of Sihon be built and established.

²⁸For fire has gone out of Heshbon, a flame from the city of Sihon; it has devoured Ar of Moab and the lords of the heights of the Arnon.

²⁹Woe to you, Moab! You are undone, O people of [the god] Chemosh! Moab has given his sons as fugitives and his daughters into captivity to Sihon king of the Amorites.

³⁰We have shot them down; Heshbon has perished as far as Dibon, and we have laid them waste as far as Nophah, which reaches to Medeba.

³¹Thus Israel dwelt in the land of the Amorites.

³²And Moses sent to spy out Jazer, and they took its villages and dispossessed the Amorites who were there.

³³Then they turned and went up by the way of Bashan; and Og the king of Bashan went out against them, he and all his people, to battle at Edrei.

³⁴But the Lord said to Moses, Do not fear him, for I have delivered him and all his people and his land into your hand; and you shall do to him as you did to Sihon king of the Amorites, who dwelt at Heshbon.

³⁵So the Israelites slew Og and his sons and all his people until there was not one left alive, And they possessed his land.

22 THE ISRAELITES journeyed and encamped in the plains of Moab, on the east side of the Jordan [River] at Jericho.

²And Balak [the king of Moab] son of Zippor saw all that Israel had done to the Amorites.

³And Moab was terrified at the people *and* full of dread, because they were many. Moab was distressed *and* overcome with fear because of the Israelites.

⁴And Moab said to the elders of Midian, Now will this multitude lick up all that is round about us, as the ox licks up the grass of the field. So Balak son of Zippor, the king of the Moabites at that time,

⁵Sent messengers to Balaam [a foreteller of events] son of Beor at Pethor, which is by the [Euphrates] River, even to the land of the children of his people, to say to him, There is a people come out from Egypt; behold, they cover the face of the earth and they have settled down *and* dwell opposite me.

⁶Now come, I beg of you, curse this people for me, for they are too powerful for me. Perhaps I may be able to defeat them and drive them out of the land, for I know that he whom you bless is blessed, and he whom you curse is cursed.

⁷And the elders of Moab and of Midian departed with the rewards of foretelling in their

King James Version

in their hand; and they came unto Balaam, and spake unto him the words of Balak.

⁸And he said unto them, Lodge here *this* night, and I will bring you word again, as the LORD shall speak unto me: and the princes of Moab abode with Balaam.

⁹And God came unto Balaam, and said, What men *are* these with thee?

¹⁰And Balaam said unto God, Balak the son of Zippor, king of Moab, hath sent unto me, *saying,*

¹¹Behold, *there is* a people come out of Egypt, which covereth the face of the earth: come now, curse me them; peradventure I shall be able to overcome them, and drive them out.

¹²And God said unto Balaam, Thou shalt not go with them; thou shalt not curse the people: for they *are* blessed.

¹³And Balaam rose up in the morning, and said unto the princes of Balak, Get you into your land: for the LORD refuseth to give me leave to go with you.

¹⁴And the princes of Moab rose up, and they went unto Balak, and said, Balaam refuseth to come with us.

¹⁵And Balak sent yet again princes, more, and more honourable than they.

¹⁶And they came to Balaam, and said to him, Thus saith Balak the son of Zippor, Let nothing, I pray thee, hinder thee from coming unto me:

¹⁷For I will promote thee unto very great honour, and I will do whatsoever thou sayest unto me: come therefore, I pray thee, curse me this people.

¹⁸And Balaam answered and said unto the servants of Balak, If Balak would give me his house full *of* silver and gold, I cannot go beyond the word of the LORD my God, to do less or more.

¹⁹Now therefore, I pray you, tarry ye also here *this* night, that I may know what the LORD will say unto me more.

²⁰And God came unto Balaam at night, and said unto him, If the men come to call thee, rise up, *and* go with them; but yet the word which I shall say unto thee, that shalt thou do.

²¹And Balaam rose up in the morning, and saddled his ass, and went with the princes of Moab.

²²And God's anger was kindled because he went: and the angel of the LORD stood in the way for an adversary against him. Now he was riding upon his ass, and his two servants *were* with him.

²³And the ass saw the angel of the LORD standing in the way, and his sword drawn in his hand: and the ass turned aside out of the way, and went into the field: and Balaam smote the ass, to turn her *into* the way.

Amplified Bible

hands; and they came to Balaam and told him the words of Balak.

⁸And he said to them, Lodge here tonight and I will bring you word as the Lord may speak to me. And the princes of Moab abode with Balaam [that night].

⁹And God came to Balaam, and said, What men are these with you?

¹⁰And Balaam said to God, Balak son of Zippor, king of Moab, has sent to me, saying,

¹¹Behold, the people who came out of Egypt cover the face of the earth; come now, curse them for me. Perhaps I shall be able to fight against them and drive them out.

¹²And God said to Balaam, You shall not go with them; you shall not curse the people, for they are blessed.

¹³And Balaam rose up in the morning, and said to the princes of Balak, Go back to your own land, for the Lord refuses to permit me to go with you.

¹⁴So the princes of Moab rose up and went to Balak, and said, Balaam refuses to come with us.

¹⁵Then Balak again sent princes, more of them and more honorable than the first ones.

¹⁶And they came to Balaam, and said to him, Thus says Balak son of Zippor, I beg of you, let nothing hinder you from coming to me.

¹⁷For I will promote you to very great honor and I will do whatever you tell me; so come, I beg of you, curse this people for me.

¹⁸And Balaam answered the servants of Balak, If Balak would give me his house full of silver and gold, I cannot go beyond the word of the Lord my God, to do less or more.

¹⁹Now therefore, I pray you, tarry here again tonight that I may know what more the Lord will say to me.

²⁰And God came to Balaam at night, and said to him, If the men come to call you, rise up and go with them, but still only what I tell you may you do.

²¹And Balaam rose up in the morning and saddled his donkey and went with the princes of Moab.

²²And God's anger was kindled because he went, and the ᵃAngel of the Lord stood in the way as an adversary against him. Now he was riding upon his donkey, and his two servants were with him.

²³And the donkey saw the Angel of the Lord standing in the way and His sword drawn in His hand, and the donkey turned aside out of the way and went into the field. And Balaam struck the donkey to turn her into the way.

AMP notes: ᵃ See footnote on Gen. 16:7.

King James Version

24But the angel of the LORD stood in a path of the vineyards, a wall *being* on this side, and a wall on that side.

25And when the ass saw the angel of the LORD, she thrust herself unto the wall, and crusht Balaam's foot against the wall: and he smote her again.

26And the angel of the LORD went further, and stood in a narrow place, where *was* no way to turn *either to* the right hand or *to* the left.

27And when the ass saw the angel of the LORD, she fell down under Balaam: and Balaam's anger was kindled, and he smote the ass with a staff.

28And the LORD opened the mouth of the ass, and she said unto Balaam, What have I done unto thee, that thou hast smitten me these three times?

29And Balaam said unto the ass, Because thou hast mocked me: I would there were a sword in mine hand, for now would I kill thee.

30And the ass said unto Balaam, *Am* not I thine ass, upon which thou hast ridden ever since *I was* thine unto this day? was I ever wont to do so unto thee? And he said, Nay.

31Then the LORD opened the eyes of Balaam, and he saw the angel of the LORD standing in the way, and his sword drawn in his hand: and he bowed down his head, and fell flat on his face.

32And the angel of the LORD said unto him, Wherefore hast thou smitten thine ass these three times? behold, I went out to withstand thee, because *thy* way is perverse before me:

33And the ass saw me, and turned from me these three times: unless she had turned from me, surely now also I had slain thee, and saved her alive.

34And Balaam said unto the angel of the LORD, I have sinned; for I knew not that thou stoodest in the way against me: now therefore, if it displease thee, I will get me back again.

35And the angel of the LORD said unto Balaam, Go with the men: but only the word that I shall speak unto thee, that thou shalt speak. So Balaam went with the princes of Balak.

36And when Balak heard that Balaam was come, he went out to meet him unto a city of Moab, which *is* in the border of Arnon, which *is* in the utmost coast.

37And Balak said unto Balaam, Did I not earnestly send unto thee to call thee? wherefore camest thou not unto me? am I not able indeed to promote thee to honour?

38And Balaam said unto Balak, Lo, I am come unto thee: have I now any power at all to say any thing? the word that God putteth in my mouth, that shall I speak.

39And Balaam went with Balak, and they came *unto* Kirjath-huzoth.

40And Balak offered oxen and sheep, and sent to Balaam, and to the princes that *were* with him.

Amplified Bible

24But the Angel of the Lord stood in a path of the vineyards, a wall on this side and a wall on that side.

25And when the donkey saw the Angel of the Lord, she thrust herself against the wall and crushed Balaam's foot against it, and he struck her again.

26And the Angel of the Lord went further and stood in a narrow place where there was no room to turn, either to the right hand or to the left.

27And when the donkey saw the Angel of the Lord, she fell down under Balaam, and Balaam's anger was kindled and he struck the donkey with his staff.

28And the Lord opened the mouth of the donkey, and she said to Balaam, What have I done to you that you should strike me these three times?

29And Balaam said to the donkey, Because you have ridiculed *and* provoked me! I wish there were a sword in my hand, for now I would kill you!

30And the donkey said to Balaam, Am not I your donkey, upon which you have ridden all your life long until this day? Was I ever accustomed to do so to you? And he said, No.

31Then the Lord opened Balaam's eyes, and he saw the Angel of the Lord standing in the way with His sword drawn in His hand; and he bowed his head and fell on his face.

32And the Angel of the Lord said to him, Why have you struck your donkey these three times? See, I came out to stand against *and* resist you, for your behavior is willfully obstinate *and* contrary before Me.

33And the ass saw Me and turned from Me these three times. If she had not turned from Me, surely I would have slain you and saved her alive.

34Balaam said to the Angel of the Lord, I have sinned, for I did not know You stood in the way against me. But now, if my going displeases You, I will return.

35The Angel of the Lord said to Balaam, Go with the men, but you shall speak only what I tell you. So Balaam went with the princes of Balak.

36When Balak heard that Balaam had come, he went out to meet him at the city of Moab on the border formed by the Arnon [River], at the farthest end of the boundary.

37Balak said to Balaam, Did I not [earnestly] send to you to ask you [to come] to me? Why did you not come? Am not I able to promote you to honor?

38And Balaam said to Balak, Indeed I have come to you, but do I now have any power at all to say anything? The word that God puts in my mouth, that shall I speak.

39And Balaam went with Balak, and they came to Kiriath-huzoth.

40And Balak offered oxen and sheep, and sent [portions] to Balaam and to the princes who were with him.

King James Version

⁴¹And it came to pass on the morrow, that Balak took Balaam, and brought him up *into* the high places of Baal, that thence he might see the utmost part of the people.

23 And Balaam said unto Balak, Build me here seven altars, and prepare me here seven oxen and seven rams.

²And Balak did as Balaam had spoken; and Balak and Balaam offered on *every* altar a bullock and a ram.

³And Balaam said unto Balak, Stand by thy burnt offering, and I will go: peradventure the LORD will come to meet me: and whatsoever he sheweth me I will tell thee. And he went to a high place.

⁴And God met Balaam: and he said unto him, I have prepared seven altars, and I have offered upon *every* altar a bullock and a ram.

⁵And the LORD put a word in Balaam's mouth, and said, Return unto Balak, and thus thou shalt speak.

⁶And he returned unto him, and lo, *he* stood by his burnt sacrifice, he, and all the princes of Moab.

⁷And he took up his parable, and said, Balak the king of Moab hath brought me from Aram, out of the mountains of the east, *saying,* Come, curse me Jacob, and come, defy Israel.

⁸How shall I curse, whom God hath not cursed? or how shall I defy, *whom* the LORD hath not defied?

⁹For from the top of the rocks I see him, and from the hills I behold him: lo, the people shall dwell alone, and shall not be reckoned among the nations.

¹⁰Who can count the dust of Jacob, and the number *of* the fourth part of Israel? Let me die the death of the righteous, and let my last end be like his!

¹¹And Balak said unto Balaam, What hast thou done unto me? I took thee to curse mine enemies, and behold, thou hast blessed *them* altogether.

¹²And he answered and said, Must I not take heed to speak that which the LORD hath put in my mouth?

¹³And Balak said unto him, Come, I pray thee, with me unto another place, from whence thou mayest see them: thou shalt see but the utmost part of them, and shalt not see them all: and curse me them from thence.

¹⁴And he brought him *into* the field of Zophim, to the top of Pisgah, and built seven altars, and offered a bullock and a ram on *every* altar.

Amplified Bible

⁴¹And on the following day Balak took Balaam and brought him up into the high places of Bamoth-baal; from there he saw the nearest of the Israelites.

23 AND BALAAM said to Balak, Build me here seven altars, and prepare me here seven oxen and seven rams.

²And Balak did as Balaam had spoken, and Balak and Balaam offered on each altar a bull and a ram.

³And Balaam said to Balak, Stand by your burnt offering and I will go. Perhaps the Lord will come to meet me; and whatever He shows me I will tell you. And he went to a bare height.

⁴God met Balaam, who said to Him, I have prepared seven altars, and I have offered on each altar a bull and a ram.

⁵And the Lord put a speech in Balaam's mouth, and said, Return to Balak and thus shall you speak.

⁶Balaam returned to Balak, who was standing by his burnt sacrifice, he and all the princes of Moab.

⁷Balaam took up his [figurative] speech and said: Balak, the king of Moab, has brought me from Aram, out of the mountains of the east, saying, Come, curse Jacob for me; and come, violently denounce Israel.

⁸How can I curse those God has not cursed? Or how can I [violently] denounce those the Lord has not denounced?

⁹For from the top of the rocks I see Israel, and from the hills I behold him. Behold, the people [of Israel] shall ᵃdwell alone and shall not be reckoned *and* esteemed among the nations.

¹⁰Who can count the dust (the descendants) of Jacob and the number of the fourth part of Israel? Let me die the death of the righteous [those who are upright and in right standing with God], and let my last end be like theirs!

¹¹And Balak said to Balaam, What have you done to me? I brought you to curse my enemies, and here you have [thoroughly] blessed them instead!

¹²And Balaam answered, Must I not be obedient *and* speak what the Lord has put in my mouth?

¹³Balak said to him, Come with me, I implore you, to another place from which you can see them, though you will see only the nearest and not all of them; and curse them for me from there.

¹⁴So he took Balaam into the field of Zophim to the top of [Mount] Pisgah, and built seven altars, and offered a bull and a ram on each altar.

AMP notes: ᵃ The literal fulfillment of this prophecy has been obvious during the more than thirty-four centuries since it was spoken. The Jews have always been separate as a nation from other peoples. Though conquered many times, they have never been absorbed by their conquerors or lost their identity. The prophecy had to become true, for "the Lord put [it] . . . in Balaam's mouth" (Num. 23:5).

King James Version

15And he said unto Balak, Stand here by thy burnt offering, while I meet *the* LORD yonder.

16And the LORD met Balaam, and put a word in his mouth, and said, Go again unto Balak, and say thus.

17And when he came to him, behold, he stood by his burnt offering, and the princes of Moab with him. And Balak said unto him, What hath the LORD spoken?

18And he took up his parable, and said, Rise up, Balak, and hear; hearken unto me, thou son of Zippor:

19God *is* not a man, that he should lie; neither the son of man, that he should repent: hath he said, and shall he not do *it?* or hath he spoken, and shall he not make it good?

20Behold, I have received *commandment* to bless: and he hath blessed; and I cannot reverse it.

21He hath not beheld iniquity in Jacob, neither hath he seen perverseness in Israel: the LORD his God *is* with him, and the shout of a king *is* among them.

22God brought them out of Egypt; he hath as it were the strength of an unicorn.

23Surely *there is* no enchantment against Jacob, neither *is there* any divination against Israel: according to *this* time it shall be said of Jacob and of Israel, What hath God wrought!

24Behold, the people shall rise up as a great lion, and lift up himself as a young lion: he shall not lie down until he eat *of* the prey, and drink the blood of the slain.

25And Balak said unto Balaam, Neither curse them at all, nor bless them at all.

26But Balaam answered and said unto Balak, Told not I thee, saying, All that the LORD speaketh, that I must do?

27And Balak said unto Balaam, Come, I pray thee, I will bring thee unto another place; peradventure it will please God that thou mayest curse me them from thence.

28And Balak brought Balaam *unto* the top of Peor, that looketh toward Jeshimon.

29And Balaam said unto Balak, Build me here seven altars, and prepare me here seven bullocks and seven rams.

30And Balak did as Balaam had said, and offered a bullock and a ram on *every* altar.

24 And when Balaam saw that it pleased the LORD to bless Israel, he went not, as at other times, to seek for enchantments, but he set his face toward the wilderness.

2And Balaam lift up his eyes, and he saw Isra-

Amplified Bible

15Balaam said to Balak, Stand here by your burnt offering while I go to meet the Lord yonder.

16And the Lord met Balaam and put a speech in his mouth, and said, Go again to Balak and speak thus.

17And when he returned to Balak, he was standing beside his burnt offering, and the princes of Moab with him. And Balak said to him, What has the Lord said?

18Balaam took up his [figurative] discourse and said: Rise up, Balak, and hear; listen [closely] to me, son of Zippor.

19God is not a man, that He should tell *or* act a lie, neither the son of man, that He should feel repentance *or* compunction [for what He has promised]. Has He said and shall He not do it? Or has He spoken and shall He not make it good?

20You see, I have received His command to bless Israel. He has blessed, and I cannot reverse *or* qualify it.

21[God] has not beheld iniquity in Jacob [for he is forgiven], neither has He seen mischief *or* perverseness in Israel [for the same reason]. The Lord their God is with Israel, and the shout of praise to their King is among the people.

22God brought them forth out of Egypt; they have as it were the strength of a wild ox.

23Surely there is no enchantment with *or* against Jacob, neither is there any divination with *or* against Israel. [In due season and even] now it shall be said of Jacob and of Israel, What has God wrought!

24Behold, a people! They rise up as a lioness and lift themselves up as a lion; he shall not lie down until he devours the prey and drinks the blood of the slain.

25And Balak said to Balaam, Neither curse them at all nor bless them at all.

26But Balaam answered Balak, Did I not say to you, All the Lord speaks, that I must do?

27And Balak said to Balaam, Come, I implore you; I will take you to another place. Perhaps it will please God to let you curse them for me from there.

28So Balak brought Balaam to the top of [Mount] Peor, that overlooks [the wilderness or desert] Jeshimon.

29And Balaam said to Balak, Build me here seven altars, and prepare me here seven bulls and seven rams.

30And Balak did as Balaam had said, and offered a bull and a ram on each altar.

24 WHEN BALAAM saw that it pleased the Lord to bless Israel, he did not go as he had done each time before [superstitiously] to meet with omens *and* signs in the natural world, but he set his face toward the wilderness *or* desert.

2And Balaam lifted up his eyes and he saw Is-

King James Version

el abiding *in his tents* according to their tribes; and the spirit of God came upon him.

³And he took up his parable, and said, Balaam the son of Beor hath said, and the man whose eyes are open hath said:

⁴He hath said, which heard the words of God, which saw the vision of the Almighty, falling *into a trance,* but having his eyes open:

⁵How goodly are thy tents, O Jacob, *and* thy tabernacles, O Israel!

⁶As the valleys are they spread forth, as gardens by the river side, as the trees of lign aloes *which* the LORD hath planted, *and* as cedar trees beside the waters.

⁷He shall pour the water out of his buckets, and his seed *shall be* in many waters, and his king shall be higher than Agag, and his kingdom shall be exalted.

⁸God brought him forth out of Egypt; he hath as it were the strength of an unicorn: he shall eat up the nations his enemies, and shall break their bones, and pierce *them* through *with* his arrows.

⁹He couched, he lay down as a lion, and as a great lion: who shall stir him up? Blessed *is* he that blesseth thee, and cursed *is* he that curseth thee.

¹⁰And Balak's anger was kindled against Balaam, and he smote his hands together: and Balak said unto Balaam, I called thee to curse mine enemies, and behold, thou hast altogether blessed *them* these three times.

¹¹Therefore now flee thou to thy place: I thought to promote thee unto great honour; but lo, the LORD hath kept thee back from honour.

¹²And Balaam said unto Balak, Spake I not also to thy messengers which thou sentest unto me, saying,

¹³If Balak would give me his house full *of* silver and gold, I cannot go beyond the commandment of the LORD, to do *either* good or bad of mine own mind; *but* what the LORD saith, that will I speak?

¹⁴And now behold, I go unto my people: come *therefore, and* I will advertise thee what this people shall do to thy people in the latter days.

¹⁵And he took up his parable, and said, Balaam the son of Beor hath said, and the man whose eyes are open hath said:

¹⁶He hath said, which heard the words of God, and knew the knowledge of the most High, *which* saw the vision of the Almighty, falling *into a trance,* but having his eyes open:

¹⁷I shall see him, but not now: I shall behold

Amplified Bible

rael abiding in their tents according to their tribes. And the Spirit of God came upon him

³And he took up his [figurative] discourse and said: Balaam son of Beor, the man whose eye is opened [at last, to see clearly the purposes and will of God],

⁴He [Balaam] who hears the words of God, who sees the vision of the Almighty, falling down, but having his eyes open *and* uncovered, he says:

⁵How attractive *and* considerable are your tents, O Jacob, *and* your tabernacles, O Israel!

⁶As valleys are they spread forth, as gardens by the riverside, as [rare spice] of lignaloes which the Lord has planted, and as cedar trees beside the waters.

⁷[Israel] shall pour water out of his own buckets [have his own sources of rich blessing and plenty], and his offspring shall dwell by many waters, and his king shall be higher than ᵃAgag, and his kingdom shall be exalted.

⁸God brought [Israel] forth out of Egypt; [Israel] has strength like the wild ox; he shall eat up the nations, his enemies, crushing their bones and piercing them through with his arrows.

⁹He couched, he lay down as a lion; and as a lioness, who shall rouse him? Blessed [of God] is he who blesses you [who prays for and contributes to your welfare] and cursed [of God] is he who curses you [who in word, thought, or deed would bring harm upon you].

¹⁰Then Balak's anger was kindled against Balaam, and he smote his hands together; and Balak said to Balaam, I called you to curse my enemies, and, behold, you have done nothing but bless them these three times.

¹¹Therefore now go back where you belong *and* do it in a hurry! I had intended to promote you to great honor, but behold, the Lord has held you back from honor.

¹²Balaam said to Balak, Did I not say to your messengers whom you sent to me,

¹³If Balak would give me his house full of silver and gold, I cannot go beyond the command of the Lord, to do either good or bad of my own will, but what the Lord says, that will I speak?

¹⁴And now, behold, I am going to my people; come, I will tell you what this people [Israel] will do to your people [Moab] in the latter days.

¹⁵And he took up his [figurative] discourse, and said: Balaam son of Beor speaks, the man whose eye is opened speaks,

¹⁶He speaks, who heard the words of God and knew the knowledge of the Most High, who saw the vision of the Almighty, falling down, but having his eyes open *and* uncovered:

¹⁷I see Him, but not now; I behold Him, but

AMP *notes:* ᵃ "Agag" was the title of the Amalekite kings, and it represents here the kingdom of the Gentiles. The Amalekites at that time were the most powerful of all the desert tribes (Num. 24:20).

King James Version

him, but not nigh: there shall come a Star out of Jacob, and a Sceptre shall rise out of Israel, and shall smite the corners of Moab, and destroy all the children of Sheth.

18And Edom shall be a possession, Seir also shall be a possession for his enemies; and Israel shall do valiantly.

19Out of Jacob shall come *he* that shall have dominion, and shall destroy him that remaineth of the city.

20 ¶ And when he looked on Amalek, he took up his parable, and said, Amalek *was* the first of the nations; but his latter end *shall be* that he perish for ever.

21 ¶ And he looked on the Kenites, and took up his parable, and said, Strong *is* thy dwelling place, and thou puttest thy nest in a rock.

22Nevertheless the Kenite shall be wasted, until Asshur shall carry thee away captive.

23 ¶ And he took up his parable, and said, Alas, who shall live when God doeth this!

24And ships *shall come* from the coast of Chittim, and shall afflict Asshur, and shall afflict Eber, and he also shall perish for ever.

25And Balaam rose up, and went and returned to his place: and Balak also went his way.

25 And Israel abode in Shittim, and the people begun to commit whoredom with the daughters of Moab.

2And they called the people unto the sacrifices of their gods: and the people did eat, and bowed down to their gods.

3And Israel joined himself unto Baal-peor: and the anger of the LORD was kindled against Israel.

4And the LORD said unto Moses, Take all the heads of the people, and hang them up before the LORD against the sun, that the fierce anger of the LORD may be turned away from Israel.

Amplified Bible

He is not near. A [a]star (Star) shall come forth out of Jacob, and a scepter (Scepter) shall rise out of Israel and shall crush all the corners of Moab and break down all the sons of Sheth [Moab's sons of tumult].

18And Edom shall be [taken as] a possession, [Mount] Seir also shall be dispossessed, who were Israel's enemies, while Israel does valiantly.

19Out of Jacob shall one (One) come having dominion and shall destroy the remnant from the city.

20[Balaam] looked at Amalek and took up his [prophetic] utterance, and said: Amalek is the foremost of the [neighboring] nations, but in his latter end he shall [b]come to destruction.

21And he looked at the Kenites and took up his [prophetic] utterance, and said: Strong is your dwelling place, and you set your nest in the rock.

22Nevertheless the Kenites shall be wasted. How long shall Asshur (Assyria) take you away captive?

23And he took up his [prophetic] speech, and said: Alas, who shall live when God does this *and* establishes [Assyria]?

24But ships shall come from Kittim [Cyprus and the greater part of the Mediterranean's east coast] and shall afflict Assyria and Eber [the Hebrews, certain Arabs, and descendants of Nahor], and he [the victor] also shall come to destruction.

25And Balaam rose up, returned to his place, and Balak also went his way.

25 ISRAEL SETTLED down *and* remained in Shittim, and the people began to play the harlot with the daughters of Moab,

2Who invited the [Israelites] to the sacrifices of their gods, and [they] ate and bowed down to Moab's gods.

3So Israel joined himself to [the god] Baal of Peor. And the anger of the Lord was kindled against Israel.

4And the Lord said to Moses, Take all the leaders *or* chiefs of the people, and hang them before the Lord in the sun [after killing them], that the fierce anger of the Lord may turn away from Israel.

AMP notes: a "This imagery in the hieroglyphic language of the East denotes some eminent ruler—primarily David, but secondarily and preeminently the Messiah" (Robert Jamieson, A. R. Fausett and David Brown, *A Commentary*). Notice that the principal time for these events is set in the prophecy for "the latter days" (Num. 24:14). "The prophecy [concerning Moab] was partially, or typically, fulfilled in the time of David (II Sam. 8:2). Moab and Edom represented symbolically the enemies of Christ and His church, and as such will eventually be subdued by the King of kings (see Ps. 60:8)" (Charles J. Ellicott, *A Bible Commentary*). "The star which the wise men from the East saw, and which led them in the way to the newborn 'King of the Jews,' refers clearly to the prophecy of Balaam (Matt. 2:1, 2)" (J. P. Lange, *A Commentary*). b After the time of David (who was forced to rescue two of his wives from Amalekite bandits, I Sam. 30:18), the Amalekites are mentioned again only in Hezekiah's time (I Chron. 4:43), before "they disappear from the field of history . . . So that the word of God here also stood fast; and the first of the surrounding tribes who impiously sought to measure their strength with the cause and people of God were likewise the first to lose their national existence" (Patrick Fairbairn, ed., *The Imperial Bible-dictionary*).

King James Version

⁵And Moses said unto the judges of Israel, Slay ye every one his men that were joined unto Baal-peor.

⁶And behold, one of the children of Israel came and brought unto his brethren a Midianitish *woman* in the sight of Moses, and in the sight of all the congregation of the children of Israel, who *were* weeping *before* the door of the tabernacle of the congregation.

⁷And when Phinehas, the son of Eleazar, the son of Aaron the priest, saw *it*, he rose up from amongst the congregation, and took a javelin in his hand;

⁸And he went after the man of Israel into the tent, and thrust both of them through, the man of Israel, and the woman through her belly. So the plague was stayed from the children of Israel.

⁹And those that died in the plague were twenty and four thousand.

¹⁰ ¶ And the LORD spake unto Moses, saying,

¹¹Phinehas, the son of Eleazar, the son of Aaron the priest, hath turned my wrath away from the children of Israel, while he was zealous for my sake among them, that I consumed not the children of Israel in my jealousy.

¹²Wherefore say, Behold, I give unto him my covenant of peace:

¹³And he shall have it, and his seed after him, *even* the covenant of an everlasting priesthood; because he was zealous for his God, and made an atonement for the children of Israel.

¹⁴Now the name of the Israelite that was slain, *even* that was slain with the Midianitish woman, *was* Zimri, the son of Salu, a prince of a chief house among the Simeonites.

¹⁵And the name of the Midianitish woman that was slain *was* Cozbi, the daughter of Zur; he *was* head over a people, *and* of a chief house in Midian.

¹⁶ ¶ And the LORD spake unto Moses, saying,

¹⁷Vex the Midianites, and smite them:

¹⁸For they vex you with their wiles, wherewith they have beguiled you in the matter of Peor, and in the matter of Cozbi, the daughter of a prince of Midian, their sister, which was slain in the day of the plague for Peor's sake.

26 And it came to pass after the plague, that the LORD spake unto Moses and unto Eleazar the son of Aaron the priest, saying,

²Take the sum of all the congregation of the children of Israel, from twenty years old and upward, throughout their fathers' house, all that *are able to* go *to* war in Israel.

³And Moses and Eleazar the priest spake with them in the plains of Moab by Jordan *near* Jericho, saying,

⁴*Take the sum of the people*, from twenty years old and upward; as the LORD commanded Moses

Amplified Bible

⁵And Moses said to the judges of Israel, Each one of you slay his men who joined themselves to Baal of Peor.

⁶And behold, one of the Israelites came and brought to his brethren a Midianite woman in the sight of Moses and of all the congregation of Israel while they were weeping at the door of the Tent of Meeting [over the divine judgment and the punishment].

⁷And when Phinehas son of Eleazar, the son of Aaron the priest, saw it, he rose up from the midst of the congregation and took a spear in his hand

⁸And went after the man of Israel into the inner room and thrust both of them through, the man of Israel and the woman through her body. Then the [smiting] plague was stayed from the Israelites.

⁹Nevertheless those who died in the [smiting] plague were 24,000.

¹⁰And the Lord said to Moses,

¹¹Phinehas son of Eleazar, the son of Aaron the priest, has turned my wrath away from the Israelites, in that he was jealous with My jealousy among them, so that I did not consume the Israelites in My jealousy.

¹²Therefore say, Behold, I give to Phinehas the priest My covenant of peace.

¹³And he shall have it, and his descendants after him, the covenant of an everlasting priesthood, because he was jealous for his God and made atonement for the Israelites.

¹⁴Now the man of Israel who was slain with the Midianite woman was Zimri son of Salu, a head of a father's house among the Simeonites.

¹⁵And the Midianite woman who was slain was Cozbi daughter of Zur; he was head of a father's house in Midian.

¹⁶And the Lord said to Moses,

¹⁷Provoke hostilities with the Midianites and attack them,

¹⁸For they harass you with their wiles with which they have beguiled you in the matter of Peor, and of Cozbi, the daughter of the prince of Midian, their sister, who was slain on the day of the plague in the matter of Peor.

26 AFTER THE plague the Lord said to Moses and Eleazar son of Aaron, the priest,

²Take a census of all the [male] congregation of the Israelites from twenty years old and upward, by their fathers' houses, all in Israel able to go to war.

³And Moses and Eleazar the priest told [the people] in the plains of Moab by the Jordan at Jericho,

⁴A census of the people shall be taken from twenty years old and upward, as the Lord com-

King James Version

and the children of Israel, which went forth out of the land of Egypt.

5 ¶ Reuben, the eldest son of Israel: the children of Reuben; Hanoch, *of whom cometh* the family of the Hanochites: of Pallu, the family of the Palluites:

6 Of Hezron, the family of the Hezronites: of Carmi, the family of the Carmites.

7 These *are* the families of the Reubenites: and they that were numbered of them were forty and three thousand and seven hundred and thirty.

8 And the sons of Pallu; Eliab.

9 And the sons of Eliab; Nemuel, and Dathan, and Abiram. This *is that* Dathan and Abiram, *which were* famous in the congregation, who strove against Moses and against Aaron in the company of Korah, when they strove against the LORD:

10 And the earth opened her mouth, and swallowed them up together with Korah, when that company died, what time the fire devoured two hundred and fifty men: and they became a sign.

11 Notwithstanding the children of Korah died not.

12 ¶ The sons of Simeon after their families: of Nemuel, the family of the Nemuelites: of Jamin, the family of the Jaminites: of Jachin, the family of the Jachinites:

13 Of Zerah, the family of the Zarhites: of Shaul, the family of the Shaulites.

14 These *are* the families of the Simeonites, twenty and two thousand and two hundred.

15 ¶ The children of Gad after their families: of Zephon, the family of the Zephonites: of Haggi, the family of the Haggites: of Shuni, the family of the Shunites:

16 Of Ozni, the family of the Oznites: of Eri, the family of the Erites:

17 Of Arod, the family of the Arodites: of Areli, the family of the Arelites.

18 These *are* the families of the children of Gad according to those that were numbered of them, forty thousand and five hundred.

19 ¶ The sons of Judah *were* Er and Onan: and Er and Onan died in the land of Canaan.

20 And the sons of Judah after their families were, of Shelah, the family of the Shelanites: of Pharez, the family of the Pharzites: of Zerah, the family of the Zarhites.

21 And the sons of Pharez were; of Hezron, the family of the Hezronites: of Hamul, the family of the Hamulites.

22 These *are* the families of Judah according to those that were numbered of them, threescore and sixteen thousand and five hundred.

23 ¶ *Of* the sons of Issachar after their families: *of* Tola, the family of the Tolaites: of Pua, the family of the Punites:

24 Of Jashub, the family of the Jashubites: of Shimron, the family of the Shimronites.

Amplified Bible

manded Moses. And the Israelites who came forth out of the land of Egypt were:

5 Reuben, the firstborn of Israel, the sons of Reuben: of Hanoch, the family of the Hanochites; of Pallu, the family of the Palluites;

6 Of Hezron, the family of the Hezronites; of Carmi, the family of the Carmites.

7 These are the families of the Reubenites; and their number was 43,730.

8 And the son of Pallu: Eliab.

9 The sons of Eliab: Nemuel, Dathan, and Abiram. These are the Dathan and Abiram chosen from the congregation who contended against Moses and Aaron in the company of Korah when they contended against the Lord.

10 And the earth opened its mouth and swallowed them up together with Korah, when that company died and the fire devoured 250 men; and they became a [warning] sign.

11 But Korah's sons did not die.

12 The sons of Simeon according to their families: of Nemuel, the family of the Nemuelites; of Jamin, the family of the Jaminites; of Jachin, the family of the Jachinites;

13 Of Zerah, the family of the Zerahites; of Shaul, the family of the Shaulites.

14 These are the families of the Simeonites, 22,200.

15 The sons of Gad after their families: of Zephon, the family of the Zephonites; of Haggi, the family of the Haggites; of Shuni, the family of the Shunites;

16 Of Ozni, the family of the Oznites; of Eri, the family of the Erites;

17 Of Arod, the family of the Arodites; of Areli, the family of the Arelites.

18 These, the families of the sons of Gad according to their numbering, totaled 40,500.

19 The sons of Judah were Er and Onan, but Er and Onan died in the land of Canaan.

20 And the sons of Judah according to their families were: of Shelah, the family of the Shelanites; of Perez, the family of the Perezites; of Zerah, the family of the Zerahites.

21 And the sons of Perez were: of Hezron, the family of the Hezronites; of Hamul, the family of the Hamulites.

22 These, the families of Judah according to their numbering, totaled 76,500.

23 The sons of Issachar after their families: of Tola, the family of the Tolaites; of Puvah, the family of the Punites;

24 Of Jashub, the family of the Jashubites; of Shimron, the family of the Shimronites.

King James Version

²⁵These *are* the families of Issachar according to those that were numbered of them, threescore and four thousand and three hundred.

²⁶ ¶ *Of* the sons of Zebulun after their families: of Sered, the family of the Sardites: of Elon, the family of the Elonites: of Jahleel, the family of the Jahleelites.

²⁷These *are* the families of the Zebulunites according to those that were numbered of them, threescore thousand and five hundred.

²⁸ ¶ The sons of Joseph after their families *were* Manasseh and Ephraim.

²⁹*Of* the sons of Manasseh: of Machir, the family of the Machirites: and Machir begat Gilead: of Gilead *come* the family of the Gileadites.

³⁰These *are* the sons of Gilead: *of* Jeezer, the family of the Jeezerites: of Helek, the family of the Helekites:

³¹And *of* Asriel, the family of the Asrielites: and *of* Shechem, the family of the Shechemites:

³²And *of* Shemida, the family of the Shemidaites: and *of* Hepher, the family of the Hepherites.

³³And Zelophehad the son of Hepher had no sons, but daughters: and the names of the daughters of Zelophehad *were* Mahlah, and Noah, Hoglah, Milcah, and Tirzah.

³⁴These *are* the families of Manasseh, and those that were numbered of them, fifty and two thousand and seven hundred.

³⁵These *are* the sons of Ephraim after their families: of Shuthelah, the family of the Shuthalhites: of Becher, the family of the Bachrites: of Tahan, the family of the Tahanites.

³⁶And these *are* the sons of Shuthelah: of Eran, the family of the Eranites.

³⁷These *are* the families of the sons of Ephraim according to those that were numbered of them, thirty and two thousand and five hundred. These *are* the sons of Joseph after their families.

³⁸ ¶ The sons of Benjamin after their families: of Bela, the family of the Belaites: of Ashbel, the family of the Ashbelites: of Ahiram, the family of the Ahiramites:

³⁹Of Shupham, the family of the Shuphamites: of Hupham, the family of the Huphamites.

⁴⁰And the sons of Bela were Ard and Naaman: *of Ard,* the family of the Ardites: *and* of Naaman, the family of the Naamites.

⁴¹These *are* the sons of Benjamin after their families: and they that were numbered of them *were* forty and five thousand and six hundred.

⁴² ¶ These *are* the sons of Dan after their families: of Shuham, the family of the Shuhamites. These *are* the families of Dan after their families.

⁴³All the families of the Shuhamites, according to those that were numbered of them, *were* threescore and four thousand and four hundred.

Amplified Bible

²⁵These, the families of Issachar according to their numbering, totaled 64,300.

²⁶The sons of Zebulun after their families: of Sered, the family of the Seredites; of Elon, the family of the Elonites; of Jahleel, the family of the Jahleelites.

²⁷These, the families of the Zebulunites according to their numbering, totaled 60,500.

²⁸The sons of Joseph after their families were Manasseh and Ephraim.

²⁹The sons of Manasseh: of Machir, the family of the Machirites (and Machir was the father of Gilead); of Gilead, the family of the Gileadites.

³⁰These are the sons of Gilead: of Iezer, the family of the Iezerites; of Helek, the family of the Helekites;

³¹Of Asriel, the family of the Asrielites; of Shechem, the family of the Shechemites;

³²Of Shemida, the family of the Shemidaites; and of Hepher, the family of the Hepherites.

³³Zelophehad son of Hepher had no sons, but only daughters, and their names were Mahlah, Noah, Hoglah, Milcah, and Tirzah.

³⁴These are the families of Manasseh, and their number was 52,700.

³⁵These are the sons of Ephraim according to their families: of Shuthelah, the family of the Shuthelahites; of Becher, the family of the Becherites; of Tahan, the family of the Tahanites.

³⁶And these are the sons of Shuthelah: of Eran, the family of the Eranites.

³⁷These, the families of the sons of Ephraim according to their number, totaled 32,500. These are the sons of Joseph after their families.

³⁸The sons of Benjamin according to their families: of Bela, the family of the Belaites; of Ashbel, the family of the Ashbelites; of Ahiram, the family of the Ahiramites;

³⁹Of Shephupham, the family of the Shuphamites; of Hupham, the family of the Huphamites.

⁴⁰And the sons of Bela were Ard and Naaman: of Ard, the family of the Ardites; of Naaman, the family of the Naamites.

⁴¹These are the sons of Benjamin according to their families; and their number was 45,600.

⁴²These are the sons of Dan according to their families: of Shuham, the family of the Shuhamites. These are the families of Dan according to their families.

⁴³All the families of the Shuhamites according to their number were 64,400.

King James Version

⁴⁴ ¶ *Of* the children of Asher after their families: of Jimna, the family of the Jimnites: of Jesui, the family of the Jesuites: of Beriah, the family of the Beriites.

⁴⁵Of the sons of Beriah: of Heber, the family of the Heberites: of Malchiel, the family of the Malchielites.

⁴⁶And the name of the daughter of Asher *was* Sarah.

⁴⁷These *are* the families of the sons of Asher according to those that were numbered of them; *who were* fifty and three thousand and four hundred.

⁴⁸ ¶ *Of* the sons of Naphtali after their families: of Jahzeel, the family of the Jahzeelites: of Guni, the family of the Gunites:

⁴⁹Of Jezer, the family of the Jezerites: of Shillem, the family of the Shillemites.

⁵⁰These *are* the families of Naphtali according to their families: and they that were numbered of them *were* forty and five thousand and four hundred.

⁵¹These *were* the numbered of the children of Israel, six hundred thousand and a thousand seven hundred and thirty.

⁵² ¶ And the LORD spake unto Moses, saying, ⁵³Unto these the land shall be divided for an inheritance according to the number of names.

⁵⁴To many thou shalt give the more inheritance, and to few thou shalt give the less inheritance: *to* every one shall his inheritance be given according to those that were numbered of him.

⁵⁵Notwithstanding the land shall be divided by lot: according to the names of the tribes of their fathers they shall inherit.

⁵⁶According to the lot shall the possession thereof be divided between many and few.

⁵⁷ ¶ And these *are* they that were numbered of the Levites after their families: of Gershon, the family of the Gershonites: of Kohath, the family of the Kohathites: of Merari, the family of the Merarites.

⁵⁸These *are* the families of the Levites: the family of the Libnites, the family of the Hebronites, the family of the Mahlites, the family of the Mushites, the family of the Korahites. And Kohath begat Amram.

⁵⁹And the name of Amram's wife *was* Jochebed, the daughter of Levi, whom *her mother* bare to Levi in Egypt: and she bare unto Amram Aaron and Moses, and Miriam their sister.

⁶⁰And unto Aaron was born Nadab, and Abihu, Eleazar, and Ithamar.

⁶¹And Nadab and Abihu died, when they offered strange fire before the LORD.

⁶²And those that were numbered of them were twenty and three thousand, all males from a month old and upward: for they were not numbered among the children of Israel, because

Amplified Bible

⁴⁴Of the sons of Asher according to their families: of Imnah, the family of the Imnites; of Ishvi, the family of the Ishvites; of Beriah, the family of the Beriites.

⁴⁵Of the sons of Beriah: of Heber, the family of the Heberites; of Malchiel, the family of the Malchielites.

⁴⁶And the name of the daughter of Asher was Serah.

⁴⁷These, the families of the sons of Asher according to their number, totaled 53,400.

⁴⁸Of the sons of Naphtali after their families: of Jahzeel, the family of the Jahzeelites; of Guni, the family of the Gunites;

⁴⁹Of Jezer, the family of the Jezerites; of Shillem, the family of the Shillemites.

⁵⁰These are the families of Naphtali according to their families; and their number totaled 45,400.

⁵¹This was the number of the Israelites, 601,730.

⁵²And the Lord said to Moses,

⁵³To these the land shall be divided for inheritance according to the number of names.

⁵⁴To a larger tribe you shall give the greater inheritance, and to a small tribe the less inheritance; to each tribe shall its inheritance be given according to its numbers.

⁵⁵But the land shall be divided by lot; according to the names of the tribes of their fathers they shall inherit.

⁵⁶According to the lot shall their inheritance be divided between the larger and the smaller.

⁵⁷And these were numbered of the Levites according to their families: of Gershon, the family of the Gershonites; of Kohath, the family of the Kohathites; of Merari, the family of the Merarites.

⁵⁸These are the families of Levi: the family of the Libnites, the family of the Hebronites, the family of the Mahlites, the family of the Mushites, the family of the Korahites. And Kohath was the father of Amram.

⁵⁹Amram's wife was Jochebed daughter of Levi, who was born to Levi in Egypt; and she bore to Amram Aaron, Moses, and Miriam their sister.

⁶⁰And to Aaron were born Nadab, Abihu, Eleazar, and Ithamar.

⁶¹But Nadab and Abihu died when they offered strange *and* unholy fire before the Lord.

⁶²And those numbered of them were 23,000, every male from a month old and upward; for they were not numbered among the Israelites,

King James Version

there was no inheritance given them among the children of Israel.

⁶³These *are* they that were numbered by Moses and Eleazar the priest, who numbered the children of Israel in the plains of Moab by Jordan *near* Jericho.

⁶⁴But among these there was not a man of them whom Moses and Aaron the priest numbered, when they numbered the children of Israel in the wilderness of Sinai.

⁶⁵For the LORD had said of them, They shall surely die in the wilderness. And there was not left a man of them, save Caleb the son of Jephunneh, and Joshua the son of Nun.

27 Then came the daughters of Zelophehad, the son of Hepher, the son of Gilead, the son of Machir, the son of Manasseh, of the families of Manasseh the son of Joseph: and these *are* the names of his daughters; Mahlah, Noah, and Hoglah, and Milcah, and Tirzah.

²And they stood before Moses, and before Eleazar the priest, and before the princes and all the congregation, *by* the door of the tabernacle of the congregation, saying,

³Our father died in the wilderness, and he was not in the company of them that gathered themselves together against the LORD in the company of Korah; but died in his own sin, and had no sons.

⁴Why should the name of our father be done away from among his family, because he hath no son? Give unto us *therefore* a possession among the brethren of our father.

⁵And Moses brought their cause before the LORD.

⁶And the LORD spake unto Moses, saying,

⁷The daughters of Zelophehad speak right: thou shalt surely give them a possession of an inheritance among their father's brethren; and thou shalt cause the inheritance of their father to pass unto them.

⁸And thou shalt speak unto the children of Israel, saying, If a man die, and have no son, then ye shall cause his inheritance to pass unto his daughter.

⁹And if he have no daughter, then ye shall give his inheritance unto his brethren.

¹⁰And if he have no brethren, then ye shall give his inheritance unto his father's brethren.

¹¹And if his father have no brethren, then ye shall give his inheritance unto his kinsman that is next to him of his family, and he shall possess it: and it shall be unto the children of Israel a statute of judgment, as the LORD commanded Moses.

¹² ¶ And the LORD said unto Moses, Get thee up into this mount Abarim, and see the land which I have given unto the children of Israel.

¹³And when thou hast seen it, thou also shalt

Amplified Bible

because there was no inheritance given them among the Israelites.

⁶³These were those numbered by Moses and Eleazar the priest, who numbered the Israelites in the plains of Moab by the Jordan at Jericho.

⁶⁴But among these there was not a man of those numbered by Moses and Aaron the priest when they numbered the Israelites in the Wilderness of Sinai.

⁶⁵For the Lord had said of them, They shall surely die in the wilderness. There was not left a man of them except Caleb son of Jephunneh and Joshua son of Nun.

27 THEN CAME the daughters of Zelophehad son of Hepher, the son of Gilead, the son of Machir, the son of Manasseh, from the families of Manasseh son of Joseph. The names of his daughters: Mahlah, Noah, Hoglah, Milcah, and Tirzah.

²They stood before Moses, Eleazar the priest, and the leaders, and all the congregation at the door of the Tent of Meeting, saying,

³Our father died in the wilderness. He was not among those who assembled together against the Lord in the company of Korah, but died for his own sin [as did all those who rebelled at Kadesh], and he had no sons.

⁴Why should the name of our father be removed from his family because he had no son? Give to us a possession among our father's brethren.

⁵Moses brought their case before the Lord.

⁶And the Lord said to Moses,

⁷The daughters of Zelophehad are justified *and* speak correctly. You shall surely give them an inheritance among their father's brethren, and you shall cause their father's inheritance to pass to them.

⁸And say to the Israelites, If a man dies and has no son, you shall cause his inheritance to pass to his daughter.

⁹If he has no daughter, you shall give his inheritance to his brethren.

¹⁰If he has no brethren, give his inheritance to his father's brethren.

¹¹And if his father has no brethren, then give his inheritance to his next of kin, and he shall possess it. It shall be to the Israelites a statute and ordinance, as the Lord commanded Moses.

¹²And the Lord said to Moses, Go up into this mountain of Abarim and behold the land I have given to the Israelites.

¹³And when you have seen it, you also shall

King James Version

be gathered unto thy people, as Aaron thy brother was gathered.

¹⁴For ye rebelled against my commandment in the desert of Zin, in the strife of the congregation, to sanctify me at the water before their eyes: that *is* the water of Meribah in Kadesh *in* the wilderness of Zin.

¹⁵And Moses spake unto the LORD, saying,

¹⁶Let the LORD, the God of the spirits of all flesh, set a man over the congregation,

¹⁷Which may go out before them, and which may go in before them, and which may lead them out, and which may bring them in; that the congregation of the LORD be not as sheep which have no shepherd.

¹⁸And the LORD said unto Moses, Take thee Joshua the son of Nun, a man in whom *is* the spirit, and lay thine hand upon him;

¹⁹And set him before Eleazar the priest, and before all the congregation; and give him a charge in their sight.

²⁰And thou shalt put *some* of thine honour upon him, that all the congregation of the children of Israel may be obedient.

²¹And he shall stand before Eleazar the priest, who shall ask *counsel* for him after the judgment of Urim before the LORD: at his word shall they go out, and at his word they shall come in, *both* he, and all the children of Israel with him, even all the congregation.

²²And Moses did as the LORD commanded him: and he took Joshua, and set him before Eleazar the priest, and before all the congregation:

²³And he laid his hands upon him, and gave him a charge, as the LORD commanded by the hand of Moses.

28 And the LORD spake unto Moses, saying, ²Command the children of Israel, and say unto them, My offering, *and* my bread for my sacrifices made by fire, *for* a sweet savour unto me, shall ye observe to offer unto me in their due season.

³And thou shalt say unto them, This *is* the offering made by fire which ye shall offer unto the LORD; two lambs of the first year without spot day by day, *for* a continual burnt offering.

⁴The one lamb shalt thou offer in the morning, and the other lamb shalt thou offer at even;

⁵And a tenth *part* of an ephah *of* flour for a meat offering, mingled with the fourth *part* of a hin of beaten oil.

⁶*It is* a continual burnt offering, which was ordained in mount Sinai for a sweet savour, a sacrifice made by fire unto the LORD.

⁷And the drink offering thereof *shall be* the fourth *part* of a hin for the one lamb: in the holy *place* shalt thou cause the strong wine to be poured unto the LORD *for* a drink offering.

⁸And the other lamb shalt thou offer at even:

Amplified Bible

be gathered to your [departed] people as Aaron your brother was gathered,

¹⁴For you disobeyed My order in the Wilderness of Zin during the strife of the congregation to uphold My sanctity [by strict obedience to My authority] at the waters before their eyes. [These are the waters of Meribah in Kadesh in the Wilderness of Zin].

¹⁵And Moses said to the Lord,

¹⁶Let the Lord, the God of the spirits of all flesh, set a man over the congregation

¹⁷Who shall go out and come in before them, leading them out and bringing them in, that the congregation of the Lord may not be as sheep which have no shepherd.

¹⁸The Lord said to Moses, Take Joshua son of Nun, a man in whom is the Spirit, and lay your hand upon him;

¹⁹And set him before Eleazar the priest and all the congregation and give him a charge in their sight.

²⁰And put some of your honor *and* authority upon him, that all the congregation of the Israelites may obey him.

²¹He shall stand before Eleazar the priest, who shall inquire for him before the Lord by the judgment of the Urim [one of two articles in the priest's breastplate worn when asking counsel of the Lord for the people]. At Joshua's word the people shall go out and come in, both he and all the Israelite congregation with him.

²²And Moses did as the Lord commanded him. He took Joshua and set him before Eleazar the priest and all the congregation,

²³And he laid his hands upon him and commissioned him, as the Lord commanded through Moses.

28 AND THE Lord said to Moses, ²Command the Israelites, saying, My offering, My food for My offerings made by fire, My sweet *and* soothing odor you shall be careful to offer to Me at its proper time.

³And you shall say to the people, This is the offering made by fire which you shall offer to the Lord: two male lambs a year old without spot *or* blemish, two day by day, for a continual burnt offering.

⁴One lamb you shall offer in the morning and the other in the evening,

⁵Also a tenth of an ephah of flour for a cereal offering, mixed with a fourth of a hin of beaten oil.

⁶It is a continual burnt offering which was ordained in Mount Sinai for a sweet *and* soothing odor, an offering made by fire to the Lord.

⁷Its drink offering shall be a fourth of a hin for each lamb; in the Holy Place you shall pour out a fermented drink offering to the Lord.

⁸And the other lamb you shall offer in the

King James Version

as the meat offering of the morning, and as the drink offering thereof, thou shalt offer *it*, a sacrifice made by fire, *of* a sweet savour unto the LORD.

9 ¶ And on the sabbath day two lambs of the first year without spot, and two tenth deals *of* flour *for* a meat offering, mingled with oil, and the drink offering thereof:

10 *This is* the burnt offering of every sabbath, beside the continual burnt offering, and his drink offering.

11 ¶ And in the beginnings of your months ye shall offer a burnt offering unto the LORD; two young bullocks, and one ram, seven lambs of the first year without spot;

12 And three tenth deals *of* flour *for* a meat offering, mingled with oil, for one bullock; and two tenth deals *of* flour *for* a meat offering, mingled with oil, for one ram;

13 And a several tenth deal of flour mingled with oil *for* a meat offering unto one lamb; *for* a burnt offering *of* a sweet savour, a sacrifice made by fire unto the LORD.

14 And their drink offerings shall be half a hin of wine unto a bullock, and the third *part* of a hin unto a ram, and a fourth *part* of a hin unto a lamb: this *is* the burnt offering of every month throughout the months of the year.

15 And one kid of the goats for a sin offering unto the LORD shall be offered, besides the continual burnt offering, and his drink offering.

16 ¶ And in the fourteenth day of the first month *is* the passover of the LORD.

17 And in the fifteenth day of this month *is* the feast: seven days shall unleavened bread be eaten.

18 In the first day *shall be* a holy convocation; ye shall do no *manner of* servile work *therein:*

19 But ye shall offer a sacrifice made by fire *for* a burnt offering unto the LORD; two young bullocks, and one ram, and seven lambs of the first year: they shall be unto you without blemish:

20 And their meat offering *shall be of* flour mingled with oil: three tenth deals shall ye offer for a bullock, and two tenth deals for a ram;

21 A several tenth deal shalt thou offer for every lamb, throughout the seven lambs;

22 And one goat for a sin offering, to make an atonement for you.

23 Ye shall offer these beside the burnt offering in the morning, which *is* for a continual burnt offering.

24 After this manner ye shall offer daily, *throughout* the seven days, the meat of the sacrifice made by fire, *of* a sweet savour unto the LORD: it shall be offered beside the continual burnt offering, and his drink offering.

25 And on the seventh day ye shall have a holy convocation; ye shall do no servile work.

Amplified Bible

evening; like the cereal offering of the morning and like its drink offering, you shall offer it, an offering made by fire, a sweet *and* soothing odor to the Lord.

9 And on the Sabbath day two male lambs a year old without spot *or* blemish, and two-tenths of an ephah of flour for a cereal offering, mixed with oil, and its drink offering.

10 This is the burnt offering of every Sabbath, besides the continual burnt offering and its drink offering.

11 And at the beginning of your months you shall offer a burnt offering to the Lord: two young bulls, one ram, seven male lambs a year old without spot *or* blemish;

12 And three-tenths of an ephah of fine flour for a cereal offering, mixed with oil, for each bull; and two-tenths of an ephah of fine flour for a cereal offering, mixed with oil, for the one ram.

13 And a tenth part of fine flour mixed with oil as a cereal offering, for each lamb, for a burnt offering of a sweet *and* pleasant fragrance, an offering made by fire to the Lord.

14 And their drink offerings shall be half a hin of wine for a bull, and a third of a hin for a ram, and a fourth of a hin for a lamb. This is the burnt offering of each month throughout the months of the year.

15 And one male goat for a sin offering to the Lord—it shall be offered in addition to the continual burnt offering and its drink offering.

16 On the fourteenth day of the first month is the Lord's Passover.

17 On the fifteenth day of this month is a feast; for seven days shall unleavened bread be eaten.

18 On the first day there shall be a holy [summoned] assembly; you shall do no servile work that day.

19 But you shall offer an offering made by fire, a burnt offering to the Lord: two young bulls, one ram, and seven male lambs a year old; they shall be without blemish to the best of your knowledge.

20 And their cereal offering shall be of fine flour mixed with oil; three-tenths of an ephah shall you offer for a bull, and two-tenths for a ram;

21 A tenth shall you offer for each of the seven male lambs,

22 Also one male goat for a sin offering to make atonement for you.

23 You shall offer these in addition to the burnt offering of the morning, which is for a continual burnt offering.

24 In this way you shall offer daily for seven days the food of an offering made by fire, a sweet *and* soothing odor to the Lord; it shall be offered in addition to the continual burnt offering and its drink offering.

25 And on the seventh day you shall have a holy [summoned] assembly; you shall do no work befitting a slave *or* a servant.

King James Version

²⁶ ¶ Also in the day of the firstfruits, when ye bring a new meat offering unto the LORD, after your weeks *be out,* ye shall have a holy convocation; ye shall do no servile work:

²⁷But ye shall offer the burnt offering for a sweet savour unto the LORD; two young bullocks, one ram, seven lambs of the first year;

²⁸And their meat offering *of* flour mingled with oil, three tenth deals unto one bullock, two tenth deals unto one ram,

²⁹A several tenth deal unto one lamb, throughout the seven lambs;

³⁰*And* one kid of the goats, to make an atonement for you.

³¹Ye shall offer *them* besides the continual burnt offering, and his meat offering, (they shall be unto you without blemish) and their drink offerings.

29 And in the seventh month, on the first *day* of the month, ye shall have a holy convocation; ye shall do no servile work: it is a day of blowing the trumpets unto you.

²And ye shall offer a burnt offering for a sweet savour unto the LORD; one young bullock, one ram, *and* seven lambs of the first year without blemish:

³And their meat offering *shall be of* flour mingled with oil, three tenth deals for a bullock, *and* two tenth deals for a ram,

⁴And one tenth deal for one lamb, throughout the seven lambs:

⁵And one kid of the goats for a sin offering, to make an atonement for you:

⁶Beside the burnt offering of the month, and his meat offering, and the daily burnt offering, and his meat offering, and their drink offerings, according unto their manner, for a sweet savour, a sacrifice made by fire unto the LORD.

⁷ ¶ And ye shall have on the tenth *day* of this seventh month a holy convocation; and ye shall afflict your souls: ye shall not do any work *therein:*

⁸But ye shall offer a burnt offering unto the LORD *for* a sweet savour; one young bullock, one ram, *and* seven lambs of the first year; they shall be unto you without blemish:

⁹And their meat offering *shall be of* flour mingled with oil, three tenth deals to a bullock, *and* two tenth deals to one ram,

¹⁰A several tenth deal for one lamb, throughout the seven lambs:

¹¹One kid of the goats *for* a sin offering; beside the sin offering of atonement, and the continual burnt offering, and the meat offering of it, and their drink offerings.

Amplified Bible

²⁶Also in the day of the firstfruits, when you offer a cereal offering of new grain to the Lord at your Feast of Weeks, you shall have a holy [summoned] assembly; you shall do no servile work.

²⁷But you shall offer the burnt offering for a sweet, pleasing, *and* soothing fragrance to the Lord: two young bulls, one ram, seven male lambs a year old,

²⁸And their cereal offering of fine flour mixed with oil, three-tenths of an ephah for each bull, two-tenths for one ram,

²⁹A tenth for each of the seven male lambs,

³⁰And one male goat to make atonement for you.

³¹You shall offer them in addition to the continual burnt offering and its cereal offering and their drink offerings. See that they are without blemish.

29 ON THE first day of the seventh month [on New Year's Day of the civil year], you shall have a holy [summoned] assembly; you shall do no servile work. It is a day of blowing of trumpets for you [everyone blowing who wishes, proclaiming that the glad New Year has come and that the great Day of Atonement and the Feast of Tabernacles are now approaching].

²And you shall offer a burnt offering for a sweet *and* pleasing odor to the Lord: one young bull, one ram, and seven male lambs a year old without blemish.

³Their cereal offering shall be of fine flour mixed with oil, three-tenths of an ephah for a bull, two-tenths for a ram,

⁴And one-tenth of an ephah for each of the seven lambs,

⁵And one male goat for a sin offering to make atonement for you.

⁶These are in addition to the burnt offering of the new moon and its cereal offering, and the daily burnt offering and its cereal offering, and their drink offerings, according to the ordinance for them, for a pleasant *and* soothing fragrance, an offering made by fire to the Lord.

⁷And you shall have on the tenth day of this seventh month a holy [summoned] assembly; [it is the great Day of Atonement, a day of humiliation] and you shall humble *and* abase yourselves; you shall not do any work in it.

⁸But you shall offer a burnt offering to the Lord for a sweet *and* soothing fragrance: one young bull, one ram, and seven male lambs a year old. See that they are without blemish.

⁹And their cereal offering shall be of fine flour mixed with oil, three-tenths of an ephah for the bull, two-tenths for the one ram,

¹⁰A tenth for each of the seven male lambs,

¹¹One male goat for a sin offering, in addition to the sin offering of atonement, and the continual burnt offering and its cereal offering, and their drink offerings.

King James Version

¹² ¶ And on the fifteenth day of the seventh month ye shall have a holy convocation; ye shall do no servile work, and ye shall keep a feast unto the LORD seven days:

¹³ And ye shall offer a burnt offering, a sacrifice made by fire, *of* a sweet savour unto the LORD; thirteen young bullocks, two rams, *and* fourteen lambs of the first year; they shall be without blemish:

¹⁴ And their meat offering *shall be of* flour mingled with oil, three tenth deals unto every bullock of the thirteen bullocks, two tenth deals to each ram of the two rams,

¹⁵ And a several tenth deal to each lamb of the fourteen lambs:

¹⁶ And one kid of the goats *for* a sin offering; beside the continual burnt offering, his meat offering, and his drink offering.

¹⁷ And on the second day *ye shall offer* twelve young bullocks, two rams, fourteen lambs of the first year without spot:

¹⁸ And their meat offering and their drink offerings for the bullocks, for the rams, and for the lambs, *shall be* according to their number, after the manner:

¹⁹ And one kid of the goats *for* a sin offering; beside the continual burnt offering, and the meat offering thereof, and their drink offerings.

²⁰ And on the third day eleven bullocks, two rams, fourteen lambs of the first year without blemish;

²¹ And their meat offering and their drink offerings for the bullocks, for the rams, and for the lambs, *shall be* according to their number, after the manner:

²² And one goat for a sin offering; beside the continual burnt offering, and his meat offering, and his drink offering.

²³ And on the fourth day ten bullocks, two rams, *and* fourteen lambs of the first year without blemish:

²⁴ Their meat offering and their drink offerings for the bullocks, for the rams, and for the lambs, *shall be* according to their number, after the manner:

²⁵ And one kid of the goats *for* a sin offering; beside the continual burnt offering, his meat offering, and his drink offering.

²⁶ And on the fifth day nine bullocks, two rams, *and* fourteen lambs of the first year without spot:

²⁷ And their meat offering and their drink offerings for the bullocks, for the rams, and for the lambs, *shall be* according to their number, after the manner:

²⁸ And one goat for a sin offering; beside the continual burnt offering, and his meat offering, and his drink offering.

²⁹ And on the sixth day eight bullocks, two rams, *and* fourteen lambs of the first year without blemish:

Amplified Bible

¹² And on the fifteenth day of the seventh month you shall have a holy [summoned] assembly; you shall do no servile work, and you shall keep a feast to the Lord for seven days.

¹³ And you shall offer a burnt offering, an offering made by fire, of a sweet *and* pleasing fragrance to the Lord: thirteen young bulls, two rams, and fourteen male lambs a year old; they shall be without blemish.

¹⁴ And their cereal offering shall be of fine flour mixed with oil, three-tenths of an ephah for each of the thirteen bulls, two-tenths for each of the two rams,

¹⁵ And a tenth part for each of the fourteen male lambs,

¹⁶ Also one male goat for a sin offering, in addition to the continual burnt offering, its cereal offering, and its drink offering.

¹⁷ And on the second day you shall offer twelve young bulls, two rams, fourteen male lambs a year old without spot *or* blemish,

¹⁸ With their cereal offering and the drink offerings for the bulls, the rams, and the lambs, by number according to the ordinance,

¹⁹ Also one male goat for a sin offering, besides the continual burnt offering, its cereal offering, and their drink offerings.

²⁰ And on the third day eleven bulls, two rams, fourteen male lambs a year old without blemish,

²¹ With their cereal offering and drink offerings for the bulls, the rams, and the lambs, by number according to the ordinance,

²² And one male goat for a sin offering, besides the continual burnt offering, its cereal offering, and its drink offerings.

²³ On the fourth day ten bulls, two rams, and fourteen male lambs a year old without blemish,

²⁴ Their cereal offering and their drink offerings for the bulls, the rams, and the lambs shall be by number according to the ordinance,

²⁵ And one male goat for a sin offering, besides the continual burnt offering, its cereal offering, and its drink offerings.

²⁶ And on the fifth day nine bulls, two rams, and fourteen male lambs a year old without spot *or* blemish,

²⁷ And their cereal offering and drink offerings for the bulls, the rams, and the lambs, by number according to the ordinance,

²⁸ And one goat for a sin offering, besides the continual burnt offering, and its cereal offering, and its drink offerings.

²⁹ And on the sixth day eight bulls, two rams, and fourteen male lambs a year old without blemish,

King James Version

30 And their meat offering and their drink offerings for the bullocks, for the rams, and for the lambs, *shall be* according to their number, after the manner:

31 And one goat for a sin offering; beside the continual burnt offering, his meat offering, and his drink offering.

32 And on the seventh day seven bullocks, two rams, *and* fourteen lambs of the first year without blemish:

33 And their meat offering and their drink offerings for the bullocks, for the rams, and for the lambs, *shall be* according to their number, after the manner:

34 And one goat for a sin offering; beside the continual burnt offering, his meat offering, and his drink offering.

35 On the eighth day ye shall have a solemn assembly; ye shall do no servile work *therein:*

36 But ye shall offer a burnt offering, a sacrifice made by fire, *of* a sweet savour unto the LORD: one bullock, one ram, seven lambs of the first year without blemish:

37 Their meat offering and their drink offerings for the bullock, for the ram, and for the lambs, *shall be* according to their number, after the manner:

38 And one goat for a sin offering; beside the continual burnt offering, and his meat offering, and his drink offering.

39 These *things* ye shall do unto the LORD in your set feasts, besides your vows, and your freewill offerings, for your burnt offerings, and for your meat offerings, and for your drink offerings, and for your peace offerings.

40 And Moses told the children of Israel according to all that the LORD commanded Moses.

30 And Moses spake unto the heads of the tribes concerning the children of Israel, saying, This *is* the thing which the LORD hath commanded.

2 If a man vow a vow unto the LORD, or swear an oath to bind his soul with a bond; he shall not break his word, he shall do according to all that proceedeth out of his mouth.

3 If a woman also vow a vow unto the LORD, and bind *herself by* a bond, *being* in her father's house in her youth;

4 And her father hear her vow, and her bond wherewith she hath bound her soul, and her father shall hold his peace at her: then all her vows shall stand, and every bond wherewith she hath bound her soul shall stand.

5 But if her father disallow her in the day that he heareth; not any of her vows, or of her bonds wherewith she hath bound her soul, shall stand: and the LORD shall forgive her, because her father disallowed her.

6 And if she had at all a husband, when she

Amplified Bible

30 And their cereal offering and their drink offerings for the bulls, the rams, and the lambs, by number according to the ordinance,

31 And one goat for a sin offering, besides the continual burnt offering, its cereal offering, and its drink offerings.

32 And on the seventh day seven bulls, two rams, and fourteen male lambs a year old without blemish,

33 And their cereal and drink offerings for the bulls, the rams, and the lambs, by number according to the ordinance.

34 And one male goat for a sin offering, besides the continual burnt offering, and its cereal offering, and its drink offerings.

35 On the eighth day you shall have a solemn assembly; you shall do no servile work.

36 You shall offer a burnt offering, an offering made by fire, of a sweet *and* pleasing fragrance to the Lord: one bull, one ram, seven male lambs a year old without blemish,

37 Their cereal offering and drink offerings for the bull, the ram, and the lambs shall be by number according to the ordinance,

38 And one male goat for a sin offering, besides the continual burnt offering, and its cereal offering, and its drink offerings.

39 These you shall offer to the Lord at your appointed feasts, besides the offerings you have vowed and your freewill offerings, for your burnt offerings, cereal offerings, drink offerings, and peace offerings.

40 And Moses told the Israelites all that the Lord commanded him.

30 AND MOSES said to the heads *or* leaders of the tribes of Israel, This is the thing which the Lord has commanded:

2 If a man vows a vow to the Lord or swears an oath to bind himself by a pledge, he shall not break *and* profane his word; he shall do according to all that proceeds out of his mouth.

3 Also when a woman vows a vow to the Lord and binds herself by a pledge, being in her father's house in her youth,

4 And her father hears her vow and her pledge with which she has bound herself and he offers no objection, then all her vows shall stand and every pledge with which she has bound herself shall stand.

5 But if her father refuses to allow her [to carry out her vow] on the day that he hears about it, not any of her vows or of her pledges with which she has bound herself shall stand. And the Lord will forgive her because her father refused to let her [carry out her purpose].

6 And if she is married to a husband while her

King James Version

vowed, or uttered ought out of her lips, wherewith she bound her soul;

7And her husband heard it, and held his peace at her in the day that he heard it: then her vows shall stand, and her bonds wherewith she bound her soul shall stand.

8But if her husband disallow her on the day that he heard it; then he shall make her vow which she vowed, and that which she uttered with her lips, wherewith she bound her soul, of none effect: and the LORD shall forgive her.

9But every vow of a widow, and of her that is divorced, wherewith they have bound their souls, shall stand against her.

10And if she vowed in her husband's house, or bound her soul by a bond with an oath;

11And her husband heard it, and held his peace at her, and disallowed her not: then all her vows shall stand, and every bond wherewith she bound her soul shall stand.

12But if her husband hath utterly made them void on the day he heard them; then whatsoever proceeded out of her lips concerning her vows, or concerning the bond of her soul, shall not stand: her husband hath made them void; and the LORD shall forgive her.

13Every vow, and every binding oath to afflict the soul, her husband may establish it, or her husband may make it void.

14But if her husband altogether hold his peace at her from day to day; then he establisheth all her vows, or all her bonds, which are upon her: he confirmeth them, because he held his peace at her in the day that he heard them.

15But if he shall any ways make them void after that he hath heard them; then he shall bear her iniquity.

16These are the statutes, which the LORD commanded Moses, between a man and his wife, between the father and his daughter, being yet in her youth in her father's house.

31 And the LORD spake unto Moses, saying, 2Avenge the children of Israel of the Midianites: afterward shalt thou be gathered unto thy people.

3And Moses spake unto the people, saying, Arm some of yourselves unto the war, and let them go against the Midianites, and avenge the LORD of Midian.

4Of every tribe a thousand, throughout all the tribes of Israel, shall ye send to the war.

5So there were delivered out of the thousands of Israel, a thousand of every tribe, twelve thousand armed for war.

6And Moses sent them to the war, a thousand of every tribe, them and Phinehas the son of Eleazar the priest, to the war, with the holy instruments, and the trumpets to blow in his hand.

Amplified Bible

vows are upon her or she has bound herself by a rash utterance

7And her husband hears of it and holds his peace concerning it on the day that he hears it, then her vows shall stand and her pledge with which she bound herself shall stand.

8But if her husband refuses to allow her [to keep her vow or pledge] on the day that he hears of it, then he shall make void and annul her vow which is upon her and the rash utterance of her lips by which she bound herself, and the Lord will forgive her.

9But the vow of a widow or of a divorced woman, with which she has bound herself, shall stand against her.

10And if she vowed in her husband's house or bound herself by a pledge with an oath

11And her husband heard it and did not oppose or prohibit her, then all her vows and every pledge with which she bound herself shall stand.

12But if her husband positively made them void on the day he heard them, then whatever proceeded out of her lips concerning her vows or concerning her pledge of herself shall not stand. Her husband has annulled them, and the Lord will forgive her.

13Every vow and every binding oath to humble or afflict herself, her husband may establish it or her husband may annul it.

14But if her husband altogether holds his peace [concerning the matter] with her from day to day, then he establishes and confirms all her vows or all her pledges which are upon her. He establishes them because he said nothing to [restrain] her on the day he heard of them.

15But if he shall nullify them after he hears of them, then he shall be responsible for and bear her iniquity.

16These are the statutes which the Lord commanded Moses, between a man and his wife, and between a father and his daughter while in her youth in her father's house.

31 THE LORD said to Moses, 2Avenge the Israelites on the Midianites; afterward you shall be gathered to your [departed] people.

3And Moses said to the people, Arm men from among you for the war, that they may go against Midian and execute the Lord's vengeance on Midian [for seducing Israel].

4From each of the tribes of Israel you shall send 1,000 to the war.

5So there were provided out of the thousands of Israel 1,000 from each tribe, 12,000 armed for war.

6And Moses sent them to the war, 1,000 from each tribe, together with Phinehas son of Eleazar, the priest, with the [sacred] vessels of the sanctuary and the trumpets to blow the alarm in his hand.

King James Version

7And they warred against the Midianites, as the LORD commanded Moses; and they slew all the males.

8And they slew the kings of Midian, beside *the rest of* them that were slain; *namely,* Evi, and Rekem, and Zur, and Hur, and Reba, five kings of Midian: Balaam also the son of Beor they slew with the sword.

9And the children of Israel took *all* the women of Midian captives, and their little ones, and took the spoil of all their cattle, and all their flocks, and all their goods.

10And they burnt all their cities wherein they dwelt, and all their goodly castles, with fire.

11And they took all the spoil, and all the prey, *both* of men and of beasts.

12And they brought the captives, and the prey, and the spoil, unto Moses, and Eleazar the priest, and unto the congregation of the children of Israel, unto the camp at the plains of Moab, which *are* by Jordan *near* Jericho.

13 ¶ And Moses, and Eleazar the priest, and all the princes of the congregation, went forth to meet them without the camp.

14And Moses was wroth with the officers of the host, *with* the captains over thousands, and captains over hundreds, which came from the battle.

15And Moses said unto them, Have ye saved all the women alive?

16Behold, these caused the children of Israel, through the counsel of Balaam, to commit trespass against the LORD in the matter of Peor, and there was a plague among the congregation of the LORD.

17Now therefore kill every male among the little ones, and kill every woman that hath known man by lying with him.

18But all the women children, that have not known a man by lying with him, keep alive for yourselves.

19And do ye abide without the camp seven days: whosoever hath killed *any* person, and whosoever hath touched *any* slain, purify *both* yourselves and your captives on the third day, and on the seventh day.

20And purify all *your* raiment, and all that is made of skins, and all work of goats' *hair,* and all things made of wood.

21And Eleazar the priest said unto the men of war which went to the battle, This *is* the ordinance of the law which the LORD commanded Moses;

22Only the gold, and the silver, the brass, the iron, the tin, and the lead,

23Every thing that may abide the fire, ye shall make *it* go through the fire, and it shall be clean: nevertheless it shall be purified with the water of separation: and all that abideth not the fire ye shall make go through the water.

24And ye shall wash your clothes on the sev-

Amplified Bible

7They fought with Midian, as the Lord commanded Moses, and slew every male,

8Including the five kings of Midian: Evi, Rekem, Zur, Hur, and Reba; also Balaam son of Beor they slew with the sword.

9And the Israelites took captive the women of Midian and their little ones, and all their cattle, their flocks, and their goods as booty.

10They burned all the cities in which they dwelt, and all their encampments.

11And they took all the spoil and all the prey, both of man and of beast.

12Then they brought the captives, the prey, and the spoil to Moses and Eleazar the priest and to the congregation of the Israelites at the camp on the plains of Moab by Jordan at Jericho.

13Moses and Eleazar the priest and all the princes *or* leaders of the congregation went to meet them outside the camp.

14But Moses was angry with the officers of the army, the commanders of thousands and of hundreds, who served in the war.

15And Moses said to them, Have you let all the women live?

16Behold, these caused the Israelites by the counsel of Balaam to trespass *and* act treacherously against the Lord in the matter of Peor, and so a [smiting] plague came among the congregation of the Lord.

17Now therefore, kill every male among the little ones, and kill every woman who is not a virgin.

18But all the young girls who have not known man by lying with him keep alive for yourselves.

19Encamp outside the camp seven days; whoever has killed any person and whoever has touched any slain, purify yourselves and your captives on the third day and on the seventh day.

20You shall purify every garment, all that is made of skins, all work of goats' hair, and every article of wood.

21And Eleazar the priest said to the men of war who had gone to battle, This is the statute of the law which the Lord has commanded Moses:

22Only the gold, the silver, the bronze, the iron, the tin, and the lead,

23Everything that can stand fire, you shall make go through fire, and it shall be clean. Nevertheless it shall also be purified with the water of impurity; and all that cannot stand fire [such as fabrics] you shall pass through water.

24And you shall wash your clothes on the sev-

King James Version

enth day, and ye shall be clean, and afterward ye shall come into the camp.

²⁵ ¶ And the LORD spake unto Moses, saying,

²⁶Take the sum of the prey that was taken, *both* of man and of beast, thou, and Eleazar the priest, and the chief fathers of the congregation:

²⁷And divide the prey into two parts; between them that took the war upon them, who went out to battle, and between all the congregation:

²⁸And levy a tribute unto the LORD of the men of war which went out to battle: one soul of five hundred, *both* of the persons, and of the beeves, and of the asses, and of the sheep:

²⁹Take *it* of their half, and give *it* unto Eleazar the priest, *for* a heave offering of the LORD.

³⁰And of the children of Israel's half, thou shalt take one portion of fifty, of the persons, of the beeves, of the asses, and of the flocks, of all *manner of* beasts, and give them unto the Levites, which keep the charge of the tabernacle of the LORD.

³¹And Moses and Eleazar the priest did as the LORD commanded Moses.

³²And the booty, *being* the rest of the prey which the men of war had caught, was six hundred thousand and seventy thousand and five thousand sheep,

³³And threescore and twelve thousand beeves,

³⁴And threescore and one thousand asses,

³⁵And thirty and two thousand persons in all, of women that had not known man by lying with him.

³⁶And the half, *which was* the portion of them that went out to war, was *in* number three hundred thousand and seven and thirty thousand and five hundred sheep:

³⁷And the LORD'S tribute of the sheep was six hundred *and* threescore and fifteen.

³⁸And the beeves *were* thirty and six thousand; of which the LORD'S tribute *was* threescore and twelve.

³⁹And the asses *were* thirty thousand and five hundred; of which the LORD'S tribute *was* threescore and one.

⁴⁰And the persons *were* sixteen thousand; of which the LORD'S tribute *was* thirty and two persons.

⁴¹And Moses gave the tribute, *which was* the LORD'S heave offering, unto Eleazar the priest, as the LORD commanded Moses.

⁴²And of the children of Israel's half, which Moses divided from the men that warred,

⁴³(Now the half that pertained unto the congregation was three hundred thousand and thirty thousand *and* seven thousand and five hundred sheep,

⁴⁴And thirty and six thousand beeves,

⁴⁵And thirty thousand asses and five hundred,

⁴⁶And sixteen thousand persons;)

⁴⁷Even of the children of Israel's half, Moses

Amplified Bible

enth day and you shall be clean; then you shall come into the camp.

²⁵And the Lord said to Moses,

²⁶Take the count of the prey that was taken, both of man and of beast, you and Eleazar the priest and the heads of the fathers' houses of the congregation.

²⁷Divide the booty into two [equal] parts between the warriors who went out to battle and all the congregation.

²⁸And levy a tribute to the Lord from the warriors who went to battle, one out of every 500 of the persons, the oxen, the donkeys, and the flocks.

²⁹Take [this tribute] from the warriors' half and give it to Eleazar the priest as an offering to the Lord.

³⁰And from the Israelites' half [of the booty] you shall take one out of every fifty of the persons, the oxen, the donkeys, the flocks, and of all livestock, and give them to the Levites who have charge of the tabernacle of the Lord.

³¹And Moses and Eleazar the priest did as the Lord commanded Moses.

³²The prey, besides the booty which the men of war took, was 675,000 sheep,

³³And 72,000 cattle,

³⁴And 61,000 donkeys,

³⁵And 32,000 persons in all, of the women who were virgins.

³⁶And the half share, the portion of those who went to war, was: 337,500 sheep,

³⁷And the Lord's tribute of the sheep was 675;

³⁸The cattle were 36,000, of which the Lord's tribute was 72;

³⁹The donkeys were 30,500, of which the Lord's tribute was 61;

⁴⁰The persons were 16,000, of whom the Lord's tribute was 32 persons.

⁴¹And Moses gave the tribute which was the Lord's offering to Eleazar the priest, as the Lord commanded Moses.

⁴²And the Israelites' half Moses separated from that of the warriors'—

⁴³Now the congregation's half was 337,500 sheep,

⁴⁴And 36,000 cattle,

⁴⁵And 30,500 donkeys,

⁴⁶And 16,000 persons—

⁴⁷Even of the Israelites' half, Moses took one

King James Version

took one portion of fifty, *both* of man and of beast, and gave them unto the Levites, which kept the charge of the tabernacle of the LORD; as the LORD commanded Moses.

48 ¶ And the officers which *were* over thousands of the host, the captains of thousands, and captains of hundreds, came near unto Moses:

49 And they said unto Moses, Thy servants have taken the sum of the men of war which *are* under our charge, and there lacketh not one man of us.

50 We have therefore brought an oblation for the LORD, what every man hath gotten, *of* jewels of gold, chains, and bracelets, rings, earrings, and tablets, to make an atonement for our souls before the LORD.

51 And Moses and Eleazar the priest took the gold of them, *even* all wrought jewels.

52 And all the gold of the offering that they offered up to the LORD, of the captains of thousands, and of the captains of hundreds, was sixteen thousand seven hundred and fifty shekels.

53 (*For* the men of war had taken spoil, every man for himself.)

54 And Moses and Eleazar the priest took the gold of the captains of thousands and of hundreds, and brought it into the tabernacle of the congregation, *for* a memorial for the children of Israel before the LORD.

32 Now the children of Reuben and the children of Gad had a very great multitude of cattle: and when they saw the land of Jazer, and the land of Gilead, that behold, the place *was* a place for cattle;

2 The children of Gad and the children of Reuben came and spake unto Moses, and to Eleazar the priest, and unto the princes of the congregation, saying,

3 Ataroth, and Dibon, and Jazer, and Nimrah, and Heshbon, and Elealeh, and Shebam, and Nebo, and Beon,

4 *Even* the country which the LORD smote before the congregation of Israel, *is* a land for cattle, and thy servants have cattle:

5 Wherefore, said they, if we have found grace in thy sight, let this land be given unto thy servants for a possession, *and* bring us not over Jordan.

6 And Moses said unto the children of Gad and to the children of Reuben, Shall your brethren go to war, and shall ye sit here?

7 And wherefore discourage ye the heart of the children of Israel from going over into the land which the LORD hath given them?

8 Thus did your fathers, when I sent them from Kadesh-barnea to see the land.

9 For when they went up unto the valley of Eshcol, and saw the land, they discouraged the

Amplified Bible

of every 50, both of persons and of beasts, and gave them to the Levites, who had charge of the tabernacle of the Lord, as the Lord commanded Moses.

48 And the officers who were over the thousands of the army, the commanders of thousands and hundreds, came to Moses.

49 They told [him], Your servants have counted the warriors under our command, and not one man of us is missing.

50 We have brought as the Lord's offering what each man obtained—articles of gold, armlets, bracelets, signet rings, earrings, neck ornaments—to make atonement for ourselves before the Lord.

51 Moses and Eleazar the priest took the gold from them, all the wrought articles.

52 And all the gold of the offering that they offered to the Lord from the commanders of thousands and of hundreds was 16,750 shekels.

53 For the men of war had taken booty, every man for himself.

54 And Moses and Eleazar the priest received the gold from the commanders of thousands and of hundreds and brought it into the Tent of Meeting as a memorial for the Israelites before the Lord.

32 NOW THE sons of Reuben and of Gad had a very great multitude of cattle, and they saw the land of Jazer and the land of Gilead [on the east side of the Jordan], and behold, the place was suitable for cattle.

2 So the sons of Gad and of Reuben came and said to Moses, Eleazar the priest, and the leaders of the congregation,

3 [The country around] Ataroth, Dibon, Jazer, Nimrah, Heshbon, Elealeh, Sebam, Nebo, and Beon,

4 The land the Lord smote before the congregation of Israel, is a land for cattle, and your servants have cattle.

5 And they said, If we have found favor in your sight, let this land be given to your servants for a possession. Do not take us over the Jordan.

6 And Moses said to the sons of Gad and of Reuben, Shall your brethren go to war while you sit here?

7 Why do you discourage the hearts of the Israelites from going over into the land which the Lord has given them?

8 Thus your fathers did when I sent them from Kadesh-barnea to see the land!

9 For when they went up to the Valley of Eshcol and saw the land, they discouraged the

King James Version

heart of the children of Israel, that *they* should not go into the land which the LORD had given them.

¹⁰And the LORD'S anger was kindled the same time, and he sware, saying,

¹¹Surely none of the men that came up out of Egypt, from twenty years old and upward, shall see the land which I sware unto Abraham, unto Isaac, and unto Jacob; because they have not wholly followed me:

¹²Save Caleb the son of Jephunneh the Kenezite, and Joshua the son of Nun: for they have wholly followed the LORD.

¹³And the LORD'S anger was kindled against Israel, and he made them wander in the wilderness forty years, until all the generation, that had done evil in the sight of the LORD, was consumed.

¹⁴And behold, ye are risen up in your fathers' stead, an increase of sinful men, to augment yet the fierce anger of the LORD toward Israel.

¹⁵For if ye turn away from after him, he will yet again leave them in the wilderness; and ye shall destroy all this people.

¹⁶And they came near unto him, and said, We will build sheepfolds here for our cattle, and cities for our little ones:

¹⁷But we ourselves will go ready armed before the children of Israel, until we have brought them unto their place: and our little ones shall dwell in the fenced cities because of the inhabitants of the land.

¹⁸We will not return unto our houses, until the children of Israel have inherited every man his inheritance.

¹⁹For we will not inherit with them on *yonder* side Jordan, or forward; because our inheritance is fallen to us on *this* side Jordan eastward.

²⁰And Moses said unto them, If ye will do this thing, if ye will go armed before the LORD to war,

²¹And will go all of you armed over Jordan before the LORD, until he hath driven out his enemies from before him,

²²And the land be subdued before the LORD: then afterward ye shall return, and be guiltless before the LORD, and before Israel; and this land shall be your possession before the LORD.

²³But if ye will not do so, behold, ye have sinned against the LORD: and be sure your sin will find you out.

²⁴Build ye cities for your little ones, and folds for your sheep; and do that which hath proceeded out of your mouth.

²⁵And the children of Gad and the children of Reuben spake unto Moses, saying, Thy servants will do as my lord commandeth.

²⁶Our little ones, our wives, our flocks, and all our cattle, shall be there in the cities of Gilead:

²⁷But thy servants will pass over, every man

Amplified Bible

hearts of the Israelites from going into the land the Lord had given them.

¹⁰And the Lord's anger was kindled on that day and He swore, saying,

¹¹Surely none of the men who came up out of Egypt, from twenty years old and upward, shall see the land which I swore to Abraham, to Isaac, and to Jacob, because they have not wholly followed Me—

¹²Except Caleb son of Jephunneh the Kenizzite and Joshua son of Nun, for they have wholly followed the Lord.

¹³And the Lord's anger was kindled against Israel and He made them wander in the wilderness for forty years, until all the generation that had done evil in the sight of the Lord was consumed.

¹⁴And behold, you are risen up in your fathers' stead, a brood of sinful men, to increase still more the fierce anger of the Lord against Israel.

¹⁵For if you turn from following Him, He will again abandon them in the wilderness, and you will destroy all this people.

¹⁶But they came near to him and said, We will build sheepfolds here for our flocks and walled settlements for our little ones.

¹⁷But we will be armed and ready to go before the Israelites until we have brought them to their place. Our little ones shall dwell in the fortified settlements because of the people of the land.

¹⁸We will not return to our homes until the Israelites have inherited every man his inheritance.

¹⁹For we will not inherit with them on the [west] side of the Jordan and beyond, because our inheritance is fallen to us on this side of the Jordan eastward.

²⁰Moses replied, If you will do as you say, going armed before the Lord to war,

²¹And every armed man of you will pass over the Jordan before the Lord until He has driven out His enemies before Him

²²And the land is subdued before the Lord, then afterward you shall return and be guiltless [in this matter] before the Lord and before Israel, and this land shall be your possession before the Lord.

²³But if you will not do so, behold, you have sinned against the Lord; and be sure your sin will find you out.

²⁴Build settlements for your little ones, and folds for your sheep, and do that of which you have spoken.

²⁵And the sons of Gad and of Reuben said to Moses, Your servants will do as my lord commands.

²⁶Our little ones, our wives, our flocks, and all our cattle shall be there in the cities of Gilead.

²⁷But your servants will pass over, every man

King James Version

armed for war, before the LORD to battle, as my lord saith.

28So concerning them Moses commanded Eleazar the priest, and Joshua the son of Nun, and the chief fathers of the tribes of the children of Israel:

29And Moses said unto them, If the children of Gad and the children of Reuben will pass with you over Jordan, every man armed to battle, before the LORD, and the land shall be subdued before you; then ye shall give them the land of Gilead for a possession:

30But if they will not pass over with you armed, they shall have possessions among you in the land of Canaan.

31And the children of Gad and the children of Reuben answered, saying, As the LORD hath said unto thy servants, so will we do.

32We will pass over armed before the LORD into the land of Canaan, that the possession of our inheritance on this side Jordan may be ours.

33And Moses gave unto them, even to the children of Gad, and to the children of Reuben, and unto half the tribe of Manasseh the son of Joseph, the kingdom of Sihon king of the Amorites, and the kingdom of Og king of Bashan, the land, with the cities thereof in the coasts, even the cities of the country round about.

34 ¶ And the children of Gad built Dibon, and Ataroth, and Aroer,

35And Atroth, Shophan, and Jaazer, and Jogbehah,

36And Beth-nimrah, and Beth-haran, fenced cities: and folds for sheep.

37And the children of Reuben built Heshbon, and Elealeh, and Kirjathaim,

38And Nebo, and Baal-meon, (their names being changed,) and Shibmah: and gave other names unto the cities which they builded.

39And the children of Machir the son of Manasseh went to Gilead, and took it, and dispossessed the Amorite which was in it.

40And Moses gave Gilead unto Machir the son of Manasseh; and he dwelt therein.

41And Jair the son of Manasseh went and took the small towns thereof, and called them Havoth-jair.

42And Nobah went and took Kenath, and the villages thereof, and called it Nobah, after his own name.

33 These are the journeys of the children of Israel, which went forth out of the land of Egypt with their armies under the hand of Moses and Aaron.

2And Moses wrote their goings out according to their journeys by the commandment of the LORD: and these are their journeys according to their goings out.

3And they departed from Rameses in the first month, on the fifteenth day of the first month;

Amplified Bible

armed for war, before the Lord to battle, as my lord says.

28So Moses gave command concerning them to Eleazar the priest and Joshua son of Nun and the heads of the fathers' houses of the tribes of Israel.

29And Moses said to them, If the sons of Gad and Reuben will pass with you over the Jordan, every man armed to battle before the Lord, and the land shall be subdued before you, then you shall give them the land of Gilead for a possession.

30But if they will not pass over with you armed, they shall have possessions among you in the land of Canaan.

31The sons of Gad and Reuben answered, As the Lord has said to your servants, so will we do.

32We will pass over armed before the Lord into the land of Canaan, that the possession of our inheritance on this side of the Jordan may be ours.

33Moses gave to them, to the sons of Gad and of Reuben and to half the tribe of Manasseh son of Joseph, the kingdom of Sihon king of the Amorites and the kingdom of Og king of Bashan—the land with its cities and their territories, even the cities round about the country.

34And the sons of Gad built Dibon, Ataroth, Aroer,

35Atroth-shophan, Jazer, Jogbehah,

36Beth-nimrah, and Beth-haran, fortified cities, and folds for sheep.

37And the sons of Reuben built Heshbon, Elealeh, Kiriathaim,

38Nebo, and Baal-meon—their names were to be changed—and Shibmah; and they gave other names to the cities they built.

39And the sons of Machir son of Manasseh went to Gilead and took it and dispossessed the Amorites who were in it.

40And Moses gave Gilead to Machir son of Manasseh, and he settled in it.

41Jair son of Manasseh took their villages and called them Havvoth-jair.

42And Nobah took Kenath and its villages and called it Nobah after his own name.

33 THESE ARE the stages of the journeys of the Israelites by which they went out of the land of Egypt by their hosts under the leadership of Moses and Aaron.

2Moses recorded their starting places, as the Lord commanded, stage by stage; and these are their journeying stages from their starting places:

3They set out from Rameses on the fifteenth day of the first month; on the day after the

King James Version

on the morrow after the passover the children of Israel went out with a high hand in the sight of all the Egyptians.

⁴For the Egyptians buried all *their* firstborn, which the LORD had smitten among them: upon their gods also the LORD executed judgments.

⁵And the children of Israel removed from Rameses, and pitched in Succoth.

⁶And they departed from Succoth, and pitched in Etham, which *is* in the edge of the wilderness.

⁷And they removed from Etham, and turned again unto Pi-hahiroth, which *is* before Baal-zephon: and they pitched before Migdol.

⁸And they departed from before *Pi-*hahiroth, and passed through the midst of the sea into the wilderness, and went three days' journey in the wilderness of Etham, and pitched in Marah.

⁹And they removed from Marah, and came unto Elim: and in Elim *were* twelve fountains of water, and threescore and ten palm trees; and they pitched there.

¹⁰And they removed from Elim, and encamped by the Red sea.

¹¹And they removed from the Red sea, and encamped in the wilderness of Sin.

¹²And they took their journey out of the wilderness of Sin, and encamped in Dophkah.

¹³And they departed from Dophkah, and encamped in Alush.

¹⁴And they removed from Alush, and encamped at Rephidim, where was no water for the people to drink.

¹⁵And they departed from Rephidim, and pitched in the wilderness of Sinai.

¹⁶And they removed from the desert of Sinai, and pitched at Kibroth-hattaavah.

¹⁷And they departed from Kibroth-hattaavah, and encamped at Hazeroth.

¹⁸And they departed from Hazeroth, and pitched in Rithmah.

¹⁹And they departed from Rithmah, and pitched at Rimmon-parez.

²⁰And they departed from Rimmon-parez, and pitched in Libnah.

²¹And they removed from Libnah, and pitched at Rissah.

²²And they journeyed from Rissah, and pitched in Kehelathah.

²³And they went from Kehelathah, and pitched in mount Shapher.

²⁴And they removed from mount Shapher, and encamped in Haradah.

²⁵And they removed from Haradah, and pitched in Makheloth.

²⁶And they removed from Makheloth, and encamped at Tahath.

²⁷And they departed from Tahath, and pitched at Tarah.

Amplified Bible

Passover the Israelites went out [of Egypt] with a high hand *and* triumphantly in the sight of all the Egyptians,

⁴While the Egyptians were burying all their firstborn whom the Lord had struck down among them; upon their gods also the Lord executed judgments.

⁵The Israelites set out from Rameses and encamped in Succoth.

⁶And they departed from Succoth and encamped in Etham, which is at the edge of the wilderness.

⁷They set out from Etham and turned back to Pi-hahiroth, east of Baal-zephon, and they encamped before Migdol.

⁸And they journeyed from before Pi-hahiroth and passed through the midst of the [Red] Sea into the wilderness; and they went a three days' journey in the Wilderness of Etham and encamped at Marah.

⁹They journeyed from Marah and came to Elim; at Elim there were twelve springs of water and seventy palm trees, and they encamped there.

¹⁰They set out from Elim and encamped by the Red Sea.

¹¹They journeyed from the Red Sea and encamped in the Wilderness of Sin.

¹²And they traveled on from the Wilderness of Sin and encamped at Dophkah.

¹³And they departed from Dophkah and encamped at Alush.

¹⁴And they set out from Alush and encamped at Rephidim, where there was no water for the people to drink.

¹⁵And they departed from Rephidim and encamped in the Wilderness of Sinai.

¹⁶And they journeyed from the Wilderness of Sinai and encamped at Kibroth-hattaavah.

¹⁷And they traveled on from Kibroth-hattaavah and encamped at Hazeroth.

¹⁸And they journeyed from Hazeroth and encamped at Rithmah.

¹⁹And they departed from Rithmah and encamped at Rimmon-perez.

²⁰And they departed from Rimmon-perez and encamped at Libnah.

²¹And they removed from Libnah and encamped at Rissah.

²²And they journeyed from Rissah and encamped at Kehelathah.

²³And they went from Kehelathah and encamped at Mount Shepher.

²⁴And they removed from Mount Shepher and encamped at Haradah.

²⁵And they set out from Haradah and encamped at Makheloth.

²⁶And they removed from Makheloth and encamped at Tahath.

²⁷And they departed from Tahath and encamped at Terah.

King James Version

²⁸And they removed from Tarah, and pitched in Mithcah.

²⁹And they went from Mithcah, and pitched in Hashmonah.

³⁰And they departed from Hashmonah, and encamped at Moseroth.

³¹And they departed from Moseroth, and pitched in Bene-jaakan.

³²And they removed from Bene-jaakan, and encamped at Hor-hagidgad.

³³And they went from Hor-hagidgad, and pitched in Jotbathah.

³⁴And they removed from Jotbathah, and encamped at Ebronah.

³⁵And they departed from Ebronah, and encamped at Ezion-gaber.

³⁶And they removed from Ezion-gaber, and pitched in the wilderness of Zin, which *is* Kadesh.

³⁷And they removed from Kadesh, and pitched in mount Hor, in the edge of the land of Edom.

³⁸And Aaron the priest went up into mount Hor at the commandment of the LORD, and died there, in the fortieth year after the children of Israel were come out of the land of Egypt, in the first *day* of the fifth month.

³⁹And Aaron *was* an hundred and twenty and three years old when he died in mount Hor.

⁴⁰And king Arad the Canaanite, which dwelt in the south in the land of Canaan, heard of the coming of the children of Israel.

⁴¹And they departed from mount Hor, and pitched in Zalmonah.

⁴²And they departed from Zalmonah, and pitched in Punon.

⁴³And they departed from Punon, and pitched in Oboth.

⁴⁴And they departed from Oboth, and pitched in Ije-abarim, in the border of Moab.

⁴⁵And they departed from Iim, and pitched in Dibon-gad.

⁴⁶And they removed from Dibon-gad, and encamped in Almon-diblathaim.

⁴⁷And they removed from Almon-diblathaim, and pitched in the mountains of Abarim, before Nebo.

⁴⁸And they departed from the mountains of Abarim, and pitched in the plains of Moab by Jordan *near* Jericho.

⁴⁹And they pitched by Jordan, from Beth-jesimoth *even* unto Abel-shittim in the plains of Moab.

⁵⁰ ¶ And the LORD spake unto Moses in the plains of Moab by Jordan *near* Jericho, saying,

⁵¹Speak unto the children of Israel, and say unto them, When ye are passed over Jordan into the land of Canaan;

⁵²Then ye shall drive out all the inhabitants of the land from before you, and destroy all their pictures, and destroy all their molten images, and quite pluck down all their high places:

Amplified Bible

²⁸And they removed from Terah and encamped at Mithkah.

²⁹And they set out from Mithkah and encamped at Hashmonah.

³⁰And they traveled on from Hashmonah and encamped at Moseroth.

³¹And they journeyed from Moseroth and pitched in Bene-jaakan.

³²And they set out from Bene-jaakan and encamped at Hor-haggidgad.

³³And they set out from Hor-haggidgad and encamped at Jotbathah.

³⁴And they journeyed from Jotbathah and encamped at Abronah.

³⁵And they traveled on from Abronah and encamped at Ezion-geber.

³⁶And they removed from Ezion-geber and encamped in the Wilderness of Zin, which is Kadesh.

³⁷And they removed from Kadesh and encamped at Mount Hor, on the edge of Edom.

³⁸Aaron the priest went up on Mount Hor at the command of the Lord, and died there in the fortieth year after the Israelites came out of Egypt, the first day of the fifth month.

³⁹Aaron was 123 years old when he died on Mount Hor.

⁴⁰The Canaanite king of Arad, who lived in the South (the Negeb) in the land of Canaan, heard of the coming of the Israelites.

⁴¹They set out from Mount Hor and encamped at Zalmonah.

⁴²And they set out from Zalmonah and encamped at Punon.

⁴³And they set out from Punon and encamped at Oboth.

⁴⁴And they traveled on from Oboth and encamped at Iye-abarim, on the border of Moab.

⁴⁵And they departed from Iyim and encamped at Dibon-gad.

⁴⁶And they set out from Dibon-gad and encamped in Almon-diblathaim.

⁴⁷And they traveled on from Almon-diblathaim and encamped in the mountains of Abarim, before Nebo.

⁴⁸And they departed from the mountains of Abarim and encamped in the plains of Moab by the Jordan at Jericho.

⁴⁹And they encamped by the Jordan from Beth-jeshimoth as far as Abel-shittim in the plains of Moab.

⁵⁰And the Lord said to Moses in the plains of Moab by the Jordan at Jericho,

⁵¹Tell the Israelites, When you have passed over the Jordan into the land of Canaan,

⁵²Then you shall drive out all the inhabitants of the land before you and destroy all their figured stones and all their molten images and completely demolish all their [idolatrous] high places,

King James Version

53And ye shall dispossess *the inhabitants of* the land, and dwell therein: for I have given you the land to possess it.

54And ye shall divide the land by lot for an inheritance among your families: *and* to the more ye shall give the more inheritance, and to the fewer ye shall give the less inheritance: every man's *inheritance* shall be in the place where his lot falleth; according to the tribes of your fathers ye shall inherit.

55But if ye will not drive out the inhabitants of the land from before you; then it shall come to pass, *that those* which ye let remain of them *shall be* pricks in your eyes, and thorns in your sides, and shall vex you in the land wherein ye dwell.

56Moreover it shall come to pass, *that* I shall do unto you, as I thought to do unto them.

34 And the LORD spake unto Moses, saying, 2Command the children of Israel, and say unto them, When ye come into the land of Canaan; (this *is* the land that shall fall unto you for an inheritance, *even* the land of Canaan with the coasts thereof:)

3Then your south quarter shall be from the wilderness of Zin along by the coast of Edom, and your south border shall be the outmost coast of the salt sea eastward:

4And your border shall turn from the south to the ascent of Akrabbim, and pass on to Zin: and the going forth thereof shall be from the south to Kadesh-barnea, and shall go on *to* Hazar-addar, and pass on to Azmon:

5And the border shall fetch a compass from Azmon unto the river of Egypt, and the goings out of it shall be at the sea.

6And *as for* the western border, you shall even have the great sea for a border: this shall be your west border.

7And this shall be your north border: from the great sea you shall point out for you mount Hor:

8From mount Hor ye shall point out *your border* unto the entrance of Hamath; and the goings forth of the border shall be to Zedad:

9And the border shall go on to Ziphron, and the goings out of it shall be at Hazar-enan: this shall be your north border.

10And ye shall point out your east border from Hazar-enan to Shepham:

11And the coast shall go down from Shepham *to* Riblah, on the east side of Ain; and the border shall descend, and shall reach unto the side of the sea of Chinnereth eastward:

12And the border shall go down to Jordan, and the goings out of it shall be *at* the salt sea: this shall be your land with the coasts thereof round about.

13And Moses commanded the children of Israel, saying, This *is* the land which ye shall in-

Amplified Bible

53And you shall take possession of the land and dwell in it, for to you I have given the land to possess it.

54You shall inherit the land by lot according to your families; to the large tribe you shall give a larger inheritance, and to the small tribe you shall give a smaller inheritance. Wherever the lot falls to any man, that shall be his. According to the tribes of your fathers you shall inherit.

55But if you will not drive out the inhabitants of the land from before you, then those you let remain of them shall be as pricks in your eyes and as thorns in your sides, and they shall vex you in the land in which you dwell.

56And as I thought to do to them, so will I do to you.

34 AND THE Lord said to Moses, 2Command the Israelites, When you come into the land of Canaan (which is the land that shall be yours for an inheritance, the land of Canaan according to its boundaries),

3Your south side shall be from the Wilderness of Zin along the side of Edom, and your southern boundary from the end of the Salt [Dead] Sea eastward.

4Your boundary shall turn south of the ascent of Akrabbim, and pass on to Zin, and its end shall be south of Kadesh-barnea. Then it shall go on to Hazar-addar and pass on to Azmon.

5Then the boundary shall turn from Azmon to the Brook of Egypt, and it shall terminate at the [Mediterranean] Sea.

6For the western boundary you shall have the Great Sea and its coast.

7And this shall be your north border: from the Great Sea mark out your boundary line to Mount Hor;

8From Mount Hor you shall mark out your boundary to the entrance of Hamath, and its end shall be at Zedad;

9Then the northern boundary shall go on to Ziphron, and the end of it shall be at Hazar-enan.

10You shall mark out your eastern boundary from Hazar-enan to Shepham;

11The boundary shall go down from Shepham to Riblah on the east side of Ain and shall descend and reach to the shoulder of the Sea of Chinnereth [the Sea of Galilee] on the east;

12And the boundary shall go down to the Jordan, and the end shall be at the Salt Sea. This shall be your land with its boundaries all around.

13Moses commanded the Israelites, This is the land you shall inherit by lot, which the Lord

King James Version

herit by lot, which the LORD commanded to give unto the nine tribes, and *to* the half tribe:

¹⁴For the tribe of the children of Reuben according to the house of their fathers, and the tribe of the children of Gad according to the house of their fathers, have received *their inheritance;* and half the tribe of Manasseh have received their inheritance:

¹⁵The two tribes and the half tribe have received their inheritance on *this* side Jordan *near* Jericho eastward, toward the sunrising.

¹⁶ ¶ And the LORD spake unto Moses, saying,

¹⁷These *are* the names of the men which shall divide the land unto you: Eleazar the priest, and Joshua the son of Nun.

¹⁸And ye shall take one prince of every tribe, to divide the land by inheritance.

¹⁹And the names of the men *are* these: Of the tribe of Judah, Caleb the son of Jephunneh.

²⁰And of the tribe of the children of Simeon, Shemuel the son of Ammihud.

²¹Of the tribe of Benjamin, Elidad the son of Chislon.

²²And the prince of the tribe of the children of Dan, Bukki the son of Jogli.

²³The prince of the children of Joseph, for the tribe of the children of Manasseh, Hanniel the son of Ephod.

²⁴And the prince of the tribe of the children of Ephraim, Kemuel the son of Shiphtan.

²⁵And the prince of the tribe of the children of Zebulun, Elizaphan the son of Parnach.

²⁶And the prince of the tribe of the children of Issachar, Paltiel the son of Azzan.

²⁷And the prince of the tribe of the children of Asher, Ahihud the son of Shelomi.

²⁸And the prince of the tribe of the children of Naphtali, Pedahel the son of Ammihud.

²⁹These *are they* whom the LORD commanded to divide the inheritance unto the children of Israel in the land of Canaan.

35 And the LORD spake unto Moses in the plains of Moab by Jordan *near* Jericho, saying,

²Command the children of Israel, that they give unto the Levites of the inheritance of their possession cities to dwell in; and ye shall give *also* unto the Levites suburbs for the cities round about them.

³And the cities shall they have to dwell in; and the suburbs of them shall be for their cattle, and for their goods, and for all their beasts.

⁴And the suburbs of the cities, which ye shall give unto the Levites, *shall reach* from the wall of the city and outward a thousand cubits round about.

⁵And ye shall measure from without the city *on* the east side two thousand cubits, and *on* the south side two thousand cubits, and *on* the west side two thousand cubits, and *on* the north side

Amplified Bible

has commanded to give to the nine tribes and the half-tribe [of Manasseh],

¹⁴For the tribes of the sons of Reuben and of Gad by their fathers' houses have received their inheritance, and also the half-tribe of Manasseh.

¹⁵The two and a half tribes have received their inheritance east of the Jordan at Jericho, toward the sunrise.

¹⁶And the Lord said to Moses,

¹⁷These are the men who shall divide the land to you for inheritance: Eleazar the priest and Joshua son of Nun.

¹⁸And [with them] you shall take one head *or* prince of each tribe to divide the land for inheritance.

¹⁹The names of the men are: Of the tribe of Judah, Caleb son of Jephunneh;

²⁰Of the tribe of the sons of Simeon, Shemuel son of Ammihud;

²¹Of the tribe of Benjamin, Elidad son of Chislon;

²²Of the tribe of the sons of Dan a leader, Bukki son of Jogli;

²³Of the sons of Joseph: of the tribe of the sons of Manasseh a leader, Hanniel son of Ephod;

²⁴And of the tribe of the sons of Ephraim a leader, Kemuel son of Shiphtan;

²⁵And of the tribe of the sons of Zebulun a leader, Elizaphan son of Parnach;

²⁶And of the tribe of the sons of Issachar a leader, Paltiel son of Azzan;

²⁷And of the tribe of the sons of Asher a leader, Ahihud son of Shelomi;

²⁸And of the tribe of the sons of Naphtali a leader, Pedahel son of Ammihud.

²⁹These are the men whom the Lord commanded to divide the inheritance to the Israelites in the land of Canaan.

35 AND THE Lord said to Moses in the plains of Moab by the Jordan at Jericho,

²Command the Israelites that they give to the Levites from the inheritance of their possession cities to dwell in; and [suburb] pasturelands round about the cities' walls you shall give to the Levites also.

³They shall have the cities to dwell in and their [suburb] pasturelands shall be for their cattle, for their wealth [in flocks], and for all their beasts.

⁴And the pasturelands of the cities which you shall give to the Levites shall reach from the wall of the city and outward 1,000 cubits round about.

⁵You shall measure from the wall of the city outward on the east, south, west, and north sides 2,000 cubits, the city being in the center.

King James Version

two thousand cubits; and the city *shall be* in the midst: this shall be to them the suburbs of the cities.

⁶And *among* the cities which ye shall give unto the Levites *there shall be* six cities for refuge, which ye shall appoint for the manslayer, that he may flee thither: and to them ye shall add forty and two cities.

⁷*So* all the cities which ye shall give to the Levites *shall be* forty and eight cities: them *shall ye give* with their suburbs.

⁸And the cities which ye shall give *shall be* of the possession of the children of Israel: from *them that have* many ye shall give many; but from *them that have* few ye shall give few: every one shall give of his cities unto the Levites according to his inheritance which he inheriteth.

⁹ ¶ And the LORD spake unto Moses, saying,

¹⁰Speak unto the children of Israel, and say unto them, When ye be come over Jordan into the land of Canaan;

¹¹Then ye shall appoint you cities to be cities of refuge for you; that the slayer may flee thither, which killeth *any* person at unawares.

¹²And they shall be unto you cities for refuge from the avenger; that the manslayer die not, until he stand before the congregation in judgment.

¹³And *of these* cities which ye shall give six cities shall ye have for refuge.

¹⁴Ye shall give three cities on *this* side Jordan, and three cities shall ye give in the land of Canaan, *which* shall be cities of refuge.

¹⁵These six cities shall be a refuge, *both* for the children of Israel, and for the stranger, and for the sojourner among them: that every one that killeth *any* person unawares may flee thither.

¹⁶And if he smite him with an instrument of iron, so that he die, he *is* a murderer: the murderer shall surely be put to death.

¹⁷And if he smite him with throwing a stone, wherewith he may die, and he die, he *is* a murderer: the murderer shall surely be put to death.

¹⁸Or *if* he smite him with a hand weapon of wood, wherewith he may die, and he die, he *is* a murderer: the murderer shall surely be put to death.

¹⁹The revenger of blood himself shall slay the murderer: when he meeteth him, he shall slay him.

²⁰But if he thrust him of hatred, or hurl at him by laying of wait, that he die;

²¹Or in enmity smite him with his hand, that he die: he that smote *him* shall surely be put to death; *for* he *is* a murderer: the revenger of blood shall slay the murderer, when he meeteth him.

²²But if he thrust him suddenly without enmity, or have cast upon him any thing without laying of wait,

Amplified Bible

This shall belong to [the Levites] as [suburb] pasturelands for their cities.

⁶Of the cities which you shall give to the Levites there shall be the six cities of refuge, which you shall give for the manslayer to flee into; and in addition to them you shall give forty-two cities.

⁷So all the cities which you shall give to the Levites shall be forty-eight; you shall give them with their adjacent [suburb] pasturelands.

⁸As for the cities, you shall give from the possession of the Israelites, from the larger tribes you shall take many and from the smaller tribes few; each tribe shall give of its cities to the Levites in proportion to its inheritance.

⁹And the Lord said to Moses,

¹⁰Say to the Israelites, When you cross the Jordan into the land of Canaan,

¹¹Then you shall select cities to be cities of refuge for you, that the slayer who kills any person unintentionally *and* unawares may flee there.

¹²And the cities shall be to you for refuge from the avenger, that the manslayer may not die until he has had a fair trial before the congregation.

¹³And of the cities which you give there shall be your six cities for refuge.

¹⁴You shall give three cities on this [east] side of the Jordan and three cities in the land of Canaan, to be cities of refuge.

¹⁵These six cities shall be a refuge for the Israelites and for the stranger and the temporary resident among them; that anyone who kills any person unintentionally *and* unawares may flee there.

¹⁶But if he struck him down with an instrument of iron so that he died, he is a murderer; the murderer shall surely be put to death.

¹⁷And if he struck him down by throwing a stone, by which a person may die, and he died, he is a murderer; the murderer shall surely be put to death.

¹⁸Or if he struck him down with a weapon of wood in his hand, by which one may die, and he died, the offender is a murderer; he shall surely be put to death.

¹⁹The avenger of blood shall himself slay the murderer; when he meets him, he shall slay him.

²⁰But if he stabbed him through hatred or hurled at him by lying in wait so that he died

²¹Or in enmity struck him down with his hand so that he died, he that smote him shall surely be put to death; he is a murderer. The avenger of blood shall slay the murderer when he meets him.

²²But if he stabbed him suddenly without enmity or threw anything at *or* upon him without lying in wait

King James Version

[23] Or with any stone, wherewith *a man* may die, seeing *him* not, and cast *it* upon him, that he die, and *was* not his enemy, neither sought his harm:

[24] Then the congregation shall judge between the slayer and the revenger of blood according to these judgments:

[25] And the congregation shall deliver the slayer out of the hand of the revenger of blood, and the congregation shall restore him to the city of his refuge, whither he was fled: and he shall abide in it unto the death of the high priest, which was anointed with the holy oil.

[26] But if the slayer shall at any time come *without* the border of the city of his refuge, whither he was fled;

[27] And the revenger of blood find him without the borders of the city of his refuge, and the revenger of blood kill the slayer; he shall not be guilty of blood:

[28] Because he should have remained in the city of his refuge until the death of the high priest: but after the death of the high priest the slayer shall return into the land of his possession.

[29] So these *things* shall be for a statute of judgment unto you throughout your generations in all your dwellings.

[30] Whoso killeth *any* person, the murderer shall be put to death by the mouth of witnesses: but one witness shall not testify against *any* person *to cause him* to die.

[31] Moreover ye shall take no satisfaction for the life of a murderer, which *is* guilty of death: but he shall be surely put to death.

[32] And ye shall take no satisfaction for him that is fled to the city of his refuge, that he should come again to dwell in the land, until the death of the priest.

[33] So ye shall not pollute the land wherein ye *are:* for blood it defileth the land: and the land cannot be cleansed of the blood that is shed therein, but by the blood of him that shed it.

[34] Defile not therefore the land which ye shall inhabit, wherein I dwell: for I the LORD dwell among the children of Israel.

36 And the chief fathers of the families of the children of Gilead, the son of Machir, the son of Manasseh, of the families of the sons of Joseph, came near, and spake before Moses, and before the princes, the chief fathers of the children of Israel:

[2] And they said, The LORD commanded my lord to give the land for an inheritance by lot to the children of Israel: and my lord was commanded by the LORD to give the inheritance of Zelophehad our brother unto his daughters.

[3] And *if* they be married to any of the sons of the *other* tribes of the children of Israel, then shall their inheritance be taken from the inheri-

Amplified Bible

[23] Or with any stone with which a man may be killed, not seeing him, and threw it at him so that he died, and was not his enemy nor sought to harm him,

[24] Then the congregation shall judge between the slayer and the avenger of blood according to these ordinances.

[25] And the congregation shall rescue the manslayer from the hand of the avenger of blood and restore him to his city of refuge to which he had fled; and he shall live in it until the high priest dies, who was anointed with the sacred oil.

[26] But if the slayer shall at any time come outside the limits of his city of refuge to which he had fled

[27] And the avenger of blood finds him outside the limits of his city of refuge and kills the manslayer, he shall not be guilty of blood

[28] Because the manslayer should have remained in his city of refuge until the death of the high priest. But after the high priest's death the manslayer shall return to the land of his possession.

[29] And these things shall be for a statute *and* ordinance to you throughout your generations in all your dwellings.

[30] Whoever kills any person [intentionally], the murderer shall be put to death on the testimony of witnesses; but no one shall be put to death on the testimony of one witness.

[31] Moreover, you shall take no ransom for the life of a murderer guilty of death; but he shall surely be put to death.

[32] And you shall accept no ransom for him who has fled to his city of refuge, so that he may return to dwell in the land before the death of the high priest.

[33] So you shall not pollute the land in which you live; for blood pollutes the land, and no atonement can be made for the land for the blood shed in it, but by the blood of him who shed it.

[34] And you shall not defile the land in which you live, in the midst of which I dwell, for I, the Lord, dwell in the midst of the people of Israel.

36 THE HEADS of the fathers' houses of the families of the sons of Gilead son of Machir, the son of Manasseh, of the fathers' houses of the sons of Joseph, came near and spoke before Moses and the leaders, the heads of the fathers' houses of the Israelites.

[2] They said, The Lord commanded [you] my lord to give the land for inheritance by lot to the Israelites; and my lord was commanded by the Lord to give the inheritance of Zelophehad our brother to his daughters.

[3] But if they are married to any of the sons of the other tribes of the Israelites, then their inheritance will be taken from that of our fathers

King James Version

tance of our fathers, and shall be put to the inheritance of the tribe whereinto they are received: so shall it be taken from the lot of our inheritance.

⁴And when the jubile of the children of Israel shall be, then shall their inheritance be put unto the inheritance of the tribe whereunto they are received: so shall their inheritance be taken away from the inheritance of the tribe of our fathers.

⁵And Moses commanded the children of Israel according to the word of the LORD, saying, The tribe of the sons of Joseph hath said well.

⁶This *is* the thing which the LORD doth command concerning the daughters of Zelophehad, saying, Let them marry to whom they think best; only to the family of the tribe of their father shall they marry.

⁷So shall not the inheritance of the children of Israel remove from tribe to tribe: for every one of the children of Israel shall keep himself to the inheritance of the tribe of his fathers.

⁸And every daughter, that possesseth an inheritance in any tribe of the children of Israel, shall be wife unto one of the family of the tribe of her father, that the children of Israel may enjoy every man the inheritance of his fathers.

⁹Neither shall the inheritance remove from *one* tribe to another tribe; but every one of the tribes of the children of Israel shall keep himself to his own inheritance.

¹⁰Even as the LORD commanded Moses, so did the daughters of Zelophehad:

¹¹For Mahlah, Tirzah, and Hoglah, and Milcah, and Noah, the daughters of Zelophehad, were married unto their father's brothers' sons:

¹²*And* they were married into the families of the sons of Manasseh the son of Joseph, and their inheritance remained in the tribe of the family of their father.

¹³These *are* the commandments and the judgments, which the LORD commanded by the hand of Moses unto the children of Israel in the plains of Moab by Jordan *near* Jericho.

Amplified Bible

and added to the inheritance of the tribe to which they are received *and* belong; so it will be taken out of the lot of our inheritance.

⁴And when the Jubilee of the Israelites comes, then their inheritance will be added to that of the tribe to which they are received *and* belong; so will their inheritance be taken away from that of the tribe of our fathers.

⁵And Moses commanded the Israelites according to the word of the Lord, saying, The tribe of the sons of Joseph is right.

⁶This is what the Lord commands concerning the daughters of Zelophehad: Let them marry whom they think best; only they shall marry within the family of the tribe of their father.

⁷So shall no inheritance of the Israelites be transferred from tribe to tribe, for every one of the Israelites shall cling to the inheritance of the tribe of his fathers.

⁸And every daughter who possesses an inheritance in any tribe of the Israelites shall be wife to one of the family of the tribe of her father, so that the Israelites may each one possess the inheritance of his fathers.

⁹So shall no inheritance be transferred from one tribe to another, but each of the tribes of the Israelites shall cling to its own inheritance.

¹⁰The daughters of Zelophehad did as the Lord commanded Moses.

¹¹For Mahlah, Tirzah, Hoglah, Milcah, and Noah, the daughters of Zelophehad, were married to sons of their father's brothers.

¹²They married into the families of the sons of Manasseh son of Joseph, and their inheritance remained in the tribe of the family of their father.

¹³These are the commandments and ordinances which the Lord commanded the Israelites through Moses in the plains of Moab by the Jordan [River] at Jericho.

Deuteronomy

Deuteronomy

King James Version

1 These *be* the words which Moses spake unto all Israel on *this* side Jordan in the wilderness, in the plain over against the Red *sea,* between Paran, and Tophel, and Laban, and Hazeroth, and Dizahab.

²(*There are* eleven days' *journey* from Horeb *by* the way of mount Seir unto Kadesh-barnea.)

³And it came to pass in the fortieth year, in the eleventh month, on the first *day* of the month, *that* Moses spake unto the children of Israel, according unto all that the LORD had given him in commandment unto them;

⁴After he had slain Sihon the king of the Amorites, which dwelt in Heshbon, and Og the king of Bashan, which dwelt at Astaroth in Edrei:

⁵On *this* side Jordan, in the land of Moab, began Moses to declare this law, saying,

⁶ ¶ The LORD our God spake unto us in Horeb, saying, Ye have dwelt long enough in this mount:

⁷Turn you, and take your journey, and go *to* the mount of the Amorites, and unto all *the places* nigh thereunto, in the plain, in the hills, and in the vale, and in the south, and by the sea side, *to* the land of the Canaanites, and *unto* Lebanon, unto the great river, the river Euphrates.

⁸Behold, I have set the land before you: go in and possess the land which the LORD sware unto your fathers, Abraham, Isaac, and Jacob, to give unto them and to their seed after them.

⁹ ¶ And I spake unto you at that time, saying, I am not able to bear you myself alone:

¹⁰The LORD your God hath multiplied you, and behold, you *are this* day as the stars of heaven for multitude.

¹¹(The LORD God of your fathers make you a thousand times so many more as ye *are,* and bless you, as he hath promised you!)

¹²How can I myself alone bear your cumbrance, and your burden, and your strife?

¹³Take ye wise men, and understanding, and known among your tribes, and I will make them rulers over you.

¹⁴And ye answered me, and said, The thing which thou hast spoken *is* good *for us* to do.

¹⁵So I took the chief of your tribes, wise men, and known, and made them heads over you, captains over thousands, and captains over hundreds, and captains over fifties, and captains over tens, and officers among your tribes.

Amplified Bible

1 THESE ARE the words which Moses spoke to all Israel [still] on the [east] side of the Jordan [River] in the wilderness, in the Arabah [the deep valley running north and south from the eastern arm of the Red Sea to beyond the Dead Sea], over near Suph, between Paran and Tophel, Laban, Hazeroth, and Dizahab.

²It is [only] eleven days' journey from Horeb by the way of Mount Seir to Kadesh-barnea [on Canaan's border; yet Israel took forty years to get beyond it].

³And in the fortieth year, on the first day of the eleventh month, Moses spoke to the Israelites according to all that the Lord had given him in commandment to them,

⁴After He had defeated Sihon king of the Amorites, who lived in Heshbon, and Og king of Bashan, who lived in Ashtaroth [and] Edrei.

⁵Beyond (east of) the Jordan in the land of Moab, Moses began to explain this law, saying,

⁶The Lord our God said to us in Horeb, You have dwelt long enough on this mountain.

⁷Turn and take up your journey and go to the hill country of the Amorites, and to all their neighbors in the Arabah, in the hill country, in the lowland, in the South (the Negeb), and on the coast, the land of the Canaanites, and Lebanon, as far as the great river, the river Euphrates.

⁸Behold, I have set the land before you; go in and take possession of the land which the Lord swore to your fathers, to Abraham, to Isaac, and to Jacob, to give to them and to their descendants after them.

⁹I said to you at that time, I am not able to bear you alone.

¹⁰The Lord your God has multiplied you, and behold, you are this day as the stars of the heavens for multitude.

¹¹May the Lord, the God of your fathers, make you a thousand times as many as you are and bless you as He has promised you!

¹²How can I bear alone the weariness *and* pressure and burden of you and your strife?

¹³Choose wise, understanding, experienced, *and* respected men according to your tribes, and I will make them heads over you.

¹⁴And you answered me, The thing which you have spoken is good for us to do.

¹⁵So I took the heads of your tribes, wise, experienced, *and* respected men, and made them heads over you, commanders of thousands, and hundreds, and fifties, and tens, and officers according to your tribes.

King James Version

¹⁶And I charged your judges at that time, saying, Hear *the causes* between your brethren, and judge righteously between every man and his brother, and the stranger *that is* with him.

¹⁷Ye shall not respect persons in judgment; *but* you shall hear the small as well as the great; you shall not be afraid of the face of man; for the judgment *is* God's: and the cause that is too hard for you, bring *it* unto me, and I will hear it.

¹⁸And I commanded you at that time all the things which ye should do.

¹⁹¶ And when we departed from Horeb, we went *through* all that great and terrible wilderness, which you saw *by* the way of the mountain of the Amorites, as the LORD our God commanded us; and we came to Kadesh-barnea.

²⁰And I said unto you, Ye are come unto the mountain of the Amorites, which the LORD our God doth give unto us.

²¹Behold, the LORD thy God hath set the land before thee: go up *and* possess *it,* as the LORD God of thy fathers hath said unto thee; fear not, neither be discouraged.

²²And ye came near unto me every one of you, and said, We will send men before us, and they shall search us out the land, and bring us word again by what way we must go up, and into what cities we shall come.

²³And the saying pleased me well: and I took twelve men of you, one of a tribe:

²⁴And they turned and went up into the mountain, and came unto the valley of Eshcol, and searched it out.

²⁵And they took of the fruit of the land in their hands, and brought *it* down unto us, and brought us word again, and said, *It is* a good land which the LORD our God doth give us.

²⁶Notwithstanding ye would not go up, but rebelled against the commandment of the LORD your God:

²⁷And ye murmured in your tents, and said, Because the LORD hated us, he hath brought us forth out of the land of Egypt, to deliver us into the hand of the Amorites, to destroy us.

²⁸Whither shall we go up? our brethren have discouraged our heart, saying, The people *is* greater and taller than we; the cities *are* great and walled up to heaven; and moreover we have seen the sons of the Anakims there.

²⁹Then I said unto you, Dread not, neither be afraid of them.

³⁰The LORD your God which goeth before you, he shall fight for you, according to all that he did for you in Egypt before your eyes;

³¹And in the wilderness, where thou hast seen how that the LORD thy God bare thee, as a man doth bear his son, in all the way that ye went, until ye came into this place.

³²Yet in this thing ye did not believe the LORD your God,

Amplified Bible

¹⁶And I charged your judges at that time: Hear the cases between your brethren and judge righteously between a man and his brother or the stranger *or* sojourner who is with him.

¹⁷You shall not be partial in judgment; but you shall hear the small as well as the great. You shall not be afraid of the face of man, for the judgment is God's. And the case that is too hard for you, you shall bring to me, and I will hear it.

¹⁸And I commanded you at that time all the things that you should do.

¹⁹And when we departed from Horeb, we went through all that great and terrible wilderness which you saw on the way to the hill country of the Amorites, as the Lord our God commanded us, and we came to Kadesh-barnea.

²⁰And I said to you, You have come to the hill country of the Amorites, which the Lord our God gives us.

²¹Behold, the Lord your God has set the land before you; go up and possess it, as the Lord, the God of your fathers, has said to you. Fear not, neither be dismayed.

²²Then you all came near to me and said, Let us send men before us, that they may search out the land for us and bring us word again by what way we should go up and the cities into which we shall come.

²³The thing pleased me well, and I took twelve men of you, one for each tribe.

²⁴And they turned and went up into the hill country, and came to the Valley of Eshcol and spied it out.

²⁵And they took of the fruit of the land in their hands and brought it down to us and brought us word again, and said, It is a good land which the Lord our God gives us.

²⁶Yet you would not go up, but rebelled against the commandment of the Lord your God.

²⁷You were peevish *and* discontented in your tents, and said, Because the Lord hated us, He brought us forth out of the land of Egypt to deliver us into the hand of the Amorites to destroy us.

²⁸To what are we going up? Our brethren have made our hearts melt, saying, The people are bigger and taller than we are; the cities are great and fortified to the heavens. And moreover we have seen the [giantlike] sons of the Anakim there.

²⁹Then I said to you, Dread not, neither be afraid of them.

³⁰The Lord your God Who goes before you, He will fight for you just as He did for you in Egypt before your eyes,

³¹And in the wilderness, where you have seen how the Lord your God bore you, as a man carries his son, in all the way that you went until you came to this place.

³²Yet in spite of this word you did not believe (trust, rely on, and remain steadfast to) the Lord your God,

King James Version

³³Who went in the way before you, to search you out a place to pitch your tents *in*, in fire by night, to shew you by what way ye should go, and in a cloud by day.

³⁴And the LORD heard the voice of your words, and was wroth, and sware, saying,

³⁵Surely there shall not one of these men of this evil generation see that good land, which I sware to give unto your fathers,

³⁶Save Caleb the son of Jephunneh, he shall see it, and to him will I give the land that he hath trodden upon, and to his children, because he hath wholly followed the LORD.

³⁷Also the LORD was angry with me for your sakes, saying, Thou also shalt not go in thither.

³⁸*But* Joshua the son of Nun, which standeth before thee, he shall go in thither: encourage him: for he shall cause Israel to inherit it.

³⁹Moreover your little ones, which ye said should be a prey, and your children, which *in that* day had no knowledge between good and evil, they shall go in thither, and unto them will I give it, and they shall possess it.

⁴⁰But *as for* you, turn ye, and take your journey into the wilderness *by* the way of the Red sea.

⁴¹Then ye answered and said unto me, We have sinned against the LORD, we will go up and fight, according to all that the LORD our God commanded us. And when ye had girded on every man his weapons of war, ye were ready to go up into the hill.

⁴²And the LORD said unto me, Say unto them, Go not up, neither fight; for I *am* not among you; lest ye be smitten before your enemies.

⁴³So I spake unto you; and you would not hear, but rebelled against the commandment of the LORD, and went presumptuously up into the hill.

⁴⁴And the Amorites, which dwelt in that mountain, came out against you, and chased you, as bees do, and destroyed you in Seir, *even* unto Hormah.

⁴⁵And ye returned and wept before the LORD; but the LORD would not hearken to your voice, nor give ear unto you.

⁴⁶So ye abode in Kadesh many days, according unto the days that ye abode *there*.

2 Then we turned, and took our journey into the wilderness *by* the way of the Red sea, as the LORD spake unto me: and we compassed mount Seir many days.

²And the LORD spake unto me, saying,

³Ye have compassed this mountain long enough: turn you northward.

⁴And command thou the people, saying, Ye are to pass through the coast of your brethren the children of Esau, which dwell in Seir; and they shall be afraid of you: take ye good heed unto yourselves therefore:

Amplified Bible

³³Who went in the way before you to search out a place to pitch your tents, in fire by night, to show you by what way you should go, and in the cloud by day.

³⁴And the Lord heard your words, and was angered and He swore,

³⁵Not one of these men of this evil generation shall see that good land which I swore to give to your fathers,

³⁶Except [Joshua, of course, and] Caleb son of Jephunneh; he shall see it, and to him and to his children I will give the land upon which he has walked, because he has wholly followed the Lord.

³⁷The Lord was angry with me also for your sakes, and said, You also shall not enter Canaan.

³⁸But Joshua son of Nun, who stands before you, he shall enter there. Encourage him, for he shall cause Israel to inherit it.

³⁹Moreover, your little ones whom you said would become a prey, and your children who at this time cannot discern between good and evil, they shall enter Canaan, and to them I will give it and they shall possess it.

⁴⁰But as for you, turn and journey into the wilderness by way of the Red Sea.

⁴¹Then you said to me, We have sinned against the Lord. We will go up and fight, as the Lord our God commanded us. And you girded on every man his battle weapons, and thought it a simple matter to go up into the hill country.

⁴²And the Lord said to me, Say to them, Do not go up or fight, for I am not among you—lest you be dangerously hurt by your enemies.

⁴³So I spoke to you, and you would not hear, but rebelled against the commandment of the Lord, and were presumptuous and went up into the hill country.

⁴⁴Then the Amorites who lived in that hill country came out against you and chased you as bees do and struck you down in Seir as far as Hormah.

⁴⁵And you returned and wept before the Lord, but the Lord would not heed your voice or listen to you.

⁴⁶So you remained in Kadesh; many days you remained there.

2 THEN WE turned, and took our journey into the wilderness by the way of the Red Sea, as the Lord directed me; and for many days we journeyed around Mount Seir.

²And the Lord spoke to me [Moses], saying,

³You have roamed around this mountain country long enough; turn northward.

⁴And command the Israelites, You are to pass through the territory of your kinsmen the sons of Esau, who live in Seir; and they will be afraid of you. So watch yourselves carefully.

King James Version

⁵Meddle not with them; for I will not give you of their land, no, not so much as a foot breadth; because I have given mount Seir unto Esau *for a* possession.

⁶Ye shall buy meat of them for money, that ye may eat; and ye shall also buy water of them for money, that ye may drink.

⁷For the LORD thy God hath blessed thee in all the works of thy hand: he knoweth thy walking *through* this great wilderness: these forty years the LORD thy God *hath been* with thee; thou hast lacked nothing.

⁸And when we passed by from our brethren the children of Esau, which dwelt in Seir, through the way of the plain from Elath, and from Ezion-gaber, we turned and passed *by* the way of the wilderness of Moab.

⁹And the LORD said unto me, Distress not the Moabites, neither contend with them *in* battle: for I will not give thee of their land *for* a possession; because I have given Ar unto the children of Lot *for* a possession.

¹⁰(The Emims dwelt therein in times past, a people great, and many, and tall, as the Anakims;

¹¹Which also were accounted giants, as the Anakims; but the Moabites call them Emims.

¹²The Horims also dwelt in Seir beforetime; but the children of Esau succeeded them, when they had destroyed them from before them, and dwelt in their stead; as Israel did unto the land of his possession, which the LORD gave unto them.)

¹³Now rise up, *said I,* and get you over the brook Zered. And we went over the brook Zered.

¹⁴And the space in which we came from Kadesh-barnea, until we were come over the brook Zered, *was* thirty and eight years; until all the generation of the men of war were wasted out from among the host, as the LORD sware unto them.

¹⁵For indeed the hand of the LORD was against them, to destroy them from among the host, until they were consumed.

¹⁶ ¶ So it came to pass, when all the men of war were consumed and dead from among the people,

¹⁷That the LORD spake unto me, saying,

¹⁸Thou art to pass over *through* Ar, the coast of Moab, *this* day:

¹⁹And *when* thou comest nigh over against the children of Ammon, distress them not, nor meddle with them: for I will not give thee of the land of the children of Ammon *any* possession; because I have given it unto the children of Lot *for* a possession.

²⁰(That also was accounted a land of giants: giants dwelt therein in old time; and the Ammonites call them Zamzummims;

Amplified Bible

⁵Do not provoke *or* stir them up, for I will not give you of their land, no, not enough for the sole of your foot to tread on, for I have given Mount Seir to Esau for a possession.

⁶You shall buy food from them for money, that you may eat, and you shall also buy water from them for money, that you may drink.

⁷For the Lord your God has blessed you in all the work of your hand. He knows your walking through this great wilderness. These forty years the Lord your God has been with you; you have lacked nothing.

⁸So we passed on from our brethren the sons of Esau, who dwelt in Seir, away from the Arabah (wilderness), and from Elath and from Ezion-geber. We turned and went by the way of the wilderness of Moab.

⁹And the Lord said to me, Do not trouble *or* assault Moab or contend with them in battle, for I will not give you any of their land for a possession, because I have given Ar to the sons of Lot for a possession.

¹⁰(The Emim dwelt there in times past, a people great and many, and tall as the Anakim.

¹¹These also are known as Rephaim [of giant stature], as are the Anakim, but the Moabites call them Emim.

¹²The Horites also formerly lived in Seir, but the sons of Esau dispossessed them and destroyed them from before them and dwelt in their stead, as Israel did to the land of their possession which the Lord gave to them.)

¹³Now rise up and go over the brook Zered. So we went over the brook Zered.

¹⁴And the time from our leaving Kadesh-barnea until we had come over the brook Zered was thirty-eight years, until the whole generation of the men of war had perished from the camp, as the Lord had sworn to them.

¹⁵Moreover the hand of the Lord was against them to exterminate them from the midst of the camp, until they were all gone.

¹⁶So when all the men of war had died from among the people,

¹⁷The Lord spoke to me [Moses], saying,

¹⁸You are this day to pass through Ar, the border of Moab.

¹⁹But when you come near the territory of the sons of Ammon, do not trouble *or* assault them or provoke *or* stir them up, for I will not give you any of the land of the Ammonites for a possession, because I have given it to the sons of Lot for a possession.

²⁰(That also is known as a land of Rephaim [of giant stature]; Rephaim dwelt there formerly, but the Ammonites call them Zamzummim,

King James Version

21A people great, and many, and tall, as the Anakims; but the LORD destroyed them before them; and they succeeded them, and dwelt in their stead:

22As he did to the children of Esau, which dwelt in Seir, when he destroyed the Horims from before them; and they succeeded them, and dwelt in their stead *even* unto this day:

23And the Avims which dwelt in Hazerim, *even* unto Azzah, the Caphtorims, which came forth out of Caphtor, destroyed them, and dwelt in their stead.)

24Rise ye up, take your journey, and pass over the river Arnon: behold, I have given into thy hand Sihon the Amorite, king of Heshbon, and his land: begin to possess *it,* and contend with him *in* battle.

25This day will I begin to put the dread of thee and the fear of thee upon the nations *that are* under the whole heaven, who shall hear report of thee, and shall tremble, and be in anguish because of thee.

26 ¶ And I sent messengers out of the wilderness of Kedemoth unto Sihon king of Heshbon *with* words of peace, saying,

27Let me pass through thy land: I will go along by the high way, I will neither turn *unto* the right hand nor *to* the left.

28Thou shalt sell me meat for money, that I may eat; and give me water for money, that I may drink: only I will pass through on my feet;

29(As the children of Esau which dwelt in Seir, and the Moabites which dwell in Ar, did unto me;) until I shall pass over Jordan into the land which the LORD our God giveth us.

30But Sihon king of Heshbon would not let us pass by him: for the LORD thy God hardened his spirit, and made his heart obstinate, that he might deliver him into thy hand, as *appeareth* this day.

31And the LORD said unto me, Behold, I have begun to give Sihon and his land before thee: begin to possess, that *thou* mayest inherit his land.

32Then Sihon came out against us, he and all his people, to fight *at* Jahaz.

33And the LORD our God delivered him before us; and we smote him, and his sons, and all his people.

34And we took all his cities at that time, and utterly destroyed the men, and the women, and the little ones, of every city, we left none to remain:

35Only the cattle we took for a prey unto ourselves, and the spoil of the cities which we took.

36From Aroer, which *is* by the brink of the river of Arnon, and *from* the city that *is* by the riv-

Amplified Bible

21A people great and many, and tall as the Anakim. But the Lord destroyed them before [Ammon], and they dispossessed them and settled in their stead,

22As He did for the sons of Esau, who dwell in Seir, when He destroyed the Horites from before them, and they dispossessed them and settled in their stead even to this day.

23As for the Avvim who dwelt in villages as far as Gaza, the Caphtorim who came from Caphtor destroyed them and dwelt in their stead.)

24Rise up, take your journey, and pass over the Valley of the Arnon. Behold, I have given into your hand Sihon the Amorite, king of Heshbon, and his land; begin to possess it and contend with him in battle.

25This day will I begin to put the dread and fear of you upon the peoples who are under the whole heavens, who shall hear the report of you and shall tremble and be in anguish because of you.

26So I sent messengers from the wilderness of Kedemoth to Sihon king of Heshbon with words of peace, saying,

27Let me pass through your land. I will go only by the road, turning aside neither to the right nor to the left.

28You shall sell me food to eat and sell me water to drink; only let me walk through,

29As the sons of Esau, who dwell in Seir, and the Moabites, who dwell in Ar, *a* did for me, until I go over the Jordan into the land which the Lord our God gives us.

30But Sihon king of Heshbon would not let us pass by him; for the Lord your God hardened his spirit and made his heart obstinate, that He might give him into your hand, as at this day.

31And the Lord said to me [Moses], Behold, I have begun to give Sihon and his land over to you. Begin to take possession, that you may succeed him *and* occupy his land.

32Then Sihon came out against us, he and all his people, to fight at Jahaz.

33And the Lord our God gave him over to us, and we defeated him and his sons and all his people.

34At the same time we took all his cities and utterly destroyed every city—men, women, and children. We left none to remain.

35Only the cattle we took as booty for ourselves and the spoil of the cities which we had captured.

36From Aroer, which is on the edge of the Arnon Valley, and from the city that is in the valley,

---

AMP notes: a All that is said here is that the Edomites and Moabites sold Israel bread and water. There is no denial, expressed or implied, of their hostility to Israel and their desire for her destruction. The passage is in entire harmony with Num. 20:17, 21, and Deut. 23:3, 4 (J. P. Lange, *A Commentary*).

King James Version

er, even unto Gilead, there was not one city too strong for us: the LORD our God delivered all unto us:

37Only unto the land of the children of Ammon thou camest not, *nor unto* any place of the river Jabbok, nor *unto* the cities in the mountains, nor *unto* whatsoever the LORD our God forbad *us*.

3 Then we turned, and went up the way to Bashan: and Og the king of Bashan came out against us, he and all his people, to battle *at* Edrei.

2And the LORD said unto me, Fear him not: for I will deliver him, and all his people, and his land, into thy hand; and thou shalt do unto him as thou didst unto Sihon king of the Amorites, which dwelt at Heshbon.

3So the LORD our God delivered into our hands Og also, the king of Bashan, and all his people: and we smote him until none was left to him remaining.

4And we took all his cities at that time, there was not a city which we took not from them, threescore cities, all the region of Argob, the kingdom of Og in Bashan.

5All these cities *were* fenced *with* high walls, gates, and bars; beside unwalled towns a great many.

6And we utterly destroyed them, as we did unto Sihon king of Heshbon, utterly destroying the men, women, and children, of every city.

7But all the cattle, and the spoil of the cities, we took for a prey to ourselves.

8And we took at that time out of the hand of the two kings of the Amorites the land that *was* on *this* side Jordan, from the river of Arnon unto mount Hermon;

9(*Which* Hermon the Sidonians call Sirion; and the Amorites call it Shenir;)

10All the cities of the plain, and all Gilead, and all Bashan, unto Salchah and Edrei, cities of the kingdom of Og in Bashan.

11For only Og king of Bashan remained of the remnant of giants; behold, his bedstead *was* a bedstead of iron; *is* it not in Rabbath of the children of Ammon? nine cubits *was* the length thereof, and four cubits the breadth of it, after the cubit of a man.

12And this land, *which* we possessed at that time, from Aroer, which *is* by the river Arnon, and half mount Gilead, and the cities thereof, gave I unto the Reubenites and to the Gadites.

13And the rest of Gilead, and all Bashan, *being* the kingdom of Og, gave I unto the half tribe of Manasseh; all the region of Argob, with all Bashan, which was called the land of giants.

14Jair the son of Manasseh took all the country of Argob unto the coasts of Geshuri and

Amplified Bible

as far as Gilead, there was no city too high *and* strong for us; the Lord our God delivered all to us.

37Only you did not go near the land of the Ammonites, that is, to any bank of the river Jabbok and the cities of the hill country, and wherever the Lord our God had forbidden us.

3 THEN WE turned and went up the road to Bashan, and Og king of Bashan came out against us, he and all his people, to battle at Edrei.

2And the Lord said to me, Do not fear him, for I have given him and all his people and his land into your hand; and you shall do to him as you did to Sihon king of the Amorites, who lived at Heshbon.

3So the Lord our God also gave into our hands Og king of Bashan and all his people, and we smote him until not one was left to him.

4And we took all his cities at that time; there was not a city which we did not take from them, sixty cities, the whole region of Argob, the kingdom of Og in Bashan.

5All these cities were fortified with high *and* haughty walls, gates, and bars, besides a great many unwalled villages.

6And we utterly destroyed them, as we did to Sihon king of Heshbon, utterly destroying every city—men, women, and children.

7But all the cattle and the spoil of the cities we took for booty for ourselves.

8So we took the land at that time out of the hand of the two kings of the Amorites who were beyond the Jordan, from the Valley of the Arnon to Mount Hermon

9(The Sidonians call Hermon, Sirion, and the Amorites call it Senir),

10All the cities of the plain, and all Gilead, and all Bashan as far as Salecah and Edrei, cities of the kingdom of Og in Bashan.

11For only Og king of Bashan remained of the remnant of the [gigantic] Rephaim. Behold, his bedstead was of iron; is it not in Rabbah of the Ammonites? Nine cubits was its length and four cubits its breadth, using the cubit of a man [the forearm to the end of the middle finger].

12When we took possession of this land, I gave to the Reubenites and the Gadites the territory from Aroer, which is on the edge of the Valley of the Arnon, and half the hill country of Gilead and its cities.

13The rest of Gilead and all of Bashan, the kingdom of Og, that is, all the region of Argob in Bashan, I gave to the half-tribe of Manasseh. It is called the land of Rephaim [of giant stature].

14Jair son of Manasseh took all the region of Argob, that is, Bashan, as far as the border of

King James Version

Maachathi; and called them after his own name, Bashan-havoth-jair, unto this day.

15And I gave Gilead unto Machir.

16And unto the Reubenites and unto the Gadites I gave from Gilead even unto the river Arnon, half the valley, and the border, even unto the river Jabbok, *which is* the border of the children of Ammon;

17The plain also, and Jordan, and the coast *thereof,* from Chinnereth even unto the sea of the plain, *even* the salt sea, under Ashdoth-pisgah eastward.

18 ¶ And I commanded you at that time, saying, The LORD your God hath given you this land to possess it: ye shall pass over armed before your brethren the children of Israel, all *that are* meet for the war.

19But your wives, and your little ones, and your cattle, (*for* I know that ye have much cattle,) shall abide in your cities which I have given you;

20Until the LORD have given rest unto your brethren, as well as *unto* you, and *until* they also possess the land which the LORD your God hath given them beyond Jordan: and *then* shall ye return every man unto his possession, which I have given you.

21And I commanded Joshua at that time, saying, Thine eyes have seen all that the LORD your God hath done unto these two kings: so shall the LORD do unto all the kingdoms whither thou passest.

22Ye shall not fear them: for the LORD your God he shall fight for you.

23And I besought the LORD at that time, saying,

24O Lord GOD, thou hast begun to shew thy servant thy greatness, and thy mighty hand: for what God *is there* in heaven or in earth, that can do according to thy works, and according to thy might?

25I pray thee, let me go over, and see the good land that *is* beyond Jordan, that goodly mountain, and Lebanon.

26But the LORD was wroth with me for your sakes, and would not hear me: and the LORD said unto me, Let it suffice thee; speak no more unto me of this matter.

27Get thee up *into* the top of Pisgah, and lift up thine eyes westward, and northward, and southward, and eastward, and behold *it* with thine eyes: for thou shalt not go over this Jordan.

28But charge Joshua, and encourage him, and strengthen him: for he shall go over before this people, and he shall cause them to inherit the land which thou shalt see.

29So we abode in the valley over against Beth-peor.

Amplified Bible

the Geshurites and the Maacathites, and called it after his own name, Havvoth-jair, so called to this day.

15And I gave Gilead to Machir [son of Manasseh].

16And to the Reubenites and Gadites I gave from Gilead even to the Valley of the Arnon, with the middle of the valley as the boundary of it, as far over as the river Jabbok, the boundary of the Ammonites,

17The Arabah also, with the Jordan as its boundary, from Chinnereth as far as the Sea of the Arabah, the Salt [Dead] Sea, under the cliffs [of the headlands] of Pisgah on the east.

18And I commanded you at that time, saying, The Lord your God has given you this land to possess it; you [Reuben, Gad, and the half-tribe of Manasseh] shall go over [the Jordan] armed before your brethren the other Israelites, all that are able for war.

19But your wives and your little ones and your cattle—I know that you have many cattle—shall remain in your cities which I have given you,

20Until the Lord has given rest to your brethren as to you, and until they also possess the land which the Lord your God has given them beyond the Jordan. Then shall you return every man to the possession which I have given you.

21And I commanded Joshua at that time, saying, Your *own* eyes have seen all that the Lord your God has done to these two kings [Sihon and Og]; so shall the Lord do to all the kingdoms into which you are going over [the Jordan].

22You shall not fear them, for the Lord your God shall fight for you.

23And I besought the Lord at that time, saying,

24O Lord God, You have only begun to show Your servant Your greatness and Your mighty hand; for what god is there in heaven or on earth that can do according to Your works and according to Your might?

25I pray You, [will You not just] let me go over and see the good land that is beyond the Jordan, that goodly mountain country [with Hermon] and Lebanon?

26But the Lord was angry with me on your account and would not listen to me; and the Lord said to me, That is enough! Say no more to Me about it.

27Get up to the top of Pisgah and lift up your eyes westward and northward and southward and eastward, and behold it with your eyes, for you shall not go over this Jordan.

28But charge Joshua, and encourage and strengthen him, for he shall go over before this people and he shall cause them to possess the land which you shall see.

29So we remained in the valley opposite Beth-peor.

King James Version

4 Now therefore hearken, O Israel, unto the statutes and unto the judgments, which I teach you, for to do *them,* that ye may live, and go in and possess the land which the LORD God of your fathers giveth you.

2 Ye shall not add unto the word which I command you, neither shall you diminish *ought* from it, that *ye* may keep the commandments of the LORD your God which I command you.

3 Your eyes have seen what the LORD did because of Baal-peor: for all the men that followed Baal-peor, the LORD thy God hath destroyed them from among you.

4 But ye that did cleave unto the LORD your God *are* alive every one of you *this* day.

5 Behold, I have taught you statutes and judgments, even as the LORD my God commanded me, that *ye* should do so in the land whither ye go to possess it.

6 Keep therefore and do *them;* for this *is* your wisdom and your understanding in the sight of the nations, which shall hear all these statutes, and say, Surely this great nation *is* a wise and understanding people.

7 For what nation *is there so* great, who hath God *so* nigh unto them, as the LORD our God *is* in all *things that* we call upon him *for?*

8 And what nation *is there so* great, that hath statutes and judgments *so* righteous as all this law, which I set before you *this* day?

9 Only take heed to thyself, and keep thy soul diligently, lest thou forget the things which thine eyes have seen, and lest they depart from thy heart all the days of thy life: but teach them thy sons, and thy sons' sons;

10 *Specially* the day that thou stoodest before the LORD thy God in Horeb, when the LORD said unto me, Gather me the people together, and I will make them hear my words, that they may learn to fear me all the days that they shall live upon the earth, and *that* they may teach their children.

11 And ye came near and stood under the mountain; and the mountain burnt with fire unto the midst of heaven, *with* darkness, clouds, and thick darkness.

12 And the LORD spake unto you out of the midst of the fire: ye heard the voice of the words, but saw no similitude; only *ye heard* a voice.

13 And he declared unto you his covenant, which he commanded you to perform, *even* ten commandments; and he wrote them upon two tables of stone.

14 And the LORD commanded me at that time to teach you statutes and judgments, that ye might do them in the land whither ye go over to possess it.

15 Take ye therefore good heed unto yourselves; for ye saw no *manner of* similitude on

Amplified Bible

4 NOW LISTEN *and* give heed, O Israel, to the statutes and ordinances which I teach you, and do them, that you may live and go in and possess the land which the Lord, the God of your fathers, gives you.

2 You shall not add to the word which I command you, neither shall you diminish it, that you may keep the commandments of the Lord your God which I command you.

3 Your eyes still see what the Lord did because of Baal-peor; for all the men who followed the Baal of Peor the Lord your God has destroyed from among you,

4 But you who clung fast to the Lord your God are alive, every one of you, this day.

5 Behold, I have taught you statutes and ordinances as the Lord my God commanded me, that you should do them in the land which you are entering to possess.

6 So keep them and do them, for that is your wisdom and your understanding in the sight of the peoples who, when they hear all these statutes, will say, Surely this great nation is a wise and understanding people.

7 For what great nation is there who has a god so near to them as the Lord our God is to us in all things for which we call upon Him?

8 And what large *and* important nation has statutes and ordinances so upright *and* just as all this law which I set before you today?

9 Only take heed, and guard your life diligently, lest you forget the things which your eyes have seen and lest they depart from your [mind and] heart all the days of your life. Teach them to your children and your children's children—

10 Especially how on the day that you stood before the Lord your God in Horeb, the Lord said to me, Gather the people together to Me and I will make them hear My words, that they may learn [reverently] to fear Me all the days they live upon the earth and that they may teach their children.

11 And you came near and stood at the foot of the mountain, and the mountain burned with fire to the heart of heaven, with darkness, cloud, and thick gloom.

12 And the Lord spoke to you out of the midst of the fire. You heard the voice of the words, but saw no form; there was only a voice.

13 And He declared to you His covenant, which He commanded you to perform, the Ten Commandments, and He wrote them on two tables of stone.

14 And the Lord commanded me at that time to teach you the statutes and precepts, that you might do them in the land which you are going over to possess.

15 Therefore take good heed to yourselves, since you saw no form of Him on the day the

King James Version

the day *that* the LORD spake unto you in Horeb out of the midst of the fire:

¹⁶Lest ye corrupt *yourselves,* and make you a graven image, the similitude of any figure, the likeness of male or female,

¹⁷The likeness of any beast that *is* on the earth, the likeness of any winged fowl that flieth in the air,

¹⁸The likeness of any *thing* that creepeth on the ground, the likeness of any fish that *is* in the waters beneath the earth:

¹⁹And lest thou lift up thine eyes unto heaven, and when thou seest the sun, and the moon, and the stars, *even* all the host of heaven, shouldest be driven to worship them, and serve them, which the LORD thy God hath divided unto all nations under the whole heaven.

²⁰But the LORD hath taken you, and brought you forth out of the iron furnace, *even* out of Egypt, to be unto him a people of inheritance, as *ye are* this day.

²¹Furthermore the LORD was angry with me for your sakes, and sware that I should not go over Jordan, and that *I* should not go in unto *that* good land, which the LORD thy God giveth thee *for* an inheritance:

²²But I *must* die in this land, I *must* not go over Jordan: but ye *shall* go over, and possess that good land.

²³Take heed unto yourselves, lest ye forget the covenant of the LORD your God, which he made with you, and make you a graven image, *or* the likeness of any *thing,* which the LORD thy God hath forbidden thee.

²⁴For the LORD thy God *is* a consuming fire, *even* a jealous God.

²⁵When thou shalt beget children, and children's children, and ye shall have remained long in the land, and shall corrupt *yourselves,* and make a graven image, *or* the likeness of any *thing,* and shall do evil in the sight of the LORD thy God, to provoke him to anger:

²⁶I call heaven and earth to witness against you *this* day, that ye shall soon utterly perish from off the land whereunto you go over Jordan to possess it; ye shall not prolong *your* days upon it, but shall utterly be destroyed.

²⁷And the LORD shall scatter you among the nations, and ye shall be left few in number among the heathen, whither the LORD shall lead you.

²⁸And there ye shall serve gods, the work of men's hands, wood and stone, which neither see, nor hear, nor eat, nor smell.

²⁹But if from thence thou shalt seek the LORD thy God, thou shalt find *him,* if thou seek him with all thy heart and with all thy soul.

³⁰When thou art in tribulation, and all these things are come upon thee, *even* in the latter days, if thou turn to the LORD thy God, and shalt be obedient unto his voice;

Amplified Bible

Lord spoke to you on Horeb out of the midst of the fire,

¹⁶Beware lest you become corrupt by making for yourselves [to worship] a graven image in the form of any figure, the likeness of male or female,

¹⁷The likeness of any beast that is on the earth, or of any winged fowl that flies in the air,

¹⁸The likeness of anything that creeps on the ground, or of any fish that is in the waters beneath the earth.

¹⁹And beware lest you lift up your eyes to the heavens, and when you see the sun, moon, and stars, even all the host of the heavens, you be drawn away and worship them and serve them, things which the Lord your God has allotted to all nations under the whole heaven.

²⁰But the Lord has taken you and brought you forth out of the iron furnace, out of Egypt, to be to Him a people of His own possession, as you are this day.

²¹Furthermore the Lord was angry with me because of you, and He swore that I should not go over the Jordan and that I should not enter the good land which the Lord your God gives you for an inheritance.

²²But I must die in this land; I must not cross the Jordan; but you shall go over and possess that good land.

²³Take heed to yourselves, lest you forget the covenant of the Lord your God which He made with you, and make for yourselves a graven image in the form of anything which the Lord your God has forbidden you.

²⁴For the Lord your God is a consuming fire, a jealous God.

²⁵When children shall be born to you, and children's children, and you have grown old in the land, if you corrupt yourselves by making a graven image in the form of anything, and do evil in the sight of the Lord your God, provoking Him to anger,

²⁶I call heaven and earth to witness against you this day that you shall soon utterly perish from the land which you are going over the Jordan to possess. You will not live long upon it but will be utterly destroyed.

²⁷And the Lord will scatter you among the peoples, and you will be left few in number among the nations to which the Lord will drive you.

²⁸There you will serve gods, the work of men's hands, wood and stone, which neither see nor hear nor eat nor smell.

²⁹But if from there you will seek (inquire for and require as necessity) the Lord your God, you will find Him if you [truly] seek Him with all your heart [and mind] and soul and life.

³⁰When you are in tribulation and all these things come upon you, in the latter days you will turn to the Lord your God and be obedient to His voice.

King James Version

³¹(For the LORD thy God *is* a merciful God;) he will not forsake thee, neither destroy thee, nor forget the covenant of thy fathers which he sware unto them.

³²For ask now of the days that are past, which were before thee, since the day that God created man upon the earth, and *ask* from the one side of heaven unto the other, whether there hath been *any such thing* as this great thing *is,* or hath been heard like it?

³³Did *ever* people hear the voice of God speaking out of the midst of the fire, as thou hast heard, and live?

³⁴Or hath God assayed to go *and* take him a nation from the midst of *another* nation, by temptations, by signs, and by wonders, and by war, and by a mighty hand, and by a stretched out arm, and by great terrors, according to all that the LORD your God did for you in Egypt before your eyes?

³⁵Unto thee it was shewed, that thou mightest know that the LORD he *is* God; *there is* none else besides him.

³⁶Out of heaven he made thee to hear his voice, that he might instruct thee: and upon earth he shewed thee his great fire; and thou heardest his words out of the midst of the fire.

³⁷And because he loved thy fathers, therefore he chose their seed after them, and brought thee out in his sight with his mighty power out of Egypt;

³⁸To drive out nations from before thee greater and mightier than thou *art,* to bring thee in, to give thee their land *for* an inheritance, as *it is* this day.

³⁹Know therefore *this* day, and consider *it* in thine heart, that the LORD he *is* God in heaven above, and upon the earth beneath: *there is* none else.

⁴⁰Thou shalt keep therefore his statutes, and his commandments, which I command thee *this* day, that it may go well with thee, and with thy children after thee, and that thou mayest prolong *thy* days upon the earth, which the LORD thy God giveth thee, for ever.

⁴¹ ¶ Then Moses severed three cities on *this* side Jordan toward the sunrising;

⁴²That the slayer might flee thither, which should kill his neighbour unawares, and hated him not in times past; and that fleeing unto one of these cities he might live:

⁴³*Namely,* Bezer in the wilderness, in the plain country, of the Reubenites; and Ramoth in Gilead, of the Gadites; and Golan in Bashan, of the Manassites.

⁴⁴And this *is* the law which Moses set before the children of Israel:

⁴⁵These *are* the testimonies, and the statutes, and the judgments, which Moses spake unto the children of Israel, after they came forth out of Egypt,

Amplified Bible

³¹For the Lord your God is a merciful God; He will not fail you or destroy you or forget the covenant of your fathers, which He swore to them.

³²For ask now of the days that are past, which were before you, since the day that God created man upon the earth, and ask from one end of the heavens to the other, whether such a great thing as this has ever occurred or been heard of anywhere.

³³Did ever people hear the voice of God speaking out of the midst of the fire, as you heard, and live?

³⁴Or has God ever tried to go and take for Himself a nation from the midst of another nation, by trials, by signs, by wonders, by war, by a mighty hand, by an outstretched arm, and by great terrors, as the Lord your God did for you in Egypt before your eyes?

³⁵To you it was shown, that you might realize *and* have personal knowledge that the Lord is God; there is no other besides Him.

³⁶Out of heaven He made you hear His voice, that He might correct, discipline, *and* admonish you; and on earth He made you see His great fire, and you heard His words out of the midst of the fire.

³⁷And because He loved your fathers, He chose their descendants after them, and brought you out from Egypt with His own Presence, by His mighty power,

³⁸Driving out nations from before you, greater and mightier than yourselves, to bring you in, to give you their land for an inheritance, as it is this day;

³⁹Know, recognize, *and* understand therefore this day and turn your [mind and] heart to it that the Lord is God in the heavens above and upon the earth beneath; there is no other.

⁴⁰Therefore you shall keep His statutes and His commandments, which I command you this day, that it may go well with you and your children after you and that you may prolong your days in the land which the Lord your God gives you forever.

⁴¹Then Moses set apart three cities [of refuge] beyond the Jordan to the east,

⁴²That the manslayer might flee there, who slew his neighbor unintentionally and had not previously been at enmity with him, that fleeing to one of these cities he might save his life:

⁴³Bezer in the wilderness on the tableland, for the Reubenites; and Ramoth in Gilead, for the Gadites; and Golan in Bashan, for the Manassites.

⁴⁴This is the law which Moses set before the Israelites.

⁴⁵These are the testimonies and the laws and the precepts which Moses spoke to the Israelites when they came out of Egypt,

King James Version

⁴⁶On *this* side Jordan, in the valley over against Beth-peor, in the land of Sihon king of the Amorites, who dwelt at Heshbon, whom Moses and the children of Israel smote, after they were come forth out of Egypt:

⁴⁷And they possessed his land, and the land of Og king of Bashan, two kings of the Amorites, which *were* on *this* side Jordan *toward* the sun-rising;

⁴⁸From Aroer, which *is* by the bank of the river Arnon, even unto mount Sion, which *is* Hermon,

⁴⁹And all the plain on *this* side Jordan eastward, even unto the sea of the plain, under the springs of Pisgah.

5 And Moses called all Israel, and said unto them, Hear, O Israel, the statutes and judgments which I speak in your ears *this* day, that ye may learn them, and keep, and do them.

²The LORD our God made a covenant with us in Horeb.

³The LORD made not this covenant with our fathers, but with us, *even* us, who *are* all of us here alive *this* day.

⁴The LORD talked with you face to face in the mount out of the midst of the fire,

⁵(I stood between the LORD and you at that time, to shew you the word of the LORD: for ye were afraid by reason of the fire, and went not up into the mount;) saying,

⁶ ¶ I *am* the LORD thy God, which brought thee out of the land of Egypt, from the house of bondage.

⁷Thou shalt have none other gods before me.

⁸Thou shalt not make thee *any* graven image, *or* any likeness *of any thing* that *is* in heaven above, or that *is* in the earth beneath, or that *is* in the waters beneath the earth:

⁹Thou shalt not bow down thyself unto them, nor serve them: for I the LORD thy God *am* a jealous God, visiting the iniquity of the fathers upon the children unto the third and fourth *generation* of them that hate me,

¹⁰And shewing mercy unto thousands of them that love me and keep my commandments.

¹¹Thou shalt not take the name of the LORD thy God in vain: for the LORD will not hold *him* guiltless that taketh his name in vain.

¹²Keep the sabbath day to sanctify it, as the LORD thy God hath commanded thee.

¹³Six days thou shalt labour, and do all thy work:

¹⁴But the seventh day *is* the sabbath of the LORD thy God: *in it* thou shalt not do any work, thou, nor thy son, nor thy daughter, nor thy manservant, nor thy maidservant, nor thine ox,

Amplified Bible

⁴⁶Beyond the Jordan in the valley opposite Beth-peor, in the land of Sihon king of the Amorites, who dwelt at Heshbon, whom Moses and the Israelites smote when they came out of Egypt.

⁴⁷And they took possession of his land and the land of Og king of Bashan, the two kings of the Amorites, who lived beyond the Jordan to the east,

⁴⁸From Aroer, which is on the edge of the Valley of the Arnon, as far as Mount Sirion (that is, Hermon),

⁴⁹And all the Arabah (lowlands) beyond the Jordan eastward, as far as the Sea of the Arabah [the Dead Sea], under the slopes *and* springs of Pisgah.

5 AND MOSES called all Israel, and said to them, Hear, O Israel, the statutes and ordinances which I speak in your hearing this day, that you may learn them and take heed and do them.

²The Lord our God made a covenant with us in Horeb.

³The Lord made this covenant not with our fathers, but with us, who are all of us here alive this day.

⁴The Lord spoke with you face to face at the mount out of the midst of the fire.

⁵I stood between the Lord and you at that time to show you the word of the Lord, for you were afraid because of the fire and went not up into the mount. He said,

⁶I am the Lord your God, Who brought you out of the land of Egypt, from the house of bondage.

⁷You shall have no other gods before Me *or* besides Me.

⁸You shall not make for yourself [to worship] a graven image or any likeness of anything that is in the heavens above or that is in the earth beneath or that is in the water under the earth.

⁹You shall not bow down to them or serve them; for I, the Lord your God, am a jealous God, visiting the iniquity of the fathers upon the children to the third and fourth generations of those who hate Me,

¹⁰And showing mercy *and* steadfast love to thousands *and* to a thousand generations of those who love Me and keep My commandments.

¹¹You shall not take the name of the Lord your God in vain, for the Lord will not hold him guiltless who takes His name in falsehood *or* without purpose.

¹²Observe the Sabbath day to keep it holy, as the Lord your God commanded you.

¹³Six days you shall labor and do all your work,

¹⁴But the seventh day is a Sabbath to the Lord your God; in it you shall not do any work, you or your son or your daughter, or your manservant or your maidservant, or your ox or

King James Version

nor thine ass, nor any of thy cattle, nor thy stranger that *is* within thy gates; that thy manservant and thy maidservant may rest as well as thou.

¹⁵And remember that thou wast a servant in the land of Egypt, and *that* the LORD thy God brought thee out thence through a mighty hand and by a stretched out arm: therefore the LORD thy God commanded thee to keep the sabbath day.

¹⁶Honour thy father and thy mother, as the LORD thy God hath commanded thee; that thy days may be prolonged, and that it may go well with thee, in the land which the LORD thy God giveth thee.

¹⁷Thou shalt not kill.

¹⁸Neither shalt thou commit adultery.

¹⁹Neither shalt thou steal.

²⁰Neither shalt thou bear false witness against thy neighbour.

²¹Neither shalt thou desire thy neighbour's wife, neither shalt thou covet thy neighbour's house, his field, or his manservant, or his maidservant, his ox, or his ass, or any *thing* that *is* thy neighbour's.

²² ¶ These words the LORD spake unto all your assembly in the mount out of the midst of the fire, of the cloud, and of the thick darkness, *with* a great voice: and he added no more. And he wrote them in two tables of stone, and delivered them unto me.

²³And it came to pass, when ye heard the voice out of the midst of the darkness, (for the mountain did burn with fire,) that ye came near unto me, *even* all the heads of your tribes, and your elders;

²⁴And ye said, Behold, the LORD our God hath shewed us his glory and his greatness, and we have heard his voice out of the midst of the fire: we have seen this day that God doth talk with man, and he liveth.

²⁵Now therefore why should we die? for this great fire will consume us: if we hear the voice of the LORD our God any more, then we shall die.

²⁶For who *is there of* all flesh, that hath heard the voice of the living God speaking out of the midst of the fire, as we *have,* and lived?

²⁷Go thou near, and hear all that the LORD our God shall say: and speak thou unto us all that the LORD our God shall speak unto thee; and we will hear *it,* and do *it.*

²⁸And the LORD heard the voice of your words, when ye spake unto me; and the LORD said unto me, I have heard the voice of the words of this people, which they have spoken unto thee: they have well *said* all that they have spoken.

²⁹O that there were such a heart in them, that they would fear me, and keep all my command-

Amplified Bible

your donkey or any of your livestock, or the stranger *or* sojourner who is within your gates, that your manservant and your maidservant may rest as well as you.

¹⁵And [earnestly] remember that you were a servant in the land of Egypt and that the Lord your God brought you out from there with a mighty hand and an outstretched arm; therefore the Lord your God commanded you to observe *and* take heed to the Sabbath day.

¹⁶Honor your father and your mother, as the Lord your God commanded you, that your days may be prolonged and that it may go well with you in the land which the Lord your God gives you.

¹⁷You shall not murder.

¹⁸Neither shall you commit adultery.

¹⁹Neither shall you act slyly *or* steal.

²⁰Neither shall you witness falsely against your neighbor.

²¹Neither shall you covet your neighbor's wife, nor desire your neighbor's house, his field, his manservant or his maidservant, his ox or his donkey, or anything that is your neighbor's.

²²These words the Lord spoke to all your assembly at the mountain out of the midst of the fire, the cloud, and the thick darkness, with a loud voice; and He spoke not again [added no more]. He wrote them on two tables of stone and gave them to me [Moses].

²³And when you heard the voice out of the midst of the darkness, while the mountain was burning with fire, you came near me, all the heads of your tribes and your elders;

²⁴And you said, Behold, the Lord our God has shown us His glory and His greatness, and we have heard His voice out of the midst of the fire; we have this day seen that God speaks with man and man still lives.

²⁵Now therefore, why should we die? For this great fire will consume us; if we hear the voice of the Lord our God any longer, we shall die.

²⁶For who is there of all flesh who has heard the voice of the living God speaking out of the midst of fire, as we have, and lived?

²⁷Go near [Moses] and hear all that the Lord our God will say. And speak to us all that the Lord our God will speak to you; and we will hear and do it.

²⁸And the Lord heard your words when you spoke to me and the Lord said to me, I have heard the words of this people which they have spoken to you. They have said well all that they have spoken.

²⁹Oh, that they had such a [mind and] heart in them always [reverently] to fear Me and keep

King James Version

ments always, that it might be well with them, and with their children for ever!

³⁰Go say to them, Get you into your tents again.

³¹But as for thee, stand thou here by me, and I will speak unto thee all the commandments, and the statutes, and the judgments, which thou shalt teach them, that they may do them in the land which I give them to possess it.

³²Ye shall observe to do therefore as the LORD your God hath commanded you: ye shall not turn aside to the right hand or to the left.

³³You shall walk in all the ways which the LORD your God hath commanded you, that ye may live, and that it may be well with you, and that ye may prolong your days in the land which ye shall possess.

6 Now these are the commandments, the statutes, and the judgments, which the LORD your God commanded to teach you, that ye might do them in the land whither ye go to possess it:

²That thou mightest fear the LORD thy God, to keep all his statutes and his commandments, which I command thee, thou, and thy son, and thy son's son, all the days of thy life; and that thy days may be prolonged.

³Hear therefore, O Israel, and observe to do it; that it may be well with thee, and that ye may increase mightily, as the LORD God of thy fathers hath promised thee, in the land that floweth with milk and honey.

⁴Hear, O Israel: The LORD our God is one LORD:

⁵And thou shalt love the LORD thy God with all thine heart, and with all thy soul, and with all thy might.

⁶And these words, which I command thee this day, shall be in thine heart:

⁷And thou shalt teach them diligently unto thy children, and shalt talk of them when thou sittest in thine house, and when thou walkest by the way, and when thou liest down, and when thou risest up.

⁸And thou shalt bind them for a sign upon thine hand, and they shall be as frontlets between thine eyes.

⁹And thou shalt write them upon the posts of thy house, and on thy gates.

¹⁰And it shall be, when the LORD thy God shall have brought thee into the land which he sware unto thy fathers, to Abraham, to Isaac, and to Jacob, to give thee great and goodly cities, which thou buildedst not,

¹¹And houses full of all good things, which thou filledst not, and wells digged, which thou diggedst not, vineyards and olive trees, which thou plantedst not; when thou shalt have eaten and be full;

¹²Then beware lest thou forget the LORD,

Amplified Bible

all My commandments, that it might go well with them and with their children forever!

³⁰Go and say to them, Return to your tents.

³¹But you [Moses], stand here by Me, and I will tell you all the commandments and the statutes and the precepts which you shall teach them, that they may do them in the land which I give them to possess.

³²Therefore you people shall be watchful to do as the Lord your God has commanded you; you shall not turn aside to the right hand or to the left.

³³You shall walk in all the ways which the Lord your God has commanded you, that you may live and that it may go well with you and that you may live long in the land which you shall possess.

6 NOW THIS is the instruction, the laws, and the precepts which the Lord your God commanded me to teach you, that you might do them in the land to which you go to possess it,

²That you may [reverently] fear the Lord your God, you and your son and your son's son, and keep all His statutes and His commandments which I command you all the days of your life, and that your days may be prolonged.

³Hear therefore, O Israel, and be watchful to do them, that it may be well with you and that you may increase exceedingly, as the Lord, the God of your fathers, has promised you, in a land flowing with milk and honey.

⁴Hear, O Israel: the Lord our God is one Lord [the only Lord].

⁵And you shall love the Lord your God with all your [mind and] heart and with your entire being and with all your might.

⁶And these words which I am commanding you this day shall be [first] in your [own] minds and hearts; [then]

⁷You shall whet and sharpen them so as to make them penetrate, and teach and impress them diligently upon the [minds and] hearts of your children, and shall talk of them when you sit in your house and when you walk by the way, and when you lie down and when you rise up.

⁸And you shall bind them as a sign upon your hand, and they shall be as frontlets (forehead bands) between your eyes.

⁹And you shall write them upon the doorposts of your house and on your gates.

¹⁰And when the Lord your God brings you into the land which He swore to your fathers, to Abraham, Isaac, and Jacob, to give you, with great and goodly cities which you did not build,

¹¹And houses full of all good things which you did not fill, and cisterns hewn out which you did not hew, and vineyards and olive trees which you did not plant, and when you eat and are full,

¹²Then beware lest you forget the Lord, Who